RELIGIONS
in Four Dimensions

Bedulu Elephant Cave, Bali, 11th century; once a Buddhist hermitage; rediscovered in 1923.

Other Books by Walter Kaufmann

NIETZSCHE: PHILOSOPHER, PSYCHOLOGIST, ANTICHRIST
CRITIQUE OF RELIGION AND PHILOSOPHY
FROM SHAKESPEARE TO EXISTENTIALISM
THE FAITH OF A HERETIC
HEGEL
TRAGEDY AND PHILOSOPHY
WITHOUT GUILT AND JUSTICE
EXISTENTIALISM, RELIGION, AND DEATH

Verse

GOETHE'S FAUST: A NEW TRANSLATION
CAIN AND OTHER POEMS
TWENTY-FIVE GERMAN POETS

Translated and Edited

EXISTENTIALISM FROM DOSTOEVSKY TO SARTRE
JUDAISM AND CHRISTIANITY: ESSAYS BY LEO BAECK
PHILOSOPHIC CLASSICS, 2 *volumes*
RELIGION FROM TOLSTOY TO CAMUS
HEGEL: TEXTS AND COMMENTARY
HEGEL'S POLITICAL PHILOSOPHY
MARTIN BUBER'S I AND THOU

Nietzsche Translations

THE PORTABLE NIETZSCHE
(*Thus Spoke Zarathustra, Twilight of the Idols,
The Antichrist, and Nietzsche contra Wagner*)
BASIC WRITINGS OF NIETZSCHE
(*The Birth of Tragedy, Beyond Good and Evil,
On the Genealogy of Morals, The Case of Wagner, Ecce Homo*)
THE WILL TO POWER
THE GAY SCIENCE

Buddhist relief, Borobodur.

Angkor.

RELIGIONS
in Four Dimensions

Existential and Aesthetic, Historical and Comparative

Text and Photographs
by
WALTER KAUFMANN

READER'S DIGEST PRESS

Distributed by Thomas Y. Crowell Company

New York
1976

Buddha, Lopburi, 12th century.

Copyright 1976 in all countries of the International Copyright Union by Walter Kaufmann. All rights reserved. First Edition. First published in 1976 in the United States by Reader's Digest Press, 200 Park Avenue, New York, New York 10017. Published simultaneously in Canada by Fitzhenry & Whiteside, Limited, Toronto. Printed and bound in Japan.
ISBN: 0–88349–104–4 (Cloth edition)
ISBN: 0–88349–105–2 (Paper edition)

Grateful acknowledgment is made to Doubleday & Company Inc., New York for permission to use the following copyrighted material: Chapter VII from *The Faith of a Heretic* (1961) by Walter Kaufmann. Copyright 1960, 1961 by Walter Kaufmann.

Grateful acknowledgment is made to The New American Library, Inc., New York for permission to use the following copyrighted material: Selected poems from *Cain and other Poems* by Walter Kaufmann. Copyright 1962, 1971, 1975 by Walter Kaufmann.

LIBRARY OF CONGRESS CATALOGING IN PUBLICATION DATA
Kaufmann, Walter Arnold.
  Religions in four dimensions.
  Bibliography: p.
  Includes index.
  1. Religions. 2. Arts and religion. I. Title.
BL80.2.K38   200   76–15367
ISBN 0–88349–104–4
ISBN 0–88349–105–2 pbk.

ORIGINATED, EDITED AND PRODUCED BY VISUAL BOOKS, INC.,
342 MADISON AVENUE, NEW YORK, NEW YORK 10017.

For Hazel,
with whom
I saw most of these sights

and Nicolas,
without whom
I might never have written this book

Prah Khan, Angkor, 12th century.

Buddhist fresco, Anuradhapura, Ceylon.

CONTENTS

Lingraja temple, Bhubaneshwar.

PROLOGUE

1

This book is a love child, born without the benefit of the clergy. It was begotten by love of men, women, and children in Asia who are poor and know suffering; love of Jews who now are dead, but who showed me religion at its best; love of images that haunt me and should haunt others, too.

The affair began innocently when I was five and was given a book written by Dhan Gopal Mukerji: *Kari the Elephant.* I was enchanted by India and read some of Mukerji's other books. In the prologue of *The Faith of a Heretic* (1961) I have related briefly how at twelve I formally abjured Protestantism and immersed myself in Judaism. But I did not mention how at thirteen I read Hermann Hesse's *Siddhartha* and came to think of the religions of India as profound alternatives to Judaism and Christianity. Martin Buber's books played some part in "saving" me from the East by focusing on religious *experience* in Judaism.

For many people the religion in which they are raised *is* religion, and they take no deep interest in other religions. Even those to whom their religion means a great deal rarely know much about its history. They are too close to it to see it as a whole, in depth, in three dimensions, not to speak of four. And religious people used to take for granted that other religions were simply wrong. Then it became fashionable to suppose that all the great religions agree on essentials. This claim, like other dogmas, was not examined closely in the light of facts. The usual approaches to religion are curiously blind. One refuses to see the major religions as alternatives that challenge us to make a choice. Yet Moses and Jesus, Zarathustra and Muhammad presented this challenge in the clearest terms, and we cannot begin to understand the religions of the East as long as we shut our eyes to the ways in which most teachers and scriptures condemn some ways and recommend others. Religions need to be seen as a whole, as living bodies that develop in relation to each other.

Becoming immersed in Judaism in Berlin in the nineteen thirties, I did not find it difficult to discover that. I could hardly have thought that all the great religions agreed. Reading Jewish history, one cannot help being struck by religious persecution, nor would anyone studying church history come to the conclusion that all the major Christian teachers have always agreed on essentials. Moreover, Judaism in Nazi Germany was not merely a matter of reading about the past. It was an existential experience that involved my whole being.

I was fortunate in getting to know both of the leading figures of German Jewry during that period, Leo Baeck and Martin Buber. They were very impressive men, but did not agree. Baeck was a liberal rabbi and not a Zionist. What was then called liberal in Germany was called conservative in the United States. Baeck observed the dietary laws and the sabbath and preached in synagogues in which men and women sat separately. Buber had a Gentile German wife, did not observe the traditional religious customs, and was a prominent Zionist.

Note: marginal reference numbers refer to color plates.

After I graduated from a German *Gymnasium* in the spring of 1938, I visited Palestine, then a British mandate, took many photographs, and returned to Berlin, where I enrolled in the "academy for the science of Judaism" (*Lehranstalt für die Wissenschaft des Judentums*). Here Baeck, whom I had known for five years, was one of my teachers, and here I also studied some Talmud—in the original. In the fall, I visited Rabbi Rudolf Seligsohn, a second cousin who had been my excellent teacher in Judaica some years back and now had a congregation in Bonn, and it was then that in a museum in nearby Cologne I saw for the first time some Eastern art. This was a profound experience that opened up a whole new dimension for me. A wooden sculpture of a Japanese Buddhist, seated, in meditation, proved unforgettable.

At seventeen I emigrated to the United States, majored in philosophy in college, minored in history, and also took courses in comparative religion, the philosophy of religion, and the psychology of religion. My graduate study was interrupted by military service, but in the spring of 1948 I began to teach annual courses in the philosophy of religion at Princeton. Ten years later I published *Critique of Religion and Philosophy*, arguing that the importance of beliefs was widely overestimated, that theology was one of the worst aspects of religion, and that it was wrong to dissociate religion from experience, as was then still customary. Now that battle, which seemed almost hopeless at the time, is won, and even my suggestion that Buddhism is in many ways much more attractive than Christianity no longer seems outrageous.

By then I had resumed contact with Baeck and Buber. Baeck died in 1956 after I had completed at his request English translations of some of his most interesting essays. These translations were published in 1958 under the title *Judaism and Christianity*. The essay that had long impressed me most was "Romantic Religion." Looking back now, it seems obvious how much one passage in particular was inscribed in my soul by the experience of the thirties and forties:

> A good deal of church history is the history of all the things which neither hurt nor encroached upon this piety, all the outrages and all the baseness which this piety was able to tolerate. . . . And a spirit is characterized not only by what it does but, no less, by what it permits. . . . The Christian religion . . . has been able to maintain silence about so much that it is difficult to say what has been more pernicious in the course of time: the intolerance that committed the wrongs or the indifference that beheld them unperturbed (275).

Baeck was a very soft-spoken man whose politeness was legendary, and he struck many people as a saintly figure. It is only in retrospect that I realize how much the pages that follow owe to him. The sentences just quoted certainly illuminate some aspects of my treatment of Hinduism, for example.

A dozen years later, in 1970, I published a new English version of Martin Buber's *I and Thou*. Our differences are more obvious than any similarities, but against the theologians of his time Buber championed the experience without which religion is but dust and ashes. In a way I work in a tradition. Yet this book breaks new ground; it attempts to do some things that have not been done before.

2

There is no subject more important than religion. It involves the most fateful questions, to which different religions give different answers. The way religion has usually been taught, from Sunday school to college, one might hardly notice that. As a result, many, if not most, people who have gone to universities know scarcely anything about religion. They may say that it is, of course, very important, but they obviously feel that it can be safely ignored. I feel that those who close their eyes to the great religions are thoughtless and, in effect, refuse to think about alternative answers to some of the most crucial questions.

This book offers a new approach to religion. It tells a story and could even be called biographical, for it relates the lives of the major religions. The way we get to know individuals is through their lives, whether they are human beings, nations, or religions. In the case of the dead everybody knows this. Michelangelo at twenty is only a small part, a segment of Michelangelo; nor is Picasso, Shaw, or Russell at ninety the whole man. We need to know the life or, since completeness is impossible and all knowledge involves selection, at least highlights that give some idea of the whole development.

That leaves open the question of whether it makes sense to deal with ten religions in one book. Plutarch, the great Greek biographer, discovered in the first century A.D. in his celebrated *Parallel Lives* how juxtaposition can add a dimension. That might be a good argument for considering two or three religions in one book, not ten. Actually, I am devoting two chapters each to five religions—Judaism, Christianity, Islam, Hinduism, and Buddhism—and one chapter to Zoroastrianism, while several other religions are considered more briefly. And there is ample precedent for taking up all or most of the major religions in one volume. Still, my approach is unusual.

The focus is on Asia, from Mount Sinai on a peninsula in the far west to Mount Fuji on an island in the far east. As we move east from Sinai, the book is almost a single story, certainly not ten. For no religion is an island, and each has defined itself in relation to others.

One reason why this is not a commonplace is that the first major attempt to construct a single story got off to a wrong start. In the early nineteenth century, Hegel, the German philosopher who impressed his historical sense on generations of scholars, believed that civilization had come from the East. From a German point of view this made sense. Athens is farther east than Berlin, and Mesopotamia is still farther east. Hegel's vastly influential account of world history began with China, then went on to India, then very briefly to Egypt and the Near East, and thence to the Greeks, the Romans, and the Holy Roman Empire of the German nation, which Napoleon had destroyed in 1806, in the Battle of Jena—the city where Hegel was just then completing his first book. Unfortunately for this brilliant scheme, India owed virtually nothing to China, and the ancient civilizations of the Near East owed nothing to either, being very much older than both cultures. Hence, as scholars developed more respect for facts, attempts to construct a single story were given up. Either one dealt with one religion only—preferably with only one aspect or phase of that—or one compiled an encyclopedic work in which all the major religions were taken up without much attention to their interaction.

But if we start in the Near East and move toward the Far East, the pieces fall into place. The pyramids of Egypt were almost as old during the age of the Upanishads, the Buddha, and Confucius, as the Buddha and Confucius would be today. In India, the Buddha is the first historical person of whose character and thought we have some knowledge and whom we can date with some confidence; in China the same consideration applies to Confucius, who was his younger contemporary. For ancient Israel, we have an unbroken record of independently confirmed dates at least as far back as the thirteenth century B.C., and a wealth of characters who come to life for us. In terms of Biblical history, 500 B.C., when the Buddha and Confucius flourished, is late.

It makes sense therefore to begin with Mount Sinai, taking up ancient Israel first, down to the Babylonian exile in the sixth century B.C. Then we turn to Zarathustra and ancient Iran, for Zarathustra probably lived in the sixth century just before the

Persians conquered Babylonia and allowed the Jews to return. Zarathustra is worth taking up, not merely because his religion still survives, but above all because he greatly influenced Christianity, Islam, and even later Buddhism. We continue our story with Judaism after the exile, stressing Israel's response to Zarathustra. Then two chapters on Christianity are followed by two on Islam. As Christianity was influenced by Judaism and Zoroastrianism, Islam was influenced by all three. And the Muslims conquered much of India.

Even up to this point, where we really have a single story, the historical dimension is not the only one to be considered. Every chapter is four-dimensional, the other dimensions being comparative, existential, and aesthetic. Since the great religious figures always rejected much, we do not begin to understand them until we compare what they offered with what they repudiated. Their refrain was always, even if they did not use the words of the New Testament: *You have been told this, but I say unto you . . .*

For a number of reasons, this polemical element is not fashionable, and a great many people manage not to see it. Religious people used to feel quite sure that other religions were wrong. Moses, Jesus, and Muhammad; Augustine, Aquinas, and Luther; and most of our forefathers had few doubts on that score. Since the age of the Enlightenment, however, and especially during the second half of the twentieth century, religion has come under so much fire from non-believers that believers have come to feel that they had better stick together. They are like the last survivors on a life raft who conclude that they had better put old quarrels aside.

Another factor that helps us understand the prevalent attitude is what in *Without Guilt and Justice* (1973) I have called decidophobia, the fear of fateful decisions. Autonomy consists in making such decisions with our eyes open to alternatives that we compare, but this is felt to be as frightening as standing on a peak without support, and most people therefore have recourse to various strategies that allow them not to look at alternatives. In the case at hand there are several popular ways of doing that.

First, one can study one religion from the inside, making sure that one never sees too much of it at one time, and avoid consideration of its rivals. Something like this has been done in Sunday schools for generations, but not only there. Then, one can study several religions, judging all of them from an unquestioned point of view. It may be some version of Christianity that furnishes the unexamined standard, or perhaps a view that one considers "scientific" and hence certain. Either way, one stands above the combat and does not experience what one studies as alternatives to one's own views. Two examples may prove helpful.

When Robert Ernest Hume, whose translation of *The Thirteen Principal Upanishads* is very respectable and still widely used, wrote *The World's Living Religions*, he gave marks to each of them. Among "Elements of Strength in Christianity" he included "The character and the teachings of its founder, Jesus Christ," while among "Elements of Weakness in Buddhism" he listed what he called, without any explanation, "Its founder's moral handicaps." Hinduism fared even worse at his hands. On the title page, Hume was identified as "Professor of the History of Religions, Union Theological Seminary, New York," and before World War II all this was considered quite as natural and reasonable as his failure to discover any "Elements of Weakness in Christianity" except for five points that were introduced each time with a phrase not used elsewhere: "The tendency in certain sections of Christendom to . . ." for example, "relapse from the founder's lofty ideal . . ." This was so blatant that after World War II it would not quite do any more, and in a revised, posthumous edition in 1959 the slur on the Buddha was omitted. White writers have to be more tactful now when writing about Asians. But if an Asian writes in comparable fashion about

Christianity, that is not felt to be embarrassing, and few readers even realize that they confront another way of avoiding any open-minded, open-eyed examination of alternatives.

Sri Aurobindo is widely considered a twentieth-century Indian saint and one of the great mystics of our time. In his book *The Upanishads: Texts, Translations, and Commentaries,* he says apodictically, without offering any argument, that when Jesus "said 'I and my Father are one,'" he was merely "expressing the deep truth that the human self and the divine self are identical" (which is the crux of the Upanishads), while the evangelists were "men of very narrow culture and scope of thought" who "misunderstood his deepest sayings." In other words, we need not choose between Christianity and Hinduism, for Jesus agreed with the Upanishads, and Christians who fail to see this are simply unable to understand their own religion.

Instead of giving any evidence for his interpretation, Aurobindo reciprocates the traditional condescension of the British toward the Indians by exclaiming: "And yet how plain the meaning is to the Oriental intelligence!" And, still in his remarks "On Translating the Upanishads," Aurobindo, who had started his career as a fervent nationalist, explains his omission of most of the texts, from which he merely offers skimpy selections, by saying that Europeans and Americans could not possibly understand most of the material, there being very little that "the West is fit to hear." We shall encounter Aurobindo again in connection with the six systems of Hinduism and, later on, in the discussion of Zen. Here it will suffice to note, first, how both Hume and Aurobindo manage to eschew the comparative dimension. Neither sees the challenge of alternatives.

Second, it is striking how impolite both of them are, and how most readers would not even notice this if one did not call attention to it. After all, Christians have long spoken far worse of Jews and Muslims as well as Indians, and to denigrate "the West" is fashionable now. But note how close Aurobindo comes to Paul Elmer More, who suggested a generation earlier that the Buddha was a stuttering Christ who said badly what only Christ could say well, and to European scholars who have claimed that the Indians do not understand their own doctrines, which are perfectly plain to a Western intelligence, or that an Indian could not possibly understand most of the Bible.

Hume and Aurobindo may appear to be extreme examples. In fact, both of them were exceptionally cosmopolitan. Hume was born in India, and Aurobindo grew up in England. In the past, most of the religious figures have spoken much more roughly of religions not their own. For religions have usually experienced each other as rivals, and as long as we ignore this whole dimension we falsify them.

One can concentrate on the historical dimension and tell a story, paying some attention to the polemics of the past, and still avoid seeing the religions as alternatives and as so many challenges to us. I have tried throughout to be comparative as well as historical. The key to this effort is the third dimension, which is existential. But before I explain that, something still needs to be said about the way our story continues once we get to India.

3

Obviously, Judaism, Zoroastrianism, Christianity, and Islam can be considered in sequence. One only has to keep in mind that a religion does not come to an untimely end as soon as a religion appears that claims to supplant it. The story of Judaism must be continued beyond New Testament times, even as the story of Christianity does not end with the writing of the Koran. But when we come to India, we have to make a fresh start, beginning with the Vedas, which were composed in Old Testament times. Then we proceed to the Upanishads and eventually to the caste system, the Gita, and Gandhi. Gandhi's reading of the Gita, which I consider here at some length, illustrates an approach very different from my own. It shows how religious people very frequently interpret texts, reading their own most cherished doctrines into books they love. This is not a peculiarity of Gandhi or of Hinduism. Jewish and Christian illustrations are given earlier in this book. But Gandhi needs to be seen not only in the context of Hinduism but also against the background of Christianity, Jainism, and Buddhism.

It is to Jainism, Sikhism, and above all Buddhism that we turn next, eventually tracing the development of Buddhism not only in India but also in the Far East, especially in China and Japan. Confucius and Lao-tze are considered in detail to allow a better understanding of what happened to Buddhism in China.

Some scholars nowadays believe that bronze may have been cast in what today is northern Thailand before it was cast in the Middle East. Others believe that it may yet prove possible to find some continuity between the culture of the cave paintings in southern France and northern Spain that may go as far back as 20,000 B.C. and the origins of civilization in the Near East. But movements from east to west or west to east in prehistoric times do not affect my argument. I would even be willing to argue elsewhere that Indian thought influenced Plato. After all, the Persians had conquered part of India before they tried to conquer Greece and were stopped at Marathon and, ten years later, at Salamis; and Greek philosophy began in the Persian empire, on the coast of Asia Minor. The points of similarity between Pythagoras and Plato on the one hand, and Indian thought on the other, are too numerous to be due to accident. I also think that it is highly probable that Buddhism had a slight influence on the New Testament. I only wish it had been greater. Any notion that culture *always* moves from west to east would be silly.

Ashoka, who ruled India in the third century B.C., said in an inscription that he sent Buddhist missionaries to Syria, Egypt, North Africa, and Macedonia. Monasticism may have its origins in India, and Buddhism may have affected some Jewish sects and the Gospels, but the West did not accept Buddhism, while Southeast Asia and the Far East did.

What is obvious is surely that Islam has to be understood against the background of Judaism, Zoroastrianism, and Christianity; that religion in India owes little to China, and that Buddhism spread east from India, first to China and then to Japan. In Asia the movement of religions was mainly from west to east.

4

My primary concern throughout is existential. I mean that it is not with beliefs and speculations, with theology and metaphysics, but with humanity. And I feel strongly that without this dimension even a good historical and comparative study would lack depth.

Too often, students of religion fail to ask what different religions do to human beings. Admirers of the Gita and of Zen often overlook all four dimensions. They ignore the historical context of both. They lack the comparative perspective and fail to see how the Gita was in some ways a response to Buddhism, and how Ch'an in China and Zen in Japan were revolts against the Indian Buddhist scriptures. Nor do they see how the Gita canonized caste, and how Zen turned a pacifist doctrine into the religion of the samurai. And their aestheticism comes nowhere near exploring the fourth dimension.

This book is mindful of the limits of all bookishness. Its treatment of Christianity may raise some hackles because people are still more sensitive about the work of scholars than they are about the *obiter dicta* of poets and mystics who are forgiven almost anything. But the handling of Christianity is of a kind with that of Hinduism and Buddhism. Religion is not merely or even mainly a matter of what people say or write in books but also of what they do in following their religion, or of what religion does to them.

While scholarly prose can contribute a great deal to the exploration of this dimension, it needs to be supplemented. One chapter, "The Third Face of India," tries to bring to life the human realities by using verse. But no reader has to wait until he gets that far to come face to face with the existential dimension. The pictures bear witness of it; their function is not exclusively aesthetic.

Some pictures illustrate points in the text or show something that is discussed, but many, if not most, are meant to convey something nowhere said in words. The text should lead to a much fuller understanding of the pictures, and the pictures to a fuller understanding of the text.

Kierkegaard, in the middle of the nineteenth century, contrasted the "existential" and the "aesthetic" as alternatives. The former he associated with commitment, the aesthetic with the attitude of the spectator who thinks in such categories as the beautiful and the profound without feeling challenged to make a choice. Unquestionably, one can look at the pictures in this book in a spirit that is aesthetic in this sense, and there is no denying that I looked for beauty and tried to enhance it by obtaining the best light and composition. How could I protest if anyone merely found my pictures, or many of them, beautiful? And yet it must be obvious that my concern is not exclusively aesthetic any more than Rembrandt's, Goya's, Daumier's, or Käthe Kollwitz's. My work is very different from theirs in almost every way, and they are also different from each other, for that matter. I only mean to point out that I share with them an existential concern or, if you prefer, a humanistic bias or—to return to the image with which I began—a love of men, women, and children.

5

Still, the pictures are not propaganda—not even in the admirable sense in which one might apply that word to some of Goya's, and Daumier's, and Kollwitz's graphic art. They are not part of a campaign against great social evils. They mean rather to bring into focus two dimensions that are often overlooked in the study of religions, the existential and the aesthetic.

About religion in general and about some particular religions, many people have preconceptions that are based on prejudice and not on any painstaking examination of the evidence. It therefore seems best to take note of some of these prejudices and to show how they are wrong. But I myself write in an existential situation and do not sit above the contest. I am a human being among others, and what I write about is not inconsequential notions that one might review and judge but the most fateful ideas that have deeply affected the lives of people. Out of many of the pictures human beings look at us or, even if their eyes are not upon us, challenge us. They are different from us, whatever we may look like, but as human as we are. And there is a continuity between the faces that confront us in the flesh and those in stone and bronze. They create a mood quite different from that in which religions are usually studied. They do not allow us even for a moment to survey the scene from Mount Olympus, or to maintain an antiquarian stance, or to be satisfied with the historical and comparative dimensions.

It is easy to admire scriptures and forget about the lives of people. It is easy to live in two dimensions. But what is the point of considering religion if it does not open our eyes to more?

6

"Aesthetic" is a term that also brings to mind art. Many of the pictures show beautiful buildings, stone sculptures, bronzes, and paintings, and two chapters deal with the relation of six religions to art. There is no need here to anticipate my conclusions about the relation of art and religion except for one point. I consider the impact of religion on art and the ways in which art illuminates religion vastly more important than theology.

Most philosophy of religion is still restricted to theological questions, like problems about proofs for God's existence. The ensuing discussions are generally parochial and utterly blind to the historical and comparative dimensions. One talks about "God" as if all men, regardless of their religion and the age they lived in, had always meant the same thing when they used some term like that. Intellectually, most philosophy of religion is sterile. Morally, it often seems to be a pastime that diverts some academics from hearing the voice of their brothers' blood.

It is surely unusual for a philosopher to include in a book on religion two chapters on art and a chapter of verse. What may be even more startling is the inclusion of hundreds of my own photographs, most of them in color. Here I do not seem to stand in a tradition but attempt something altogether new. Let me conclude this prologue by explaining why.

Occasionally, though not often, I have shown guests color slides that included a few Buddhas or heads of Buddhas. When I was asked where these sculptures were, my answer, "right here in this room," was met with disbelief. Photography can help people to see more.

Showing friends two pictures of a Japanese Noh mask, I have found them unwilling to believe that both were of the same mask, even if they had seen the mask itself. I had fallen in love with the mask and had bought it because its expressions, which change as one moves it, are so extraordinary. Yet one can see only one expression at a time. Photography enables us to see four on one page.

168–171

Some few people have such fine visual memories that they can summon up at will what they saw years ago. I need photographs, but with their help I can live in many dimensions. I naturally saw the people whom I photographed, but in some cases only for a second. Then they disappeared, and there were others. In many places, and especially in India, I kept seeing more than I could possibly absorb, and could not meditate on faces that were gone almost as soon as seen. Photographs of them allow me to live with these people until they become part of my world.

Often I photograph what does not last, perhaps a fleeting expression, a momentary grouping, or a sculpture that seems to be timeless with its moss or lichen and discolored stone, like the Buddha at Borobodur in central Java; but when I returned a few years later it had fallen victim to the multi-million-dollar restoration of the site. Even what seems timeless generally does not last, and it is only in pictures that it survives at least for a time.

142,144

One motive for taking pictures is quite independent of results. When one film I took in India was lost, it was no total loss. Taking the photographs had been a wonderful experience that I vividly remember. "Never let the fruits of work be your motive," says the Gita, but its ethos of doing the duty of one's caste, regardless of the outcome, is not mine. Part of my joy in taking pictures is that this is not in any way my duty. It is rather like writing poetry. So is my other writing.

Crossing the Atlantic in a hurricane in January, 1939, as I emigrated to the United States, I had no camera and wrote poems instead, which I had not done for a few months. Now my experience is generally the opposite when I travel. I stop writing and take pictures. To me it seems that I need to do something creative, but somebody else might feel that there is something wrong with always needing to *do* something. Would it not be better to sit still sometimes, absorbed in contemplation? The miracle of photography is its fusion of creative work and contemplation. It is a way of seeing creatively. Photography can involve the discovery of a way of seeing in which the You confronting me reveals itself. That it is possible much later to share this revelation with others is another miracle.

What I am trying to say in this book could not be said in any other way, neither in words alone nor in images alone. Mixed media are in fashion, and yet this mixture of a scholarly text that aims to make the reader see the great religions in some new ways with photographs of the Third World, of its art, temples, and people, including children who have never thought about religion, is not very much like any previous blend. Does it make sense nevertheless?

The point of philosophy and scholarship, as I understand them (see section 5 of my *Critique*) is also the point of photography: to see better and to help others to do likewise. That is not the usual view of philosophy and scholarship. Indeed much of it is a training in blindness, or at the very least a training in microscopy that keeps people from seeing things whole, in depth, in four dimensions. I have come to believe that the most important thing a scholar or a poet can hope or try to teach is vision or, to put the point more modestly, to see better. This book is part of a battle against blindness. Hence the pictures.

Bangkok.

Amenophis II, Karnak.

I
ANCIENT ISRAEL

Background—Egypt—Hammurabi—God—Moses—
The Chosen People—Political Influence—A Higher Law—
The Ideal Society—Called to Be Free

Step pyramid, Saqqara, 28th century B.C.

Until the nineteenth century, it was customary to consider the Old Testament as if it did not have any historical or literary background; it was studied as the revelation of God, as an absolute beginning, completely self-sufficient. In the eighteenth century, the sustained criticism of the Enlightenment led to a gradual decrease in respect for the Hebrew Scriptures, and interest in them diminished, too. But it was only after the publication of Darwin's *Origin of Species*, in 1859, that an altogether new approach to the Old Testament was widely accepted: an evolutionary approach that first broke down the unquestioned barrier between the Bible and its background, and eventually all but drowned the Bible in its background until no distinctive feature at all was perceived any more.*

A hundred years after the concept of evolution first gained wide currency, it has become easy to recognize the foolishness of some of the excesses perpetrated in its name. Some of these excesses actually antedate Darwin, but spread like wildfire as soon as they could feed on his ideas.

As far as any background is concerned, the crucial point that should never be forgotten in the history of ideas can be put into a single sentence: one may have been influenced profoundly by others and yet be strikingly original and even revolutionary.

What makes the study of history fascinating is, among other things, the perception of discontinuity in the context of continuity. The historically ignorant believe in absolute novelty; those with a smattering of history are apt to believe in no novelty at all; they are blinded by the discovery of similarities. Beyond that, however, lies the discovery of small, but sometimes crucial, differences.

Ancient Israel was deeply influenced by two older civilizations—probably the two oldest civilizations on the earth, excepting that of the so-called Cro-Magnon men who perished 20,000 years ago, leaving superb drawings of animals on the walls of some caves in southern France and northern Spain. The first high civilizations that seem to be continuous with subsequent cultures are probably those of Egypt and Mesopotamia, which can be traced back approximately to 4000 B.C.

The Old Testament emphasizes the relation of Israel to both cultures. It places the Garden of Eden near, if not in, Mesopotamia; it speaks of the Tower of Babel; and it relates that Abraham, the ancestor of Israel, was born and brought up in Ur of the Chaldeans. After leaving his native Mesopotamia, Abraham is said to have traveled widely in what later became the land of Israel, and he is also said to have visited Egypt. His grandson, Jacob, who was named Israel after his nocturnal struggle with an angel whom he defied, saying, "I will not let you go unless you bless me," is said to have migrated to Egypt with his children and his children's children. And the Bible relates that the children of Israel remained in Egypt for several generations before Moses, a Hebrew versed in the wisdom of Egypt, led them out of the land of slavery into the desert of Sinai where he gave them laws and precepts that set them apart from all the nations of the world. That was in the thirteenth century B.C., if not earlier.

1–8

In the next generation the Hebrews began their conquest of the promised land where they were to live, midway between Egypt and Mesopotamia. In 586 B.C. Nebuchadnezzar, king of Babylonia, sacked Jerusalem and led a large portion of the Jews into the so-called Babylonian exile, from which they were liberated by the Persians in

---

* With a few changes, this chapter has been taken over from Kaufmann, *The Faith of a Heretic*. The other fourteen chapters and the pictures have not been published before.

538 B.C. At that time, many of them returned to Israel and rebuilt their temple in Jerusalem—which was eventually destroyed by the Romans in A.D. 70.

That ancient Israel was deeply influenced by Egypt and the various Mesopotamian cultures, from the Sumerians down to the Babylonians and Assyrians, should therefore have been taken for granted long before archaeological discoveries and detailed comparisons left no doubt about it. But in fact it had not been taken for granted during the many centuries in which the approach to Scripture was theological and supernaturalistic rather than naturalistic and historical. The discovery of the historical background of ancient Israel was therefore accompanied by a militant sense of opposition to what had previously been believed, and—as often happens in such cases—it was pushed to utterly absurd extremes; it became the fashion to deny all originality to the Old Testament. This view is easily as fantastic as the assumption of earlier times that there was no connection at all between the Hebrew Scriptures and the cultures of Egypt and Mesopotamia.

8

The civilization of ancient Egypt is not only as old but also easily as remarkable as any the world has seen. If we date its approximate beginning around 4000 B.C., we find that it endured for about 4,000 years. The gigantic step pyramid at Saqqara, the world's first large stone structure, whose originality, verve, and power are still fascinating to behold, and the slightly later, still vaster pyramids at Giza were as old when the Parthenon and the other temples on the Acropolis in Athens were built as the Parthenon is today, but in Egypt magnificent temples were still built centuries after the completion of the Parthenon. Admirable paintings and sculptures were produced in Egypt over a period of more than 3,000 years.

If we compare Egypt with Israel, what strikes us first of all is the great difference; in many ways, ancient Israel might well be understood as the diametric opposite of ancient Egypt. In Egypt, *sculpture and painting* flourished; in Israel, both were expressly prohibited—according to tradition, by Moses himself. In Egypt, man's concern with the *life after death* was as intense as it ever was anywhere: the pyramids were tombs; the finest paintings and many of the most remarkable sculptures were found in the tombs in the Valley of the Kings, across the Nile from Luxor and Karnak, hundreds of miles upstream from Giza and Saqqara; and the treasures found in the tomb of Tutankhamen, a relatively insignificant king, give us some idea of the contents of other tombs which were robbed thousands of years ago. In ancient Israel, we find no concern whatsoever with the afterlife: for Moses, death is the end, and it is only in the very latest passages of the Old Testament, in Hellenistic times, that we find a few intimations of immortality. In Egypt, we find *a profusion of gods*, many of them half human, half animal; in Israel, we find none of all that. Moses expressly repudiates all belief in many gods.

These three differences are not only obvious but they far outweigh any similarities. For all that, there are continuities. First, we find in Egypt, albeit restricted to a special class, a love of learning and respect for wisdom. Here the difference in similarity was expressed in a single imperative by Moses: "You shall be unto me a kingdom of priests." And again: "You shall be holy." Not one class but all. Every man is called upon to make something of himself. Perhaps this was the most revolutionary idea of world history. In the countries to which the Old Testament has spoken either directly or by way of Luther's revival of the call for "the priesthood of all believers," this idea may appear to be a commonplace; elsewhere—for example, in Egypt, not only in Moses' time but also in Luther's and ours—one can appreciate the revolutionary impact of these words.

Freud's desk, London.

Secondly, we find in Egyptian architecture and sculpture an embodiment of the sublime that has never been surpassed. In parts of the Old Testament this sublimity has been transmuted into prose and poetry. This point does not depend on any ambiguity of "sublime." The similarity is genuine and deep and could be circumscribed in other words. Perhaps nowhere else in the ancient world, and nowhere at all except under the influence of the Hebrew Bible, do we encounter such a fusion of austere simplicity and overwhelming power. (The King James Bible and the Douay Version, with their more ornate and baroque flair for magnificence and rhetoric, are misleading in this respect; and some modern versions go out of their way *not* to be sublime.)

There remains one similarity which, since its relatively recent discovery, has attracted far more attention than any other: in the fourteenth century B.C., according to the accepted chronology, there was a monotheistic Pharaoh in the eighteenth dynasty in Egypt. After ascending to the throne as Amenophis IV, he renounced and forbade the worship of Amon and the other gods, changed his name to Akhenaton, insisted that only Aton should be worshiped, and moved the capital to what today is known as Tell el-Amarna—the place where some remarkable sculptures and reliefs and a fine hymn to Aton were unearthed by Ludwig Borchardt around 1900, almost 3,300 years later. The notion that the Hebrews might have acquired their monotheism from the heretical Pharaoh was too intriguing not to have been taken up by at least a few writers, of whom Freud, the founder of psychoanalysis and himself a Jew, is by far the best known. He was not deterred by the established fact that Akhenaton's innovations barely survived his early death and were ruthlessly suppressed long before the end of the fourteenth century; indeed, the very name of Aton was scratched out on all accessible works of the period. Freud speculated that, for this very reason, a surviving adherent of the Aton cult might have found himself forced to leave Egypt and, if he wanted adherents, to turn to another people. Freud himself thought of his work on this subject, *Moses and Monotheism*, as perhaps no more than "a historical novel"; and the details of his argument do not stand up.

There is also the possibility that Akhenaton derived his monotheism from the Hebrews whose presence in Egypt at that time is claimed by the Bible and admitted by Freud and most scholars. Immanuel Velikovsky has argued that Akhenaton lived long after Moses. But even if he did not, it seems plain that he could not have influenced Moses.

Again the difference in similarity should not be overlooked. Akhenaton's monotheism consists of a quantitative reduction of traditional polytheism: of the many traditional gods he recognizes only one, Aton, the sun. It is the sun that awakens all life and that alone deserves worship. In the Five Books of Moses, any worship of the sun is scorned. The word used for the sun, *shemesh*, is written just like the word for servant, *shamash* (the vowels not being written); and in the creation story in Genesis the sun is created together with the moon to serve man as an instrument that makes possible the calculation of days, months, and years.

Hebrew monotheism cannot be understood as a quantitative reduction of any traditional polytheism or as an exclusive declaration of loyalty to one of the established gods; all the established gods of the nations are set aside, and the whole lot of them is considered beneath comparison with God, who not only does not happen to be identified with the sun but who is not at all an object in this world. No object in this world deserves worship: not the sun and moon and stars, which Plato, many centuries later, still considered divine; not the Pharaoh nor any other human being; nor any animal. Only God who is utterly unlike anything in the world. Man alone, according to the First Book of Moses, is made in God's image and breathes his spirit. And that means every man and every woman, not just some king, emperor, or hero, or one family or people only.

Karnak.

On reflection, all this is so different from the religion of Akhenaton that no likelihood at all remains that Hebrew monotheism was derived from the worship of Aton. Moreover, it is "debatable"—as Professor John Wilson has noted in his preface to Akhenaton's famous hymn to Aton in *Ancient Near Eastern Texts Relating to the Old Testament* (Pritchard, 1950, 1955)—whether the Amarna religion can really be "called monotheistic." For only the Pharaoh and his family worshiped Aton, while the courtiers worshiped Akhenaton himself. Incidentally, "the great majority of Egyptians was ignorant of or hostile to the new faith" (369).

Finally, few Pharaohs, if any, were so possessed with the desire to make images of the things in this world, from reliefs of the disk of the sun to the beautiful birds and flowers found on the floor of the Pharaoh's palace and the magnificent sculptured likenesses of the Pharaoh and his family and the men at his court, which now grace the museums of Cairo and Berlin.

Our archaeological discoveries in Egypt leave the originality of the religion of Moses as stunning as it ever seemed. The experience of Egypt may have awakened the Hebrews to a haunting sense of the sublime, to dissatisfaction with the ephemeral, to respect for learning—and to a lasting revulsion against any concern with the afterlife, against polytheism, and against idolatry and any form at all of sculpture.

We must leave open the possibility that faith in the God of Abraham antedated the sojourn in Egypt. What the Bible claims, and what we have no good reason to doubt, is that the Hebrew religion was hammered out in response to the experience of Egypt—not by way of accepting the religion of Egypt but rather as an enduring reply to it.

9

Several generations before the Hebrews went to Egypt, Abraham is said to have come from Mesopotamia, and around 1900 it was fashionable in some quarters to juxtapose *Bibel and Babel*—to cite the title of an essay of that time—and to deny the originality of the Bible. One of the motifs in the birth story of Moses is encountered earlier in a story about a Mesopotamian king, Sargon, and the story of Noah and the flood bears some marked similarities to the far earlier Mesopotamian epic of Gilgamesh. Such literary influences are undeniable but, if one stops to think about them, of rather limited importance. Nobody would think of denying the originality of Shakespeare, Goethe, or Sophocles on similar grounds. What matters is how such motifs are used.

Far more interesting is the question whether the so-called Law of Moses was significantly influenced by the Code of Hammurabi. Hammurabi was a king of Babylonia, probably from 1728–1686 B.C. He may be the man referred to in Genesis 14 as "Amraphel, king of Shinar." His law code was discovered in the winter of 1901–1902 in the course of excavations at Susa (the Shushan of Esther and Daniel) in southern Persia, where an Elamite raider had taken the diorite stela about the twelfth century B.C. The stela, topped by a bas-relief showing Hammurabi with the sun god Shamash, was found by French archaeologists who took it to the Louvre in Paris.

The code is not the earliest code of laws known to us, but in its preservation and comprehensiveness it has no equal of comparable antiquity, save only the Law of Moses, which is younger. Hammurabi's laws are framed by a poetic prologue and epilogue and deal with the following matters: accusations, witnesses, and judges; theft and robbery; a military feudal system; field, garden, and house; tradesmen and female wine sellers; articles left with another person for safe-keeping; family relationships; injuries; ships; rents; and slaves. In this central portion there are no digressions, and the arrangement is far more systematic than in the comparable sections of the Five Books of Moses. This, added to the many parallels in detail, led early scholars to underestimate the striking originality of the Mosaic legislation. Confronted with such an unusually significant and unexpected discovery, these scholars could scarcely have been expected to react differently; and the tremendous influence of the Code of Hammurabi on the Law of Moses cannot be doubted. Indeed, Hammurabi and his successors succeeded in extending the influence of Babylonia as far as Palestine, and the cultural hegemony of Babylonia outlasted its political dominion. It would therefore be tedious to catalogue parallels or, for that matter, minor differences. Are there any *major* differences? Do we find any radically new point of departure in the Mosaic legislation?

The two central principles of Hammurabi's code are, first, *ius talionis* (the conception that justice in criminal cases consists in precise retaliation) and, second, that the law *is* a respecter of persons and that different standards must be applied to people of different social status. Both of these principles are anathema to most contemporary penologists, and retaliation is widely considered all but synonymous with the Law of Moses. The arguments of T. H. Green, Bernard Bosanquet, and other apologists for *ius talionis* notwithstanding, both of these principles have a common presupposition: they distinguish insufficiently between human beings and material objects. And the crucial difference between the Code of Hammurabi and the Law of Moses is that in the latter the unique worth of man as such is proclaimed and implicit—for the first time in human history.

The Code of Hammurabi recognizes three classes of people: an aristocracy, commoners, and slaves. Accordingly, it generally provides three kinds of punishment, depending, for example, on whether an injury has been inflicted on a member of the aristocracy, a commoner, or a slave. The slave is considered less as a human being than as a piece of property, and so are the sons and daughters even of a noble. The way in which the principle of retaliation is applied suggests that the body of the noble himself, too, is considered as essentially a material object.

Here are a few illustrations, accompanied in each case by a contrast with the Law of Moses. The man who has destroyed an eye or broken a bone of another man's slave has to pay one half his value; he merely has to compensate the owner for the damage done to his property. In the same vein, there is no penalty whatsoever for destroying an eye or breaking a bone of one's own slave. This should be compared with Exodus 21:20 and 21:26 ff. Here the man who as much as breaks a tooth of his own slave must let him go free for his tooth. In the Law of Moses, the slave is first of all a human being and has to be treated as such.

According to the Code of Hammurabi, if a man either helps a fugitive slave "escape through the city gate" or harbors him in his house "and has not brought him forth at the summons of the police, that householder shall be put to death" (15 ff.). Compare this with Deuteronomy 23:15 f.: "You shall not give up to his master a slave who has escaped from his master to you; he shall dwell with you, in your midst, in the place which he shall choose within one of your towns, where it pleases him best; you shall not oppress him."

In the Law of Moses, being a slave is an accidental condition. This is further emphasized by constant reminders that the children of Israel had been slaves in Egypt themselves and should therefore know how it feels to be a slave. On the Sabbath the slave, too, should rest, and every Sabbath thus becomes a celebration of the brotherhood and equality of human beings.

The contrast in this respect between Hammurabi and Moses is most neatly illustrated by Hammurabi's last law (282): "If a male slave has said to his master, 'You are not my master,' his master shall prove him to be his slave and cut off his ear." In Exodus 21 we find a faint but, no doubt, deliberate echo of this law—an echo that seems designed to bring out the deep difference between the two legislations: "When you buy a Hebrew servant, he shall serve six years, and in the seventh he shall go out free, for nothing. . . . But if the servant plainly says '. . . I will not go out free' . . . his master shall bore his ear through with an awl; and he shall serve him for life."

Hammurabi considers a man's children, too, not as human beings in their own right but as his property. If a man strikes the daughter of another man, "if that woman has died, they shall put his daughter to death" (210). A man's daughter may thus be put to death merely to impose a severe fine on the father. The fine becomes less severe if the woman killed in the first instance was the daughter of a commoner (one-half mina of silver); and if she was a slave, the fine is still lower (one-third mina).

Similarly, if a man builds a house for another man, and he builds it badly and the house collapses—if it causes the death of the owner, the builder is to be put to death; but "if it has caused the death of a son of the owner of the house, they shall put the son of that builder to death" (229 ff.).

To such provisions there is no parallel in the Law of Moses, which insists, with striking originality, that there is only one God and that all men alike are made in his image and therefore altogether incommensurable with things or money.

The law of talion, to be sure, appears in the Law of Moses, too, but in an almost polemical manner. The Mosaic phrase, "an eye for an eye," might be said to conceal a revaluation of Hammurabi's values. Consider the three Old Testament passages in which the phrase occurs, and the first two will make plain the new spirit, while the third brings out an interesting continuity.

The first occurrence of "life for life, eye for eye, tooth for tooth" is in Exodus 21, where it is immediately followed by the provision already cited: "If he knocks out his servant's or his maid's tooth, he shall let them go free for the tooth's sake." This provision shows immediately what is amply borne out by the entire Law of Moses, that the principle of retaliation was never applied mechanically and in accordance with the letter of the phrase. Rather, the emphasis was on the spirit; to wit, that an injury is an injury and that the law is no respecter of persons. Or, to put it positively, the words of the ancient, pre-Mosaic law of talion are employed to announce the new principle of equality before the law.

This interpretation is corroborated by the second Biblical passage in which the phrase occurs, in Leviticus 24, where the ancient formula is followed by this declaration: "You shall have one law for the stranger and for the native; for I am the Lord your God."

The third passage, finally, in Deuteronomy 19, echoes and expands a similar law in the Code of Hammurabi:

> If a malicious witness rises against any man to speak evil of him . . . the judges shall inquire diligently, and if the witness . . . has accused his brother falsely, then you shall do to him as he had meant to do to his brother; so you shall purge the evil from your midst. And the rest shall hear, and fear, and shall never again commit any such evil in your midst. Your eye shall not pity: it shall be life for life, eye for eye, tooth for tooth, hand for hand, foot for foot.

In Hammurabi's similar law, there is no reference to the intention of the witness; the man who accuses another of murder and then cannot prove his charge is put to death.

It is customary today to decry "an eye for an eye" as the epitome of legal barbarism. But to arrive at a judicious evaluation one should compare this last application of the ancient principle with, say, public morality in the United States of America during the decade after World War II: does it manifest higher moral standards when a United States senator who advised one of his colleagues to accuse as many people as possible to increase his chances of making at least some of his accusations stick was widely admired for his exemplary honesty and integrity?*

It is a popular myth that the principle of talion was left behind by Jesus' counsel that one should love one's enemies. In fact, the passage in which Jesus repudiates the ancient maxim, "an eye for an eye, and a tooth for a tooth" is the one in which he proceeds: "But I say to you, resist not evil . . . and if any one would sue you and take your coat, let him have your cloak as well." Where he rejects talion, he rejects the courts altogether; but where he speaks of the divine judgment, he returns to talion again and again; for example, to cite the Sermon on the Mount once more: "For with the judgment you judge, you will be judged; and the measure you give will be the measure you get" (Matthew 5 and 7). Elsewhere the New Testament goes far beyond both Moses and Hammurabi by holding out eternal punishment for calling a man a fool or for not accepting the teachings of Jesus' apostles.

Until quite recently, the idea of retaliation was all but inseparable from the Western sense of justice. Jesus' counsel to love one's enemies is on an entirely different plane; it is a maxim for personal relations, on a level with the Mosaic injunction, "If you meet your enemy's ox or his ass going astray, you shall bring it back to him" (Exodus 23:4; cf. also verse 5 and many similar passages). In personal relations Hammurabi did not advocate retaliation either, and in their law courts Christian countries have not distinguished themselves from non-Christian countries by renouncing the principle, "life for life," or the underlying conception of retaliation.

It is only in recent times that modern penologists have moved away from the whole conception of retaliation to advocate a penal system based on the primacy of reform. And it is instructive that so many Christian writers have opposed this recent development, which is associated mainly with stubbornly un-Christian thinkers like Jeremy Bentham and George Bernard Shaw, who emphasized the inefficiency of retaliation; with Friedrich Nietzsche, whose Zarathustra says, in his discourse "On the Tarantulas," *"that man be delivered from revenge, that is for me the bridge to the*

---

* So serious a charge should not be left at the level of insinuation. In his "Letter from Washington" in *The New Yorker* of April 22, 1950, Richard Rovere wrote, in part:

> These things have been accompanied by a sophisticated callousness and mischief-making that is probably most strikingly symbolized by Senator Robert A. Taft's advice to Senator McCarthy, given several weeks ago, to go on making his accusations, in the hope that "if one case doesn't work out, another one may." The temper of the period can be gauged not only by the fact that this remark received almost no censure in the press and none at all in Congress but also by the fact that Senator Taft, who always enjoyed a formidable and by no means undeserved reputation for fairness and probity, found it possible to make it in the first place.

A fuller treatment may be found in William S. White's *The Taft Story*, in the chapter on "The Sad, Worst Period." White's political orientation is very different from Rovere's, and his biography is informed by an enormous sympathy for Taft. His evaluation of Taft's attitude toward McCarthy, however, is well summed up by the chapter heading. (See especially 84–86, 193, and 219 f.)

Since Taft is the only senator in American history to have been honored with a huge public monument in Washington, D.C., comparable to those erected in honor of Washington, Jefferson, and Lincoln, this little footnote memorial seems appropriate—not as a posthumous indictment but as an invitation to reflect on different standards of public morality. For the monument does not honor his very dubious judgment—his isolationism during the early part of World War II or his assurance right after the war that, if only the OPA were abolished, prices would come down—but his supposedly exemplary integrity.

1

2

3

4

6

7

8

11

highest hopes"; and with Albert Camus, who tried to show in his "Reflections on the Guillotine" that "capital punishment . . . has always been a religious punishment" and is irreconcilable with humanism. A generation earlier, Shaw had pointed out in his Preface to *Major Barbara* that "the only editor in England who renounces punishment as radically wrong, also repudiates Christianity."

Pope Pius XII put the matter very clearly in 1953. He took issue with those "modern theories" which "fail to consider expiation of the crime committed . . . as the most important function of the punishment." Against them he cited Matthew 16:27 and Romans 2:6 and 13:4, concluding:

> The function of protection disappears completely in the after-life. The Omnipotent and All-Knowing Creator can always prevent the repetition of a crime by the interior moral conversion of the delinquent. But the supreme Judge, in His last Judgment, applies uniquely the principle of retribution. This, then, must be of great importance (117 f.).

To return to Hammurabi, the most striking parallel to the Law of Moses is not to be found in his legislation but in the prologue and epilogue where Hammurabi declares that he is giving his laws "in order that the strong might not oppress the weak, and that justice might be dealt the orphan and the widow."

10

The conceptions of God and of man in the Old Testament differ sharply from those current in Egypt and Mesopotamia: they are distinctive, novel, and original, and they have exerted a decisive influence on Western thought.

What distinguishes the God of the Old Testament from the gods of Egypt and Mesopotamia, the *Rigveda*, the *Iliad*, and the *Edda* is not by any means adequately suggested by the one word "monotheism." The difference is not merely quantitative; the gods of Homer are far more similar to human beings than they are to the God of the Old Testament. Unlike the gods of polytheism, and unlike the god Aton of Pharaoh Akhenaton, the God of ancient Israel is altogether separate from the world that he made, and he did not make it in human fashion, either after a fight with rival gods, demons, or dragons, or after a struggle with recalcitrant material, but in a manner as unique as he is himself—by saying, "Let there be." He is not an object among objects but the sovereign subject who engages in the pure unimpeded activity of speech.

He cannot be seen—he cannot be made the passive object of vision—but he speaks to man, actively. It is not possible to make an image of him: one cannot make an image of one who is essentially not an object. Nor does anything in nature represent or resemble him, unless it were man who is made in his image and who breathes his spirit.

This relation of God to man is of the essence of the religion of the Old Testament. This religion is not metaphysical, not speculative, not mythical: it does not concern itself with the nature of God as he may be, as it were, in himself; it does not speculate about his activities before the creation of the world or, quite generally, insofar as they do not affect man; it does not relate myths about his private life. The religion of the Old Testament is concerned with God only as a Thou or You, only as related to man, only as addressing man and as addressable by man. His deeds are a subject of concern and related only insofar as they constitute an address to man. Of other deeds, nothing is said; God is not an object of interest, study, or entertainment.

The conception of this God and his relation to man leads to a revolutionary new conception of man. Neither man in general nor any kind or race of men is a brother or cousin of the apes that so closely resemble him, or of any other animal or object in nature. Having been created in the image of a God who transcends nature, and breathing his spirit, man is raised out of nature and endowed with a supranatural dignity.

This dignity is not restricted to one man, one family, or one people, but is a quality of man as such: for all men are descended from a single couple—from Adam and Eve and, again, after the flood, from Noah and his wife. Thus all men are brothers.

Two of the three great ideas of the French Revolution are readily traced back to the Old Testament: equality and fraternity. What of the third idea, liberty? At least implicitly, this idea, too, is central in the Old Testament. Having been created in the image of God, no man is merely an object or should be treated merely as an object; every man has a supranatural dignity; all men are brothers. It would seem to follow that no man should treat another man as a slave and deprive him of his liberty.

Logic is the weak side of history, and it sometimes takes centuries before apparently obvious implications are realized. American history furnishes a ready example with its noble declaration, in 1776: "We hold these truths to be self-evident, that all men are created equal, that they are endowed by their creator with certain unalienable rights, that among these are life, liberty, and the pursuit of happiness." When these words were proclaimed to the world—and their Biblical inspiration meets the eye—their author was a slaveholder, and the country on whose behalf he was speaking was one of the few civilized countries left in which slavery was still legal. It is a long and arduous road indeed that leads from pride in such a principle to its full realization, effectively guaranteed by law.

That the implications of the Biblical conception of man regarding slavery were grasped at least to some extent even in Old Testament times is plain from the passages cited by way of contrast with the Code of Hammurabi. Since there is no Hebrew word for "slave" other than *ewed*, which means "servant," it is not an easy thing to say whether some form of slavery persisted through most of the time covered by the Old Testament or not. In theory at least, the institution of the Sabbath, on which the slave, or servant, was to rest, too, and the Sabbath year, in which any Hebrew slave was to go free (unless he wanted so badly to remain a slave that he subjected himself to the previously mentioned ceremony of having one ear pierced), and the institution of the Jubilee, every fiftieth year, in which non-Hebrew slaves, too, may have been meant to go free, would seem to have gone far toward abolishing slavery. That inhumanity nevertheless found frequent expression is obvious, but no other sacred scripture contains books that speak out against social injustice as eloquently, unequivocally, and sensitively as the books of Moses and some of the prophets.

In the religion of the Old Testament a keen social conscience is central. This is one of the distinctive features that set the Old Testament apart, quite radically, from the New Testament and the Koran, from the Upanishads and the Bhagavadgita, from the *Tao Teh Ching* and the Dhammapada. And in the Old Testament this social conscience is by no means unrelated to the belief in God; rather, it is the most significant implication of this belief.

In the third Book of Moses, Chapter 19, we read: "You shall not hate your brother in your heart, but you shall reason with your neighbor, lest you bear sin because of him. You shall not take vengeance or bear any grudge against the sons of your people, but you shall love your neighbor as yourself: I am the Lord." And again: "When a stranger sojourns with you in your land, you shall not do him wrong. The stranger who sojourns with you shall be to you as the native among you, and you shall love him as yourself; for you were strangers in the land of Egypt: I am the Lord your God."

Malachi, the prophet, cries out: "Have we not all one father? Has not one God created us? Why then are we faithless to one another?" (2:10). And Job says: "If I have rejected the right of my manservant or my maidservant, when they contended with me; what then shall I do when God rises up? When he makes inquiry, what shall I answer him? Did not he who made me in the womb make him? And did not one fashion us in the womb?" (31:13–15).

11

One of the most important points about God and man in the Old Testament involves the person of Moses. The so-called "higher critics" of the Old Testament, who dominated the field for almost a century, beginning in the early second half of the nineteenth century, claimed that monotheism had developed very slowly and that it did not attain full purity until the time of the prophets.

This whole question is very involved, and one cannot do justice to it in passing. What needs to be shown is that the presuppositions of the "higher criticism" are untenable, that it contains a crucial self-contradiction, and that its methods are extremely unsound. Having tried to show this in detail in Chapter X of my *Critique of Religion and Philosophy*, I can refer interested readers to that book, and come to the point at issue in the present context.

There is ample evidence in the Old Testament—and its authors actually make a point of the fact—that the superstitions and even the idols of neighboring nations often gained a foothold in ancient Israel. No claim whatever is made that all the people from the time of Moses on were pure and dedicated monotheists or that their behavior came up to the highest moral standards. On the contrary, the Old Testament records Moses' epic struggle with his stiff-necked people; and Judges, Kings, and the books of the prophets relate the sequel, which is essentially similar. It took time before the whole people rose, even in theory, to the height of Moses' vision, and, of course, the people never became a nation of Moseses.

Two things, however, are extremely striking. First, in spite of occasional appearances of idolatry, beginning with the golden calf, the theory that objects in this world are gods and merit worship never seems to have gained ground. One gets the impression that some of the people sometimes fell into the habits of the nations among whom they lived and thoughtlessly adopted their practices. What the prophets attack is this unthinking, stupid inconsistency, never a rival creed, and least of all any belief that the traditional religion of Israel either contains or is indifferent to such ideas as, say, that the sun and moon are gods. This fact suggests most strongly that the monotheism of Israel was not derived from that of Akhenaton, and that it was not arrived at gradually by way of a slow process of exclusion.

The second point is even more striking. In India, the Jina and the Buddha, founders of two new religions in the sixth century B.C., came to be worshiped later by their followers. In China, Confucius and Lao-tze came to be deified. To the non-Christian, Jesus seems to represent a parallel case. In Greece, the heroes of the past were held to have been sired by a god or to have been born of a goddess, and the dividing line between gods and men became fluid. In Egypt, the Pharaoh was considered divine.

In Israel, no man was ever worshiped or accorded even semidivine status. This is one of the most extraordinary facts about the religion of the Old Testament and by far the most important reason for the Jews' refusal to accept Christianity and the New Testament.

It is extraordinary that the prophets never had to raise their voices against any cult of Moses or the patriarchs. One explanation, theoretically possible but incompatible with the evidence, would be that Moses never lived and was merely the fiction of a later age. But not one of the prophets makes the slightest claim to be an innovator; all remind the people of what they have long known and rebuke them for unthinkingly betraying standards and ideas long accepted. And there is no first prophet: before Amos came Elisha and Elijah and Micaiah and whole groups of prophets—Kings is full of them—and, before them, Nathan; and, before him, Samuel; and so forth. Yet there is not the slightest evidence that any one of them was the creator of the religion of ancient Israel or even a man who radically changed it. Everything points back at least to the time of Moses.

Why, then, was Moses never deified or worshiped—unlike Lao-tze, Confucius, and the Buddha and the Jina, and the Pharaohs of Egypt? The most obvious explanation is that he himself impressed his people with the firm idea that no human being is divine in any sense in which the rest of mankind isn't.

Being a stiff-necked and critical people, they may have been quite willing to believe that he was not a god, that no Jew is a god, and certainly no Gentile. But it seems clear that Moses himself was unequivocal on this point—as, indeed, the Buddha was, too—and that Moses, unlike the Buddha, succeeded in imprinting it forever in the minds of his followers.

It could not have been hard for a man in his position to suggest to at least some of his most ardent followers that he himself was in some sense divine and without flaw. On the contrary, the image he created of himself was that of a human being, wearing himself out in the service of God and Israel, trying against all odds to wed his people to his God, modest, patient, hard to anger, magnificent in his wrath, but completely unresentful, capable of the deepest suffering, the quintessence of devotion—humane to the core.

He went away to die alone, lest any man should know his grave to worship there or attach any value to his mortal body. Having seen Egypt, he knew better than the Buddha how prone men are to such superstitions. Going off to die alone, he might have left his people with the image of a mystery, with the idea of some supernatural transfiguration, with the thought that he did not die but went up to heaven—with the notion that he was immortal and divine. He might have created the suspicion that, when his mission was accomplished, he returned to heaven. Instead he created an enduring image of humanity: he left his people with the thought that, being human and imperfect, he was not allowed to enter the promised land, but that he went up on the mountain to see it before he died.

The Jews have been so faithful to his spirit that they have not only never worshiped him but, alas, have never pitted him against the other great men of the world by way of asking who compared with Moses. To be sure, after relating the story of his death, they added: "There has not arisen a prophet since in Israel like Moses." But they have not confronted the world with this man to stake out a claim for him. One speaks of Jesus and the Buddha, of Confucius and Socrates, perhaps also of Francis of Assisi, but one does not ask: Does not Moses belong with them? Was he perhaps, man for man, simply as a human being, more attractive, greater, more humane?

What the Jews have presented to the world has not been Moses or any individual, but their ideas about God and man. It is a measure of Moses' greatness that one cannot but imagine that he would have approved wholeheartedly. It would have broken his heart if he had thought that his followers would build temples to him, make images of him, or elevate him into heaven. That he has never been deified is one of the most significant facts about the ideas of God and man in the Old Testament.

The troublesome question remains of how the elaborate ritual law of the last four Books of Moses is related to Moses. Traditional Judaism has assumed, as have Jesus, Paul, and traditional Christianity, that these laws were given by Moses. Goethe even suggested that the Ten Commandments did not derive from Moses, while a more ritualistic set of ten commandments, which he found in Exodus 34, did. Many of the "higher critics" agreed with Goethe. The admission that a sublime morality was taught by Moses in the thirteenth century B.C. would have been fatal to their evolutionary construction of the Old Testament. The morality they admired they ascribed to the great pre-exilic prophets, whom we shall consider shortly. The detailed ritual law they assigned to the postexilic period; for, in brief, it does not seem at all plausible to assign it to the years in the desert, long before there was any real state, not to speak of a settled agricultural community, which seems to be presupposed by these laws. Moreover, neither the historical nor the prophetic books of the Old Testament seem to presuppose all of this legislation.

The reasons for dissociating Moses from the highly intricate ritual law are to my mind almost conclusive and establish an overwhelming probability. The reasons, on the other hand, for not ascribing to him the Ten Commandments or the moral principles traditionally associated with him strike me as utterly implausible; indeed, one is generally not confronted with any reasons at all, but merely with the presupposition that sublime moral ideas *must* be late. This assumption is surely false. Quite typically, we encounter a supreme moral challenge at the beginning of a new religion, and, more often than not, this is later subjected to compromise and dilution rather than improvement. Confucius and Lao-tze, the Buddha and Jesus furnish examples in this vein. If it should be objected that none of them stand at the beginning of a new civilization and that all four of them draw on past developments, the same consideration applies to Moses.

For all that, the problem remains whether Moses really tried to impress a high morality on his people. So far, it has merely been suggested that he well might have; that this cannot be ruled out a priori; and that, if he did, there would be many parallels in the history of religion. The question we must ask now can be expressed in Job's words: "If it is not he, who then is it?" Somebody must have originated this morality. The Bible critics answer: the prophets.

We are asked in effect to believe that, in the eighth century, Amos and Hosea, independent of each other and without the least awareness of their originality—in fact, emphatically disclaiming any originality—came up all at once with the same moral demands. These were echoed almost immediately by Isaiah and Micah who, rather oddly, also seemed to think that their people had long been told what they were reminding them of, and that it was truly shameful and inexcusable that Israel should have forgotten, or rather failed to live up to, these ancient standards.

The point here is not merely that the prophets must have known better whether their moral standards were original with them than any "higher critic" could. After the Exile, the practice of ascribing books to ancient authors to heighten the prestige of the works became common, and there are excellent reasons for considering Proverbs, Song of Songs, Ecclesiastes, and Daniel cases in point. It might therefore be asked whether the prophets might not have employed the same ruse, pretending that ideas original with them were ancient. There are at least two good answers to this.

The first of these may sound subjective and intuitive to anyone who has not read the great pre-exilic prophets, but it may well be conclusive for anyone who has: the indignation of these men is inseparable from their unquestioning conviction that Israel has betrayed, violated, broken the faith with norms known since the Exodus from

Egypt. The second answer has already been given: the whole phenomenon of pre-exilic prophecy, of the almost simultaneous appearance, independently of each other, of men appealing to the same standards of morality, can hardly be explained if we are to suppose that these standards were original with them. It can be explained by considering Moses one of humanity's greatest teachers. That this does not deprive the prophets of their glory will be seen as soon as we come to consider them in detail. (Cf. also my *Critique*, § 90: "Religion and Progress.")

At this point it will suffice to cite a single passage from Jeremiah:

> I did not speak to your fathers, and I did not command them on the day that I led them out of the land of Egypt, about burnt offerings and sacrifices. But this is what I commanded them: Listen to my voice, and I shall be God for you, and you shall be a people for me; and walk in all the way that I command you, that it may be well with you. . . . From the day that our fathers came out of the land of Egypt to this day, I sent to you all my servants the prophets, day upon day; yet they did not listen to me, or incline their ear, but stiffened their neck (7:22 ff.).

12

It is widely supposed that the conception of the chosen people is diametrically at odds with the humanistic strain in the Old Testament, and what has so far been pointed out is often altogether ignored or at the very least held to represent a relatively minor motif. It has become fashionable to ignore whatever in the New Testament may seem unedifying, especially the many passages on hell and eternal torment, while emphasizing out of all proportion whatever in the Old Testament is questionable from a moral point of view.

Plainly, the Old Testament, written over a period of a thousand years and containing history and poetry as well as proverbs and laws and stories, is not in its entirety a book of moral instruction. It contains, for example, the Book of Joshua, which relates the conquest of Palestine and ascribes to God the command to slaughter "both men and women, young and old, oxen, sheep, and asses, with the edge of the sword." But to find the spirit of the religion of the Old Testament in Joshua is like finding the distinctive genius of America in the men who slaughtered the Indians. Many nations have their Joshuas, and the chance to make a unique contribution to humanity has often been bought with the sword; the genius of a people shows itself in what is done later to realize this costly opportunity.

In the Old Testament itself, the idea of the chosen people is not offered by way of justifying lower moral standards, as if it were claimed that, being chosen, one need not live up to standards intended only for the mass of men. On the contrary, the conception of the chosen people is inseparably linked with the twin ideas of a task and of an especially demanding law.

In two definitive passages, Amos, the first prophet to compose poetic speeches that were committed to writing, proclaims: "You only have I known of all the families of the earth; therefore I will punish you for all your iniquities" (3:2). And:

> Are you not like the Ethiopians to me, O people of Israel? says the Lord. Did I not bring up Israel from the land of Egypt, and the Philistines from Crete, and the Syrians from Kir? Behold, the eyes of the Lord God are upon the sinful kingdom, and I will destroy it from the surface of the ground; except that I will not utterly destroy the house of Jacob, says the Lord (9:7–8).

Not utterly; for, as Isaiah puts it a little later when he names his son Shear-jashub: a remnant shall return—that is the meaning of the name. What matters is not the glory of the people; most of them, almost generation after generation, shall be destroyed. What matters is the task: maintaining and spreading what has been revealed to them, namely, the belief in God and the morality that goes with it. And that is why a remnant shall return, lest the flame be extinguished entirely.

This theme runs through the books of the ancient Hebrew prophets—and, beyond that, through most of the Hebrew Bible. The structure of the Hebrew Bible has been changed in the Christian version of it, which ends with the prophets. The Hebrew Bible has three parts. The first consists of the Five Books of Moses. The second part is the Prophets, divided, in turn, into two parts: the first part is historical and comprises the books of Joshua, Judges, Samuel, and Kings; the second and central part consists of the prophets proper—that is, of Isaiah, Jeremiah, Ezekiel, and the Twelve. Some of the Twelve are easily as impressive as Ezekiel, but their books are far shorter than those of the Big Three. The last part comprises the so-called Scriptures: Psalms, Proverbs, Job, Song of Songs, Ruth, Lamentations, Ecclesiastes, Esther, Daniel, Ezra, Nehemiah, and Chronicles. The Hebrew Bible ends with the end of the Babylonian exile, when a remnant returned to Jerusalem; and the last words are the words of Cyrus, King of Persia: "The Lord, the God of heaven, has given me all the kingdoms of the earth, and he has charged me to build him a house at Jerusalem, which is in Judah. Whoever is among you of all his people, may the Lord his God be with him. Let him go up."

Christianity had no use for this conclusion when it put together its canon, over a hundred years after the destruction of the second temple in A.D. 70—a destruction it had come to view as a definitive punishment for the Jews' alleged rejection of Jesus. The Christians put the prophets at the end of the Old Testament. In this manner, the prophets ceased to appear as the central portion of the Hebrew Scriptures and became the transition from the Old to the New; and instead of the last sentence of the Hebrew Bible, which pronounced a blessing and a promise, one got this conclusion: "Lest I come and smite the land with a curse."

The supranationalistic, cosmopolitan, humanistic motif runs through the Hebrew Bible from the creation to the words of the King of Persia who, in the Hebrew view, is an instrument of God. The culmination of this motif may be found in the vision of the messianic kingdom, which will be considered shortly. But it is also noteworthy that two whole books of the Old Testament are given over all but completely to this motif: Ruth and Jonah.

The point of the Book of Ruth cannot be fully grasped if it is forgotten that she is a Moabitess, and that the feeling of ancient Israel about Moab is epitomized in the story in Genesis which relates that Moab was born to one of Lot's daughters after she had made her father drunk and spent the night with him. The point of the Book of Ruth is that Ruth, the Moabitess, became the great-grandmother of King David, the national hero. If there were any racist-minded jingoists in ancient Israel, this book must have shocked them rather more than the claim that George Washington or Robert E. Lee had a black great-grandmother would shock a bigot in the United States. Immediately, the question arises what special merits and resulting dispensation made it possible for Ruth to become a member of the chosen people. But the conception of the chosen people is not racial but spiritual. No dispensation was needed, no ritual, no baptism. Ruth simply said to the mother of her deceased Hebrew husband: "Where you go, I will go, and where you lodge I will lodge; your people shall be my people, and your God my God; where you die, I will die, and there will I be buried. May the Lord do so to me and more also if even death parts me from you." These unprompted words were sufficient. No more is said. No further problem is even acknowledged.

In the Book of Jonah we are confronted not with a woman from Moab but with Nineveh, the capital of the Assyrians who destroyed Samaria and the kingdom of Israel, who led the ten northern tribes into an exile from which they were never to return, and who came within a hair's breadth of capturing Jerusalem and destroying the southern kingdom, too. How the design of the Assyrian king was frustrated unexpectedly is the theme of one of Byron's *Hebrew Melodies*, "The Destruction of Sennacherib."

In the Bible, Jonah is sent to Nineveh to prophesy its imminent destruction as a punishment for its wickedness. He refuses, flees on a ship, is brought back in the belly of a great fish, and finally goes and utters his prophecy. Then the people of Nineveh repent, and God forgives them. They do not become Jews. They are not circumcised or baptized. They simply repent. That is enough. God decides not to destroy Nineveh. Jonah, displeased, protests that this is what he foresaw in the first place: "I knew that thou are a gracious God and merciful." That is why Jonah had fled. Why now must he bear the humiliation of having been forced to make a prophecy and then to see it refuted by the event? "It is better for me to die than to live." But God replies, after a short humorous episode: "Should not I pity Nineveh, that great city, in which there are more than a hundred and twenty thousand persons who do not know their right hand from their left, and also much cattle?" Joshua is not unique: the lore of the nations abounds in men more or less like him. But in what other tome of sacred scriptures do we find a book like Jonah?

It might be supposed that, if the foregoing analysis is right, the Jews would surely have endeavored to make proselytes, converting others to their own religion. And they did. An odd reference to this well-established fact is found in one of Jesus' most extreme denunciations of the Pharisees, in the Gospel according to Matthew: "You traverse sea and land to make a single proselyte" (23:15). Soon after Jesus' time, the Romans, provoked by the Jews' refusal to accept their pagan rule, first destroyed Jerusalem and then, when the Jews rebelled rather than accept the presence of an image of the emperor as god in the place of their former temple, the Romans, among other things, put an end to any further missionary activities by the Jews. Later the Christian church of Rome continued this ban, and again and again surpassed in ferocity anything the Romans had done by way of persecuting the remnant of Jewry. Still later, Luther urged the German princes to burn all synagogues and to drive all Jews out of the country. Gradually, the Jews became resigned, as Christians came to be under Hitler, to the ethos of standing fast, clinging to their religion without surrendering on any point of substance and, of course, without making proselytes.

This ethos was beautifully formulated by the Lutheran pastor Niemöller in a sermon delivered less than two weeks before the Nazis arrested him. He chose as his text the words of Jesus: "You are the salt of the earth." And he told his listeners, who, defying all threats by the government, crowded his church to hear him, that it was their task to keep themselves pure, lest the salt lose its savor: in their present situation this advice made no sense whatsoever, but that should not concern them; that was God's concern. Their task was to hold out, and some day God might find some use for his salt.

To reproach the Jews for not making more proselytes is like reproaching Niemöller for not making more proselytes in those days before his arrest. When it was feasible, the Jews made proselytes—in the Roman empire, among the Khazars in the Crimea, and elsewhere. But it is harder to persuade men to submit to circumcision than it is to baptize them; it is harder to convert to the law than to trust in grace; and those who demand works will always make fewer converts than those who stress faith and the remission of sins.

13

The influence of Old Testament ideas concerning the state has been second only to that of the ancient Hebrew conceptions of God and man. The three main points concerning this influence can be made briefly. They concern the origin of the state, the value of the state, and the vision of an ideal society.

Regarding the origin of the state, the first thing to note is. that, according to the Old Testament, the state has an origin within history and is not the natural condition of man. The Hebrew Bible believes in the priority of the individual. This point is made twice: first, in Genesis where we find man in Paradise, without any state; then again in the Book of Judges in which we encounter this refrain, which also concludes the book: "In those days there was no king in Israel; every man did what was right in his own eyes."

The condition portrayed in the doubtless very early Book of Judges is one of attenuated anarchy. Only under foreign attack, or when foreign oppression becomes too severe, do the tribes rally now and then under a charismatic leader who, after his military triumphs, enjoys such prestige that the people come to him to arbitrate what differences may arise between them. Such men, and occasionally also women, like Deborah, are called judges and fill the otherwise vacant spot of a ruler until they die. Then the people relapse into their former state, approximating anarchy, until their enemies get the better of them and another leader rises and eventually becomes their judge.

Against this background, we find highly explicit doubts about the value of the state in the Old Testament. In the Book of Judges itself we encounter a fable whose prime intent is clearly antimonarchical, and this point was not lost on such close students of the Old Testament as Cromwell and Milton. But in the twelfth century B.C., to which this fable takes us back, there were no republics, and the issue revolves around the people's desire to form a state "like all the nations."

Abimelech, one of the sons of Jerubbaal, one of the judges, went out after his father's death and said to the people of Shechem: "Which is better for you, that all seventy of the sons of Jerubbaal rule over you, or that one rule over you?" And eventually ". . . he slew his brothers the sons of Jerubbaal, seventy men, upon one stone; but Jotham, the youngest son of Jerubbaal, was left; for he hid himself."

Jerubbaal had not confined himself to a single wife, any more than Jacob, or David, or Moses, who married a second, Ethiopian wife—and his brother and sister, Aaron and Miriam, were severely punished by God for reproaching him. But that aspect of the Old Testament has had scarcely any influence on the history of Europe and America— except, of course, for the early Mormons—while the following fable has had more influence.

Jotham came out of hiding and told the people of Shechem his memorable fable:

> The trees once went forth to anoint a king over them; and they said to the olive tree, "Reign over us." But the olive tree said to them, "Shall I leave my fatness, by which God and men are honored, and go to sway over the trees?" And the trees said to the fig tree, "Come you, and reign over us." But the fig tree said to them, "Shall I leave my sweetness and my good fruit, and go to sway over the trees?" And the trees said to the vine, "Come you, and reign over us." But the vine said to them, "Shall I leave my wine which cheers God and men, and go to sway over the trees?" Then all the trees said to the bramble, "Come you, and reign over us." And the bramble said to the trees, "If in good faith you are anointing me king over you, then come and take refuge in my shade; but if not, let fire come out of the bramble and devour the cedars of Lebanon."

Jotham ran away and was heard from no more, but his fable, in Judges 9, has re-
verberated through history. (Abimelech was killed in a battle, three years later, when he
tried to take a tower "and a certain woman threw an upper millstone upon Abimelech's
head, and crushed his skull. Then he called hastily to the young man his armor-bearer,
and said to him: Draw your sword and kill me, lest men say of me, 'A woman killed him.'
And his young man thrust him through, and he died.")

The point of the fable is that nobody but an unproductive parasite would wish to
be king in the first place, and that any people is better off without a king than with
such a tyrant. This view is almost as far removed as possible from any belief in the divine
right of kings. But the First Book of Samuel goes even further.

Samuel was a judge for a long time, and when he became old he made his sons
judges. But his sons accepted bribes and perverted justice. Then the elders of Israel
assembled and said to Samuel: "Behold, you are old, and your sons do not walk in your
ways; now appoint for us a king to govern us like all the nations." In its context, this
request seems understandable enough, though it is hardly surprising that it displeased
Samuel, and that "Samuel prayed to the Lord." It is the following lines that go beyond
even Jotham's fable: "And the Lord said to Samuel, 'Listen to the voice of the people
in all that they say to you; for they have not rejected you, but they have rejected me
from being king over them.'"

Here—and not only in this passage—the earlier, premonarchic condition of Israel
is idealized: it was not anarchy but the kingship of God. The institution of human kings,
on the other hand, and the establishment of a state after the model of "all the nations,"
is considered as a betrayal of God.

God's answer to Samuel continues: "According to all the deeds which they have
done from the day I brought them up out of Egypt even to this day, forsaking me and
serving other gods, so they are also doing to you. Now then, listen to their voice; only,
you shall solemnly warn them, and show them the ways of the king who shall reign over
them." The Bible relates further that Samuel told the people what God had told him,
and that he offered them this picture of human kingship:

> These will be the ways of the king who will reign over you: he will take your
> sons and appoint them to his chariots, and to be his horsemen, and to run before
> his chariots; and he will appoint for himself commanders of thousands and com-
> manders of fifties, and some to plow his ground and to reap his harvest, and to
> make his implements of war and the equipment of his chariots. He will take your
> daughters to be perfumers and cooks and bakers. He will take the best of your
> fields and vineyards and olive orchards and give them to his servants. He will take
> the tenth of your grain and of your vineyards and give it to his officers and to his
> servants. He will take your menservants and maidservants, and the best of your
> young men, and your asses, and put them to his work. He will take the tenth of
> your flocks, and you yourselves will be his servants.

The fable of Jotham and Chapter 8 of First Samuel are extreme, and the rest of
the Hebrew Bible does not deny all value whatsoever to the state or to kingship. But
the Hebrew Bible consistently denies any claim of the supremacy of the state in human
affairs or of the superiority of kings as such. Above the state and king and any government there is a higher moral law by which states, kings, governments, and any laws
that they enact are to be judged. The influence of this idea can hardly be overestimated.

14

The quintessence of this higher law was condensed into a classical sentence by the
prophet Micah, in the eighth century B.C.: "He has told you, man, what is good and
what the Lord requires of you: only to do justice, to love mercy, and to walk humbly

with your God" (6:8). Amos and Hosea had made much the same points, insisting passionately on their social implications.

Unlike most representatives of religion in other civilizations, the prophets were not concerned about religious ritual. Their demands and their social criticism were moral. Indeed, the concern about ritual was one of the things they persistently denounced in the name of the overriding importance of social justice. Micah introduces his bold summary of what God demands with four rhetorical questions: "With what shall I come before the Lord, and bow myself before God on high? Shall I come before him with burnt offerings, with calves a year old? Will the Lord be pleased with thousands of rams, with ten thousands of rivers of oil? Shall I give my first-born for my transgression, the fruit of my body for the sin of my soul?" And then, as a bold antithesis, he proclaims the words cited above. What is wanted is not any ritual at all, but justice, mercy, and humility.

Amos, a little earlier, had been, if possible, still more explicit:

> I hate, I despise your feasts, and I take no delight in your solemn assemblies. Even though you offer me your burnt offerings and cereal offerings, I will not accept them, and the peace offerings of your fatted beasts I will not look upon. Take away from me the noise of your songs; to the melody of your harps I will not listen. But let justice roll down like waters, and righteousness like an ever–flowing stream (5:21 ff.).

In the name of him "who made the Pleiades and Orion, and turns deep darkness into the morning, and darkens the day into night, who calls for the waters of the sea and pours them out upon the surface of the earth, the Lord is his name," Amos denounces those who "trample upon the poor and take from him exactions of wheat" and those "who afflict the righteous, who take a bribe, and turn aside the needy" (5:8 ff.).

Isaiah, Micah's great contemporary, cries out (in Chapter 1):

> What to me is the multitude of your sacrifices?
> says the Lord;
> I have had enough of burnt offerings of rams
> and the fat of fed beasts;
> I do not delight in the blood of bulls,
> or of lambs, or of he-goats.
> When you come to appear before me,
> who requires of you this trampling of my courts?
> Bring no more vain offerings;
> incense is an abomination to me. . . .
> Wash yourselves; make yourselves clean;
> remove the evil of your doings from before my eyes;
> cease to do evil,
> learn to do good;
> seek justice,
> abolish oppression;
> defend the orphan,
> plead for the widow.

The kings, too, are judged by the same standards, and no man, however admired, is exempt from judgment by the standards of this higher law. Indeed, the Hebrew Bible goes out of its way to emphasize that the greatest national heroes had their faults. Jacob, who was renamed Israel and, according to tradition, gave his name to his children and children's children, is no exception; nor is Moses; nor David; nor Solomon. The Hebrew Bible excels in its unforgettable portrayals of human greatness, but it never fails to stop this side of idolatry.

A hundred years before Amos, Elijah applied the same standards to King Ahab, and about 1000 B.C. the prophet Nathan applied them to David, after the king had asked Joab, his general, to place Uriah, the Hittite, in an exposed place where he might get killed, so the king would be free to marry Uriah's beautiful wife, Bathsheba.

The law that asserted against the norms current in the ancient world, "You shall have one law for the stranger and for the native; for I am the Lord your God" (Leviticus 24:22), would not brook any exception on behalf of kings or nobles. And it tells us a great deal about ancient Israel that the Law of Moses should include the injunction: "You shall not be partial to the poor or defer to the great" (Leviticus 19:15; cf. Exodus 23:3). The first part of that law would not have occurred to many legislators.

15

We are ready for the ancient Hebrew conception of an ideal society. Much of what should be said about this has by now been said; both in the Five Books of Moses and in the Prophets we constantly encounter the vision of a society in which the poor, the orphan, the widow, and the stranger are treated with special consideration; a society in which justice rolls down like water, and righteousnes like an ever-flowing stream; a society based on justice, mercy, and humility. It is perhaps more often recognized that this ideal permeates the prophetic books than it is admitted, as it ought to be, that the Five Books of Moses are inspired by the same vision and seek to implement it with a wealth of detailed legislation.

What the prophets add is the great vision of the messianic kingdom which is found in both Isaiah 2 and Micah 4:

> It shall come to pass in the latter days
> that the mountain of the house of the Lord
> shall be established as the highest of the mountains,
> and shall be raised up above the hills;
> and all the nations shall flow to it,
> and many peoples shall come, and say:
> Come, let us go up to the mountain of the Lord,
> to the house of the God of Jacob;
> that he may teach us his ways
> and we may walk in his paths.
> For out of Zion shall go forth the Torah,
> and the word of the Lord from Jerusalem.
> He shall judge between the nations
> and shall decide for many peoples;
> and they shall beat their swords into plowshares,
> and their spears into pruning hooks;
> nation shall not lift up sword against nation,
> neither shall they learn war any more.

In Micah, two further verses follow:

> But they shall sit every man
> under his vine and under his fig tree,
> and none shall make them afraid;
> for the mouth of the Lord of hosts has spoken.
> For all the peoples walk
> each in the name of its god,
> but we will walk in the name of the Lord our God
> for ever and ever.

What distinguishes this conception from myths of a golden age among the Greeks and among other people is that the prophets stress the abolition of war and the establishment of a peaceful international community—and that they envisage this in the future and not, as other nations who spoke of golden ages, in the distant past. On paper these differences may seem small, the more so because the vision of the prophets has become a commonplace in the twentieth century. It is hard to do justice to the originality of men who, in the eighth century B.C., untutored by the horrors of two world wars, poison gas, and atom bombs, and without the frightening prospect of still more fearful weapons of destruction, insisted that war is evil and must some day be abolished, and that all peoples must learn to dwell together in peace.

In retrospect we may say that they merely spelled out explicitly what was implicit in the ancient Hebrew conception of God and man. There is nothing wrong with putting it that way, provided we remember how long it has taken the mass of men to perceive the very same implication.

16

One implication of almost everything that has been quoted here from the Hebrew Bible, and quite especially of the commandments, "You shall be holy" (Leviticus 19:2) "You shall be to me a kingdom of priests" (Exodus 19:6), is that man is called upon to raise his stature; that no man is a mere machine or instrument. We are called upon to be more than animals; we are summoned to freedom—whether it makes us happy or not.

Aldous Huxley created a deliberately nightmarish utopia in *Brave New World* (1932). His point was that we are on the best way toward creating a society of happy imbeciles, and that we might yet achieve a society in which everybody would be happy at a slightly subhuman level. Would anything be wrong with that? Many of us hope and think that, human nature being what it is, freedom and the fullest possible development of man's creative powers, in a society based on humanity, mercy, and humility, would promote the greatest possible happiness. This faith is obviously rooted in ancient Israel. But suppose that it were possible to ensure the greatest possible happiness of the greatest possible number either by reducing man's creative powers, whether by drugs that reduced men to blissful imbecility or by operations that reduced their intelligence. What then?

Those of us who feel that happiness, however important, is not the ultimate consideration and that it would be an impermissible betrayal to sell our birthright for a mess of bliss are probably haunted by the challenge of the Hebrew Bible. Here a voice was raised that has aroused a large portion of mankind, albeit a distinct minority, from their pre-Israelitic slumber.

II

ANCIENT IRAN

Zarathustra's Setting—His Dualism—His Eschatology—
His Sacraments and Nietzsche's Comments—Zoroastrianism—
Mani—Manichaeism—The Problem of Evil—
The Spread of Manichaeism

Persepolis.

17

The great prophet of ancient Iran is known to many Westerners only as a name used by Nietzsche in *Thus Spoke Zarathustra.* Some people suppose that his real name was Zoroaster, but that is merely the Greek form. His Persian name was Zarathushtra. The ancient Greeks believed that he had lived around 6000 B.C. In modern times some historians have argued for dates between the eleventh and the eighth centuries, but by now most scholars agree that he lived in the sixth century as the Zoroastrians themselves insist. According to their tradition, his ministry began two hundred and fifty-eight years before Alexander the Great conquered the Persian Empire— about 588, a year or two before the Babylonians sacked Jerusalem. R. C. Zaehner, one of the leading authorities on Zoroastrianism, has suggested that the prophet may have lived from 627 to 551. Jack Finegan, in *Archaeology of World Religions,* holds with those who think that the king whom Zarathustra converted and who then protected him was probably the father of Darius I, and he tentatively gives the prophet's dates as 570 to 493.

Both scholars accept the tradition that Zarathustra died at the age of seventy-seven, which may well be true, but the evidence we have does not enable us to come up with precise dates for his life. The two hundred and fifty-eight years before Alexander come from the Bundahish, a work of the ninth century A.D. that also furnishes a list of all the kings who are said to have reigned during these years. Unfortunately, this list is quite different from the historical records of the kings of Persia. It also contains two successive reigns of approximately one hundred years each. Hence many scholars take the two hundred and fifty-eight years with a grain of salt. Still, it seems highly probable now that Zarathustra came along after Amos and Hosea, Isaiah and Micah, and even a little later than Jeremiah. Whatever his exact dates may have been, he evidently lived during the Babyonian exile of the Jews and was a contemporary of the Second Isaiah, the Jina, and the Buddha—and perhaps also of Confucius, who was born in 551.

Cyrus, who conquered Babylon and allowed the Jews to return to their homeland, was probably not yet a follower of Zarathustra, but Darius I, under whose reign (521–486) the temple in Jerusalem was rebuilt, certainly was. Darius is mentioned repeatedly in the Bible, in the Books of Ezra and Nehemiah, Haggai and Zechariah, and Daniel. The remains of his great palace at Susa and the extensive ruins of Persepolis, which he founded as the ceremonial capital of his empire, still bear witness to the magnificent architecture and sculpture of his reign. Persepolis was destroyed by Alexander but is still one of the greatest sites of ancient splendor. No comparable ruins of equal antiquity are to be found anywhere in the world outside the Near East.

Stonehenge and other European sites that are older have nothing like the sculptured friezes of Persepolis. But after defeating the army of Darius I at Marathon in 490 B.C., and after their triumphs over the navy and army of his son Xerxes, a decade later, the Greeks built the Parthenon and the other buildings whose ruins still grace the Acropolis of Athens.

The tombs of Darius and his successors, the so-called Achaemenid kings—or rather kings of kings, for their empire included many old kingdoms—are still to be seen at Naqsh-i-Rostam, near Persepolis, hewn into the face of a rock that rises verti-32 cally out of an austerely beautiful plain. The tombs are simple and were adorned with 34 friezes only in the third century A.D., by the so-called Sassanian kings of Persia. But in a relief on one of the lofty columns at Persepolis we behold Darius himself standing under a parasol—a symbol that we shall discuss in section 113—and above that appears 33 the emblem of Ahura Mazda, Zarathustra's god.

The religion founded by Zarathustra barely survives in the modern world. His native Iran was conquered and converted by the Muslims in the seventh century A.D., and it is only in India, in and around Bombay, that a sizable community of Zoroas-trians survives—a little more than 100,000 people. They are usually referred to as Parsees because of their Persian origin. Although the Parsees are widely respected for their intelligence and industry, their influence on the thought and culture of non-Parsees has not been so great that Zarathustra would need to be discussed here on that account. But his influence on Christianity and Islam has been immense. His influence on Judaism was also considerable although not quite so great, for reasons that will be considered in the next chapter.

To grasp the prophet's impact one must consider the political realities of the last thousand years of antiquity. Cyrus' son and successor, Cambyses, conquered Egypt in 525 B.C. For 2,500 years—as long a span of time as separates us from this event—Egypt and Mesopotamia had been the two great rival civilizations of the Near East. Now they were united in a single empire—the largest empire the world had ever seen. Upon Cambyses' sudden death, the empire threatened to fall apart, but Darius, the founder of the Achaemenid dynasty, held it together. His dominion also included the Greek settlements in Asia Minor where Greek philosophy was born in the sixth cen-tury B.C. While the Persian attempt to conquer Greece failed and only a small part of India (now part of Pakistan) was integrated into the empire, cultural cross fertiliza-tion did not stop at the borders. By 330 B.C. Alexander the Great had conquered the Persian empire and was on his way to the Indus, and his dominion included Greece.

Zarathustra lived at the dawn of an age of unprecedented syncretism, and since his religion was for a while the official religion of the Persian empire, everybody in that whole vast area was exposed to it. In this melting pot, which became even larger as the Roman empire expanded, some of Zarathustra's ideas came to be very widely accepted. But their country of origin was not stamped upon them, and one did not necessarily associate them with Zarathustra or with ancient Iran, for they did not seem strange or exotic. On the contrary, they seemed so plausible and pleasing that they were soon taken for granted, and the two major religions born in that part of the world after Zarathustra's time, Christianity and Islam, adopted some of his central notions.

Zarathustra's impact was not due to any great subtlety, nor did he have a complex system of which different aspects influenced different people. The same ideas were accepted widely, and their enormous appeal was due to their simplicity. Scholars agree that we have the prophet's own ideas, largely in his own words, in the seventeen hymns of the Gathas. These are found in chapters 28–34, 43–51, and 53 of the Yasna, a collection of liturgical texts that constitutes one of the three parts of the Avesta. The other two parts are the Yashts (hymns that accompanied sacrifices to various deities) and the Videvdat (law against demons that ordains rites of purification). Only the Gathas were composed by Zarathustra himself.

He tried to reform his ancestral religion, but not by appealing to any earlier teacher or texts. He relied entirely on the revelations of his god Ahura Mazda. *Ahura* means "lord," and *Mazda* means "wise." In the name of the Wise Lord, the prophet rejected the polytheism and the animal sacrifices of his ancestors—a religion that was probably very similar to that found in the ancient Vedas of India. In India the Vedas became canonical and authoritative, and Hindu teachers always professed to interpret them without presuming to criticize them. The Jina and the Buddha did not accept the authority of the Vedas, nor did they claim that any god had revealed anything to them. Zarathustra represents an altogether new departure from the old Indo-Iranian religion.

18

Zarathustra's influence is inseparable from his dualism. There are two kinds of people, and the prophet calls himself an "enemy of the followers of the Lie [*druj*] and a powerful support for the followers of the Truth [*asha*]" (Yasna 43:8). Ahura Mazda commands us to exert ourselves in our words, our thoughts, and our deeds to "do evil to the followers of the Lie" (33:2). There are also two kinds of deities. This distinction was part of the ancient religion of the Indo-Iranian people. Zarathustra's *ahuras* and *daevas* correspond to the Vedic *asuras* and *devas*. In India the former gradually 135 came to be considered mere demons, while the *devas* were regarded as gods; and the English word "divinity," the Latin *deus*, and Greek *theos*, as well as "theology" and "theosophy," "theism" and "deism," all come from this same ancient root. Zarathustra, however, has it the other way around. The *ahuras* are divine, and the *daevas* are demons whom he associates with the followers of the Lie. He belonged to a pastoral community, and the *daevas* were worshiped by nomadic tribes that raided the cattle and performed bloody sacrifices, using cows that were sacred to Zarathustra's people. He succeeded in projecting these simple and scarcely unusual circumstances into a cosmic vision that cast an enduring spell upon humanity.

There are two great parties in the world, according to Zarathustra, one good and one wicked, and we are summoned to side with the good and fight against evil. We are called upon to make a momentous choice, but the decision is easy because all good is on one side, and all evil on the other. Precisely this simplicity has proved irresistible to simple minds. It hallows hatred, glorifies an inhuman self-righteousness that denies the enemy all moral qualities, and assures those who oppose the wicked of a glorious final triumph.

Zarathustra has sometimes been called a monotheist, on the assumption that the *daevas* are not really gods and that Ahura Mazda is so far superior to all the other *ahuras* that they are, as it were, mere angels, and the Christian belief in angels may indeed have one of its sources here. But that leaves us with the problem of the origin of evil. Here the Gathas are not as clear as they might be. They speak of "the two spirits of whom at the beginning of existence the Holy One said to the Evil One: Neither our thoughts nor our teachings, nor our wills, nor our choices, nor our words, nor our deeds, nor our beliefs, nor our souls agree" (45:2). This theme is developed more fully in what is perhaps the most important of all the Gathas: Yasna 30, which has been called "The Twin Gatha" because it pictures the two spirits as twins. Verses from it are quoted in almost all accounts of Zoroastrianism, but quoting it in its entirety will serve to give a better idea of the Gathas and of Zarathustra.

Vohu Manah means "good mind" but is personified throughout the Gathas and has therefore been left untranslated, like Ahura Mazda.

The Twin Gatha

1. To all who listen I will
   proclaim what those who are wise
   must remember: hymns for Ahura
   and songs of Vohu Manah,
   the joy that those who recall them
   will see in the light with Truth.

2. Hear with your ears what is best
   and behold in the light two ways.
   Each man must choose between them,
   each must decide for himself,
   thinking how he may prevail
   at the time of the final test.

3. The two primeval spirits,
   revealed in a dream as twins,
   the Better One and the Evil One
   in thought and word and deed—
   the sensible choose well between them;
   not so the fools.

4. These two spirits met in the beginning
   and ordained life and death
   and that in the end the worst
   existence should await
   the followers of the Lie,
   and the best mind the fighters for Truth.

5. Of these two spirits, the Liar
   elected to do the worst;
   clothed in the firmest firmament,
   the Most Holy Spirit chose Truth,
   as do all who by righteous deeds
   want to please Ahura Mazda.

6. Between Lie and Truth, the *daevas*
   did not choose right, for folly
   overcame them as they took counsel,
   and the *daevas* chose the worst mind
   and rushed to fury to use it
   to ruin human existence.

7. With dominion, with Vohu Manah,
   and with Truth, the breath of life
   comes to the bodies and makes
   them supple so that in the final
   retribution through molten metal
   they will prevail as the first.

8. When the evil, O Mazda, receive
   their punishments, Vohu Manah
   will establish your dominion
   for all of those, Ahura,
   who have delivered the Lie
   into the hands of Truth.

9. We want to make this existence
   glorious for you. O Mazda
   and you other Ahuras, and you,
   O Truth, grant help that our thoughts
   may collect themselves
   where insight still falters.

10. Then will destruction come
    to the delight of the Lie,
    while those who have won a good name
    will receive their promised reward
    in the good abode of Vohu
    Manah, Mazda, and Truth.

11. When you remember, O man,
    the commandments of Mazda—well-being
    and suffering—enduring torment
    for the followers of the Lie
    and salvation for the fighters for Truth,
    all will be well henceforth.

If Zarathustra was truly a monotheist, then the twin spirits—the Evil One and the Good or Holy One—must both have issued from Ahura Mazda. Although this view has its defenders, the Gathas are far from proclaiming it; on the contrary, they suggest repeatedly that the two spirits confronted each other "at the beginning of existence." They even leave room for speculation about the relation of the better spirit to the Most Holy One, and of the Evil One to the Lie. But such scholastic subtleties seem a far cry from the poetic vision of the Gathas. In English the word "monotheism" first occurs in the late seventeenth century, and it was only in the course of the nineteenth century that a great many scholars began to use it constantly—less as a descriptive term than as an encomium. Monotheism was supposed to be good, and anything less than that—or rather any belief in more than one god—was held to be inferior. It is scarcely an exaggeration to say that those who insist on Zarathustra's monotheism have not found any evidence that others have failed to see; they are voicing their admiration for Zarathustra. In the same spirit, prolonged contact with the British led many educated Hindus to insist that they were not polytheists but monotheists; and it led the Parsees to modify their religion, which had come to involve belief in two gods, one good and one evil, and to insist that they, too, are monotheists.

It is precisely the contrast between the Gathas and later Zoroastrianism that provides some reason for calling Zarathustra a monotheist. The belief in two great gods, Ohrmazd and Ahriman, the god of goodness and light and the god of evil and darkness, which is widely associated with Zarathustra's name, is actually found only after his death. It was only then that Ahura Mazda became Ohrmazd and Angra Mainyu, the Evil Spirit, Ahriman. In the Gathas Ahura Mazda is not opposed by any god of comparable stature, and his relationship to the twin spirits is left unclear. Indeed, no god besides Ahura Mazda is named in the Gathas—not even Mithra, whose cult must have been ancient even in the prophet's time, seeing that Mitra is an important deity in the Vedas. We therefore must not call Zarathustra a polytheist or a believer in two great gods, but for all that he was a dualist. His dualism was basically moral but also had a cosmic dimension. He summoned men to do Ahura Mazda's bidding by fighting against evil, meaning evil men, evil cults, and evil spirits—including above all the Evil One. But it is altogether wrong to attach a great deal of significance to the distinction between monotheism and polytheism, as if the former were good and the latter evil. Anyone who thinks in such terms is a dualist and uses simplistic categories that permit little understanding of religions. And the notion that one can save this scheme by allowing for shades of gray, as it were, and giving marks to religions according to how many gods they recognize—with Hinduism and presumably also ancient Greece at or near the bottom of the scale and Zoroastrianism near the top—is surely grotesque.

"The deepest difference between religions is not that between polytheism and monotheism. To which camp would one assign Sophocles? Even the difference between theism and atheism is not nearly so profound as that between those who feel and those who do not feel their brothers' torments" (Kaufmann, 1961, section 46).

19

In this perspective, Zarathustra's eschatology assumes immense importance. It is thoroughly dualistic, as the Twin Gatha, for example, shows clearly. In the end men will be tested, apparently by passing through molten metal, and the wicked will be punished with enduring torment, while the fighters for Truth will be rewarded. As the point is put in another Gatha (45:7): "Immortal shall be the soul of the follower of Truth, but enduring torment awaits those who cleave to the Lie. Thus Ahura Mazda has ordained with sovereign power." The conception of enduring torment in what is sometimes called "the House of the Lie" is a recurrent theme of Zarathustra's religion, and Zaehner argues convincingly that, "Unlike later Zoroastrianism in which the souls of the damned are released in the last days, the Prophet seems to have regarded the torments of the damned as being eternal" (1961, 57).

In Zarathustra's eschatology, each individual will come to a bridge where he is tested in molten metal and fire (46:10 f., 51:9 ff.) before departing for his eternal destiny of either bliss or misery. Ahura Mazda's holiness will manifest itself in his perfect retributive justice as he metes out evil for the evil and good for the good.

> Then I saw, Ahura Mazda,
> your holiness, as in the beginning
> when existence was born you ordained
> that deeds and words be requited,
> with evil for the evil, but good
> for the good, at the world's final turning (43:5).

Zaehner says: "Oddly enough, the torments of hell are more fully described than the joys of heaven" (1961, 57). But what *is* odd is that anyone, and quite especially a Roman Catholic scholar, should consider this odd. After all, Christian writers, too, have shown far more imagination in their evocations of hell than in their far rarer attempts to describe the joys of heaven, and few Christians who still believe in heaven and hell could give as detailed an account of heaven as they could give of hell. In the eleventh canto of Homer's *Odyssey* Sisyphus and Tantalus are tormented, but there is no mention of any wrongs they might have done. It remained for a later age to explain and justify their torments. But what is even far more striking is that in Homer's account there are no rewards whatever. Homer, of course, was no dualist, and the *Iliad*, the great epic that deals with the Trojan war and is structured around a series of contests, is one of the world's greatest monuments of an antidualistic spirit.

Christian attempts to picture the rewards of goodness have rarely got beyond such phrases as listening to angels who play on harps or—at a higher level of sophistication—being close to God. In the Thomistic *Summa Theologiae* (III, 94:1) we find one of the few images that is less vapid and more detailed: "In order that the bliss of the saints may be more delightful for them and that they may render more copious thanks

to God for it, it is given to them to see perfectly the punishments of the damned."
The Supplement to the *Summa*, in which these words are found, may have been added after the death of St. Thomas Aquinas, but the idea is found already in Tertullian, one of the greatest and most influential of the early fathers of the Christian church, who developed it at great length in his treatise *On Spectacles*, around A.D. 200.

He urged his readers not to attend such frivolous affairs while promising them that on "that last day of judgment, with its everlasting issues" there will be far greater spectacles for them to "admire," to "enjoy," and to "exult" over. They will see "many illustrious monarchs, whose reception into the heavens was publicly announced, groaning now in the lowest darkness with great Jove himself," and "governors of provinces, too, who persecuted the Christian name, in fires more fierce than those with which in the days of their pride they raged against the followers of Christ." Philosophers who denied the existence of the soul or the bodily resurrection will also be seen in the fire, along with actors who will be lither of limb in the flames than they ever were on the stage. The charioteer whom the blessed did not go to see in mundane spectacles will now be seen "all glowing in his chariot of fire," and "the wrestlers, not in their gymnasia, but tossing in the fiery billows." Tertullian goes on to say that perhaps "even then I shall not care to attend" to such trifles "in my eager wish rather to fix a gaze insatiable on those whose fury vented itself against the Lord." Nor need the followers of Christ wait for the day of judgment when they will be "exulting in such things as these," for "even now we in a measure have them by faith in the picturings of imagination."

The Reverend Sydney Thelwall, whose Victorian translation has been quoted here, considers this long passage in the last chapter of Tertullian's treatise "a beautiful specimen of lively faith and Christian confidence" and quite fails to see why Edward Gibbon, in his great *History of the Decline and Fall of the Roman Empire*, should have seen fit to "censure" it. Whether one is appalled by Tertullian's inhumanity and by the whole idea of eternal torture, or whether one considers it a beautiful part of the Christian faith, one should ask where these ideas come from. The answer is, in one word, Zarathustra.

The idea of a judgment after death is found in Egypt much earlier, in connection with the cult of Osiris. There are pictures of the weighing of the heart of the deceased and at least some fantasies about the mishaps that may be encountered in the afterlife. At Abydos one can still see on the walls pictures of people walking upside down, but this has been explained in terms of the charms offered for sale by Egyptian priests, who found in this business an "unlimited opportunity for gain. Their imagination grew increasingly fertile in the issuance of ever new spells, which of course they sold to increasing numbers of credulous buyers. This practice undoubtedly contributed much to heightening the popular dread of the dangers of the hereafter and spread the belief in the usefulness of such means for meeting them" (Breasted, 1933, 241) One might meet serpents or crocodiles and therefore needed a charm for repulsing serpents and crocodiles. One might encounter fire and hence must not be without a charm for going forth from the fire; and to be quite safe, better also a charm for entering the fire. Still, one might stray

> into the place of execution of the gods, but from this he was saved by a spell of "Not Entering Into the Place of Execution of the Gods"; and lest he should suddenly find himself condemned to walk head downward, he was supplied with a "Spell for Not Walking Head Downward." These unhappy dead who were compelled to walk in this inverted posture were one's most malicious enemies in the hereafter. Protection against them was vitally necessary. It is said to the deceased: "Life comes to thee, but death comes not to thee. . . . They (Orion, Sothis, and the Morning Star) save thee from the wrath of the dead who go head

downward. Thou art not among them. . . . Rise up for life, thou diest not; lift
thee up for life, thou diest not."

The belief in the efficacy of magic as an infallible agent in the hand of the
dead man was thus steadily growing, and we shall see it ultimately dominating the
whole body of mortuary belief as it emerges a few centuries later in the Book of
the Dead (242).

Moses and the prophets had developed a religion that was centrally concerned
with ethics and left no room whatsoever for torture either in this life or in the hereafter; indeed, they did not recognize any hereafter. Christianity and Islam followed
Zarathustra in dividing humanity into two camps—the followers of the Truth and the
Lie—and in looking forward to the eternal bliss of the former and the eternal torment
of the latter. This moral and eschatological dualism became central in the New Testament and in the Koran. Indeed, "moral" dualism is not quite accurate: failure to embrace "the Truth"—as seen by Zarathustra, or Jesus, or Muhammad—and opposing it,
however courageously and, one might suppose, nobly in the name of one's own religion
is considered quite sufficient to incur eternal torment. It is interesting that Western
scholars who have written about Zarathustra are generally full of praise for him and
not at all shocked by this aspect of his faith. Apparently, nineteen centuries of Christianity have inured them entirely to the prophet's inhumanity.

The ultimate fate of the majority of mankind has been of much less concern to
most writers on Zarathustra than the precise relationship of the Holy Spirit to the
Evil One and of both to Ahura Mazda. Just so, Christian theologians and historians of
Christianity have shown incomparably more interest in the exact relationship of God
the Son to God the Father and of both to the Holy Spirit than in the moral implications of the doctrine of hell. And Western philosophers down to the present have
demonstrated the same attitude even in their discussions of the problem of evil—
meaning the question of how human suffering can be reconciled with faith in an omnipotent and infinitely good and merciful and just God. Most academics have always
found theological and metaphysical subtleties more interesting than the torments of
their fellow men.

Before we return to the problem of evil in connection with Manichaeism, we must
round out our account of Zarathustra. In addition to his dualism and his eschatology
he formulated a third conception that became immensely influential.

20

Zarathustra provided a remarkable shortcut to salvation: "the *Yasna*, a word
which literally means 'sacrifice.'" He denounced the ancient sacrifices "in which a
bull was slain and the fermented juice of a plant called *Haoma* consumed; yet it is
precisely the drinking of this *Haoma*-juice which has for time immemorial constituted
the central act of the Zoroastrian ritual." While there is no clear textual evidence to
show that the prophet himself instituted this rite, there is reason to believe that it must
go back to him because it "was never disputed by any party at any later time." This
sacrament provided a royal road to salvation, and the juice itself—like *Soma* in the
Vedas—was considered divine. As a god, it is Ahura Mazda's son. "In the ritual, the
plant-god is ceremonially pounded in a mortar; the god, that is to say, is sacrificed and
offered up to his heavenly Father. . . . After the offering, priest and faithful partake
of the heavenly drink, and by partaking of it they are made to share in the immortality
of the god." Zaehner (1959, 222) concludes: "The conception is strikingly similar to
that of the Catholic Mass."

Considering the three great pillars of Zarathustra's faith, one might also recall

Nietzsche's cutting comment on the Law of Manu, the Hindu scripture in which the caste system is developed at length: "*Aryan influence* has corrupted all the world." The overt racism of this remark in a late note (*Will to Power*, #142) that Nietzsche himself did not publish is mitigated by its complex irony. In the first place, he is reversing an anti-Semitic cliché, and in another note of the same period he says: "Contra Aryan and Semitic. Where races are mixed, there is the source of great cultures. . . . Maxim: to have nothing to do with anyone who has any share in the mendacious race swindle" (XVI, 373 f.). It is as if he had meant to say: If one speaks in these stupid terms at all, just look at what the so-called Aryans have bequeathed to us. And if that term is applicable to anyone, it is, of course, appropriate to the ancient Indians and Iranians, and above all to Zarathustra and Manu. Indeed, Iran means Aryan. But this does not exhaust the irony of Nietzsche's comment. In one of his last books, *The Twilight of the Idols*, Nietzsche included a chapter on "The 'Improvers' of Mankind" in which he dealt at some length with Manu and the caste system and especially with the treatment of the outcastes before he exclaimed: "These regulations are instructive enough: here we encounter for once *Aryan* humanity, quite pure, quite primordial— we learn that the concept of 'pure blood' is the opposite of a harmless concept."

Nietzsche did not include Zarathustra in his indictment of "Aryan humanity," but one may wonder why he chose the Persian prophet as a mouthpiece for his own philosophy, if only in one major work. He had a number of reasons, including his need for the name of a prophet about whom almost none of his readers would know anything, thus precluding irrelevant and disturbing associations. Moreover, Nietzsche obviously liked the sound of the phrase, *Also sprach Zarathustra*, "Thus spoke Zarathustra," which recurs again and again in his book. But that was not all, and Nietzsche himself said in his last book, *Ecce Homo:*

> I have not been asked, as I should have been asked, what the name Zarathustra means in my mouth . . . Zarathustra created this most calamitous error, morality [or the moralistic world view that sees the world and human history as a contest of good and evil]; consequently, he must also be the first to recognize it. . . . After all, the whole of history is the refutation by experiment of the principle of the so-called "moral world order" . . . Zarathustra is more truthful than any other thinker. His doctrine, and his alone, posits truthfulness as the highest virtue . . . The self-overcoming of morality, out of truthfulness . . . that is what the name of Zarathustra means in my mouth.

Nietzsche's claim about Zarathustra's truthfulness is highly questionable. Section 46 of Nietzsche's *Antichrist*, written a few weeks before *Ecce Homo*, ends: "The noble scorn of a Roman, confronted with an impudent abuse of the word 'truth,' has enriched the New Testament with the only saying *that has value*—one which is its criticism, even its *annihilation:* 'What is truth?'" What did Jesus say in John 18? "I have come into the world, to bear witness to the truth. Everyone who is of the truth hears my voice." Whereupon "Pilate said to him, 'What is truth?'" Jesus' use—or abuse—of the word "truth" in this passage is surely entirely Zoroastrian, and it is wholly misleading to say that Zarathustra "posits truthfulness as the highest virtue." Zarathustra assumed that those who were persuaded by him and followed him were followers of the Truth and would be rewarded, while those who did not were followers of the Lie and would be tormented in all eternity.

21

After Zarathustra's death his eschatology was changed in two important respects. In the Gathas the word *Saoshyant* is sometimes applied to the prophet himself and sometimes to a king who will establish the rule of right in the future. When the king-

dom did not come, the advent of the "Savior" was postponed until it came to be expected only at the end of time. Then he would establish a new world that is not
subject to decay and corruption, the dead would rise again, and the Lie would perish
(Yasht 19). At the same time the vision of the final triumph became more humane
than the vision of Zarathustra had been and than that of Jesus was to be. The Savior,
a distant descendant of the prophet, was now expected to reunite the bodies of the
dead with their souls, to purge them from sin in a sea of molten metal—and then "the
whole human race will enter paradise where they will rejoice for ever and ever." Only
Ahriman "and his hosts will be cast into hell where they are either totally annihilated
or made powerless for all time" (Zaehner, 1959, 219). Thus all of humanity was to
be saved.

When Angra Mainyu, the Evil Spirit of the Gathas, became Ahriman, the god of
darkness and evil and the cosmic adversary of Ohrmazd, he still did not equal the
power of the god of light and good, but it was believed that he would not be vanquished
entirely until the end of the time. And the doctrine of universal salvation for all men,
which was later repeatedly rejected by the Christian churches as a heresy, is accepted
by Zoroastrianism.

22

The history of religions is full of ironies. It is not the least of these that Zarathustra's dualism is now chiefly remembered as the central doctrine of Manichaeism.
Indeed, this dualism is not only considered the quintessence of Manichaeism but
virtually synonymous with Manichaeism—although Mani, the founder of Manichaeism,
was martyred by Zoroastrian priests.

Ancient Iran recovered from Alexander's conquest and did not become part of
the Roman empire, like Egypt and Palestine, for example. In 249 B.C. Arsaces I liberated
Iran from the rule of the Seleucid dynasty that had succeeded Alexander the Great and
that continued to rule over the area west of Iran, including Palestine until the Maccabees gained their independence from Antiochus Epiphanes. Arsaces founded the kingdom of Parthia which continued under the Arsacid dynasty until A.D. 226. But this
dynasty took no great interest in Zoroastrianism.

In 226 Ardashir I, the grandson of a priest named Sasan, founded a new dynasty,
the Sassanians, and a neo-Persian empire. He invaded India and levied tribute on the
Punjab. Then he declared war on Rome and conquered Armenia. He was succeeded
by a very remarkable king, Shapur I (240?–271). Shapur waged two major wars against
Rome. Both times he invaded Mesopotamia and Syria, but the first time he was driven
back by the emperor Gordian. In the second war, however, Shapur defeated and captured the Roman emperor Valerian, who remained a prisoner until his death. A relief
34 at Naqsh-i-Rostam, where the Achaemenid kings are buried, shows the captive Valerian
before Shapur. That Shapur should have chosen this ancient site to commemorate
his victory shows his deliberate attempt to revitalize the proud tradition of the Achaemenid kings of kings, and it is not surprising that under his successors Zoroastrianism
became the official religion of the Sassanian empire. But this did not happen during
Shapur's reign. He took an interest in a prophet who appeared during his own reign:
Mani.

Mani was born in Babylonia in 216. He experienced his call to be a prophet quite
early in life, and it was in northwestern India—modern Pakistan—that he made his
first attempts to gain converts. The region was predominantly Buddhist at that time,
Gandhara art was flourishing there, and Buddhism was still actively looking for con-

verts. There is abundant evidence that Buddhism made an enormous impression on Mani. Possibly, his "conception of the highest being as a four-faced God" (Widengren, 46) was influenced by Hindu representations of Brahma; but that is only my guess.

Mani returned to Iran for the coronation of Shapur, who subsequently sent letters to lesser kings and governors to facilitate Mani's missionary activities. Mani also succeeded in converting two brothers of Shapur, but there is some doubt about the king's attitude. It has been suggested that he may have encouraged a free flow of religious ideas, giving equal protection to Jews and Christians, Hindus and Buddhists. He certainly refused to make Manichaeism the state religion, and while his inscriptions prove that he considered himself a Zoroastrian, he resisted the efforts of Karter, the leading dignitary of that faith, to make Zoroastrianism the state religion. Shapur's favorite son and first successor seems to have continued his father's religious policies, but he died after a reign of less than a year and was succeeded by Shapur's eldest son, who immediately began to cleanse the empire of all Ahrimanic or devilish beliefs and practices. Manichaeism was proscribed, and Mani himself was charged with having "taught against our law." Geo Widengren explains in his *Mani and Manichaeism* (39): "The recognized Zoroastrian faith, administered by the Magi [the hereditary priestly caste], was always designated as 'law.' Such offenses against the religious creed were regarded in later Sassanian justice as 'Offences against God' and punishable by death. Probably this was the case in the earlier Sassanid period also." Mani was found guilty and taken to prison in heavy chains: three around his wrists, three around his ankles, and one around his neck. Thus he died at the age of sixty, after twenty-six days in prison.

Christianity was the product of a syncretistic age in which many different religious traditions had come together. Mani, however, was an archeclectic who deliberately tried to synthesize the major religions he knew. J. G. Davies (161) quotes Mani's own statement in the *Kephalaia* (154), one of Mani's works that has survived in a Coptic translation:

> The writings, wisdom, apocalypses, parables and psalms of all previous religions, gathered from all parts, have come together in my religion, in the wisdom that I have revealed. As one river mixes with another and forms one great stream, so also the ancient books have been united to my writings and there has thus been formed one great wisdom, to which nought can be compared that has been preached to any previous generation.

Widengren argues that during one stage of his career Mani went through a "*Mithraic period*" and wished to be regarded as the representative of the god Mithras, but that "Mani from a certain time onwards felt himself primarily to be *Christ's representative*," and in his extant letters he constantly speaks of himself as "Mani, Apostle of Jesus Christ" (36 f.). Mani's "Christian exposition of his message was meant for the West, the Buddhist one for the East," while "the Zoroastrian cast of his system" was meant for the Iranian empire. Widengren may seem too unkind in putting it that way, but he is surely right when he goes on to say that "the Christian and Buddhist elements" may be regarded as "trimmings" that could be eliminated "with no harm to the system," while the Zoroastrian elements are "constituent parts" that could not be removed without destroying the system. When this distinction is kept in mind, the references to Jesus and the Buddha do indeed "give an impression of having been selected for tactical reasons." Moreover, for Mani "Buddhism was *Mahayana* Buddhism, Zoroastrianism the religion of the Median Magi, which meant Zervanism, and Christianity was Gnosticism, especially in the form supported by Bardesanes and Marcion" (72 f.). In other words, Mani cared little and knew less about the original form of any of these three religions and in each case drew on the version that he had happened to encounter.

Moreover, Zervanism, Gnosticism, and Mahayana Buddhism were themselves products of syncretism. Buddhism will be considered later, but Zervanism and Gnosticism must be explained briefly at this point. That is a hazardous undertaking, for the literature on Gnosticism is growing steadily, and while that on Zervanism is less abundant, Zaehner, for example, has devoted to it half of his big book on *The Dawn and Twilight of Zoroastrianism*; that is, most of Part II: "Twilight." (He transcribes the name as "Zurvanism.")

In later Zoroastrianism, the twin spirits of the Twin Gatha were equated with Ohrmazd and Ahriman. Hence it could no longer be said that both had issued from Ahura Mazda, but one did want to know from where they had come. Zervanism suggested a single source, which Zaehner ascribes to Indian influence, because he associates the quest for "the One behind the manifold" with the Hindus; "and it is quite probable that Zurvanite speculation owes a great deal to India here" (211). This seems questionable because the One of the Hindus is not only beyond diversity, it is also beyond time. The Zervanites, however, taught that the One was *Zervan*, which is time. While this seems a far cry from the Upanishads of India, it does bring to mind Goethe's early poem, "Prometheus," in which the titan challenges his archenemy, Zeus:

> I honor you? For what?
> Have you ever eased the suffering
> of the oppressed?
> Have you ever stilled the tears
> of the frightened?
> Was I not welded to manhood
> by almighty Time
> and eternal Fate,
> my masters and yours?

But while *Zervan* is generally rendered as "time," nothing about Zervanism is as simple as that, and at one point Widengren says that it was "an hermaphrodite space-time godhead" (44). Moreover, Mani's debt to Zervanism is disputed. While Widengren stresses it, the article on Mani and Manichaeism in *The Encyclopedia of Philosophy*, for example, insists that "The chief characteristic of Mani's system is a consistent dualism which rejects any possibility of tracing the origins of good and evil to one and the same source."

There is no question about Mani's profound debt to Gnosticism, although there are many disputes about Gnosticism itself, beginning with the time of its origin. The major question is whether it developed early enough to have exerted a profound influence on the New Testament, or whether the term can be applied only to a heretical Christian movement. But there is no doubt that Gnosticism was deeply indebted to Zoroastrianism, and that its fusion of the ancient Persian religion with Christianity helped to shape Manichaeism. Gnosticism was extremely eclectic and drew inspiration from so many different sources that it is difficult to sum up the central doctrines. J. G. Davies, however, has put the matter very succinctly:

> Syncretistic in character, it claimed to mediate a gnosis or knowledge that would bring salvation. Although the details of this redemptive myth differed from group to group, its underlying structure remained the same. It affirmed a complete antithesis of spirit and matter; it postulated a primordial catastrophe in heaven when the original man fell and his being was shattered into a myriad fragments. These elements were seized upon by demons as nuclei to create a world out of the chaos of darkness and they still survive as the souls of men. Although stupefied and held in bondage by the evil powers, they yearn to ascend to their

former home in eternity. The supreme deity, who is at an infinite distance from evil matter, takes pity on these imprisoned sparks of light and sends a saviour, who descends to overcome the demons and ascends in triumph . . . (33 f.).

The question about the age of Gnosticism is partly semantic, for there is agreement that these ideas were current before the Gospels were written, and Manichaeism is really a form of Gnosticism.

23

The basic conflict for Mani is that between good and evil, truth and error, light and darkness. The principle of the good he called God, and the principle of evil Matter. The soul is a spark imprisoned in the body, and death is a release that allows the soul to return home. This brings to mind the ancient Orphic play on words quoted by Plato: The body (*soma* in Greek) is the soul's tomb (*sema*).

In the beginning light and darkness were separate, but the dark resented the light and attacked it. Then the light, which Mani calls "the Father of Greatness," called (Christians might say "created") "the Mother of Life," and she in turn called "the first man" or "Primeval Man," who went out to fight the forces of evil, darkness, Matter. But the Prince of Darkness and his legions defeated him and stripped him of his armor, which consisted of the five elements of light, and they devoured these elements as well as his very soul. Primeval Man had allowed all this to happen of his own free will; he had deliberately sacrificed himself, knowing that the dark would be unable to digest the light. Manichaean hymns often deal with the dire situation in which Primeval Man found himself at that point and recall his prayer to the Father of Greatness, who thereupon called a second redeemer, "the Living Spirit." Then the Living Spirit went forth to the edge of darkness and, in Mani's own words:

> The Living Spirit cried with a loud voice, and the voice of the Living Spirit was as a sharp sword, and it laid bare the form of Primeval Man and said to him: Peace be with you, excellent among the evil, lustrous in the dark, god among beasts of wrath that know nothing of their glory. And Primeval Man answered: Come in peace . . .

Accompanied by the Mother of Life, the Living Spirit reached out with his right hand and raised Primeval Man from the dark, returning him to his abode of light. But the five elements of light and the soul of the Primeval Man still remained captive. The Living Spirit liberated them, too, flayed the forces of darkness, and used their skins to fashion the sky, their bones to make mountains, and their excrement to make the earth. Of the purest particles of light, the Living Spirit made the sun and moon, and of those which had been defiled only a little, the stars.

After Primeval Man and the Living Spirit, the Father of Greatness brought into being the Third Messenger, the father of the Twelve Virgins of Light, who are the twelve signs of the zodiac. And then an immense cosmic wheel drew up toward the sun and moon the particles of light that had been defiled most.

> During the first half of the month the rescued particles of light rose in a pillar of light, known as the "column of glory," towards the moon which, filled and swollen with particles of light, became full. During the second half of the month the particles of light were conducted from the moon to the sun and thence to the paradise of light. Behind these . . . concepts, are the old Indo-Iranian ideas concerning the purgation of the human soul by way of this ascent to the lunar and solar spheres. The notion of the column of light stretching from earth to heaven and consisting of mounting particles of light is simply the ancient idea of the

Milky Way which is made up of the souls of the dead rising unceasingly to the firmament of fixed stars. In late antiquity this mythical interpretation dominated eschatology generally. Mani in this instance adopted a train of thought that was common property during antiquity and originated in Iran and the Middle East (Widengren, 55 f.).

The Third Messenger was a hermaphrodite. As he traversed the heavens, riding the moon, he excited the forces of darkness, the so-called Archons, by appearing to the males among them as a beautiful nude woman, and to the females as a radiant, nude youth. Then the male Archons ejaculated the particles of light that they had retained until then, and the seeds of light fell upon the earth and developed into plants that continue to harbor some of the light. The female Archons, being pregnant, gave premature birth to demons that fed on some of the plants, and so they, too, came to harbor light.

Then the forces of evil struck back. They decided to concentrate as much light as was still within their power. A male demon absorbed all the male demons, a female demon all the female demons, and they copulated. Their offspring were the first man and woman, Adam and Eve. The bodies and the lust of human beings are their heritage from the forces of evil, but their souls are their heritage from the light. Initially, however, Adam knew nothing of the light within him, nor did he see or hear anything. He was unconscious until the Redeemer appeared, and the Redeemer was a manifestation of the Third Messenger. He is sometimes called Ohrmazd, sometimes the Son of God, sometimes Jesus.

Not only is light good and dark evil, but woman is the instrument of the forces of darkness, and sex is evil. Eve seduced Adam, and sexual intercourse means the triumph of darkness as every birth means another captive soul. But the Redeemer reappears now as Zarathustra, now as the Buddha, now as Jesus—and finally as Mani. Mani teaches men what is needful for salvation: various sacraments and abstention from sexual intercourse and from eating anything that has a soul—that is, vegetarianism. The elect who practice this ethic will go to paradise when they die, while ordinary Manichaeans who live less ascetically must wait longer to be redeemed.

24

Some modern scholars have suggested that Manichaeism is more rational than the Christian faith; for given an omnipotent God whose goodness, justice, and mercy are infinite, the problem of evil is unanswerable and we simply cannot account for the suffering we encounter in the world. But taking Manichaeism as a whole, it is difficult indeed to find it particularly rational; and to avoid an unanswerable problem of evil, we certainly do not need Mani's speculations. Zoroastrianism will do—and often the word "Manichaeism" is used very loosely to mean a radical dualism that sees history as a perennial contest between the children of light and the children of darkness. It is easy to understand Zaehner's claim that "the 'classic' dualism of the Pahlavi books [the scriptures of later Zoroastrianism] is perhaps the most rational solution of the problem of evil ever devised" (1959, 219); but this claim, too, is untenable.

The problem of evil is unanswerable if one believes that there is only one god and that he is omnipotent as well as infinitely good, merciful, and just. But as soon as one denies one or more of these premises, the problem disappears. The belief in two great gods, one good and one evil, is merely one way of doing that. Polytheism is another. Belief in only one god who is omnipotent but not infinitely good, just, and merciful is a third way. Belief in a god who has these moral qualities but who is not omnipotent is a fourth. Belief in no god at all, a fifth.

The claims about the unique rationality and plausibility of Manichaeism or Zoro-astrianism do not stand up under examination and merely serve to cover up the real appeal of these doctrines: it is their inhumanity that answers to a profound human need. It reduces moral complexities to simplistic choices that make themselves. There is no need to analyze the pros and cons of multiple alternatives; there are only two ways, one good and the other evil, and our opponents are followers of the Lie and children of darkness, while our party, our religion, our movement, our country, our side is composed of the followers of the Truth, who are children of light. Moreover, we know that in the end we shall prevail, while they deserve torment, and any punishment we inflict on them is only a foretaste of their ultimate penalties. Need one wonder about the perennial appeal of doctrines that make so many complexities so simple, so many difficult choices so easy, and promote at the same time self-righteousness, hatred, and hope?

25

In Egypt and Syria Manichaeism was widely accepted while Mani was still living, and from there it spread to North Africa and to Spain, to Asia Minor and Greece, to Italy and Gaul. By 297, a mere twenty years after Mani's death, the Roman emperor Diocletian considered it necessary to send an edict against the Manichaeans to his African proconsul Julianus. He described them as a plague that had spread from hostile Persia and was poisoning Rome and the world. "The tracts and their authors together with the ringleaders were to be burned, their followers to lose their lives and have their property confiscated by the State. Persons holding a position in society who had adhered to this disgraceful sect or succumbed to the Persian doctrine were condemned to compulsory labour in the mines . . ." (Widengren, 118). That very same year the Egyptians rebelled against Roman rule, and it is considered possible that the revolt was engineered by Manichaeans. At the same time, an Arabian prince defended the Manichaeans.

A little more than a hundred years later, Augustine became a Manichaean, although by that time the Christians and the Manichaeans were fierce rivals, but later Augustine changed his mind and wrote a tract against the Manichaeans. Still, the Zoroastrian influence is unmistakable in Augustinian Christianity—and even in the Gospels and in Paul's epistles.

In the East, Manichaeism spread to Samarkand, Tashkent, and beyond central Asia to China. The planets have Iranian names in China, and it has been surmised that Manichaeans may have introduced China to the Western planetary calendar. In 732 the emperor of China proclaimed an edict against Manichaeism, but later in the eighth century the Uigurian Turks, who held parts of eastern China, adopted Manichaeism as their state religion and clung to it for several centuries. "Inside China Manichaeism from the eleventh to the fourteenth century enjoyed high favour above all in the province of Fu Kien. But as a religion it went in China also the way of syncretism and two of Mani's works were even adopted into the Taoist canon" (Widengren, 134).

Under Islam the Manichaeans did not fare so well. The Muslims persecuted them ruthlessly (Widengren, 129). Not surprisingly, the religions that had absorbed Zarathustra's and Mani's dualism were most intolerant of Manichaeism.

The Manichaeans' attitude toward Christianity was simple. They approved of the many "Manichaean" elements in the New Testament, including the antithesis of flesh and spirit, while repudiating as a falsification of Jesus' teaching whatever did not agree with their own doctrine. They liked the parable of the tares in the Gospel according to Matthew, chapter 13, where a man sowed good seed but his enemy came and sowed weeds among the wheat. Then the master said to his servants: "Let both grow together until the harvest, and at harvest time I will tell the reapers: Gather the weeds first and bind them into bundles to be burned, but gather the wheat into my barn." As the Manichaeans saw it, the New Testament itself contained many tares. For the Old Testament they had no use whatever. Like Marcion, an influential dualist born about A.D. 100, and like the leading Gnostics, the Manichaeans saw clearly that the Old Testament was essentially anti-"Manichaean."

Iranian bronze stag, 500 B.C.

III

THE JEWS SINCE JEREMIAH: EXILE AND RETURN

Jeremiah and the Second Isaiah—Ezekiel and Apocalyptic Literature—
Satan—The Completion of the Hebrew Bible—The Pharisees—
Hillel—Text: The Fall of Masada—Early Diaspora:
Septuagint, Philo, Yokhanan ben Sakkai—
Rabbi Akiba—Talmud and Midrash—
From the Eleventh Century to the Twentieth—
The Birth of the New Israel—
The Wars of 1956, 1967, and 1973—
Problems

Tiberias.

26

It is some measure of the age of the Jewish religion that one tends to consider as "late" the literature that came into being during and after the Babylonian exile. The last prophecies of Jeremiah date from the first years of the exile, but he and his thought and style had been formed earlier and one thinks of him as belonging with the great pre-exilic prophets. It was of the utmost significance that a man of such stature was at the height of his powers when Jerusalem and the first temple were destroyed in 586 B.C., and that he interpreted the events leading up to these disasters and the exile that followed in consistently Mosaic, monotheistic terms. God, who had led Israel from Egypt, had now punished her for her iniquities. Yet the Book of Jeremiah is pervaded by compassion, and the prophet wrote some of the greatest poetry of suffering.

> Cursed be the day
> on which I was born!
> The day when my mother bore me,
> let it not be blessed!
> Cursed be the man
> who brought the news to my father,
> A son is born to you!
> making him glad.
> Let that man be like the cities
> that the Lord destroyed without pity;
> let him hear a cry in the morning
> and an alarm at noon.
> That he did not kill me in the womb,
> that my mother might have been my grave . . . (20)

A later age ascribed to Jeremiah not only his own book but also the Book of Lamentations over the destruction of Jerusalem.

Even so, the trauma of the exile might well have left the Jewish people prone to assume that their religion was somehow inferior to that of their conquerors—or later, their liberators, the Persians. And if their religion had not been formed so largely before that time, it would surely have been quite impossible for them to resist that temptation. (Consider, for example, Plato's contempt for democracy after Sparta had defeated democratic Athens; or the attitude of the Japanese toward the West after their defeat in 1945.) It remains astonishing that the Jews, though liberated by the Persians, who even allowed them to return to Jerusalem and rebuild the temple, resisted Zarathustra's dualism much more successfully than the other people of the Near East. This seems to have been due in some measure to the emergence of an extraordinary prophet who responded to the new doctrine with poetic speeches whose force and eloquence have never been excelled. There is no version of Zarathustra's Gathas that does not look pale and wooden besides the verses of the so-called Second Isaiah, whom we encounter in chapters 40 to 55 of the Book of Isaiah. We know nothing whatever about him and cannot even be sure that his name was Isaiah, but it is arguable that since his death the world has not seen a religious poet or prophet who could brook comparison with him.

> Comfort, comfort my people!
> says your God.
> Speak to the heart of Jerusalem
> and shout to her
> that her trials are ended,
> her debt is paid,
> she has received from the hand of the Lord
> double for all her sins.
>
> A voice cries:
> In the desert even
> a path for our God.
> Every valley shall be raised,
> every mountain, every hill be made low,
> the crags become level
> and rough places plain.
> The glory of the Lord is revealed,
> all flesh beholds it,
> for the mouth of the Lord has spoken.
>
> A voice says: Cry!
> And he says: What shall I cry?
> All flesh is grass,
> all its grace like the flowers of the field.
> The grass withers, the flower fades
> as the breath of the Lord comes upon them.
> Thus the people is grass.
> The grass withers, the flower fades,
> but the word of our God will stand for ever. . . .
>
> He feeds his flock like a shepherd,
> he brings home the lambs in his arms,
> carries them at his bosom
> and gently leads those with young. . . .
>
> Behold, nations as a drop on a bucket,
> they have as much weight as dust on the scales;
> behold, isles he raises like mist.
> Lebanon is not enough for fuel,
> nor its beasts for a burnt offering.
> All the nations are as nothing before him . . .
>
> Why do you say, Jacob,
> and speak, Israel:
> Hidden is my path from the Lord,
> and my right ignored by my God!
> Do you not know, have you not heard,
> the eternal God is the Lord,
> created the ends of the earth,
> never weary, never faint,
> unfathomable in understanding.
> He gives strength to the weary. . . .

This seems to have been his first speech, proclaiming the impending end of the exile. Nothing like that had happened before; no other people who had been uprooted from their homeland, after the Assyrians or Babylonians had destroyed their capital cities and their temples, had ever survived and returned. But the prophet's voice reaches out far beyond the immediate occasion, however sublime, and strikes chords that reverberate through millennia.

> But you Israel, my servant,
> Jacob, whom I have chosen,
> you seed of Abraham who loved me,
> you whom I took from the ends of the earth
> and called from its farthest corners,
> saying to you:
> You are my servant,
> I have chosen you and not cast you off.
> Fear not, for I am with you . . .
>
> Behold put to shame and disgraced
> all who burnt up against you;
> reduced to nothing, lost
> your opponents. . . .
>
> I awakened one from the North, and he has come
> from the rising of the sun and calls on my name
> to come upon princes as if they were mortar,
> like a potter pounding his clay.

It is God who reduced the great empire of the Babylonians to nothing; under his breath the Babylonians have faded away, and Cyrus, coming from the northeast, was sent by the Lord. But is it Cyrus of whom the prophet is speaking later in chapter 42?

> Behold my servant whom I uphold,
> my chosen in whom my soul delights,
> I have given my spirit upon him
> to issue right to the nations.
> He does not cry or shout
> to make his voice heard in the streets;
> a bruised reed he breaks not,
> and a dim wick he does not blow out. . . .
>
> Thus speaks God, the Lord,
> who created the heavens . . .
> I, the Lord, have called you in justice,
> taken your hand and given you
> as a covenant to the people,
> a light to the nations
> to open blind eyes,
> to free the prisoner from the dungeon,
> from captivity those who dwell in darkness.

Of whom is the prophet speaking in chapter 53?

> Despised and shunned by men,
> a man of suffering, familiar with sickness,
> people hid their faces from him,
> he was despised and we thought him of no account.
> Yet it was our sickness he bore
> and our suffering that he endured.

We thought him afflicted,
smitten by God and debased.
But he was wounded for our transgressions,
he was bruised for our iniquities,
the punishment upon him was for our good,
and with his stripes we were healed.
All of us went astray like sheep,
each in his own way,
while the Lord laid on him
the iniquity of us all.
He was oppressed and debased
and did not open his mouth,
like a lamb led to the slaughter
and like a sheep that is silent before its shearers
and did not open his mouth.

The passion of Jesus in the Gospels was formed in the image of these verses and those that follow, and Christians have long read passages like these as prophecies of Christ. Some Jewish interpreters have suggested that the Second Isaiah was speaking of one of his own contemporaries, while others have thought that he meant that the sufferings of Israel were vicarious and that the Jewish people were somehow atoning for the iniquities of the nations. We cannot know whom the prophet meant, but after hearing him we should experience human suffering differently—without self-righteousness, with reverence and compassion.

Here was no mere epigone of Moses and Elijah, Amos and Isaiah; here was flesh of their flesh and blood of their blood—a voice worthy of inclusion in the Book of Isaiah. The old God was not dead, yielding his place to Zarathustra's god.

I, I am the Lord,
and besides me no savior (43:11).

I am the first and I am the last,
besides me there is no god (44:6).

I am the Lord and there is no other,
and besides me there is no god. . . .
I am the Lord and there is no other
who forms light and creates darkness,
who makes peace and creates evil (45:5 ff.).

27

The prophet Ezekiel, who was an older contemporary of the Second Isaiah, was no less original and in some ways more of a harbinger of the future. Much of the time, he turned his back on the reality of the exile and devoted himself to detailed descriptions of his visions. In the night of apparently hopeless exile he saw the rebuilt temple so clearly and could picture it so minutely that his speeches—much more often in prose than in poetry—probably went far toward maintaining the morale of his people. Some of the other things he saw, notably fantastic animals, clearly show the influence of Babylonian and Iranian art.

Like Amos and Hosea, almost two hundred years earlier, he marks a new departure. They had composed great poetic speeches without waiting to be consulted, and their central thrust had been moral. With Ezekiel a new type of literature begins: apocalyptic books that describe visions of things to come. In this genre Zarathustra's eschatology was to gain considerable influence. By this time, however, Judaism could look back upon an imposing literature, and the ancient traditions were far from being merely of the past. The Second Isaiah provided a living link to a stunning heritage, and so did many other less imposing figures. As a result, the new apocalyptic literature remained rather a marginal phenomenon in Judaism, and only one book that is partly of this type was eventually accepted into the canon of the Hebrew Bible: Daniel, parts of which were probably written later than any other part of the Hebrew Bible.

The whole book is postexilic, and the last chapters were added in the early second century B.C., the time of the Maccabees. Daniel is only partly written in Hebrew; parts of it are Aramaic. The first six chapters relate the adventures of Daniel at the courts of Nebuchadnezzar, the Babylonian king who had destroyed the temple, Darius, and Belshazzar. Here Daniel appears in the third person. But in the last six chapters (7–12), Daniel relates in the first person four apocalyptic visions of the future of four kingdoms; and in the last chapter there are two verses that reflect Zarathustra's eschatology: "And many of those who sleep in the dust of the earth shall awake, some to everlasting life, and some to shame and everlasting contempt. And the wise shall shine like the brightness of the firmament, and those who have led many to righteousness, like the stars for ever and ever" (2–3). Even here there is no reference to torments of hell. Perhaps Isaiah 26:19 is also a late insertion: "Your dead shall live, my corpses shall rise. Awake and sing with joy, you that dwell in the dust." But this verse need not be taken so literally. In any case, the eighth-century Isaiah did not believe in any life after death, as chapter 38 shows, nor did the Second Isaiah; and scholars do not ascribe the end of the Book of Isaiah to either of them, least of all the last verse, which does not even seem to connect well with what has gone before: "And they go out and look at the corpses of those who rebelled against me, for their worm will not die and their fire not be quenched, and they will be an abhorrence to all flesh."

The two verses in Isaiah, though probably very late and written under Zoroastrian influence, did not have to be interpreted literally, while Daniel was known to have been written too late to be included with the prophets; the Hebrew Bible, unlike the Christian, places Daniel among the so-called Writings, near the end of the canon, followed only by Ezra, Nehemiah, and Chronicles. Like these books, Daniel did not have the prestige of the earlier books.

Upon reflection, it is stunning to note how little influence Zoroastrianism gained on Biblical Judaism. We find three or four verses that suggest some sort of afterlife or resurrection, and no development at all of the "Manichaean" theme of heaven and hell. Through an age of unprecedented syncretism, the Jews resisted the galloping eclecticism of the Near East to an almost incredible extent, though, of course, not with complete success.

Well before New Testament times there were large Jewish communities in Egypt as well as Mesopotamia, many Jews were fluent in Greek and some wrote Greek books, and there were many sects with different ideas. But we must distinguish between "normative" Judaism, to use George Foot Moore's useful phrase, and fringe phenomena. The taste that decided on what merited inclusion in the Hebrew Bible had been formed by Moses and the prophets—the great prophets from Amos and Hosea, Isaiah and Micah, down to Jeremiah and the Second Isaiah. The apocalyptic literature in which the influence of Zarathustra's eschatology is undeniable would not have survived if Christians had not taken a fancy to some of these books and translated them into various tongues; and after World War II some material that was decidedly more syncretistic and "Manichaean" than the Hebrew Bible was found among the Dead Sea scrolls. These finds are of enormous interest and importance for our understanding of the New Testament background and of nonnormative Judaism. But it should not be forgotten that such books were not accepted into the canon; and while some teachers were revered by the Jews, as Hillel and Akiba were, many others were not remembered at all and remain unknown even after the Dead Sea scrolls have increased our knowledge of the heterogeneity of Judaism in the Hellenistic and Roman periods.

28

There is no devil in the Hebrew Bible, but under Zoroastrian influence a new figure, Satan, was introduced in three books. The word is older and simply means opponent or adversary (see Numbers 22:22, 32; I Samuel 29:4; II Samuel 19:23; I Kings 5:18, 11:14, 23, 25; and Psalms 109:6). In three postexilic passages, however, "the adversary" seems to be a nonhuman individual. The Book of Zechariah belongs to the period immediately after the end of the exile. The third chapter begins: "And he let me see Joshua, the high priest, standing before the messenger of the Lord, and the adversary stood at his right to speak against him. Then the Lord said to the adversary: The Lord will rebuke you, adversary; the Lord who has chosen Jerusalem will rebuke you. Is not this a brand saved from the fire?" The adversary never even opens his mouth after that, nor is he mentioned again.

In the second of our three passages, Satan's appearance is limited to a single verse that is, however, of some interest. In II Samuel 24:1 the anger of the Lord flares up against Israel and he tells David to count the people. David counts them—there are 1,300,000 men of military age—and then repents, too late, because counting the people was forbidden; and the Lord strikes the people with three days of pestilence. This story at the end of Samuel is puzzling and evidently offended the moral sense of a later age. In retelling the story in Chronicles a few centuries later, after the exile, an attempt was made to remove the offense: "And an adversary stood up against Israel and he told David to count Israel" (I, 21:1). Again, nothing further is heard of the adversary; there is only this one reference that, no doubt, made the story less offensive to shallow minds not only in those days but down to our own time. But for the uncompromising monotheism of the Hebrew Bible, which is not placed in question either here or in Zechariah, the problem remains—along with the ancient prophetic response to it:

> Shall a trumpet be blown in the city
> and the people not be afraid?
> Shall there be evil in a city
> and the Lord has not done it? (Amos 3:6)
>
> Do not evil and good proceed
> from the mouth of the Most High? (Lamentations 3:38)
>
> I make peace and create evil (Isaiah 45:7).

And when Job's wife says to him: "Do you still cling to your integrity? Curse God and die!" he replies: "Like foolish women you speak. Shall we receive good at the hand of God and not evil?" (2:10)

It is in the Book of Job that the adversary has the biggest role he ever acquired in the Hebrew Bible, and it is not very big. He appears only in chapter 1:6–8 and 12 and at the beginning of chapter 2. By verse 10 of chapter 2 he is discounted totally. Neither Job nor his friends ever question God's power. What Job does question is God's justice, while his friends insist that God is just and that Job's suffering therefore proves that Job must have done wrong—which as a matter of fact, we are told, he has not. In the end the Lord rebukes Job's friends: "for you have not spoken of me what is right as my servant Job has." Thus the Book of Job is downright anti-Zoroastrian and anti-Manichaean. The absence of any reference to rewards and punishments after death should also be noted.

Some recent scholars have argued that the body of the book must have been composed before the exile and that the prologue with Satan in it was added later. However that may be, Satan, the adversary, is used as a literary device to set the stage for a profound discussion of the problem of innocent human suffering. When God says that Job is blameless or flawless, Satan retorts: "Does Job fear God for nothing?" Has he not every reason to be good? As soon as God will touch his possessions, "he will curse you to your face." Then God does bring disaster upon Job, and Job only says: "Naked I came from my mother's womb, and naked shall I return. The Lord has given, and the Lord has taken away; blessed be the name of the Lord." When God points out to Satan that he was wrong, Satan replies: "Skin for skin! All a man has he will give for his life. But reach out with your hand and touch his bone and flesh, and he will curse you to your face." Then "the Lord said to Satan: Behold, he is in your power; only spare his life. And Satan went forth from the presence of the Lord and afflicted Job with loathsome sores from the sole of his foot to the crown of his head." After that (2:7), Satan is mentioned no more, and in the forty chapters after this the idea that God might not be responsible for Job's suffering is never considered even for a moment. Here the book is at one with Amos and the Second Isaiah.

A literary device, of course, need not be trivial, and the prologue in heaven with which the book begins displays a narrative power and skill that have rarely been matched in world literature. The economy of style, the compression of a maximum of meaning into a couple of pages, the vivid simplicity that invites endless reflections —all this is worthy of the author of Genesis and may help us to understand why some rabbis attributed the book to Moses (Babylonian Talmud, Baba Batra 14b). Even as a great actor can make much of a very small role, the author of Job succeeds in giving us in a few lines an unforgettable conception of the adversary. Goethe leaned heavily on the prologue to Job when he composed his own "Prologue in Heaven" for his *Faust*. What is more, his whole conception of Mephistopheles—his very un-Manichaean and un-Christian "devil"—may be seen as a development of these few lines.

What is at stake in the Book of Job, however, is not merely a conception of the world, although even on that score the work may be unsurpassed. The world of Job is the world of human experience—of pestilences, floods, and famines, of quakes and other natural disasters, of Auschwitz and Treblinka. It is not an orderly world postulated or construed by theologians and philosophers, and it is utterly removed from all such complicated speculations as those, for example, found in Mani's books. Job's is an uncanny world in which there is nothing like a proportion between an individual's wickedness and suffering; it is a world in which great evildoers often flourish while the virtuous are smitten—a world of which a human being with compassion simply can't make moral sense. For all that, neither Job nor the author of the book is prepared to renounce his humane ideas and to agree that whatever is, is right. Job stubbornly refuses the wisdom of his friends who keep insisting that suffering proves some prior guilt. Most of the theologians and philosophers who have commented on the book have failed to note not only that Job questions God's justice and is upheld by the Lord in the end but also that the implications of the book are not confined to theology and metaphysics. What is at stake no less is our attitude toward human suffering. Job's steadfast insistence that there cannot be any presumption that suffering is just implies that we must not harden our hearts to the misery of our fellow men as if they merely got what they deserved. While the book has usually been read badly, this humane attitude toward suffering has remained part of normative Judaism and has become so deeply ingrained among Jews that millions of them have retained it even after giving up their belief in God.

29

The Book of Jonah has already been considered in the chapter on Ancient Israel (section 12) along with the Book of Ruth. Both are thoroughly anti-Manichaean and may well belong to the period immediately after the exile. But Jonah needs to be recalled here because its central themes supplement what has just been said. The people of Nineveh, the archenemy, are human beings first of all, and their sufferings are as real as ours and merit compassion even when they *are* deserved. Moreover, as soon as they truly repent and decide to change their ways, they should be forgiven, and it is inhuman to insist that their punishment should continue. Jonah, unlike Daniel, was placed among the prophets. His book is read in every synagogue on Yom Kippur, the Day of Atonement, which is the highest holiday of the Jewish year, and according to the Talmud, Job was always recited by the high priest shortly before Yom Kippur. Ruth is read on Shavuot (Pentecost)—and Ecclesiastes during Sukkot (the feast of tabernacles).

Ecclesiastes is one of the great oddities of the Hebrew Bible. It begins "The words of the preacher, David's son, king in Jerusalem. Vanity of vanities, says the preacher, vanity of vanities! All is vain." Being ascribed to King Solomon certainly helped the book to win inclusion in the canon, but in New Testament times some rabbis still objected to a few books included among the so-called Writings, the third and last part of the Hebrew Bible; notably Ecclesiastes and the Song of Songs, which was also ascribed to Solomon. By that time it was not unusual to ascribe books to ancient authors, and that was not enough to decide the matter. Hence it tells us a great deal about the liberality of spirit among the rabbis of that time that these two books were included in the canon.

Why, one should ask, were these books canonized when so many others were not? Two major reasons come to mind. First, the rabbis evidently knew a gem when they saw it. Ecclesiastes (Kohelet in Hebrew) and the Song of Songs were simply too fine, too obviously inspired to be set aside. Indeed, Rabbi Akiba defended the Song of Songs, saying that it was the holiest of all books. In time, it generated a rich mystical-erotic literature—largely among Gentiles. Secondly, the profound disillusionment of Kohelet and what might strike many a reader as despair and skepticism, and the eroticism of the Song of Songs plainly did not seem as offensive to the rabbis as did the Manichaean apocalypses that the early Christians liked so much—and some aspects of Christianity.

30

The rearrangement of the books of the Hebrew Bible in the Christian Old Testament has already been discussed in section 12 of the chapter on Ancient Israel. It may seem to make sense to place Ruth after Judges because she is said to have lived at the time of the judges, and to follow up Kings with some of the other historical books from the "Writings." And once that is done, it may even be understandable that Job, Psalms, Proverbs, Ecclesiastes, and the Song of Songs should appear after these books in the Christian Bible. Nevertheless, the fact that the Christian Old Testament ends

Caves where Dead Sea Scrolls were found.

with the prophets is extremely unfortunate, and not only for the reasons mentioned earlier. This arrangement also seems to corroborate the Christian notion that during the centuries before Jesus appeared Judaism had stagnated in legalistic disputes. The arrangement of the Hebrew Bible shows at a glance that during this period the Jews produced a literature that need not fear comparison with the books of the New Testament.

For all that, Judaism did change gradually but drastically. In Greece the period during which great literature of the first order was created did not last long. The first Greek philosophers lived at the time of the Babylonian exile, in the sixth century; Herodotus and the great tragic poets as well as Thucydides and Socrates in the fifth century; and the works of Plato and Aristotle were written in the fourth. This span of two hundred and fifty years must be extended back into the seventh or eighth century to allow for Homer and Hesiod. But after 406, the year when Euripides and Sophocles died, there was no more poetry of that order, and after Plato and Aristotle there were no more philosophers of their rank.

The Hellenistic age was dominated by eclecticism, editorial efforts, and scholasticism. In Israel the editorial efforts resulted in the final canon of the Hebrew Bible, and the motivation behind that was largely to resist the flood of syncretism.

The Jewish scholasticism of the Hellenistic and Roman periods had the same motivation and was more legalistic than philosophical or theological, although "legalistic" is a prejudicial and somewhat misleading term, the more so because it is often taken to imply a contrast with moral concerns. It would be fairer to say that the concern of the rabbis was more practical than theoretical, more with questions about how one was to live than with what one might believe. In another age, their distinctive national literature might have been sufficient to insure not only a proud sense of national identity but also survival. But in that period survival was as unlikely as it had been in the Babylonian exile. Jewish survival against staggering odds was due in very large measure to the success of the rabbis in spelling out in painstaking detail a way of life that precluded assimilation.

During the first century A.D. there was still considerable variety in life styles as well as beliefs among the Jews. The Sadducees did not believe in any life after death, while the Pharisees believed in it and spoke occasionally of "the world to come," without spelling out any detailed visions. The torments of the damned had no place in normative Judaism, but there were also sects that liked apocalypses. Some were more or less monastic and ascetic, and little was known about them until some of their scrolls were discovered in caves near the Dead Sea. The Pharisees were anything but monolithic; their intellectual life involved constant discussion, especially about practical questions, and the mode of argument was largely exegetical. One pitted interpretations of verses and words in Scripture against each other, and while there was some element of playfulness in much of this, one never doubted the ultimate seriousness of the whole enterprise as well as its practical relevance.

What was gradually hammered out in this way was, to give a few examples, a liturgy (which is to say, the order of prayers), a Sabbath law (which is to say, what was and was not permitted on the Sabbath—and on other holidays), and dietary laws, defining with precision what one could and could not eat.

The basic dietary laws were to be found in Leviticus 11. Some animals had been pronounced kosher or clean, and others unclean. "Whatever parts the hoof and is cloven-footed and chews the cud, you may eat." The Torah followed up this simple rule with a few examples of animals that fulfill one of these conditions but not both and are therefore forbidden, and the pig is merely one of these, along with the camel and the hare. "Whatever in the waters has fins and scales, whether in the sea or in the rivers, you may eat"; but again both conditions must be met, and therefore lobsters, crabs, shrimps, scallops, oysters, and all sorts of other seafood are ritually unclean, although these creatures are not named specifically. Regarding birds there is no general rule, but a few are singled out as forbidden. These include eagle and osprey, falcon and kite, raven and ostrich, hawk and sea gull, owl and ibis, pelican and vulture, stork, heron, and hoopoe. Except for some locusts and grasshoppers, insects as well as bats, reptiles, crawling things, and "whatever has many feet" are forbidden, no less than animals found dead.

Reading these laws, one gets the impression that they could have been prompted at least in part by an aesthetic sense and a concern for health. Two of the most fateful prohibitions suggest an aesthetic-moral inspiration and seem to be based at least in large measure on humane feeling. First, the law in Leviticus against eating blood (17:12 ff.):

> No person among you shall eat blood, nor shall the stranger who sojourns among you eat blood. And whoever among the children of Israel or the strangers among them hunts and captures any beast or bird that may be eaten, shall pour out its blood and cover it with earth.

The rabbis took this to mean that all meat was forbidden unless the animal had been slaughtered in an especially prescribed ritual manner that was designed to make sure that one would not eat blood. Hence a Jew could not buy meat from Gentiles or eat even the meat of otherwise clean animals at the table of a Gentile.

Another dietary law that had enormous consequences is not to be found in Leviticus but twice in Exodus (23:19, 34:26), and once in Deuteronomy (14:21): "You shall not boil a kid in its mother's milk." This is as close as the Torah comes to forbidding—as the rabbis did—the cooking together or eating together of milk and milk products on the one hand and meat and meat products on the other.

The extension and multiplication of dietary rules as well as many other laws may well defy any simple explanation. After all, it was not the work of one man whose reasons one might perhaps hope to reconstruct but the labor of many generations over a period of several centuries. But it is hard to escape the conclusion that a central purpose in all of this was to prevent the assimilation and demise of the Jewish people. And once this immense enterprise of laying down rules for all occasions was begun, it became—like scholastic philosophy in the Middle Ages, or like chess—a kind of madness. Here was an obsession that was essentially constructive and permitted, even fostered, the development of intellectual agility and subtlety.

The survival of the Jewish people as a separate entity was made possible by the ark of the law; for the Jews were threatened by the danger of drowning in the flood of syncretism. Moreover, after the destruction of the second temple, and especially in the Christian world, many Jews found themselves in the position of a despised and hated minority that was frequently subjected to inhuman treatment. In such circumstances many people lose their self-respect and any interest in their own culture; they lose their heritage along with their pride. It is obvious that this did not happen to the Jews—owing to the heroic measures taken by the rabbis who constructed for their people a world of their own, based on the Hebrew Bible but not stopping with it.

We might find it more interesting if the Jews had gone on producing books that one might put beside their Bible; if they had kept creating radically new things instead of conserving their heritage. But in the first place other people and religions did not produce books like the Hebrew Bible during the Middle Ages either, and the scholastic philosophies of Christians and Muslims, Hindus and Buddhists, invite comparison with what the rabbis did. And then the spread of all of these religions—whether by conquest or dispersion—posed the problem of keeping a common identity. To prevent endless fragmentation it seemed essential to cultivate their common traditions.

It does not follow from any of this that the rabbis who were regarded most highly considered legal details more important than moral matters. A look at the two rabbis who were, respectively, Jesus' and Paul's most eminent contemporaries among the Pharisees—Hillel and Akiba—shows that the opposite is true.

31

Hillel was born in Babylonia but studied in Jerusalem and became the most revered and influential rabbi during the forty years from 30 B.C. to A.D. 10 if not of the whole post-Biblical period. His views prevailed on a great many specific points, and he also formulated seven principles for the exegesis of the Bible. First, minor cases permit inferences to major cases. Second, words with similar meanings in different laws suggest that these laws must be considered together. Most of the remaining principles also concern similarities between passages and the application of what is said in one to the others, but the seventh principle enjoins regard for the context. Roughly a hundred years later, Rabbi Ishmael elaborated these principles, suggesting thirteen hermeneutical rules.

Hillel's impact was not least a function of his personality. The Babylonian Talmud relates that a man once made a large bet with a friend that he could make Hillel lose his temper. Then he waited till the sabbath was approaching and Hillel was getting ready for it, went to Hillel's house, and yelled: "Is Hillel there?" Hillel came out and the man asked him a pointedly stupid question, but Hillel gave him a kind and informative answer. A few minutes later, the man called him back, and he kept trying to irritate Hillel, but Hillel's patience remained unshaken. Finally, the man rebuked him because on his account he had lost a large sum of money, but Hillel replied that it would have been worse if he had lost his temper (Shabbat 31a).

On the same page we find an even much more famous story in a similar vein:

> A Gentile came to Shammai and said to him: I will become a convert if you teach me the whole Torah [or Law: the Five Books of Moses] while I stand on one foot. But Shammai chased him away with the rod he had in his hand. Then the man went to Hillel, who accepted him, saying: What is hateful to you, do not do to others; that is the whole Law, the rest is commentary; go and learn!

With his legendary patience he combined a rare gift for aphorisms. The aphorism just quoted is usually given without its tripartite ending, yet Hillel did not merely say what Confucius had said five hundred years earlier; he went on to suggest that this was the soul of Judaism—but not as easy to understand as one might suppose. For all its simplicity, the great rule requires a commentary that spells out its implications and its applications in diverse circumstances, and there is no way around study.

Shammai was the most distinguished rabbi of the time besides Hillel, and both men had many followers. The Babylonian Talmud tells two great stories about their rivalry (Erubin 13b). *Halakha* means law and is distinguished from *haggada*, which means stories and reflections.

> For three years the school of Shammai and the school of Hillel argued: one said the halakha was to be decided according to it, the other said the halakha was to be decided according to it. Then a heavenly voice was heard and said: the one and the other are words of the living God, but the halakha is to be decided according to the school of Hillel. But if the one and the other are words of the

> living God, why was it granted to the school of Hillel that the halakha was de-
> cided according to it? Because it was peaceable and modest and studied not only
> its own views but also those of the school of Shammai; even more, it placed the
> words of the school of Shammai before its own. . . . This teaches you that when
> a man humbles himself, the Holy One, Blessed be He, exalts him . . .

The story recognizes the ambiguity of Scripture and the fact that two or more different interpretations can be equally tenable. But to develop a defensible theory is not everything, and when a choice must be made between equally arguable alternatives, it cannot be made by appeal to the text. In matters of law, the moral qualities of the interpreter might tip the balance; and nowhere is self-righteousness more out of place than in difficult moral and legal questions. Nowhere are humility and respect for rival views more seemly.

Many people associate such faith in argument and patience, in humility and respect for others with a rather bland optimism. Hence the next story may come as something of a surprise, at least to those who do not know Jeremiah and Job.

> The Rabbanan taught: For two and a half years the school of Shammai and
> the school of Hillel argued: one said, it were better for man not to have been cre-
> ated than to have been created, and the other said, it was better for man that he
> was created than that he should not have been created. Then they took a vote and
> agreed that it would indeed have been better for man not to have been created,
> but that, since he has been created, he should ponder his [past] actions. Some
> read: he should deliberate his [future] actions.

Hillel and Shammai contributed a great deal to the codification of the so-called oral law or oral tradition. Early in the third century A.D. the law finally received its final written form. It is called *Mishna,* and during the following two centuries the *Gemara* developed around it, chapter for chapter, recording the discussions of the rabbis in a terse style that is so condensed that prolonged study is required to master it. The Mishna and Gemara together are called the Talmud, and there are two versions of that—the Babylonian Talmud, which is meant when reference is made simply to half million words, the latter of 750,000. In the original, the Mishna is printed, bit by "the Talmud," and the Jerusalem Talmud. The former is said to consist of two and a bit, in the middle of each page, and the Gemara around it. The pagination is the same in all editions, and the whole text is available in six volumes; a good German version by Lazarus Goldschmidt fills twelve bulky volumes, and various English translations many more.

One tractate of the Mishna has no Gemara. It is called Avot or Pirke Avot, meaning the Fathers, or the Sayings of the Fathers. The second chapter of it records some of Hillel's sayings (5–6):

> Do not separate yourself from the community. Until the day of your death
> do not believe in yourself. Do not judge your neighbor until you have stood in his
> shoes. Do not say anything incomprehensible, [thinking] one will understand it
> later. Do not say you will study when you have leisure; perhaps you will never
> have leisure.

> The uninformed cannot stand in awe of sin; the ignorant cannot be pious;
> the timid do not learn; the impatient do not teach; and those who immerse them-
> selves in business do not become wise. Where men are lacking, strive to be a man.

Hillel also appears in the first chapter, which provides some historical context and is of special interest.

> 1. Moses received the Torah on Sinai and transmitted it to Joshua, Joshua to the
> elders, the elders to the prophets, and the prophets transmitted it to the men of the
> great assembly. These men said three things: Be deliberate in passing judgment,

train many students, and build a fence around the Torah [protecting it against violation of its laws by demanding more].

2. Simon the Just was one of the last men of the great assembly. He said: The world rests on three pillars—the Torah, worship, and works of charity.

3. Antigonos of Sokho received it from Simon the Just. He said: Do not be like servants who serve their master, expecting rewards, but be like servants who serve their master without expecting·rewards; only the reverence of heaven be over you. [He was the first of the Sadducees, and they did not believe in any life after death.] . . .

12. Hillel and Shammai received it from them. Hillel said: Be one of the disciples of Aaron, loving peace and striving for peace, loving men and leading them to the Torah.

13. He also said: Whoever wants to make his name great will destroy it; whoever does not grow shrinks; whoever does not learn is guilty of death; and whoever uses the crown [the Torah, according to most interpreters; others have suggested that Rome may be meant] wastes away.

14. He also said: If I am not for myself, who will be? And if I am only for myself, what am I? And if not now, when?

It was during the lifetime of Hillel that Jesus was born. For the Jews of the first century A.D. the teaching and crucifixion of Jesus did not seem earthshaking at all, nor did the Romans take the slightest notice of it in their annals. For the Jews the cataclysmic event of the first century was the destruction of Jerusalem and the second temple by the Romans in A.D. 70, after three years of war. The temple was burnt on the ninth day of the month of Ab, the anniversary of the destruction of the first temple by the Babylonians in 586 B.C. But though they were confronted with the power of the Roman Empire, which extended all the way around the Mediterranean and included Egypt, North Africa, Spain, Gaul, southern Germany, Italy, the Balkans, Greece, and Asia Minor, the Jews continued their fight. The last fortress to hold out against the Romans was Masada, situated on a hill that rises from the western shore of the Dead Sea, 1,300 feet below sea level, to a little more than 300 feet above sea level. It is an austere place in the desert, not far south of the caves where the Dead 11 Sea scrolls were found in the twentieth century.

Thanks to Flavius Josephus, we possess a moving account of the fall of Masada in A.D. 73. He was a Jew and lived approximately from A.D. 38 to 100. At the beginning of the war with the Romans he was commander in Galilee in the north, but when a stronghold he defended was taken by the Romans he won the favor of the Emperor Vespasian and adopted the emperor's family name, Flavius. He was present at the destruction of Jerusalem and later wrote several books in Greek, including *The Jewish War*. His account of the fall of Masada in chapters 8 and 9 of the last book (VII) is of exceptional interest for a number of reasons. This was an epoch-making event that marked the end of the ancient Jewish state, and these pages show us aspects of Jewish living and dying that are not dreamed of in accounts that are based solely on the Talmud, not to speak of the New Testament. Moreover, this is one of the great tales of human valor that has left its mark upon twentieth-century Israel, and it also contains some references to India.

32

Text: The Fall of Masada

"We have long decided, my brave comrades, to serve neither the Romans nor anyone else except God, who alone is the true and just lord of men. The time has come to prove our resolve by deeds. Let us not disgrace ourselves now. Formerly, we would not submit to slavery even when it was not perilous; and now we should accept slavery deliberately along with the vilest torments that await us if we let the Romans catch us alive? We were the first to revolt against them and are the last still fighting them. I consider it a great boon granted us by God that we can die well as free men, unlike those who were defeated unexpectedly. We know that the dawn means capture, but we can still choose to die nobly with those we love. For our enemies, though they would dearly love to take us alive, cannot prevent this any more than we can defeat them in battle. . . .

"Our wives shall die unabused, our children without knowing slavery. Then, let us do each other the last favor, and let us die wrapped in freedom. Only let our possessions and the fortress go up in flames first; for it will surely be a blow to the Romans if they can neither lay their hands on us nor find any loot. Only food let us leave them, to bear witness after our death that we were not conquered by want but kept our old resolve to choose death rather than slavery."

Thus spoke Eleazar, but not all who heard him reacted alike. Some were eager to do what he had said and almost seemed elated at the thought of such a noble death; but others had softer hearts and felt compassion for their wives and children. . . .

"Given our education, we should give other men an example of readiness to die. But if anyone needs foreign examples, consider the Indians who go in for philosophy. These brave men suffer life on earth reluctantly as a time of service due to nature and look forward to the release of their souls from the fetters of their bodies. Even when no calamity weighs on them, they still tell others, motivated only by their longing for the immortal, that they are about to depart. Nor would anyone hinder them; on the contrary, everybody felicitates them and gives them messages for dead relatives; so firm and confident is their belief in the reunion of souls. After listening to these messages, they surrender their bodies to the fire in order to part the soul from the body in the greatest possible purity, and they die amidst hymns of praise. Those loving them escort them to their deaths more cheerfully than other people part from friends who go on a long journey. They weep for *themselves* but count the dead happy for entering the ranks of the immortals. Should we not be ashamed if we show less spirit than the Indians and through our lack of courage slander the laws of our fathers which are the envy of the world?

"But even if we had been raised from childhood on the opposite belief, that the greatest boon of man is life, and death a disaster, our situation should still teach us to accept it bravely since God's will and necessity bid us to die. . . .

"You know that there is not a town in Syria that has not slaughtered its Jewish inhabitants though these had been more hostile to us than to the Romans. Without even bothering to invent the least pretext, the people of Damascus stained their city with a revolting bloodbath, butchering eighteen thousand Jews with their wives and children. Those tortured to death in Egypt are said to exceed sixty thousand. These Jews died wretchedly, being abandoned defenseless to their enemies in foreign countries. But those who took up arms against the Romans at home seemed to have every hope of success. Weapons, walls, impregnable fortresses, and courage that faced all the dangers of the war of liberation without fear, led the whole people to revolt. But all this helped for only a short while and after filling us with high hopes proved only to be the beginning of a chain of disasters. Fortress upon fortress was conquered and captured as if they had been built only to make the triumph of the Romans more glorious and not to protect us. Those who fell in battle did well, for they died with their swords in their hands in defense of liberty. But who would not pity the legions captured by the Romans? Who would not rather die gladly than share their fate? Some of them died on the rack or tortured with fire and whips; others, half eaten by savage beasts, were kept alive for another repast, providing amusement and a diversion for their tormentors. But none are more wretched than those who are still living, longing for death but unable to die.

"And where is the great city, the mother city of the whole Jewish people, fortified with so many walls, protected by so many ramparts and magnificent towers, the city that could hardly hold the mass of our arms and that contained so many myriads of defenders? Where is she now that was once believed to have been founded by God? Her very foundations are destroyed, and her only memorial now is the camp of those who ravished her. Decrepit old men sit by the ashes of the temple, and a few women have been kept there to satisfy the wanton lust of the enemy.

"Who, thinking of all this, could wish to go on living even if he could do so in safety? Who is such a coward and enemy of his country that he is not sorry that he is still living now? If only all of us had died before seeing the holy city razed by the enemy and the sacred temple impiously destroyed! We were deceived by the not ignoble hope of revenge. That hope gone, abandoned to our distress, let us hasten to die well. Let us have compassion for ourselves, for our children and our wives, while it is still in our power to act compassionately. For we were born for death and have begotten children for death; and even those who are most fortunate cannot escape death. But outrage and slavery and having to look on as wife and children are dragged off to abuse—such evils are not imposed on anyone by nature and necessity but are born of cowardice and come only to those who refuse to die instead.

"Proudly relying on our strength, we revolted against Rome and only recently refused their invitation to surrender. Can anyone fail to foresee their wrath if they took us alive? Pity the youths who are strong enough to survive prolonged torture! Pity the old whose age cannot stand up to such torments! Should a man see his wife dragged away to be violated and hear the voice of a child cry "Daddy" when his own hands are bound? No, while those hands are free and can still hold a sword, let them serve us with honor. Unenslaved by the enemy, let us die and part from life as free men with our wives and children. This is what our laws command us, this is what our wives and children implore us to do. It is God who confronts us with this necessity, while the Romans hope for the opposite; they fear that even one of us might die before capture. Let us therefore hasten to leave them not the anticipated pleasure of taking us alive but the shock of finding us dead and awe at our courage."

. . . In the end, no man proved too weak for the daring deed; all killed their loved ones. In their dire need it seemed the least evil to them to slaughter their wives and children with their own hands. Unable to endure their pain at what they had done and feeling that they would wrong the dead if they survived them even for a short while, they quickly piled up their possessions and set fire to them and then chose ten men by lot to kill all the rest. Then each lay down beside his wife and children, spread his arms over them and offered his throat to one of the ten. No sooner had they killed all of their comrades without hesitation than they drew lots in turn to determine who should kill the other nine and then himself. They trusted each other completely that every one would comply both in suffering and in action. Thus nine more died by the sword, and the last lone survivor looked once more over the multitude of the prostrate bodies to see whether anyone was left who might still need his help to die; and when he found that all were dead, he set fire to the palace, and with all his strength drove his sword through himself and fell beside his family.

They died, convinced that not a soul was left alive to fall into Roman hands. But one old woman as well as another who was related to Eleazar and more intelligent and educated than most women had escaped with five children to hide in a subterranean aqueduct while the men were entirely preoccupied with the slaughter. The dead numbered nine hundred sixty, including women and children, and this happened on the fifteenth of the month Xanthikos.

Expecting armed resistance, the Romans got ready at dawn . . . But when they did not see any enemies but everywhere uncanny emptiness, fire inside, and silence, they were at a loss to understand what might have happened. Finally, they shouted as if to give a signal to shoot, hoping that this might bring out some of the defenders. The women heard the shout, immediately came out of their subterranean hiding place, and told the Romans in detail what had happened, and one of them in particular was able to relate precisely what had been said and done. But the Romans paid little attention to her because they could not believe such amazing fortitude. They exerted themselves to extinguish the flames and soon found a way into the palace. But when they actually saw the multitude of the dead, they did not exult over them as enemies but admired the nobility of their resolution and the utter contempt of death shown by so many.

33

The fall of Masada marked the end of a war that had lasted almost seven years. The men of military age that remained in the country were deported as slaves, and many of them died in Rome as gladiators. The precious things found in the temple in Jerusalem, including the famous seven-armed candelabra, had been shipped to Rome earlier, and the images of these treasures still adorn the triumphal arch of Titus in the Foro Romano. Jerusalem was destroyed so thoroughly that one could scarcely believe that she had once been a large city. The Romans also abolished the office of the high priest and the synhedrion or supreme court. But all of this meant neither the end of Palestinian Jewry nor the beginning of the Diaspora, the dispersal of the Jews among the nations. The dispersal had begun much earlier. When Cyrus had given the Jews permission to return from the Babylonian exile, most of them chose to stay in Babylonia, which became a major Jewish settlement and eventually, around A.D. 200, a great center of Jewish studies. Many Jews also settled in Egypt, not only in Alexandria in the north but also as far south as the island of Elephantine, centuries before Jerusalem was destroyed. There also were Jewish communities in Rome and throughout the empire.

By the third century B.C., the Jews of Alexandria felt the need for a Greek translation of the Torah. Legend has it that this version was commissioned by King Ptolemy Philadelphus of Egypt, during the first half of the century, and the Christian church fathers were to claim that the whole of the Hebrew Bible was rendered into Greek at that time. Scholars do not rule out the possibility that the king may have encouraged the enterprise, but they insist that the Prophets and Writings were done into Greek only during the second century. The translators' grasp of Hebrew was not always adequate, and the texts they translated sometimes differed from the Hebrew Bible that became canonical a little later, the so-called Masoretic recension. This Greek Bible became the Old Testament of the early Christians, and down to the twentieth century Christian scholars have assumed that the Septuagint (that is, the Greek Old Testament) is earlier and more reliable than the Masoretic text. There were no Hebrew manuscripts of the Bible that were as old as the earliest Greek manuscripts. There were three ancient Greek manuscripts (called the Vaticanus, Sinaiticus, and Alexandrinus), but they often do not agree. By 1952, Aage Bentzen, a Scandinavian scholar, argued in his two-volume *Introduction to the Old Testament* that the Masoretic text is far more reliable than the Septuagint, the Samaritan text, and all other ancient texts and translations (I, 101). Since the discovery of the Dead Sea scrolls, which include a scroll of Isaiah and other Biblical material, there is no longer much room for doubt on this score.

It was also in Alexandria that the first great Jewish philosopher, Philo (about 25 B.C. to A.D. 40), appeared. When the Roman emperor Caligula (37–41) demanded that he be worshiped as a god, the Jews protested and sent a delegation to Rome, headed by Philo. His writings have survived and he has come to be considered a pioneering thinker. In a way, his philosophy was not strikingly original, for he drew liberally on Plato and the Stoics. But he was the first to read these philosophies into the Bible and to synthesize the revelation of God with the wisdom of the Greeks, making extensive use of allegorical interpretations. Thus he fashioned the philosophy and theology that flourished until the age of Descartes. He also made much of the dualism of spirit and matter (which survives even in Descartes), and he argued that the cleft between God and the world was so great that God used a mediating principle, the *logos*, an idea taken up at the beginning of the fourth Gospel in the New Testament.

Both the Septuagint and Philo's philosophy made a great impression on many Gentiles. So did the Jewish conception of God, the Jews' religious services in their synagogues, and the Jewish religion as a whole. Many Gentiles were converted; others became, as it were, fellow travelers or, in the language of those days, God-fearing Gentiles. Around A.D. 120, Juvenal, the poet, deploring the erosion of ancient Roman customs, cited as a typical example the way in which so many become more and more Jewish, accepting first the Sabbath and then the God who is worshiped without images, then the dietary laws, and finally even circumcision (Satire 14). This process of proselytizing continued until Christianity became the state religion of the empire. Much as the Christians had suffered from persecution by the Romans—as the Jews had, too, from time to time—the Romans were incomparably more tolerant in religious matters than the Christians. And the Christians were especially intolerant of the Jews, whom they regarded as rivals whose religion had been superseded by Christianity.

The man who did the most to shape the religious life of the remnant that remained in the Holy Land was Yokhanan ben Sakkai. According to tradition, he was carried out of Jerusalem in a coffin during the siege of the city, and then gained an audience with the Roman commander, who granted his request to establish an academy for Jewish studies in Yavne, on the coast of the Mediterranean. Henceforth this academy became the cultural center of Palestinian Jewry. The most intelligent lived more and more in their studies, hoping for the re-establishment of the state. With the fall of the temple, all sacrifices were abolished, and Yokhanan cited the prophetic derision of sacrifices; what God wanted was love and humility.

Gnostic doctrines and apocalypses—"Manichaean" in their outlook although Mani had not yet been born—were flourishing throughout the Near East but were firmly rejected by Yokhanan and the rabbis who followed him. Some of them even forbade the study of such books. The Pharisees were separatists—that is the literal meaning of the name—in the sense that they opposed assimilation, or death by drowning in the flood of syncretism. Their overwhelming desire was for the survival of their people and religion with a separate identity. The crucial difference between the Pharisees and the Sadducees was that the latter took their stand on scripture and rejected the oral tradition and "oral law" of which the Pharisees made a great deal; and the Tannaim, the teachers who succeeded the Pharisees after the fall of the temple, went still much further in their devotion to the study and eventually the codification of the oral tradition.

34

Among those who lived through the destruction of Jerusalem and then of Masada was Rabbi Akiba (about 40–135). In some ways it was Rabbi Ishmael, Akiba's contemporary, who followed in the paths of Hillel, for it was Ishmael who developed the hermeneutical principles of Hillel and insisted that the Torah speaks in "the language of men" and must be interpreted in a relatively straightforward way. Akiba's exegeses assumed, in effect, that common sense did not suffice because in the Bible every detail, no matter how small, is full of significance.

In the Mishna we find this passage in the tractate "Blessings" (9:5): "Man must give praise for the bad no less than for the good, for it is written [Deuteronomy 6:5]: You shall love the Lord, your God, with your whole heart, etc. With your whole heart: [that means,] with both your impulses, with the good impulse and with the evil impulse. With your whole soul: [that means,] even when he takes your soul." The Gemara on this passage tells us that it was Akiba who explained "with your whole soul" in this way, because these words would not be in the text if they did not convey something important that was not said in the preceding words.

The Gemara goes on to relate that:

> Once the infamous government had given an order that the Israelites should no longer study the Torah. Then Papos ben Yehudah met Rabbi Akiba as he held public meetings for the study of the Torah. Then he said to him: Akiba, are you not afraid of the infamous government? He replied: I shall tell you a parable to which this is comparable. A fox once walked along the bank of a river, and when he saw fish congregating everywhere, he said to them: what are you fleeing? They replied: The nets that men put out for us. Then he said to them: Then come on land, and we, I and you, shall dwell together as my ancestors once dwelled together with your ancestors. Then they replied to him: Is it you that is reputed to be the cleverest animal? You are not clever but stupid. If we are afraid even in the element in which we have our life, how much more in the element in which we die! Thus it is with us, too: If it has come to that even now when we sit and study the Torah of which it is written [Deuteronomy 30:20], "for it is your life and the length of your days," how much more if we go and withdraw from it!

A few days later, Akiba was apprehended. After a long imprisonment, he was led to his execution at the time of day when the liturgy calls for the reading of the so-called *Shma*: "Hear, Israel, the Lord our God, the Lord is One. And you shall love the Lord, your God, with your whole heart and with your whole soul . . ." This is how the Talmud relates his death:

> His flesh was ripped off with iron combs, but he took upon himself the yoke of the kingdom of heaven. His students said to him: Master, so far? He replied to them: My whole life I have grieved over the verse in Scripture, with your whole soul—even when he takes your soul; for I thought, when shall this opportunity be given to me, and I shall do it. And now that it is given, I should not do it? He prolonged the word "One" so long that his soul expired on "One."

Akiba was ninety-five when he was tortured to death by the Romans. He had loved God with his whole heart and soul, and the study of the Torah had been his life. He would no more consider giving it up than Socrates would cease questioning his fellow citizens. And if the penalty for such persistence was death, Akiba, like Socrates, found the choice easy to make because neither of them felt any unseemly dread of death. Yet Akiba's way of life and conception of truth were obviously very different from Socrates', much less individualistic and much more tradition-directed. When Akiba spoke of "the element in which we have our life," he meant the Jews and by no means only or even mainly himself. After the destruction of Jerusalem more than ever before, the survival of the Jews depended on continued study of the Torah, and this was how they did in fact survive until modern times.

Akiba's exegesis of the words "with your whole soul" is moving, suggestive, unforgettable, but—it may be objected—surely not what Moses (or whoever the author may have been) had meant. Akiba and his contemporaries would not have considered this an objection. They were not after the human author's meaning and granted that, even if it had been Moses himself, he had not had in mind the things that Akiba and those trained by him derived from the texts. A story in the Talmud makes this point beautifully (Menahot 29b):

> Rabbi Yehuda said in the name of Rav: When Moses climbed the mountain he found the Holy One, blessed be he, sitting there and fashioning little crowns for the letters. Then he said to him: Lord of the world, for whose sake are you doing that? He replied: there is a man who will come to be after many generations, called Akiba ben Joseph; he will one day present heaps and heaps of doctrines concerning every little hook. Then he said before him: Lord of the world, show him to me. He replied: turn around. Then he turned around and sat down

behind the eighth row, but he did not understand their conversation and was dismayed. When Akiba came to a point about which his students asked him how he knew, he replied to them that this was a doctrine given to Moses on Sinai. Then Moses was calmed; and he turned back and stepped before the Holy One, blessed be he, and said before him: Lord of the world, you have such a man and give the Torah through me! He replied: Be still, that is how it entered my mind. Then he said before him: Lord of the world, you have shown me his knowledge of the law; show me his reward too. He said: turn around. Then he turned around and saw Akiba's flayed flesh weighed in a butcher's shop. Then he said before him: Lord of the world, this is the Torah, and this its reward? He replied: Be still, that is how it entered my mind.

As Jeremiah and Job and the Second Isaiah had insisted, the virtuous often suffer outrageously while the wicked flourish. But by Akiba's time most Jews believed in a life to come, which permitted at least a vague hope for some reward after death. I say "vague" not merely because men have rarely succeeded in picturing the joys of heaven very well, but because the Talmud of Jerusalem (Haggiga 77a) says that it was Akiba who said: "Whoever ponders four things—what is above, what is below, what is before, and what is after—it would be better for him if he had never been born" (Mishna, Haggiga 2:1). The same reverent agnosticism also finds expression in a saying that is cited twice in the Babylonian Talmud (Berakhoth 34b and Sanhedrin 99a): "All the prophets prophesied only about the messianic days; but as for the future world—apart from you, O God, no eye has seen it [Isaiah 64:3]."

In this spirit, Akiba and the other great rabbis did not indulge in dreadful descriptions of the torments of hell, as did the Gospels and the last book of the New Testament, not to speak of Tertullian and later Christian preachers. Of course, Akiba and the Pharisees did not join the Sadducees in denying any life after death altogether, and the last verse of the Book of Isaiah did pose a problem for him. It has already been quoted in section 2: "And they go out and look at the corpses of those who rebelled against me, for their worm will not die and their fire not be quenched, and they will be an abhorrence to all flesh." All kinds of apocalypses could simply be ignored or repudiated, but this verse was in the Hebrew Bible and required exegesis. What the writer, whoever he was, might have meant is far from clear but was not in any case crucial for Akiba. In his bold way, he turned to the preceding verse: "From new moon to new moon and sabbath to sabbath, all flesh comes to worship before me, says the Lord." And Akiba said: "The punishment of the wicked in Gehinnom lasts twelve months; for it is written: it will be from new moon to [the same] new moon." This extraordinary interpretation was accepted in the Mishna (Eduyyoth 2:10) and is assumed elsewhere in the Talmud as well (for example, Sabbath 33b and 152b). But this still leaves us with twelve months of torment and evidently distressed Akiba, for he taught that Isaiah 5:14 meant that the underworld (Sh'ol) had opened its mouth not, as modern scholarship has it, "beyond measure" but rather "for lack of an observance"; and then he argued: "It does not say for the lack of observances, but of an observance; only those who possess no good deeds at all will descend into the netherworld" (Finkelstein, 1936, 186; cf. Makkoth 24a and Sanhedrin 81a).

It would be difficult to find a more extreme example of exegetical thinking—of reading one's own ideas into a revered text to get them back endowed with authority. It would be no less difficult to find a more striking example of anti-Manichaean humanity. For who could say even of such colossal villains as Hitler or Stalin that they had never done any good deed at all?

Legends are revealing, too. The following story bears witness to the humanity not only of Akiba, whose life and teachings inspired it, but also of those who told and retold the legend, which has come down to us in many versions.

Akiba once walked through a graveyard and saw a charcoal burner running around like a frantic beast of burden, carrying wood. Akiba said to him: "My son, why such heavy toil? If you are a bondsman, and your master imposes such a yoke upon you, I shall redeem you and set you free. If you are poor, let me help you." But the man replied: "I am of the dead: day after day I am fated to gather wood and to be burnt." Akiba asked him what he had done. "I was a tax-collector, and I favored the rich and was a scourge to the poor. I even seduced an affianced virgin on the Day of Atonement [when even marital intercourse is forbidden]." Akiba asked him if there was no remedy for him. At first the man replied that there was none, but then added on second thought: "I did hear them say that my punishment would be relaxed if I had a son who could stand up in the congregation and proclaim publicly: Bless ye the Lord who is worthy to be blessed. But I had no son. Yet on my death I left my wife with child, but whether she bore a boy or girl I do not know. And if she did bear a son, who would teach him?" Akiba asked his name and his wife's, and then traveled from town to town asking for her. One day he came to a village where the wife was known. The people remembered her husband with horror, and the boy, it turned out, had not been circumcised. Akiba fasted for forty days, and a heavenly voice was heard: "Because of this boy you fast?" Akiba replied: "Yes." And he taught the boy the alphabet, and he taught the boy Scripture, and he taught him to stand up in the congregation to say: "Bless ye the Lord who is worthy to be blessed." Then the charcoal burner appeared to Akiba in a dream and told him that he had been rescued from hell, and Akiba replied by citing a psalm: "O Lord, your Name is for ever; your memorial, O Lord, for all generations" (Montefiore, 591 f.).

35

Akiba lost his life after the last major revolt of the Jews against Rome had failed, in A.D. 135. There had been occasional uprisings since the fall of Masada, and there were more to come when the Romans were fighting the Persians or Parthians. But the fight led by Bar Kokhba, whom Akiba saw as the Messiah, was far greater and raised much bolder hopes than any subsequent rebellion against Rome. It had been triggered by the resolve of the Emperor Hadrian to place a statue of the emperor on the site of the temple, as an object of worship. This had struck the Jews as intolerable, and when petitions failed they had resorted to arms. Initially, they were successful, but in the end Rome was able to bring in far larger forces and to drown the revolt in blood. That done, a Jupiter temple was built on the ancient temple square in Jerusalem, Jews were forbidden to as much as enter the city, and the Jewish religion became an object of persecution for a few years. But that stopped about 140, under the reign of the emperor Antoninus Pius, and after that there was peace for a while.

The head of the academy was called Nasi (prince), and Yudah Hanasi (135–210), the most renowned Nasi, was able to use these years to complete the Mishna. He was a descendant of Hillel, and with him the age of the Tannaim, the successors of the Pharisees, came to an end. They were followed by the Amoraim, who completed the Talmud. The Palestinian or Jerusalem Talmud was finished around 400, and the Babylonian Talmud a hundred years later, though some minor additions were made still later.

Both "Mishna" and "Talmud" are words derived from roots that mean "to learn" or "study." The Tannaim who did so much to define normative Judaism were men who worked for a living, taught without receiving any compensation for it, and

Synagogue ruins, Bir'am, Galilee, 3rd century.

lived to learn and teach. Many of their Biblical interpretations were collected in various volumes of Midrashim. "Midrash" is derived from a root meaning "inquire," and these inquiries concerned the meaning of words and passages in the Bible. The most important Midrash is the Midrash Rabbah, which deals with the Five Books of Moses and the Five Scrolls or Megillot, that is: the Song of Songs, Ruth, Ecclesiastes, Esther, and Lamentations. By no means all of this collection and of various other ones goes back to the Tannaim; much of it belongs to later times, and the Midrash Rabbah on Exodus and Numbers may even have been compiled as late as the twelfth century.

In the year 212, under the emperor Caracalla, all of the people living in the Roman empire, including the Jews, became citizens. But a century later, when Christianity became the official religion of the empire, Constantine and his successors turned against the Jews, passing special laws concerning them, and by 438 Jews had been removed from all important offices and positions of honor. The discrimination was not racial but religious and actually was one of the forms in which Christian Rome exerted pressure on the Jews to become Christians. The Jews enjoyed some respite when Julian the Apostate became emperor in 361 and tried to restore the ancient "paganism" of Rome, but the respite did not last, as Julian died less than two years later.

Farther east, in the Persian empire, the adoption of Zoroastrianism as the official religion after the death of Shapur also led to religious persecution. As we saw in our discussion of Manichaeism (section 22), not only that religion was proscribed and Mani himself martyred, but the king of kings tried to cleanse his empire of all Ahrimanic or devilish—that is, non-Zoroastrian—beliefs and practices. The Romans could be incredibly cruel, but there is no hatred like that among hostile brothers.

Muhammad, as we shall see later, illustrates the same sad theme, but in this respect his influence did not extend much beyond his native Arabian peninsula. The countries that were conquered by his followers and converted to Islam proved to be infinitely more hospitable to Jews than most Christian countries were before the eighteenth and nineteenth centuries.

Until Islam arrived on the scene in the seventh century, and even for a period after that, Palestine and Babylonia remained the chief centers of Jewish intellectual life. Eventually great Jewish scholars and poets appeared in Europe, too, especially in Muslim Spain; but it was not only in their prayers and least of all only in the synagogues that the Jews recalled the Psalmist's cry: "If I forget you, Jerusalem, let my right hand wither!" (137:5).

36

Rabbi Shlomoh Yitzhaki (1040–1105), better known by his initials as Rashi, founded an academy in Troyes in France and wrote commentaries on the whole Hebrew Bible as well as the Babylonian Talmud. He died before completing the latter work, but his grandson finished it. Orthodox Jews study his commentaries along with the texts to this day.

Meanwhile, Spain witnessed a much more spectacular flowering of Jewish culture. At least a few of the greatest names should be mentioned here. Shlomoh ben Yudah ibn Gabirol (about 1021–1058) was a poet and philosopher who wrote both in Hebrew and in Arabic. It remained for Solomon Munk, a Jewish Orientalist born in Silesia who became a professor at the Collège de France, to discover in 1845 that Gabirol was also the man who is often cited by the Christian scholastic philosophers as Avicebron. His most important philosophic work, "The Fountain of Life," written in Arabic, survived only in a Latin version as *Fons Vitae*, except for some excerpts that have also come down to us in a Hebrew translation of the thirteenth century.

Yudah ben Halevi (about 1075-1141) was a physician but became famous as a great Hebrew poet and as the author of *Kuzari*, a dialogue, originally written in Arabic, between a Jewish scholar and a Khazar king whom he converts to Judaism. His best known poem is an elegy "To Zion." He went to Jerusalem, and it is said that an Arab killed him at one of the city gates where he was reciting his elegy. The decision to go to Jerusalem was not unusual. Another great Jewish scholar, Saadyah ben Joseph (882-942), who was born in Egypt, also went there, although he moved on to Babylonia where he became Gaon (head) of the great academy at Sura.

Rabbi Moses ben Maimon (1135-1204), known also (by his initials) as Rambam and as Maimonides, was born in Cordova. He, too, went to the Holy Land, and is buried outside Tiberias, but he spent most of his life in Egypt, was the personal physician of Saladin, and wrote some of his books in Arabic, others in Hebrew. His commentary on the Mishna, finished in Egypt in 1168, was Arabic but translated more than once into Hebrew. His two major works were both written in Hebrew: *Mishneh Torah*, a distillation of the law, completed in 1180, and *Moreh Nevukhim* (A Guide for the Perplexed), 1190, which is perhaps the major work of Jewish philosophy before Spinoza. Moses ben Maimon's epitaph in Tiberias represents the ultimate encomium: "From Moses to Moses there was none like Moses."

Moses ben Nahman (or Ramban, or Nahmanides) was born in Spain in 1194 and became the most eminent Jewish scholar in the whole country. But he did so well in a public disputation in Barcelona in 1263 that he was forced to leave. Not only did he, too, go to the Holy Land, but he insisted that the resettlement of the land of Israel was commanded by the Bible.

Moses de Leon (1250-1305) lived in Guadalajara and, later, in Avila. He wrote a great deal but is now chiefly remembered as the author of a book that he did not claim to be his: the Zohar, the major work of Jewish mysticism and the fountainhead of the so-called Kabbalah (literally: tradition or what is received). Tradition has it that the book was written by Shimeon bar Yohai's circle in the second century, but modern scholarship has identified Moses de Leon as the author. Soon Tsfat (Safed) in Galilee, 28,30 not far from Tiberias, became the center of Jewish mysticism; it is 2,780 feet above sea level, while Tiberias lies 680 feet below sea level. It was at Tsfat that Isaac Luria (1534-1572) settled. Born in Jerusalem, he became the leading kabbalist of his time and founded a school that survived him.

A little earlier, Joseph Karo (1488-1575), who was also a kabbalist, had moved to Tsfat. He was born in Spain, and when the Jews were expelled in 1492 his family had first moved to Turkey, where he became a rabbi. He is chiefly remembered for his authoritative codification of rabbinical law in *Shulhan Arukh*, written in Tsfat and published in Venice in 1564-1565. Ismar Elbogen (1874-1943), a liberal Jew who wrote a history of the Jewish liturgy as well as a history of the Jews in Germany, says in his very brief, terse, and rich *History of the Jews since the Destruction of the Jewish State* (German, 1920, 84): "It was a calamity that a book not considered especially valuable by its author was elevated to the rank of a masterpiece. The Shulhan Arukh was virtually conceded equal value with the Talmud and for centuries served along with it as the center of studies. . . ." Orthodox Jews are not likely to share the judgment that this was a disaster. In any case, it is noteworthy how much the land of Israel remained the center not only of Jewish prayers and dreams but also of Jewish life and studies.

It was only in the modern age that the Jews made such monumental contributions to European culture that the twentieth-century Zionist movement becomes something of a riddle. Those with no special interest in Jewish studies are not likely to have ever heard of Isaac Luria and Joseph Karo. They are much more likely to have heard of their contemporary, Nostradamus (1503–1566), the great astrologer of Jewish origin who stayed in France. His book of rhymed prophecies was proscribed by a papal court in 1781 because it seemed to prophesy the fall of the papacy. But by then Goethe had immortalized Nostradamus in the opening scene of his *Faust*. Incomparably greater and more influential is Michel de Montaigne (1533–1592), who might be called the father of French philosophy and of modern skepticism. His mother belonged to a Jewish family that had fled to Toulouse from the Iberian peninsula. Montaigne's essays are not only among the authentic masterpieces of French literature but also exerted an incalculable influence on modern thought.

A century later we have Baruch Spinoza (1632–1677) in Holland—a philosopher who is widely ranked with Plato, Aristotle, and Kant. His *Tractatus theologico-politicus* (1670) is one of the fountainheads of modern political theory—and of Bible criticism. His most important work *Ethica* was published in the year of his death in a volume of *Opera posthuma* that also included his Hebrew grammar.

Another century later, Moses Mendelssohn (1729–1786) spearheaded the emergence of the Jews as a major cultural force in Germany. For a hundred fifty years—from the publication of Mendelssohn's major philosophical work, *Jerusalem or On Religious Power and Judaism* (1783), which influenced Hegel, until the Nazis came to power in 1933—the Jews participated in the cultural life of Germany in a way that had no real precedent or parallel in France or England, not to speak of eastern Europe. Again, only those conversant with Jewish studies are likely to know that it was also in Germany that *die Wissenschaft des Judentums*, the scientific, scholarly study of Judaism, was founded and flourished during these years. The men who worked in this field are overshadowed by the many more famous Jews who distinguished themselves above all in music, literature, and science: Felix Mendelssohn (1809–1847) and Giacomo Meyerbeer (1791–1864), Jacques Offenbach (1819–1880) and Gustav Mahler (1860–1911); Heinrich Heine (1797–1856) and Franz Kafka (1883–1924); Karl Marx (1818–1883), Sigmund Freud (1856–1939), and Albert Einstein (1879–1955).

It would serve no purpose here to adduce the names of hundreds of other musicians, writers, and scientists, or to add the names of men and women who distinguished themselves in other fields. One way of giving at least some idea of the extraordinary nature of this great explosion of creative talent is to consider the Nobel Prizes awarded annually since 1901. During the first seventy years of its existence, the Nobel Prize for physics went to eighteen Jews and four men who were half-Jewish. In physiology and medicine, which are treated as a single field, the figures were sixteen and seven; and Freud never got the prize.

These figures are the more remarkable because such international recognition naturally comes more readily to those who are not outsiders. It is therefore understandable that during the first twenty years the prize-winners—including also those in chemistry, literature, and peace, which were the other three recognized categories—included eight Jews and five half-Jews. Those awarded the prize from 1952 through 1970 included twenty-six Jews and three half-Jews, not counting Paul Samuelson who won the prize in economics, which was awarded for the first time in 1970, and has gone to several other Jews since then.

It is no wonder that the world thinks of the Jews in the twentieth century as part of the civilization of Western Europe and the United States. Does it follow that they are a foreign element in the ancient land of Israel? Such an emotionally charged question cannot be discussed at length here, but a few more figures may help to place it in perspective.

37

Although it is widely supposed that Jerusalem was a Muslim city until Nazi persecution gave Zionism a strong boost and greatly increased Jewish immigration into the Holy Land, this is actually false. The eleventh edition (1911) of the *Encyclopaedia Britannica*, which is still widely admired for its meticulous scholarship, says at the end of the article on Jerusalem: "The population in 1905 was about 60,000 (Moslems 7,000, Christians 13,000, Jews 40,000)." In other words, two thirds of the population were Jewish, and there were almost twice as many Christians as Moslems.

It is not easy to get impartial and reliable figures for earlier periods. But according to Baedeker's *Palästina und Syrien* (1891), the population of Jerusalem at that time was a little over 40,000, including 28,000 Jews, 7,560 Muslims (this figure includes quite a few Africans), 4,150 Greek Orthodox Christians, 2,000 Roman Catholics, 560 Armenian Christians, 300 Protestants, 100 Copts (Egyptian Christians), and 75 Ethiopian Christians. Thus there seem to have been roughly equal numbers of Christians and Muslims; but the Jews constituted two-thirds of the population then, too.

Moving closer to the present, a German encyclopedia published in 1930, a few years before the Nazis came to power, gives the population of Jerusalem as 84,000, more than 60,000 of these being Jews. But it was not until 1948 that the Jews were able to establish an autonomous state in the Holy Land—the first since A.D. 70.

In some ways the Zionist movement that culminated in the establishment of the state of Israel was the child of nineteenth century European nationalism. In this sense, Israel is one of a large number of new states founded after World War II, including India, Pakistan, Bangladesh, Nigeria, and literally dozens of other "new" countries. To these we could even add some of the new states established after World War I: Yugoslavia and Czechoslovakia, Poland and Finland, and the Baltic republics, which were subsequently re-annexed by the Soviet Union. It was the break-up of the Austro-Hungarian, Russian, and Turkish empires after World War I and of the British and French empires after World War II that opened up the possibilities for ever so many peoples to claim the right to have states of their own. In many cases it was extremely difficult to draw plausible borderlines. Tens of millions of people had to be moved, and generally they were not compensated in any way for their lost property but were considered lucky if they got away alive, and there were exceedingly bloody wars attending, or soon after, the establishment of many new states. Case after case shows how there is no hatred to compare with that between hostile brothers.

What had been the history of Palestine? It is one of the oldest civilized centers in the world. Jericho, a few miles north of the Dead Sea, is sometimes said to be the oldest city anywhere, and the history of Jerusalem seems to go back to about 2,000 B.C. or roughly the time of Abraham and Hammurabi. The Jews conquered Jericho no later than the thirteenth century B.C., much of the rest of the country soon after that, and Jerusalem in the eleventh century. Their entirely credible tradition has it that their ancestors had dwelled in the country long before that, in the early part of the second millennium B.C., before they achieved nationhood. King David, in the eleventh century, ruled over a large kingdom that extended far to the east of the Jordan river, indeed east of Damascus and what is now Amman. His son Solomon built the first temple. Under

Jerusalem sky.

Solomon's son the kingdom was divided in 933 B.C. between a northern kingdom of Israel and a southern kingdom of Judah, and after that the borders were never again as far-flung as under David and Solomon. But under the Maccabees and under Herod, the land included a little more than the area between the Jordan and the Mediterranean. From A.D. 73 until 395 the land belonged to Rome; then the Roman empire was divided between Rome and Byzantium, and for a little more than two centuries Palestine belonged to the Byzantine empire.

In 636 it was conquered by the Arabs, who went on to conquer Egypt, North Africa, and Spain, as well as Syria, Mesopotamia, and Persia. In 1099 Christian Crusaders, coming from Europe, conquered Jerusalem, and for two centuries the Holy Land was fought over by Christians and Muslims. (The Crusades will be considered in chapter V, the major churches and mosques in Jerusalem in chapter XIII.) The fall of Acco (Acre), the last Christian stronghold, in the year 1291 marked the end of the Crusades. The final defeat of the Crusaders was administered by the Mamluks, Muslim warriors who were not Arabs but had been slaves in Egypt under Arab rule. Their first dynasty, the Bahrites (1250–1382), were chiefly Turks and Mongols, while the second dynasty, the Burjites (1382–1517) were Circassians, originally from the region between the Black Sea and the Caucasus. In 1516 the Turks conquered Palestine, and it remained part of their empire until 1918.

In 1917 Lord Balfour, the British foreign secretary, promised the Jews, who had furnished a legion that during World War I fought with the British against the Turks, that the British would establish a national home for the Jews in Palestine. In the peace treaty, Palestine was placed under British administration as a "mandate," while Syria and Lebanon were placed under French administration. The British played off the Arabs against the Jews, even as they played off the Muslims against the Hindus in India. In this way they exacerbated existing tensions and probably increased—and obviously did not forestall—the bloodshed that followed upon their eventual departure. They were quite unwilling to leave until World War II had weakened them so much that they had to relinquish their empire everywhere.

The United Nations, founded immediately after that war, passed a resolution in November 1947 to partition Palestine and establish two states, one Arab and one Jewish. On May 14, 1948, the State of Israel proclaimed its independence and was promptly recognized by the United States, the U.S.S.R., and most of the rest of the world. But the regular armies of Egypt and Iraq (ancient Mesopotamia, the home of the Assyrians and Babylonians), Syria and Lebanon, and the new state of Transjordan, on the east bank of the river, invaded the new state in an avowed effort to destroy it. Although the British had left arms with the Arab population while trying to disarm the Jews, neither the native population nor the Arab armies from outside the country did very well, and when all these countries except Iraq eventually signed armistice agreements with Israel without, however, recognizing her right to exist, Israel was larger than she had been in May 1948. Only the Arab Legion of Transjordan, commanded by a British officer, managed to hold on to part of Jerusalem and large areas on the west bank of the Jordan, which were annexed. Transjordan then changed its name to Jordan. The part of the holy city that Jordan acquired was the so-called old city, which includes the holy places of Christianity, Islam, and Judaism.

Henceforth, Jews were forbidden access to Jordan, including the old city, and Americans and Europeans had to produce baptismal certificates or other proof to show they were not Jewish before they could get visas for Jordan. The synagogues in the Jewish quarter of the old city were demolished. Thousands of old Jewish gravestones between the city wall and the Mount of Olives that faces it were torn up and used to build a road across a cemetery in which Jews had been buried since pre-Christian times, and tombstones with Hebrew inscriptions were used to build army barracks on the road to Jericho.

India, who in past centuries had suffered worse from Muslim invaders, had a government that appreciated this opportunity to show some friendship for Muslims; for after partition India still had a Muslim population of about 50,000,000. The pope, who had far more followers among the Arabs than among Jews, also did not feel moved to protest. Nor did the United Nations. To the Jews it seemed like the Nazi experience all over again. Nobody cared; nobody did anything; nobody was even outraged.

To understand how the Jews felt, one has to know something of the fate of the Jews in Europe. Our concern here is mainly with Asia, and in any case the bloody annals of Christian persecutions of the Jews, from the Crusades and the Inquisition to Luther and the pogroms of Tsarist Russia, tell us more about Christianity than about Judaism. But the Nazis' attempt to destroy the Jewish people was motivated by a secular ideology, directed at the Jewish "race," and did not exempt Jews who had embraced Christianity. Germany was known widely as the country of "poets and thinkers," and students from other continents, including America as well as Asia, came to study at the German universities. When Hitler commenced his persecution of the Jews in 1933, however, there was no widespread protest in Germany—or elsewhere. Although anti-Semitism had become official policy and the establishment of concentration camps and torture was common knowledge, all the great nations sent athletes to the Olympic games in Berlin in 1936. World War II began September 1, 1939, with Germany's lightning attack on Poland. By the time the war ended in the total defeat of Germany in May 1945, the Nazis had killed six million Jews, mostly in extermination camps such as Auschwitz where gas chambers had been set up to liquidate human beings in huge numbers day after day after day.

Large numbers of Germans were involved in this enterprise, which involved rounding up the Jews throughout western Europe and in Poland, Russia, and the rest of eastern Europe, but most Germans knew less about it than did the governments of England and the United States. Yet neither the camps themselves nor the rail networks that led to them were bombed, and the information was not made public until the war was over. While the primary responsibility for this unprecedented atrocity obviously lay with Hitler and his henchmen, the Jews who survived this nightmare had an overwhelming feeling that the rest of the world did not greatly care what happened to them.

The establishment of the state of Israel and its quick recognition by so many countries briefly raised the hope that the horrors of the recent war had reached the conscience of the civilized world. But during the war of independence Israel fought alone against overwhelming odds. When the war was over and Jordan, having acquired the old city of Jerusalem under British leadership, desecrated synagogues and cemeteries and refused to allow Jews to come anywhere near the Western Wall (or Wailing Wall) in Jerusalem, the last remnant of the ancient temple, or the tombs of Abraham, Isaac, and Jacob in Hebron—the Christian world did not protest. And again, when Arab terrorists crossed the borders into Israel and killed Jews aimlessly, the Christian world did not protest. Only when Israel retaliated in order to deter her enemies from this campaign did the United Nations raise its voice in protest.

Meanwhile, there was widespread concern about the fate of the Arab refugees who had fled from the state of Israel. Some Arab leaders had urged the Arabs to leave the country in order to facilitate the wholesale slaughter of the whole population by the invading Arab armies. Some Jewish terrorists—men strongly opposed by Prime Minister David Ben Gurion and his government—had tried to frighten the Arabs so that they would leave. Jordan and Egypt kept these refugees in barely human quarters in camps and refused to let them out and to absorb them into their economies. They succeeded in reaching the heart of the pope, of the United Nations, and of large numbers of decent people everywhere with the plight of these unfortunate people. What was not widely noted was that roughly equal numbers of Jews had fled from Arab countries to Israel, and were not kept in camps but welcomed as citizens. As boundary lines were redrawn during the decade after World War II, more than 40,000,000 people were uprooted and moved* without any international protests and with no widespread sense of outrage. Only in this case did persistent propaganda succeed in giving the impression that the state of Israel was responsible for the plight of the refugees who were living wretchedly in camps, while nothing was said about the Jews driven out of Arab countries.

38

In the aftermath of Israel's war of independence, the monarchy was overthrown in Egypt, and eventually Gamal Abdel Nasser emerged as the leader of his country, with aspirations to become the leader of the Arab world. Nothing seemed more likely to gain him this position than a victorious war against Israel in which he would avenge the humiliation of the Arab armies and destroy the new state. To understand what happened next, one has to realize that Israel as well as France and England gradually came to see the Egyptian leader as a man bent on imitating the German *Führer*, Hitler. His use of the title "Leader" (which means *Führer*) suggested the parallel, no less than his attempts to whip up anti-Jewish (by no means only anti-Zionist) feeling in Egypt and his broadcasts aimed at other Arab countries, calling for the extermination of the Jews in Israel. His defenders sometimes claimed that Nasser's rhetoric did not mean much and that Arabs have a way of talking rather picturesquely without meaning what they say, but people in Israel, France, and England, including Anthony Eden, who was then prime minister and who had resigned from Chamberlain's government to protest the appeasement of Hitler, remembered that many people had used precisely the same argument about Hitler and had been terribly wrong. In retrospect it was painfully clear that Hitler should have been stopped when that was still relatively easy.

Moreover, Egypt had offered a haven to many Nazi war criminals, and it was gradually becoming obvious that these men were influencing Nasser. To give a single example, in the spring of 1956 visitors to Cairo were sometimes taken to the ministry of propaganda and given an official but undated little book, called *Selected Studies* (No.. 1): *Egypt Between Two Revolutions* by Mohamed Moustafa Ata, translated by Dr. M. Yehia Eweis. The cover was black, white, and red, the colors of imperial Germany, adopted by Hitler, and the black eagle on the cover looked rather like the German emblem. Inside, a picture of Nasser was captioned "The Leader," and the leader principle (Hitler's *Führerprinzip*) was defended at length (125–30). Even "the fatherland" was there (149), along with the assurance that Nasser was "a man of pure Egyptian blood" (156), which presumably was not intended to suggest that he was not an Arab but merely a mindless repetition of a Nazi cliché. Other such clichés included "an easy prey to Jewish brokers" (18), "the Jewish firm of Rothchild [*sic*]" (21), the "stab in the back" (38) to rationalize a failure, and ominous threats, like this one:

---

* See *Encyclopaedia Britannica*, 1974 ed., vol. 15: "Refugees."

The Egyptians thus proved that they never abandon their right to avenge themselves from those who had inflicted misery and humiliation upon them. Their spirit of revenge never subsides, and they are capable of patiently awaiting [sic] the opportunity . . . (39)

With its borders drawn right through the middle of Jerusalem and but a few miles from Tel Aviv, with hostile armies poised at the eastern frontier of Israel, a mere fifteen miles from the Mediterranean in the west, and with terrorists constantly killing Jews with the open encouragement of Egypt, Israel was not eager to wait for the day that Nasser might consider most opportune for a swift and fatal attack. After reaching an agreement with the governments of France and England, Israel launched a pre-emptive strike against Egypt in October 1956, reached the Suez Canal in a few days, and then France and England joined in, hoping to topple Nasser. At that point the U.S.S.R., which had just invaded Hungary, threatened to interfere, President Eisenhower, who was running for re-election against Adlai Stevenson, demanded an immediate end to the fighting, and Nasser was saved. When the United Nations subsequently insisted that Israel give up all the territory she had conquered and return the Sinai peninsula to Egypt, with a United Nations Emergency Force stationed between the hostile countries to keep peace, Nasser managed to make the whole affair appear as an enormous victory. To be sure, he had to make some solemn promises in return, but he considered it safe to assume—and he was right—that nobody but Israel would care if he broke them. One of these promises was to keep open the Straits of Tiran at the southern end of the Red Sea. Israel has a port, Elat, at the northern end.

Egypt, like the other Arab countries, still refused to make peace with Israel or to recognize her. They all insisted that they were still at war with Israel, supported raids across the borders, and Egypt in particular kept exhorting the Arabs in Israel over the radio to take up arms. On May 14, 1967, Egypt began to assemble troops in the Sinai peninsula, near the border of Israel. Two days later she asked the United Nations Emergency Force that was stationed there to keep the peace, to withdraw; and it was withdrawn. On May 22, Egypt blockaded Elat by closing the Straits of Tiran. Both according to international law and in its overt intent, this was an act of war. The next day Canada and Denmark requested the Security Council of the United Nations to deal with the situation, but on May 24, the Soviet representative succeeded in keeping the Council from taking up the subject. The Egyptian representative, Ambassador Mohammad Awad el-Kony, justified Nasser's blockade on the 29th, saying: "There is not a shadow of a doubt as to the continued existence of the state of war between the Israelis and both the Arabs of Palestine and their brethren in the Arab countries." He insisted that "a state of overt war has been existing" and that therefore Egypt had "the legitimate right" to blockade the straits "with respect to shipping to an enemy."

Israel waited in vain for the United Nations or at least some governments that had made specific promises to her to act. Nobody lifted a finger to help while Nasser continued his preparations for war and noted with satisfaction that nobody had any mind to stop his attempt to destroy Israel once and for all. On June 5 Israel surprised the Egyptians with a swift attack. Immediately, the Syrians attacked Israel from the north. Israel warned the king of Jordan repeatedly to stay out of the war, but he saw his chance either to destroy Israel altogether or at least to enlarge his kingdom and attacked. Within six days, however, Israel vanquished the armies of all three countries, conquering the whole Sinai peninsula, the old city of Jerusalem, the whole west bank of the Jordan, and the strategic Golan heights from which the Syrians had been shelling civilian settlements in northern Israel off and on for years. At that point, the Security Council did meet to address itself to the situation and called for an immediate end to the fighting.

Israel annexed the old city of Jerusalem and gave Arabs no less than Jews the freedom of the whole city; visitors regardless of their religion were allowed everywhere, except that the temple area was closed to visitors during the hours of worship in the mosques to make sure that the Muslims would be undisturbed. The Israeli government's attitude was that they would not go back to the old borders, but that the borders were negotiable as long as the Arab countries would recognize Israel and concede her right to live in peace within secure borders. Only one acquisition was not considered negotiable: Jerusalem must remain undivided. The whole city must be in Israeli hands, but with free access to holy places for members of all religions. Against this view, the Arab nations argued, with Soviet support, that no nation must ever be allowed to keep any territory acquired by force of arms. The irony of this stand taken by Islamic nations and by the Soviet Union does not need to be labored. It is sufficient to quote *Pravda*, the leading Soviet newspaper, which defended the Soviet Union's annexation of various territories as follows (September 2, 1964):

> A people which has been attacked, has defended itself, and wins the war is bound in sacred duty to establish in perpetuity a political situation which will ensure the liquidation of the sources of aggression. It is entitled to maintain this state of affairs as long as the danger of aggression does not cease. A nation which has attained security at the cost of numerous victims will never agree to the restoration of previous borders. No territories are to be returned as long as the danger of aggression prevails (Draper, 26).

The Arab nations could not reconcile themselves either to the loss of any territory or to negotiations with Israel, a country they still refused to recognize. After six and a half years of peace or armed truce, they launched a surprise attack on Israel on the eve of Yom Kippur, 1973. The twenty-five-hour fast starts in the evening, at sundown, and millions of Jews who are not too meticulous about other holidays fast on this day, the highest holiday of the year, and spend it in the synagogue. The Arabs achieved a stunning surprise and initially did so well that the Soviet Union, which had furnished Syria alone with more tanks than the British had had at their command in World War II to stop the Nazis under Rommel in North Africa, once again kept the Security Council from interfering and actually called upon all Arab countries to join in the war against Israel. But although Israel had been shockingly unprepared and did very badly in the first couple of days, she quickly turned the tide and crossed the Suez Canal into Egypt while at the same time starting on the road to Damascus. At that point, the Security Council ordered an immediate cease-fire. Jordan had sent only a token force to help the Syrians and did not attack Israel outright; hence Israel had ignored Jordan.

It took the deep shock of the opening days of the Yom Kippur war to bring home to millions of Jews a desperate situation that they had forgotten after the Six Day War of 1967. When the Six Day War started, most Jews all over the world feared that it might mean the destruction of Israel, and that the world would once again stand by idly without doing anything to stop the massacre. When that war ended, most of them soon forgot that fear and came to think that Israel's armed forces were so superb and the courage of the people so great that Israel need never be afraid again. Now it suddenly dawned upon Jewry both in Israel and elsewhere that time was against them; that the Arabs could simply keep trying without ever risking very much; that no lost war need stop the Arabs for very long since the Soviet Union or some other country would quickly rearm them again—while Israel might be finished if she lost just once. No argument about legal or moral rights and no appeal to history had much bearing on this simple fact.

What followed from it? If Israel could not trust in her armed forces to provide security and if the very concept of secure borders was becoming less meaningful every day as modern technology was absorbed by the Arab countries, where could Israel place her trust? In the United Nations which had never yet acted to save her at times of desperate need, interfering only when Israel's armed forces were doing well? Israel had only one vote, while the Arab countries had many and were moreover supported by non-Arab Muslim countries, by the Soviet Union and China, and by many African nations. (Twenty-six countries are predominantly Muslim, and in China, India, and the Soviet Union at least ten percent of the population are Muslim.) Could Israel trust the promises of an American government that might not stay in office long? Plainly, she could not count on anybody.

39

It will never do to see the establishment of the state of Israel in 1948 merely in terms of nineteenth-century European nationalism. The longing for a return to the ancient Biblical home of the Jewish people and especially for Jerusalem is inseparable from religion. Theodor Herzl, the Viennese Jewish journalist whose little book *Der Judenstaat* (The Jewish State, 1896) marked the beginning of political Zionism, was not a religious man, and he actually considered the question whether Uganda might perhaps be a more feasible place for such a state than the Holy Land. But the psychic energy that led to the birth of Israel did not come from Vienna and western Europe; it came from eastern Europe and centuries of religious longings.

For thousands of years the Jews had lived in the Bible with their hearts and souls, developing their liturgy around the Bible and creating a large religious literature on the basis of the Bible, and the locale of almost all Biblical books was the land of Israel. Every square mile of the land was familiar and full of associations, and Jerusalem was the center of the Jews' dreams as well as their prayers. One day there would be a Jewish state in the ancient land again. Yet this wish was profoundly problematic, and not only because there were Arabs in Palestine.

Before the Nazis came to power, many German Jews felt that they were Germans whose religion was Jewish. To many people, and especially Jews in other countries, this seems ridiculous in retrospect, but this is how most Jews in France and England, in the United States and many other countries felt and still feel in relation to their countries. To complicate matters, many of these Jews no longer believe in the religion of their ancestors, though they are proud to be Jews. Even if they do not feel that it would be treason for them to become "like all the nations," even if they do not feel that they somehow owe it to their fathers, who suffered so much for so many centuries, to remain different from other people, very large numbers of them feel that the state of Israel must somehow be a very different and special country. But how?

This question is so difficult to answer that it is not surprising that many Jews have accepted the simple answer given by the Orthodox—that in Israel the laws developed by the Pharisees and Tannaim and codified in the Talmud and Shulhan Arukh should enjoy a special status. The Sabbath should be kept throughout the land at least to the extent that there should be no public transportation on that day, and the dietary laws should be kept at least in official places, in the army, and on Israel's air line. Since no political party ever won an absolute majority during the first quarter century of the existence of the new state and all governments were always coalition governments, the Orthodox religious party actually succeeded in winning some such concessions. But in Haifa, for example, there was bus service on the Sabbath, and some taxis were available on the Sabbath elsewhere, too; many restaurants do not abide by the dietary laws, it is easy to buy food that is not kosher, and anybody is free to eat as he pleases and to drive on the Sabbath. The Orthodox rabbinate, however, gained a monopoly on performing marriages; there are no civil marriages; and thus a Jew and a Gentile cannot get married in Israel unless the Gentile is converted by an Orthodox rabbi.

Of course, many Jews are not Orthodox. Among those who are religious there are two other large groups: Conservative and Reform. Oddly, the Conservative congregations in the United States are very similar to the Jewish congregations in Germany before World War II that called themselves liberal. Indeed, with every passing decade the Conservatives are becoming more liberal than the liberals in Germany were. The basic idea is to have services Friday evenings and Saturdays, in keeping with the tradition, and to have these services in Hebrew, although now more and more English material is introduced. Men and women used to sit separately in congregations of this type, though the women were brought into the service a little more than in Orthodox congregations. In recent years the Conservatives have begun to accord women more and more equal treatment. Reform Jews went further than liberal congregations did, dispensing with Hebrew in some cases and, in Germany, where most of the population used to work Saturday mornings, holding Sabbath services on Sunday. It was all a matter of degree, varying from place to place and decade to decade, and as Reform congregations came to introduce a little more Hebrew again while conservative Jews brought in more English, the lines got blurred. Orthodox services came far closer to being the same everywhere, from eastern Europe to California, than did the other two types, which varied far more from one country to another. For Jews returning to Israel from many different places, including Morocco, Yemen, and Iraq, the kind of services developed in the Western world by Conservative and Reform congregations could not provide any common bond, and this helped the Orthodox rabbinate to retain its monopoly on marriages and to try to preclude recognition of conversions by Conservative or Reform rabbis.

There are significant differences among Orthodox Jews, too. Many of them no longer grow beards and would hardly seem Orthodox to their grandparents or great grandparents, if they were still living. Nor do they seem Orthodox to the Jews who live in the Meah Shearim quarter of Jerusalem (established in 1874), who still wear not only beards but also *peot* as well as the long black gaberdines that strike others as relics of the European Middle Ages. *Peot*, literally "corners," is the name given to the hair over the temples when it is never cut. The custom is derived from Leviticus 19:27: "do not round off the corners of your heads." The Talmud did not take this to mean that the hair must be allowed to grow very long, and this custom first developed in Hungary and Galicia, as well as Yemen. There are Jews in Israel who are even more Orthodox than most of the Jews of Meah Shearim. The Natorei Karta go so far that they refuse to recognize the state of Israel because Jews should wait for the Messiah; they strongly disapprove the secular nature of the state, and they refuse to use the Hebrew language for everyday purposes.

There is no need here to consider the myriad problems faced by the new state, but some of the problems posed for it by the Jewish religion point up the dilemmas of Judaism in the modern world. The Hebrew Bible is unquestionably the greatest creation of the Jewish religion, but a modern Jew can hardly be expected to believe all of it, and it is quite arguable that it was not really meant to be believed, that much of it is obviously poetry and ancient stories. Maimonides insisted that a great deal should be understood allegorically. But if one takes one's stand on the Hebrew Bible alone and reads it that way, one is not left with any distinctive religion. What remains is one of the great treasures of humanity, a book full of ideas that have left their mark upon Western civilization, a work that those who are at home in Hebrew can appreciate even more than those who do not know this language—but nothing that establishes a unique

Meah Shearim, Jerusalem.

identity. Orthodox Jews feel that their religion, which is based not only on the Bible but also on the Talmud and the Midrash and the rich traditions that developed through the centuries, does confer a distinctive religious identity, which is true, but most modern Jews no longer wish to live that way and feel that for anyone who no longer believes in the ancient God, it makes no sense to live that way. Many Jews do not see how they could possibly believe in God any more after Auschwitz. Nor does Auschwitz stand alone. Other camps come to mind, and not only millions of murdered Jews but also slaughters in India and Pakistan—for the sake of religion—and in Biafra, Vietnam, and Bangladesh, as well as the fate of millions of black people who are starving to death in Africa.

An Orthodox Jew who is not simply horrified by such blasphemous thoughts may answer: Our religion has kept our people alive for more than three thousand years, and our fathers and mothers have often preferred death to forsaking it. How can we give it up now when the price of retaining Orthodox Judaism is at most a minor inconvenience? We must keep the faith even if in our time God should have hidden and should not care to address us. Perhaps He will speak again to our children. And as for Israel, a secular state in which Judaism is no more privileged than Islam or Christianity, and all offices are open equally to Jews and Gentiles, could easily cease to be specifically Jewish, and it could even happen that the Jews might once again—here, too—become a minority. And then the old dream would have come to naught.

To this one might reply: If Israel became a state with an established religion that discriminated against those who did not share that, while treating as second-class citizens those of different descent who have no desire to convert to Judaism, then the ancient dream has come to nothing. So far, of course, this has not happened; the largest political parties are secular, and all the prime ministers and presidents of Israel have been secularists. If Israel has failed to give the world a shining example of how minorities ought to be treated, there were extenuating circumstances as long as terrorism was such an acute problem and her neighbors refused to sign peace treaties with Israel and to recognize her right to exist. Still, becoming more humane is more important than orthodoxy, and in our time organized religion has become profoundly problematic. Yet if we decide that we should give it up, we must also realize that at that point not only God but much else that had long seemed timeless and untouched by change will disappear. Ancient and distinctive ways of life are quickly disappearing, and in another generation people everywhere may well look very much alike.

Visual images are needed to make us realize the greatness of this loss. It is not confined to one area of the world, to one people or one religion. We find the same problem in Iran and Afghanistan, in India and Ceylon, Nepal and Thailand, Cambodia, Indonesia, China, and Japan. Soon what seemed timeless will survive only in photographs, in literature, and in the arts.

IV

THE NEW TESTAMENT

*Matthew and Luke on Jesus as a Moral Teacher—
The Earliest Gospel (Mark)—The Gospel According to John—
Paul—His Ethic—Did Paul Found Christianity?—
The Christian Bible*

Samaritan priest with Samaritan Torah.

40

Christianity was the first major religion that was born during the great age of syncretism. Judaism and Zoroastrianism, Hinduism and Buddhism, Confucianism and Taoism are far older, but Buddhism underwent a thorough transformation during this age, as we shall see. Among the great world religions, only Islam is much younger than Christianity and almost equally eclectic. It is anything but a coincidence that Islam, Christianity, and late, syncretistic Buddhism were eventually adopted by hundreds of millions outside the countries of their origin.

In the mid-twentieth century some Christian theologians spoke a good deal about recovering early, pre-Hellenistic Christianity. But that quest was rather like the alchemists' hunt for the philosophers' stone or a search for wooden iron. In the area where Christianity originated, the Hellenistic age began with Alexander's conquest, around 330 B.C. The age of syncretism had begun more than two hundred years earlier with the creation of the Persian empire, and in New Testament times the Roman empire had further enlarged the melting pot. All the books of the New Testament were written in Greek, mostly by Jews who were at least bilingual—or trilingual if we count Aramaic and Hebrew as different languages; and some of them probably knew Latin as well. To say that the religion by which they were influenced most was Judaism would be an egregious understatement. Their religion *was* Judaism. But their Judaism was not normative Judaism. It was not the Judaism of the Sadducees who denied any life after death, nor was it the separatist Judaism of the Pharisees who bent their efforts toward preventing the amalgamation of non-Jewish ideas and practices. The Judaism of the early Christians was less homogeneous than these two central strains; it was more sectarian and much more hospitable to all kinds of foreign influences.

The early Christians were people who believed not only in a life after death but also that the world might soon come to an end and that the final judgment might well be at hand. They felt at home not in the prophetic demands for social justice, nor in the biblical scholarship of the Pharisees, but in the apocalyptic books that dealt with the end of things and offered frightening images of damnation. The central concern of those who had come to listen to Jesus and of those who, after his crucifixion, cherished his memory was with salvation—their own salvation. According to the Gospels, it had not been necessary for Jesus to convert people to his rather Zoroastrian or "Manichaean" world picture with its heaven and hell and its day of judgment. He preached that the end was at hand, and many who were frightened and wondered what one needed to do to be saved came to hear him.

The language in which Jesus preached was Aramaic, the dialect spoken by ordinary Jews in those days. He did not know Greek and, unlike Paul and the evangelists, preached only to Jews. He constantly referred to the Hebrew Bible and quoted from it, and, like John the Baptist whose ministry had barely preceded his, he reminded those who listened to him of various prophecies. Sometimes this was deliberate, at other

times it was simply due to the fact that people in those days—and especially those influenced by apocalyptic books—were looking for portents everywhere. When John the
Baptist appeared near the site where the Dead Sea scrolls were found, in the Judean
desert, not far from the monastic community of Qumran, whose ruins have been excavated since World War II, some Jews thought that he was the one of whom Isaiah
had spoken when he said: "A voice cries in the desert." What the Second Isaiah had
actually said, as we have seen, was:

> A voice cries:
> In the desert even
> a path for our God.

But the Pharisees often took greater liberties when interpreting Scripture, and so did
the evangelists and Paul and, according to the Gospels, Jesus as well.

In some ways the world in which Jesus and his original audience lived was defined
by the Hebrew Bible. It was certainly unthinkable without that. But the world of
Jesus was also remarkably different from the world of Moses and the great prophets.
They had been concerned with *this* world, with social justice, and they had wanted
their people to build an ethical society. Moses, as pictured in the Torah, was looking
forward to the time when, long after his own death, his people would live under his
laws in the promised land that he himself was to see only from a mountain top. Amos
and Hosea, outraged by their people's betrayal of this dream, exhorted them to implement it now. Even after Alexander's conquests had deprived much of the Near
East of autonomy and more and more people came to feel that the realization of whatever dreams they had was certainly beyond their power, normative Judaism did not
swim with the rising tide of otherworldliness. Israel clung to her autonomy and, after
losing it temporarily, regained it under the Maccabees in 165 B.C.; and this event was
commemorated henceforth by a new annual festival, Hanukkah. Even under Roman
rule enough remained of autonomy to make it possible for normative Judaism in the
age of Hillel and Jesus to maintain the ancient emphasis on social justice and to
resist the growing preoccupation with the end of things.

In many ways, of course, the world of Hillel was different from that of the pre-
exilic prophets and even from that of the Second Isaiah, Job, and Jonah. Political and
social realities had changed, and study of the Scriptures as a large part of the rabbis'
way of life was something that had developed only after the Babylonian exile. In the
Hebrew Bible itself we do not yet find this preoccupation with exegetical thinking,
nor the rabbinical concern with details of the law. Insofar as Jesus, according to the
Gospels, was much less concerned with fine points of the law, it could be said that he
was closer to the prophets than were the Pharisees. But according to the Gospels,
Jesus' conception of salvation was otherworldly and opposed to all messianic hopes
for *this* world—not only to chauvinistic dreams but also to swords beaten into plowshares and the abolition of slavery. It is not only in the Gospel according to John (18:36)
that the "kingdom is not of this world." Moses and the prophets had been concerned
with the neighbor and the stranger, the orphan and the widow, the poor and oppressed.
Man was told to love them and to treat them humanely—for their sake and for God's,
and not for his own, to escape damnation. In the Gospels, social injustice and oppression are of no concern, and heaven and hell have been moved into the center.

For all that, Jesus and his audience were Jews and not Zoroastrians. Consider how
the third of the four Gospels introduces what is perhaps the most famous of all the
parables attributed to Jesus (Luke 10):

> Behold, a lawyer stood up to put him to the test, saying: Teacher, what shall
> I do to inherit eternal life? He said to him: What is written in the Law? How

do you read? And he answered: You shall love the Lord, your God, with all your heart, and with all your soul, and with all your strength, and with all your mind; and your neighbor as yourself. And he said to him: You have answered right; do this, and you will live.

It should be noted first of all that "the Law" of the New Testament is the Torah, the Five Books of Moses, although the Torah contains a great deal besides laws, and the First Book of Moses, Genesis, contains scarcely any laws at all. Still, the Greek word used to translate *Torah* was *nomos*, "law." In the same vein, the Gospels call those who devoted much of their life to study of the Torah and of the rest of the Hebrew Bible "lawyers." This is thoroughly misleading, and the German Bible simply renders *nomikos* as *Schriftgelehrter*, which is, literally, "Scripture scholar." The evangelists constantly impute bad motives to men of this type and to representatives of normative Judaism generally. This could be due to one or more of three main reasons.

First, this could be historically accurate. Second, the evangelists may have felt, as they looked back on the ministry and crucifixion of Jesus and the refusal of the great majority of Jews to believe in his resurrection and to accept him as the Messiah, that his rejection by the Jews was in a large measure the fault of these men. Since the world view of the envangelists was rather "Manichaean," this second reason might well have led them to tar all representatives of normative Judaism with the same brush, picturing them as the enemy. In literature designed at least to a considerable extent for propaganda in the original and literal sense of that word—to propagate the faith among pagans, very much including unsophisticated and anti-intellectual people—this was also a very effective way of telling a story, presenting it as a contest between good and evil.

Third, the Gospels we have were all written, or at least received their final form, after the fall of Jerusalem, at a time when the Romans had reason to consider the Jews enemies. Hence the followers of Jesus who believed that he had been the Messiah (*Christos*, in Greek) had ample reason to insist that they were not Jews and that they, too, considered the Jews their enemies. Nowhere is this tendency more apparent than in the extraordinary way in which the evangelists coped with the fact that Jesus had been crucified by Pilate, the Roman procurator. They suggested that Pilate had been a kind man who had had nothing against Jesus, and that they had nothing against Pilate and the Romans; it had all been the fault of the Jews. In the long run, this falsification of history cost the Jews dearly. But while we have no testimony outside the New Testament regarding Jesus' life and death, we do have independent witnesses about Pilate, well summarized by Jack Finegan in *Light from the Ancient Past*. Of the first six procurators of Judea, Pilate seems to have been the most ruthless. He killed Jews and Samaritans in such large numbers that eventually he was replaced. There is no need here to spell out the details; but a contemporary accused him of "corruptibility, violence, robberies, ill-treatment of the people, grievances, continuous executions without even the form of a trial, [and] endless and intolerable cruelties" (257).

One would never have gathered that from the Gospels. But once the lines were drawn in this way, with the Jews and not Pilate thirsting for blood, the Manichaean tendency of the evangelists had free rein. Scholars who have made a study of the normative Judaism of that period are agreed that the New Testament offers an utterly misleading picture of that, too. Again it will suffice to cite Gentile scholars: R. Travers Herford's *The Pharisees* and *Judaism in the New Testament Period*, and George Foot Moore's three-volume work on *Judaism in the First Centuries of the Christian Era*.

It is doubly remarkable that when Jesus, according to Luke, answers the "lawyer's" question with a question—"What is written in the Torah?"—the Jewish scholar replies by citing the two great commandments from Deuteronomy 6:5 and Leviticus 19:18.

The first imperative follows immediately upon the most famous and central Jewish prayer, the so-called *Shma* (that is, "hear"), which begins: "Hear, Israel: The Lord is our God, the Lord is One." The words of the first of the two commandments are part of the *Shma* and recited by Orthodox Jews every morning and every evening. (In Mark 12, Jesus cites the words from the Torah and includes the *Shma*; "and the scribe said to him: You are right, Teacher; you have truly said that he is one, and there is no other but he; and to love him with all the heart, and with all the mind, and with all the strength, and to love one's neighbor as oneself, is much more than all whole burnt offerings and sacrifices.")

As for love of the neighbor, Leviticus 19 also commands love of the stranger. In Luke 10, Jesus accepts the two great commandments of love of God and the neighbor, saying: "Do this, and you will live." As we shall see, the Gospels do not agree on this crucial point, but here Jesus sides with normative Judaism and agrees with the "lawyer," saying: "You have answered right."

Luke continues: "But he wanted to justify himself and said to Jesus: And who is my neighbor?" Thereupon Jesus tells the parable of the Good Samaritan: On the road from Jerusalem to Jericho a man is attacked by robbers who beat him and leave him half-dead. Soon a priest travels the same way, and then a Levite as well. Both see the poor man lying by the road but pass by. Then a Samaritan comes by and takes care of him in a compassionate and generous way. And Jesus asks: "Which of these three, do you think, proved a neighbor to the man who had fallen among robbers?" Luke goes on: "He said: The one who showed him mercy." Where the evangelists relate that Jesus took this line, they generally recognize that he was at one with the Jewish tradition. Yet even in these passages his ethos is not simply that of Moses and the prophets. What mattered to Jesus and his audience, but not to Moses and the prophets, was what an individual might do to gain salvation.

The four Gospels in the New Testament offer us four versions of Jesus, and although there are areas of agreement, especially between the first three Gospels which seem to have shared some sources, they also differ in many ways. But questions do not arise only where the Gospels actually contradict each other. The celebrated parable of the Good Samaritan is to be found in only one of the four. Thus we have two options.

If Jesus had really told this parable, then it would be revealing that three of the evangelists had no use for it and did not record it. It is also possible that he never did tell this story but that in time some people who liked it attributed it to him. We may never know the answer, but it is important to realize that most readers and preachers tend to choose from the Gospels what they like, and that the Jesus of most books that pose as biographies of Jesus is a mouthpiece for the author's ethic.

The preoccupation with individual salvation is amply attested by all four Gospels. On another occasion, also in Luke (18), Jesus is said to have answered the question, "what shall I do to inherit eternal life," by reciting five of the Ten Commandments: "Do not commit adultery, do not kill, do not steal, do not bear false witness, honor your father and mother." His questioner replied: "All these I have observed from my youth." Then Jesus said: "One thing you still lack. Sell all you have and distribute it to the poor, and you will have treasure in heaven; and come, follow me." Now this was certainly not in keeping with normative Judaism, nor was it Zoroastrian. This commandment is closer to the sects of those days that expected the end of the world before long, and the influence of Buddhism cannot be ruled out. But what is different from Moses and the prophets is not only the radicalism of the demand; it is also the motivation, which is to accumulate "treasure in heaven."

Luke says that the man given this answer

> became sad, for he was very rich. Jesus, seeing this, said: How hard it is for the
> rich to enter the kingdom of heaven! It is easier for a camel to go through the eye
> of a needle than for a rich man to enter the kingdom of God. Those who heard
> this asked: Who, then, can be saved? But he said: What is impossible with men
> is possible with God. Then Peter said: Behold, we have left everything and fol-
> lowed you. And he said to them: Truly, I say to you, there is no man who has left
> house or wife or brothers or parents or children for the sake of the kingdom of
> God, who will not receive many times as much in this world, and in the world to
> come eternal life.

The first half of the final promise (about *this* world) requires some very bold
interpretation to be saved from being false as well as absurd (many times as many
wives or brothers or parents?), and in the statement of the conditions for the rewards
the "or," repeated four times where one would expect "and," is puzzling. The questioner has been told that he should distribute all he has among the poor, but the disciples seem to be told that it is quite enough to leave one's wife or one's children, or
one's parents, or one's brothers, as long as one does it in order to be saved. As for the
rich, it is apparently impossible for them to be saved; but God can do the impossible.
Hence it would seem that He can save even the rich if He wants to, but it is not at all
clear whether in that case He first makes the rich give all they have to the poor, or
whether He might cause them instead to leave their wives for the sake of salvation, or
whether God might choose in some cases to save a rich man although that man never
parted from anything at all to gain treasure in heaven. Parting from one or more of the
people mentioned seems to be a sufficient condition for salvation, provided this is
done for the sake of salvation, and hence a prudent person would clearly be well
advised to choose this path and not to bank on God's choosing to do the impossible.
But thoroughgoing concern for the welfare of others without any regard for one's own
treasure in heaven is not commended at all. Indeed, our passage clearly suggests that
whoever exerts himself to help the poor for *their* sake does *not* fulfil the conditions of
salvation.

Remember the maxim of Antigonos of Sokho (section 31 above): "Do not be
like servants who serve their master, expecting rewards . . ." Moreover, many Jews in
Jesus' time still did not believe in any afterlife and much less that the world was about
to come to an end.

The passages in Luke discussed here do not stand alone. The same basic problems are raised, for example, by the so-called Sermon on the Mount. Modern scholarship has long ceased to believe that Jesus ever delivered this sermon on a mount.
It is agreed that Matthew collected many of the master's most striking sayings in
chapters 5 through 7 of his Gospel. This "sermon" begins with nine "beatitudes."
Each announces a personal reward, and this poem ends: "Rejoice and be glad, for your
reward is great in heaven." Throughout the "sermon" promises and threats alternate
continually, and what is threatened is not merely that one "will never enter the kingdom
of heaven" but "judgment" and "hell fire" and that "your whole body should be cast
into hell." At the same time, the demands of this "sermon" are easily as radical as those
in Luke, and many of them also turn up in different contexts in Luke's Gospel. Once
again, these extreme demands raise the question: Who, then, can be saved? Will all
who do not comply with them be cast into hell? Many passages in the "sermon" suggest
precisely that, but if the evangelists and the other early Christians had accepted that
view, they would certainly have made few converts, and Christianity would never even
have come close to being adopted as the official religion of the Roman empire.

The "Manichaean" emphasis on heaven and hell proved to be effective from
a missionary point of view. The threat of damnation lent the new faith a sense of

urgency, and the prospect that those who did not embrace this faith—one's enemies and oppressors, the rich, and all who were evil—would meet with dire punishments was gladly heard. A saying that found a place in Matthew 10:14 f. and 11:34, in Mark 6:11, and in Luke 10:10 ff. was that of Jesus comforting his disciples: "If anyone will not receive you or listen to your words, shake off the dust from your feet as you leave that house or town. Truly, I say to you, it shall be more tolerable on the day of judgment for the land of Sodom and Gomorrah [a proverbial designation for the greatest evildoers of all time] than for that town."

The Hebrew Bible relates that when God told Abraham that he was about to destroy Sodom and Gomorrah, Abraham raised his voice against God to say that it would be shameful for God if there should be a few decent people in those cities and he killed them along with the wicked (Genesis 18). Job also argued with God and insisted that his ways were not just. Jeremiah, without claiming that Jerusalem had been innocent, still mourned over her destruction. The author of the Book of Jonah insisted that even the people of Nineveh, the archenemy, should be forgiven all of their outrages as soon as they repented. The Pharisees made allowances for the just among the Gentiles and in any case did not revel in dreams of hell. Nor do we find any teaching of eternal torment—much less any exultation over this prospect—in the Buddha, Confucius, or Lao-tze. Yet many people, including non-Christians, believe that Jesus was mankind's greatest moral teacher, that he had a more exalted conception of neighbor love than anyone before him, and that he discovered the infinite value of every human soul.

According to the Gospels, Jesus believed that God would torment the mass of men in all eternity, and this did not bother Jesus. Moreover, Jesus, as pictured in the Gospels, was totally indifferent to the social order—to oppression, slavery, and torture; for he believed that this world was of no account and would shortly come to an end anyway. Those who are *phronimos* ("prudent"; many English translations have "wise") are concerned to "lay up for yourselves treasures in heaven, where neither moth nor rust consumes and where thieves do not break in and steal," to quote the "sermon on the mount"; while those who are concerned about *this* world are *moros* ("foolish" or "moronic").

Ernst Troeltsch, who was a Protestant theologian before he gave up theology to become a philosopher, was right when he said in the most comprehensive and scholarly book ever written on *The Social Teachings of the Christian Churches* that the ethic of Jesus in the Gospels amounts to "unlimited and unconditional individualism"; that "of an ideal for humanity there is no thought"; and that "any program of social renovation is lacking" (39, 41, 48). It is therefore no wonder that no agreement can be had on where Jesus stood on specific moral questions, such as pacifism or the courts.

It is, however, a striking feature of his teaching that many of his formulations do not seem to have been meant literally. He often alternates between hyperbole and parables. But if he thought that his teaching might save people from eternal torment, and felt compassion for those who came to hear him, why did he speak in such a manner that even the disciples and the evangelists were unsure about what was needful?

In the "sermon" he says: "Till heaven and earth pass away, not an iota, not a dot will pass from the law until all is accomplished. Whoever therefore relaxes one of the least of these commandments and teaches men so, shall be called least in the kingdom of heaven. . . . Unless your righteousness exceeds that of the Pharisees, you will never enter the kingdom of heaven." One might suppose that those "called least in the kingdom" had at least entered it and been saved, but the sequel suggests that being "called least in the kingdom" may be a euphemism for eternal damnation. Still in the same "sermon on the mount," Jesus exceeds the demands of the Pharisees by insisting that it is by no means sufficient not to kill people—the Pharisees, of course, had never suggested that this was sufficient, but they did not go on to say, as Jesus did: "Whoever says, 'You fool!' shall be liable to hell fire." Jesus himself said far worse things about the Pharisees again and again, and one is left to wonder once again whether he could have meant what he said, and almost all of the most renowned teachers of Christianity have called their opponents worse things than fools.

Also in the "sermon on the mount," Jesus says:

> You have heard that it was said: You shall not commit adultery! But I say to you that whoever looks at a woman and covets her has already committed adultery with her in his heart. If your right eye troubles you, tear it out and cast it away from you; it is better for you that one of your members should perish than that your whole body should be cast into hell.

Here Jesus quotes one of Moses' Ten Commandments and suggests that it is not sufficient. The text we have ignores the fact that the last of the Ten Commandments says specifically: "You shall not covet your neighbor's wife! And you shall not desire your neighbor's house, his field, or his manservant, or his maidservant, his ox, or his ass, or anything that is your neighbor's!" But Jesus goes much further. The Ten Commandments seem to say, and at the very least permit the interpretation, that one should not *nurture* such desires. Jesus condemns even a single lustful glance at any woman at all as the equivalent of adultery and as a sin deserving of eternal punishment in hell. Again, one recalls the disciples' query: "Who, then, can be saved?" Jesus' implicit answer is anything but reassuring and has led exegetes to wonder whether he meant what he is reported to have said.

Nietzsche commented in *The Antichrist* (section 45): "It is not exactly the eye that is meant." The eye is no "member" (*melos*); the male sexual organ is. Is Jesus then exhorting men troubled by lust to castrate themselves? Origen (about 185–254), who was the greatest Bible scholar among the early Christians and prepared a parallel edition of six Hebrew and Greek versions of the Hebrew Bible (the Hexapla), did castrate himself to achieve sexual purity. He headed important schools, first in Alexandria and later in Caesarea, and has been called the most influential Christian theologian before St. Augustine. Presumably, he was moved not only by the passage in the "sermon" but also by Matthew 19:12, which distinguishes "eunuchs who have been made eunuchs by men, and . . . eunuchs who have made themselves eunuchs for the sake of the Kingdom of heaven. He who is able to accept this, let him accept it." Today this is not quoted as often as the two verses immediately following, which have been sentimentalized: ". . . Let the children come to me . . . for to such belongs the Kingdom of heaven." Surely, the remark about the children belongs with the material cited here. See also 18:3: Unless one becomes as a child, one cannot be saved. Yet Origen's example was not followed widely and his relatively humane teaching about hell was not accepted. Still it seemed quite clear to many Christians that Jesus had condemned sexual desire and that he had threatened all who fostered it, or at the very least those who indulged it, with hell fire. Hence monasticism gained an important place in Christianity while in normative Judaism it had had no place at all.

If one of the church fathers, or indeed any Christian teacher before the Protestant Reformation, rivaled Origen's Biblical scholarship, it was St. Jerome (about 347–420). Working in a monastery in Bethlehem, he translated the Bible into Latin, working from the Hebrew Scriptures and checking an older Latin version of the Gospels against the Greek original. To this day, his Latin version is the Roman Catholic Bible. His many other works include an essay in praise of virginity, and his sentiments are summed up in two striking aphorisms: "Marriage peoples the earth, but virginity peoples heaven"; and, again contrasting virginity and matrimony, "a cup is for drinking, and a chamber

pot for the secretions of nature" (Coulton, 444). This ethos is as remote from normative Judaism as Jerome's maxim, "when a man has once been washed in Christ, there
is no need that he should wash again" (554). This denigration of sex and the body we
have found in Mani; it can be found in Gnosticism before him, and it was easy to derive
it from some of Jesus' sayings, whatever Jesus' own ethos may have been.

There is always room for doubt about Jesus' meaning. The Gospels attribute to
him hyperbole that may not be meant to be taken literally, enigmatic parables, and plain
evasion and equivocation. But the radical sayings that condemn sex as evil and consign
most men to hell without any sign of compassion are not balanced by equally clear state-
ments that would bring Jesus closer to the views that most modern readers would like to
find in him. Although in the "sermon" he says, after forbidding all oaths, "Let your
speech be yes if yes, no if no; for whatever is more than this comes from the evil one,"
what the Gospels record of his own speech was rarely forthright and straightforward.

One of the striking exceptions appears in the "sermon" directly before this admonition: "Whoever divorces his wife, except on the grounds of unchastity, makes her
an adulteress; and whoever marries a divorced woman commits adultery." This statement appears not only in Matthew 5:32 but also in 19:9 and—*without the clause*
"except on the grounds of unchastity"—in Mark 10:11–12 and in Luke 16:18. But although Protestants insist that the Roman Catholic church has strayed far from the
Gospels and that Protestantism involves above all else a return to the Bible, most of
them condone divorce, notably including liberal Protestants who pride themselves on
their regard for scholarship and truthfulness.

When it is a matter of getting around a disagreeable commandment or prohibition, Protestant theologians no less than Catholic theologians have been quite as
ingenious as any "lawyer." In this respect they resemble the exegetes of other religions,
from the rabbis to Gandhi, whose interpretation of the Gita will be considered in
chapter IX. What may be distinctive in Protestantism, including liberal Protestantism,
is the degree of self-righteousness. While doing what others do, one pours contempt
on them for doing it; first on the Pharisees, then on the Catholic church, and finally on
almost everyone except liberal Protestants. For well over a century this was done so
vigorously that by the middle of the twentieth century, when most of the educated
public in formerly Protestant countries no longer had any firsthand knowledge of the
Bible, liberal Protestant claims about Jesus and the New Testament were accepted as
common sense. Jesus is still widely considered a moral genius whose extremely liberal
and progressive ethic was—just like one's own—and thus the best the world had ever
seen. We shall see that even Gandhi shared this view. There is a consensus that Jesus was
right, but not about what he meant.

Many people feel sure that Jesus was martyred for his moral liberalism by men
who were infinitely less humane. Yet according to the Gospels, Jesus believed, as the
Pharisees and Sadducees did not, that the end of the world was at hand; he believed, as
they did not, that the mass of men was headed for eternal torment; and there is no
evidence that this conviction troubled him.

41

The first three Gospels—Matthew, Mark, and Luke—are much more similar to
each other than they are to the fourth Gospel, and they are often discussed together
as if they presented a common view of Jesus. For the sake of convenience they are
therefore called "the synoptic Gospels." Mark is the oldest of the three, but was written
later than the Epistles of Paul in the New Testament. Most scholars are agreed that
the first version of this Gospel was written in Rome around A.D. 65 and drew on Peter's

recollections; also that Matthew and Luke drew on Mark as well as some other sources. Some German scholars have postulated another written source (called *Q* for short; the German word *Quelle* means source); this was supposed to be a collection of Jesus' sayings from which Matthew and Luke might have derived the many sayings that both of them report, usually in very different contexts, and that are not to be found in Mark. Many of the sayings that appear in the "sermon on the mount" in Matthew, for example, appear in Luke either in a sermon in a plain or as the climaxes of stories found only in Luke. But the *Q* hypothesis has been abandoned by most scholars, and what is "in" now is "oral tradition."

J. G. Davies offers some interesting statistics about the relation of Mark to the two later synoptic Gospels. "Of Mark's 661 verses Matthew reproduces the substance of over 600 in language largely identical with Mark, while Luke does the same for more than fifty per cent of Mark." Moreover, "the order of Mark's narrative is mainly reproduced by Matthew and Luke," and where one does not follow him, the other one usually does. In addition, Matthew and Luke have in common "some 200 verses" not found in Mark. "There are left some 400 verses peculiar to Matthew and some 500 peculiar to Luke" (10 f.).

Still, it should not come as any surprise that the image of Jesus in the earliest Gospel is rather different from that in Matthew and Luke on whom we have concentrated so far. Luke after all begins his Gospel by saying explicitly: "Inasmuch as many have undertaken to compile a narrative of the things accomplished among us . . . it seemed good to me also . . . to write an orderly account for you, dear Theophilus, that you may know the truth . . ." He was aware of many earlier accounts and clearly felt that they left much to be desired. Biblical scholars are agreed that the author of the Gospel according to Luke also wrote The Acts of the Apostles, which is the fifth book of the New Testament, and that he was close to and had traveled with Paul, who is the hero of Acts. It is also widely believed that Luke, unlike Mark and Matthew, was a Gentile. But Matthew and Luke share more than their sources; both also have a pronounced interest in Jesus' moral teachings although we have seen that this concern has been exaggerated by some modern readers. Still, when we turn to the oldest of the four Gospels which tradition as well as modern scholarship link to the witness of Peter who, unlike Paul, had known Jesus, it comes as a surprise to observe how extraordinarily little emphasis there is on any moral teaching.

Mark begins with John the Baptist and has him baptize Jesus in the Jordan, whereupon "the spirit immediately drove him [Jesus] into the desert; and he was in the desert forty days and was tempted by Satan" (1:12 f.). Then Jesus called some of his disciples to follow him, went to Capernaum (Kfar Nahum) on the shores of the Sea of Galilee (Yam Kinneret), and taught in the synagogue there on the Sabbath. "And they were astonished at his teaching, for he taught them as one having authority, and not as the scribes did" (1:22). Mark does not report what Jesus taught. Matthew placed this sentence at the end of the "sermon on the mount," very probably because he felt that after the sayings he had collected there, the remark about the astonishment of the people was particularly appropriate.

Actually, Matthew's placement of this comment makes it even weightier by suggesting that Jesus' most radical sayings did not astonish his Jewish hearers particularly, as they were used to an enormous variety of opinions. What did astonish them was his conception of himself, his manner, his assumption of authority.

Mark, after ignoring the content of Jesus' teaching and observing the people's reaction, goes on to report a miracle: Jesus encountered a man possessed by an unclean spirit and commanded the spirit to quit him, which he did with a loud cry. Then the people were amazed that even the unclean spirits obeyed him, "and immediately his

fame spread throughout the surrounding region of Galilee" (1:28). Thus Jesus became known, according to Mark, for his miracles and his manner and not for his moral
message.

Right away, Jesus performed another miracle, and when evening came, that very
same day, "they brought to him all who were sick or possessed with demons" (1:32).
"And he went throughout all Galilee, preaching in their synagogues and casting out
demons" (1:39). The first chapter of Mark closes with yet another miracle: Jesus
cures a leper.

The first chapter sets the tone for Mark's record of Jesus' ministry in Galilee. The
master is, as much as anything, an exorcist and a worker of miracles. There is no chapter without a miracle, but there are many without any moral teaching. Mostly he
exorcizes demons and heals diseases, but he also stills a storm on the Sea of Galilee,
raises a twelve-year-old girl from the dead—she is said to have died a few moments
earlier, but Jesus says, "the child is not dead but sleeping"—and he walks on the Sea
of Galilee. In chapter 2 he gives offense by saying to a man: "My son, your sins are
forgiven." At that point, says Mark, the scribes sitting there "thought in their hearts:
Why does he utter such blasphemy? Who can forgive sins but God alone?" At first
glance one might ask how Mark could know what they thought; but on second thought
one can hardly doubt that, if Jesus had really said that, the scribes must have thought
precisely that.

In chapter 8, finally, Jesus asks his disciples—he has ordained twelve—"Who do
men say that I am? And they told him: John the Baptist [who had been beheaded by
then]; and others say: Elijah; and others: one of the prophets. And he asked them:
But who do you say that I am? Peter answered him: You are the Messiah [literally,
the anointed one, which is in Greek *ho christos*, and in English 'the Christ']. And
he charged them to tell no one about him."

The final sentence recurs often in Mark and brings to mind a passage in Mark 4,
where Jesus has told a parable that his disciples did not understand. When they asked him
about it, he told them: "To you has been given the secret of the kingdom of God, but
for those outside everything is in parables, so that seeing they will see but not perceive,
and hearing will hear but not understand, lest they should turn back and be forgiven."
The lack of compassion is startling and reverberates through the refrain: "he charged
them to tell no one."

To be sure, Jesus is quoting from the sixth chapter of Isaiah, which relates how
the prophet received his call and which is also the source of the tremendous three-
fold *kadosh* ("holy") in the Hebrew liturgy that reappears in the Catholic mass as
Sanctus, sanctus, sanctus. Yet there are at least three profound differences between
the impact of these striking words in Isaiah and in Mark. First of all, Jesus' belief in
hell and eternal torment makes these words infinitely crueler; he takes pains to keep
people from being saved. Second, God commands Isaiah: "Go forth and say to this
people: Hearing, hear and do not understand! Seeing, see and do not perceive! . . ."
The prophet is to say this to the people and not behind their backs. Finally, Isaiah does
not want to go, but his lips are touched with a live coal and he is called to go and given
this message; but he has no sooner heard it than he says to God: "Until when, Lord?"
He is immediately struck by the cruelty of these words, and the idea that this should
continue forever is unthinkable for him: *ad matai adonai,* until when, Lord? is a humane
plea. The prophet's humanity is beyond question; but what about God's? His answer is
cruel: "Until the cities are desolate, without inhabitants . . ." He hints at the devasta-
tion of the land by the Assyrians—and his words are as cruel as was the event; the God
of the Hebrew Scriptures is as cruel as life and history are, but no more so. He is not a
utopian god, above the clouds, divorced from what happens on earth. Neither does his

cruelty extend beyond what happens on earth. "Shall there be evil in a city and the Lord has not done it?" (Amos 3:6). The world is cruel, and neither the prophets nor Job see any way of acquitting the Lord of this cruelty. But they are mindful of it, deeply troubled by it, and do not extend it beyond the evidence of our eyes to a site of eternal damnation.

In Mark 11 Jesus enters Jerusalem. His Galilean ministry is ended. But his entry into the city is associated with one last miracle. "He was hungry. And seeing, far off, a figtree in leaf, he went up to it to see if he might find anything on it. But when he came to it, he found nothing but leaves, for it was not yet the season for figs. And Jesus responded saying to it: Let no man eat fruit from you hereafter in all eternity! And his disciples heard it." The next morning, "they saw the figtree dried up from the roots." One of the disciples, Peter, called Jesus' attention to it, and Jesus, far from rueing his ill temper and his curse of an innocent tree, did not heal or restore it; he answered: "Have faith in God! Truly, I say to you, whoever says to this mountain, raise yourself up and cast yourself into the sea, and does not doubt in his heart but believes that what he says will come to pass, what he says will happen to him."

In between the cursing of the tree and the withering of the tree, there are four verses relating that Jesus

> entered the temple and began to drive out those who sold and those who bought in the temple, and he overturned the tables of the moneychangers and the seats of those who sold pigeons; and he would not allow anyone to carry anything through the temple. And he taught and said to them: Is it not written, my house shall be called a house of prayer for all nations? But you have made it a den of robbers.

The "den of robbers" comes from Jeremiah 7:11, the "house of prayer for all nations" from Isaiah 56:7. Some Christians have found "Christ chasing the moneychangers out of the temple" a superbly edifying spectacle, and it is—for better or worse—the only forceful action ascribed to Jesus in the Gospels. The evangelists record that he associated with the "publicans" whom most Jews shunned—the "collaborators" who collected taxes for the Romans—and that he said expressly, "Give to Caesar whatever is Caesar's, and to God what is God's" (Mark 12:17 and Matthew 22:21 and Luke 20:25).

No oppression or social wrong seems to have outraged him as much as the stalls outside the temple (in the court, not inside the temple building). But this is almost of a piece with his wrath at the figtree for not bearing fruit out of season to still his hunger. As long as there were sacrifices, there had to be stalls where worshipers who came from out of town could buy pigeons if not some other small animals, as well as stalls where those who came from other countries could change money.

According to Mark, "as he [Jesus] was walking in the temple, the chief priests and the scribes and the elders came to him and said to him: By what authority are you doing all this?" In reply, "Jesus said to them: I will ask you a question; answer me and I will tell you by what authority I do all this. John's baptism, was that from heaven or from men? Answer me. And they argued with one another" and could not agree. "So they answered: We do not know. And Jesus said to them: Neither will I tell you by what authority I do all this." End of chapter 11.

From chapter 12 some passages have already been quoted. It is of some interest that Jesus here tries to refute the Sadducees, "who say there is no resurrection." For once Jesus neither answers with a question nor tells a parable; he argues—like a Pharisee: "Have you not read in Moses' book about the bush how God said to him: I am the God of Abraham and the God of Isaac and the God of Jacob [Exodus 3:6]. He is not a God of the dead but of the living. You err greatly."

In the next chapter Jesus tells his disciples, casually and without any compassion, that Jerusalem will be destroyed—an event that had taken place when the Gospel received its final form. He merely says: "Do you see these great buildings? Not one stone will remain upon another, unbroken." Four of his disciples ask Jesus: "When will all this happen, and what will be the sign . . . ?" At this point Jesus moves close to the apocalyptic literature of the age and cites Daniel 12:11, showing far more interest in portents than in suffering humanity and no concern whatever for the many who will not be saved.

Chapters 14 and 15 relate Jesus' passion and crucifixion. Up to this point Jesus appears as a miracle worker who has a very exalted conception of himself and *seems* to agree when Peter calls him the Messiah. He is certainly not portrayed as an especially admirable or attractive person. When he says in chapter 13 that "they will see the Son of Man coming in clouds with great power and glory," it is clear that he knows Daniel 7:13, but not at all whether he means himself. He prophesies the end but not necessarily his own return—also in Mark 9:1: "Truly, I say to you, there are some standing here who will not taste death before they see the kingdom of God come with power." The obvious reaction to these prophecies is surely that Jesus was a false prophet.

Still, some of his sayings no less than many of his parables have a haunting quality and stay in the mind; many bits have a strange beauty even if they are morally disturbing, and the imagery is often inspired. But much of what is impressive is not new but collected from a variety of Jewish and Hellenistic sources—whether by Jesus himself or by those who soon attributed these words to him. (See Billerbeck and Strack.) If all we knew of Jesus were chapters 1 through 13 of Mark, Jesus would never have been considered more than a minor Jewish prophet. Nor do the next two chapters add any sayings or teachings that can begin to explain the impact of the Gospels on humanity. The remaining dicta are of a kind with what has gone before.

As he sat in Bethany in the house of Simon the leper, a woman came and used much precious ointment to anoint him. Some felt that this was wasteful and that the ointment might have been sold for a great deal of money that could then have been given to the poor. But Jesus commended her and said: "The poor will always be with you, and you can do good to them any time; but I will not always be with you. She has done what she could; she has anointed my body beforehand for my burial."

At his last meal with his disciples—"the last supper"—he predicted that one of them would betray him, and then he called himself "Son of Man." After blessing and breaking the bread, he said: "Take; this is my body." And of the wine he said, after the blessing: "This is my blood of the covenant, which is poured out for many." Thus, according to Mark, he transformed the traditional Jewish ceremony of the blessing of bread and wine into sacraments, but with a minimum of explanation.

20   Then he prayed at Gethsemane, on the slope of the Mount of Olives, not far from the temple, but his disciples, whom he had asked to stay awake with him, kept falling asleep. Meanwhile he pleaded with God: "Abba, Father, everything is possible for you; remove this cup from me; yet not what I will but what you will!"

A crowd came to arrest him, carrying swords and clubs, led by one of the twelve disciples, Judas, "the betrayer." This betrayal is stressed a great deal, but it is never made clear in what sense Judas betrayed Jesus, except that "the betrayer had given them a sign, saying: The one I shall kiss is the man; seize him and lead him away safely." The symbolism of the betrayal with a kiss, by a person who had up to that moment been very close to the master, is so powerful that it has blotted out the question of why it should have been necessary to point out to those who came to arrest Jesus which one he was. After all, he had allegedly attracted a great deal of attention for a long time;

he had created a commotion before the temple; and he had argued again and again with Pharisees and Sadducees. But *this is the crux of the Gospels; their power is inseparable from their symbolism.*

What Jesus does and says in the last pages of Mark's Gospel is not particularly admirable or inspiring. "One of those who stood by drew his sword and struck the high priest's servant and cut off his ear. And Jesus said to them: Have you come out as against a robber, with swords and clubs to capture me?" He shows no compassion for the servant and does not try to heal him or comfort him; he thinks of himself. But when Mark continues, "and they all abandoned him and fled," the image of the totally forsaken Jesus casts a spell.

The disciples are placed in a dreadful light. Not only did the eleven that might be considered the first Christians sleep when Jesus asked them to wake with him, not only did all of them flee when he was arrested, but that same night Peter fulfilled Jesus' prophecy that "before the cock crows twice, you will deny me three times." When a maid asked him whether he had not been with Jesus, he three times denied knowing him. Yet Matthew (16:18) was to claim that Jesus had called Simon, his disciple, "Peter" (*Petros* in Greek, *Kepha* in Aramaic), explaining: "On this rock [*petra*] I will found my church." An admirable or heroic type? Hardly. But precisely this made the Gospels more appealing. With God all things were possible, and he could elect mediocre people while making sure that many who might have seemed far superior would go to hell. That held out hope for millions.

Meanwhile Jesus had a hearing before "all the chief priests and the elders and the scribes." And when

> the high priest asked him, Are you the messiah, the son of the Blessed? Jesus said: I am, and you will see the Son of Man sitting at the right hand of Power and coming with the clouds of heaven. And the high priest tore his coat and said: Why should we need further witnesses? You have heard his blasphemy. What is your decision? And they all condemned him as deserving death.

At the literal level, it is significant that, although many people suppose that Jesus was a great liberal who collided with the Pharisees because allegedly they prized the ritual law above all while he stressed pure morality, all four evangelists agree that Jesus was condemned for blasphemy, for what he said about himself, and not for breaking any law. And The Acts of the Apostles, the book that follows upon the Gospels in the New Testament, makes it abundantly clear that the disciples initially upheld the ritual laws. What determined whether one was a follower of Jesus or not was not one's way of life or one's morality but what one thought of Jesus; specifically, whether one believed that he was the Messiah, that he was raised from the dead, and that he would return at the right hand of Power.

According to the Gospels, Jesus was no mere man who might be judged by the same standards that are used in judging his opponents. He was a miracle worker not in the sense in which an enlightened modernist might think of miracle workers—either as frauds or as deluded and superstitious men. He was thought of as having supernatural powers that his opponents, except for Satan, lacked, and this was not an incidental fact about him but a point Mark never forgets. What he relates is *a drama in which two cosmic forces clash.*

Jesus was brought to trial and crucified by Pilate, the Roman governor. Pilate crucified Jews in such huge numbers that the Jews as well as the Romans lost track of the victims, and both quickly forgot Jesus. Yet the trial is an image of immense symbolic power, infinitely suggestive, and it was the genius of the evangelists to realize that the crucifixion, though an everyday event in those days, was a symbol in whose name worlds

Jesus (1500) in Braunschweig cathedral, Germany. The 12th century crucifix in the same cathedral suggests no suffering and is known as the *Triumphkreuz*.

could be conquered. The idea of gods who had suffered and been resurrected was old, but the image of the Messiah on the cross remains one of the most impressive religious symbols of all time. Hinduism and Buddhism have images of no less power, and Christianity has never made much headway where those symbols reigned. But Judaism has no visual image to compare with the crucifix, nor did the other religions of the Roman empire.

The proliferation of crucifixes belongs to a later age, and they have no place in many Christian churches. But what matters at this point is not the embodiment of the image in wood or stone. *The image of Christ on the Cross is*—the play on words is called for—*the crux of the Gospels.* The brief exchange between Jesus and Pilate is subordinate to that. "Pilate asked him: Are you the king of the Jews? And he answered him: You have said it. . . . But Jesus made no further answer" (Mark 15). What follows is an attempt to acquit Pilate and the Romans of all responsibility, as if the evangelists said outright to the Romans: We have nothing against you; we blame you for nothing; we are not your enemies; our enemies are the people who have fought you, the Jews. Had it not been for that line the Roman empire would hardly have found Christianity so congenial that eventually it became the official religion. The evangelists were very prudent in their treatment of the Romans. But the brief exchange with Pilate was needed to explain the inscription on the cross: IESUS NAZARENUS REX IUDAEORUM, Jesus of Nazareth, king of the Jews.

On the literal level, one may speculate that this formula provided the meeting ground for the Jewish charge of blasphemy and the Roman governor's interest in the matter. The representatives of normative Judaism felt that Jesus' manner and conception of himself were intolerable; Pilate may have thought that if the man had called or proclaimed himself king of the Jews he was a threat to the imperial authority. It is not likely that Pilate gave the matter much thought at all. At times the Romans crucified so many people that the stench filled the air. On that particular day, it seems, only two other men were crucified, and according to Mark both reviled him.

Again, the symbolic image transcends the literal level. The crucified king strikes ancient chords, bringing to mind the theme that Mary Renault has summed up succinctly in the title of her first novel about Theseus, *The King Must Die.* But in the Gospels this old theme is fused with the imagery of the servant of God in Isaiah 53, the man not recognized for what he was while he suffered. He is crucified between two robbers, and the scene is embellished with motifs from the 22nd Psalm as well as Isaiah 53 until it becomes a masterpiece of syncretism in which Greek and Jewish elements are fused with Zoroastrian dualism and ancient Near Eastern lore.

On the literal level, the barrenness of Mark's moral imagination and the lack of moral force in his version of Jesus are astonishing. The horror of the cross is that death comes slowly; but this might have provided great teacher or the world's greatest moral genius with an extraordinary opportunity to say something uniquely memorable that would be forever associated with the Messiah on the cross. According to Mark his only words from the cross were the first words of the 22nd Psalm: "And at the ninth hour Jesus cried with a loud voice: *Eli, Eli, lama sabachthani?* which is translated: My God, my God, why have you forsaken me? And some of those who stood there said when they heard this: See, he is calling Elijah." None of his disciples were there, according to Mark, only some women who had followed him. Matthew follows Mark very closely in these respects, while Luke and John both omit the quotation from the 22nd Psalm and attribute different sayings to the master—Luke three of them, John four, but there is no overlap at all. The only one of these seven words from the cross that is morally very impressive is Luke's: "Father, forgive them; for they know not what they do" (23:34). Perhaps there is no more beautiful line in the whole New Testament, but it is not to be found in many ancient manuscripts, as is duly noted in a footnote of the Revised Standard Version, and Morton Scott Enslin among others has called it "more or less doubtful" (208). We cannot even be sure that this line goes back to Luke, much less that it was spoken by Jesus. But if the answer to both questions should be no, someone would still deserve credit for inserting it here. It is similar to the beautiful story of the woman caught in adultery, at the beginning of John 8, with its splendid line: "Let him who is without sin among you be the first to cast a stone at her." The whole story is missing in the earliest manuscripts and was inserted only later. But to its glory, the New Testament does contain sayings like these.

Mark still records that a Jew who was "a respected member of the council, who was also himself looking for the kingdom of God, took courage and went to Pilate, and asked for the body of Jesus," which he then placed "in a tomb that had been hewn out of the rock, and he rolled a stone against the door of the tomb." Two women "saw where he was laid." Thus ends chapter 15.

The last chapter was originally very short: a mere eight verses. The day after the Sabbath, the two women went to the tomb, found that the stone had been rolled away, and saw a young man in a white robe sitting inside. He told them: "He has risen, he is not here." And he told them to inform the disciples that they would see him again in Galilee. But they fled and "said nothing to anyone, for they were afraid." Thus the earliest versions of the oldest Gospel ended with a rather weak suggestion that Christ had been resurrected. But later twelve more verses were added in some versions, and the other Gospels also presented a stronger case. The first Christians were those who believed that Jesus had risen from the dead and would soon return with Power.

By the time the last twelve verses were added to the Gospel according to Mark, as a coda, they believed much more than that. First, it had by then become accepted as fact that at first the risen Christ had appeared to a woman who was not believed when she told others, then "in another form to two of them, as they were walking into the country," but that they also encountered unbelief. Eventually he had appeared "to the eleven themselves as they sat at table, and he upbraided them for their unbelief and hardness of heart because they had not believed those who saw him after he had risen."

Secondly, there were the final words of the risen Christ to the eleven:

> Go into all the world and preach the gospel to all creatures. *Whoever believes and is baptized will be saved; but whoever does not believe will be damned.* [Emphasis added.] And these signs will attend those who believe: in my name they will cast out demons, speak in new tongues, and handle serpents; and if they drink anything deadly it will not harm them; they will lay their hands on the sick who will get better.

Finally, in the next verse Jesus is called "Lord" and the reader is told that after these words "he was taken up into heaven and sits on the right hand of God." In the Revised Standard Version these last twelve verses are printed in small type as a footnote because they are not found in the earliest manuscripts, but for Christianity they have been more important than the first thirteen chapters of Mark. Now at last the old question, "what must I do to be saved?" was given a clear and unequivocal answer: "Whoever believes and is baptized will be saved; but whoever does not believe will be damned"—no matter how moral a life he has led. Morality and humanity are out of the picture. Their place is taken by a "Manichaean" world view in which Christians are saved and non-Christians damned. For the belief that is required is clearly the belief that the risen Christ is Lord and sits on the right hand of God, and this belief must be sealed by baptism—by formal conversion.

42

In the fourth Gospel, that according to John, the cosmic drama is stressed from the start:

> In the beginning was the *Logos* [usually rendered as "the Word"], and the Logos was with God, and God was the Logos. He was in the beginning with God; all things were made through him, and without him was not anything made that was made. In him was life, and life was the light of men. The light shines in the darkness, and the darkness has not overcome it.

The opening words hark back to the opening words of the Torah ("In the beginning God created the heavens and the earth"); and the primacy of the word, of speech, points to the same source, for in the Hebrew Bible God creates the world solely by means of his sovereign commands, of which the first is: "Let there be light. And there was light. And God saw that the light was good; and God separated the light from the darkness. And God called the light day, and the darkness he called night."

Yet the tone of the opening of John is very different from that of Genesis: more philosophical, more Greek, more Zoroastrian—or in one word, Gnostic. Almost every sentence seems to be soaked in syncretism. "And the Logos became flesh and dwelt among us, full of grace and truth."

To discount this "prologue" and concentrate on Jesus' sayings in the pages that follow is to miss the point of this Gospel—and of all the Gospels. On such a "naturalistic" reading, Jesus would emerge as a rather unattractive human being, who constantly speaks of himself, saying things like: "I am the light of the world; whoever follows me will not walk in darkness but will have the light of life" (8:12); and "You are from below, I am from above; you are of this world, I am not of this world. I told you that you would die for your sins, for you will die in your sins unless you believe that I am he" (23 f.); "Why do you not understand what I say? It is because you cannot bear to hear my word. You are of your father the devil, and your will is to do your father's desires. He was a murderer from the beginning and has nothing to do with the truth . . . Because I tell the truth, you do not believe me" (43 ff.); "Truly, truly, I say to you, if anyone keeps my word he will not see death in all eternity" (51).

His constant "truly, truly, I say to you" may be tedious, but it is certainly not meant to be "naturalistic"; it comes closer to the refrain of a liturgical drama. The whole style of this Gospel is not designed to work up gradually to a posthumous vindication in the form of a few sentences in which it is said that Jesus has risen from the dead. To appreciate this Gospel one must know from the start—and therefore is told at the outset—that Jesus was the Logos that was with God from the beginning, and that the Logos became flesh. No sooner does John the Baptist see Jesus than he exclaims: "Behold the Lamb of God who takes away the sin of the world" (1:29)—and then, "this is the Son of God" (1:34). Still in the first chapter, we are also told, without having to wait for the encounter with Pilate or the inscription on the cross: "Rabbi, you are the Son of God; you are the king of Israel" (49). In response, Jesus says: "Truly, truly, I say to you, you will see heaven opened and the angels of God ascending and descending upon the Son of Man." End of chapter 1.

The point made in the coda of Mark's Gospel, "Whoever believes and is baptized will be saved; but whoever does not believe will be damned," is one of the central motifs of John's Gospel:

> Unless one is born of water and the spirit, one cannot enter the kingdom of God (3:5).

> Whoever does not believe is condemned already because he has not believed in the name of the only Son of God (3:18).

Whoever does not believe the Son shall not see life, but the wrath of God abides on him (3:36).

Whoever does not honor the Son does not honor the Father who sent him (5:23).

This is the work of God, that you believe in him whom he has sent (6:29).

This is the will of my Father, that every one who sees the Son and believes in him shall have eternal life (6:40).

Whoever believes has eternal life (6:47).

I am the living bread that came down from heaven; whoever eats of this bread will live for ever (6:51).

Truly, truly, I say to you, unless you eat the flesh of the Son of Man and drink his blood, you have no life in you; whoever eats my flesh and drinks my blood has eternal life, and I will raise him up on the last day. For my flesh is food indeed, and my blood is drink indeed. Whoever eats my flesh and drinks my blood abides in me and I in him (6:53–56).

Whoever eats me will live because of me. This is the bread that came down from heaven . . . whoever eats this bread will live for ever (6.57 f.).

For those who had wondered what one had to do to be saved, and whether anyone could satisfy God's demands, this simple recipe was glad tidings indeed. But perhaps it seemed too good to be true and hence had to be repeated again and again to be believed. What was needed for salvation was nothing but belief in the Son of God, baptism, and the eating of the sacramental bread and the drinking of the sacramental wine, while all who had lived exemplary lives without such faith and sacraments were condemned already. Nor did even one disciple object by quoting Abraham's words to God: "Shame on you if you did such a thing, to slay the just with the wicked, letting the just fare like the wicked! Shame on you if the judge of the whole earth should not do right!" (Genesis 18:25). Not one of them interceded, as Abraham had done for Sodom and Gomorrah, and asked: Master, what of all those who lived before you appeared among us? And what of those who live far away and never heard your words? And, master, might there not be some—are there not many—among those who have heard you who are perhaps put off by your manner?

Least of all did one of them say: Master, if that is God's way and you see nothing wrong in it, I will not believe in you, nor will I eat your body and drink your blood to gain eternal life. I would rather go into oblivion where there is no remembrance of you and your God, sleeping for ever in the dust. And if that cannot be, if those whom you do not raise up must suffer the wrath of God, then let me dwell among them and, if I have the strength, I shall try to comfort them.

What is extraordinary is less that this simple humanity is lacking in the Gospel according to John than that most Christian theologians have quite failed to notice this and have made the most sweeping claims for the humanity of the Gospels in general and of John in particular. Those who know Luther will scarcely be surprised that he should have called John "a master above all other evangelists" (VII, 2,008) or that he said, "one might even call him alone an evangelist" (XI, 1,462). What is astonishing is that so many *liberal* Protestants have said that this Gospel is preeminently the Gospel of love. Having been told that before they ever read it, they may have found confirmation in this famous verse: "A new commandment I give to you, that you love one another; even as I have loved you, that you also love one another. By this all men will know that you are my disciples, if you have love for one another" (13:34 f.). But a reader with critical faculties must surely ask: What is new about this commandment? After all, the commandment to love one's neighbor, and the stranger as well, goes back to Leviticus 19 and was central in the teachings of the most respected Pharisees, such as Hillel. Moreover, Jesus' disciples will be distinguished by the fact that they love *one another*, while their attitude toward unbelievers is closer to Zarathustra's than it is to Hillel's.

It is no different with the other celebrated verses in which love is mentioned: "God so loved the world that he gave his only Son, that whoever believes in him should not perish but have eternal life. . . . Whoever believes in him is not condemned; whoever does not believe is condemned already because he has not believed in the name of the only Son of God" (3:16 ff.). And: "This is my commandment, that you love one another as I have loved you. Greater love has no man than this, that a man lay down his life for his friends. You are my friends if you do what I command you" (15:12–14). Surely, it is possible for a man or woman to have greater love than that, and many people have given their lives for others who were not their friends. Indeed, this is an appalling abuse of the word "friends" (*philoi*). Those who do whatever a man commands them are not therefore his friends, and a friend does not necessarily do whatever he is commanded. One who sacrifices himself for those who believe in him while he feels no concern whatever for the mass of men who do not believe in him is hardly in a position to say of himself: "Greater love has no man than this."

What is at stake here is not a minor error. Compassion for unbelievers is implicitly condemned and proscribed. *Liberal* Protestants have persuaded themselves and millions of educated people who did not consider themselves especially religious, as well as some Jews and Hindus, that when Augustine argued expressly against compassion for the damned, or when Luther used invective against his enemies, these men, however laudable in other ways, behaved in a regrettably "un-Christian" manner. This odd use of the labels "Christian" and "un-Christian" is widespread. But it is totally indefensible unless one is prepared to say also that much of the New Testament is un-Christian, that a great many, and quite possibly most, of the sayings of Jesus recorded in the Gospels are un-Christian, and that the Gospel according to John is un-Christian in its central tendency. Now this might not be a reduction to the absurd if the central message or *kerygma* of the fourth Gospel were profoundly at odds with the other three; but it is not. This Gospel merely puts the point much more crisply and poignantly—and repeats it again and again and again. "I am the way and the truth and the life; no one comes to the Father but by me" (14:6). The other Gospels do not refute this *kerygma*; they also state it. Indeed, they go into more detail about hell than John did; and none harps on hell more than Matthew (See Mark 3:29, 6:11, 9:43–48; Matthew 3:12, 5:22, and 29 f., 8:12, 10:15, 11:20 ff., 13:40 ff. and 50, 16:18, 18:8, 22:13, 23:33, 24:51, 25:30 and 41 and 46; Luke 3:17, 12:5, 13:27 f., and 16:19–31). The last book of the New Testament is The Revelation, or Apocalypse, which the title and tradition ascribe to St. John; here the pious imagination runs amuck in describing hell and wallowing in cruelty.

C. G. Jung's comments on the last book of the Christian Bible are interesting:

> . . . there grew up a terrifying picture that blatantly contradicts all ideas of Christian humility, tolerance, love of your neighbor and your enemies, and makes nonsense of a loving father in heaven and rescuer of mankind. A veritable orgy of hatred, wrath, vindictiveness, and blind destructive fury that revels in fantastic images of terror breaks out and with blood and fire overwhelms a world which Christ had just endeavored to restore to the original state of innocence and loving communion with God.

One might have supposed that such a renowned psychologist would not so mindlessly repeat the clichés of liberal Protestantism. One might have thought that a man who was once Freud's most distinguished disciple and then became profoundly interested in Oriental religions would at least have reread the Bible with an open mind before writing, in his late seventies, his *Answer to Job* in which these sentences are found (section XIII). Seeing how widespread this untenable conception of what is Christian and what is un-Christian has come to be, one can hardly discuss these issues without some polemic, unless one simply ignores views that are still common.

If liberal Protestantism is dead now, it is survived by its falsifications of history. Millions still see the Old Testament and the New much as the liberal Protestants did. They prided themselves on their intellectual conscience and often wrote as if they were the first to bring to Biblical studies the standards of decent scholarship. Yet they were quite as involved in exegetical thinking as their predecessors. That is not to say that they were children of darkness and evil. Many of the moral ideas that they read into the New Testament were humane, and some of them even sought to find in the Gospels a concern for social justice.

43

In 1881 Nietzsche argued in *The Dawn* that "the apostle Paul" was really "*The first Christian*," and that without him "there would be no Christianity; we should scarcely have heard of a small Jewish sect whose master died on the cross." A great many people have come to accept this view, and at least the first sentence of Nietzsche's argument would seem to be borne out by The Acts of the Apostles, the book that in the New Testament follows upon the four Gospels:

> That the ship of Christianity threw overboard a good deal of its Jewish ballast, that it went, and was able to go, among the pagans—that was due to this one man, a very tortured, very pitiful, very unpleasant man, unpleasant even to himself. He suffered from a fixed idea—or more precisely, from a fixed, ever-present, never resting question: what about the Jewish law? and particularly the fulfillment of this law? In his youth he had himself wanted to satisfy it, with a ravenous hunger for this highest distinction which the Jews could conceive—this people who were propelled higher than any other people by the imagination of the ethically sublime, and who alone succeeded in creating a holy god together with the idea of sin as a transgression against this holiness. Paul became the fanatical defender of this god and his law and guardian of his honor; at the same time, in the struggle against the transgressors and doubters, lying in wait for them, he became increasingly harsh and evilly disposed to them, and inclined toward the most extreme punishments. And now he found that—hotheaded, sensual, melancholy, malignant in his hatred as he was—he was himself unable to fulfill the law; indeed, and this seemed strangest to him, his extravagant lust to domineer provoked him continually to transgress the law, and he had to yield to this thorn.
> Is it really his "carnal nature" that makes him transgress again and again? And not rather, as he himself suspected later, behind it the law itself, which must constantly prove itself unfulfillable and which lures him to transgression with irresistible charm? But at that time he did not yet have this way out. . . .
> Luther may have had similar feelings when, in his monastery, he wanted to become the perfect man of the spiritual ideal; and just as Luther one day began to hate the spiritual ideal and the pope and the saints and the whole clerisy with a true, deadly hatred—all the more the less he could own it to himself—so it was with Paul. The law was the cross to which he felt himself nailed: how he hated it! how he resented it! how he searched for some means to annihilate it—not to fulfill it any more himself!
> And finally the saving thought struck him, together with a vision—it could

scarcely have happened otherwise to this epileptic. . . . Paul heard the words: "Why do you persecute *me?*" The essential occurrence, however, was this: his *head* had suddenly seen a light: "It is *unreasonable*," he had said to himself, "to persecute this Jesus! Here after all is the way out; here is the perfect revenge; here and nowhere else I have and hold *the annihilator of the law!*" . . . Until then the ignominious death had seemed to him the chief argument against the Messianic claim of which the adherents of the new doctrine spoke: but what if this were necessary to get rid of the law?

The details of Nietzsche's imaginative reconstruction of Paul's psychic history are controversial. (Rather oddly, some people suppose that "psychohistory" was invented in the mid-twentieth century—not only long after Nietzsche but even after Freud.) Nietzsche's conclusion, however, is widely credited: "This is the first Christian, the inventor of Christianity. Until then there were only a few Jewish sectarians."

What is clear from The Acts of the Apostles is that the disciples, notably including Peter and James, the brother of Jesus, considered it essential to keep the Jewish laws, including not only the observance of the Sabbath but also the dietary laws and circumcision. Further, Paul had not been one of the disciples, nor had he known Jesus; and after the crucifixion he actually persecuted the followers of Jesus. His name in those days was Saul, and Acts says of him: "Saul laid waste the church, and entering house after house, he dragged off men and women and committed them to prison" (8:3)—although according to Acts, his teacher Gamaliel, the leading Pharisee of the time, had said: "Keep away from these men and let them alone; for if this plan or this undertaking is of men, it will fail; but if it is of God, you will not be able to overthrow them" (5:38 f.). Saul was "breathing threats and murder against the disciples of the Lord" (9:1). One may wonder whether there really ever was any such Jewish persecution of the first followers of Jesus as is implied in this story, but Acts certainly gives a frightful picture of Paul before his conversion. He

> went to the high priest and asked him for letters to the synagogues in Damascus so that if he found any belonging to the Way, men or women, he might bring them bound to Jerusalem. Now as he journeyed and approached Damascus, suddenly a light from heaven flashed around him; and he fell to the ground and heard a voice saying to him: Saul, Saul, why do you persecute me? And he said: Who are you, Lord? And he said: I am Jesus whom you are persecuting . . . (9:1–5; cf. 22:3 ff.).

That was Saul's conversion, after which "for three days he was without sight" (9:9). Many scholars suppose, as Nietzsche did, that he was an epileptic. He changed his name to Paul and became the most zealous missionary of the budding church. As an apostle to the Gentiles he had no equal. And when he saw his missionary work endangered by the disciples' insistence on the preservation of the Jewish law, he argued insistently for its relaxation. Paul is the hero of Acts, but for the doctrine he preached we must turn to his Epistles.

Four of Paul's letters, all four of unquestioned authenticity, convey his teaching: the Epistle to the Romans and the rather similar Epistle to the Galatians, as well as the two letters to the Corinthians. Paul had not heard Jesus preach; and if his preaching had been ethical in part, Paul did not consider that to be of any crucial importance. As he said in his First Epistle to the Corinthians, "When I came to you, brethren . . . I decided to know nothing among you except Jesus Christ, and him crucified" (2:1 f.). And: "We preach Christ crucified, to the Jews a *skandalon,* to the Greeks a folly" (1:23). *Skandalon* is usually rendered either as an offense or as a stumbling-block; more rarely, in theological contexts, as a scandal.

Paul is suggesting that to those who are not followers of Jesus, his crucifixion seems to prove that he had no special powers or authority; but in fact "Christ died for our sins in accordance with the Scriptures," the allusion being to Isaiah 53. The crucified Messiah took upon himself the punishment for our sins and thus became our Saviour. What is required of us is the faith that he died for us. The antinomy of law and faith is central in Paul. Since the Messiah or Christ died for our sins, we need no longer satisfy the law; what is required for salvation is faith in Christ.

The heart of Paul's message is a verse in one of the minor prophets of the Hebrew Bible, Habakkuk, whose brief book comprises only three short chapters. In the original language and context, the meaning of verse 4 of chapter 2 is none too clear, but Paul's version of it is not startling: "the just man shall live by faith" (Romans 1:17 and Galatians 3:11). In Hebrew *emunah* meant firmness, truthfulness, reliability, faithfulness; not belief that anything was the case or had happened. But among the Jews of Paul's time far bolder exegeses were not uncommon; and this last half of a verse in a very minor prophet became for Paul the epitome of his *kerygma*. Of course, Habakkuk was not suggesting any opposition between law and faith, between doing and believing, but Paul evidently had not derived his doctrine from Habakkuk; he merely found in him a convenient proof text.

While Jesus, according to the Gospels, had taught as one having authority and had only very occasionally deigned to argue and to "prove" his points by citing Scripture—much more often he had pointed to his miracles as proof that he had authority—Paul argues constantly. One would think that his arguments must strike almost any reader as poor: a reader not versed in rabbinical literature as simply outlandish, and readers versed in it as obviously open to a host of counter-arguments. But in the Christian churches Paul was quickly canonized, and his arguments were received uncritically. For Luther, Paul—and quite especially his use of the half-verse from Habakkuk—became the cornerstone of the Reformation, and in Protestant churches Paul's arguments have been read from the pulpit so frequently that generations of Protestants would no more think of questioning them than they would question their most cherished convictions.

From Deuteronomy 27:26 Paul quotes: "Cursed be whoever does not uphold the words of this Torah to do them!" This is the last of an imposing series of twelve curses that begins: "Cursed be the man who makes a graven or molten image, an abomination to the Lord, a work made by a craftsman's hands, and puts it up in secret!" Here are the other curses: "Cursed be whoever dishonors his father or his mother!" "Cursed be whoever removes his neighbor's landmark!" "Cursed be whoever leads the blind astray on their path!" "Cursed be whoever violates the rights of the stranger, the orphan, and the widow!" The next four curses are pronounced on anyone who has sexual intercourse with his father's wife, with his sister or half-sister, with his mother-in-law, or with any beast. Then: "Cursed be whoever slays his neighbor in secret!" And: "Cursed be whoever takes a bribe to slay an innocent human being!"

Moses ordained, according to this passage in Deuteronomy, that on the day when the children of Israel should cross the Jordan river into the promised land, these curses as well as a series of blessings should be pronounced most solemnly. After every curse, the refrain is repeated: "And all the people shall say: Amen." And immediately after the last curse, which Paul quotes, the blessings begin.

Paul, however, not only quotes out of context in order to make his point; he also inserts a crucial word in the curse he quotes, changing "the words of this Torah" to "*all* things written in the book of the law."

> All who rely on works of the law are under a curse; for it is written: "Cursed be whoever does not abide by all things written in the book of the law to do them!" But that nobody is made just before God through the law is evident, for "the just man shall live by faith." But the law does not rest on faith,

for "whoever does them shall live by them" [Leviticus 18.5]. Christ redeemed us from the curse of the law, by becoming a curse for us—for it is written "Cursed be whoever hangs on a tree" [the allusion is to Deuteronomy 21:23, which in context says something rather different]—that Abraham's blessing might come upon the Gentiles in Jesus Christ, that we might receive the promised spirit through faith" (Galatians 3:10–14).

This short quotation may give at least some idea of Paul's mode of argument. It may also serve to call attention to the central flaw of his argument. He postulates that before the Crucifixion the only way to be saved was to "abide by all things written in the book of the law"; he assumes further that this condition was impossible to fulfill and that therefore one was condemned to live under "the curse of the law." Thus it seems that prior to the Crucifixion no one could be saved, because no one, neither Jew nor Gentile, could satisfy all the laws. We were all sinners, but now Christ has died for our sins, and if we believe this we are saved.

Paul's assumptions, however, are flagrantly at odds with the spirit of both the Hebrew Bible and the Pharisees. The whole notion of a judgment in which some are saved while the rest of mankind is damned is alien to Moses, and the notion that everyone who transgresses any commandment whatsoever, no matter how small, is damned is, in one word, Pauline. In the Hebrew Bible and among the rabbis there never seems to have been the slightest doubt that God could at any time freely forgive those who repented. The Book of Jonah taught emphatically that this forgiveness extended to Gentiles as well as Jews, that no conversion was required, and that even the most outrageous evildoers—not merely those guilty of some small transgression—were in fact forgiven by God as soon as they truly repented. But Paul simply could not acknowledge this without conceding that—in the pregnant words he used to rule out alternatives—"then Christ died in vain" (2:21).

Paul's God is anything but a paradigm of love and forgiveness. He first gave the Jews a law they could not possibly keep, and damned all who failed to keep every least commandment. He apparently also damned all Gentiles. Then, after well over a thousand years had passed since the giving of the law, God decided to save a few human beings, but saw no way of doing even that without a human sacrifice. Since such a sacrifice was necessary—Paul does not tell us why it should have been—God decided that Jesus Christ should be tormented and crucified after instituting certain sacraments; and henceforth those would be saved who believed all this and ate and drank what they themselves believed to be the flesh and blood of Christ.

It may seem as if a more unlikely story would have been hard to invent. Paul claims to have been raised a Pharisee; his epistles abound in quotations from the Septuagint; and some recent studies have demonstrated his heavy debts to rabbinical Judaism. But in the context of either the Hebrew Bible alone or of normative Judaism, his major arguments simply do not make sense. One has to recall the syncretism of the age in which he lived and his eagerness to convert Gentiles.

44

Before we consider the full measure of the impact of this syncretism on Christianity, something needs to be said at least briefly about Paul's ethic, and then also about the question whether he really was "the first Christian" and the true founder of Christianity. As for his ethic, it seems plain that his message at first stressed faith so much that it invited an "antinomian" reading. *Nomos* means "law," and Paul's teaching unquestionably was "antinomian" in the literal sense of that word. But the term is technical and suggests the belief that Christian faith supersedes moral laws, that the believer will be saved because he has faith, even if his conduct is immoral. Those whom Paul had converted evidently understood him to be saying that, but confronted with their conduct, Paul, with his Jewish upbringing, was deeply shocked. In brief, the theme he stressed henceforth was that we are redeemed by faith, but that the person who has faith will not be immoral. Of course, he will not keep all the laws, but neither will he fornicate and murder. On one occasion, in the famous thirteenth chapter of his First Epistle to the Corinthians, Paul not only sings the praises of love but actually extols it above faith:

> If I have all faith, so as to remove mountains, but have not love, I am nothing. If I give away all I have, and if I deliver my body to be burned, but have not love, I gain nothing. . . . Thus faith, hope, love abide, these three; but the greatest among them is love.

Nietzsche's comment, in a note published posthumously in *The Will to Power* (section 175) is of considerable interest: "The principle of *love* . . . was neither Greek nor Indian, nor Germanic. The song in praise of love that Paul composed is nothing Christian but a Jewish outburst . . ." "Nothing Christian" is not judiciously put, but it would be too weak to say "nothing distinctively Christian," as if the point were merely that this exaltation of love was Jewish no less than Christian. These verses are at variance with the central thrust of Paul's message as well as the evangelists', not to speak of The Revelation of St. John and the church councils. Moreover, this hymn on love is extraordinarily unspecific, and where it does become a little more specific it falters: "Love bears all things, believes all things, hopes all things, endures all things" (7). One feels like asking: What is so good about doing that, and what does it have to do with love? To say that a love that believes all things is greater than faith is not as humane as that comparison sounds out of context; evidently the love praised here includes faith— and, if we accept the plain meaning of the words, the most promiscuous, uncritical, and indiscriminate faith.

Elsewhere in Paul we do find more specific moral teachings. Romans 13 begins: "Let every one be subject to the governing authorities; for there is no authority that is not from God, and what authorities there are, are ordained by God. Whoever therefore resists the authorities, resists what God has ordained; and whoever resists will be condemned." It would be hard to exaggerate the influence of these words from the Roman Empire down to Lutheranism.

No less great was the impact of chapter 7 of The First Epistle to the Corinthians:

> It is good for a man not to touch a woman. Yet to avoid fornication, let every man have his own wife, and every woman her own husband. . . . Do not refuse one another except perhaps by agreement for a season that you may devote yourselves to prayer; but then come together again lest Satan tempt you to incontinence. I say this by way of concession, not of command. I wish that all were like myself; but each has his own special gift from God, one of one kind, one of another. To the unmarried and to widows I say that it is good for them to remain single as I do. But if they cannot be continent, let them marry; for it is better to marry than to burn. . . .
>
> Every one should remain in the state in which he was called. Were you a slave when called? Never mind. But if you can be made free, use it rather. ["use it rather" is what the King James Bible says. The Revised Standard Version elaborates: "avail yourself of the opportunity." The New English Bible concedes in a footnote that Paul's meaning could be just as well: "choose rather to make good use of your servitude." In context, the whole thrust of the passage is in any case that it is no matter whether one is free or slave; what matters is salvation.] . . .
>
> I mean brethren: the appointed time has grown very short. Lef those who

have wives live as though they had none, and those who weep as though they wept not, and those who rejoice as though they rejoiced not, and those who buy as though they possessed nothing, and those who deal with the world as though they had no dealings with it; for the form [*schema:* also rendered as "fashion" or "nature"] of this world is passing away.

Yet I wish that you were free of care. The unmarried care for the things of the Lord, how they may please the Lord; but those who marry care about what is of the world, how they may please their wives. . . .

45

The question of whether Paul was "the inventor of Christianity" and whether without him "we should scarcely have heard of a small Jewish sect whose master died on the cross," as Nietzsche claimed, is difficult if not impossible to answer because Paul's Epistles are older than the four Gospels and all of the rest of the New Testament. According to tradition, he died as a martyr in Rome, but it is not known how or when. The article on Paul in *Harper's Bible Dictionary* notes that Luke, who is credited with Acts as well as the Gospel that bears his name, "must have known about Paul's death, but he did not record it, because to have ended his book by narrating how Chrisitanity's chief hero had been put to death as an enemy of the state would have alienated Roman readers, and defeated his purpose of commending Christianity to the Roman world." In any case, Paul seems to have died before the destruction of Jerusalem, while the Gospels we know, as well as Acts and the rest of the New Testament, were all written later—and go out of their way not to alienate Roman readers, while stressing that the Christians hate the Jews quite as much as the Romans do.

It is therefore thoroughly misleading to treat the Gospels as if they showed us what Christianity might have been had it not been for Paul. Paul was Luke's hero, and in their present form, the other Gospels are influenced by Paul, too. What is more, the whole idea of writing gospels *in Greek*, for a Gentile audience, is due in large measure to Paul's influence. On the other hand, it is plain that some of those who had known Jesus, as well as some who had been close to those who had known him, felt a need for a kind of witness that was essentially different from Paul's preaching; they wanted to put down in writing the story of Jesus' last year. What clearly concerned them most was—in Paul's words—"Christ crucified." But for them this was not merely a cosmic event through which salvation had become possible at least for a few; it was also a passion narrative that involved the Master's human suffering.

It is striking that in leading up to the Crucifixion Mark saw no need to go back more than about a year, and John followed his example after writing a prologue that takes us back to the beginning of time. Matthew and Luke both reached Jesus' baptism by John the Baptist at the beginning of chapter 3 but furnished some background material first. Matthew went to some length to prove that Joseph, the husband of Mary, the mother of Jesus, was descended from King David, but then went on to say that Joseph was not the father of Jesus, who was begotten by the Holy Ghost. Then he mentioned that Jesus was born in Bethlehem (like David) and told how Herod tried to kill him and actually did kill all children in Bethlehem, while Jesus' parents fled with him to Egypt and eventually returned from there to Nazareth. But there is nothing here that deals with Jesus as a child, a young man, or indeed with any aspect of his life or character prior to his baptism by John.

With one exception, this is also true of Luke who supplied in his first two chapters a story about the conception of John the Baptist, a wonderful speech made to Mary by the angel who announced to her that she would give birth to Jesus, a marvelous reply by Mary, a meeting between the two pregnant mothers, a great song uttered by the father of John the Baptist, and the celebrated story of the birth of Jesus in a manger.

Much of this has no parallel in the Hebrew Bible, but Luke's annunciation story is modeled on the annunciation of Samson in the Book of Judges, and Matthew's tale about the king who killed all the children is obviously inspired by the pharaoh who killed all the Jewish children when Moses was born, at the beginning of Exodus.

Luke went on to relate that Jesus was circumcised and claimed further—and this is the one exception—that when Jesus was twelve and the family had gone up to Jerusalem for the Passover, as they did every year, they looked for him for three days before they found him in the temple among the teachers, listening and asking questions; "and all who heard him were amazed at his understanding and his answers."

The first chapters set the tone for what follows; the evangelists used their imagination very creatively without feeling restricted by any anxiety about historical fact, and there is no reason to believe that their standards changed suddenly at some later point. Not only did they feel free to tell little stories to lead up to some saying, but we need have no doubt that they unhesitatingly ascribed to the Master any saying that seemed good enough to them to be worthy of him, just as they felt free to ascribe to "the Jews" or to a "lawyer," "scribe," or "Pharisee" any epithet or motive that seemed appropriate for an opponent of Jesus.

Under these circumstances, we cannot reconstruct the real Jesus with any certainty. Almost all attempts to find him have ended up with portraits that the writer considered ideal; all sayings that offend the writer are dismissed as unauthentic; and in the end liberals give us a liberal Jesus, socialists a socialist Jesus, and so forth. Not knowing what there was before Paul wrote his Epistles—the account in Acts is intensely partial to Paul —we cannot be sure what might have happened without Paul. But it seems clear that the little Christian sect in Jerusalem had no future among the Jews; it is obvious that it could never have become the state religion of the Roman Empire without first making it much easier to be a Christian than it had always been to be a Jew; and that Paul and John found a way of making it easy by stressing belief and sacraments.

Some modern writers have insisted that faith (*pistis*) in the New Testament must not be understood as belief, and they have tried to establish a contrast between faith in Christ and belief that something is the case, claiming that the former is the essence of Christian faith. But this is untenable. John constantly uses the verb "believe," and both John and Paul insist on belief that several propositions are true: faith in Christ means among other things belief that Jesus was the Christ, sent by God, that he died for our sins and was resurrected, that those who believe this and are baptized and eat his flesh and drink his blood are saved, and that no one comes to the Father but through Christ. What is true is that all this should not be believed in the way in which one might believe that there are black swans in Australia. Christian faith, according to the evangelists and Paul, is a profound emotional experience, more similar to the belief that a wonderful and beautiful person whom we adore returns our love. It is the joyous acceptance of glad tidings that makes one see the whole world in a different light.

Paul was the first writer who had this tremendous experience in a flash, all at once, and then bore witness of it at length. The evangelists did not bear such personal witness, and none of them comes to life for us as a person, least of all as a world historical individual who changed the course of history. Still, it does not follow, even if we grant that without Paul Christianity might have remained a minor sect, that Paul's endeavors would have made of it a world religion even if there never had been any evangelists. As it was, the defects of Paul's logic and the whole quality of his argumentation were more than balanced for millions of readers by the Gospels. Even if many theologians found more grist for their mills in Paul, it was the Jesus of the Gospels who cast a spell over ordinary believers.

46

Christianity was the second major religion that was based on a book. Initially, this book consisted of four Gospels, Acts, twenty-one epistles by various authors, and Revelation. It was a short book, full of quotations from and allusions to the Jewish Bible, for most of the authors and principals had been Jews who tried to make sense of whatever happened by relating events to Scripture; and in the beginning it was considered all-important to insist that in ever so many ways Christ had fulfilled as many prophecies in Scripture as possible. Men vied with each other in finding instances even where there did not seem to have been any prophecies. To give one example among many: the twenty-second Psalm contains the outcry, "they divide my garments among them, and for my raiment they cast lots." All four evangelists have this "prophecy" fulfilled during the Crucifixion.

All this had an odd result. Taken by itself, the new book—the New Testament—did not make any sense; it remained esoteric; it became essential to include with it as part of the same book—the Bible—the Jewish Bible, as the Old Testament. For the first Christian community in Jerusalem, the Hebrew Scriptures were the Bible; and the decision was rather to add the New Testament to it. But this need not have been binding for the new churches that sprang up as Paul reached out to more and more Gentiles. The decision to keep the Jewish Bible as part—indeed, much more than three quarters—of the Christian Bible was made more or less inevitable by the nature of the Gospels and Epistles. As a result, the very people who meant in some sense to transcend the Hebrew Bible because they considered it dated by their glad tidings actually brought it about that the Jewish Bible reached people all over the earth, was translated into all languages, and eventually changed much of humanity.

The books of the Hebrew Bible had been written over a period of more than a thousand years and represent a rich selection from the literature of a remarkable people. This accounts for the great diversity of styles and contents. The books of the New Testament were written within a hundred years and are, superficially considered, incomparably less heterogeneous, but on closer inspection they represent an astonishing grab bag that all but compels the reader to make his own selection. Originally, there were many more than four Gospels, and only the Gospels enjoying the strongest support in crucial communities were canonized, but later generations had to choose one account or another—and the typical reader chooses from each of the four what he likes best without even noticing the many contradictions. But in a smaller measure that is what each of the first three evangelists had done in the first place, and then Paul offered a very different approach, and James, Jesus' brother, argued against Paul in his Epistle, insisting that "Man is justified by works and not by faith alone."

The great variety of points of view in the New Testament, not to speak of the Christian Bible as a whole, had two immensely important results. First, it offered something for almost every taste, including a large number of very striking sayings, haunting parables, and unforgettable stories. In this respect, no other religion in the Roman Empire had so much to offer. At the same time, the new religion seemed to *require* very little, although it *allowed* for martyrdom and soon also monasticism. Secondly, given such immense variety, it became incumbent on the new church, if it wanted to survive, to make some centralized decisions before long about what was and what was not acceptable. The choice of books to be included in the canon did not solve this problem, and eventually church councils decided what precisely one had to believe in order to be saved. But not only did these councils stray far from the concerns of the evangelists and Paul, but the realities of the Christian religion were something else again, almost as far from the disputes of the theologians as they were from the milieu of the Christian Bible.

A student of comparative religion whose knowledge of Christianity was based entirely on the New Testament would be baffled on coming to any "Christian" country—not only in the twentieth century but also in any other age, modern, medieval, or ancient. Most Western students think of the religions of Asia in terms of their Scriptures without ever thinking of the gap that separates Christianity as a living force—in the countries in which it still is a living force—from the Christian Scriptures. Also, when addressing themselves to the question of how Christianity spread and reached millions, Christian scholars rarely ask whether one might not be able to learn a great deal about that by paying some attention to the ways in which Islam and Buddhism converted hundreds of millions of people. We shall here consider Christianity first; then Islam; then the religions of India; and eventually the spread of Buddhism in the Far East.

Mosaic, Torcello cathedral, near Venice, 1200.

V

POST-BIBLICAL CHRISTIANITY

Syncretism—Constantine and the Creed of Nicaea—
Julian the Apostate—The Two Great Schisms—The Crusades—
The Inquisition—Francis of Assisi—The Reformation

Wedding procession enters church, Tule, Mexico.

47

In the middle of the twentieth century some Protestant theologians in the United States were suddenly struck by the notion that "God is dead"—as they read Nietzsche, in translation. Actually, as Nietzsche knew, the notion of the dead god is far older than Christianity. When the New Testament was written, this idea was already older than the New Testament is today. In fact, the concept is so ancient that we do not know where it came from, but we find it in both Egypt and Mesopotamia. In Egypt it was the great god Osiris who was killed and dismembered by his brother Seth. But his death was virtually a rite of passage through which he passed to assume a greater role than ever. Osiris's sister and wife, Isis

> collected his dismembered body, and caused it to be mummified by Anubis [the god represented in Egyptian art with the head of a jackal]. She then conceived Horus from her dead husband, and as the young god he revived his father . . . But although she was, therefore, ultimately responsible for the restoration of Osiris, he remained the dead god living in his son [Horus, one of the most important of all the gods of ancient Egypt] and the Pharaoh, in spite of the exalted position he attained as the judge and "king of the dead," and when his cult had been solarized, "lord of the sky" (James, 81 f.).

There are many myths about Osiris. The Egyptians thought of him as having brought civilization to Egypt. The story of his dismemberment may be a rationalization of the fact that so many places claimed to have relics of the god, but the belief that his head, if not the whole god, was buried at Abydos was widely shared, probably even before the pyramids were built. By the end of the fifth dynasty, in the middle of the third millennium B.C., the dead Pharaoh became Osiris, and by the end of the Middle Kingdom, in the eighteenth century B.C., it was believed that upon dying everyone became Osiris. But before Osiris became the king of the underworld, he had probably long been associated with fertility. E. O. James reproduces a picture that shows "stalks of wheat growing from the mummy of Osiris watered by a priest" (137). This is from a very late temple at Philae, but at Abydos there is a far older relief that shows the god lying on his back with an erection, and this motif is not uncommon. James also remarks that "Osiris is frequently represented in the act of rising from his bier (figure 7), and on the bas-reliefs which accompany the inscription at Denderah the culmination of the festival is shown to have occurred on the last day (thirtieth) when the ithyphallic god, swathed as a mummy, is represented gradually raising himself up . . ." (136). Thus Osiris was associated with the phallus, as was Dionysus, and there was an annual festival in his honor when the time came for planting. Indeed, as early as the fifth century B.C., Herodotus identified Osiris with Bacchus or Dionysus, and by late antiquity the cult of Osiris had spread through the Mediterranean world.

The cult of Isis spread with that of Osiris, but her immense appeal was not based solely on her embodiment of fidelity beyond death. There are innumerable images of her as the mother with the young Horus sitting on her lap. Sometimes, not always, she is shown nursing him.

Another motif that recurs in Egyptian art is Osiris as the judge of the dead. They are led before him, and he weighs the heart of each.

Similar ideas are found in Mesopotamia. We have parts of Sumerian myths involving a goddess who was the queen of heaven, Inanna by name, and much fuller accounts in Akkadian about the goddess Ishtar. Our sources for Ishtar go back only to the first millennium B.C. They relate at length how she descended into the underworld to raise from the dead her husband, the young god Tammuz. Again there was an annual festival associated with this event, celebrating "the revival of life in nature and mankind" (James, 80).

All this makes it understandable that Paul thought that "Christ crucified" was "to the Greeks a folly"—but not the Resurrection. The god raised from the dead was a familiar theme to the Gentiles in late antiquity. We may think of the Resurrection as a unique miracle, the ancient world did not. After recording Jesus' last cry from the cross, Matthew says: "he gave up the ghost. And behold, the curtain of the temple was torn in two, from top to bottom, and the earth shook, and the rocks were split; the tombs also were opened, and many bodies of the saints who had fallen asleep were raised, and coming out of the tombs after his resurrection [two days later?] they went into the holy city and appeared to many" (27:31–33). Matthew evidently considered resurrections unusual but by no means unique. Unless we assume that the other three evangelists considered them so commonplace that they did not even find them worth mentioning because it was not only on that Sunday that many dead people took a stroll in Jerusalem, this passage throws light on Matthew's historical reliability. He felt free to invent what he considered fitting.

The virgin birth may be a case in point. It is never mentioned by Mark, John, or Paul, but only by Matthew and Luke. Anyone familiar with Greek mythology knows that many heroes were thought to have been borne by virgins, Zeus being the father, and that Heracles, the greatest hero of all, who after his death ascended to heaven, was begotten by Zeus with Amphitryon's wife. To the Jews, the idea that Jesus was literally begotten by God and thus himself a demigod or God, was blasphemy, but to many Gentiles the God who had the form of a handsome youth seemed more humane and attractive than the austere and totally invisible God of the Jews. Even in the twentieth century a Christian scholar still complains that when Islam replaced Christianity in large parts of the Byzantine empire, "God, who had been revealed to the Mediterranean people through the Incarnation of His Son, who had been seen by them face to face, became once more a remote and inaccessible Being raised high above the miseries and vicissitudes of earthly life, inscrutable in his dealings with men" (Zernov, 84).

Moreover, the cult of virgin goddesses was popular in the Mediterranean world. Classical Greece alone offers two great examples: Athene and Artemis. The Mary of the Gospels has hardly anything in common with them and yet was venerated before long as "the Virgin," "the Mother of God," and "the Queen of Heaven."

Nothing in the New Testament suggests that Mary, the mother of Jesus, might be a proper subject of worship. Not even the two evangelists who took Isaiah 7:14—"Behold, a young woman shall conceive and bear a son, and call his name Immanuel" (to cite the Revised Standard Version)—for a prophecy that a virgin would conceive and bear a son, ever suggested that the virgin herself was anything but a human being. Indeed, Luke has Jesus rebuke his mother (2:49), and John has him address her twice, rather rudely, as "woman"—on the first occasion, to say: "What have I to do with you, woman?" (2:4).

Nothing in the New Testament would seem to commend the worship of saints, or a cult built around relics, or the conception of Purgatory. Where, then, did these ideas originate? Plainly, the New Testament was merely one source of Christianity and not the only one. The New Testament was a product of syncretism, but as Christianity spread it absorbed more and more of the ideas of the people who adopted it. After World War II the Roman Catholic church began to admit that some saints who were worshiped ardently had never lived. In fact, pre-Christian pagan cults survived in this form not only in Italy and the Old World but also in Mexico and the New World. Similarly, the cult of Mary did not spring from the Gospels, but Christianity made room for the cult of the great mother, the queen of heaven, Isis, and named her Mary.

In his First Epistle to the Corinthians (9:20 ff.) Paul had said of himself:

> To the Jews I became as a Jew, in order to win Jews; to those under the law I became as one under the law, though not being myself under the law, that I might win those under the law. To those outside the law I became as one outside the law—not being without law toward God but under the law of Christ —that I might win those outside the law. To the weak I became weak, that I might win the weak. I have become all things to all men that I might by all means save some. I do it all for the sake of the gospel, that I may share in its blessings.

This is an extraordinary passage, exceedingly different from the ethos of Moses and the prophets. They had tried to teach their people to have backbone and to be uncompromising, and post-Biblical Judaism became very rigid and separatist. Paul went to the opposite extreme of becoming all things to all men. One might call this the chameleon principle: conform yourself to your environment. And he explained why he did this: to save people, on the assumption that if he did that he, like a good salesman, would reap his reward. While it is obvious that a little misrepresentation and ingratiation may help to sell a bill of goods to large numbers of people, one may wonder whether those won over by such means will really be saved. But if all that is required for salvation is belief in Christ and the sacraments there is no profit in being a purist.

According to tradition, Paul became a martyr. We do not know the circumstances, but there is no reason to believe that he considered it possible to be saved without faith and sacraments. Thus there was a point beyond which he and many others would not compromise. They would not disavow their beliefs about Jesus Christ. Moreover, it is possible that even in Paul's time some people had come to believe that the surest way of being saved was to become a martyr. Soon, many thousands would elect that path, again without any clear authority for it in Scripture.

In the matter of adapting Christianity to the beliefs and practices of those whom they desired to convert, however, Paul and his followers did not show much backbone. At this point they were extremely permissive. The price did not seem too high for gaining vast numbers of converts, and the strategy worked. But we may wonder about Jesus' saying: "What would it profit a man if he gained the whole world but his soul was harmed?" Was not the soul of Christianity harmed in the process? But Jesus' sayings are rarely unambiguous, and the Revised Standard Version translates Mark 8:36—and this is entirely defensible: "What does it profit a man, to gain the whole world and forfeit his life?"

48

The other ways in which Christianity transcended—or strayed from—the Bible are too numerous to be considered here at length. For a while the desire to be martyred was so fierce among so many that a Roman procurator asked Rome for instructions on how to deal with such large numbers of fanatics. But even then martyrdom was merely one way among many, and it was never decreed that this was required of Christians.

Much the same consideration applies to monasticism, which became popular in the fourth century. Christianity made room for it without requiring it. It also became the custom for priests in the West, but not in the East, to remain celibate. Since precisely many of the most intelligent elected to become monks or priests, these institutions became a genetic disaster. Christian scholars and intellectuals died without progeny—a kind of natural selection in reverse.

The permissiveness of the churches eventually led to such divergencies that some people considered it necessary to decide what precisely one must believe in order to be saved. In other words, the time came to define dogmas, and the work was begun at the first church council, in Nicaea in Asia Minor, in A.D. 325. The genius for orderliness and centralized authority was contributed by the Roman emperor Constantine, who embraced Christianity in 312 and called the Council of Nicaea. The significance of the council, however, can be appreciated only in the context of Constantine's reign.

He was born in Naissus, the modern Nis, in Serbia—now Yugoslavia—about sixty miles from the Bulgarian border, probably around A.D. 288. "He was the illegitimate son of Constantius I and Flavia Helena (described by St. Ambrose as an innkeeper)."* His father was a distinguished general who in 293 became Caesar, but at that time there were two Caesars and two men with the title of Augustus, and when the father assumed command of the western provinces, his little son was left, virtually as a hostage, at the court of the Roman emperor, Diocletian, in Nicomedia, not far from the site where Constantine later founded Constantinople. In the year 303, Diocletian launched the last great persecution of Christians in the Roman empire. In 305 both he and Maximianus Augustus resigned; Constantius and Galerius became Augusti; and Constantius asked Galerius to return young Constantine to him. It seems that Constantine actually had to flee to get away. He reached his father at Bononia (the modern Boulogne) from where he was about to cross to Britain to repel an invasion. Victorious, Constantius died at the site of modern York the following year, and the army promptly proclaimed young Constantine Augustus. But for many years after that he was still engaged in wars to defend and strengthen his position. The single most decisive battle was that at the Milvian Bridge across the Tiber, near Rome (also called the battle of Saxa Ruba), where Constantine in 312 defeated and killed his chief rival, Maxentius, the son of Maximianus. With this victory, Constantine became unchallenged ruler of the western part of the Roman Empire; it took another dozen years before he became sole emperor. Constantine made Christianity the official religion of the empire.

Eusebius, born in Palestine around 263 and bishop of Caesarea from about 314 10 until his death in 339, baptized Constantine on his deathbed in 337. But Constantine had embraced Christianity much earlier, although there is no agreement among scholars about the seriousness and depth of his faith in the early years after his conversion. Eusebius, best remembered for his pioneering history of the church, was also an important Christian apologist and wrote a biography of Constantine. In this "life" he claims to have been told by the emperor himself that before the decisive battle at the Milvian Bridge he had seen a flaming cross in the noonday sky along with the words *En touto nika:* "In this [or by this] win!" Although Eusebius wrote in Greek, the words are usually quoted in Latin: *Hoc signo vinces* (in this sign win). Having won, he became a Christian. Jones notes that Eusebius published this story only after the emperor's death, "and it was evidently unknown to him in the shape given above when he wrote the

---

* Henry Stuart Jones, "Constantine I" in the *Encyclopaedia Britannica,* in the celebrated eleventh edition. My account draws on many other sources as well.

Ecclesiastical History. . . . A well-informed contemporary . . . tells us that the sign was seen by Constantine in a dream; and even Eusebius supplements the vision by day with a dream in the following night."

What is really much more extraordinary than the tale of the miraculous vision is the fact that the decisive turn in the history of Christianity was brought about by a Roman emperor who was persuaded by a huge military victory that Christianity was true and that the cross should henceforth be his emblem. For him, of course, taking up the cross did not involve turning his back on war, empire, and victory. He placed his tri- umphal arch in Rome next to that of Titus, which had celebrated the destruction of Jerusalem, but made it far more opulent—three arches in one—and went on to wage campaigns for the Empire. The battle at the bridge invites comparison with the victory that prompted Ashoka, emperor of India, to embrace Buddhism (see the beginning of chapter XII). We shall also have to remember Constantine in connection with the Crusades and our discussion of Christianity and the arts, for it was he who "discovered" Jesus' tomb in Jerusalem and had a church built over it.

The first church council and the creed of Nicaea should be seen against this back- ground. Any notion that Christianity might be distinguished by an ethic was by now beneath consideration. It was a matter of belief, which made it urgent, at least to the orderly mind of a Roman emperor, to spell out precisely what one must believe in order to be saved. The matter was doubly urgent because two great theologians of the period disagreed about it. Arius (about 256–336), a Libyan who had become a priest in Alex- andria, taught that God had created the *Logos* in the beginning, before all other things, and that hence there was a profound difference between the essence or nature (*ousia*, in Greek) of God the Father, who was eternal and uncreated, and the Son, who was neither. Athanasius (about 297–373), who in 328 became patriarch of Alexandria and eventually a saint, insisted that the Father and the Son were of the same essence (*homo- ousion*). At the council Athanasius prevailed, and it was decided that all who believed as Arius did would be damned, and should be. Here is the Creed of Nicaea:

> We believe in one God, the all-sovereign Father, maker of all things visible and invisible;
> And in one Lord Jesus Christ, Son of God, begotten of the Father, only begotten, that is, of the essence of the Father, God from God, Light from Light, true God from true God, begotten not made, of the same essence as the Father, through whom all things were made both in heaven and on earth; who for us men and our salvation came down and was made flesh, becoming human, suffered, and on the third day rose and ascended into heaven, and will come to judge the living and the dead;
> And in the Holy Spirit.
> But those who say: Once he was not; or: Before he was begotten he was not; or: He came into being out of nothing; or who claim that the Son of God is: of another substance or essence, or created, or changeable, or mutable—these the Catholic and Apostolic church anathematizes.

With this creed, we are closer to the world of medieval scholasticism than to the "man of suffering" in Isaiah 53. The Passion has been reduced to one word—"suffered" —and the moral teachings that abound in the first three Gospels have been spirited away entirely. What is affirmed is faith in God the Father, in the Son of God, and in the Holy Spirit, and the momentous issue that is moved into the center is the precise rela- tionship of the Son to the Father—above all, the insistence that they are of the same essence. While all this is closer to Paul than to Isaiah, and Paul already required propo- sitional belief, we have traveled a long way from Paul as well, who wrote to the Romans: "If you confess with your lips that Jesus is Lord and believe in your heart that God raised him from the dead, you will be saved" (10:9). Less than three centuries later, this was no longer nearly enough, and Arius and his adherents who confessed and believed this and more besides were still anathematized.

The creed of Nicaea was not the first one, although the notion that the so-called Apostles' Creed was composed by the apostles has long been discredited by scholars, and we have no textual authority for it that is as old as the Creed of Nicaea. In different churches different creeds had become traditional, and the Creed of Nicaea was based on the Creed of the church of Caesarea, which was proposed to the council by Eusebius and modified and greatly enlarged to rule out the Arian heresy. The Creed of Nicaea was then made obligatory for all churches.

49

The one great but brief interruption in this development of intolerance occurred when Flavius Claudius Julianus became emperor in 361. He tried to restore paganism and is therefore remembered as Julian the Apostate. He was a nephew of Constantine, whose son and successor, Constantius II, appointed Julian as his successor. The Jews were not alone in enjoying some respite from intolerance during his two-year reign, as noted in the chapter on the Jews, for he issued a general edict on toleration. Although Julian had abandoned Christianity, he did not wish to persecute the Christians any more than any other religious group:

> . . . Let the people live in harmony. Let no one be at variance, or do wrong to another; neither you that are in error to those who worship the gods as is right and proper, in the manner handed down from earliest antiquity; nor let the worshipers of the gods destroy or plunder the house of those who are misled by ignorance rather than deliberate choice. Men should be taught and won over by reason, not by blows, insults and corporal punishments. I therefore most earnestly admonish the adherents of the true religion not to injure or insult the Galilaeans [that is, the Christians] in any way, either by physical attack or by reproaches. Those who are in the wrong in matters of supreme importance are objects of pity rather than of hate (Bettenson, 29).

When Julian was killed in a skirmish against the Persians, tolerance died with him; Christianity was restored as the official religion, and no similar plea prevailed for well over a thousand years. Indeed, as long as there seemed to be a chance that persecution might succeed it flourished, and it was abandoned only when Europe had been utterly exhausted by the slaughters of the Thirty Years' War (1618–1648) and become persuaded that the killing was futile.

Julian's views about the worship of Jesus and the martyrs are also worth recalling:

> Unfortunately, you do not abide by the tradition of the apostles. . . . Neither Paul, nor Matthew, nor Luke, nor Mark had the audacity to say that Jesus is God. But the worthy John, realizing that by that time a vast number of people in many of the Greek and Italian cities were infected with the disease, and hearing, I fancy, that the tombs of Peter and Paul were being worshiped (privately, no doubt, but still worshiped), John, I say, was the first to have the audacity to make this assertion.
> This evil was inaugurated by John. But who can find a fitting denunciation of this additional innovation of yours, the introduction of many recent dead bodies [as objects of worship], besides that original dead body? You have filled all places with tombs and monuments (Bettenson, 29).

This is a "pagan" upbraiding Christians!

Julian also gave the Jews permission to reconstruct their temple in Jerusalem. Work was actually begun in 363, but when he died later that year it had to cease, and his Christian successors resumed discrimination against the Jews and banished them from Jerusalem. When the Persians conquered Jerusalem in 614, they allowed the Jews to return, but in 629 the Christians ousted the Persians—and the Jews.

50

It would serve little purpose here to explore or summarize the many controversies over doctrines that arose during the following centuries and regularly led to the solemn damnation of heresies. Only two of these disputes have to be mentioned because they precipitated the two great schisms that split Christendom long before the Protestant Reformation.

Many people suppose that Christianity was one before Luther divided it in two, and they ignore the differences between Lutheranism, Calvinism, and Anglicanism, and between, say, French, Italian, and Irish Catholicism. Much less do they realize that at least one third of Christendom is neither Protestant nor Catholic but divided among various Eastern churches.

The Orthodox Eastern church is merely one of these and is subdivided into many semiautonomous or "autocephalous" churches. The Greek term means that each has its own head, and there is no central authority as in the Roman Catholic church. The oldest patriarchates are those of Alexandria, Antioch, Constantinople, Jerusalem, and Mt.
6–7 Sinai. (The abbot of St. Catherine's monastery at the foot of Mt. Sinai is a patriarch.) But there are many other "autocephalous" Orthodox churches, including those of Albania, Bulgaria, Cyprus, Finland, Greece, Japan, Poland, Rumania, and—by far the largest of them—the Russian Orthodox church. The languages used in the rituals of these churches differ. That used in the Russian ritual is Old Church Slavonic.

Eastern churches that are not Orthodox include the Coptic churches of Egypt and Ethiopia, the Jacobite churches of Syria, Iraq, and India, and the Armenian church. All of them are Monophysite, meaning that they believe that Jesus had only one nature, and that this was divine. This "heresy" has to be understood against the background of Nestorianism, which originated early in the fifth century when Nestorius denied that Mary could be called *theotokos* (God-bearer, or Mother of God), seeing that she bore Jesus as a human being. In response, two church councils explained and insisted that Jesus had two distinct natures joined in one person and partaking of the divine substance. The Monophysites did not agree and were solemnly excommunicated at the Council of Chalcedon in 451. This was the first of the three major schisms of Christianity, and these very ancient churches are neither Orthodox nor Catholic nor Protestant. In many Western countries they may not be very visible; in Jerusalem and the Near East they are. Moreover, the Christians who influenced Muhammad were neither Catholic nor Orthodox.

The schism between Roman Catholic Christianity and Orthodox Christianity did not become final and irrevocable for another six hundred years. The fiercest controversy was about one word, *filioque*, which means "and the son." The question was whether the Holy Spirit issued from the Father or from the Father "and the Son." Perhaps one needs to be a theologian or a metaphysician to see what is at stake here besides words. But one does not need to be either to feel reminded of Matthew's account of Jesus' lengthy vituperation of the Pharisees in which he says among other things: "Woe to you, scribes and Pharisees, hypocrites! for you . . . have neglected the weightier matters of the law, justice and mercy and faith . . . You blind guides, straining out a gnat and swallowing a camel!" (23:23 f.).

The Eastern churches could cite John 15:26, where Jesus says: "When the *para-*

kletos comes, whom I shall send to you from the Father, the spirit of truth that proceeds from the Father, he will bear witness of me." The King James Bible renders the Greek term "the Comforter," the Revised Standard Version has "the Counselor," the Roman Catholic "Jerusalem Bible" has "the Advocate," while C. G. Jung sprinkled his *Answer to Job* with references to "the Paraclete." The term is found only a few times in the New Testament, in the fourth Gospel and in the First Epistle of John (2:1), but according to John 14:26 it seems to be an epithet for the Holy Spirit: "But the *parakletos*, the Holy Spirit, whom the Father will send in my name, he will teach you everything and remind you of everything I have said to you." One may wonder whether he ever did. Even if it was he who taught Western theologians to argue against those in the East that the clause "that proceeds from the Father" refers to "the sending of the Spirit into the world rather than the eternal 'proceeding,' "* it would seem that the men who defined Christian dogmas at church councils, East as well as West, forgot a great many things that Jesus had said according to the Gospels, notably including the remark about straining out a gnat—not to speak of all the things that even the evangelists failed to remember.

Of course, the famous *filioque* clause was not the only reason for the schism between East and West, although this word seems to have been discussed longer and more frequently than any other issue. The church of Rome also came to insist on the celibacy of the clergy while the Eastern churches had many married priests and did not see any reason for changing this institution. Peter, whom the Western church considered the first bishop of Rome and thus the first pope, had been married according to the New Testament. From the Eastern point of view, "Germanic emperors" and popes of German and French birth who were strangers to the Mediterranean world, assumed falsely that their own customs "represented the authentic Apostolic tradition, and they pressed two of their innovations, the *filioque* addition to the creed and compulsory celibacy of the clergy, upon the unwilling southerners. When they had achieved their victory in Italy the reformers decided to impose the same novelties upon the Greeks, and this naturally provoked the greatest indignation in Byzantium," the capital of the eastern Roman Empire, also known as Constantinople. And in a footnote, Nicholas Zernov adds: "The decrees against married clergy were passed by the reforming synods of Augsburg 952, Poitiers 1000, Goslar 1019, Pavia 1022, Selingstad 1023, Bourges 1031, Rome 1047. Finally Pope Gregory VII excommunicated all married priests in 1074" (*Eastern Christendom*, 98).

One might suppose that really the issue of celibacy must have been more decisive than the *filioque* clause. Yet when "the last attempt at reconciliation with the papacy was made on the eve of the fall of the Empire," at the Council of Florence in 1439, "Five main items were selected for deliberation, the *Filioque* clause, purgatory, papal primacy, Eucharistic bread [whether it should be leavened or unleavened], and the words of consecration of the elements for Holy Communion," and "Consideration of the *Filioque* clause took the longest time" (128). The attempt at reconciliation failed, and in 1453 the Muslim Turks conquered Constantinople and put an end to the eastern Roman Empire. Another seventy years later, Luther had split the Western church, and before long Christendom was splintered into a multitude of denominations.

The passions generated by minute differences, both in the East and the West, were sincere, immense, and bitter, and the energy spent on such controversies almost defies belief. But in the end the lines that were drawn coincided geographically with boundaries that were far older than these issues. The Roman Empire had been divided among Constantine's sons into an eastern and western empire, and eventually the East-

---

* See the footnote commentary in the "Jerusalem Bible."

ern church did not wish to recognize the primacy of Rome. And in northern Europe the countries that had not been under Roman rule eventually seceded from the church of Rome and became Protestant, and after long and bloody wars the Germans in the south and in the Rhineland, who had lived under Roman rule fourteen centuries earlier, remained Roman Catholic, while the rest of Germany became Lutheran, and the religious boundary coincided with the ancient Roman *limes* or border fortifications.

51

One might suppose that when Islam appeared on the scene in the seventh century and within a hundred years wrested from the Christians Palestine, Egypt, North Africa, and Spain, posing a further threat to the eastern empire by also conquering Iraq and Iran, the Christians might have come to see their differences in a larger perspective, feeling that the many things they had in common were far more important. But what happened much later at the Council of Florence, a mere fourteen years before the Muslims conquered Constantinople, was altogether typical. The squabbling among the Christians facilitated the expansion of Islam, and the bizarre complexities of Christian controversies over the relation between God the Father and the Son, and over the relation of the Holy Spirit to both, must have made the sublime simplicity of Muslim monotheism doubly appealing to many minds.

The one major response of Christianity to Islam was an attempt to reconquer the Holy Land, and especially Jerusalem. It is customary to explain the Crusades as a development of the institution of penitentiary pilgrimages which, in the case of Christianity, can be traced back to the eighth century. By that time Christians were confessing their sins to priests who made forgiveness contingent upon some penance, such as fasting, flagellation, or a pilgrimage. By the tenth century the goal of such pilgrimages was sometimes Jerusalem. "Pilgrims who were travelling to Jerusalem joined themselves in companies for security, and marched under arms; the pilgrims of 1064, who were headed by the archbishop of Mainz, numbered some 7,000 men. When the First Crusade finally came, what was it but a penitentiary pilgrimage under arms—with the one additional object of conquering the goal of pilgrimage?" Thus asks no less a scholar than Ernest Barker, writing an article the length of a short book for the eleventh edition of the *Encyclopaedia Britannica*, perhaps unaware of the irony of his question.

A superb German reference work—an earlier edition furnished the basis for William L. Langer's *An Encyclopaedia of World History*—prefaces its detailed account of the Crusades with this general remark, which also represents a widespread view:

> In the Crusades the unity of the Christian occident, which sacrifices blood and treasure for a religious idea, gains its most magnificent expression. Christian knighthood joins across all national barriers and finds here the highest goal of its ideal striving. The prestige of the papacy, which brought about the Crusades, reaches its highpoint. The final failure of these endeavors dealt the position of the Roman church a blow from which it never recovered and marks the beginning dissolution of the *universitas Christiana* (Ploetz, 1960, 448).

These are not eccentric opinions but expressions of a widely shared consensus that precede very detailed scholarly accounts. Yet there is no question about the facts. The First Crusade began with a pogrom "in the towns of the valley of the Rhine, during which some 10,000 Jews perished as first-fruits of crusading zeal," to cite Barker, who spares us the dreadful details (527); and his description of the capture of Jerusalem in 1099 is also mercifully brief, compared with his lengthy account of the antecedents: "The slaughter was terrible; the blood of the conquered ran down the streets, until men splashed in blood as they rode. At nightfall, 'sobbing for excess of joy,' the crusaders came to the Sepulchre from their treading of the winepress, and put their blood-stained hands together in prayer. So, on that day of July, the First Crusade came to an end" (529). That the Jews of Jerusalem were burnt alive in their largest synagogue, Barker did not consider worthy of note. Neither did Raymond in one of the eyewitness accounts of the capture that have come down to us; but his description still gives one a better sense of what happened.

> Now that our men had possession of the walls and towers, wonderful sights were to be seen. Some of our men (and this was more merciful) cut off the heads of their enemies; others shot them with arrows, so that they fell from the towers; others tortured them longer by casting them into the flames. Piles of heads, hands, and feet were to be seen in the streets of the city. It was necessary to pick one's way over the bodies of men and horses. But these were small matters compared to what happened at the Temple of Solomon [meaning the Al Aqsa mosque], a place where religious services are ordinarily chanted. What happened there? If I tell the truth, it will exceed your powers of belief. So let it suffice to say this much, at least, that in the Temple and porch of Solomon, men rode in blood up to their knees and bridle reins. Indeed, it was a just and splendid judgment of God that this place should be filled with the blood of the unbelievers, since it had suffered so long from their blasphemies. The city was filled with corpses and blood. . . .
> Now that the city was taken, it was well worth all our previous labors and hardships to see the devotion of the pilgrims at the Holy Sepulchre. How they rejoiced and exulted and sang a new song to the Lord! . . . This day, I say, will be famous in all future ages, for it turned our labors and sorrows into joy and exultation; this day, I say, marks the justification of all Christianity . . . (Krey, 261 f.).

23

Another eyewitness relates how eventually the Christian leaders "ordered all the Saracen dead to be cast outside because of the great stench, since the whole city was filled with their corpses," and how these were arranged "in heaps, as if they were houses. No one ever saw or heard of such slaughter of pagan people, for funeral pyres were formed from them like pyramids, and no one knows their number except God alone" (262).

Most of the population of Jerusalem was exterminated. Old accounts often mention 70,000 dead, but a modern historian has estimated that this figure is much too high and "some twenty or thirty thousand inhabitants perished" (Prawer, 15). Some Jews were not killed but sold into slavery by the Christians, mostly to Europe but some also in Ashkelon, which was still Muslim. These slaves, both in Europe and in Palestine, were quickly redeemed by Jewish communities. The city now being depopulated, the Crusaders moved Christian Arabs into the Jewish quarter of Jerusalem ("Jeru-Salem" in *Encyclopaedia Judaica*, 1415).

This was the high point of the Crusades and the beginning of the kingdom of Jerusalem. Next to that, the greatest triumph was the capture of Constantinople in 1204, the climax of the Fourth Crusade. This marked the beginning of the Latin empire of Constantinople, which endured until 1261. Barker notes that, "like the First Crusade, the Fourth Crusade also . . . was a French enterprise" (539), and he has a good deal to say about it but devotes only three words to the climax: "Constantinople was captured" (540). Ploetz's incomparably more concise summary at least mentions "merciless plundering; many works of art perish" (451). Nicholas Zernov, writing about *Eastern Christendom* (1961), goes into a little more detail. But first consider the attitude of the Eastern church, and of Zernov, toward the capture of Jerusalem.

The final schism between the Eastern and the Western churches had come in 1054; the First Crusade began in 1096. Naturally, the Eastern church was apprehensive about the approach of the pope's armies but tried to obtain agreement that the Holy

Land must be restored to the Eastern church, from which it had been wrested by the Muslims. For a long time any truly vital clash between Eastern and Western Christendom was avoided, and the treatment of the non-Christian population of Jerusalem in 1099 did not lead to controversies, like that over the *filioque* clause. To this day, what draws a protest from Zernov is only the fact that "the entire population suffered at the hands of the invaders, the Crusaders showing no respect for the lives and property of Christians" (105).

Two pages later he describes how the Crusaders entered Constantinople

> on Good Friday, 1204, and for three days savagely sacked the great capital of the Christian East, which had never before been conquered. The looting of Constantinople is one of the major disasters of Christian history. The city contained innumerable and irreplaceable treasures of classical antiquity and of Christian art and learning. All the best that the Mediterranean world possessed was gathered there. For three days, a wild crowd of drunken and blood-thirsty soldiers killed and raped; palaces, churches, libraries and art collections were wantonly destroyed; monasteries and convents were profaned, hospitals and orphanages sacked. A drunken prostitute was placed on the Patriarch's throne in the Cathedral of St. Sophia and sang indecent songs to the applause of the Crusaders, whilst the Knights [whose "ideal striving" should not be forgotten] were busy hacking the high altar to pieces; it was made of gold and adorned with precious stones.

Christian scholars have often said falsely that the great library of Alexandria, with its unique collection of ancient manuscripts, was burnt by the Muslims, who are thus held responsible for our loss of most of Aeschylus and Sophocles and untold other treasures, but they rarely mention the sack of Constantinople. At most, it is said that this was how the Greek bronze horses came to St. Mark's church in Venice.

Pope Innocent III, during whose "crowded and magnificent pontificate" this sack occurred, had made this "Crusade his ultimate object, and [had] attempted to bring it back to its old religious basis" (Barker, 539). He had not foreseen the capture of Constantinople and was furious at first, but quickly reconciled to the new Latin empire of Constantinople. Still, this was not enough, and he next called for a new kind of Crusade, against the Albigenses in what now is southern France. The name is derived from Albi, a town about forty-five miles northeast of Toulouse. They were also known as Cathars (the purified) and had originally come to the region south of Albi from the Byzantine empire. They were Christians but heretics inasmuch as they were more or less Manichaean dualists, denied purgatory and eternal damnation, rejected masses for the dead and oaths, and believed that eventually all souls would be saved. Matter was evil in their view, the body a prison, and sexual intercourse sinful, because "it either condemned an existing soul to another period of imprisonment in matter [some of them believed in the transmigration of souls] or it involved a new soul in this evil world. . . . Jesus was an emanation from God, but he was not God. Neither was he a man; his apparent body was merely an illusion, for pure spirit could have no contact with matter"; and the Church had misunderstood his saving truths. The *perfecti* among them renounced the world and lived in poverty and chastity, while the mass of believers (*credentes*) "could enjoy the society of the 'perfect' without being perfect themselves; they could hope to achieve salvation without repeated acts of penance and reception of the sacraments" (Strayer, 28 f., 34).

In 1208 Pope Innocent III called for a Crusade against these very peaceable heretics,

> offering the lands of the count of Toulouse and other supporters of heresy to those who would conquer them. . . . Never was a Crusade so attractive, never were crusading vows easier to fulfill. . . . Remission of sins was certain and the Crusade could take the place of all other penance. The chances for plunder were good . . . Best of all, a crusader had to serve only forty days to secure all

the indulgences granted to participants in the Holy War. This forty-day rule is one reason why no one can estimate the size of the crusading army; it was constantly increasing and diminishing as contingents came and left (52 f.).

In 1209 the Crusaders conquered the town of Béziers and killed all inhabitants, Catholics as well as heretics, women as well as children. Reporting to the pope, his legate "said cheerfully that neither age nor sex was spared and that about twenty thousand people were killed. The figure is certainly too high; the striking point is that the legate expressed no regret about the massacre, not even a word of condolence for the clergy of the cathedral who were killed in front of their own altar" (62 f.). Actually, the papal legate added: "our men . . . making a huge slaughter, pillaged and burned the whole city, by reason of God's wrath wondrously kindled against it." When the castle of Bram fell, the Crusaders "tore out the eyes of more than 100 of the defenders, and cut off their noses" (Coulton, 1938, 99; cf. Strayer, 70). When Minerve fell, the papal legate tried to convert the Albigensians in the city, who replied: "We abjure the Roman Church; ye labor in vain; neither life nor death shall separate us from the sect whereunto we hold." And "still more obstinate did he find the heretickesses." So they were all burnt alive. A phrase that recurs in the reports is: "our Crusaders burned innumerable heretics with prodigious joy"—*cum ingenti gaudio* (Coulton, 100 f.). Yet it was only with the fall of Montségur in 1244 that the Albigensians suffered their final defeat—and France achieved full dominion south of the Loire and became "for the next five centuries the most powerful, the wealthiest, and the most populous state in Europe. Neither the pope nor the crusaders who answered his summons had planned to increase the authority of the French king, and yet the aggrandizement of France was one of the most durable results of the Crusades" (Strayer, Preface).

In 1212 Stephen of Vendôme preached a Children's Crusade. Thousands of children embarked in Marseille—and were sold into slavery in Alexandria.

Innocent's ardor was not abated. By 1215 he called for the Fifth Crusade—the Albigensian Crusade and the Children's Crusade do not count. This time Cairo was to be conquered, but was not, and after four years a truce was signed.

In 1227 the emperor Frederick II launched the Sixth Crusade, caught a fever and returned, was excommunicated by Pope Gregory IX (Innocent had died in 1216), resumed his Crusade the following year, and when he had left, Gregory proclaimed a Crusade against the emperor's Sicilian lands. Meanwhile Frederick, already king of Jerusalem by marriage, obtained by negotiation Nazareth and Bethlehem as well as Jerusalem and a corridor from the Holy City to the sea. When the patriarch of Jerusalem refused to crown him as king of Jerusalem, he crowned himself in the church of the Holy Sepulchre in 1229. Since then, no monarch has been crowned in Jerusalem.

After that, Louis IX of France still attempted a Seventh Crusade (1248–1254) and an Eighth (1270), without accomplishing much. Some writers count the Fifth and Sixth Crusades as one and recognize only seven, a number that is holier. When Acco (Acre) fell to the Muslims in 1291, a little less than two hundred years after the First Crusade, this madness stopped. But meanwhile the pogrom with which it had begun and above all the Albigensian Crusade had proved that there were easier ways of expressing one's religious zeal.

52

Most historians admire Innocent III. They call him a towering personality, a splendid jurist, a brilliant administrator, and even a really good man. Yet after the great massacre at Béziers he wrote a letter to Simon de Montfort that begins with

Capuchin catacombs, Palermo, where about 8,000 corpses are lined up in various poses.

"Praise and thanks to God for that which He hath mercifully and marvellously wrought through thee, and through others whom zeal for the orthodox faith has kindled to this work, against His most pestilent enemies." He also promised his help in "extirpating the remnants of heretical iniquity"; and "At the same time he wrote urgent letters to the Emperor Otto, to the kings of Aragon and Castile, and to many abbots and other prelates, pressing them to help Montfort. . . . These letters are noticeable for the first appearance of that word *exterminare* which . . . plays so important a part in papal policy" (Coulton, 103).

Six years later, in 1215, the year of the Magna Carta in England, Innocent convened the Fourth Lateran Council, which institutionalized religious persecution. The decrees passed in 1215 stipulate that "Catholics who assume the cross and devote themselves to the extermination of heretics shall enjoy the same indulgence and privilege as those who go to the Holy Land." Moreover, every bishop or a representative shall make regular visits to every parish "in which there are said to be heretics . . . and he shall compel three or more men of good reputation, or even, if need be, the whole neighborhood, to swear that, if any of them knows of any heretics or of any who frequent secret conventicles or who practice manners and customs different from those common amongst Christians, he will report them to the bishop" (Bettenson, 189). Jews were compelled henceforth to wear yellow badges on their clothing to facilitate instant recognition—and harassment.

The emperor Frederick II, "one of the most notorious free-thinkers of his day," quickly promised his collaboration and by 1224 "condemned all future heretics to the stake."* Yet the man who is generally credited with having created the Inquisition is Gregory IX, pope from 1227 to 1241. As soon as he became pope, "he gave full support and encouragement" to Conrad of Marburg, who always believed all accusations of heresy and of whom a chronicler reports that "no chance of defence was offered, no delay was granted for deliberation, but the accused must either at once confess guilt and be brought to penance, or deny it and be burned." In 1231, Gregory burned a group of heretics in Rome. But what was ultimately more important was that he used all the laws he could find against heresy and, where it seemed necessary to him, introduced stringent new laws, and it was he who developed the methods of the Inquisition. The most important among these were torture and the terror one could generate with that, although it was only Innocent IV, Gregory's successor, who published a papal bull that officially authorized torture in cases of heresy. Of course, torture was not altogether new, and St. Augustine already had "commended flogging to elicit the truth" (Coulton, 153). But the systematic use of torture and terror on a large scale, and the use of these devices to secure denunciations, were the achievement of the thirteenth century—the celebrated High Middle Ages.

"No man was safe from his neighbors, his servants, or even his children" (Coulton, 292). "Gregory IX had found the correct formula. . . . Since one of the essential signs of real repentance was to name everyone whom the penitent thought might be either a heretic or an associate of heretics, and since mere suspicion created such a presumption of guilt that those accused could clear themselves only by confession and revealing more names" (Strayer, 148), heretics hardly stood a chance, and thousands of people quite innocent of heresy suffered the same fate.

The Albigensian Crusades and the Inquisition were a great success. No Albigensians survive. Of course, "secular governments learned how easy it was to suppress opposition," and the techniques developed by the popes "were used by European states of the later Middle Ages. Modern totalitarian governments have made few innovations; they have

* Coulton, 111 f. The quotations that follow are also from Coulton.

simply been more efficient" (Strayer, Preface). Writing before Spain became a totalitarian state in 1939, Coulton said of Spain under Ferdinand and Isabella, when the Spanish Inquisition was at the height of its power and the Jews were expelled: "Spain was now the most efficient Totalitarian State in Europe, or in the World" (290). Indeed, one cannot begin to understand the origins of totalitarianism until one realizes that the Inquisition provided the great model.

Did the Inquisition have anything to do with Christianity, or was it more or less an accident that Innocent and Gregory were popes, and that the Fourth Lateran Council was attended by about 1,300 bishops, abbots, and other prelates? Was the recourse to torture a betrayal of Christianity and a relapse into paganism, or derived in any significant way from the New Testament? For a long time it has been fashionable to absolve, if not Christianity, at least the New Testament. But if God tortures unbelievers in all eternity, then it is arguable that Gregory was much more charitable than Jesus who, according to the Gospels, contemplated this prospect with equanimity. To let heretics lead other men astray is cruel, and to torture them for a few days to save them from eternal torment is anything but cruel.

Nevertheless, modern liberals feel so uncomfortable in the presence of suffering that many of them simply cannot understand how medieval Christians could inflict torture on others—and turn out in large numbers to see heretics being burned. But the belief in hell fostered altogether different attitudes. It was widely assumed that the blessed in heaven would watch the tortures of the damned. Tertullian's detailed account of this notion has been cited in connection with Zarathustra's eschatology; it was written around A.D. 200. Four hundred years later, Pope Gregory the Great, whose *Dialogues* lent powerful support to the belief in angels and devils and promoted the worship of relics, reaffirmed the belief that the blessed would rejoice in the torments of the damned. He was proclaimed a saint. In the twelfth century, Peter Lombard composed his celebrated and vastly influential *Sentences*, which immediately became the principal theological text in the universities. He gave a detailed account of St. Gregory's position and emphatically endorsed it, pointing out that the story about Lazarus and the rich man in Luke 16 proves Gregory right (Coulton, 19). His reading of Luke seems correct.

St. Thomas Aquinas (1225–1274) did not only agree; he also argued at length in his *Summa Theologica* that heretics deserve "to be severed from the world by death. For it is a much graver matter to corrupt the faith which quickens the soul than to forge money." Heretics should be admonished first, but if stubborn should be delivered "to the secular authority to be exterminated." In support, he cited St. Jerome: "Cut off the decayed flesh, expel the mangy sheep from the fold, lest the whole house, the whole paste, the whole body, the whole flock, burn, perish, rot, die. Arius was but one spark in Alexandria, but as the spark was not at once put out, the whole earth was laid waste by its flame." In his very next article (II, II, IX:4), Thomas quotes from the "sermon on the mount": "Love your enemies; do good to them that hate you." But we must distinguish, says St. Thomas, between spiritual and

> temporal good, such as life of the body, worldly possessions, good repute . . . for we are not bound by charity to wish others this good . . . Hence if the presence of one of these goods in one individual might be an obstacle to eternal salvation in many, we are not bound out of charity to wish such a good to that person, rather should we desire him to be without it, both because eternal salvation takes precedence of temporal good, and because the good of the many is to be preferred to the good of one.

St. Thomas was a Dominican, born four years after the death of St. Dominic. Dominic, a Spaniard, had asked Innocent for permission to convert the Tatars but had been sent instead to preach to the Albigenses, and in 1216 he had founded his Order of

Preachers. There had been other orders before. St. Benedict had founded a monastry on Monte Cassino in the sixth century, and later the Cluniacs and Cistercians had followed this model. But in 1232, when Thomas was five, Pope Gregory IX entrusted the Dominicans with the sacred task of being the bloodhounds of the Lord and rooting out heresy.

53

Francis of Assisi (about 1182–1226) was an Italian like Thomas and a younger contemporary of Dominic. When he founded his order, he simply put together a few precepts from the Gospels as "The Rule" of the order. In 1219 he visited the Holy Land but had to return when his order was plagued by serious dissensions. He resigned his active leadership but, with the help of some lawyers, worked out a much more detailed Rule, which was approved by Pope Honorius III in 1223.

While Francis was praying a year later, he is said to have received the stigmata— the wounds that Jesus had received when crucified, in his hands, feet, and side—and Francis is said to have suffered intensely from them until his death two years later. While no nails are mentioned in the Gospels, and Jesus is depicted in many northern Renaissance paintings as tied to the cross with ropes, John 20:27 suggests stigmata.

Here are some quotations from the Rule of St. Francis:

> 2. . . . And I warn and exhort them lest they despise or judge men whom they shall see clad in soft garments and in colors, enjoying delicate food and drink; but each one shall rather judge and despise himself.
> 3. . . . But I advise, warn and exhort my brothers in the Lord Jesus Christ, that, when they go into the world, they shall not quarrel, nor contend with words, nor judge others. But let them be gentle, peaceable, modest, merciful and humble . . .
> 7. . . . They must beware lest they become angry and disturbed on account of the sin of any brother; for anger and indignation hinder love in ourselves and others.
> 8. All the brothers shall be bound always to have one of the brothers of the order as minister general and servant of the whole brotherhood, and shall be strictly bound to obey him. . . .
> 9. . . . I also exhort these same brothers that in all their preaching their language shall be pure and careful, to the advantage and edification of the people; preaching to them of vices and virtues, punishment and glory; and let their discourse be brief; for the words which the Lord spoke upon earth were brief.
> 10. The brothers who are the ministers and servants of the other brothers shall visit and admonish their brothers and humbly and lovingly correct them; not teaching them anything which is against their conscience and our Rule. But the brothers who are subjected to them shall remember that, before God, they have discarded their own wills. Wherefore I strictly charge them that they obey their ministers in all things which they have promised God to observe, and which are not contrary to their conscience and to our Rule. . . . They shall . . . take care . . . that they love those who persecute, revile and attack us. For the Lord saith: "Love your enemies, and pray for those that persecute you and speak evil against you; Blessed are they that suffer persecution for righteousness' sake, for of such is the kingdom of Heaven; He that is steadfast unto the end shall be saved."
> 11. I strictly charge all the brethren not to hold conversation with women so as to arouse suspicion, nor to take counsel with them. . . .

One might love Francis of Assisi even if he had said nothing but "let their discourse be brief; for the words which the Lord spoke on earth were brief." But what strikes one like lightning out of a leaden and oppressive sky is the theme of love. In the

450 pages of Bettenson's *Documents of the Christian Church*, this is its only appearance. Nevertheless, a common reaction to Francis is that he was a true Christian—unlike Tertullian and Augustine, Constantine and Innocent, the Crusaders and inquisitors, Luther and Calvin. On the face of it, it would make more sense to suggest that his rule that "anger and indignation hinder love in ourselves and others" is Buddhist. We shall find it in the Dhammapada, centuries before the New Testament, and will discuss it later in that context. Do we find it also in the New Testament? Certainly, Francis wished to find it there, but this idea about anger and indignation is neither stated there by Jesus nor embodied by him; on the contrary, unlike the Buddha, he appears angry and indignant much of the time.

The New Testament quotation at the end of Rule 10 is really three different quotations; there is no place where the theme of the first one is sustained at any length, and the reason Jesus gave in the Gospels for loving one's enemies was: "For if you love those who love you, what reward have you? Do not even the tax collectors do the same?" 123 (Matthew 5:46). The whole tenor of Francis of Assisi is different and really at times much closer to the Buddha than it is to Jesus. Still, here, too, there are deep differences. The Franciscan ardor that finally culminated in the ecstasy in which he is said to have received the stigmata seems worlds removed from the Buddha. That Francis should have loved all creatures, including not only the birds to whom he preached—actually and not only in Giotto's beautiful painting—but also the vermin that he tolerated on his body, again brings to mind India rather than the New Testament, but not so much the Buddha as many Jain saints. But that in the end he asked forgiveness of his own body—"brother body"—for having loved it so little, that crystallizes his own distinctive sweetness, which is, when one sees him as a whole, different from the great figures of India as well as the great Christians. That instead of merely trying to perfect himself he founded an order and tried to convert others to his sentiments, that he tried to change the world by creating an institution in which love would be cultivated and made a force among men—was doomed to be no more than a momentary flash in a dark sky. Within a few decades after the death of Francis, his order vied with the Dominicans to implement the Inquisition.

> The practice of employing Dominicans and Franciscans together led to quarrels and scandals, and Clement IV [a mere forty years after Francis' death] had to forbid the inquisitors to prosecute each other. It was found wiser to define the boundaries of their jurisdictions; thus in Italy the north was assigned to Dominicans, the center to Franciscans. Both orders seem to have carried out their duties in the same spirit . . . (*The Cambridge Medieval History*, volume VI, 752).

Few writers on Francis mention this. Fewer still give any evidence of having felt the poignant tragedy of this event. That it should have happened is heartbreaking; that almost no one seems to have been bothered by it is shattering.

It seems scarcely credible that Gregory IX, who became pope a year after the death of Francis and proclaimed him a saint the following year, in 1228, had actually been a close associate of Francis. Indeed, the very pope who burned heretics in Rome and developed the Inquisitorial system had assisted Francis in formulating the rule of the order. Francis had not wanted to formulate any elaborate rule; he was "not minded to become an executioner" and did not wish to enforce anything with threats of punishment. He did not even want buildings but thought that the members of his order, instead of withdrawing from the world into a community that would own things, should go out into the world in absolute poverty. Gregory, perceiving that sufficient emphasis on obedience might turn the order into a valuable instrument of the papacy, left out things that Francis wished to include, and included things Francis did not like. In his testament, written shortly before his death, Francis protested against the way his order was changing but, after canonizing him, Gregory declared that the testament had no binding force.

As soon as Francis was canonized, vast sums of money were poured into the construction of a fine monastery and a very beautiful lower church and upper church over his sepulcher. By 1253 the buildings were finished and then adorned with some of the finest frescoes of the Western world, depicting scenes from the life of the saint. It has often been said that Giotto, who painted some of these frescoes, humanized painting. Francis, no doubt, would rather have humanized Christianity.

54

Many people believe that during the Middle Ages the church made a travesty of Christianity and that it remained for Martin Luther to recall Christendom to its authentic inspiration. For although Luther began his career as a monk, he took a public stand against the sale of indulgences and, when summoned to Worms in the Rhineland to recant, refused to acknowledge the authority of popes and councils and would not recant unless refuted from Scripture. His initial protest, in the form of ninety-five theses that he offered to defend in public debate, marks the beginning of the Protestant Reformation, and many Europeans consider that date, 1517, the end of the Middle Ages and the dawn of the Modern Age. Luther's stand at Worms, in 1521, sealed the schism. To save him from the fate of Johann Hus, the Bohemian reformer who had been burnt as a heretic at the Council of Constance in 1415, a friendly elector kidnapped Luther on his way home from Worms and hid him at the Wartburg, where he translated the Bible into German, from the original Hebrew and Greek. Printing was then in its infancy. The first book printed in Europe was the Gutenberg Bible, in Latin, in 1453, the year Constantinople was conquered by the Turks. But fifteenth-century books were extremely expensive. Luther was the first writer who availed himself of the immense potentialities of printing to reach a very large public. He published a steady stream of short tracts that were reprinted as soon as they were sold out. And he succeeded in acquainting large numbers of Germans with the Bible. Moreover, the power of his language has rarely been equaled in any tongue, and his German Bible, which had been preceded by a few earlier translations, caught something of the spirit of the originals. Hence it is true in some sense that Luther demanded and really brought about a return to the Bible.

Yet he was anything but another St. Francis. Indeed, it would be difficult for anyone to be more different from St. Francis than Luther was; yet the other great Protestant reformer, John Calvin, was. For Luther at least shared with the saint a warmth of feeling, even a consuming ardor, while there was something ice cold about Calvin. Insofar, however, as Francis abhorred the idea of judging anyone and exhorted Christians to beware of anger and of indignation, while insisting above all on love, both Luther and Calvin are his antipodes. For Luther the saving insight was that man, according to St. Paul, is saved by faith and not by works. Jesus' strenuous commandments were meant to teach us that we are incapable of pleasing God with works and therefore must rely exclusively on faith in Christ. "The law is fulfilled not insofar as we satisfy it, but insofar as we are forgiven for not being able to do anything" (XXII, 377). This reasoning applies not only to the most extravagant demands in the "Sermon on the Mount"; it also applies, according to Luther, to the Ten Commandments, which prohibit murder, theft, and bearing false witness, for example. "The hearts that are filled with God's bliss do not fulfill the Ten Commandments; but Christ has brought about such a violent

salvation that he deprives the Ten Commandments, too, of all their claims" (VII, 1516).
And in a letter to his friend and close associate in the Reformation, Philip Melanchthon,
Luther wrote on August 1, 1521, from the Wartburg:

> If you are a preacher of grace, do not preach a fictitious but a true grace; and if
> the grace is true, carry a true and not a fictitious sin. God does not work salvation
> for fictitious sinners. Be a sinner and sin vigorously [*esto peccator et pecca
> fortiter*]; but even more vigorously believe and delight in Christ who is victor
> over sin, death, and the world. . . . It is sufficient that we recognize through
> the wealth of God's glory the lamb who bears the sin of the world; from this sin
> does not sever us, even if thousands, thousands of times in one day we should
> fornicate or murder.

This was glad tidings indeed, especially in an age when faith was not that hard to
come by. Of course, a person with an intellectual conscience might have difficulties
with the Christian faith, but Luther's advice on that was good news, too, for most
people—and again bears witness of his linguistic genius. "There is on earth among all
dangers no more dangerous thing than a richly endowed and adroit reason, especially
if she enters into spiritual matters which concern the soul and God. For it is more possible to teach an ass to read than to blind such a reason and lead it right; for reason
must be deluded, blinded, and destroyed" (V, 1,312). This is a theme that keeps re-
curring in Luther's writings, and the reason for calling reason "she," in English, too, is
that Luther thought of her as "the devil's bride" and a "whore" (XII, 1,530; VIII,
2,048).

> Christ says: Take, eat, this is my body; Drink ye all of it, this is my blood.
> No, no, they say; it is not his body and blood, for Christ sits on the right side
> of God. They would judge the word according to their reason. Fie on you! That
> is like teaching hens to lay eggs, and teaching cows how to calve, trying to teach
> our Lord God how to preach. Would we like it so well if our servants and maids
> behaved like this towards us? (XIII, 1,688).

What has become of Luther's grand refusal to recant unless refuted from Scripture? Unquestionably, he took his stand on the New Testament, and specifically on
Paul's Epistles and the Gospel according to John. But he also said that John was far
superior to the other evangelists and that "one might even call him alone an evangelist" (VII, 2,008; XI, 1,462). And since James, Jesus' brother, says in his Epistle, "Man
is justified by works and not by faith alone," Luther says that this Epistle is utter
straw (XIV, 105).

It follows that those who share Luther's beliefs will be saved even if they are
mass murderers, while the rest of mankind is damned and will suffer eternal tortures
in hell, regardless of the excellence of their works. The pope is, to Luther's mind, the
Antichrist, and the church of Rome must be defied because it leads men to damnation.
Luther was quite as intolerant as those who devised the Inquisition, and the power of
his language often manifests itself in tirades of abuse against the enemies of God.

The splintering of Protestantism into a multitude of sects goes back to Luther's
outrage at Ulrich Zwingli, a Swiss reformer, a year younger than Luther, who insisted
that the bread and wine of the sacraments were symbols and did not really contain the
flesh and blood of Christ, as Luther taught. As for the Jews, Luther initially hoped to
convert them and published a short book with the title, *That Jesus Christ Was Born
a Jew* (1523). At the outset he said: "Our fools, the popes, bishops, sophists, and monks,
the crude ass heads, have hitherto treated the Jews in such a manner that anyone who
was a good Christian would have felt like becoming a Jew."

When the Jews did not embrace his version of Christianity, he was furious and
published books against them. In "On the Jews and their Lies" (1543) he asked: "What

shall we Christians do now with this depraved and damned people of the Jews? . . . I will give my faithful advice: First, that one should set fire to their synagogues. . . . Then, that one should also break down and destroy their houses. . . . That one should drive them out of the country." As it happened, it was on Luther's birthday, November 10, 1938, that Luther's countrymen last set fire to the synagogues in Germany. But Luther was even more pitiless in his attitude toward the German peasants, when they revolted. In 1525 Luther wrote:

> There are to be no bondslaves since Christ has freed us all? What is all this? This makes Christian freedom carnal! . . . Read St. Paul . . . This article goes straight against the Gospel and advocates robbery so that each robs his master, who owns it, of his body. For a bondslave can be a Christian and have Christian freedom just as a prisoner and a sick man can be Christians even without being free. This article wants to make all men equal and turn the spiritual kingdom of Christ into a worldly, external kingdom, which is impossible (XVI, 85).

No doubt, Luther felt that the peasants' uprising endangered his Reformation, which depended on the sympathy of the German princes and on their aversion to Rome, which for years had carried away some of the wealth of their lands and interfered in their affairs. But Luther was not betraying any principle for political advantage. His position was consistent and of a piece with the view he expressed to Christian prisoners of war who had been reduced to slavery by Turkish Muslims: "You are robbing and stealing your body from your master who has bought it or acquired it in some other way so that it is no longer yours but his property, like cattle or other possessions."* Like the Catholic church and the New Testament, Luther was far from protesting against slavery.

It was during his life time that Ferdinand and Isabella the Catholic expelled from Spain all Jews who refused conversion, instituted the Inquisition, and after Columbus's discovery of the New World, introduced black slavery into the West Indies. It was during his life time, too, that Spanish conquerors, with the aid of the Inquisition, exterminated the indigenous civilizations of Mexico and Peru and destroyed countless works of art and manuscripts because they were un-Christian.

In 1555, nine years after Luther's death, his former associates concluded the Augsburg settlement with the German Catholics, which stipulated that each prince could determine the religion of his subjects, provided it was either Lutheran or Catholic, and the members of the other faith could leave the land. But it was only after the Thirty Years' war between the two religions (1618–1648) had devastated Germany and many other lands and decimated the population that Christians gradually grew weary of religious fanaticism.

Calvin was no more humane than Luther. When Michael Servetus, a Spanish physician and surgeon of great distinction who had published works criticizing the doctrine of the Trinity, was fleeing from the Inquisition, having actually escaped from one of its prisons, Calvin seized him and had him executed in Geneva in 1553. Calvin wanted to have him beheaded, but the town council had him burned.

Eventually, Calvinism became established in Scotland, and in 1643 the Assembly of Divines there drew up the Westminster Confession, to which all Presbyterian ministers henceforth had to subscribe and still did after World War II. This Confession gives at least some idea of Calvin's theology—and not only of *his* ideas.

> By the decree of God, for the manifestation of His glory, some men and angels are predestinated unto everlasting life, and others foreordained to ever-

---

* Quoted by Troeltsch, 581 f.

Thinker, Colima, Mexico, about 100 B.C.

lasting death. . . . Neither are any redeemed by Christ . . . but the elect only. The rest of mankind God was pleased . . . to pass by, and to ordain them to dishonor and wrath. . . .

Works done by unregenerate men—although, for the matter of them, they may be things which God commands . . . are sinful and cannot please God.

The Baptist Confession of Faith, drawn up in London in 1646, also made belief in dual predestination mandatory, and this clause was retained in the Second Confession of 1677.

Not only liberal Protestants but legions of other people of good will have long assumed that Christianity was, perhaps even above all other religions, a religion of love. But the belief in the eternal damnation of the vast majority of mankind, including those Christians who did not share whatever was considered the orthodox interpretation of the Christian faith, was not a marginal excrescence that had no effects on what was done. On the contrary, where Christians were in a position to persecute those who did not share their own faith they have often, if not generally, done so.

The relation of Christianity to the arts will be considered in chapter XIII.

Jerusalem, old city.

VI

MUHAMMAD AND THE KORAN

Muhammad's Early Life and His View of Women—
His Call, the Hijra, and Comparison with Moses—
The Koran—God and the Devil, and the Prophet's Attitude
Toward Jews and Christians—Hell and Heaven, Comparison
With Calvin, Slavery and War

Tangiers, Morocco.

55

Islam is generally acknowledged to be the third great monotheistic religion. Like Judaism it insists that God is one and not a trinity. It is based on a book that is said to have been revealed to Muhammad by God: the Koran, written in Arabic in the seventh century A.D. Many Biblical figures and stories are mentioned in the Koran, including not only Moses and David but also Jesus, and Muhammad had many contacts with Jews and Christians. But he considered Jesus a prophet and in no sense God, and he did not accept the Bible. Islam recognizes the authority of only one God, called Allah; one prophet, Muhammad; and one book, the Koran.

Muhammad was born in 570 or soon after, in Mecca, a town about fifty miles inland from Jidda, which is almost exactly at the midpoint of the Red Sea coast of the Arabian peninsula. But for him, few people would ever have heard of Mecca, although it was even then the site of an important sanctuary that contained a black stone that had fallen from heaven, as well as many idols. Two months before Muhammad's birth, his father had died, and when he was six, his mother died. His grandfather decided to bring him up, but died two years later. Then an uncle reared him and is said to have done so very lovingly.

There are stories about prophecies preceding Muhammad's birth, voices addressing his mother when she carried him, and miracles attending his birth. But scholars do not question the fact that when he was about twenty-five he married Khadijah, a wealthy widow who had employed him as a camel driver. She was fifteen years his senior and had already had two husbands when she proposed to him. He is said to have loved her dearly, and he took no other wives as long as she was living. That he took many after that is also agreed, but evaluations differ widely. These two are fairly typical. Tor Andrae's *Mohammed*, originally published in German in 1932, was immediately translated into Italian, Spanish, and English and widely acclaimed as the best short study. The book is sympathetic, but four pages from the end the author suddenly explodes:

> Undoubtedly a prophet who declares that women and children belong to the enticements of worldly life, and who nevertheless accumulates a harem of nine wives, in addition to various slave women, is a strange phenomenon when regarded from the standpoint of morality. The situation is not improved by the fact that up to Khadijah's death, that is, until Mohammed was fifty years old, he was content with one wife. At the height of his career, when he was already an ageing man, he gave free rein to his sensual impulses.

In *Islam*, Caesar E. Farah offers a very different view, although he includes in his list of "Recommended Reading" Andrae's "brilliant exposé of Muhammad's life and doctrine."

Further insight into his personality and character can be derived by a glance into his domestic life. This is one facet of Muhammad where authorities concede he set an example of virtue emulated by so many millions of believers in subsequent times. . . . Muhammad's marriages after Khadijah's, yielding about eleven wives in all, were due partly to political reasons and partly to his concern for the wives of his companions who had fallen in battle defending the nascent Islamic community. In spite of the calumnies heaped upon him by his detractors who, among other things, described him as a voluptuary and wife-hungry, a study of Muhammad's marital inclinations reveals that, besides the political considerations for acquiring more than one wife following the death of Khadijah, pity and elementary concern prompted him in later years to take on wives who were neither beautiful nor rich, but mostly old widows. . . . In these post-Khadijah marriages, he is not known to have cohabited with any but 'A'ishah, the only virgin wife he ever married (67 ff.).

Neither of these writers seems very persuasive on this issue. The former begins his tirade by saying: "No doubt the trait of Muhammad's character most offensive to the Christian Occident is his sensuality." The latter is plainly an apologist who tries to meet this charge by insisting that the women in question were not "beautiful," leading one to wonder how he could possibly know that and who is to judge, and by claiming that we have no proof that the Prophet actually cohabited with his wives, which raises the embarrassing question of what would count as evidence. And Farah further undermines our confidence by claiming, erroneously, that "It was a commonplace for the nobility among Christians and Jews to contract plural marriages." What is true is that neither the Hebrew Bible nor the New Testament condemns polygamy. Other defenders of the Prophet have said that during the first part of his life he gave us an example of monogamy, and then an equally fine example of polygamy.

What may be offensive to some people in the Christian Occident seems less important in a way than what seemed offensive to Christians and Jews in Muhammad's time. They knew that Abraham, Jacob, and Moses had had more than one wife, and that more recently—about one thousand and six hundred years ago—David and Solomon had had many. But a prophet who proclaimed solemn revelations made to him by God, recorded in the Koran, permitting him to have more wives than anybody else, may have been difficult for them to take seriously.

O prophet! To you we have made lawful your wives to whom you paid their dowries and slaves whom Allah has placed under your thumb [literally: your right hand], the daughters of your uncle on your father's side, the daughters of your aunt on your father's side, the daughters of your uncle on your mother's side, and the daughters of your aunt on your mother's side, who emigrated with you, and any believing woman who gives herself to the prophet and whom the prophet desires to marry—a privilege for you alone and not for other believers (33:50).

There is much more like this, especially in the thirty-third sura, and it must have struck the Jews as being a far cry from Amos and Jeremiah, and the Christians as rendering absurd the Prophet's claim that he was superseding Jesus. The question of how many if any of the Prophet's wives were beautiful is surely a red herring. Not only are repeated marriages for political considerations not necessarily more attractive than marriages based on feeling, but slaves did not count, and they still did not count when Allah finally told his prophet that enough was enough: "No further wives are permitted to you henceforth, nor even exchanging your wives against others, no matter how much their beauty might please you, except for the slaves under your thumb. And Allah observes everything" (33:52).

The Jewish religion had certainly not treated women as the equals of men, nor had

Christianity. But in the Hebrew Bible one found an abundance of great women, including Moses' sister, Miriam, and Deborah, the prophetess and judge—both of them composed great songs that are among the oldest parts of the Bible—Yael and Ruth, Huldah and Esther. In the post-Biblical age, the prophetesses had no successors, but marriage was monogamous and in the home the mother enjoyed special authority. One of the Ten Commandments began "Honor your father and your mother," and in the Third Book of Moses (19:3) we find: "Every one of you shall revere his mother and father." In rabbinical law, whether one was a Jew or not depended on the religion of one's mother—and does to this day. On the whole, women fared worse in Christianity, although the church canonized many women as saints and accorded Mary something like the status of the Great Mother of the syncretistic cults that had spread through the Roman Empire. But the place of women in Islam was far below their standing in Judaism and Christianity.

Writers on Islam generally do not blame the Prophet for the degradation of women in Islamic countries, pointing to two other factors instead. First, and this is also relevant to his own marriages, the status of women among the Arabs was wretched in Muhammad's time, and he improved it. Thus polygamy, for example, was unlimited, and he limited other men to no more than four wives at one time, not counting slaves; but divorce was not made difficult in the Koran, and a man could have a great many wives in the course of his life. All this is a commonplace, but apologists stress the Prophet's deep concern for women, which we need not doubt, and make no reference to verse thirty-four in the fourth sura: "Men are in charge of women . . . Hence good women are obedient . . . As for those whose rebelliousness you fear, admonish them, banish them from your bed, and scourge them." Second, many writers on Islam have said that while the Prophet did what he could to improve the status of women, "it was not long before most of the rights accorded to women and of the restrictions imposed on their guardians were substantially curtailed by the ingenuity of Muslim casuists" (Gibb, 34); or in the words of Fazlur Rahman, "The later Muslims did not watch the guiding lines of the Qur'an and, in fact, thwarted its intentions" (36).

The Koran does not claim, as Christians have often alleged, that women have no souls. Nor can the institution of purdah be charged to the Prophet. Still, it is rather astonishing that this term is not as much as listed in the indices of many books on Muhammad and Islam nor mentioned in the passages that deal with the status of women. Yet it was Islam that brought purdah to the countries it conquered, and even in the twentieth century it is still to be found in North Africa, Arabia, Iran, Afghanistan, Pakistan, and Bangladesh, although more and more young women give it up. Purdah originally meant the curtain that screens women from the sight of men. The institution involves special quarters for women, but the term is now used more often for the covering of the face that allows a woman to look out, barely, while keeping men from seeing her, and that has been obligatory for Muslim women whenever they ventured to leave home. Andrae says that "the duty of wearing a veil . . . was later adopted from Persian and Syrian Christians" (78). In the twentieth century most Muslim women have given up this custom, and many wear modern Western dresses and no longer take pains to conceal at least the whole of their body, from the neck to the feet.

Those who have lived or traveled in Muslim countries can hardly fail to be aware of this, but many do not know that in spite of the many ways in which women were discriminated against, once saint worship developed in Islam there were many women saints. "The tomb of the Sitta Nafisa is one of the most sacred spots in Egypt, and the miracles which were wrought by the saint in her lifetime and after her death are the subject of a whole cycle of legend. . . . In the flourishing days of Moslem monasticism

41

there were many convents for women" (Moore, 494). What is more surprising is that even in the High Middle Ages some Muslim women gained fame as scholars.

It is time to return to Muhammad, but it seemed best to discuss the treatment of women in Islam in connection with his marriages. And it would have been perverse to ignore these, for few aspects of his life have attracted so much attention. It is at this point that he differs most obviously from his predecessors in Judaism and Christianity, not to speak of the Jina and the Buddha.

56

Our sources for the life of Muhammad are, in addition to the Koran, manifold "traditions" (*Hadith*), written like reports, that begin with pedigrees in the form of: I have heard from X, who heard from Y, who heard from Z, who heard the Prophet say . . . There is general agreement that many of these traditions are authentic and that many are spurious, but on particular Hadiths there is often disagreement. The testimony of the Koran about the life of the Prophet, however, is accepted not only by Muslims but also by most Western scholars.

According to tradition, the Prophet was illiterate, and the Biblical material in the Koran shows that he had not read the Bible nor had a Bible at hand. His knowledge of the Bible was plainly second-hand and oral; he knew what Jews and Christians had told him, but not necessarily what was actually in the Scriptures and what was later Jewish or Christian lore. Moreover, Jews and Christians have often charged that he also made simple mistakes and, for example, confused Miriam, the sister of Moses, with Mary, the mother of Jesus. Muhammad, in turn, accused the Jews and Christians of having falsified their scriptures.

He experienced his call when he was about forty years old, very suddenly. Every one of the one hundred and fourteen suras that comprise the Koran is identified as belonging either to the period when he lived in Mecca (most of them) or the time, later on, when he lived in Medina (twenty-two of them, but in bulk much more than half of the book). It is therefore possible to determine what themes predominated in his early prophecies. He proclaimed that the divine judgment was at hand, that there was only one God, Allah, and that idolatry would be punished in the eternal flames of hell. Since Mecca was the center of the cult he denounced, with the black stone even then a great attraction for pilgrims but surrounded by many idols, the wealthier elements in the town, who had a vested interest in the old religion, did not like the new teaching at all. Muhammad managed to convert a few individuals, but beyond that he gained a following only among the lower classes, not by any means large or powerful enough to guarantee, or even to make likely, the survival of his reforms.

Then Muhammad received an invitation to come to Medina, a town roughly 275 miles due north of Mecca, a little over a hundred miles inland from the Red Sea. The town was originally called Yathrib and had been settled by Jews before Arabs had moved in and taken over the government. At that time, two Arab tribes were contesting the rule of the town, "with the Jews maintaining an uneasy balance of power. The latter, engaged mainly in agriculture and handicrafts, were economically and culturally superior to the Arabs, and were consequently disliked" (Lewis, 40). The Arabs of Medina invited Muhammad in the hope that he might arbitrate their disputes since he obviously was a powerful personality with rare gifts as a leader of men. They probably had no very strong feelings about his religious ideas one way or the other and did not fully accept them until much later. Of course, not everyone favored the invitation, and there were protracted negotiations before Muhammad finally made the move from Mecca to

Medina in the year 622. This move has often been pictured as a flight, but scholars say that there was no need for that at all and that Muhammad waited until enough of his followers had preceded him to Medina so that he would immediately have their support. However that may be, the move from Mecca to Medina, the so-called *Hijra*, marks the beginning of the Muslim era, and Muslims date events as having occurred so many years after the Hijra.

For the rest of his life, Muhammad was concerned with legislation as much as with theology, and he occupied his immigrant followers by conducting raids on caravans, and eventually wars, until he finally succeeded in conquering Mecca. Two years later he died after a short illness, in the arms of one of his wives, in 632. "Much righteous indignation has been expressed by European writers at the spectacle of an Apostle of God leading the faithful in predatory raids on merchant caravans; but in the conditions of the time and to the moral ideas of the Arabs brigandage was a natural and legitimate occupation." And Bernard Lewis (44) goes on to explain that these raids helped to blockade Mecca and thus advanced its eventual submission to Islam, while at the same time they increased the wealth and prestige of the community in Medina. After a great victory over a Meccan caravan in 624, the Medina suras began to deal more and more with problems of government, the distribution of booty, and other practical problems.

Clearly, Muhammad was very different from Jesus. That seems undeniable even if one does not see the matter at all the way Andrae does when he concludes his *Mohammed*, saying: "But if we would be fair to him we must not forget that, consciously or unconsciously, we Christians are inclined to compare Mohammed with the unsurpassed and exalted figure whom we meet in the Gospels . . . And when it [his historical personality] is measured by such a standard, what personality is not found wanting?"

We have dealt with the conception of Jesus implicit in these lines in the chapter on the New Testament, but for all that, the contrast between Muhammad and Jesus is great, if not nearly so vast as that between Muhammad and the Buddha. Among the great Christians, Muhammad may seem to resemble Calvin most of all because Calvin, too, was the ruler of a city and therefore confronted with practical concerns; both made much of the sublimity and sovereign power of God, who had predestined some for salvation and others for damnation, and both demanded submission to God's sovereign decree. But Calvin was very much a northerner, icy rather than ardent, severe and ascetic, while Muhammad was in all of these respects his diametric opposite.

Was he then more like Moses with whom he shares the desert setting, the uncompromising monotheism, and the practical concern with legislation? Our accounts of both men speak for themselves and show how they differed. But one additional feature they share. Both impressed upon their followers that they were not divine but merely messengers of God. God was so great that by comparison they themselves were essentially like their fellow men, distinguished only by their mission to serve as God's mouthpiece. Neither of them wished to be worshiped. These similarities are certainly not accidental. As Goitein has pointed out, Moses is "the predominant figure in the Koran. . . . Compared to Jesus, who is mentioned only four times in the Koran during the Meccan, that is, the formative, period of Muhammad's career, Moses' name occurs there over a hundred times." And "the stories about Moses are not confined to certain chapters, but pervade the whole Koran and the idea of Moses, the Prophet with a Book, possessed Muhammad to such an extent that he" also became a prophet with a book. "The very name of Christ (in Arabic, *al-Masih*, messiah) became known to Muhammad—or at all events, was mentioned by him—only after he migrated to al-Medina" (55 f.). To appreciate the differences no less than the similarities between Muhammad and Moses one must, of course, turn to the Koran.

57

The Koran is not at all like either the Hebrew Bible or the New Testament. Much of the Hebrew Bible consists of stories and histories that are clearly meant to be read continuously and that are often so gripping that one is carried along by the narrative. The books are divided into chapters, and the chapters into verses, but in large parts of the Hebrew Bible these divisions plainly represent afterthoughts and were imposed later on material that is essentially continuous. The Psalms are different; here each chapter represents a separate poem, and there is obvious continuity only within each psalm. The prophetic books are occasionally like this, too; a chapter may be a more or less self-contained unit, but generally some attempt has been made to arrange these units so as to present a sequence. Only the Book of Proverbs is simply a collection of sayings.

In the New Testament, each of the four evangelists gave his Gospel the form of a story that was meant to be read straight through; the Book of Acts is a history; and the Epistles are letters that are also meant to be read from beginning to end. The order of the whole is: first the four versions of Jesus' ministry, then the history of what happened after his death, then the letters written by some of the principals in that history, and finally the Apocalypse or Revelation of St. John.

Anyone who approaches the Koran with these models in mind and tries to read it straight through in an effort to find out about the life of the Prophet and the origins of Islam is not only bound to be disappointed and frustrated but apt to find the book unreadable. The first sura consists of seven short verses that mark the opening, but the remaining one hundred and thirteen suras are arranged roughly in order of their length, beginning with the longest suras, most of which were written late in the Prophet's life, and ending with the shortest, which belong to the first years of his mission. Thus the second sura, called "The Cow," has two hundred and eighty-six verses, of which many are quite long. It was composed in Medina, as were the next three suras, "The Family of Imran" (Amram, the father of Moses), which has two hundred verses, "Women," which has one hundred and seventy-seven (or one hundred and seventy-five according to the traditional numbering), and "The Table," which has one hundred and twenty. The next two suras are said to have been revealed in Mecca, much earlier, the two after that again in Medina, and so forth. In bulk, the first twenty suras comprise about half of the Koran. Of the last forty-nine, which are very short, all but two are Meccan and supposed to be very early. Many of the last suras comprise only half a dozen very short lines, or even less. Moreover, most of the suras "are a mosaic of passages of revelation, uttered by Mohammed at different times and on different occasions, somewhat un-evenly compiled from oral and written records. It seems possible that the work of com-pilation was begun in his lifetime, but it was completed only some years after his death" (Gibb, 1959, 179).

In his *Mohammedanism*, Gibb explains further that "the generally received ac-count" describes the compilation of the Koran "a few years after his death from 'scraps of parchment and leather, tablets of stone, ribs of palm branches, camels' shoulder-blades and ribs, pieces of board and the breasts of men.' To this, probably, is to be ascribed much of the unevenness and the rough jointing which characterize the present composition of the longer suras" (46).

Few scholars question the authenticity of the Koran. No other major religion has a holy scripture that received its final and authoritative recension within twenty years of the prophet's death. By 650, the third caliph sent copies of the definitive text to the major cities, and the consonantal text of the Koran has remained unchanged ever since. Seven ways of reading it by supplying different vowels have been accepted as orthodox, but the divergences are minor, and all modern texts agree on one of these. The verbal inspiration of the Koran is part of the Muslim faith. Scholars who do not believe that the Koran was revealed to Muhammad by Allah do not doubt for the most part that the Prophet himself believed that it had been; much less do they doubt that the Koran goes back to Muhammad.

Still, it follows from what has been said that the Koran is not a book in the traditional Western sense. When we approach it as if it were, we naturally find that it does not brook comparison with Genesis or Jeremiah. Moreover, what comes across in translations into Western languages is not remotely comparable to the best translations of the Bible. The Koran was not supposed to be translated. In a way it defies translation. A comparison of many different translations into European languages reveals that most of them generally agree very closely about the meaning, but none of the translations is very impressive, and where it is very close to the Hebrew Bible it generally suffers by comparison. What kind of a book is the Koran, then? And what is the secret of its immense appeal to hundreds of millions of people?

First of all, the Arabs, to whom it was presented, originally did not have an imposing literature of their own. They had nothing to pit against the Jewish or Christian Bible. Their religion is usually described as idolatry, which is accurate enough, and the Koran denounces idolatry again and again with the utmost contempt, following in the footsteps of the Hebrew Bible. The harm to which this led when the Muslims invaded India was tragic. The Muslims' notion that the Hindus and Buddhists were idolaters might suggest that the religion of the Arabs that Islam replaced was also associated with a highly sophisticated and refined civilization. It was not. The Koran did not have to compete with an indigenous literature; it more nearly filled a vacuum.

Secondly, the call Muhammad received was not to write but to recite; and whether he was sensual or not, and whether sensuality is hateful or not, the Koran should not be considered in exclusively cerebral terms, apart from its sensuous quality —initially its sound and later also its visual appearance. The Koran was meant to be heard and has an aesthetic dimension that is lost in translation. George Foot Moore, an exceptionally admirable scholar, once made a noble attempt at "an imitative translation of an early Sura (93)" in order to give the reader at least "some notion of the form" which he described as "the rhymed sing-song in which the heathen soothsayers were wont to couch their responses" (390); but his version does not seem any more comparable to Isaiah than do unrhymed translations:

> By the bright day
> And the night without ray,
> Thy Lord forsakes not nor casts thee away.
> The hereafter the present will more than repay;
> Thy Lord will give, nor say thee nay.
> Found he thee not an orphan and became thy stay,
> Found thee wandering and set thee on the way,
> Found thee poor and did thy wants allay?
> Therefore the orphan do not thou gainsay,
> Nor the beggar drive away;
> But the goodness of thy Lord display.

Or consider the five lines in which Muhammad is said to have received his first revelation. One need not wonder that the Jews, knowing Isaiah's account of his calling (Isaiah 6), were not converted; neither should one assume that any of our translations capture what beauty there is in the original of the beginning of sura 96:

Recite in the name of your Lord who created,
created man from a clot of blood.
Recite! Your Lord is most glorious,
Taught through script,
Taught man what he knew not.

The sensuous aspect of the Koran is most obvious to those who do not know Arabic when they see how verses from the Koran have been used in decorating mosques. And Islam without mosques would almost be like Judaism without Scripture.

Islam is a profoundly aesthetic religion to which one cannot be fair as long as one judges it only in cerebral terms. But, of course, it has an intellectual dimension, too, and part of the appeal of Islam has been that it offered men a relatively short book, said to be revealed by God and divided into suras that could be recited, listened to, and read in short pieces. At the same time it provided ample work for scholars who have studied it on and on, and it did not require anyone to believe a great many things that it is difficult to believe. The only miracle, according to Muhammad, was that the Koran was revealed to him. He himself claimed no supernatural powers or feats, and it was only after his death that

> the popular imagination seized on hints and allusions in the Koran and elaborated them into miracles (as, for example, the splitting of the moon to confound his Meccan adversaries) or other supernatural interventions in his life. The most famous is the lengthy narrative of the "Night-journey" (*isrā'*) to Jerusalem, followed by an "Ascension" (*mi'rāj*) to paradise in the course of a single night, when, under the guidance of Gabriel, he is said to have met and talked with the Prophets who had preceded him and to have been granted the ineffable Vision of God.

This story, which was later "accepted as an article of orthodox belief" (Gibb, 1959, 179), assumed importance when it became the basis for the Muslims' interest in Jerusalem.

58

The central theme of the Koran is its stark and uncompromising monotheism. There is only one God, and he is one; not, as the Christians would have it, three in one. Here one should recall the controversies into which Christianity had been plunged for centuries when Muhammad appeared, including disputes about the precise relationship of the Son to the Father, and of the Holy Ghost to both. The relative simplicity of the Muslim conception of God helps to account for the enduring appeal of Islam down to the twentieth century.

Of course, at this point Islam merely returns to Judaism, but by also dispensing with the complexities of the Jewish law, Islam far surpassed the appeal of Judaism as well. Indeed, one might suppose that nothing more needs to be said to account for the rapid spread of this new religion and its great attractiveness. But it will not do to present Islam as a kind of liberal Judaism or as merely an early version of Unitarianism. To show this, it may be best to begin by considering very briefly Muhammad's attitude toward the Jews.

His debt to them was enormous. He did not sit down with their Bible to study it along with the Midrash and the Talmud to decide what he might retain. He was illiterate, and his revelations came upon him in trances that many scholars believe were associated with epileptic fits because his descriptions of them suggest something like that. Needless to say, if he was an epileptic that would not discredit his revelations

12

13

14

15

16

17

18

19

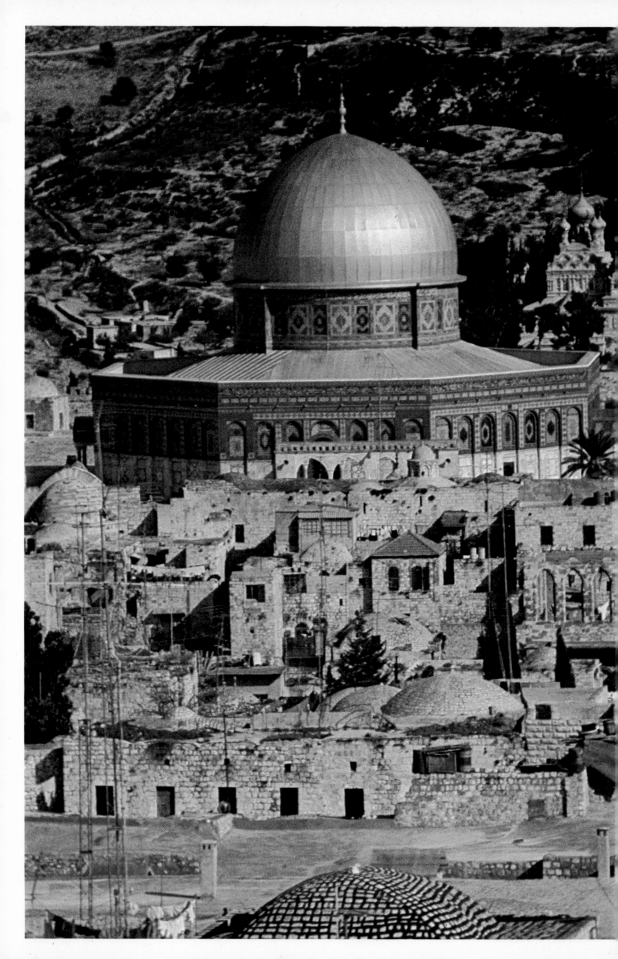

21

22

23

24

25

27

28

29

30

31

32

34

35

38

39

40

41

42

43

44

45

any more than Dostoevsky's indubitable epilepsy discredits his novels. If God can speak to men in their dreams, why not during a fit? But the point is that his messages came to him in an involuntary way, and he did not consciously choose and pick the elements of Judaism that appealed to him. Yet there is no doubt that he was deeply influenced by what he had heard of Jewish ideas. Above all, his God is the God of the Hebrew Bible. In the West it is customary to call him Allah, as even the most popular English version of the Koran by Mohammed Marmaduke Pickthall does, using the Arabic term, but one should not suppose that this is a proper name like Zeus or Mars or Vishnu; it is simply the Arabic way of saying God and corresponds to the Hebrew *elohim*.

Since Muhammad's contact with the Hebrew Bible was indirect, his conception of God was colored by the Judaism of his time. "The title, al-Rahman, 'the merciful,' which in one period of his ministry Mohammed used as a proper name for God by preference to all others, is a foreign word, borrowed from the Jews, and the emphasis on the attribute of mercy, especially on God's forgiving grace, is of the same origin" (Moore, 395). God is indeed called *el rahum*, merciful God, not only in his famous account of himself in Exodus 34:6 but also in Deuteronomy 4:31, and the word *rahum* is applied to him another ten times in the Hebrew Bible but used as a name for God only in the apocryphal book of the Wisdom of Jesus ben Sirach. Other forms derived from the same root, notably including *rahamim*, "mercy," are applied to God again and again in the Jewish Bible, more than sixty times. But the form *rahman*, "merciful," which Muhammad picked up, is attested only in post-Biblical literature, is used as God's name in the Talmud, and was common in Muhammad's day.

Muhammad's conception of Allah as enthroned "in the highest heaven, seated upon a lofty throne, surrounded by angelic ministers, some of whom continually adore him, while others go to and fro, revealing his word or doing his will upon earth" (Moore, 395) again owes something to the Bible, notably Isaiah 6, Ezekiel, and Psalms, but as filtered through the popular imagination of his time. This is even plainer in his conception of *Iblis* or *Shaitan*, obviously derived from the Hebrew Satan and the Greek *diabolos*, as an angel whose pride caused his fall and who is now a devil, an adversary, a tempter. Consider the passage in the second sura (34 ff.) where both terms make the first of their many appearances:

> Then we said to the angels: Prostrate yourselves before Adam, and they prostrated themselves, all except Iblis; he refused in his pride, for he was an unbeliever.
> Then we said to Adam: You and your wife shall dwell in the garden and eat freely in it as you wish; but do not approach this tree lest you become wrongdoers.
> But Satan led them astray . . .

The Jewish influence is as plain in some of Muhammad's commandments as it is in his theology. Consider sura 17:22 ff.:

> Place no other god beside Allah . . .
> And the Lord has decreed that you serve none but him, and treat your parents kindly if they become old with you, one or both; do not say Fie to them or scold them but speak to them with reverence. . . .
> Your Lord knows well what is in your hearts, whether you are righteous, and he forgives those who return.
> Give what is right to your kinsman and to the poor and the wanderer . . .
> Slay not your children, fearing poverty; we shall provide for them and you. Slaying them is a great sin.
> And shun fornication, for it is an abomination and a wicked way. . . .
> Do not touch what belongs to the orphan . . .
> Give full measure when you measure, and weigh with true scales . . .

Moreover, Muhammad, when still in Mecca, during the first period of his mission, commanded his followers to face toward Jerusalem when they prayed, and he adopted the highest holiday of the Jewish calendar, Yom Kippur, as a day of atonement and fasting. It is scarcely surprising that he expected the Jews to accept him as a prophet and to embrace his teaching. Even Luther expected the Jews to be converted by his version of Christianity, although he placed faith in Christ at the center of his teaching and firmly believed in the Trinity. If even Luther, who was such a learned man, could expect that, how much more Muhammad, whose early revelations were so much closer to Judaism!

Yet the Jews felt that they did not need an illiterate Arab prophet to present to them in Arabic as an altogether new series of revelations what God had revealed to them in their own language more than a thousand years earlier. They knew their own Bible well and were put off by all the things that struck them as misunderstandings and confusions. Muhammad, for example, seemed to mix up the stories of Moses, Esther, and the Tower of Babel by having Pharaoh ask Haman to build for him a tower so tall that he could climb up to the God of Moses (28:38).

When Muhammad came to Medina and found that the many well-to-do Jews there rejected his religion, his doctrines changed. Henceforth the *kibla*, the direction taken during prayer, was changed from Jerusalem to Mecca, the old Arab sanctuary that Muhammad hoped to conquer one day. (When he did conquer it, he smashed the idols but kept much of the old ritual.) The day of prayer was changed from the Jewish Sabbath to Friday. Yom Kippur ceased to be a holiday, and Ramadan, the month of fasting, was introduced. Of the Jewish dietary laws, he kept only a few, notably the prohibition against pork and blood. In the process Islam was transformed. In the Koran Jerusalem is never named expressly, but the change of the *kibla* is discussed in the second sura (142 ff.): "The fools among men will ask: What has turned them from the *kibla* they used to observe? Reply: To Allah belong east and west . . ." Formerly, Muhammad explained, he had wanted to see who followed him and who did not; for no Arab adopted the first *kibla* when he prayed, except his followers. But henceforth everyone should turn in the direction of Mecca. Tradition has it, and scholars agree, that the first *kibla* was to Jerusalem, the second to Mecca. At that point Islam began to appeal to Arab feelings and traditions. Instead of simply deriding the Arabs' old religion, the Prophet now could claim some continuity with it; it only needed to be purified. The relationship to Judaism and Christianity was undeniable; but the revelations granted to Muhammad surpassed those of all previous prophets, and Islam now claimed to supersede both Judaism and Christianity, as Christianity had claimed earlier that it superseded Judaism.

If all this seems reasonable enough and one recalls further that after his arrival in Medina Muhammad found work for his followers by raiding caravans and blockading Mecca, prompted in part by his desire for revenge against those who had not accepted his religion, it is hardly astonishing that Muhammad also attacked the Jews, dispossessed them, drove them from Medina, waged war against them elsewhere, killed large numbers of them, and—in the long run this proved even more unfortunate—said some very unkind things about them that became part of the Holy Scripture of Islam. Perhaps they had said some very unkind things about him first without foreseeing that his retorts would soon be accepted as divine revelation by people from Spain in the West to the borders of India in the East, and eventually even much further east than that. And when he killed Jews, that also was recorded in the Koran. If the giving of the Koran to Muhammad, bit by bit, was a miracle, it seems no less a miracle that although the Koran was accepted as divine revelation by the Muslims they did not treat the Jews far worse than they did.

As for the Christians, Muhammad's strict monotheism involved him in polemics against the Trinity and against any claim that Jesus was God or the son of God. Two interesting examples are found in the long sura "Women." (It will have been noted by now that the names of the suras give no adequate notion of their contents.)

> O people of the Scripture! Do not go too far in your religion, nor say anything about Allah save the truth. The messiah, Jesus, son of Mary, is only a messenger of Allah and his Word that he accomplished through Mary, and a spirit from him. Therefore believe in Allah and his messengers and do not say, Trinity. Cease for your own good! Allah is one God; he is too sublime to have a son. His is whatever is in the heavens and on the earth, and Allah is defense enough (171).

Earlier in the same sura, revealed in Medina, Muhammad denounces the Jews, saying that they had already asked Moses, "Let us see Allah plainly!" He accuses them of having been sinful ever since, down to their terrible slanders of Mary, the mother of Jesus.

> . . . they said: We have slain the messiah, Jesus son of Mary, the messenger of Allah. But they did not slay or crucify him, it merely appeared that way to them. Truly, those who dispute about this are in doubt about it; they have no knowledge but merely an opinion. Really, they did not slay him. But Allah raised him up to himself. Allah is powerful and wise (157 f.).

Here Muhammad accepts the view of Jesus known as docetism that was held by many Gnostics. In a sense he denies the Crucifixion, while he affirms the virgin birth. As in the case of Judaism, his ideas are by no means always biblical but reflect the views of his informants. And "recent research has conclusively proved that the main external influence . . . can be traced back to Syriac Christianity" (Gibb, 37). This was also a prime source for his anti-Jewish polemics, which are occasionally rather startling, as when he says: "The Jews say, Ezra [Usayr] is the son of Allah, and the Christians say, the messiah is the son of Allah . . ." (9:30). Here he would seem to be right about the Christians but incredibly misinformed about the Jews, who never accorded Ezra any unique status, much less the place that the Christians gave to Jesus.

For all his polemics against Jews and Christians, however, Muhammad did not place the "people of the Scripture" on the same plain with the idolaters. Indeed, while the immediately preceding verse in the Koran exhorts the faithful to fight against the Jews and Christians, it does not demand their extermination; they should be fought only "until they pay their tribute willingly, being humbled." In Gibb's succinct summary: "idolatry is not to be tolerated; Jews and Christians, on the other hand, are not to be molested provided they acknowledge the supremacy of the Muslim state and pay the stipulated tribute, a concession subsequently extended to Zoroastrians also" (1959, 180). The reasons for the inclusion of the Zoroastrians should become plain in the next section.

59

"Mohammed's definition of an infidel is one who calls the judgment-day a lie; to such he promises a convincing experience of it," says Moore (398 f.). Here are the Prophet's own words from sura 22:19–23:

> These two are opponents who dispute about their Lord. But for those who disbelieve there are garments of fire, and boiling fluid will be poured over their heads.
> What is in their bodies and their skin will melt.
> And there are iron rods for them.

> Whenever in their agony they wish to escape, they are brought back. Taste the torment of burning!
> But those who believe and do good works Allah will lead into gardens under which rivers are flowing; they will be adorned with bracelets of gold and with pearls, and their garments will be of silk.

Here we encounter the heritage of Zarathustra. There are two types, the good and the wicked, those who side with the Prophet and those who oppose him, and on the day of judgment two very different fates await them as the wicked are plunged into fire. The Muslims themselves recognized this kinship when they conquered Iran and came into contact with the Zoroastrians, but Muhammad got these ideas from Jews and Christians. The conception of hell was by then a commonplace in the Near East, but "many of the details about the process of the Judgement and . . . the . . . torments of Hell, as well as several of the special technical terms employed in the Koran, are closely paralleled in the writings of the Syriac Christian fathers and monks" (Gibb, 39). Muhammad's description of heaven as an oasis obviously owes something to his Arab background and his experience of the desert.

The dualism of believers and unbelievers, heaven and hell, is central in Muhammad's message. He predicated his whole appeal on the imminence of the day of judgment, and threats of hell punctuate his pronouncements.

> Fear the fire prepared for unbelievers; its fuel are men and stones.
> Proclaim glad tidings for those who believe and do good works that they will have gardens under which rivers are flowing, and whenever they are regaled with fruits from them they say: these are the same we had before, thus attesting to the similarity. They are also provided with immaculate women who stay with them eternally (2:24 f.).

> Truly, those who do not believe our verses we shall fry in the fire. Whenever their skins are done, we shall exchange them for fresh skins to make them taste the torture. Truly, Allah is all powerful and all wise.
> But those who believe and do good works we shall lead into gardens under which rivers are flowing, and they shall dwell there for ever and ever. They are also provided with immaculate women, and we shall offer them plentiful shade (4:56 f.).

> Whoever slays a believer on purpose, his reward is hell where he shall dwell eternally . . . (4:93).

That is the style of Medina. The next quotation comes from a sura (98) that some assign to Medina and others to Mecca, and the last lines definitely illustrate the Meccan style.

> Truly, the unbelievers among the people of the Scripture and the idolaters will dwell in the fire eternally. They are the worst of creatures.
> Those who believe and do good works are the best of creatures.
> Their reward with their Lord: the gardens of Eden underneath which rivers are flowing . . .
> Enter the gardens, you and your wives, to be glad! . . .
> Truly, the sinners are immortal in the torment of hell.
> It does not abate for them, there is no hope for them
>   (43:70, 74 f.).

The conception of hell is very much like that of Christianity, while the conception of heaven is obviously influenced by the region in which Muhammad lived. As it happens, the Prophet's teachings were accepted only where the promise of "plentiful shade" was appealing. But it required a world historical battle to stop the Muslims at the Pyrenees (Charles Martell, the grandfather of Charlemagne, defeated them between

Tours and Poitiers in 732); it took the power of the eastern Roman Empire to keep Islam out of eastern Europe; and after Constantinople had fallen to the Muslim Turks, it took many battles, some of them at the gates of Vienna, to keep them from conquering central and northern Europe.

If Muhammad's conception of heaven was rather un-Calvinistic not only in promising shade, Muhammad, like Calvin nine hundred years later, suggested that it was Allah who had granted belief and salvation to some while he abandoned others to unbelief and eternal torment. "The idea of predestination in the Koran is not derived from abstract reflections on the implications of God's sovereignty, but is the practical solution of a problem thrust upon Mohammed by his experience," says Moore (396), meaning that there seemed to be no other explanation for the fact that only a few people believed him while so many rejected his convincing revelations. That may be true, but the implicit contrast with Calvin should not be pushed too far. The theme of predestination was available to both in the New Testament and in post-Biblical Christianity, and neither of them had to invent it. Moreover, the Koran seems to waver between assertions of predestination and free will, leaving ample room for bitter controversies in later Islam.

Gibb has stressed the side of Muhammad that brings to mind Calvin:

> The fear of God's "wrath to come" dominated his thought throughout his later life. . . . The characteristic sign of the Believer is ever-present fear of God, and its opposite is "heedlessness" or "frivolity." This antithesis was never absent from Muhammad's mind, and it forms the recurrent motive of early Muslim asceticism, which in this certainly reflected the central element in his teaching. That God is the omnipotent master and man His creature who is ever in danger of incurring His wrath—this is the basis of all Muslim theology and ethics. Forgiveness is only to be obtained by the grace of God; man cannot win it for himself by merit; but to be worthy to attain it requires of man unrelenting self-control and the service of God by means of good works and especially by prayer and alms-giving (39).

One might add that gambling and drinking alcohol are strictly forbidden in the Koran. But the Prophet's attitude toward sex was deliberately un-Christian. Gibb refers to Muhammad's "often-quoted phrase 'No monkery in Islam'" (45), but what is even more important is that the Prophet so obviously did not consider sex sinful in any way. Still, not only adultery but also fornication he considered major sins. Here his legislation seems to favor those who can afford to have four wives and many slaves.

Slavery is condoned in the Koran, but it has often been pointed out that in Arabia in those days the slave was a member of the household and Muhammad did not know slavery in the form it took in the Roman Empire or, much later, on the plantations in the South of the United States of America. Nor did he know the slave trade in which Muslims became so prominent later on. Still, he did make a sharp distinction between the four wives a man was permitted and his slaves, with whom he could also sleep if he wished, there being no limit to those.

In the fourth sura Muhammad commanded kind treatment of parents, close relatives, orphans, the poor, and several other groups, including slaves (36), and he also ordained that "whoever has killed a believer without meaning to, must free a slave who is a believer besides paying the blood money to the family unless they remit it" (92). It would be difficult to improve on Moore's succinct formulation: "he accomplished notable reforms; unfortunately he gave the finality of revelation to their limitations" (400).

Given Muhammad's dualistic eschatology, which promises eternal bliss to those who are believers and—it should be noted—do good works, but eternal torment to unbelievers, regardless of their works, his attitude toward war is not surprising. Once again, the essentials are stated in the fourth sura:

> Let those fight for the way of Allah who exchange this life for the life to come. Whoever fights for the way of Allah and is killed or victorious will receive a glorious reward (74).

> Those who believe, fight for the way of Allah, but the unbelievers fight for the way of idols. So fight the minions of Satan . . . (76).

Passages about war and the slaying of all idolaters abound in the Koran, but it will suffice to cite sura 47:4–8:

> When you meet the unbelievers, smite them in the neck until you have laid them low, and then draw tight the fetters; then pardon or ransom until war sheds its burdens. So. If Allah wished he could avenge himself; but he prefers to test some of you by means of others. And those slain for the way of Allah, he will not let their work wane.
> He will guide them and improve them,
> And lead them into the garden he promised them.
> O believers, when you help Allah he helps you and makes firm your stand.
> But for the unbelievers, perdition . . .

Camel market, Luxor, Egypt. The paintings record the owner's *hajj*.

VII

ISLAM AFTER MUHAMMAD

The Conquests of the First Century—The Shia and Islamic Philosophy—Sufism—The Five Pillars of Faith—Color and Slavery—The Turks and the Mongols, the Mogul and the Ottoman Empires—The New States Since 1917—Machismo

Tangiers, Morocco.

Muhammad died in 632 and was buried in Medina. Abu Bakr, his intimate friend for many years and one of his fathers-in-law, assumed the title of *khalifa*, which means "deputy" (of Muhammad) and is generally rendered as caliph in European languages. At first, most of the Arabian tribes did not recognize his authority and fell away. Within a year, however, Abu Bakr was master of Arabia, and when he died an Arab army was on its way to conquer Syria. As his successor he appointed Omar, who ruled for ten years before he was murdered in 644. Omar's ten-year reign was marked by spectacular conquests. His armies defeated the forces of both the Byzantine and the Sassanian empires; they conquered Damascus and, almost bloodlessly, Jerusalem (in 638), and then the

10 whole of Palestine (Caesarea held out until 640). Iraq, Iran, and Egypt were conquered soon after.

It has often been claimed that the Muslims burned the magnificent library in Alexandria with its irreplaceable collection of ancient manuscripts because their leader reasoned that if these manuscripts said what was also in the Koran they were superfluous, and if they did not they were heretical, but this is a Christian myth of which no trace can be found before the thirteenth century. When the Muslims conquered Egypt, the great library was no longer in existence.

In their expansion, the Arabs were unquestionably unified and inspired by their new faith, which gave them a sense of pride and mission. They were helped by the deep dissatisfaction of the people whom they conquered with the empires to which they belonged. The Byzantine Empire was resented both in Asia and in Egypt, and the Persian Empire was very unpopular as well. But the victories that made the conquests possible in the first place were military and must be charged to superior generals as well as high morale.

Omar was assassinated and succeeded by Othman (644–656). Historians rank him far below his predecessors. When the eastern Roman Empire retook Alexandria, using its navy, in 645, the Muslims reconquered it the following year, and Othman not only managed to hold on to his empire but began the conquest of North Africa. But his nepotism made him many enemies, and finally he, too, was assassinated.

His successor was Ali, Muhammad's cousin and son-in-law, who had been passed over three times. His five-year reign was marked by internal dissension. He was widely held responsible for the murder of Othman. He left Medina, which had been the capital until 656, and made Kufa, a great garrison town in Iraq, his capital. But Muawiya, who had been appointed governor of Syria by Omar, and confirmed in that position by Othman, his relative, disputed Ali's authority. There was a battle, there were attempts at arbitration, and in the course of these disputes the Kharijites, a group of extremists, revolted against Ali. Even before one of them succeeded in assassinating Ali, in 661, Muawiya had managed to seize control of Egypt and to raid Iraq (Mesopotamia) at will. Upon Ali's death, he became caliph and founded the Omayyad dynasty that remained in power until 750. Later Arab historians denied the title of caliph to the rulers of this dynasty, except for Omar II (717–720), and called them kings. Whatever their title, their accomplishments are imposing. Abd al-Malik (685–705) built the Dome of the

Rock in Jerusalem, also known as the Mosque of Omar, which is not only the oldest 20,22
surviving mosque in the world but also one of the most beautiful buildings of all time.
His successor, Walid I, built the Great Mosque of Damascus and the original Al Aqsa 23
mosque in Jerusalem. It was also during the reign of Walid that Spain was conquered
by the Muslims (711–715).

When Muhammad appeared on the scene, the Arabs had not really entered history.
They lived on the margins of the civilized world, mainly in the desert of Arabia, and had
no especially remarkable art or religion of their own. Within a hundred years of his
death, they were the masters of an empire comparable to the Roman Empire before its
division, and they brought to it a religion comparable to Christianity and sponsored an
architecture whose perfection has rarely been equaled and never excelled. This was not
by any means a case of barbarians bursting into lands with higher cultures and destroying priceless treasures, leaving a wake of ruins behind them, like the Huns and various
Germanic tribes and, much later, the Mongols. The Arabs proved more tolerant than the
empires they displaced, Christian as well as Zoroastrian, and at a time when the art of
these empires was for the most part epigonic, imitative, unoriginal, the Muslims introduced a new style. One may search far and wide for any real parallel; the only one that
seems at all close is the advent of the Persian Empire in the sixth century B.C., about
twelve hundred years earlier.

The similarities are considerable, and the ruins of Persepolis still stand as a monu- 33
ment of the sudden emergence of a new religion, a new culture, a new pride, and great
originality. But the Persian Empire lasted a mere two hundred years; then Alexander
conquered it. The second Persian Empire withstood the expansion of Rome and retained its independence until the Muslims conquered it, but it never recaptured the
dynamism of the first. And the usual view is that the legacy of ancient Iran comes to
little more than some imposing ruins and a small community of Parsees in and near
Bombay. Actually, the Persian legacy looms large in the New Testament and the Koran,
and the rapid spread of Islam not only brings to mind the conquests that followed upon
the appearance of Zarathustra, but it also spread some of the Persian prophet's most
characteristic ideas wherever it reached.

After 750, when the Omayyad dynasty was followed by the Abbasid caliphate, which
lasted over five hundred years, until 1258, the Muslim empire ceased more and more to
be Arab; the two great cultural centers were Spain, where the Omayyads continued in
power and eventually, in the tenth century, insisted that they, and not the Abbasids,
were the true caliphs, and Persia. Mansur, the second of the Abbasid caliphs, chose for
his capital a new city, Baghdad, built on the site of a Persian village. This was in Mesopotamia, on the west bank of the Tigris, but close to the ruins of Ctesiphon, the old
capital of the Sassanian dynasty of Persia. And the new Baghdad, whose Muslim name
was Madinat as-Salam, was actually built with the stones of the old Persian capital. Not
only did Baghdad become world famous as the capital of Islam, but it was in Persia that
Islamic art developed in new ways. It was here that some of the most beautiful mosques 35–39
were built in a distinctive new style; that a new kind of painting was created, as well as
pottery and rugs; and when the Muslims finally pushed into India, it was in the Persian
style that they built in northern India, not in the older Arab style.

61

Persia also became the center of the Shia, by far the most important dissident sect
in Islam, and of Sufism, the very influential mystical movement in Islam. The great
majority of Muslims, estimated at perhaps 85 percent, are Sunnites, while about fourteen

percent are Shiites. The latter include the Persians and some of the people in adjacent Iraq. No brief definition of the difference between these two major denominations of Islam can give an adequate idea of the differences. As Nietzsche once said in another context, in his *Genealogy of Morals* (II:13), "only that which has no history is definable." And the Shia has a very long and intricate history and, like Sufism, was not born in Iran.

Two distinctive ideas might be considered the defining characteristics of the Shia, but they are mutually contradictory. The first provided the occasion for the schism and constitutes an abiding difference between Sunnites and Shiites. The latter considered Ali the rightful successor of Muhammad, and after Ali his sons, who were the grandsons of the Prophet—and, like Ali, were assassinated. The Shiites claimed that Ali had been designated caliph by Muhammad himself, although the Koran does not say so, and that the succession must remain in the family. "To this day it is the mark of orthodoxy among the great body of the followers of Ali (Shia) to curse Abu Bekr, Omar, and Othman, in the public prayers in their mosques" (Moore, 432); for the Shiites did not consider the Omayyad dynasty legitimate. For the majority of Muslims, an imam (leader) is simply the man who leads the others in prayer on Friday or a religious teacher. For the Shiites, the imam is the true deputy of the Prophet, and they developed the notion of the hidden imam, who is not recognized by his contemporaries, as well as the concept of the Mahdi, the imam who will return one day as a messiah to restore the caliphate to its true nature. Meanwhile, many an imam was recognized, and it came to be believed that the imam was an infallible authority, free of sin; some even claimed that he was Allah incarnate.

The other idea that is sometimes said to define the Shia is quite incompatible with all of this unless it is stated more carefully than is often the case. It is said that the Shiites reject the oral tradition, as if they, unlike the Sunnites, took their stand exclusively on the Koran. But Sunna does not mean oral tradition; it means "way," "custom," or "tradition," and what the Shiites reject is obviously some of the customs and traditions of the Sunnites, though by no means all of them. They are not by any means obviously closer to the teachings of the Koran. In the years after the Prophet's death there had developed the custom of deciding many questions by consensus. It was through a consensus of those most immediately concerned—using a modern term, one might call them the power elite—that it was determined Abu Bakr should succeed the Prophet, and then Omar, then Othman, and only then Ali; and after him, Muawiya. The Shiites rejected the concept of consensus and were more authoritarian. No doubt, a great many different factors contributed to the schism, including regional jealousies. Thus some South Arabians were among those who would not recognize Muawiya and his successors in Damascus. But it has often been remarked that one of the central motifs of the Shia was furnished by the ancient Persian notion of a hereditary monarchy.

The Omayyads tolerated the Shiites although the Shiites considered them illegitimate. "This toleration, however, soon disappeared under the Abbasids when the Shia had helped wrest the caliphate from the Umayyads in 750. One hundred years later in 850 the caliph al-Mutawakkil became particularly harsh with the Shia, destroying their venerated shrines" (Farah, 176). Thus the very dynasty that resided in Baghdad, which was built with the stones of the old Iranian capital, and which relished the splendor of a court that brought to mind the ancient emperors of Iran, turned upon the dissidents who, also under Persian influence, claimed that their own imams had divine authority. In response, the Shiites had recourse to dissimulation (*taqiyah*), pretending to believe what they did not believe.

The most prominent sect among the Shiites are the Twelvers. Of the early Shiite imams four had died of poison, while most of the others had either been killed in war or executed for sedition.

> The twelfth . . . simply disappeared in 878 in the cave of the great mosque at Samarra without leaving any heir. Hence he has become known as the *Muntazar* (awaited) Imam whose return will usher in the golden era of true Islam shortly before the end of this world. Thus the messianic concept so dear to Christianity finds an equivalent of a sort among the Persians of today, as it had with their spiritual predecessors of yesteryears like the Zoroastrians and related sectarians. . . . The Twelvers' variety of Shiism was formally and forcibly imposed on a then predominantly Sunni Persia by the early Safawid Shahs in the year 1502. These Shahs subsequently claimed themselves to be descendants of the seventh Imam (Farah, 177).

Meanwhile the Sunnite caliphate continued until it was formally abolished by Kemal Atatürk, the first president of modern Turkey, in 1924. By then the leadership of the Muslim world had long passed from the Arabs, first to the Persians and then to the Turks.

The great Saladin, who conquered Jerusalem in the twelfth century and, instead of imitating the bloodbath of the Crusaders not quite a hundred years earlier, gave them a lesson in generosity, was a Kurd, from Mesopotamia. Suleiman the Magnificent, who surrounded the old city of Jerusalem with the great wall that still stands, was a Turkish sultan, and his empire reached far into Europe, although his siege of Vienna in 1529 proved unsuccessful. The pressure he brought to bear upon the German emperors may have facilitated the religious secession of the German princes who supported Luther.

In philosophy the Arabs played an important part, but so did the Persians and the Jews. In the age of Muhammad there had not been much Arabic literature, not to speak of philosophy, but early in the ninth century one of the caliphs founded a "house of wisdom" that was above all a center for translations of Greek philosophy and science. Generally, Syriac versions were used instead of the original Greek texts, and almost all of the translators were Christian Arabs, but within a century they created philosophic Arabic. The first extremely important Muslim philosopher was Avicenna (980–1037), a Persian from Bokhara who wrote a few books in Persian and many more in Arabic. He drew on Plato and Aristotle, the Stoics and the Neoplatonists in developing a system of his own. Later philosophers writing in Arabic included Avicebron (really Yudah ibn Gabirol, in the eleventh century) and Maimonides (in the twelfth), both of them Jews. The most important Arabic philosopher was Averroës, born in Cordova like Maimonides and his contemporary. He considered Aristotle the philosopher par excellence (as St. Thomas did after him, under his influence) and wrote commentaries on his works. He wrote in Arabic but was considered highly unorthodox, and most of his writings survive only in Hebrew and Latin translations. These men and others like them laid the foundations for Christian scholasticism and, if only indirectly, for Descartes and Spinoza; and it was partly through the Muslim world that medieval Europe rediscovered Greek philosophy.

62

Meanwhile Islam became less and less homogenous, both politically and religiously. Among the religious developments the most noteworthy is Sufism, which developed in the ninth century. By then asceticism had gained many adherents among Muslims. In many regions there were people who were terrified by the prospect of eternal damnation.

Some were influenced by the monastic tradition in Christianity but also by many other traditions, including not only Gnosticism and Zoroastrianism but also Buddhism. Although some scholars have wondered whether the origin of the name "Sufism" is to be found in the Greek word for wisdom, *sophia*, there is wide agreement that the term comes from *suf*, "wool," and originally referred to the undyed wool used for monastic garments.

Sufism was not founded by any one person, but one of the important figures in its development was al-Hallaj who composed a hymn to Muhammad that illustrates this syncretism: "All the Lights of the Prophets proceeded from his Light; he was before all, his name the first in the Book of Fate; he was known before all things and all being, and will endure after the end of all. . . . All knowledge is a drop from his ocean, all wisdom a handful from his stream, all times an hour from his life" (Gibb, 102). He was executed in 922 for proclaiming in Baghdad, "I am the Truth"—*ana al-haqq*. This was a quotation from the Gospel according to John, but it was a far cry from the Koran.

Actually, the martyr's meaning may have been closer to the Upanishads and Indian thought than to John's Jesus. What Sufism suggests is not that al-Hallaj was God become man but rather that each of us is God, who is One, and that we can even now try to experience this unity. The mystical union of the soul with God was called *fana*, and al-Hallaj said of it:

> I am He whom I love, and He whom I love is I.
> We are two spirits dwelling in one body.
> When you see me you see Him,
> And when you see Him, you see us both.*

This emphasis on love is characteristic of Sufism but did not by any means begin with al-Hallaj, any more than it ended with him. Sufism has been characterized as a revolt against intellectualism and legalism, which had become prominent in Islam, but it certainly was not a return to the Koran. On the contrary, it was even much more eclectic than early Islam had been and proved immensely hospitable to all kinds of foreign ideas.

Gibb has pointed out that while "true Koranic asceticism condemned celibacy: 'Ye that are unmarried shall marry' . . . Koran (xxiv:32)," and virtually all the early Sufis in the tenth century were married, two hundred years later one of the most important Sufis wrote: "It is the unanimous opinion of the leaders of this doctrine that the best and most distinguished Sufis are the unmarried, if their hearts are unstained and their minds free from sin and lust" (106). What is even more striking is that "in the teeth of the Koran, tradition, rationalism, and orthodox theology (which regarded the invocation of saints as trespassing into polytheism by derogating from the worship of God alone) the worship of saints crept into the Islamic fold and eventually swept everything before it" (107).

The man who has been given credit above all others for the fact that Sufism gained a central place in Islam is al-Ghazali (1058–1111). He was a Persian but wrote most of his works in Arabic. Gibb has called him "a man who stands on a level with Augustine and Luther in religious insight and intellectual vigour" (108), while conceding that "through the breach which he made there would rush in a full tide of popular religious practice and heterodox intellectual conceptions by which his ideals would be debased . . . Sufism swept over the whole body of Islam . . . it became an almost hopeless task for the theologians to attempt to stem the popular tide" (110 f.).

---

* Quoted from Nicholson, *Mystics of Islam*, 151, by both Moore, 448, and Farah, 211. I have changed "thou" to "you."

The most celebrated Persian poets from Omar Khayyam (around 1100) to Jalal-al-Din al-Rumi and Sadi (both thirteenth century), Hafiz (fourteenth), and Jami (fifteenth) were all Sufis. The poems of Hafiz, however, invite more literal readings as celebrations of earthly love and wine. Goethe, like many Western scholars after him, read Hafiz that way and paid lavish tribute to him in poems of his own. Indeed, his discovery of Hafiz prompted Goethe to publish a collection of poems under the title *West-Eastern Divan* (1819). Although Goethe was then seventy, the poems were so splendid and his enthusiasm so contagious that his *Divan* triggered a great deal of German interest in Oriental poetry. Friedrich Rückert (1788–1866) gained the greatest reputation as a virtuoso translator of verse; he also became a professor of Oriental philology, and one of his students, Max Müller, who became a professor at Oxford, not only published splendid English versions of the major Upanishads and the Dhammapada but also edited *The Sacred Books of the East*, in fifty volumes—one of the greatest monuments of nineteenth-century scholarship. To return to Hafiz and Sadi: both were born and buried in Shiraz, where their tombs are still to be seen—roughly forty miles from Persepolis.

Islam makes much more of tombs than Judaism, though much less than Christianity, and to anyone who knows the biblical account of Moses' death—God buried him east of the Jordan, and "no man knows the place" (Deuteronomy 34:6)—it comes as a shock that the Muslims venerate his tomb, in the Judean desert west of the Jordan. The Hebrew Bible also relates that Elijah ascended to heaven in a storm, but the Muslims revere his tomb near the Golan. And they venerate "Abel's tomb" outside Damascus.

No other Asian country left as deep an imprint on Islam as did Iran, but regional traditions entered into Islam wherever it spread. Writing as an anthropologist, Clifford Geertz has shown vividly in his short and elegant book, *Islam Observed: Religious Development in Morocco and Indonesia* (1968), how Islam in these two countries is scarcely the same religion. It sometimes seems like a veneer over ancient local cults. As he puts it, writing about Indonesia: "The peasantry absorbed Islamic concepts and practices, so far as it understood them, into the same general Southeast Asian folk religion into which it had previously absorbed Indian ones, locking ghosts, gods, jinns, and prophets together into a strikingly contemplative . . . animism" (13).

Geertz himself suggests that the same observation applies to the spread of Hinduism and Buddhism, and it would be wholly in the spirit of his inquiry to ask whether it does not also apply to the peasantry of southern Italy or Ireland. And when at the end of his book he gives us the image of a highly educated French-speaking Moroccan student, flying to New York to study at an American university, frightened by the flight and the new life that awaits him, passing "the entire trip with the Koran gripped in one hand and a glass of scotch in the other," it seems easy to transpose the image into Buddhism, Christianity, or another religion. The religions that were adopted by the most people paid the highest price.

63

Are there nevertheless ideas and practices shared by Muslims everywhere? Of course, there are. First of all, the *shahada* or profession of faith: *la ilaha illa'llah muhammadun rasulu'llah*, which Gibb renders, "There is but one God, Mohammed is the Apostle of God" (48). He goes on to point out that this *shahada* is not to be found in the Koran in this form, although the two halves of it are. He adds that verse 136 of sura 4, to which we have had occasion to turn again and again, is often taken by Muslims as a short *credo*: "O believers, believe in Allah and his messenger and the scripture that he revealed to his messenger and the scripture he revealed earlier. Whoever disbelieves in Allah and his angels and his scriptures and his messengers and the Last Day, has gone far astray."

Muslims the world over share an allegiance to the Koran. To be sure, many Muslims drink alcohol in flat defiance of the Koran or worship saints, but Jews, Christians, and Buddhists are in no position to be astonished at that; and the common allegiance to the Koran unquestionably establishes a strong bond.

Unlike Jews, Christians, and Buddhists, the Muslims were convinced that their holy scripture must not be translated into other tongues. Wherever they brought the Koran, it was written and recited in Arabic. Thus the language established a further bond even if large numbers of Muslims did not understand it. Here the difference between the Muslims of North Africa and those of central Asia and Indonesia is considerable, and Geertz points out that in Indonesia Arabic was "a very foreign language" that, even among the religious scholars, "probably not one person in a hundred ever really mastered." Nevertheless the Koran was chanted in Arabic, with thick regional accents, and students "gained what understanding of the texts they might from vernacular summaries and annotations dictated by teachers whose grasp of the original was in most cases not much greater than their own" (70). Still, the book and the sacred language established a shared loyalty.

Then there are the five daily prayers, at dawn, at noon, midafternoon, after sunset, and in the early part of the night, each of which "consists of a fixed number of 'bowings' (called *rak'ah*), the 'bowing' itself consisting of seven movements with their appropriate recitations," the two most striking of the seven being two prostrations with the face to the ground. The morning prayer consists of two *rakahs*, the evening prayer of three, and the other three of four each. "Although neither the ceremonies nor the five set times of prayer are precisely stated in the Koran, it is certain that they were well established before Mohammed's death" (Gibb, 54 f.). Such an essentially simple ritual constitutes a powerful bond.

Another very striking ritual is the fasting during the month of Ramadan, the ninth month of the lunar year. During this month, which in the Muslim calendar does not always come in the same season but moves around, one is not supposed to have any food or drink during daylight. Fortunately, the Muslims never conquered those regions where the midnight sun shines.

A third ritual is the *Hajj*, the pilgrimage to the Kaaba in Mecca. Here Islam modified, slightly, the ancient ritual of the idolaters who worshiped at the Kaaba long before the Prophet's birth.

> The traditional ceremonies of going in circuit around the Kaaba, running between the two small eminences of Safa and Marwa in the vicinity, assembling on the ninth day of the [twelfth] month at the hill of Arafat (some twelve miles east of Mecca), offering sacrifices of sheep and camels at Mina on the way back to Mecca—all these were retained and prescribed in the Koran. Other traditional usages, including the kissing of the Black Stone set in one of the walls of the Kaaba, and the stoning of the pillars representing the Devil in the vicinity of Mina, though not mentioned explicitly, were observed by Mohammed in his pilgrimages, and so were incorporated into the Muslim rite. . . . Although the Pilgrimage constitutes a religious obligation on every Muslim, the obligation is explicitly limited by possession of the necessary means . . . (Gibb, 57).

Thus a Muslim living not too far from Mecca might make the pilgrimage annually, while those living further away might hope to make it at least once in their lives, and the peasants of Java not at all.

The Five Pillars of the Faith are the *shahada,* or profession of faith, the daily prayers, the giving of alms, the fasting during Ramadan, and the *Hajj.* What is meant by the giving of alms is really not that, although voluntary giving is also meritorious, but a poor tax "of one-fortieth of the annual revenue in money or kind. It is to be exacted from all who, whether voluntarily or under constraint, enter into the brotherhood of Islam; but it is not a tax. Rather it is to be regarded as a loan made to God, which He will repay many-fold" (Gibb, 56).

It would be absurd to claim that these five pillars, no more and no less, are what all Muslims have in common, just as it would be absurd to lay down similar criteria for Judaism or Christianity. One could add many other points, such as circumcision, which is not mentioned in the Koran, and the prohibition of eating pork, which is, and something will also have to be said about mosques. The point here is mainly to suggest that despite the immense differences between Muslims in different parts of the world it should not be supposed that they have nothing in common but the name of their religion.

64

Islam has often been presented as singularly egalitarian and color blind; yet the Muslims had quite a reputation, not so long ago, as slave traders. The Koran neither inculcates contempt for those whose skin color is dark nor condemns slavery. In both respects it does not greatly differ from the Bible. The question is what happened after the Prophet's death when Islam spread to many different countries and was adopted by people of different races.

The practice of slavery continued, as it did in the Christian world, and color prejudice persisted. Bernard Lewis's well-documented and beautifully written *Race and Color in Islam* shows how common color prejudices have been not only among the rank and file but also among the leading figures. What may come as a surprise to many readers is the notion expressed succinctly by one writer in the ninth century: "If the country is cold, they are undercooked in the womb; if the country is hot they are burnt in the womb" (33). In other words, deviation from the norm with which one was familiar was considered abnormal, and contempt was expressed not only for those who, in the words of a tenth-century writer, are "overdone in the womb until they are burnt, so that the child comes out something between black and murky, malodorous, stinking, woolly-haired, with uneven limbs, deficient mind and depraved passions, such as the Zanj, the Ethiopians, and other blacks who resemble them," but also for those who have "blond, buff, blanched and leprous coloring, such as the infants dropped from the wombs of the women of the Slavs and others of similar light complexion" (34).

These estimates were reflected by—or rather were reflections of—the practice of white as well as black slavery. Yet

> White slaves were rarely used for rough labor, and filled higher positions in domestic and administrative employment. Both blacks and whites were used as eunuchs, but the blacks soon predominated. . . . An Arabic description of the court of the caliph in Baghdad at the beginning of the tenth century speaks of 7,000 black and 4,000 white eunuchs. Later white eunuchs became rare and costly (68).

Military slaves were employed in even far larger numbers.

As in Christendom, these matters did not change drastically until very recently, and what brought about the changes was not religion but the pressures of secular liberalism.

The importation of black slaves into the central Islamic lands began at the time of the conquest and has continued without interruption to the present century. . . . With the Russian annexation of the Caucasian lands (*ca.* 1801–1828) the main source of supply of white slaves for the Islamic world was stopped. Deprived of their Georgians and Circassians, the Muslim states turned elsewhere, and a large-scale revival of slaving in black Africa took place

through Egypt, Morocco, and Tunisia, "and across the Red Sea and Indian Ocean to Arabia, Iraq, Persia and beyond" (81).

Lewis quotes long nineteenth-century descriptions of Muslim harems and cites a book of 1802 that relates how "between 100 and 200 African boys were castrated every year at Abu Tig in Upper Egypt, on the slave caravan route from the Sudan to Cairo." A eunuch fetched double the price of an ordinary male slave. Twelve years later a Swiss traveler found two other places in upper Egypt where blacks were castrated before being sold. At the lesser place, many of the eunuchs were "sent as presents by the Negro sovereigns to the great mosques at Mekka and Medina"; at the main center, which was in a predominantly Christian village, "the operators . . . were two Coptic monks" whose profession was "held in contempt even by the vilest Egyptians." Theirs was "the great *manufactory* which supplies . . . Turkey with these guardians of female virtue" (85).

Two final quotations: "Apart from commercial channels, the supply [of slaves] was augmented through the practice by which a wealthy pilgrim brought a retinue of slaves from his own country and sold them one by one—as a kind of travelers' checks— to pay the expenses of his pilgrimage" (88). And why did the blacks not leave more of a trace in the non-black world? Not only because so many of the black males had been castrated but also because the mortality rate was so high. In Tunisia around 1810 hardly any black children reached adulthood, and in Egypt, in the middle of the nineteenth century, a British observer reported that "five or six years are sufficient to carry off a whole generation of slaves, at the end of which time the whole has to be replenished" (89).

65

It may seem odd that Islam should ever have been considered egalitarian, but then many people have also associated Christianity with democracy. It remains true that before the twentieth century Islam was strikingly international, and it is only in our time that it brings to mind Arab nationalism. For the last thousand years it was not specifically Arabic, although the Koran, which was not translated, was written in that language, and many medieval philosophers, including Persians and Jews, wrote some of their most important works in Arabic. Similarly, Christian scholastics in the Middle Ages wrote in Latin, whether they were Italian, German, French, or Scottish.

The cultural leadership of the Persians has already been mentioned. In the course of the ninth century, the caliphs at Baghdad relied more and more on an army composed of Turkish slaves and mercenaries, and gradually the caliphs became mere puppets of the Turks. During the next century, a Persian local dynasty, the Buwayhids, gained power and, as secular "sultans," continued to use the caliphs as figureheads.

By the eleventh century the Turks were entering the world of Islam, not only as individuals recruited by capture or purchase, but by the migration of whole tribes of free nomadic Turks . . . The consolidation of the Sung regime in China after an interregnum of disorder cut off the route of expansion into China

and forced the Central Asian nomads to expand westwards. These Turkish invaders of Islam . . . are usually known as Seljuqs, after the name of the military
family that led them (Lewis, 1950, 147).

They accepted Islam, conquered most of Persia, and in 1055 conquered Baghdad. They
took Jerusalem in 1072, but the Fatimids of Egypt ousted them, and it was from the
latter that the Crusaders wrested the holy city in 1099. As mentioned earlier, Saladin,
who ousted the Crusaders from Jerusalem, was not an Arab either but a Kurd. Meanwhile, the Turks conquered large parts of Anatolia from the Byzantine Empire, lands
that no Muslim had been able to take previously, and Anatolia is still Turkish.

Early in the thirteenth century, during the "crowded and magnificent pontificate"
of Innocent III, at the time of the Children's Crusade and the Albigensian Crusades,
Jenghiz Khan united some of the nomadic Mongols of eastern Asia and conquered an
empire larger than any the world had ever seen. He entered Persia in 1221 but died
six years later. His successors got as far as Silesia, where they defeated the armies that
tried to stop them at Wahlstatt, in 1241—but then, instead of uniting Europe, they withdrew. Their empire included China and Korea, large parts of Indochina but not Thailand or Angkor, Tibet but not India, almost all of Siberia and Russia, Iran and Iraq.
They also invaded Anatolia, but in 1260 the Mamluks defeated them in a major battle
near Ain Harod in the valley of Jezreel, where Gideon, one of the judges of Israel, had
assembled his forces to fight the Midianites in the eleventh century B.C. A few years
later Kublai Khan defeated the Sung dynasty in China and established the rule of his
own Mongol Yüan dynasty, which ruled China until 1368, when it was succeeded by
the Ming dynasty. It is arguable that of all the dynasties of China only the Sung produced finer paintings than the Yüan. The Mongol dynasty also distinguished itself by
building roads and canals, establishing a fine postal system, and facilitating communica-
tions and trade with the West. Gunpowder and printing are said to have been introduced
to Europe from China during this period, and it was also under the Mongol dynasty
that Marco Polo visited China.

A Christian scholar writing about Eastern Christendom has remarked that "The
Mongol Empire which spread from the China Sea to the Black Sea . . . offered a
unique opportunity for Christians to convert Asia to their religion." And he has sought
"some explanation" for the Mongols' "ultimate conversion to Islam" (Zernov, 124 ff.).
Actually, by no means did all of them become Muslims; and by the time some of them
did, the vast empire had broken up. But Zernov has argued that Eastern Christianity
demanded too much:

> Conversion to the Russian Church would have meant giving up their national
> customs. . . . The Russians were intensely ritualistic; they observed the Old
> Testament distinction between clean and unclean food, and the Mongol habit
> of eating any kind of meat . . . revolted them. They treated the Tatars as im-
> pure . . . Islam was more accommodating. Its simple rules of faith and conduct
> . . . impressed the Mongols,

who retained their own tribal ways. The conversion of the Mongols "closed Asia to
Christianity for many centuries to come. . . . Tamerlane (1363–1405), the last great
military leader of the Mongols, was a fanatical Moslem, and in his devastating march
across Asia he virtually exterminated Christianity." Some scholars believe that he may
have killed 80,000 people in Delhi alone after capturing it, and they believe the story
that he built pyramids of the skulls of his victims. They add, however, as Zernov does
not, that he was no less brutal with fellow Muslims.

When trying to explain the spread of Islam in the seventh and eighth centuries,
Zernov claims similarly that "The chief attraction of Islam was that," unlike Chris-

tianity, "it did not demand seemingly superhuman efforts"; and he makes much of
Christian ascetics and of monasticism. One may wonder about some of Zernov's
alleged facts, notably his claim that Islam "drastically lowered the cultural, social and
artistic life of the Eastern nations whose passionate intellectual curiosity and all-
absorbing preoccupation with theological speculations were arrested by the acceptance
of final truth as proclaimed in the *Koran*" (83 f.). After all, the cessation of the Christian disputes about the one or two natures of the Son, his relation to the Father, and
the question whether the Holy Ghost issued from both or not, may not really have been
such a devastating loss, and the two great mosques built in Jerusalem around A.D. 700
scarcely suggest a drastic lowering of artistic standards. If there is nevertheless a grain
of truth in Zernov's rather emotional explanations and the success of Islam was indeed
furthered by its initial simplicity and its less strenuous demands, it is surely striking
that the same considerations apply much more clearly to the way in which the spread
of Christianity far outstripped that of Judaism a few centuries earlier; and there is
hardly any denying that the rapid spread of Christianity, at least in the Western
empire, was accompanied by a very drastic lowering of the artistic and cultural life.
Obviously, a religion that does not demand much while basking in the reflected glory of
a few exemplars who have made incredible demands of themselves will always be more
appealing to large masses of people than a religion that requires much of every convert.
But the triumphs of Christianity and Islam, as well as their defeats, also owed much to
the luck of battle, to some brilliant generals, and to simple accidents.

When the Mongols appeared in the Near East, the Muslim empire had long
ceased to be one, and the Arabs were no longer a great power. It was not only in Iran
that the Turks had become more important; in the middle of the thirteenth century
the Mamluks, originally Turkish military slaves, became the rulers of Egypt, and their
sultans ruled effectively in that whole part of the world from 1250 until 1517, when the
Ottoman Turks replaced them for another four hundred years. Earlier, the Ottoman
Turks had conquered Constantinople and put an end to the Eastern, or Byzantine,
empire in 1453. When the Ottoman empire was split up after World War I, along
with the Austro-Hungarian, Russian, and German empires, there had not been an
Arab state anywhere for almost a thousand years.

Whether it was Mongols or Turks who conquered northern India and converted
the population to Islam is still disputed. The first Muslim kingdom in India was the
Delhi sultanate, established in the twelfth century, but there is some doubt about the
ethnic identity of the invaders. Baber, however, the founder of the so-called Mogul
empire in India, was a descendant of Jenghiz Khan and Tamerlane. He conquered Kabul
41–45   and established a kingdom in Afghanistan in 1504, captured Delhi and Agra in 1525,
and eventually ruled over most of northern India. He was succeeded by his son Humayun, who preferred the arts to war. After a grave military defeat in 1540, at the hands
of Sher Khan, Humayun found asylum in Iran. After the death of Sher Khan's son,
Humayun invaded India with Persian support and regained his empire.

His son, Akbar (1542–1605), succeeded him in 1556. Akbar greatly enlarged the
empire until it included most of northern and central India, down to the Godavari
River, as well as Afghanistan and Baluchistan. Although illiterate himself, he made
Delhi, Agra, and Fatehpur Sikri great centers of arts and letters. He loved Persian
culture and eventually proclaimed a new, highly eclectic creed that fused elements of
Islam with ideas taken from Hinduism, Zoroastrianism, and Christianity. He was not
only interested in many religions but also tolerant. The Muslims, however, did not like
his new religion, and it disappeared soon after his death. His son Jahangir also cultivated
the arts, notably including miniature painting; and Jahangir's son Shah Jehan built the
Taj Mahal in Agra as a memorial for his favorite wife, who had died in 1629. Com-

pleted in 1648, it is generally considered one of the most beautiful buildings in the world. The architect was a Turk, and the calligrapher who designed the inscriptions a Persian.

By that time there were already some English factories on the east coast of India, and in 1640 the British had acquired Madras. During the reign of Aurangzeb, the son of Shah Jehan, the British crown acquired Bombay, in 1661. "Half a century after the death of Aurangzeb, when rich Bengal was acquired, nothing, not even an Act of Parliament, could stop the masters of the sea and the Gangenetic valley from becoming the rulers of India" (Spear, 335).

66

When the Ottoman empire was broken up after World War I, Iraq, Transjordan, and Palestine were assigned to the British as mandates, to be administered under the League of Nations, while Syria and Lebanon became French mandates. By then the British empire was far larger than any previous empire had ever been. Egypt became independent in 1922, at first only nominally; Iraq ten years later; and Syria and Lebanon after the defeat of France in World War II. Meanwhile Ibn-Saud had succeeded in uniting under his rule the whole Arabian peninsula, except for Yemen, the Aden Protectorate, and Oman—all in the far south. "It was the first time after the rise of Islam that such an extensive area had been organized into one state," says Hitti in *The Near East in History* (466); and his reputation as perhaps the greatest modern Arab historian leads one to ask what he might have meant, seeing that the claim would be so obviously wrong even if he had said, "into one Muslim state." As Hitti's own map of the Ottoman empire shows, that had been far larger. Presumably he meant "one Arab state," and, of course, not "after the rise of Islam" but rather "since the decline of Arab power, more than a thousand years ago." And here, after all that time, was not only one huge Arab state, Saudi Arabia, but suddenly there were several Arab states. It is impossible, and also quite irrelevant for our purposes, to say how many, because some of the new states in North Africa, including Egypt, have populations that speak Arabic but are ethnically quite mixed.

Muslim countries include, in addition to those mentioned, Morocco and Algeria, Tunisia and Libya, Sudan and Jordan, Turkey and Iran, Afghanistan and Pakistan, Bangladesh, Malaysia, Indonesia, Chad, the Gambia, Malawi, Mali, Mauritania, Niger, Senegal, Somalia, and Albania. All these countries, except for Turkey, Iran, and Albania, have only recently emerged from European rule—French, British, or Dutch—and their Christian masters neither tried hard to convert them to Christianity nor behaved in such a way that the Muslims were converted by example. As independence came to them, most of them took Islam, as they understood it, very seriously—much more so than most Christian countries, except for Ireland, took their religion. And some of the Muslims, like some of the Irish, killed and were killed in large numbers for the sake of their religion.

The birth of Pakistan was the most striking example. The Muslims insisted on the partitioning of India because they did not want to have to live in a predominantly Hindu state, even if it was secular. There never had been any Pakistan, and the name was chosen as an acronym: *P* for Punjab, *A* for Afghans, *K* for Kashmir, *S* for Sind; and the name means "Land of the Pure" (Spear, 807). The idea was to fuse regions with large Muslim populations and to engineer a vast population exchange. Punjab and Bengal were both split in two along religious lines, although the Muslim and Hindu Bengalis speak the same language, which is very different from the language of the

Muslims, Hindus, and Sikhs of the Punjab. Moreover, Muslim Bengal, which became East Pakistan, was separated by a thousand miles of Hindu India from West Pakistan. Pakistan was not eager to have many Hindus in the "Land of the Pure," and about 15,000,000 people had to leave their homes. How many people were killed in the process is uncertain, as reliable statistics about numbers of people are hard to come by in India, but the figure was in the hundreds of thousands.

The arguments on which the case for Pakistan was based and the insistence on vast population exchanges offer a stark contrast to the rhetoric of the Muslims regarding Israel. "The Muslims felt that if Pakistan was to bring prosperity to their people, Sikhs who owned the best wheat lands of the Punjab would have to be dispossessed. Chaudhri Rahmat Ali, who first conceived Pakistan, stated this categorically:

> Avoid minorityism, which means that we must not leave our minorities in Hindu lands, even if the British and the Hindus offer them the so-called constitutional safeguards. For no safeguards can be substituted for the nationhood which is their birthright. Nor must we keep Hindu and/or Sikh minorities in our lands, even if they themselves were willing to remain . . . For they will never be of us. Indeed, while in ordinary times they will retard our national reconstruction, in times of crisis they will betray us . . .*

Half of the Sikhs lived in the part of the Punjab claimed by Pakistan. All who survived the massacres wound up in India, leaving behind some of the best agricultural land in the whole subcontinent. Pakistan offered them no compensation, nor did other Muslim countries raise their voices in protest. The rest of the world was too preoccupied with other problems, like that of the Palestinian refugees, to care. The reaction of the Sikhs themselves, which was very different from that of the Palestinians, will be considered when we take up the Sikhs in chapter XI. The reason for bringing up the subject here is that the partition of India was precipitated by Islam, and the mutual massacres were based on religious hatreds.

People who do not take religion seriously may find it difficult to believe that there were no linguistic or racial differences, but in the Punjab people who spoke the same language and were of the same stock killed each other in vast numbers, and the only common element of the overwhelming majority of the people of Pakistan was, and was meant to be, Islam. To be sure, one point that the Punjabi Muslims had used against the Hindus was that their color prejudices, embodied in the caste system, were inhuman. But the Muslims of West Pakistan never treated the Muslims of East Pakistan as their own equals. The Bengalis in the East were smaller and darker, and West Pakistan exploited them unmercifully.

Actually, the population of East Pakistan was greater, but when it won a huge election victory in 1971 its demands were nevertheless turned down by the government in West Pakistan. President Yahya "loosed the Punjabi army on the East in a terror campaign that eventually took the lives of more than 1 million Bengalis and drove 9.8 million into exile in India."** While President Nixon, who liked President Yahya, encouraged him to expect help, Yahya tried to exterminate the intelligentsia and the potential leaders of East Pakistan; but eventually India intervened, East Pakistan gained its independence and assumed the name of Bangladesh, and Sheikh Mujib, its first president, "estimated a death toll of about 3 million."*** The Pakistan that remained was no longer by far the most populous Muslim state in the world. Incidentally, no

---

* Singh, vol. 2, 267, quoting Rahmat Ali, *The Millat and its Mission; Muslim League Attack on Sikhs and Hindus*, 8.
** *Newsweek*, 6 December 1971. Quoted in Roy Chowdhury, *The Genesis of Bangladesh*, 96.
*** Ibid., 96.

Arab state supported the Bengalis. "Algeria and Libya, Saudi Arabia and Jordan—radical and reactionary alike—joined in denouncing . . . the struggle for Bengali liberation, while proclaiming Islamic solidarity with West Pakistan."*

67

There is actually a term that illuminates not only Arab relations with Israel but a great deal of Arab behavior and perhaps also that of the Muslims of Pakistan: *machismo*. It is a word not generally associated with Muslims but with Mexicans and Spaniards. Since it is not listed in most dictionaries and encyclopedias, some explanation may be in order. James Norman, having lived in Mexico for over ten years, put it this way:

> In most cultures . . . the man who must constantly prove that he is tough and forceful is regarded as childish or adolescent. In Mexico the reverse is true. The cult of *machismo* (maleness) is pursued with passion, dedication, and terrible compulsion. It colors countless aspects of Mexican behavior. It is basically a defense mechanism against insecurity; an overcompensation, an attempt to emulate the ways of the father, the Spanish conqueror. It appears in many forms. . . . When a Mexican says, "My house is your house," we accept it as a sign of wonderful hospitality. Mexican psychologists say it goes beyond hospitality and may be another way of proving one's maleness . . . At times the mechanism is a retreat into fantasies: the creation of marvelous projects that are not feasible; political and social plans that may not be workable, including handsome constitutions and laws. Visitors in Mexico are occasionally confused or dismayed by Mexicans who make grandiloquent statements or promises, then forget about them. . . . [All this] has led to adhesion to chieftains and strong personalities, on the part of the population, rather than to adhesion to principles (118 f.).

Reading this, one may well wonder whether the author is not speaking of Egypt or some other "Arab" country.

Could it be, one asks, that the Arabs brought their lavish and proverbial hospitality to Spain, and the Spaniards to Mexico? Could it be that before the Mexicans' attempt to emulate the ways of the Spanish conqueror the Spaniards tried to imitate the ways of the Muslim conqueror?

If the quintessence of the *machismo* of Mexico and Spain is to be found in the bullfighter who proves his manhood by playing with death and is rewarded with shouts of *macho!* ("there's a man!"), this particular ritual did not originate among the Arabs and may well have some connection with the similar rituals of Crete in the second millennium B.C. and the spectacles in which Roman audiences delighted long before Muhammad was born. But the Romans pitted slaves and captives against beasts of prey or against each other, and they fully expected the men to die. They certainly did not make heroes of them; much less did they model themselves on men of this type, as Spaniards and Mexicans have done for centuries. The compulsion to prove one's manhood by playing with death, by killing while bravely risking one's life, did not come from Rome and might well owe something to the Muslims. Again, the most striking examples in recent years are furnished not by Mexicans or Spaniards but by Arab highjackers and terrorists.

On a trivial level, Mexican *machismo* is illustrated by drivers who see themselves as matadors and prove their manhood by constant brushes with death. But here, too, many motifs come together, including a profound lack of respect for other human beings

---

* *Encyclopaedia Britannica*, 15th ed., vol. 9, 777.

and especially women; and again one used to see in Egypt, too, what some writers have stressed about Mexico: drivers who deliberately aimed their cars at women and expected the passengers' applause when the women shrieked as they dodged death. *Machismo* has been associated with a social life that men live exclusively with men, and here, too, Muslim society could well have been the paradigm.

We must not project into the eighth century attitudes found in the twentieth. The *machismo* of so many modern Mexicans and Arabs seems inseparable from centuries of oppression. It involves a retreat into fantasy and a concern with appearances and "face" rather than substance. One wonders if the conquerors of Palestine, Iran, and Spain could possibly have felt the need to prove their manhood, which presumably was above doubt. Perhaps the Spaniards had that need—and proved their manhood when they came to Mexico by being quite as ruthless with the idolaters and their impious idols as any Muslim had ever been. The Koran did not teach the faithful how to cope with persecution and oppression, and when the Muslims themselves became a subject people their very male religion seems to have plunged them, too, into *machismo*.

Other people have not usually reacted to oppression in this way. Hindus, Jews, and blacks, for example, did not, and the rather striking differences between the *machismo* of the leaders of Pakistan, at least until 1973, and the lack of it among the leaders of India seems to call for a religious explanation. The Indian leaders, to be sure, had many faults, but *machismo* was not one of them, and there is some significance in the fact that at the time of Bangladesh's war of independence, the prime minister of India was a woman, which would have been utterly unthinkable in Pakistan, whose head of government at the same time was a *macho*. Again, the cockiness of many Israelis should not be confused with *machismo*, and it is revealing that Israel also had a woman prime minister at a time when that would have been quite impossible in Saudi Arabia, Egypt, Syria, Jordan, or Libya.

It may still be objected that *machismo* is to be found among American blacks. But that is a recent development and began only with Malcolm X and the Black Muslims. Then some of the black leaders discovered Frantz Fanon's book, *The Wretched of the Earth*, which was written out of his Algerian experience and turned *machismo* into an ideology.

Neither the policies of Pakistan during its first quarter of a century nor Arab attitudes, especially regarding Palestine, can be understood apart from *machismo*. This is not to deny that there have been manifold provocations, but not everybody would have reacted to them in the same way. Often arguments seem to have been wholly secondary, and what was primary was the need to prove one's manhood.

Like Judaism and Christianity, Islam must face up to modern secularism, but so far no liberal ideology seems to match the appeal of Marxism for young ex-Muslim intellectuals. If they find Marxism attractive while they reject other Western ideas, this could be because Marxism has become so Manichaean that it seems closer to the Muslim heritage than does liberalism.

We have noted earlier that Islam is a profoundly aesthetic religion to which one cannot be fair as long as one concentrates entirely on ideas and moral issues. Hence the account given here needs to be supplemented with an attempt to disclose other dimensions of Islam. This will be done in chapter XIII, which places this religion in a rather different light. Meanwhile, some of the pictures may convey something of its beauty.

VIII

ANCIENT INDIA

*The Four Religions of India—The Vedas—The Upanishads—
Brahman and Atman—Moral Implications—Salvation—
The Six Systems and the Major Deities*

Durga slays Mahishasura, a buffalo demon. Mahabalipuram, 7th century.

68

India has given birth to at least four great religions: Hinduism and Buddhism, which have been accepted by hundreds of millions, and Jainism and Sikhism, which have far fewer followers. If a Westerner should feel that their differences are negligible and that they are all much the same, a Hindu or Buddhist might well say with equal right that the four great religions that were born in the Middle East are much the same. Actually, Judaism began by rejecting earlier religions, and after the Babylonian exile defined itself in opposition to the faith of Zarathustra; and Christianity experienced Judaism as a rival, and later also Islam. Islam, in turn, meant to supersede both Judaism and Christianity. All this is not to say that these religions have nothing in common. In many ways they are certainly closer to each other than they are to the religions born in India. But their differences are hardly negligible. It is similar with the religions that came out of India; they have to be understood in relation to each other, but some of their differences run very deep.

The Jewish Bible, the New Testament, the Koran, and Zarathustra's extant hymns taken together are a small fraction of the length of the sacred books of India. Our concern here will be mainly with Indian religious literature rather than Indian history, in which the Indians themselves have taken very little interest. Their religions are not historical in their outlook, like Judaism and its progeny, and some reasons for this difference will be found in their sacred books. Nor did they wage religious wars and crusades, trying to exterminate one another. Their rivalries, which are important, can be understood without paying much attention to dynasties, dates, and battles.

There would be some advantage in taking up the Indian religions in a single chronological sequence to show vividly how they interacted. But it will be less confusing if after dealing with their common heritage we consider Hinduism first and then, in a separate chapter, Buddhism, which will eventually take us beyond India to China and Japan. Jainism and Sikhism will be dealt with briefly at the beginning of chapter XI, in sections 79 and 80.

Hinduism, Jainism, and Buddhism are as philosophical as they are unhistorical. They are concerned pre-eminently with what is timeless. This concern has taken three main forms: a search for certain experiences, philosophical reflections, and sculpture. The *experiences* in question involve no consciousness of time and were, and are, taken for intuitions of a reality that is timeless. The *philosophies*—and there are many of them—seek to offer the knowledge that is considered a prerequisite for such experiences. The *art* developed much later, is illustrated in these pages, and will be discussed in chapter XIV.

Still, one observation on art in India may help to provide a much-needed perspective on ancient India. There was an old civilization in the Indus valley of which archaeological digs, especially at Harappa and Mohenjo Daro, give us at least some idea. This civilization had contacts with and was influenced by the Sumerians and the ancient Babylonians. The people built cities and used stone; they made sculptures and they had a script comprising about 270 signs.

Their best known and most frequently reproduced sculpture is a small statue, barely over four inches tall, showing a very slim nude girl in an animated pose, her right hand on her hip, her left arm, entirely covered with bangles, hanging down almost to her left knee, which is raised very slightly. It has been variously described in scholarly books as being made of bronze or copper. The breasts are small, and the whole type is very different from later Indian sculptures of women. Whether she is a dancer is uncertain. Another sculpture that has elicited much comment is a male torso of similar size, but made of stone. Just enough remains of the left leg to show that the thigh must have been horizontal, while the right thigh points down, and some interpreters have therefore called it a dancing god. If this identification should be right, we should have here a prototype of the dancing Shiva, of which no examples are known until about two thousand years later. But it need not be a dancer, and there is no evidence that it is a god. One other statuette found here is of exceptional interest. It shows a bearded man with an ornamented robe; his facial expression is very dignified, and his eyes look rather Mongolian. The face of the nude girl looks Negroid. The date of these pieces and others, including interesting seals, is not known, but there is agreement that this civilization perished in the sixteenth century B.C. The Aryan invaders' treatment of the native population of India will be considered later in connection with the caste system.

What needs to be emphasized now is that from about 1550 B.C. until after the invasion of Alexander the Great we have no evidence of any art in India, except literature. No temples, no other stone buildings, no sculpture, nor even an inscription survives. There is nothing until the third century; not much, but some of it superb, before the time of Jesus; and most of the glories of Indian architecture and sculpture are medieval. The Aryan invaders who composed the Vedas and Upanishads could have used wood and other perishable materials, but they probably did not build cities or temples and did not make images. They were warriors, and the Vedas throw some light on their battles, in which initially they massacred their enemies. Nor are there any written records dating from the period between 1550 B.C. and the inscriptions of Ashoka, a Buddhist king, around 250 B.C. He used two different scripts, of which one is unquestionably derived from the Hebrew-Aramaic alphabet and the other probably also from a Semitic script. In the Vedas and Upanishads no reference is ever made to writing, which is quite extraordinary in view of their bulk. Such references occur only in the later Sutras and in the Buddhist scriptures.

Hence one is led to wonder whether the pronounced lack of interest in history could be due at least in part to illiteracy, for usually a sense of history is tied to literacy. A. L. Basham considers it certain that the people who composed the Vedas were illiterate (33). At first glance, this suggestion is bound to seem odd because they have left us such a vast literature. But for some decades now scholars have become more and more convinced of the importance of oral traditions. Actually, some features of this large literature may be more understandable if one keeps in mind that it was not put into writing until very much later.

The thousand years from the sixteenth century to the sixth are a dark age and, in Basham's words, "almost an archaeological blank" (30). Scholars have sought to fill this void by saying that the Vedas and Upanishads were composed during this period. But what reasons remain for dating the Aryan invasion so early? This was plausible as long as it was assumed that the Indus valley culture was destroyed by the Aryans; but most scholars have come to agree that it perished before the Aryans arrived. And once Zarathustra is no longer dated in the second millennium but in the sixth century, we should seriously consider the possibility that the Aryan invasion occurred later than used to be thought and that the Vedas are younger. But nothing I am about to say hinges on that.

69

The Vedas are composed in Sanskrit. It was only toward the end of the eighteenth century that an Englishman discovered that Sanskrit was related to Greek and Latin, French, German, and English, and particularly close to ancient Persian. Now this linguistic family is often called Indo-German or Aryan to distinguish it from other families, like the Semitic, which includes Hebrew and Arabic, and the Mongolian, which includes Chinese and Japanese.

The Vedic religion was brought to India by people who called themselves Aryans and probably came from the Iranian highlands. Where they came from originally is a matter for conjecture, but that they shared a common heritage with the Persians and the Greeks is attested not only by their language but also by the names of their gods. The Vedic Dyaus Pitar, for example, brings to mind the Greek Zeus Pater and the Roman Jupiter. The Vedic goddess of the dawn, Ushas, is related to the Greek Eos, and the Vedic Varuna, who is also called Asura, to the Greek Uranos and the Persian Ahura Mazda. The Vedic Mitra shares more than his name with the Persian Mithra. All this makes it doubly interesting to see how very differently the Indians developed this heritage.

To this day, many educated Indians believe that the Vedas are 10,000 years old, and that they are far older than any other literature anywhere is almost a commonplace. Yet scholars have come to agree that the Rigveda was composed between 1500 and 900 B.C., and the other Vedas a little later than that. In other words, much of the literature of ancient Egypt and Mesopotamia is far older, some of it by well over a thousand years, even if we accept these dates. Some are as old as the oldest portions of the Hebrew Bible, and no other Indo-Germanic texts are that ancient.

The Vedas comprise four collections: the Rigveda, the Samaveda, the Yajurveda, and the Atharvaveda. All of them were parts of sacrificial rites, performed by priests. One priest recited one or another of the 1,017 hymns of the Rigveda (there are 10,580 verses in all). Another priest chanted something from the Samaveda. This collection comprises "1549 verses (or with repetitions 1810)," of which all but 75 are also found in the Rigveda. A third priest, while actually performing the sacrifice, muttered or chanted something from the Yajurveda, which contains "both prose sacrificial sentences (*yajus*) and verses, the latter of which are in great measure taken from the material of the Rigveda." There was a fourth priest, who supervised the whole ritual and had to know all three collections "and to whom the Atharvaveda [the fourth collection] is only referred for the sake of appearance, in order to help to raise it to the dignity of a fourth Veda, which was for a long time refused to it" (Deussen, 6 f.).

The Yajurveda is thought to have been compiled after the Rigveda, and the Atharvaveda is younger than both. It "consists mainly of magical spells and incantations in verse" and is of interest to scholars chiefly as a clue to "animism and sympathetic magic" (Basham, 232); but Aurobindo, the great twentieth-century mystic, found in it a source of profound wisdom. About one sixth of its seven hundred and sixty spells and incantations come from the Rigveda.

Maurice Bloomfield, who translated *Hymns of the Atharva-veda* for *The Sacred Books of the East,* omitted most of the "hymns," saying: "Since not a little of the collection rises scarcely above the level of mere verbiage, the process of exclusion has not called for any great degree of abstemiousness" (lxxii). Few scholars now would adopt that tone; and fewer still are in a position to pass judgment. The pendulum has swung back since this Victorian verdict; many students believe that less "civilized" people had a wisdom that we lack; and "magic" is no longer a term that instantly suggests superstition.

Bloomfield divided the material he translated in terms of what was desired, and distinguishes charms to cure diseases and possession by demons, prayers for long life and health, imprecations against demons, sorcerers, and enemies, charms pertaining to women, to royalty, charms to secure harmony, influence in the assembly, prosperity—including success in gambling—expiation, and prayers and imprecations in the interests of the Brahmins (the priestly class, which will be discussed later in connection with the caste system). Finally, he includes nine "theogonic and theosophic hymns," which—at least in translation—seem too long, verbose, and repetitious to be quoted here. Perhaps nothing in his tome comes across better in translation than this spell (102):

Charm to Arouse the Passionate Love of a Woman

May the disquieter disquiet you! Do not hold out on your bed! With the terrible arrow of love I pierce your heart.

The arrow, winged with longing, barbed with love, whose shaft is straight desire—with that, well-aimed, shall love pierce your heart.

With that well-aimed arrow of love which parches the spleen, whose plume flies forward, which burns, I pierce your heart.

Consumed by burning ardor, with parched mouth, come to me, pliant, pride laid aside, mine alone, speaking sweetly, devoted to me!

With a goad I drive you from your mother and your father, so you will be in my power and come up to my desire.

All her thought, O Mitra and Varuna, drive out of her! Then, having deprived her of her will, put her into my power alone!

I have revised the translation slightly and omitted obtrusive parenthetical explanations along with some archaisms—also in the other quotations in this chapter. In the fourth stanza, for example, Bloomfield's version reads in part: "do thou (woman) come to me, pliant, (thy) pride laid aside."

This charm may illustrate a general point. In a way, the Vedas and Upanishads are esoteric lore intended for the initiated only or, to be more specific, for Brahmins. Accordingly, each of the four Vedas consists not only of a *Samhita* or collection of *mantras* (verses, chants, or sacrificial sentences) but also of *Brahmanas*, "whose most direct purpose generally is, to teach the practical use of the materials presented in the Samhita," although they frequently exceed this immediate purpose (Deussen, 7). And the Upanishads are conceived as appendices to the Brahmanas. Finally, the Vedic literature still comprises the *Sutras*, which represent attempts to systematize doctrines. These in turn are divided into three kinds: some deal with public worship, others with domestic rituals, while the *Dharmasutras* deal with laws and caste, and the Laws of Manu, which will be considered at length later, is derived from them.

In other words, this is not a literature designed to express personal feelings. It does not bear the imprint of different individuals. It does not record historic events. It is worlds removed from the songs of Miriam and Deborah, which celebrate historic victories, from David's lament over the deaths of Saul and Jonathan, or from the outbursts of the Hebrew prophets. It is no less different from the Koran, Paul's epistles, and the Gospels. It is emphatically not addressed to a wide and heterogeneous audience. It is not meant to be understood at all, except by priests who also receive the benefit of lengthy instructions. Nevertheless, very occasionally some lines or even a whole charm or hymn speak straight to the heart.

It should be apparent by now how different the whole atmosphere of the Vedas is from Homer and the beginnings of Greek literature, in spite of the similarities between the names of some of the gods. Nor did these differences decrease with time. In ever so many ways, the religion, literature, architecture, and sculpture of India are all utterly remote from the striking simplicity of Sophocles or a Doric temple. The luxuriant abundance of India dwarfs even the Gothic and the Baroque. One might say that in India we encounter Dionysus unrestrained by Apollo.

There are legions of gods. Occasionally we are told in the Vedas that there are thirty-three—eleven each on the earth, in the air, and in the heavens—but in India precise figures are usually contradicted by any number of conflicting figures. (That is true to this day even when it comes to statistics.) Others have estimated that there are literally millions of gods in Indian religion. The Vedic gods seem to have been associated with natural phenomena to begin with; Varuna, for example, with the sky; Mitra with the sun; Agni with fire; Indra with the storm. But the gods refused to be confined to their appointed places. The sky is everywhere, sees everything, is pure and infinite; but the storm also reaches everywhere, is omnipresent, boundless, and cleanses impurity. The gods do not remain distinct, and often are addressed jointly and even identified outright. Moreover, there are many sky gods, many sun gods, many storm gods; and in addition to the higher gods there are lesser gods, elfish beings, hostile demons; and some heroes are deified, as is Soma, a psychedelic drink and the plant from whose juice it is made (hemp, perhaps, or a mushroom). The whole ninth book of the ten books of the Rigveda consists of hymns to Soma, and references to it abound in other hymns as well, especially in those to Indra. (There is a complete English translation in two volumes by R. T. H. Griffith.)

A few very short quotations may illustrate some of these points. Thus the Rigveda attributes to Varuna "power that no man deceives" (I:15,6); associates him with lawfulness, presumably because the orbits of the heavenly bodies are a paradigm of that; and then says: "May we be made sinless in your heavenly law" (I:24,15).

In the hymns to Indra, the original association of the god with storms is often evident. "Even heaven and earth bow down before him; before his breath the mountains tremble" (II:12,13). Some of the many mythical feats attributed to him seem to have the same source. He is ever active and often aggressive. "Only the active conquers those who dwell in peace and thrives; not for the niggard are the gods" (VII:32). Indra is "Lord of heaven" (VIII:87,6); but he is also associated with Soma juice.

I in my grandeur have surpassed heaven and all this spacious earth. Have I not drunk of Soma juice? . . .
In one flash will I smite the earth in fury here or there. Have I not drunk of Soma juice? (X:119)

One gathers that Soma juice was offered to the god, and that his behavior occasionally suggested that he had drunk it. The verse quoted above, ending "before his breath the mountains tremble," continues: "Known as the Soma drinker, armed with thunder, who wields the bolt, he, men, is Indra."

Originally, Varuna and Indra almost seem opposites. But then we are told: "I Varuna am Indra" (IV:42). And this identification of different gods is one of the central and striking features of the Rigveda and proved to be immensely influential.

A pantheon that seems almost chaotic can be arranged on paper in all kinds of tables. But it is more to the point to realize that this lavish and apparently confused abundance facilitated the triumph of the spirit over any ossified, departmentalized magic.

Varuna is not simply the sky god who can be propitiated by minutely designated rites of which the Vedic hymns form an important part; he transcends any one function and therefore sets no limits to those who reach out beyond the tedium of routine. The hymn to Varuna or Indra, or one of the other gods—but chiefly these two—can express fervor, and occasionally striking metaphors leap out of a jungle of rhetoric.

Thus a hymn to Soma (IX:69) begins:

> Laid like an arrow on the bow, the hymn has been loosed
> like a young calf to the udder of its dam.
> As one who comes first with full stream she is milked;
> thus Soma is impelled to this man's holy rites.

The remainder, more like the last two lines than like the first two, celebrates Soma juice in a manner of which two relatively lively stanzas may give some idea:

> He flows about the sheep-skin, longing for a bride:
> he loosens Aditi's daughters for the worshiper.
> The sacred drink has come, gold-tinted, well restrained;
> like a strong bull he shines, whetting his manly might.
>
> The bull is bellowing; the cows are coming near:
> the goddesses approach the god's own resting place.
> Soma has passed on through the sheep's fair bright fleece
> and has endued a garment newly washed.

In another stanza we encounter "the beams of Surya," the sun god, to whom the great temple at Konarak was dedicated more than 2,000 years later. Then, like many hymns to Varuna, Indra, and the other gods, this hymn, too, ends with a volley of requests:

> Pour out upon us wealth in goods, in gold, in steeds,
> in cattle and in corn, in great heroic strength . . .
> Bring splendid treasures to the man who lauds you.
> O heaven and earth, with all the gods protect us.

Westerners may feel more comfortable with these stanzas from a hymn to Varuna (VII:86):

> With my heart I commune on the question how
> Varuna and I may be united.
> What gift of mine will he accept unangered?
> When may I calmly look and find him gracious?
>
> Eager to know my sin, I question others:
> I seek the wise, O Varuna, and ask them.
> Even the sages gave me the same answer:
> Surely, Varuna is angry with you.
>
> What, Varuna, has been my chief transgression
> that you would slay the friend who sings your praises? . . .
>
> Free us from sins committed by our fathers;
> from those through which we have ourselves offended.
> O king, loose, like a thief who feeds the cattle,
> as from a cord a calf, set free Vasishtha.
>
> Not our own will has betrayed us but seduction,
> thoughtlessness, Varuna, wine, dice, or anger.
> The old are near to lead astray the younger:
> even sleep does not remove all evil-doing. . . .

Perhaps the most impressive poem in all the Vedas is hymn 129 in Book X of the Rigveda. (Book X is later than the rest of the Rigveda.) Most scholarly translations give hardly an inkling of its grandeur. Paul Deussen, who was, with Max Müller, the greatest nineteenth-century Sanskritist, translator, and interpreter of Indian thought, published a superb German version—as literal as Griffith's but in rhymes. Here is my own attempt, omitting the fourth and fifth stanzas, which contain some very obscure lines. It may be worth pointing out that Griffith has "warmth" in the last line of the third stanza. The Sanskrit word is *tapas*, which generally refers to ascetic austerities, even in the Vedas, and Hindus believe no less than Jains that ascetic practices generate great heat that confers mysterious power, not only over oneself. Hence even the gods fear the great ascetics. Deussen translates the line at issue *Das Eine durch der Glutpein Kraft geboren*, literally: "The one born through the strength of ardor-pain," or "flame-pain." The skeptical conclusion of the hymn is authentic and not the result of poetic license.

The Creation

Both being and not-being were not yet,
no air was then, nor any sky.
Who kept the world or bounded it?
Where was abyss and where the sea?

No day was there, nor was there night,
no death was then nor immortality,
then breathed in windless, pristine might
the One without duality.

The whole world was a lightless field,
an ocean in a dark domain.
Then what had so far been concealed,
The One arose through power born of pain. . . .

Who, then, could be the arbitrator
To tell about creation's source?
The gods came into being later.
Who knows from where it took its course?

He by whom all was first begot,
Who looks from heaven's apogee,
Who made it, or perhaps did not,
He knows it—or not even he?

70

After the age of the Vedas came the age of the great commentaries; first, the Brahmanas, which are concerned with ritual, and then, a little later, the Upanishads, which are concerned with knowledge. The bulk of this literature is of lavish proportions; there are over two hundred Upanishads* of which Max Müller, in *The Sacred Books of the East*, translated twelve, in two volumes. In 1931 Robert Ernest Hume published a new translation of *The Thirteen Principal Upanishads* in a single volume; and since then many selections have appeared, including several in soft covers.

The word *Upanishads* means "sessions" or "seminars." They offer instruction and are often cast in the form of a dialogue between a priestly sage and a student who is slow to understand. Most scholars believe that the earliest and most important Upanishads (Brihad-Aranyaka and Chandogya) go back to the seventh century and antedate

---

* Radhakrishnan, 37. He adds that the traditional number is a hundred and eight.

the Buddha. In Biblical terms, they come soon after Amos and Hosea, Isaiah and Micah, but before Jeremiah and the Babylonian exile, and the outlook of the Upanishads is in important respects the opposite of that of the prophets. The prophets predicted disasters that were inevitable *if* the people persisted in their perilous ways, and though their moral demands were in one sense timeless, in another sense time was of the essence. When Jonah cried, "Yet forty days, and Nineveh shall be overthrown," it would never do for the inhabitants of that city to ignore the element of time. Repentance and reform must come now or never. In keeping with this message, the Book of Jonah is very short.

Most of the other prophetic books are a little longer, but compared to the Upanishads they are terse and urgent. The people's fate is at stake and will be decided here and now. Insofar as the perspective of the Hebrew Bible extends beyond the decisive present moment, it is defined by unique events that happened just once, at a certain time; above all, the exodus from Egypt and the revelation at Mt. Sinai.

In the Upanishads, there is no people and there is no history, there is only the individual, concerned—one is tempted to say—about his salvation. Insofar as salvation was what was sought, it was liberation from the endless transmigration of souls. This conception is not yet found in the Vedas, but it is found in some of the Upanishads, including the Brihad-Aranyaka and Chandogya. Initially, the idea was not that one was reborn in another body immediately after death. The good soul would first go to various places, including a stay on the moon, before passing on to space and then to air, finally returning to the earth in the rain to become food and be reborn. When it is put that way, it may sound rather strange, but the doctrine that gradually developed is surely less difficult to believe than the idea that immortal souls are created out of nothing whenever a baby is born and at death pass into hell or heaven—or the grave (most Christians are not quite sure what they believe)—from which they are eventually resurrected, given back their bodies, judged, and then sent back to hell or heaven. The belief that eventually came to be accepted by the three major religions of India was that our soul has lived in innumerable bodies before our birth and will be reborn after our death. Its migrations are governed by *karma*, a moral law in accordance with which those who live like pigs are reborn as pigs, and others are reborn as worms or insects or as human beings—and what kind of human being we are is the result of our previous life. One's conduct or, in moral terms, one's guilt or merit becomes attached to the soul in some way and determines its destiny.

We know from Jainism and Buddhism that the imagination that has really absorbed this notion of eternal life in the form of ever-new lives may long for salvation in the form of a final release from this wheel. It is a reasonable interpretation of the Upanishads to say that their central concern is with the knowledge that makes this liberation possible. Since there is no sense of urgency in the Upanishads, and the instruction tends to be extremely slow and repetitious, one can say further that this is surely due to the fact that when one has already lived so many times there is no hurry, and if one does not attain salvation in this life, one may at least hope that, having tried earnestly, one will be reborn closer to one's goal.

This seems right as far as it goes, but perhaps a little too reasonable. In the first place, one does not gain the impression in reading many Upanishads that the central concern of all the sages and their students is with transmigration, which comes up rarely. The central concern, at least most of the time, is with a certain piece of esoteric knowledge and an experience that is its corollary, and while both could be desired merely as a means to salvation, that is not the impression one gets generally. It therefore seems quite probable that we are confronted, at least initially, with a social system in which it was considered proper for some people to leave home between childhood and

marriage in order to wait on a teacher and listen to his instruction. The concept of esoteric lore was of very ancient standing in India, and we need not suppose that such
wisdom was always sought or given only as an indispensable condition of salvation from
rebirth.

The doctrine of the four stages of life may have gained its full form only later, but
it lends some support to this theory. For it was said that during the first stage one should
live with a teacher, as suggested; then one should marry and bring up children; after the
birth of one's grandchildren one should become a hermit in the forest; and finally one
should close one's days as a homeless wanderer.

One crucial factor in the development of the esoteric tradition in India has gone
unnoticed—the function of illiteracy. The only way to acquire learning was to receive it
orally from a teacher, and the teacher was above criticism and could always claim that
he had been misunderstood. Judging from the Vedas and Upanishads, the teachers—
Brahmins all of them—did not have any large body of knowledge to impart. In Vedic
times they knew how to handle the proper *mantras*, or spells, and how to perform the
sacrifices. By the time of the Upanishads they claimed to have another kind of esoteric
knowledge—and made the most of it. One who lived with a Brahmin and waited on him
might hope that eventually this secret knowledge would be imparted to him, provided
he was of high caste.

By way of contrast, the children of Israel possessed the art of writing even in the
time of Moses and the judges; they were called upon to be "a people of priests"—all of
them; and their prophets spoke to all and moreover wrote down and disseminated their
ideas. In ancient India, illiteracy, the caste system, elitism, and the esoteric tradition
belong together.

The wisdom that was imparted slowly and unhurriedly involved the claim that the
temporal world with its diversity was like a veil drawn over ultimate reality. This notion
could also explain—or rationalize—the repetitious style of the Upanishads.

In *The Age of Imperial Unity*, volume 2 of *The History and Culture of the Indian
People*, published in Bombay under the general editorship of R. C. Majumdar, we find
at least some recognition of this along with some pertinent reflections: "The knowledge
of writing might have been expected to introduce a great change in the system of education, but this does not appear to have been the case. There is abundant evidence to show
that the teaching continued to be mainly oral, and the study of manuscripts was positively condemned" (584). It is difficult to escape the conclusion that when writing
finally came to be known in India the Brahmins realized that it endangered their
position.

The Indian historian goes on to note that some passages in the Buddhist scriptures
suggest that even when "the art of writing was in vogue, the sacred books were not
written but committed to memory, even though the monks realized the danger that a
portion of the canon might thus altogether be lost"; and he finds it "difficult to explain
this attitude." Eventually, he concedes: "In the case of the Brahmanas, the growing
desire to withhold the sacred *mantras* from the people and retain teaching as an exclusive privilege for themselves might act as an incentive to oral teaching by the exclusion
of books. But the same motive could not possibly operate in the case of the heterodox
sects like the Buddhists" (585).

So far from invalidating our theory, the example of the Buddhists removes the most
powerful objection to it; namely, that it would simply have been impossible to commit
as vast a literature as that of the Vedas and Upanishads to memory, and that therefore
the people who composed them must have possessed the art of writing. If, like the
Brahmins, the Buddhists initially favored oral transmission, instead of immediately

seizing on the art of writing when it became available, this would only show how deeply ingrained the notion had become in India that religious teaching had to be done orally. Among the Buddhists this notion would have been reinforced by the example of the Buddha and his early followers. Religion is conservative and does not break lightly with such a precedent. Moses, according to the tradition, had written and spoken of writing again and again, which is entirely believable, seeing that he was said to have received his education in Egypt, where the priests had long possessed the art of writing. His demand that his people should become a people of priests meant among other things that they should all become literate, that they should all study, and that they should not regard priests as in any way superior beings.

Admirers of Indian thought sometimes stress that it heightens our awareness. This is surely a half-truth. In the Upanishads there is little or no awareness of whole dimensions of human existence that were considered crucially important in ancient Israel: history; oppression of the poor, the widow, and the stranger; wrongs that cry out for correction now. In the Upanishads, whatever is temporal is of no importance. The teacher, having found peace through his wisdom, no longer feels under any pressure of time. The style of the instruction reflects the peace that passes understanding and aims to inculcate a new state of mind.

The idea that time and change are unimportant and unreal poses problems. One of these is that it rules out any belief in transmigration. One can, of course, try to square these two doctrines in some way, and philosophers eventually rose to this challenge. But it is not really probable at all that the doctrine of the unreality of time, and the timelessness of ultimate reality, was developed in the first place as a means to save initiates from rebirth, while the uninitiated were condemned to transmigration. It is much more likely that the notion of the timelessness of ultimate reality was older and came from a distinctive experience. The teacher was willing to initiate the student into his experience, which was surely sought for its own sake at first.

It seems a reasonable guess that similar experiences had already been induced in Vedic times by Soma juice and possibly other drugs as well. By the age of the Upanishads, however, some priests had mastered the art of attaining states of timeless consciousness without drugs. The teaching we find in the Upanishads is based on such experiences and almost certainly was supplemented by all kinds of exercises.

It may be objected that if the temporal world were merely an illusion, it would make no sense for the teacher to believe that there is any student and that there are any questions and answers. Surely, there is something odd about long lectures that are intended to convince the listener that neither he nor the lecturer exist. Shankara, the greatest commentator on the thought of the Upanishads as well as India's most celebrated philosopher, argued in effect that the temporal world is not *merely* an illusion and that we must distinguish degrees of reality. Some of the greatest Western philosophers—notably, Plato, Kant, Schopenhauer, and Bradley—also taught that the world of sense experience is in some sense illusory, and they also had to make some qualifications.

Shankara wrote his commentaries early in the ninth century. About three hundred years later, Ramanuja, whose reputation as a philosopher is second only to Shankara's, argued that the world was not an illusion. And there were different philosophies even in the age of the Upanishads, which will be considered later on.

It is easy to romanticize the forest sages whose teachings are recorded in the Upanishads. But they were the world's first scholastic philosophers. They belonged to a school of thought that differed with other schools but was sure it had the truth; they accepted the Vedas as authoritative and professed to interpret them when they read their own ideas into them; and they lived in a social system, the caste system, that was highly questionable but, unlike the Jaina and the Buddha, they did not question it. For all that, they were the first to develop the haunting doctrine of appearance and reality, which remains one of the most fascinating philosophical ideas of all time.

71

The two central concepts of the Upanishads are *Brahman* and *Atman*. Brahman is ultimate reality, the One that is encountered beyond change, time, and diversity. The world is a veil that conceals Brahman from the uninitiated. The word *Brahman* is much older than this use of it and in the Vedas refers to some great magical power. The Brahmin was originally one who had this power. Some writers transcribe "Brahmin" in ways that make for confusion of the two words, but it is essential to keep them apart, and to distinguish both from *Brahma* (with the accent on the second syllable and the second *a* pronounced like that in balm or cart), who is a god.

80   How can we transcend change, time, and diversity to reach Brahman? The Upanishads imply that no god can be of the slightest help to us. This is clearly a striking departure from the Vedic religion. But even as far back as the Rigveda we encountered "the One without duality" and the notion that whatever god is addressed becomes the gateway to the one and only ultimate reality. Much of the Upanishads could be considered an elaborate explication of the forty-sixth stanza of the fifty-two that make up hymn 64 in Book I of the Rigveda:

> They call him Indra, Mitra, Varuna, Agni,
> and he is heavenly, nobly-winged Garutman.
> To what is one, sages give many a title;
> they call it Agni, Yama, Matarisvan.

The Upanishads call the ultimate essence of a human being Atman. This word is related to the German *Atem* ("breath"), and the Indians originally assumed that man's essence was his breath. After all, when he stops breathing he dies. A. C. Bouquet notes (119) that "A discourse proving that breath is the vital constituent of any human being is found in five Upanishads." He mentions this to show how the Upanishads abound in parallel passages, but his observation also throws light on Atman.

The obvious English translation would be "spirit," which comes from the Latin *spiritus*, which means breath and wind as well as spirit. So do Greek *pneuma* and Hebrew *ruah*. Yet Atman has generally been translated as either "soul" or "self." It seems far better not to translate the term at all instead of introducing irrelevant connotations. Still, it may be helpful to note that "spirit" is sometimes almost a synonym of "gist," and "gist" is another form of *Geist*, the German word for "spirit." The Atman is our essential gist, a reality that underlies all accidental attributes, the spirit that is veiled by appearances. If only we could transcend all these changeful appearances, we would encounter Atman in ourselves. And Brahman? *Tat tvam asi*, that you are. Atman is Brahman, Brahman is Atman. You yourself are the ultimate reality, but you are not what you seem. The gist of you is not to be found in your body, which differs from other bodies, or in anything diversified, temporal, or subject to change.

' What is needful is knowledge, not sacrifices, but this knowledge does not consist of a large quantity of information, nor is it the kind of cumulative knowledge that is gradually assembled by the sciences. The knowledge that matters is simple and can be expressed in few words. But who will understand these words? It is one thing to repeat a scientific formula like $E = mc^2$ and quite another thing to understand it and appreciate its implications. Such understanding requires the willingness to discipline one's mind, taking some time to follow complicated expositions.

The difficulty in the case of the teachings of the Upanishads is partly similar to this —but only partly. The two major difficulties are these: on the face of it, the doctrine of the Upanishads flatly contradicts common sense by denying the reality of the common-sense world; and the most important implications of this doctrine are not theoretical but practical, for the main point of accepting the doctrine is to lose interest in this world and to become progressively absorbed in the eternal. This emancipation from worldly concerns, this alienation from any interest in fame, riches, health, love, and gods is not accomplished by a single demonstration but, according to the Upanishads, by a prolonged immersion in the highly repetitive lore of the Upanishads.

There is little argument in the Upanishads, but much that requires elucidation. This may be shown by quoting a famous passage from the Brihad-Aranyaka Upanishad, which is widely considered the most important of all Upanishads. In section 3:7, Yajnavalkya (pronounced, more or less, as Yágaválkya), one of the greatest sages, is asked to explain the conception of Atman and replies:

> He who, dwelling in the earth, yet is not earth, whom the earth does not know, whose body the earth is, who controls the earth from within—He is your Atman, the ruler within, the immortal.
>
> He who, dwelling in the waters, yet is not the waters, whom the waters do not know, whose body the waters are, who controls the waters from within—He is your Atman, the ruler within, the immortal.
>
> He who, dwelling in the fire, yet is not the fire, whom the fire does not know, whose body the fire is, who controls the fire from within—He is your Atman, the ruler within, the immortal.
>
> He who, dwelling in the atmosphere . . .
> He who, dwelling in the wind . . .
> He who, dwelling in the sky . . .
> He who, dwelling in the sun . . .
> He who, dwelling in space . . .
> He who, dwelling in the moon and stars . . .
> He who, dwelling in the ether . . .
> He who, dwelling in the darkness . . .
> He who, dwelling in the light . . .
> Thus far with reference to the divinities . . .
> He who, dwelling in all things . . .
> He who, dwelling in breath . . .
> He who, dwelling in the tongue . . .
> He who, dwelling in the eye . . .
> He who, dwelling in the ear . . .
> He who, dwelling in the mind . . .
> He who, dwelling in the semen . . .
> He is the unseen seer, the unheard hearer, the unthought thinker, the unknown knower. There is no hearer but he. There is no thinker but he. There is no knower but he. He is your Atman, the ruler within, the immortal.
>
> Thereupon Uddalaka Aruni held his peace.

And so did not only the man who had asked Yajnavalkya for an explanation but also generations of Hindu scholars ever since. This kind of answer does not encourage further questions, argument, or critical discussion, but commentaries.

Another one of Yajnavalkya's discourses, which is related twice in the Brihad-Aranyaka Upanishad, both in section 2:4 and in section 4:5, has an unusual biographical setting, but the mode of instruction is the same.

Yajnavalkya had two wives, Maitreyi and Katyayani. Of the two, Maitreyi was conversant with Brahman; Katyayani had just a woman's knowledge in that matter.

Yajnavalkya was about to commence another mode of life.

He said: Maitreyi! Truly, I am about to leave my house. Behold! Let me make a settlement for you and that Katyayani.

Maitreyi said: My Lord, if this whole earth filled with wealth were mine, would I then be immortal or not?

No, no! said Yajnavalkya. Like the life of the rich would your life be. Of immortality there is no hope through wealth.

Then Maitreyi said: What should I do with that through which I do not become immortal? What you know, my Lord, explain to me.

Yajnavalkya replied: Although you, my Lady, were truly dear to me, you have increased your dearness. Behold, then, Lady, I will explain it to you. But as I am expounding it, ponder thereon.

Then he said: Truly, not for love of a husband is a husband dear, but for love of the Atman a husband is dear.

Truly, not for love of a wife is a wife dear, but for love of the Atman a wife is dear.

Truly, not for love of sons . . .
Truly, not for love of wealth . . .
Truly, not for love of cattle . . .
Truly, not for love of Brahminhood . . .
Truly, not for love of Kshatrahood . . .
Truly, not for love of worlds . . .
Truly, not for love of the gods . . .
Truly, not for love of the Vedas . . .
Truly, not for love of beings . . .
Truly, not for love of all . . .

Truly, it is the Atman that should be seen, that should be listened to, that should be thought on, that should be pondered on, O Maitreyi.

In the Atman's being seen, listened to, thought on, known, all this is known. . . .

As one cannot seize the sounds when a drum is beaten, but by seizing the drum or the beater of the drum the sound is seized. . . .

As clouds of smoke issue from a fire laid with damp fuel, so truly, Maitreyi, from this great Being has been breathed forth that which is Rig-Veda, Yajur-Veda, Sama-Veda . . . Ancient Lore, Sciences, Upanishad, Verses, Aphorisms, Explanations, Commentaries, Sacrifice . . . this world and the other world, and all beings . . .

As all waters are united in the sea, all touches in the skin; all tastes in the tongue . . .

As a mass of salt is without inside, without outside, entirely a mass of taste, even so, truly, this Atman, without inside, without outside, is entirely a mass of knowledge.

Arising out of these elements, into them also one vanishes away. After death there is no more knowledge. Thus say I. Thus spoke Yajnavalkya.

Then said Maitreyi: Here my Lord, you have landed me in utter bewilderment. Truly, I do not understand him.

Then he said: O Maitreyi, I said nothing bewildering. Truly, this Atman is imperishable and indestructible.

For where there is duality, as it were, there one sees another; there one smells another; there one tastes another . . . there one knows another. But where Atman alone is all, how and whom would one see? then how and whom would one smell? . . . how would one know him by means of whom one knows all?

That Atman is not this, not that [neti, neti]. It is unseizable, for it cannot be seized; indestructible, for it cannot be destroyed; unattached, for it does not attach itself; is unbound, does not suffer, is not injured.

How could one know the knower?
Thus you have been instructed, Maitreyi. Truly, this is immortality.
After speaking thus, Yajnavalkya departed.

Whether his wife was still bewildered, is not recorded. The sage did not take any chances that she might ask further questions. Neither he nor the other sages of the Upanishads were concerned to stimulate critical reflection; rather he said to his wife—and this remained the motto of the Upanishads—: "ponder thereon."

72

Strictly speaking, there is no Upanishadic view of anything; since the Upanishads contain the traditions of centuries of discussion, we find divergent views on many matters. Even so, the amount of agreement on essentials is striking, and on Brahman and Atman there is agreement, on the whole.

Moreover, the Upanishads are speculative in their basic orientation rather than moral. In this they stand directly opposed to the books of the Hebrew prophets, which are moral rather than speculative. In the Upanishads morality is a side issue, touched on as an implication.

Two of these *moral implications* deserve special mention. The first is a corollary of the belief in reincarnation, which the Chandogya Upanishad formulates in section 5:10,7 as follows: "Those whose conduct has been good will quickly attain a good birth, the birth of either a Brahmin, or a Kshatriya, or a Vaishya. But those whose conduct has been stinking will attain a stinking birth, the birth of either a dog, or a swine, or an outcaste [*Chandala*]."

Here the caste system that had become increasingly articulate since Vedic times receives not only a religious sanction but a moral rationalization that would have outraged the Hebrew prophets. The Brahmins, the priests, now stand at the top of the social ladder; next come the Kshatriyas, or warriors, then the Vaishyas—while the outcaste, to whom the Old Testament might have referred as "the stranger in your midst," asking for special consideration for him along with the poor, the orphan, and the widow, is ranked with the dog and the swine. It is implied that he *deserves* the wretched existence forced on him by the callousness of priests and warriors. Even as St. Augustine argued a thousand years later that the damned in hell deserve no pity or prayers because they have received their just deserts, the Upanishads imply that the outcaste has received his just deserts for his presumed sins in a previous life in which he must have been guilty of "stinking conduct." The mode of argument is that of Job's friends, roundly condemned in the Hebrew Bible: where there is suffering there must have been guilt, for the world is governed by justice. But the outcaste is not condemned eternally, without any possibility of reprieve, like the damned of Christianity; he may gradually climb to salvation through the transmigration of souls.

The other moral implication of the Upanishads is encountered on an entirely different plane—cosmic rather than social—but it, too, could become a sanction for callousness and cruelty. Atman-Brahman, being beyond all distinctions, all multiplicity, all duality, is also beyond good and evil. Moral distinctions, like all distinctions, belong to the world of appearance, *maya*, illusion. To cite the Brihad-Aranyaka Upanishad (4:4,22):

Atman is not this, not that [*neti, neti*]. It is unseizable, for it cannot be seized.
It is indestructible, for it cannot be destroyed. . . . It is not injured.
Him [who knows this] these two do not overcome—neither the thought, I did

wrong, nor the thought I did right. He overcomes both. What he has done and what he has not done do not burn him.

This has been declared in the verse:
This eternal greatness of a Brahmin
Is not increased by deed [karman], nor diminished.
One should be familiar with it. By knowing it,
One is not stained by evil action.

This is part of the instruction Yajnavalkya gives a king. At the end of a later section (5:14), which extols the mystical significance of an obscure prayer, the same point is summarized more briefly: "Even so, although he commits very much evil, one who knows this, consumes it all and becomes clean and pure, ageless and immortal."

In the relatively short Kaushitaki Upanishad (3:1), Indra himself says, right after we are told that "Indra is truth":

Know me only. This indeed I deem most beneficial for man—to know me. I slew the three-headed son of Tvashtri [a feat often celebrated in the Vedas]. . . . And not a single hair on me was injured!

So he who knows me—by no deed whatsoever of his is his life injured, not by the murder of his mother, not by the murder of his father, not by theft, not by the killing of a Brahmin. If he does any evil, his face does not turn pale.

To attain the proper knowledge, to be sure, one has to subject oneself to considerable mental discipline, and a great deal of thought and meditation are indispensable. The Upanishads do not encourage the licentious to persist in their licentiousness but call upon everyone who takes them seriously to change his life. The new life that is demanded involves above all else superiority to the illusory temptations of this world and, to put it positively, self-control of the very highest order. The short, important, and impressive Katha Upanishad therefore does not at all contradict the passages cited when it says (1:2,24):

Not he who has not ceased from bad conduct,
Not he who is not tranquil and composed,
Not he whose mind is not at rest,
Can obtain Atman by knowledge.

This stanza, moreover, should be taken in conjunction with the immediately preceding one which has struck some Western scholars as an anticipation of Calvin's doctrine of election:

This Atman cannot be gained by the Veda,
Nor by understanding, nor by much learning.
He whom the Atman chooses, by him the Atman can be gained (Cf. Mundaka Upanishad 3:2,3).

As Yajnavalkya taught, Atman is "the unseen Seer, the unheard Hearer, the unthought Thinker, the ununderstood Understander"—the subject in all things, but different from all things insofar as they are objects; Atman never is, nor ever can be made, an object. Therefore Atman cannot be an object of instruction, of the intellect, of learning. If a man is to reach Atman, it must be Atman that does the reaching.

But Shankara understood the last line of the quotation to say that those who choose only Atman, to the exclusion of all else, gain Atman. In any case, intelligence, instruction, learning, mental discipline, and meditation are not disparaged; on the contrary, they are considered necessary conditions of salvation. But they are not held to be sufficient conditions. A high degree of moral purity—judged by standards that were very different from those of the Hebrew Bible—was also widely considered a necessary, though not a sufficient, condition. But the ideal man is not held to be necessarily a moral man. Whoever has had the liberating experience of the unity of Atman and Brahman—what is wanted ultimately is this experience rather than any abstract knowledge—knows that he will not be reborn, and for the rest of his earthly life he may be moral or not, as he pleases. He is beyond good and evil.

But if time and change and diversity are unreal, then the rest of us are not really reborn either. Why, then, should we fret? Why should we not, all of us, live without regard for moral standards and, if it pleases us, without regard for learning and mental discipline, since the fashion of this world is all illusory? To this objection the Upanishads answer in effect that we can say all this, but that short of learning, mental discipline, and meditation we can never really come to believe it; we remain caught, as it were, in a bad dream or even in a succession of nightmares. The sage, on the other hand, wakes up. Or, to use an image found in the Upanishads: the ultimate experience of Unity is like dreamless sleep. More often, the Upanishads distinguish waking, dreaming, dreamless sleep, and "the fourth" state.

In one sense, a nightmare is an illusion; in another, it is painfully real. It is important to distinguish my dreams from my waking life; but it does not follow that in fact I never did dream. Similarly, it is clearly justifiable to juxtapose two kinds of experience—on the one hand, the experience of multiplicity which includes both the world of sense experience and the world of our dreams, and on the other hand, the experience of Unity. And just as few people would hesitate to say that the world of waking life is more important than the world of our dreams and in that sense the "real" world, while our dreams are "illusory," the Indian mystic says that the world of diversity is less important and in that sense "illusory," while the Unity which he experiences sometimes with great intensity is infinitely more important and in that sense "real." He trusts that after death the nightmare of diversity will be dispelled entirely for him, and he hopes to encounter unbroken Unity, while the rest of humanity goes from nightmare to nightmare. We sleep on and on, while the sage wakes up when he dies.

It may be well to conclude this account of the Upanishads with two exceptionally fine passages. The first comes from the Katha Upanishad (1:3) and may remind those who know Plato's *Phaedrus* of his use of the image of a charioteer:

> Know Atman as sitting in a chariot, the body as the chariot, the intellect [*buddhi*] as the charioteer, and the mind as the reins.
>
> The senses are called the horses, the objects of the senses what they range over. When he is in union with the body, the senses, and the mind, then wise men call him the enjoyer.
>
> Whoever has no understanding and whose mind is not firmly held, his senses are uncontrolled like the vicious horses of a charioteer.
>
> But whoever has understanding and whose mind is always firmly held, his senses are under control, like the good horses of a charioteer.
>
> Whoever has no understanding, is unmindful and always impure, never reaches that place but enters into the round of births.
>
> But whoever has understanding, is mindful and always pure, reaches that place from which he is not born again.
>
> He whose understanding is his charioteer and who holds the reins of the mind, he reaches the end of his journey, and that is the highest place of Vishnu.
>
> Beyond the senses there are their objects, beyond the objects there is the mind, beyond the mind there is the intellect, the great Atman is beyond the intellect.
>
> Beyond the great there is the undeveloped, beyond the undeveloped there is the person [*purusha*]. Beyond the person there is nothing—this is the goal, the highest road.
>
> This Atman is hidden in all beings and does not shine forth, but is seen by subtle seers through their sharp and subtle intellect.

> A wise man should keep down speech and mind; he should keep them within the Atman which is knowledge; he should keep knowledge within the Atman which is the great; and he should keep that within the Atman which is the quiet.
> Rise, awake! . . .

Whether Plato was influenced by this passage, however indirectly, we do not know. The whole problem of possible Indian influence on the two world theories of the Greeks (Parmenides and Plato) and the idea of transmigration in Greek philosophy (Pythagoras and Plato) remains unresolved, although it seems highly probable that there was such an influence.

The last passage to be quoted here from the Upanishads also stresses that philosophy is a means to salvation—which is true for Plato, too, although he did not conceive of salvation in the same way. Moreover, in this passage from the Chandogya Upanishad (8:13-15) the refusal to hurt others (*ahimsa*) is considered one of the distinctive features of those who have attained salvation. This is the conclusion of one of the most highly regarded Upanishads:

> From the dark I go to the varicolored. From the varicolored I go to the dark. Shaking off evil, as a horse its hairs; shaking off the body, as the moon releases itself from the mouth of Rahu; I, a perfected soul [*krtatman*], pass into the uncreated Brahma-world—yes, into it I pass!
> Truly, what is called space is the accomplisher of name and form. That within which they are, is Brahman. That is the immortal. That is the Atman.
> I go to Prajapati's abode and assembly hall.
> I am the glory of the Brahmins, the glory of the princes, the glory of the people.
> I have attained glory.
> May I, who am the glory of glories, not go to hoary and toothless, yes to toothless and hoary and driveling [old age]!
> Yes, may I not go to driveling!
> Thus spoke Brahma to Prajapati; Prajapati, to Manu; Manu, to human beings.
> Whoever has learned the Veda according to rule from the family of a teacher, in time left over from doing work for the teacher; whoever, after having come back again, continues Veda-study in a home of his own in a clean place and produces [sons and pupils]; whoever has concentrated all his sense upon the Atman; he who is harmless [*ahimsant*] toward all things except at holy places [at animal sacrifices]—whoever lives thus throughout his span of life, reaches the Brahma-world and does not return hither again—yes, he does not return hither again!

73

The conception of salvation in the Upanishads and in almost all of Indian thought, including Jainism and Buddhism no less than Hinduism, is the opposite of the Christian notion. The Indian seeks salvation from life everlasting, while the Christian desires life everlasting. But the Christian imagination has never succeeded very well in picturing eternal life in any way that would make the desire for it reasonable. Somehow, the prospect of extinction when one died had become oppressive to some people in the Near East during the centuries before Jesus appeared, and the Pharisees, like many of those who sought Jesus's advice, hoped for immortal life. In India people had a more concrete and detailed notion of eternal life; it meant endless incarnations in one body after another, with no prospect of rest, cessation, peace.

Seeing how millions of Indians live today, one naturally wonders whether life in the seventh and sixth centuries B.C. was particularly wretched, and whether the wish for an end to eternal rebirths was begotten by despair. After all, we do not find it in the Vedas; we do find it in the Upanishads and in the Jaina's and the Buddha's teachings. What happened, we ask, in between? But we do not know. It seems plausible to posit physical reasons for a spread of hopelessness, but no evidence has come to light. Moreover, it is plain that the development of otherworldliness in the Near East coincided with—and presumably was prompted in large measure by—oppression. As people upon people lost their independence to large empires and no longer had control of their affairs, this-worldly hopes gave way to other-worldly hopes—but not a growing hope for an end to life when one died. Of course, those who believe the Christian promise are not likely to believe that the desire for life in another world was prompted by despair; but the question of whether this promise is true is really independent of the question of why such large numbers of people even among the Jews, who had dispensed with such hopes through most of the Biblical period, came to long for life in another world.

In any case, Indian philosophy, which is older than any other philosophy, including that of the Greeks, was born of the desire for release from time and endless transmigration. It was begotten by the quest for knowledge that was needed for salvation. So was Christian philosophy, which issued from the need to define precisely what one must believe in order to be saved.

Those who find such motives uncongenial ought to ask themselves what other motives have ever led large numbers of people to occupy themselves with philosophy. In the ancient Greco-Roman world the most important alternative was certainly the quest for a good and happy life in this world, happiness usually being understood in an extremely refined way. This was the motivation of Aristotle and the Stoics and the Epicureans, for example. If many or even most contemporary philosophers find that motive unworthy, too, because it is unprofessional and a decent philosopher should not be motivated by fear of living badly any more than by the fear of hell or rebirth, one must retort that such a stress on fear is ill-advised. As a defender of Indian philosophy has put the matter rather well: "The subtleties of modern philosophy should on these terms be necessitated by the fear of being regarded as less clever than one's colleagues, or the fear of not getting tenure" (Staal, 174). No doubt, large numbers of people have unedifying motives in all ages, while genuine philosophers become absorbed in problems and are carried forward by an interest that will not be denied.

In the Upanishads we do not yet encounter individual philosophers with distinct intellectual personalities. Yet it was here that philosophy originated in reflections on the Vedas that were prompted by the search for redemption. The way of life of the forest sages was a far cry from the warlike life found in the Vedas. The sages were Brahmins and still performed ancient rituals, including sacrifices, but they did not expect salvation from the gods. They had learned from the Vedas that Indra was Varuna, and Varuna Mitra, and that the multiplicity of the gods was only apparent, as ultimately there was only One. They had also learned from the magnificent hymn on the creation that "the gods came into being later." That was no sufficient reason for disregarding the proprieties, but in order not to be reborn one needed more than ritual and sacrifices. What was needed was knowledge, but even that was not enough. Since it is clear from the texts that the sages practiced meditation, it seems evident that what was wanted was an experience in which one did not come to know Atman as an object but was seized by him—a mystical union. Redemption was originally an experience.

In this experience, multiplicity and time were left behind. Here was "the One without duality." In Vedic times, Soma juice led to altered states of consciousness. In the Upanishads, intellectual discipline is required for the attainment of the mystical union, and so is meditation, as well as a high degree of self-control and apparently life in the forest, ministering and listening to a sage who has had the experience. Those who have had it and presumably keep having it expect not to be reborn.

These ideas furnished the background against which the Jaina and the Buddha de-

veloped their doctrines, which will be considered in another chapter. They also marked
the beginning of Hindu philosophy, and something needs to be said about that.

74

The philosophy that most directly developed the ideas of the Upanishads is the
Vedanta. Since Europeans first became deeply interested in Indian thought in the early
nineteenth century, the Vedanta has been studied and talked about far more than any
other Indian system, but it is actually only one of six traditional systems of thought, all
of which are considered orthodox and somehow complementary. We have not traced
the development of Jewish, Christian, or Muslim philosophy, and cannot here explore
Indian philosophy, which is every bit as subtle and complex. But all six systems require
mention to provide a better perspective for the Upanishads and later Indian thought,
including Jainism and Buddhism.

In India, too, the Vedanta has had and still has as much prestige as any of the six,
if not more. Shankara, who died in A.D. 820 in his thirties, was its greatest exponent;
Vivekananda, Aurobindo Ghose, and Radhakrishnan, who became president of India,
have been more recent representatives of this school. Those coming to Vedanta by
way of its modern interpreters should keep in mind how heavily these men were influenced by Western thought. Vivekananda (1863–1902), who gained a considerable
following in the United States and Europe, was a disciple of Ramakrishna (1836–1886),
a Bengali like himself, who had reached his doctrine after immersing himself not only
in Hinduism but also in Islam and Christianity. For all that, his central teaching that
all religions are acceptable ways to the one God owed far more to the Upanishads than
it did to Christianity and Islam.

Aurobindo, as he is usually called, was born in Bengal in 1872, but was brought up
in England, where he lived for fourteen years and attended the universities of London
and Cambridge. It was only after his return to India in 1893 that he immersed himself
in Indian studies. Eventually the British jailed him as a leader of a terrorist organiza-
tion, and in prison he experienced a profound conversion. After his release in 1910 he
founded an ashram (retreat) in Pondicherry, in southern India, and wrote books that
made a deep impression on people in many countries. When he died in 1950, some
considered him the greatest mystic of his time.

Sarvepalli Radhakrishnan was born in southern India in 1888 but spent many years
at Oxford and became interested in British idealism. Like many Indian philosophers,
he felt an affinity for Hegel and F. H. Bradley, whose *Appearance and Reality* has
seemed as attractive to modern Vedantists as it has been uncongenial to contemporary
Anglo-American philosophers. It was Bradley who called his ethic one of self-realization,
meaning the fullest possible development of one's talents and personality so as to contribute the maximum to one's society. The application of the same term to the Upanishads makes for confusion.

The serious student of Vedanta still has to go back to Shankara, who was born a
Brahmin in the deep south of India, near Cochin, and traveled widely—but only in
India. His commentaries on the Brahma Sutra and on ten major Upanishads present
often bold interpretations that remove apparent contradictions and add up to a consistent system known as Advaita Vedanta, or nondualistic Vedanta. "Vedanta" means
literally the end of the Veda. Shankara taught that the world was *maya* and that ultimate reality was One, meaning that the gods, too, are ultimately unreal, but he also
recognized other levels of less ultimate truth—and did this not only in the course of
brilliant arguments but was also a fervent Shaivite.

By his time, religion in India had changed enormously since the days of the

Upanishads when, for all we know, the Brahmins had no temples nor any idols. Certainly there were none made of stone. But by the ninth century, temples, carvings, and statues abounded, and most of the temples were dedicated either to Vishnu or Shiva. 73 Vishnu is a minor deity in the Rigveda, and Shiva is not mentioned at all but was later identified with Rudra, one of the less important Vedic gods. In Shankara's time, as now, most Indians were devoted mainly to either Vishnu or Shiva, without denying the other gods. One way of reconciling Vishnu and Shiva was the *Trimurti*, the Hindu trinity, which comprises Brahma (not to be confused with Brahman) as creator, Vishnu as preserver, and Shiva as destroyer. It naturally invites comparison with the Christian Trinity, but A. L. Basham is surely right in remarking that "the parallel is not very close, and the Hindu trinity, unlike the Holy Trinity of Christianity, never really 'caught on'" (310). It did result in one of the finest and most famous Indian sculptures. On the island of Elephanta near Bombay, there is an immense head with three faces at right angles, probably fashioned within a hundred years of Shankara's death, but even that stands in a Shiva temple; there are very few temples dedicated to Brahma; and most Indians prefer to concentrate on one god or goddess when they worship.

The most important of these besides Shiva and Vishnu is a goddess who has several names and is said to be "Shiva's consort," Parvati. Less often, she is called Uma. She is also worshiped as "the mother," but is not very much like the Christian "Mother of God" or the Great Mother of the pre-Christian cults. For she is also associated with terrifying power and cruelty and is then called Durga, or Kali. She is worshiped by most traditional Hindus, and some sects consider her the supreme deity. Often she is simply called Devi (goddess). Lakshmi, Vishnu's consort, is not nearly so important.

Shiva, too, has his terrifying aspect, yet is not by any means only the destroyer. He also preserves and is so strongly associated with creativity that he is most often worshiped in the form of the *lingam*, a very simple, stylized phallic symbol. This seems to be a sur- 77,79 vival from the Harappa culture. The greatest gods of the Vedas, Varuna, Indra, or Mitra, no longer have any significant place in worship. But there are many other gods of whom Ganesha, Shiva's son, is probably the best known because he is so easy to recognize by his elephant head.

All this may seem a far cry from Vedanta, but it is not. It seems a safe surmise that the Indians have so many gods because the country is so large, the indigenous population in different regions had their gods, and the invaders, who composed the Vedas, theirs; and in some cases one simply said that two or three or even four gods were the same and merely had a number of different names. It is not really such a long way from this idea to Ramakrishna's notion that Hinduism and Islam and Christianity and all the other great religions really worship the same God. Or to Shankara's doctrine that all diversity is deceptive and that ultimate reality is One. To get agitated about differences between cults or religions only shows that one is not enlightened. Salvation comes through knowledge gained by thought and meditation—not one alone but both.

It should be plain by now how the traditional dichotomy of monotheism and polytheism is unhelpful. Realizing that their British conquerors despised polytheism, some Hindus have insisted that Hinduism is monotheistic; but that is misleading, too. Many Hindus do believe in many gods, but the Vedantists are obviously neither monotheists nor polytheists, nor will it do to call Shankara a pantheist. Like Sophocles, he was above such crude distinctions.

Another label that does not fit Shankara and many other Hindus is "idolater." Images of Shiva and Brahma are illustrated and discussed in this book; Shiva will also 73,80 be encountered in chapter X; and the whole question of "idols" will be taken up in the discussion of religions and the arts. Meanwhile the Vedanta needs to be seen in the context of the other five orthodox systems.

Vishnu, Prambanan, Java, 9th century.

Shiva's sons: Ganesha on a rat; Karttikeya on a peacock. Wood.

The six systems are usually arranged in three pairs, and Vedanta is paired with *Mimamsa*. It started out as an exposition and defense of the Vedas against any criticism, maintaining that they were eternal and authoritative. Then it came to include the cultivation of logic and semantics, as well as law, and by Shankara's time it was merging with the Vedanta.

Another pair that merged in the Middle Ages need not concern us here because it comes so close to being secular philosophy: *Nyaya*, mainly concerned with logic and the theory of knowledge, and *Vaishesika*, a physical theory that developed the idea that nature is made up of atoms. This theory was developed in India before it appeared among the pre-Socratics, and the Buddha's older contemporary, the Jina, shared it. So did some later Buddhist schools.

Of the last two systems, the *Sankhya* may be as old as the Upanishads. Like Jainism, it leaves no room for gods and is dualistic. While it recognizes twenty-five basic principles, it will suffice to mention two. Prakriti and purusha are usually rendered as "matter" (or "nature") and "person." Almost everything, including the other basic principles, is derived from matter, but persons are not, and there are infinitely many of them, all of them eternal and as independent of matter as matter is of them. In the Middle Ages, however, Prakriti was understood by some sects as the consort of Purusha, and the genesis of things was then explained in less philosophical terms.

Yoga may be even better known than the Vedanta. The name is related to the English "yoke" and suggests union as well as severe discipline. This was spelled out in terms of eight stages. It would be difficult to improve on Basham's succinct summary (326):

> 1. Self-control (*yama*), the practice of the five moral rules: non-violence, truthfulness, not stealing, chastity, and the avoidance of greed.
> 2. Observance (*niyama*), the regular and complete observance of the above five rules.
> 3. Posture (*asana*), sitting in certain postures, difficult without practice, which are thought to be essential to meditation. The most famous of these is . . . the "Lotus Posture" . . .
> 4. Control of the breath (*pranayama*) . . .
> 5. Restraint (*pratyahara*), whereby the sense organs are trained to take no note of their perceptions.
> 6. Steadying the Mind (*dharana*), by concentration on a single object, such as the tip of the nose, the navel, an icon, or a sacred symbol. [This also illuminates "idolatry."]
> 7. Meditation (*dhyana*), when the object of concentration fills the whole mind.
> 8. Deep meditation (*samadhi*), when the whole personality is temporarily dissolved.

This is *rajayoga* (royal yoga). *Mantrayoga* (yoga of spells—or sounds) relies on the repetition of magical syllables or phrases; *hathayoga* (yoga of force) relies on exercises and very difficult postures, "and sometimes advocated sexual union as a means of salvation." *Layayoga* (yoga of dissolution), which is "often identified with hathayoga," involves a physiological theory that Western physiologists consider simply false; and so does Basham, adding that the subject needs further study "by open-minded biologists and psychologists, who may reveal the true secret of the yogi" (327); for it cannot be denied that some yogins have performed remarkable feats.

One can also question yoga, and to some extent the other systems, too, from quite another point of view. One may wonder whether such extreme preoccupation with oneself is commendable. If it should seem priggish to even raise such a doubt, one can readily grant that this path seems more attractive than that chosen, say, by Innocent III, when he launched the Albigensian Crusade, or by Gregory IX when he unleashed the Inquisition. But other comparisons come to mind; with the Hebrew prophets, for example, and their concern for the treatment of the poor. There obviously is no reason why one could not do some yoga and also try to do something for others. But it is plain that this has not been emphasized either in the Vedas or in the Upanishads; and raja-yoga, mantrayoga, and hathayoga do not stand alone among the traditional Indian systems in diverting attention from social evils and teaching select individuals to find salvation for themselves. There are other forms of yoga, such as *karmayoga* and *bhakti-yoga*, which stress, respectively, action and ardent devotion to a god; and we shall have occasion to consider them when we come to the Gita. But before we do that, we must consider the caste system; for the criticism suggested here has to be seen in that perspective.

Aryan invader, ca. 3rd century. Gandhara protrait in stucco from Hadda.

IX

HINDUISM:
CASTE, THE GITA, AND GANDHI

Caste and Women—The Gita—Gandhi

Shiva Nataraja, Tanjore.

75

Hinduism without caste is a little like Christianity without God. Both kinds of "expurgation" have been attempted, but neither has caught on. Most Christians and Hindus seem to feel that what would remain after such surgery would no longer be their religion.

Since the Vedic age the caste system has been central in Indian life, and Hinduism .is built around it. The Jina and the Buddha rejected the system, as the Sikhs, too, have done, at least in theory, in modern times, but Hinduism would not go along with them. On paper, of course, it is easy to have Hinduism without caste, but that only goes to show how far removed from the realities many accounts of Hinduism are.

"Caste" is a term of European origin. It is derived from the Latin *castus*, which means "pure," and was used by the Portuguese when they came to India. The Indian word is *varna*, which means "color."

The most comprehensive account of the caste system is found in the Laws of Manu. Manu is mentioned in the Upanishads, but there is no agreement about the date of the metrical version in which his law has come down to us. Some scholars date it as early as the third century B.C., others as late as the first century A.D. But there is agreement that this version is based on earlier versions with much the same content, and the basic structure that is codified here reaches back long before the age of the Buddha.

Its foundations are to be found in the Rigveda; for example, in hymn 90 of the tenth book, which is about Purusha, who is said at the outset to have "a thousand eyes, a thousand feet." "This Purusha is all that ever has been and all that will be." But then "the gods prepared the sacrifice with Purusha as their offering." The crucial verses are eleven and twelve:

> When they divided Purusha,
> how many portions did they make?
> What do they call his mouth, his arms?
> What do they call his thighs and feet?
>
> The Brahmin was his mouth,
> of both his arms was the Rajanya made,
> his thighs became the Vaishya,
> from his feet the Shudra was produced.

This is the only place in the Rigveda where Shudras are mentioned, and there has been some debate about the age of this passage, but here we have the four original varnas; only the Rajanya were later called Kshatriya.

There is a similar passage in the Laws of Manu in which Manu, after fashioning the world, "caused the Brahmin, the Kshatriya, the Vaishya, and the Shudra to proceed from his mouth, his arms, his thighs, and his feet" (I:31). Men were not created equal, are not all descended from a single couple, and are not all made in the image of the deity, and they are to remain unequal. Varna is hereditary, and the central conception of the system is stated succinctly in the Laws of Manu (X:4–5):

> The Brahmin, the Kshatriya, and the Vaishya varnas are the twice-born, while the fourth, the Shudra, has one birth only; there is no fifth.
> In all varnas only those begotten in the direct line on wedded wives, equal (in varna and married as) virgins, are to be counted as belonging to the same varna (as their fathers).

Actually, there are far more than four varnas in India. Megasthenes, a Greek writing around 300 b.c., noted seven, and scholars feel certain that even then there were many more.* But it seems best to consider the proliferation of castes later and to begin with the basic four, or rather with the dichotomy between the three twice-born varnas and the Shudra. This most fundamental distinction originated in the Vedic age, at the time of the Aryan invasion of India. A distinction frequently encountered in the literature of that time is that of "the Aryans, white-skinned, good-featured, making sacrifices and worshipping gods like Agni, Indra, Varuna, etc., from the Dasas or Dasyus, who were"— omitting the Sanskrit terms also given by Dutt—"black-skinned, flat-nosed, of unintelligible speech, not sacrificing, worshipping no god, and following strange customs" (50 f.). Basham thinks it safe to assume that these Dasas were the survivors of the Harappa culture (32).

Initially, these Dasas were massacred. But while Dasa originally meant "enemy," Dasi, the feminine form, never meant the wife of the enemy; it always meant a female slave. "This shows that at first captives were taken of women only, the males not being spared, and that at a later stage male Dasas were also acquired as slaves" (Dutt, 51). For later Dasa came to mean slave and then gave way to another term, Shudra. The origin of the word "Shudra" is uncertain, but it may originally have been "the name of some prominent Dasa tribe conquered and reduced to slavery by the Aryans." The fate of these people is summed up in these words of the Aitareye Brahmana (VII:29): a Shudra "may be driven away or slain at will."

In the Vedas, then, we have a dichotomy between two kinds of people, the light-skinned and the black-skinned, the Aryans and the non-Aryans; and at that time there seems to have been no restriction on intermarriage between Aryans (57). One is reminded of Zarathustra's dualism, but the dark enemy of the Vedas is not encountered in the Gathas; it is the indigenous population of India. That these people worshiped no god is very unlikely. It is much more probable that Shiva and the other Hindu gods and goddesses who are not mentioned in the Vedas were eventually taken over from the native population. It is also virtually certain that Indian art and architecture owes more to the Dravidian non-Aryans than to the Aryan invaders. But we shall come to that in the chapter on art.

The tripartite division of the conquerors corresponds very closely to the three classes in Plato's *Republic*, composed much later, in the fourth century b.c. This is certainly based on occupations, and it is not clear whether there was any ethnic foundation for these differences. We do find the view that the Brahmins are white, the Kshatriya red, and the Vaishyas darker, and it is also plain that the Vaishyas are considered inferior to the first two varnas. But there is evidence that the Brahmins and the Kshatriya did not agree about who deserved primacy, any more than the medieval popes and emperors did. The Brahmins were the priests, while the Kshatriya were the kings and

---

* See the section on "Caste in Greek Accounts" in Dutt.

warriors. In the sacred texts, the Brahmins are supreme—because the sacred texts were written by Brahmins.

The first way in which the system of the four varnas required amplification was to account for those who did not belong to any of the four categories, the outcastes. Manu derives them from miscegenation. If a Brahmin woman has a child by a Shudra, that child is a "Chandala, the lowest of men" (X:16).

Almost equally base is the Svapaka, who is thought to be descended from a Kshatriya and an Ugra woman, and the Ugra in turn are supposed to be the offspring of a Kshatriya and a female Shudra and "resembling both a Kshatriya and a Shudra, ferocious in manners and delighting in cruelty" (X:9). Here are Manu's provisions for the Chandalas and Svapakas: Their dwellings "shall be outside the village," and

> Their dress shall be the garments of the dead, they shall eat their food from broken dishes, black iron shall be their ornaments, and they must always wander from place to place.
> . . . their transactions shall be among themselves, and their marriages with their equals . . .
> By day they may go about for the purpose of their work, distinguished by marks at the king's command, and they shall carry out the corpses (of persons) who have no relatives; that is a settled rule.
> By the king's order they shall always execute the criminals, in accordance with the law, and they shall take for themselves the clothes, the beds, and the ornaments of (such) criminals (X:51–56).

While it is possible that the children of Brahmin women and Shudra fathers were "exposed"—not, as Oedipus was in Greece, in order to die, but by being abandoned to the outcastes who were dwelling outside the village—it seems highly improbable that this was the origin of the Chandalas. As the children of Israel expressed their opinion of Moab and Ammon by saying that they were descended from the daughters of Lot who made their father drunk and then cohabited with him, Manu derived these outcastes from what he considered a similar abomination. It seems to be a safe surmise that these people were ethnically different from the Shudras and despised "even" by them. They almost certainly were nomadic tribes. In fact, they are encountered as early as the Yajurveda as

> savage races, who had been on a very low culture-level, lived in a repulsively dirty fashion and followed the primitive professions of hunting and fishing when they were first met by the conquering Aryans. . . . The great contempt with which these peoples were treated becomes somewhat more explicable if we remember that, besides being of extremely dirty habits and low culture, they belonged to a Pre-Dravidian stock, probably Munda-Monkhmer race, who had remained unabsorbed by the Dravidians, and had been treated as pariahs even by the latter (Dutt, 89 f.).

To the modern mind, the very idea of considering people unclean, of refusing to eat with them, and of feeling that physical contact with them is to be avoided seems outrageous. But the modern traveler to India is still asked again and again by liberal friends: Did you get sick? And he quickly discovers that if he has any regard for his health, he cannot share the food and drink of most people. Unquestionably, one element in Manu's system is a simple regard for hygiene. But if it should be true that some of these savages who were classified and treated as outcastes were Mon-Khmer people, it is noteworthy that the Buddha images created by the Mon-Khmer in Thailand and Cambodia, beginning around the seventh century A.D., are among the finest works of art ever created.

125,127,129, 134–140

Here are some of Manu's provisions for the Shudras, who are discussed at great length in his law:

> A Brahmin may compel a Shudra, whether bought or unbought, to do servile work; for he was created by the self-existent to be the slave of a Brahmin.
> A Shudra, though emancipated by his master, is not released from servitude; since that is innate in him, who could set him free from it? (VIII:413 f.)
> A wife, a son, and a slave, these three are declared to have no property; the wealth they earn is for him to whom they belong.
> A Brahmin may confidently seize the goods of (his) Shudra; for as he can have no property, his master may take his possessions.
> (The king) should carefully compel Vaishyas and Shudras to perform the work (prescribed) for them; for if these two swerved from their duties, they would throw this world into confusion (VIII:416–18).

Indeed, if the two lower classes did not do their appointed work, the whole society would collapse. In verse 417 one may wonder whether the translator's parenthetical addition of "his" is justified, or whether a Brahmin is entitled to rob, or forcibly expropriate, any Shudra at all. But the problem does not arise, because every Shudra is supposed to be somebody's slave, and if one were free, then any Brahmin could make him his own slave at will. In a footnote, the translator informs us that three important commentaries explain the word "confidently" in the same verse as meaning "without fearing that he commits the sin of accepting a present from a Shudra." But Manu holds out hope for the Shudra:

> To serve Brahmins learned in the Vedas, householders, and famous (for virtue) is the highest duty of a Shudra, which leads to beatitude.
> (A Shudra who is) pure, the servant of his betters, gentle in his speech, and free from pride, and always seeks a refuge with Brahmins, attains (in his next life) a higher caste (IX:334–5).

It will have been noted that a wife is ranked with a slave. Dutt deals at length with the position of women. Here it will suffice to cite some of the main points.

> The Brahmin sages in the later Samhitas and Brahmanas evinced a brutal spirit towards the weaker sex and impressed a permanent mark of degradation upon the position of women. . . . The position of women has suffered a great decline since the Rigvedic period, and this has gone hand in hand with the increasing severity of caste rules and ceremonial purity. First of all, probably on account of the large accession of [a] black non-Aryan female element into the harems and households of the Vedic Aryans in the second stage of their conquest . . . women in general came to be associated with ceremonial impurity, an idea unknown in the days of the Rigveda. Hence the grouping together of a woman and a Shudra in the Brahmana literature . . . (101).

The second point is that polygamy was the rule. But it is noteworthy that in ancient times widows could be wed, while later this was forbidden and widows were actually burned on their husbands' funeral pyres. And when the British put an end to that custom, the life of widows in India became a kind of hell on earth.

Introducing some selections from the Laws of Manu, in *A Source Book in Indian Philosophy*, Radhakrishnan has said: "A high place is given to women" (172). But Dutt's comments are far more accurate:

> It is a pleasure in the midst of the general depreciation of woman in the Indian religious and legal literature to come across some rare passages embodying very noble sentiments towards the female sex, such as Manu III. 55–61 . . . It cannot be denied that even in such passages women are honoured as potential mothers and obedient wives, and they do not much take away from the general cynical tone . . . (197).

Moreover, the following two verses are also from the Laws of Manu:

> A wife, a son, a slave, a pupil, and a (younger) brother of the full blood, who have committed faults, may be beaten with a rope or a split bamboo.
> But on the back part of the body, never on a noble part; he who strikes them otherwise will incur the same guilt as a thief (VIII:299–300).

Manu's provisions for the twice-born still remain to be considered:

> Brahmins who are intent on the means (of gaining union with) Brahman and firm in (discharging) their duties, shall live by duly performing the following six acts, in their order.
> Teaching, studying, sacrificing for himself, sacrificing for others, making gifts, and receiving them are the six acts for a Brahmin.
> But among the six acts for him, three are his means of subsistence: sacrificing for others, teaching, and accepting gifts from pure men.
> From the Brahmin to the Kshatriya: three acts (incumbent on the former) are forbidden: teaching, sacrificing for others, and, thirdly, the acceptance of gifts.
> The same are likewise forbidden to a Vaishya, that is a settled rule; for Manu, the lord of creatures, has not prescribed them for those two.
> To carry arms for striking and for throwing (is prescribed) for Kshatriyas as a means of subsistence; to trade, (to rear) cattle, and agriculture for Vaishyas; but their duties are liberality, the study of the Veda, and the performance of sacrifices (X:74–9).

In an emergency, a Brahmin may support himself like a Kshatriya; and if worse comes to worst, members of the two higher castes may maintain themselves by "living by a Vaishya's mode of subsistence," provided they observe certain exceptions.

The overall division of society that Manu codified and imposed on India is relatively simple, in spite of the wealth of detail. There are a class of priests, a class of soldiers, and a class of men who farm and trade; beneath these three classes, there is a class of slaves; and beneath that, on the fringes of society, are all kinds of outcastes. The sages' most noble duty consists of teaching and studying the Vedas. The Vedas are considered not only sacred but also full of miraculous powers:

> A Brahmin who retains in his memory the Rigveda is not stained by guilt, though he may have destroyed these three worlds, though he may eat the food of anybody.
> He who, with a concentrated mind, thrice recites the Riksamhita, or Yajur-veda, or Sama-veda together with the secret (texts, the Upanishads), is completely freed from all sins.
> As a clod of earth, falling into a great lake, is quickly dissolved, even so every sinful act is engulfed in the threefold Veda (XI:262–264).

It will be noted how a rather problematic idea we encountered in the Upanishads has here been vulgarized.

Even if a few of these ideas developed after the time of the Buddha, this system was a feature of the time in which he lived and helps us to gain some notion of the independence of his spirit, and that of the Jina. The following two verses represent the reaction of the lawgiver to the teachings of the Buddha and the Jina:

> All those traditions and all those despicable systems of philosophy which are not based on the Veda, produce no reward after death . . .
> All those (doctrines), differing from the (Veda), which spring up and perish, are worthless and false, because they are of modern date (XII:95–6).

It would be easy to give a very different, and highly misleading, impression of the Laws of Manu by citing a few sentences out of context, leaving out of account the overall structure. Thus two verses out of the section dealing with the ascetic are occasionally quoted without as much as a mention of the fact that they deal with the ascetic only.

The section on the ascetic consists of ninety-seven verses. Here, too, caste distinctions are observed; only the twice-born may become ascetics. The verses sometimes cited to give a glowing impression of the spirit of the whole book are marked with an asterisk below:

> Let him not desire to die, let him not desire to live; let him wait for (his appointed) time, as a servant for the payment of his wages.
> Let him put down his foot purified by his sight, let him drink water purified by (straining with) a cloth, let him utter speech purified by truth, let him keep his heart pure.
> * Let him patiently bear hard words, let him not insult anybody, and let him not become anybody's enemy for the sake of this (perishable) body.
> * Against an angry man let him not in return show anger, let him bless when he is cursed, and let him not utter speech, devoid of truth, scattered at the seven gates.
> Delighting in what refers to the Soul, sitting (in the postures prescribed by the Yoga), independent (of external help), entirely abstaining from sensual enjoyments, with himself for his only companion, he shall live in this world, desiring the bliss (of final liberation). . . .
> His vessels shall not be made of metal, they shall be free from fractures; it is ordained that they shall be cleansed with water, like (the cups called) Kamasa, at a sacrifice. . . (VI:45–9 and 53).

Insulting other men or defaming them is quite generally forbidden; but the penalties are graded, depending on the caste both of the offender and the offended. A very few examples may suffice: "A Brahmin shall be fined fifty (panas) for defaming a Kshatriya; in (the case of) a Vaishya the fine shall be twenty-five; in (the case of) a Shudra twelve" (VIII:268). If this is rather like the law of Hammurabi, what follows is different:

> A once-born man (a Shudra), who insults a twice-born man with gross invective, shall have his tongue cut out; for he is of low origin.
> If he mentions their names and castes with contumely, an iron nail, ten fingers long, shall be thrust red-hot into his mouth.
> If he arrogantly teaches Brahmins their duty, the king shall cause hot oil to be poured into his mouth and into his ears (VIII:270–2).
>
> A low-caste man who tries to place himself on the same seat with a man of a high caste, shall be branded on his hip and be banished, or (the king) shall cause his buttock to be gashed.
> If out of arrogance he spits (on a superior), the king shall cause both his lips to be cut off; if he urinates (on him), the penis; if he breaks wind (against him), the anus (VIII:281–2).

The Laws of Manu end: "A twice-born man who recites these Institutes, revealed by Manu, will be always virtuous in conduct, and will reach whatever condition he desires" (XII:126).

Thus we are saved from the popular assumption that the great religious figures of the world agree about moral questions. Nor can their striking differences be taken care of by arranging them chronologically, as if less humane views were always early and more humane attitudes gradually replaced them. Those responsible for the present metrical form of the Laws of Manu considered the teachings of the Buddha despicable, and Moses and Amos, who lived centuries before the Buddha, disagreed on essentials with both him and Manu.

Of course, we do not know how often the gruesome punishments mentioned in the

Laws of Manu were actually administered, and it is very probable that they were applied far less frequently than the tortures of the Inquisition. But they help to define a milieu in which the "crimes" they were presumably intended to prevent could hardly have occurred often.

As for the red-hot iron nail, it may come as a surprise to the many admirers of Saint Thomas More, the author of *Utopia* (1516), that he said in his *Confutations* that heretics should have their tongues bored with a red-hot iron. In the midseventeenth century, James Naylor rode into Bristol naked on a donkey, claiming to be Christ, and was actually punished in precisely this way.* It would seem that this was considered a particularly fitting punishment for blasphemy in England as well as in India, although there was some difference of opinion about what counted as blasphemy.

The greatest difference between the Laws of Manu, as described so far, and the realities of the system not only in our time but for many centuries now is that there are so many more castes than the original four plus the various kinds of outcastes. Manu already distinguished between the four varnas, insisting that there were no more than four, and *jatis*, of which he distinguished about fifty, as well as *vratyas*. The jatis he derived from mixtures of the varnas and the vratyas from degradations caused by the failure to observe prescribed rites. Thus he recognized five kinds of Vratya Brahmins, seventeen kinds of Vratya Kshatriyas, including the Greeks and the Chinese (!), and six kinds of Vratya Vaishyas. "Yet it will not do to reject Manu's views as absolutely stupid and nonsensical. That new social groups are produced by intertribal marriages can still be observed among some of the aboriginal tribes in India . . ."; and Dutt goes on to give many relevant examples.

In sum, the difference between the light-skinned Aryan invaders and the dark-skinned non-Aryan native population prompted the dichotomy between the twice-born and the Shudras; tribal differences contributed their share to the endless complexities of the caste system; and the division of labor did not merely accompany these differentiations but led to unending subdivisions. Hence the aspect of the caste system of which many people are most immediately aware is the occupational difference from group to group (5 ff.); and the total number of castes and subcastes now is said to be 3,000 or more. Moreover, as Basham points out (150), in the largely non-Aryan, Dravidian south of India, there have been almost only Brahmins, Shudras, and untouchables, but the Shudras, being most numerous,

> were divided into two great caste groups, known as the right and left hands. The great animosity and rivalry which still exists between these groups is at least a thousand years old. On the right are the trading castes, some weaving castes, musicians, potters, washermen, barbers, and most of the cultivating and labouring castes; on the left are various castes of craftsmen, such as weaver and leather workers, cowherds, and some cultivating castes. We have no evidence how this strange bisection of society arose.

Naturally, relatively liberal sentiments have occasionally found expression within this system, notably in this passage of the Mahabharata, the greatest Indian epic. Yaksha asks: "Of what does Brahmindhood really consist: of descent, conduct, the study of the Veda, or learning?" And the answer (III:313), quoted by Dutt (216), is: none of these. "Character is, no doubt, the basis of Brahmindhood. . . . A man without character, though he may have learned all of the four Vedas, is not better than a Shudra. He that offers the fire sacrifice and at the same time curbs his senses is known to be a Brahmin." But no Shudra could possibly offer the fire sacrifice.

---

* Information from Richard Marius, one of the editors of More's collected works.

That the caste system obtained such a stranglehold on Indian life is due in large measure to the most famous and influential part of the Mahabharata, the Bhagavadgita.

76

The Bhagavadgita (Song of the Lord), or Gita (song) for short, is beyond compare the most popular, beloved, and influential of all the many sacred scriptures of the Hindus. It is also available in a great many translations—many of them rather free— and hence so widely known that there is no need to try to proportion the length of this discussion to its importance. On the contrary, an extremely concise summary of some of the most central points of the Gita is likely to be more helpful than a detailed chapter-by-chapter account.

At the beginning of the Gita, Arjuna, a great hero of unquestioned courage, with his army ready for battle, decides not to fight. He has no wish for victory or pleasure and does not want to kill those ranged against him—not for anything in the world. Even though they should slay him, he would not fight back to slay them.

This is truly extraordinary and shows how far Indian thought had come since the age of the Vedas. One can hardly help wondering at this point whether Arjuna has been overcome by the ethic of the Buddha, and whether Lord Krishna's exhortation, which makes up the bulk of the Gita, is a plea to forsake this despicable ethic and return to the ways of the Vedas. But Arjuna has a special reason for not wishing to fight; those opposing him are his kinsmen. There is no need here to explore the context of the Gita in the Mahabharata, which explains how this situation came about. What is relevant is that Arjuna does not argue against all war but against this particular battle.

At this point, toward the end of the first chapter, Arjuna seems to digress. Where family ties are broken, he argues, the women become corrupt; and once that happens, there will be a mixing of castes, which leads to hell (1:40–42).

Then Krishna answers him, urging him to fight. The Gita is so familiar that many people fail to be struck by the fact that one of the most sacred scriptures of India should be cast in the form of an exhortation to go to battle. Surely, one would expect the opposite—that a man wishing to fight is persuaded to seek peace. Now it is obviously possible to interpret a sacred text to say almost anything one wishes to hear; and in the case of the Gita, as in that of the Gospels, contemporary examples are not hard to find. But we should not be totally unmindful of the significance of a book in its historic context and of its influence on many generations of believers, who thought that war meant war, and caste meant caste, and hell meant hell. Nor is it at all clear that they did not.

Khrishna argues that the soul is immortal and keeps moving from body to body. "Therefore fight, O scion of Bharata! Whoever thinks that this slays and that that is slain, lacks knowledge. He is never born, nor does he die; nor having been once, does he cease to be. He is unborn, eternal, changeless, primeval. He is not slain when the body is slain" (2:18 ff.). This is surely a straightforward argument that comes directly to the point and, appealing to central ideas of the Upanishads, sanctions killing and—one might suppose at this stage—murder or any other atrocity. Many readers have lost the capacity for being shocked, but at this point one ought to ask oneself whether this exhortation could not also be addressed to Stalin or the henchmen of Auschwitz. *Go ahead and kill! You are not really killing anyone. It is all right to torture others.* Surely, a reader ought to ask himself whether the Gita condones total callousness toward the feelings of our fellow men.

Krishna next appeals to Arjuna's duty as a Kshatriya. It is the duty of his varna to fight; and if he does not, people will speak evil of him, and his honor will suffer. It is odd that other men's bodies and killing them are mere appearances and not real, and that one can kill them without qualms, but that one's varna and its traditional duties, one's honor and what other people might say about one, should deserve so much consideration.

The next argument sounds more like the Koran than like the things people say about the Gita: "If you are slain in battle, you will go to heaven; but if you win, you will enjoy the earth!" (2:37). But the next verse introduces a new note: "Regarding pleasure like pain, gain like loss, victory like defeat, fight the battle! Then sin will not stain you." We are after all much closer to the Upanishads than to the Koran. But the next verse brings another surprise: "This is the wisdom of Sankhya; now listen to Yoga . . ." If one recalls that these are two of the six traditional systems of philosophy, and if one further associates the Upanishads with the Vedanta, one may suddenly wonder whether everything said so far is meant to be no more than an exposition of one system, and whether Krishna is now saying in effect: *On the other hand, you can also look at things quite differently.* But it would be a mistake to suppose that only the Vedanta is an interpretation of the Upanishads; nor should one forget that the six systems are held to be compatible and complementary. Zaehner's very scholarly translation is rather free at this point, which would be no serious fault in any case because he offers a careful and erudite commentary; but in this case he also manages to bring out very strongly—probably too strongly—the complementary nature of the two philosophies: "This wisdom (*buddhi*) has [now] been revealed to you in theory; listen now to how it should be practised." This seems a bit too neat, but there certainly is no reversal at this point, no even partial renunciation of what has been said so far.

The doctrine presented now can be stated very briefly, and is stated briefly again and again. "To work you are entitled, never to its fruits. Never let the fruits of work be your motive, nor become attached to inaction" (2:47). "He whose mind is untroubled in the midst of sorrows, and who does not long for pleasures, from whom passion, fear, and anger have departed, he is called a steadfast sage" (2:56). "Work is better than inaction" (3:8). "Therefore, without attachment, always do the work that needs to be done; for by doing work without attachment man attains to the highest" (3:19).

This is totally consistent with the stress on the impermanence, if not illusoriness, of the body. Be not attached to the fashion of this world, which passes away. Only one may wonder why one should be active. This is the *karmayoga* with its stress on work or action (*karma*). One may also wonder whether the emphasis on detachment is a sufficient safeguard against the dangers mentioned earlier, and on reflection, it is clear that it is not. If one's duty involves harming others, or not helping others in need, or even killing or torture, such work can certainly be done without attachment. But that is small comfort for the victim.

No very persuasive reason is given as to why one should be active. Zaehner calls chapter 3 "Why?" and then answers his own question with a heading he inserts: "Work and Bodily Life are Inseparable." Radhakrishnan uses a heading "Why then work at all?" and follows it with a heading "Life is work." These ideas are indeed found in the text but are hardly compelling answers. The Gita, however, is not a mathematical article that offers a new proof. It is more reasonable to see it as a response to Buddhism. The Buddha had argued that the questions discussed in the Upanishads did not tend toward edification. Here were seminars for Brahmins and Kshatriyas who were interested in elusive concepts and pursued them in the forest, but he made salvation available to simple people who had no mind for metaphysical subtleties but could still become monks or nuns. Now the Gita proposes a doctrine of salvation that is in the Vedic tradition of heroism and in many ways close to the Upanishads, but that makes redemption available to all, including simple people. You do not have to withdraw into the forest; you do not have to practice hathayoga and do difficult exercises; you need not become a monk; you can stay in this world and do your job; and you can still be saved if you achieve detachment.

This is not the standard interpretation of the work, nor is there any standard interpretation. All sorts of doctrines have been read into the Gita. But in the process most readers seem to have overlooked its plain meaning. There is much more in it than this, but this is the central idea.

The appeal to the mass of men is formulated very strikingly. "Better one's own duty done badly than the duty of another done well. Better is death while doing one's own duty; the duty of others is perilous" (3:35). It would be difficult to overestimate the importance of this verse, which is repeated once more in almost the same words in the last chapter (18:47). It sanctified the caste system and did its share to persuade men to be content with their wretched duties, no matter how mean and demeaning. It taught men that it was sinful to aspire higher, wicked to say: *I have a talent for another job and could do that much better than a lot of people who have that job and do it badly.* The Bhagavadgita sealed the doom of the downtrodden, held out no hope for talent, condemned all ambition, all worldly aspiration, including the desire for a job in which one might find some fulfillment. "Better one's own duty done badly than the duty of another done well." *Stick to your wretched job; but there is hope for you, if only you will learn detachment.* You, too, can be saved. Meanwhile, the caste society was saved from the threat of Buddhism.

One crucial element remains: *bhaktiyoga*, which relieves the austerity of the doctrine of detachment, which could hardly have become very popular, however it must appeal to many educated people in all ages. *Bhakti* is loving devotion—not to the fruits of work or to anything worldly but to a deity, to Krishna in this case. Krishna is Vishnu incarnate, and while he is by no means Vishnu's only incarnation, in the Gita he personifies all the power and the glory of the divine. When he reveals his majesty to Arjuna, Arjuna's hair stands on end (11:14). Then, in the next chapter, Krishna proclaims that the best yoga is intense devotion to him. Now the ice is broken and he speaks also of compassion: "Whoever hates no being, is friendly and compassionate, done with thoughts of 'I' and 'mine,' indifferent to pain and pleasure, and forgiving, ever content and controlled, firmly determined, his mind and understanding absorbed in me—my devotee is dear to me" (12:13 f.). Four verses in a row end: "is dear to me." Love is reciprocated.

In the next chapter there is still some exposition of Brahman and of Prakriti and Purusha, and in chapter 16:16 ff. Krishna speaks of hell and damnation without any ultimate reprieve.

> Bewildered by many fancies, caught in the net of delusion, obsessed with the satisfaction of their desires, they fall into a foul hell. . . . Full of selfishness, force, and arrogance, lust, and anger, these malicious people despise me as they dwell in their bodies and in those of others. These envious haters, the lowest of men, I hurl ever into devilish wombs, birth upon birth. Caught in devilish wombs, deluded birth upon birth, they never attain me and sink to the lowest state.

In the final chapter, Arjuna is told again to fix his mind entirely on Krishna, and he will prevail, "but if in selfishness you will not listen, you will perish" (58). This is surely less distinctive than the emphasis on detached action, which is then suffused with bhakti.

The devotion to the deity is obviously no adequate safeguard at all for other men. Men have nailed their fellow men to crosses from a sense of duty and, no doubt, in some cases merely from that, with perfect detachment, and some of them may have felt devotion to some deity in the process, as some of the henchmen of the Inquisition unquestionably did. "Those devotees who worship other gods with faith, worship me, but in the wrong way" (9:23). That is surely generous but does not provide any safeguard. That also applies to our last quotation from the Gita: "Even if one commits the most abominable actions, if he is devoted to me unflinchingly, he must be considered righteous, for his resolve is right. Quickly his soul will be justified and win eternal rest. You may rest assured, Arjuna, those devoted to me perish never" (9:30 f.).

The Gita has many dimensions. It offers philosophical instruction but is also a powerful poem; it is full of religious ideas and also contains a theophany—Krishna appearing to Arjuna in his divine aspect—and it is a rich book that millions of people have read again and again and lived with. Such a work cannot be summed up in a few pages. Whatever is said about it briefly must at least be supplemented with the concession that there is much more to it than that. Here, the moral and social dimension has been stressed, and that may well be the most problematic and vulnerable side of the Gita.

77

Instead of attempting a brief survey of Indian history, let us leave some of that to the sections on Indian art, and conclude the present chapter with a section on Gandhi, emphasizing his interpretation of the Gita. In our time the world's religions have produced two world-historical saints: Gandhi and Pope John XXIII. Pope John seems to have been utterly lovable and hardly controversial as a human being. Gandhi seems to have been a much more complex figure, and widely different views have been put forward regarding him as a person; but he was surely one of the major religious figures of the last thousand years, and he was a remarkable thinker. Our concern here will be with his ideas, not his personality or politics.

What Gandhi is remembered for above all is nonviolent resistance and his condemnation of violence. On the face of it, his central doctrine would seem to contradict the teaching of the Gita, which apparently sanctions war even when it involves killing one's own kinsmen, provided only that one is detached and has one's mind on Krishna. This difficulty did not escape Gandhi, and he addressed himself to it repeatedly; for example: "Now about the message of the Gita. . . . Thus, according to the Gita, all acts that are incapable of being performed without attachment are taboo. This golden rule saves mankind from many a pitfall. According to this interpretation murder, lying, dissoluteness and the like must be regarded as sinful and therefore taboo."

The last sentence surely goes against the Gita. It seems quite possible to murder and lie without attachment, in the line of duty. But Gandhi proceeds to read into the Gita the ancient Jain and Buddhist doctrine of *ahimsa* (nonviolence) that the Gita seems expressly designed to reject.

> Thinking along these lines, I have felt that in trying to enforce in one's life the central teaching of the Gita, one is bound to follow Truth and *ahimsa*. When there is no desire for fruit, there is no temptation for untruth or *himsa*. Take any instance of untruth or violence, and it will be found that at its back was the desire to attain the cherished end. [The Gita says that this need not be so.] But it may be freely admitted that the Gita was not written to establish *ahimsa*. It was an accepted and primary duty even before the Gita age. [Indeed, and the Gita taught that *ahimsa* was *not* necessary.] . . .
> But if the Gita believed in *ahimsa* or it was included in desirelessness, why

did the author take a warlike illustration? When the Gita was written, although people believed in *ahimsa*, wars were not only not taboo, but nobody observed the contradiction between them and *ahimsa*.*

In brief, believing in nonviolence and loving the Gita, Gandhi felt that the Gita must teach nonviolence—just as generations of Christians have felt that the Bible must teach their morality. Nor is it enough to note that Gandhi's attempt to read his own moral message into the Gita is not one whit more absurd than was Albert Schweitzer's attempt to read his moral ideas into the Gospels,** or to find a few other comparable examples; what Gandhi illustrates at this point is the exegetical thinking that is almost inseparable from the religious mentality. This is what Jews and Muslims as well as Hindus and Buddhists have done for centuries.

Since Gandhi lived in an age in which this mode of thought was not by any means universal, the oddity of his reading of the Gita was brought home to him again and again. In *My Non-Violence* a section bears the title: "Central Teaching of the Gita." Asked, "Is the central teaching of the Gita selfless action or non-violence?" he replied:

> I have no doubt that it is *anasakti*—selfless action. Indeed I have called my little translation of the Gita *Anasaktiyoga* and *anasakti* transcends Ahimsa. He who would be anasakta (selfless) has necessarily to practise non-violence in order to attain the state of self-lessness. Ahimsa is therefore a necessary preliminary, it is included in *anasakti* . . .

It is objected:

> Lord Krishna actually counters the doctrine of Ahimsa. For Arjuna utters this pacifist resolve:
>> Better I deem it, if my kinsmen strike,
>> To face them weaponless, and bare my breast
>> To shaft and spear, then answer blow with blow.
> And Lord Krishna teaches him to answer blow with blow.

Gandhi replies:

> There I join issue with you . . . Those words of Arjuna were words of pretentious wisdom. "Until yesterday," says Krishna to him, "you fought your kinsmen with deadly weapons without the slightest compunction. Even today you would strike if the enemy was a stranger and not your own kith and kin!" The question before him was not of non-violence, but whether he should slay his nearest and dearest.

True; but Krishna could have taken this occasion to preach a more inclusive compassion and a doctrine of nonviolence; but he did more nearly the opposite.

On another occasion, in 1936, Gandhi admitted:

> Hinduism, as it is practised to-day or has even been known to have ever been practised, has certainly not condemned war as I do. What, however, I have done is to put a new but natural and logical interpretation upon the whole teaching of the Gita and the spirit of Hinduism. Hinduism, not to speak of other religions, is ever evolving. It has no one scripture like the Koran or the Bible. Its scriptures are also evolving and suffering addition. The Gita itself is an instance in point.

It gave new meaning to ancient concepts and spelled out implications of earlier writings that might not have been noted before. Just so, says Gandhi,

> I have endeavoured, in the light of a prayerful study of the other faiths of the world, and what is more, in the light of my own experiences in trying to live the

---

* *The Gospel of Selfless Action or the Gita According to Gandhi* by Mahadev Desai, 35, 39.
** See Kaufmann, 1961, section 60.

teaching of Hinduism as interpreted in the Gita, to give an extended but in no way strained meaning to Hinduism, not as buried in its ample scriptures, but as a living faith speaking like a mother to her aching child. What I have done is perfectly historical. I have followed in the footsteps of our forefathers. At one time they sacrificed animals to propitiate angry gods. Their descendants, but our less remote ancestors, read a different meaning into the word "sacrifice" . . .*

Rarely has this point been put so beautifully. What has not been so rare is the re-interpretation of originally pacifist doctrines to make them compatible with a warlike ethos. That has been one dimension of Zen Buddhism, as will be shown when we come to that. More ironically still, it was what happened to Gandhi's own teaching.

The attitude expressed by Gandhi in the last long quotation sums up much of religious liberalism, and his "study of the other faiths of the world" is noteworthy. The crux of the matter is always that one reads into one's own favorite scripture what one likes best in other traditions. In Gandhi's *Speeches and Writings* there is a section on "The Genesis of Passive Resistance." He was asked, "Surely the *Bhagavad Gita* came first?" And he replied: "No." He had known it, of course, but

It was the New Testament which really awakened me to the rightness and value of Passive Resistance. When I read in the "Sermon on the Mount" such passages as "Resist not him that is evil but whosoever smiteth thee on thy right cheek turn to him the other also" and "Love your enemies and pray for them that persecute you, that ye may be sons of your Father which is in heaven," I was simply overjoyed and found my own opinion confirmed where I least expected it. The *Bhagavad Gita* deepened the impression and Tolstoy's "The Kingdom of God is within you" gave it a permanent form (1,072).

Louis Fischer, who knew Gandhi and all but worshiped him, remarked in his *The Life of Mahatma Gandhi*:

As Gandhi read his deepest convictions into the *Gita*, so he wove his own notions into Ruskin [and perhaps also into the New Testament?]. Those books appealed to him most which were closest to his concept of life, and, where they deviated, he brought them closer by interpreting them. "It was a habit with me," Gandhi once wrote, "to forget what I did not like and to carry out in practice whatever I liked" (76).

As for Tolstoy, Gandhi read him right, but Tolstoy himself read the way Gandhi said *he* did. And a great many people who quite lack the genius of Gandhi and Tolstoy feel that this is surely the best way to read—especially religious texts.

Gandhi's fight against the degrading aspects of the caste system and especially the treatment of the so-called Untouchables was probably as important as anything he did —and also was most certainly not inspired by the Gita. Indeed, the combination of this deep concern with the insistence on nonviolence suggests most strongly that Gandhi's real inspiration, although he was evidently unaware of this, was the Buddha. But it is an interesting psychological phenomenon that he could no more admit this to himself than Schweitzer could admit that his desire for the realization of the kingdom of God in this world came from the Hebrew prophets. Schweitzer's loyalty to the New Testament demanded that he not present his own advance over what he took to be dated aspects of it as implying that the prophets, centuries earlier, had been morally superior, at least in some crucial ways. Similarly, Gandhi's loyalty to the Gita would not allow him to admit the superiority of the Buddha: "Religious faith cannot be understood apart from faithfulness, fidelity, loyalty. It is loyalty that determines allegiance to Judaism, Christianity, Hinduism, or Buddhism. Acceptance of specific propositions as well as

---

* *Harijan*, 3rd Oct. 1936, in *Selected Writings*, 45.

religious experiences, whether mystic or prophetic, are secondary. What is primary is
. . . loyalty to a tradition . . ."*

Had he appealed to Buddhism, Gandhi would have been totally ineffective in
India, and he would have been finished politically. But there is no reason to doubt his
word when he said:

> I can describe my feeling for Hinduism no more than for my own wife. . . .
> Not that she has no faults. . . . But the feeling of an indissoluble bond is there.
> Hinduism, as I know it, entirely satisfies my soul, fills my whole being, and I
> find a solace in the *Bhagavad Gita* and *Upanishads* that I miss even in the Ser-
> mon on the Mount. . . . When I see not one ray of light on the horizon I turn
> to the *Bhagavad Gita* and find a verse to comfort me; and I immediately begin
> to smile in the midst of overwhelming sorrow. **

That is the relationship of a religious person to his favorite scripture and his own tradition, and out of gratitude for all the comfort, or simply as part of the whole relationship, he credits it with all that he finds best.

Here are two other illustrations, both very brief. In a selection from his own works
that he included at the end of *A Source Book in Indian Philosophy*—an imposing collection that begins with the Vedas—Radhakrishnan, the Vedantist, says: "When the
Vedas are regarded as the highest authority, all that is meant is that the most exacting
of all authorities is the authority of facts" (616). Loath to break with a tradition that
has regarded the Vedas as the supreme authority for close to three thousand years, but
living in an age that proclaims the authority of facts, Radhakrishnan sees no need to
choose one or the other. Nor is he content to say that when he pays allegiance to the
authority of the Vedas, he merely uses those words to proclaim his respect for facts.
Instead he implies that this is what was always meant.

This is no odder than Paul Tillich's declaration: "That symbol is most adequate
which expresses not only the ultimate but also its own lack of ultimacy. Christianity expresses itself in such a symbol in contrast to all other religions . . ." And on the very
next page of his *Dynamics of Faith* (98) he goes on to say with an extraordinary dis-
regard for the authority of facts: "Doctrinal formulations did not divide the churches
in the Reformation period." Actually, Luther repudiated Ulrich Zwingli, the Swiss
Reformer, because Zwingli took the sacraments for symbols of Christ's flesh and blood,
while Luther, with whose church Tillich would not break, insisted that they were no
mere symbols but truly Christ's flesh and blood. On the other hand, symbols that
express not only the ultimate but also their own lack of ultimacy are found in Judaism
and Buddhism as well as Hinduism—quite especially in the Vedanta of Shankara.

Let us now turn to the substance of Gandhi's version of what he called *My Non-
Violence*. His doctrine was not quite what it is widely believed to have been.

> Ahimsa is the highest ideal. It is meant for the brave, never for the cow-
> ardly. To benefit by others' killing and delude oneself into the belief that one
> is being very religious and non-violent, is sheer self-deception.
> A so-called votary of non-violence will not stay in a village which is visited
> by a leopard every day. He will run away and, when someone has killed the leop-
> ard, will return to take charge of his hearth and home. This is not non-violence.
> This is a coward's violence. The man who has killed the leopard has at least
> given proof of some bravery. The man who takes advantage of the killing is a
> coward. . . .
> In life it is impossible to eschew violence completely. The question arises,
> where is one to draw the line? The line cannot be the same for everyone. . . .

---

* Kaufmann, 1958, section 78: "Religion and Loyalty." See also section 80, "Loyalty and Truth."
** *Young India*, 10–6–21 and 8–6–25.

Meat-eating is a sin for me. Yet, for another person, who has always lived on meat and never seen anything wrong in it, to give it up simply in order to copy me will be a sin.

This is pushing relativism rather far. Still it is a fact, even if it is not widely known, that "The Rigvedic people, including the Brahmins, were fond of meat-eating" and that "Yajnavalkya, the greatest sage and philosopher of his time," actually enjoyed eating beef,* which orthodox Hindus consider a heinous sin. But the crucial issue for us here is what precisely Gandhi's doctrine of nonviolence comes to. He continues:

If I wish to be an agriculturist and stay in the jungle, I will have to use the minimum unavoidable violence in order to protect my fields. I will have to kill monkeys, birds and insects which eat up my crops. If I do not wish to do so myself, I will have to engage someone to do it for me: There is not much difference between the two. To allow crops to be eaten up by animals in the name of Ahimsa while there is a famine in the land is certainly a sin. Evil and good are relative terms. What is good under certain conditions can become an evil or a sin under a different set of conditions (239 f.).

It might be thought that this relativity ceases when it comes to the killing of human beings. But Gandhi himself said:

On the three occasions, the Boer War, the Zulu "Rebellion," and the Great European War of 1914, that I participated in war, I was bound, in the circumstances in which I found myself, to adopt the course I did. My conduct was actuated in the interests of non-violence. . . .

A girl who attacks her assailant with her nails or teeth is "almost" non-violent, because there is no premeditated violence in her. . . .

Violence is any day preferable to impotence. There is hope for a violent man to become non-violent. There is no such hope for the impotent. [Gandhi said the same about cowardice and cowards.] . . .

Vengeance is any day superior to helpless submission. He who cannot protect himself or his nearest and dearest or their honor by non-violently facing death, may and ought to do so by violently dealing with the oppressor. He who can do neither of the two is a burden. . . .

Here Gandhi seems to be saying clearly that under certain circumstances participation in war is justifiable, and that his own was. Yet after these direct quotations from Gandhi, N. B. Parulekar continues:

To questions, however, Gandhiji [the ending, often used, indicates great respect for Gandhi] answered and made it clear that he never permitted violence . . .

"I am an out and out believer in 'ahimsa' and as such am an uncompromising opponent of violent methods even to serve the noblest of causes. . . . I am also uncompromisingly against all war. I do not justify war under any conditions. . . ."

"But I belong to a world which is partly based on violence and it is true that we shall perhaps never be able to do without violence altogether. Hence I do advocate training in arms for those who believe in the methods of violence. I would rather have India resort to arms in order to defend her honor than that she would, in a cowardly manner, become or remain a helpless witness to her own dishonor. Under Swaraj [self-rule] too I would not hesitate to advise those who would bear arms to do so and fight for the country" (68 ff.).

If it seems clear that Gandhi contradicts himself, one may wonder how probable it is that great religious figures of the past, including those whose words have come down to us in sacred scriptures, did *not* contradict themselves. Gandhi published a good deal

---

* Dutt, 54 f. Cf. "Beef-eating in the Sutras," 160–66.

over his own name and lived in a climate of opinion in which it was possible for his followers to press him occasionally with all due respect, and it is greatly to his honor that he allowed people to question him like this and tried to answer them. According to the Gospels and the Koran, Jesus' and Muhammad's manner was very different; nor can one imagine anyone reverently but persistently questioning Jeremiah, Isaiah, or Moses. A believer will say that some of these men, unlike Gandhi, were revealing the word of God. A nonbeliever may wonder whether we cannot perhaps learn something about them by studying Gandhi.

The last quotation offers a strange contrast to Gandhi's appeal to Great Britain on July 2, 1940, printed in the same volume.

> I appeal for cessation of hostilities . . . because war is bad in essence. . . . Invite Herr Hitler and Signor Mussolini to take what they want of the countries you call your possessions. Let them take possession of your beautiful island . . . If these gentlemen choose to occupy your homes, you will vacate them. If they do not give you free passage out, you will allow yourself man, woman and child, to be slaughtered . . . (56 f.).

Yet in 1947, "In a Christmas Day broadcast, Gandhi approved of India's action in sending troops to Kashmir to repel the tribal invaders. He condemned suggestions to partition the state between India and Pakistan. He regretted the fact that Nehru had submitted the dispute to the United Nations" (Fischer, 489).

It was hardly Gandhi's finest moment when, a month before he was assassinated by a Hindu fanatic, he proclaimed that beautiful Kashmir was worth fighting for. His position regarding war had been inconsistent all along, but this broadcast made it all too easy even for his followers and friends, including those governing newly independent India, to set his teachings aside altogether.

By July 1963, Radhakrishnan, the Vedantist philosopher, was president of India, with his official residence in the former British viceroy's palace. To a visitor who had recently spent ten months in Israel, the choice of this building with its extreme Victorian opulence seemed symbolic in itself. Those at the head of the Israeli government had chosen to create a new life style. Thus one might have tea with David Ben-Gurion, the first prime minister of Israel, be asked spontaneously to stay for supper, go into the kitchen with his wife to get it, and afterward witness a friendly argument over whether it was his or her turn to do the dishes. But Gandhi, who had fought for India's independence wearing a simple loin cloth—Churchill had contemptuously called him a naked fakir—lived to see the first president move into the viceroy's palace. And here Radhakrishnan received visitors in the afternoon, giving twenty minutes to each, and a philosopher coming to Delhi was apt to be told to his surprise that he was expected at 5 p.m. on Saturday. Asked how he felt about the relevance of Gandhi's doctrine of nonviolence to India's foreign policy—at a time when posters on the streets referred to the Chinese as dogs—Radhakrishnan replied that Gandhi himself had realized toward the end of his life that his ideas were unworkable and not relevant, and he referred specifically to Gandhi's recognition that India had to fight for Kashmir. He also asked whether his visitor did not wish to see the viceroy's palace and instructed the naval attaché, who sat at the desk as a receptionist, to dispatch an officer to serve as a guide. Only one feature of the palace was unforgettable. There was no room without at least one picture of Gandhi. That seemed symbolic of the fate of great religious teachers.

49

50

51

53

54

32

57

58

59

62

60

63

61

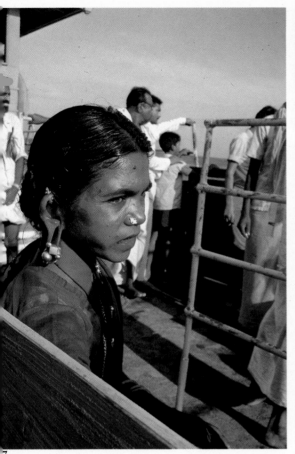

67

68

69

72

73

74

76

77

78

79

82

83

84

86

87

88

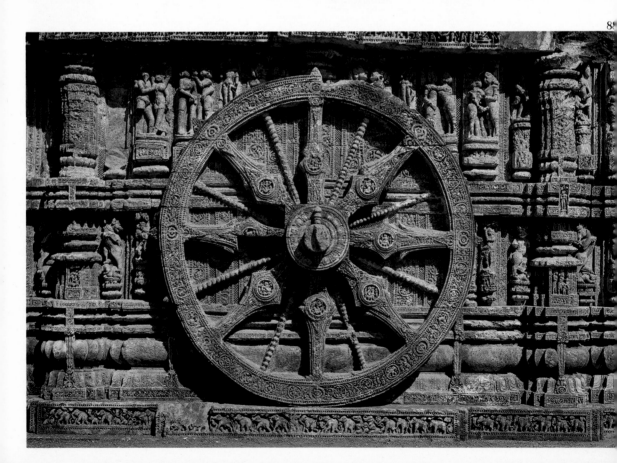

2

94

95

100

101

102

103

104

X

THE THIRD FACE OF INDIA

*Introduction—Northern India—Rajasthan Traffic—Manu/Moses—
Close to the Earth—December—One That Got Away—Itinerary—
Breeding—Radios—The Cape—Kerala—Shiva's Wreath—
Matu Pungal (Bull Festival)—Golden Advice—Orissa—
The Hamster Wheel—Déjà Vu—Calcutta—Great God!—
The Cobra—Peace—Hermits—Your Swastikas*

Calcutta.

The first face of India is seen in her ancient scriptures. Many people know only this face and do not know it very well, being familiar only with some very free translations. For some readers India means above all wisdom, and there is no denying that some of her scriptures are exceptionally profound. But to think of India only in terms of old books is a little like associating some Western country mainly with the New Testament. Such texts are not irrelevant, but they do not prepare anyone for modern realities. They neither mirror nor were ever meant to mirror the realities of any period.

The second face of India may be seen in the pictures in this book. They are bound to strike different people very differently, but they were selected largely for their beauty —to show how India is an endless feast for the eyes and in purely aesthetic terms, if you unhinge your moral sense, a paradise. There may be more impressive landscapes elsewhere, but the colors and variety of the human scene are unsurpassed. In their often brilliant sarees many of the poorest women look and carry themselves like queens in fairytales.

Many people simply fail to see this; they are so depressed by the poverty. Of course, one could take pictures to frame an indictment; but that is not how these pictures were taken. They were intended to make what is beautiful endure. But to persist in a wholly aesthetic orientation and to be simply enchanted by the beauty of the desperately poor and starving would involve a cruel refusal to think.

The pages that follow represent an attempt to cope with the third face of India, with her misery and heartbreak. These pages are extremely problematic, but so is the third face. Some lines may give offense. So does the third face. If poems were supposed to be, by definition, governed by an aesthetic sense, with thoughts permitted to enter only if they are content to play a wholly secondary role, then what follows is decidedly not poetry. For the central intention of these pages is precisely to supplement the aesthetic orientation of the visual images. That is not to say that this chapter is purely intellectual and devoid of feeling. What calls for some explanation is rather that the feeling is not always compassion but often outrage or at least extreme exasperation. That is less true in the early pages; the sense of irritation becomes greater after a visit to Buddhist Ceylon, beginning with "The Cape."

One of India's leading novelists and short story writers, R. Prawer Jhabvala, who was born in Europe, remarks in the introduction to her collection, *An Experience of India*, that Westerners tend to pass through several phases when they come to India: first, uncritical enthusiasm; then, "everything Indian not so marvellous"; and finally, "everything Indian abominable." For some, she says, that is the end of it, while others go through this cycle again and again, as she does herself. Meeting Westerners, she says, she usually can tell quickly at what stage they are. All this is as perceptive as it is charming. Yet none of the poems that follow can be classified that way.

If the poem on the bull festival deals with what was felt to be "abominable," it was written after taking pictures for several hours of what was beautiful. There are no pictures of the horribly maimed in this book, but after not taking such pictures one may still be haunted by the sight and seek verbal expression. "Golden Advice" is petulant, but the point is plainly that it is so difficult in India to be left alone to enjoy, admire, and enter into the spirit of the temples and their sculptures—in this case, at Tanjore. Wherever you look at carvings in India, chances are that someone who knows nothing about Indian sculpture will come up to tell you, "This is Shiva and Parvati, sir!" And then he will stick to you like a leech, keeping up his chatter, giving you no peace, and expect in the end to be paid for his services. Paying right away would be no help; he would only redouble his efforts to get more. The only other country where this is, or used to be, that bad is Egypt, where ignorant "guides" love to point out again and again and again the jackal-headed god Anubis, whom a three-year-old would have no trouble picking out.

These poems bear witness of a tension between eternal beauty and everlasting profanation. The second part of "Shiva's Wreath" should illuminate the first, but those for whom the dancing Shiva has never been one of the most sublime religious symbols   73 of all time may still fail to understand it. The central contrast in "Shiva's Wreath" is one of the main themes of this whole book, but some readers will probably find this theme more accessible elsewhere. A later poem, "The Cobra," may help.

Two glosses on "Great God!" The umbrella or parasol as a symbol of royalty may seem absurd, but see the next poem and the pictures of Darius and the Naga Buddha.   33 The symbol will be discussed further in the context of Buddhist art. *Mahadé* means great god, and one of Goethe's greatest ballads begins with this word and ends: "Immortals raise lost children to heaven in fiery arms." That did not help to lessen the shock when the crowd bestowed this epithet on a maharaja.

India has many faces, and to claim that the third face is the only one would be slander. Still it seemed wrong to present only the first two faces—not because something would be left out—after all, completeness is impossible—but because it would be heartless. Obviously, similar poems could be written about Western countries, perhaps about any country at all. Nor have brutalities in other parts of the world been ignored in these pages. It is only because no other country in the world is represented in these pages with so much that is beautiful that these poems may be needed to remind us that India has more than one face.

All three faces can be seen in four dimensions, but in the treatment of the Scriptures the historical and comparative dimensions meet the eye, while in the pictures the aesthetic dimension is most obvious. In both cases the existential dimension is present also, but in the poems that follow it cannot be missed.

Northern India

Straight level roads
  fade into haze
Always a silent
  stream of thin men
  occasional cows
  donkeys and sheep
  and bubbling children
Emerald and purple
  turbans and rags
  ride ringing cycles
  into the mist.

There is none
  of the unending
  fields and roads
  and teeming lanes
  without ruby-and-amethyst-robed
  caryatids
  with porphyry-smooth skin
  their heads
  proudly supporting
  what heaven
  there is.

Cripples slither like snakes
Vultures wait in the trees
  for sleepers that starve in the dust
  in crowded streets
  not to awaken
Death is outnumbered
  by laughing children
Rainbow-colored
  young women smile
None of the old do
Cycles fade into mist.

Rajasthan Traffic

In the streets
cows are most common
after people and cycles
followed by
donkeys and sleeping dogs
buffaloes, trucks,
.cars, sheep, and goats
(counting herds as one).

On the roads
all of these along
with camels and chipmunks
peacocks and monkeys
a horse a day
and elephants
many
only on the road to Jaipur.

Crows scatter like sparks
but some pigeons are slow
and beside a dead dog
lies a flattened vulture.

Manu

Hard
relentless
and cutting

the glass
of your wisdom
served
only the fewest

leaving the mass
to eat
dust

But for your wisdom
the roads to hell might be paved.

Moses

In your book
only the snake
eats dust
while the curse of man
is work

Whomever you reached
you raised
from the earth

In glorious unwisdom
you fashioned
for those whom you chose
an incandescent hell.

Close to the Earth

Nowhere else
do so many men
live so close to the earth
and dust
and dozens of species
of animals.

Cities
are bulwarks
from which the inhabitants
break out
and raid
the countryside.

Bedouins *own* camels
sail through the desert
build tents
to keep out
the sand
Bedouins are islands.

But these villages
are the sea
in which animals
earth
and men
are teeming.

December

When the sun struck the earth
and was bloodied
flattened and buried
the sky paid no heed

but now it mourns
robed in gold.

One That Got Away

A child absorbed in his homemade strings
makes music on Mount Abu.
A Sikh ex-sergeant explodes:
> Straighten up
> can't you see
> the gentleman
> wants to take
> your photo
> you bum.

55–63

Itinerary

Amrítsar, Delhi, and Amber,
Jaípur, Chitórgarh, Udaípur,
Nágda, Eklíngji, Abú,
Ellóra, Ajánta, Aurángabad,
Bombáy and Kanyakumári;
Trivándrum, Thékkady, Mádurai,
Trichy, Srírangam, Tánjore,
Madrás, Mallapúram, Hyderabad,
Konárak, Bhubanéshwar (Oríssa),
Calcutta, Benares, Sarnáth.

Breeding

Pink piglets
striped piglets
miniature boars

Literature
rock temples
bronze figurines

cebu and
buffalo calves

deities
no one can count

infants on
children's arms
pups in a huddle

infants on
children's arms
six in one seat

kites and
parakeets

no sense of
distance is left.

how many
birds in a
banyan tree?

In all their
languages
no one knows No.

Every banyan
wants to make minyan.

Radios

As fast as tigers
circle their cages
radios are carried
through zoos and museums.

Doing Ajanta
while listening to ball games
Indians are rushing
past Vishnu and Buddha.

Even before
the land was so crowded
silence had to be
sought in the woods.

Now meditation
survives
only in
stone.

The Cape

"At Kanyakumari
three seas meet
and because this is no port of call
there is no place like this"
—said Gandhi—
"and the waters
are virgin
like the goddess."

Where Gandhi's ashes
were immersed in the sea
a shrine has been built
that looks like an ice-cream parlor
at Kanyakumari
where three seas meet
and what little beach is left
is the village latrine.

"When we first read
of Kanyakumari
we thought it was
a wild and forsaken place
where three seas meet."
Replied my Indian friend
"That was years ago
but it is all right now."

Where Vivekananda
sat two years
on a rock
off Kanyákumari
saw the mountains
on the mainland
and the sun rise from
and set in the sea

Where he sat in silence
and heard the waves
dashing against the rock
off Kanyakumari
they have built a lavishly
hideous temple
and ferries vomit
thousands of visitors.

Signs proclaim
only in English:
Please keep silence!
But guides keep blabbering
over the babel
of Indian languages.
Oh please keep silence
at Kanyakumari.

Where three seas meet
a poor woman
half naked
picks clams and shells
under huge boulders
for food and necklaces
and one can swim
off Kanyakumari.

Kerala

Kérala State
in the tropical South
is more literate
cleaner
and Communist.

Hills exceed bicycles.
In the roads
no cows
less dirt
dust and people.

Most people work
few squat
skins are much darker.

Blacks are not Negroid
and there is no correlation
one way or the other
between fairness
and beauty.

Some older women
still work on the roads
with bare breasts.

Young women carry
heavier loads
of rocks
on their heads
and laugh.

The three poems that follow are discussed in the opening section of this chapter.

Shiva's Wreath
I

"On Srirangam Island
in Jambukeshwaram Temple
non-Hindus are not permitted
past the flagpost
but can see the sculptures
of elephants monkeys and birds
carved by 16th Century sculptors"
—says the guidebook.

I saw a live elephant
eating hay in the temple
and he paused for an instant
to touch my hand with his trunk.
I was looking at
the carved elephant and the bird
on the twilit pillars
but had not yet found the monkey

when a priest rushed me
to the shrine of Shiva
unlocked the padlock
bade me step up
took a garland
of faded flowers
from the neck of the god
and draped it on me.

He asked for a gift for the priest
but returned half a rupee
and asked for two.
I returned the flowers
no longer fragrant
and went on not heeding the priest
who followed to ask for one rupee
for Shiva's priest.

I saw Shiva dance
draped in a leopard skin
men were praying to him
some were bowed over oil lamps
while others ceaselessly circled
the sacred flames
in Jambukeshwaram Temple—
and on my way out found the monkey.

73

II

The coin I withheld
clinks in my mind:
was I mean?

What I sought was silence
not a priest's chatter
about small change.

Here was Dionysus
draped in a leopard skin
Bacchae in ecstasy

timeless tragedy
Nietzsche's vision
the dancing god

sculpted eternity
summons to solitude
changelessly moving.

There
incarnate corruption
a priest.

Matu Pungal (Bull Festival)

In Tamil Nad
small bulls are painted
particolored
one is held by a rope
by several men
with the help of a tree.

A large crowd
of young men
attacks the bull
but as soon as he
is given some leeway
they scatter in terror.

Then the bull
is pulled back
and the wave returns
to sweep over him
throw him down
and sprawl all over him.

This ballet continues
till all are tired
A new bull appears
with a hundred more heroes
but most of the crowd
pays no attention.

While the men
play the bulls
children ride homemade
ferris wheels
women sit
on the hillside and chat.

A man taking pictures
gets more attention
than the annual bull fights
and a man in the dust
without hands and feet
gets none.

Golden Advice

One more
"This is Shiva and Párvati, sir!"
and I'll scream
"You are Anubis-Jackal!"

It is not so much that these beggars
like those in Egypt
know even less than I do
but that they give you no peace.

As soon as they start
"This is bull!"
you must say
"No English"—

delightfully ambiguous sounds
but they never doubt your meaning:
their faces fall as they ask
"You are not knowing even a little English?"

"No English!"
They leave
in search of another victim
and silence returns.

Orissa

In Bhubaneshwar (Orissa)
and east to the Bay of Bengal
the sarees are monochrome
in hues drenched in dust.

Greens look like cornstalks
too close to the road
orange and pink like the soil
blue and purple like dusk.

The roads are almost bare
unless a blackfaced monkey
completes his dance before
he leaps away knocking down signs.

The beach of the bay is vast
surf both ways to the horizon
a few thatched huts in the sand
no village or filth in sight.

Two miles from the Bay of Bengal
Konarak's ruins rise:
the Black Pagoda—no color
but a paean of joy in stone.

Elephants, horses, lions,
love play, cymbals, and drums
a celebration of sex
and Surya the god of the sun.

By the road to Bhubaneshwar
hundreds of ponds and paddies
reflect the evening sky
glowing orange and pink and purple.

The Hamster Wheel

Everywhere women carry
sand or rocks on their heads
and men and women are building
houses and roads and schools.

But in twenty-one years the people
of India have doubled adding
two hundred million more.

Death by disease and starvation
has been checked and soon there will be
a billion people in India.

No program keeps pace with this flood
everywhere roads are eroded
and buildings are going to seed.

The Rambagh Palace in Jaipur
the Lake Palace in Udaipur
now hotels whose glamour is legend

and hundreds of lesser places
the Cricket Club in Bombay
the Ambassador cars made in India

are all more or less decrepit:
death has been checked—not decay.

Déjà Vu

Of seven thousand temples
in Bhubaneshwar (Orissa)
a hundred survive.

The Lingraja is largest.
All but one of the others
are copies in varying sizes.

The Parasu Rameshwara
is small and a little older
and the tower is slightly different.

The sculptures at the Rajrani
are the best but nothing is done
only once. Carvings like bronzes

are multiplied as with a stencil.
Who could count all the elegant
elephants at Konarak?

The images are reborn
whenever a temple is built
there is no release from rebirth.

There is no direction or aim
no task but to do one's duty
day after day without sabbath.

The Gita says it is better
to do one's own office badly
than to do another man's well.

The future is like the past
their sculptures, their books, and their lives
are repetitive like the seasons.

Bhubaneshwar. / Kailasanatha, Ellora.

Calcutta

In the Grand Hotel one forgets.
It is a fortress designed
to keep out India.
A few steps from the Sikh doormen
two boys are sleeping
under a blanket of flies.

Around the first corner
a man brushes his teeth
with water from a puddle
and women wash clothes in the gutter.

Cows abound on Chowringhee
the broad main street
while goats eat the garbage on side streets.
No picture can capture the smells
the electronic blare
and the car horns that sound like sick cows.

Coolies run by with rickshaws.
Beggars are looking for foreigners.
With a smaller child on her arm
a four-year-old girl is dancing.

Great God!

The Maharaja of Ramnagar
has a palace south of Benares.
North of Benares lies Sarnath
where the Buddha preached his first sermon.

The government guides take tourists
in buses with wheels but no springs
or shock absorbers to Sarnath
and then to see Ramnagar.

The outer court of the palace
is filled with rubbish and junk
but in the inner court soldiers
beat drums and boys march with bayonets.

The Maharaja of Ramnagar
appears in a business suit
from what looks like a shed in the rear
and is followed by an umbrella.

He makes Namaste and he salutes
the soldiers that present rifles
and as he enters his old sedan
the crowd shouts Mahadé—

great god! And an Indian tourist
says to a foreigner, Please
you took a snap of the great king,
please send me a picture to Ranchi

I am an analyst and I want
a picture of the king because
I saw the king at Ramnagar.
Sarnath is far away.

93

94

The Cobra

Darius, king of kings, upon a pillar 33
still stands under a parasol
amid the ruins of Persepolis.

The Buddha sits alone, no lackeys,
upon a serpent's coils, and in the shadow
of seven-headed hooded death he smiles
and lets the jungle feed on crumbling temples.

The fatal cobra twined around his arm,
destructive flames encircling him—unmoved, 73
Lord Shiva dances, crushing underfoot
the blindness that dwarfs us.

Peace

Nowhere else is one tempted so often to say
Leave me in peace!
Nowhere else is this desperate plea so futile.

While you are eating, a flock of waiters is hovering
hummingbirdlike
reaching for things while asking if you are finished

telling you rice is rice and that Memsahib should
have some more meat.
Rearranging the silver, they dream of bakshish.

Look at some friezes or sculptures: unwanted guides
proudly reveal
either the obvious or what is palpably false.

That does not bother some Indian gentlemen who
puncture this flood
with their courtly refrain: Carry on!

Are these people totally blind to what here
has become stone?
Serenity seems to touch no chord in their souls.

Since the thirteenth century art has gone downhill.
Temples that were
built in the last fifty years are public nightmares:

richly dressed idols and electronic noise
leave you no peace
willy-nilly you hear the Ramáyana

as if sufficient volume could cure the scratch.
But the devout
feel at home with the noise and do their prostrations.

Buddha's heretical doctrine was welcomed in
nearby Ceylon
and in Thailand: both are different worlds.

He preached compassion, a sense of distance, and peace.
Cleanliness, too.
India has turned her back on all four.

Hermits

When Captain Oberoi's plane
was hijacked to Pakistan
and crew and passengers were
detained in Lahore for two days

two hundred people swarmed
into his wife's small house
stayed with her two days and nights
and the telephone rang all the time.

Indians like being in crowds
and the dailies are full of their clashes
near Trichy with spears and aruvals
in Benares with barrages of rocks

in Calcutta gangs prefer knives.
The carnage is dwarfed by the birth rate.
The hermits and teachers of peace
have left to lecture abroad.

What one reads in too many books
of the ancient wisdom of India
is insipid Victorian hash
covered up with Sanskrit curry.

What is ancient indeed is their faith
in caste and that fair skin is good
inhumanity to one's inferiors
and contempt for critical thought

hovering, scraping, and groveling,
whining, pleading, and dirt.
But ancient, too, is the poise
of the women on every road

carrying brass on their heads
that catches the sunlight like torches
carrying loads, looking regal
goddesses carrying rocks.

As long as you think of their plight
the country is a vast nightmare.
It is also a riot of colors
and a festival for the eyes.

Your Swastikas

Your swastikas are not as innocent as we were taught.
Sure, they appeared in the friezes of temples before
Germany made them the symbol of her contempt
for the idea that we are brothers. But you
closed all your temples to outcastes and built your whole life
on the denial of brotherhood and on the rock
of varna or color which people now translate as caste.
Broadmindedness in the marriage ads that mar
newsprint along with horoscopes *still* consists
in saying that difference in *sub*caste is no crucial bar.

The varnas of Manu as well as the ancient conceit
that *fair* skin only is beautiful have survived
Gandhi's martyrdom and his heroic attempt
to spread the gospel of Tolstoy which he claimed to find
in the Gita which actually teaches caste
and that it's noble to kill without any aim
except devotion to duty and love of him
who bids the noble to prove their nobility thus.
Soldiers should soldier and kill in accordance with caste
Brahmins should teach and slaves ought to slave: that is caste.
And Gandhi was killed in the name of this ancient faith.
Your swastikas are not as innocent as we were taught.

Ganesha under a nine-headed Naga (16th century) and Ganesha with Shiva's trident in his hand and on his head, his rat on his right, a sweet for the rat in front, ca. 1700, folk art. 2 bronzes from Punjab.

XI

JAINISM, SIKHISM, BUDDHISM

Jainism—Sikhism—The Buddha—His Four Noble Truths—
The Pali Scriptures: Women, "The Rhinoceros," and "Goodwill"—
The Dhammapada—Mahayana Buddhism—Tantrism

Naga Buddha, museum, Lopburi.

79

In the sixth century B.C. two new religions arose in India: Jainism and Buddhism. Both were heretical insofar as they did not accept the authority of the Vedas. Both represented protests against the religion of the Upanishads which underwent important changes in response to these two challenges, and the Bhagavad Gita needs to be seen as an attempt to answer Buddhism and Jainism. Moreover, both Jainism and Buddhism rejected the caste system. Nevertheless, the two new religions and Hinduism lived side by side in India, and for hundreds of years, down to the ninth century, they built their cave temples next to each other at Ellora. Eventually, Buddhism lost ground in India, and now hardly any Buddhists are left in the land in which the Buddha himself preached. But meanwhile Buddhism had converted large masses of people in Ceylon and Thailand, in Indochina, China, and Japan. And at Angkor in Cambodia it is often difficult to tell what temples and sculptures are Hindu and what is Buddhist.

Jainism never made many converts abroad, but it survived in India where in the middle of the twentieth century it had about 1,500,000 adherents out of a total population of roughly 400,000,000. Again it is noteworthy that at Khajuraho, one of the great temple sites of India, the Jains and the Hindus built their temples, with superb carvings, in the same area, around the year 1000. On Mount Abu, the four great temples are 56–63 all Jain, but on a hill not far away there are Hindu temples.

Jainism is named after the Jina (pronounced "gin"), meaning the conqueror, as Buddhism is named after the Buddha, which means the enlightened one, and Christianity after Christ, which is also an epithet and not a proper name. Actually, the followers of the Jina call him Mahavira, "great hero," because they believe that he was merely the last of twenty-four Jinas. Most scholars consider him an older contemporary of the Buddha and believe that he was born in northern India in 599 B.C. and died in 527.

His personal name was Vardhamana, and his father, Siddhartha, was a prince. He was raised accordingly, married, and had a daughter. When he was thirty, however, after his parents' death, he left his family and became an ascetic. There were many ascetics and ascetic groups by that time, and he apparently adopted the practices of a group founded by Parshva, who is said to have died in 776 B.C. The Jains consider Parshva the twenty-third Jina or *tirthankara*, which means pathmaker. Scholars accept his historicity but have doubts about the other twenty-two tirthankaras.

Vardhamana's asceticism was very austere. He moved about, as many ascetics did, begging for his food and initially wore a single garment that he never changed; but after about a year he shed it and is believed to have spent the rest of his life without wearing anything. While his life was in some respects quite similar to the Buddha's, it is usually easy to tell whether a statue represents one or the other. The Jina is shown nude, while the Buddha always wears a simple monk's robe.

After thirteen years of self-mortification, Vardhamana found enlightenment, nirvana, and thus became a Jina. He then taught for almost thirty years and gained a large following. At the age of seventy-two he starved himself to death. Some consider him a younger contemporary of the Buddha and believe that he died in 468 B.C.

His teaching was remarkably philosophical and based on no appeal to scripture or divine revelation. In a sense, he did not deny the existence of the gods; but his religion is often called atheistic because he in effect denied their divinity. They can be of no help whatsoever to us and are decidedly inferior to the tirthankaras. There are two kinds of substance: *jivas* and *ajivas* (the *i* in both words is pronounced like the *ee* in *keen*, while the *a*'s are short like the vowel sound in *but*). Jivas are souls or spirits (literally, lives), while ajivas is inorganic matter, which is believed to consist of atoms. Rebirth is governed by *karma*, which is given a materialistic interpretation. During each life a karma body forms around the soul and determines in what incarnation it will spend its next life. The soul's passions generate a sticky substance, and the material atoms that flow in through sense experience stick to it, forming the karma body.

To prevent rebirth, one must eradicate the passions and gradually eliminate sense experience. Hence the need for asceticism and austerities. In the end, the ascetic who has eliminated his karma body may starve himself to death, as Mahavira did, without any fear of rebirth. Starving oneself to death earlier would obviously be futile. The soul that is not reborn enters nirvana.

How nirvana is to be understood is always a difficult question because it has been conceived differently by different religions and sects and, of course, by different individuals. But in Jainism nirvana has often meant eternal bliss above the highest heavens, inactive and omniscient.

The Jains also speak of "three jewels": right faith, right knowledge, and right conduct, and right conduct involves five restraints: ahimsa and no lying, stealing, sexual activity, or property. Jainism has also stressed moderation, meditation, and alms-giving for those who do not become ascetics. Laymen, however, cannot gain nirvana, while Hinduism considers it possible if rare.

Ahimsa—the practice of nonviolence and the prohibition against killing animals as well as human beings—was enjoined on lay followers as well as monks. Not only vegetarianism was made a rule for all but also the prohibition against tilling the soil lest one kill earthworms. As a result, the Jain lay folk tended to move into towns where a great many of them became merchants and, owing at least in part to their frugality, self-control, and high rate of literacy, became wealthy and, being pious, built spectacular temples. Those at Ellora and Mount Abu—the latter, symphonies carved out of marble —are illustrated in this book and discussed in section 112 below, but the lavish temple in Calcutta almost seems a gaudy showcase to display precious metals and an incredible array of jewels. Of course, all this wealth has been given away, but it still provides a numbing contrast to the life of the founder and the ascetics who followed in his steps. Why, one is almost bound to ask oneself, do Jains need any temples? After all, Mahavira said: "Man! You are your own friend. Why do you wish for a friend beyond yourself?"* He disparaged the concern with gods, but in time he himself was worshiped, and the idols representing him are rarely works of art that suggest ultimate serenity, as do many Buddha images.

56, 60–63

Mahavira and the Buddha were the first to elevate ahimsa into a general rule of life and to found monastic orders, and we do not know for sure which of them did it first. As for ahimsa, we do know that Mahavira carried asceticism much further than the Buddha and that this led to more extreme attitudes toward tiny animals. To

---

* Akaranga Sutra, 1:3.3, SBE, vol. 22, 33. Cf. 22, 152.

Marble pillar, Dilwara temple, Mount Abu.

this day one can see Jain monks in India wearing face masks to prevent the death of minute organisms by inhalation, and carrying whisks as they walk across country, to brush worms and insects from their path. One can also read about ascetics who tolerated all kinds of vermin on their bodies, as Mahavira may have done when he did not change his robe for thirteen months, but this is no reason for supposing that the Jain middle class has low standards of cleanliness. In his Gifford Lectures on *The Living God*, Archbishop Söderblom recalled

> the pious amazement of the monks, when the murdered Thomas à Becket's clothes were taken from his body, and they perceived the crawling crowds of insects on his body. They had not known that he was as holy as that.
> Cardinal Bellarmine answered with scholastic exactitude the question whether one is allowed to kill the vermin on the body, which the medieval mystics, often sublime in their philosophy, had denied. The cardinal said that they ought to be permitted to bite undisturbed, for man had got eternal happiness, but they only this life. One may contrast the Avesta, where it is a pious and meritorious work, used also as a penance, to kill obnoxious insects and other evil animals, or the Book of Daniel [4:33], where long hair and long nails, the pride of ascetic Hindu holiness, are considered as belonging to the punishment of Nebuchadnezzar: "till his hair was grown like eagles' feathers, and his nails like birds' claws" (84).

Monks have developed similar austerities in the East and the West, and the example of Francis of Assisi, who also tolerated vermin on his body, may remind us that the ethos of ahimsa has had at least one great representative in Christian Europe. But in Jainism it has been much more prevalent, and Heinrich Zimmer related in his *Philosophies of India* that in Bombay the following custom could still be observed:

> Two men come along carrying between them a light cot or bed alive with bedbugs. They stop before the door of a Jaina household, and cry: "Who will feed the bugs? Who will feed the bugs?" If some devout lady tosses a coin from a window, one of the criers places himself carefully in the bed and offers himself as a living grazing ground to his fellow beings. Whereby the lady of the house gains the credit, and the hero of the cot the coin (179).

Who is closest to the spirit of Mahavira: men like these or the architects and sculptors of Mount Abu? Or the Jain philosophers who developed elaborate cosmologies and subtle theories of knowledge? There is no obvious answer, but on reflection none of them seems very close to him.

As for the cosmologies, it will suffice to note that they postulate

> an infinite number of cycles, each consisting of a period of improvement . . . and one of decline . . . Each . . . is to all intents and purposes like the last, containing twenty-four *Tirthankaras*, twelve Universal Emperors . . . altogether sixty-three Great Men . . . At the peak period men are of enormous size and live to a tremendous age. . . . At present the world is rapidly declining. . . . The process of decline will continue for 40,000 years, when men will be dwarfs in stature, with a life of only twenty years, and will dwell in caves, having forgotten all culture, even to the use of fire. Then the tide will turn . . . Unlike the cosmology of the Buddhists and Hindus, that of the Jainas involves no cataclysms of universal destruction (Basham, 290).

In keeping with this general idea, Mahavira was said to have been ten and a half feet tall and to have died at seventy-two, while Parshva was thirteen and a half feet tall and died at the age of one hundred. The height and age of the preceding twenty-two tirthankaras are also given in the Jain scriptures and become more and more enormous as one goes back. The first of the line, Rishabha was supposed to have been 3,000 feet tall, and he lived to eighty-four lakhs of purvas, which is 8,400,000 times 8,400,000 years. But that was very long ago; the time that elapsed between his death and that of the second tirthankara was 50 lakhs of krores of sagaras, which is 5,000,000 times 10,000,000 times a 100,000,000 palyas; and one palya is the time required to empty a receptacle that is nine miles wide and deep and filled with new lamb's hairs, grown within seven days, when one hair is removed every hundred years (Finegan [1966], 190 f.). The intervals between the tirthankaras, like their height and age, have grown progressively shorter; that between the twenty-second and Parshva was only 84,000 years, and that between Parshva and Mahavira 250.

Jain theory of knowledge is quite another matter. There are five kinds of knowledge: Ordinary knowledge, which includes memory and inference, and scriptural knowledge, which is always preceded by ordinary knowledge but involves words, signs, or symbol, are the two forms of "mediate" knowledge, while the remaining three are immediate. First, "extraordinary knowledge," which is clairvoyant knowledge of things at a spatial or temporal distance, is fallible like the first two types. The remaining two types are not. One of them is "mental knowledge," which is telepathy; the other is "perfect knowledge." So far things are relatively simple. From here on they become extremely subtle. There are always seven points of view; we use judgments in seven different ways; and we should recognize the manysidedness of reality. The doctrine of *syadvada* holds that our knowledge needs to be qualified by "somehow" or "in a certain sense" or "maybe" (Radhakrishnan, 250–71).

Although Jainism is an old religion, one might suppose that it was rather compact and homogeneous, seeing that it has relatively few followers and that virtually all of them are Indians, and most of them live in India. Nevertheless, even Jainism bears out that a great religion that survives for a long time does so in part by making room for very different kinds of people. It has many mansions, ranging from the polished marble of Mount Abu, with its marble ceilings cut to look like lace, to the vermin-ridden cot of Bombay, from the wild intoxication with huge numbers to the subtle skepticism of *syadvada*. Add to this that most Jains have never been to Mount Abu or to Ellora or to Khajuraho, have never gone deeply into philosophy, and keep their homes extremely clean. But if even Jainism with its million and a half adherents cannot be reduced to a neat concept or a few revealing generalizations, how could one hope to do anything like that for Islam or Christianity, Hinduism or Buddhism? Lacking perfect knowledge that is all-inclusive, and could not be communicated in writing in any case, we should learn from the Jains, if we did not know it before, that we need to recognize the manysidedness of reality and the need for more than one perspective.

80

This may be the best place for a brief account of Sikhism. Once we get into Buddhism, there is no stopping until we reach Japan. Chronologically, the Sikhs belong between the Gita and Gandhi, but since we concentrated on Gandhi's reading of the Gita, an exposition of Sikhism would have been an interruption at that point.

Sikhism is a relatively new religion, as old as Lutheranism. It was founded by Guru Nanak (1469–1539), who felt that Hinduism and Islam had a great deal in common and wished to bring them together. He proclaimed, "There is no Hindu, there is no Muslim," and traveled all over India and even as far as Mecca and Medina, preaching against fanaticism and intolerance, against the caste system and reliance on ritual. He gained many followers and eventually picked Angad to succeed him as the second guru. Angad compiled Nanak's writings and eventually picked one of his disciples to succeed him. The fourth guru, Ram Das, laid the foundations of the great Sikh temple in Amritsar. His son and successor Arjun (1563–1606), "invested it with 48 the special sanctity it has for the Sikhs today" and also "compiled the Granth Sahib by collecting the writings of the preceding gurus and those of Hindu and Muslim saints, adding to them his own. The Granth Sahib became the sacred scripture of the Sikhs in preference to the holy books of the Hindus or the Muslims."* Arjun also built two other temples and eventually was martyred by the Mogul emperor Jehangir. Arjun stressed the differences between Sikhism and Islam and Hinduism and succeeded in giving the new religion a distinct identity.

Besides him and Nanak, the founder, the tenth and last guru, Gobind Singh, was the most influential. His father was martyred by another Mogul emperor for refusing conversion to Islam. Guru Gobind decided to transform the Sikhs into a fighting force, and though he was not especially successful in battle, he did succeed in transforming the Sikhs. Many Hindu fighters had had the surname Singh, which means "lion." Gobind made his followers shed their surnames, which indicated their castes, and had all men assume the last name Singh, and all women take Kaur ("princess") as their last name. He also introduced "the five Ks, namely, to wear the hair and beard unshorn (kesh); to carry a comb (kangha) in the hair; to wear a pair of shorts (kuchha); to wear a steel bangle (kara) on the right wrist; and always to carry a sabre (kirpan). . . ."

He prohibited smoking and alcohol and introduced some other rules. Thus he forged a group that felt like a single family and united some of the features of traditional asceticism (including the unshorn hair and beard) with an emphasis on soldiering and great courage. "It is also likely that, by making his followers easily recognisable by virtue of their turbans and beards, the Guru wanted to raise a body of men who would not be able to deny their faith when in danger but whose external appearance would invite persecution and in turn breed courage to resist it."

Having done all that, he did not name a successor but expressly declared that henceforth there would be no more gurus; the sacred book would take their place. He refrained from including his own writings in it; they became the Dasam Granth and are still cherished by the Sikhs but not revered as much as the Granth Sahib. Eventually, he was murdered by one of his Muslim retainers, but he left his mark as few men did.

While other religions are always in danger of losing their identity when they become very liberal and tolerant, the gurus created a highly visible and strongly felt identity for the Sikhs. Not only others recognize a male Sikh wherever they see him, 47 Sikhs obviously do, too. While every one of them has the same last name, Singh, not every Singh is a Sikh. But when you see him, you know whether he is one.

The God in whom the Sikhs believe is the abstract principle of truth, which is held to be one, omnipresent in the universe, not born, "nor does he die to be reborn again," as the most popular prayer, written by Nanak, puts it. The third guru expressed a less lovely sentiment:

> Those who worship strange gods,
> Cursed shall be their lives, cursed their habitations.
> Poison shall be their food—each morsel,
> Poisoned too shall be their garments.
> In life for them is misery,
> In life hereafter, hell (16).

The tendency toward fatalism in Islam was explicitly rejected. "With your own hands carve out your destiny," said Nanak. The doctrine of transmigration and karma is accepted, but we can break out of the cycle when we are human beings. One's life determines "whether one is condemned to go through the 8,400,000 forms of life (a conven-

---

* Singh, 6 f. This whole section is based on his work.

tional figure [familiar to us from Jainism]) or attain salvation by the fusion of one's light with the light of God [shades of Gnosticism]" (18).

Singing hymns and chanting and repeating *Satnam, Wah Guru* ("the true name, the wondrous guru") have a prominent place in Sikhism. But the gurus were merely human teachers, and the tenth guru insisted:

> I was ordained to establish a sect and lay down its rules.
> But whosoever regards me as Lord
> Shall be damned and destroyed.

There is no worship of men in this religion. If anything is worshiped, it is a book, the Granth, which contains the writings not only of the gurus but also of great Hindu and Muslim teachers. In many homes, parts of it are read every day, and on special occasions it is read from cover to cover by readers who take turns, a process that takes two days and nights. When no outside help is available, there sometimes are seven-day readings.

The so-called Golden Temple of the Sikhs in Amritsar is square. It is located in a 48 large square tank of water, surrounded by a huge court. The water comes right up to the walls of the temple, which is reached over a causeway, more than 200 feet long. Inside, the Granth is chanted by a relay of readers. The sense of simplicity and peace and beauty might well have pleased the gurus. One can sit on the floor and listen. One can also go up some stairs, look down on the reading from above, and find a huge old open copy of the Granth, which consists of more than 6,000 verses. There are no idols.

In some other ways the gurus have been less successful. They repeatedly condemned the caste system in no uncertain terms. The founder said:

> Some are ignoble among the noblest
> and pure among the despised.
> The former you shall avoid,
> and be dust under the feet of the latter.

The other gurus composed verses in the same vein and also derided quite specifically the caste practices concerning food that "went under the garb of hygiene" (23). Nevertheless, "The 'caste system' current today divides the Sikhs into three: agriculturists (Jats), non-agriculturists and Harijans"; and there is still some discrimination against the Harijans (24).

Even more striking is the departure from the strict pacifism of the first five gurus, whose writings form the bulk of the Granth. After the execution of the fifth and ninth gurus the last guru turned his followers into warriors, saying: "When all other means have failed, it is righteous to draw the sword." After that, the Sikhs gradually acquired the reputation of being the best soldiers of India.

Close association with Hindus has left its mark on Sikhism. The Sikhs have long been concentrated in the Punjab, in the north, where they won the respect of the Hindus among whom they lived. The Hindus in that region revered the gurus and often "brought up one or more of their sons as Sikhs and gave their daughters in marriage to Sikh men." This may have been a factor in the re-entry of caste into Sikhism; it certainly helps to account for the re-emergence of the taboo against eating beef. Indeed, the Sikhs became as zealous as anyone in their protests against the killing of cows. All kinds of other Hindu rites and practices have reappeared among the Sikhs; and in 1839, when Ranjit Singh, a very powerful and still extremely popular Sikh ruler, died, "some of his widows were cremated with him" (27). Yet during his reign he had never passed a death sentence.

All this has led Khushwant Singh, author of a scholarly two-volume *History of the Sikhs*, a sympathetic expositor of Sikhism, and a fine novelist and journalist, to muse:

> A Sikh's long hair and unshorn beard are in effect the only things which mark him out as different from the Hindu. His name, family associations, deportment, religious practices—in fact nothing else, serves the same purpose. Therein lies the secret of the concern of orthodox elements over the increasing practice amongst certain sections to discard these external symbols of their faith. The orthodox are willing to overlook defections of the spirit but not of the form. There is nothing like the same insistence on the carrying of the other "Ks" as there is on the unshorn hair. It leads to incongruities like the absolute insistence on abstinence from tobacco (one rarely finds Sikhs smoking in public) with but little censure on the consumption of alcohol. The only explanation is that non-smoking differentiates the Sikhs from the Hindus more than non-drinking (27).

On paper, Sikhism is obviously incomparably closer to Islam than it is to Hinduism. But this only goes to show once again that written accounts concentrating on doctrine often give an utterly misleading impression of the realities, and it is one of the many beauties of Khushwant Singh's writings on the Sikhs that he has an eye for the realities, not only in his novels.

Most Sikhs have long lived in the Punjab, and the people of that state have a common language, Punjabi, which is spoken by the Sikhs, the Muslims, and the Hindus of the region. Yet when the great partition of 1947 was made, the Punjab was divided. Roughly 2,500,000 Sikhs lived in the part given to Pakistan, and about the same number in the part given to India. When the fighting and migrations were all over, all the surviving Sikhs were in India, none in Pakistan. Those who fled the new Muslim state had to leave behind their homes, their very rich agricultural lands, their temples, and virtually all their possessions. The Muslims who moved in the opposite direction were mostly landless tenants. Yet Pakistan did not offer the Sikhs any compensation, and neither the other Muslim countries nor the rest of the world insisted that there could not be any lasting peace until the Sikhs were either given back their land or compensated for it. The Sikhs themselves did not become terrorists, nor did India keep them in camps, nor did the Sikhs wait for the United Nations or some other agency to take care of them. Khushwant Singh, himself one of the refugees, says this about his people:

> *The Sikhs are India's best farmers.* In their home state of the Punjab they make an acre yield four to five times more than an acre yields elsewhere. Lands in other parts of India which had been abandoned as barren, weed-infested, swampy or malarial, have been reclaimed by Sikh refugees ousted from Pakistan and turned into the most productive in the country. By contrast, the lands which they had tilled in what is now Pakistan, and which were considered the very best in India have lost much of their productivity through water-logging and neglect (xiii).

Even readers who may wonder whether he is not perhaps exaggerating will still have to concede that people can maintain their pride under such trying circumstances in rather different ways. Complaining that one does not belong where one had fled, insisting that one must be given back what one once had, and meanwhile supporting and applauding "freedom fighters" who deliberately kill women and children at point-blank range is not the only way.

It is also remarkable that all the Sikhs left Pakistan, although their beliefs are closer to Islam than to Hinduism. This was due in part to the fact that the whole idea of Pakistan was to have a Muslim state. It was also a reflection of a long and extremely bloody history of hatred between Sikhs and Muslims. The Muslims had executed several of the early leaders of the Sikhs, along with their children; the Sikhs, seeking revenge, had put large numbers of Muslims to the sword; the Muslims had retaliated, and all this bloodshed had not been forgotten. Finally, the Sikh's overwhelming preference for India tells us something about India, too.

Hinduism has a fabulous capacity for reabsorbing heretics. If even Jainism has many mansions, Hinduism is certainly misunderstood if one reduces it to the views of one sect or philosophy. Of course, there is intolerance in Hinduism, too, and the caste system is a case in point. It is doubly remarkable that protests against Hindu intolerance, like Jainism and Sikhism, have been unable to resist the gradual re-infiltration of caste. What is even more astonishing is that Buddhism all but disappeared in India because its followers were eventually reabsorbed into Hinduism.

81

Buddhism is the oldest of the three religions that converted hundreds of millions of people who are ethnically quite different. The Buddha himself sent out missionaries, more than five centuries before Jesus and Paul, more than eleven before Muhammad. Even so, the immense spread of Buddhism came much later, in the age of syncretism. The Buddha himself antedates that age and was not an eclectic. His doctrine was of one piece and extremely simple. But he himself was quite as remarkable as his teaching. His personality was as impressive as any in world history. When his doctrine had been changed almost beyond recognition, his spirit still found expression in bronze and stone. 123ff.

He was born at the foot of the Himalayas in what is now Nepal. Most scholars agree that this was in 563 B.C., and that he died at eighty in 483. His name was Siddhartha Gautama (in Sanskrit, Gotama in Pali; the earliest Buddhist scriptures are in Pali). Gautama was the son of a prince who, according to legend, had received a prophecy that his son would become either a great emperor or a great teacher. To make sure that his son would become an emperor, the father raised him in a magnificent palace, surrounded by a large park, and tried to make sure that nothing would sadden or disillusion him. 105–120

The legends, unlike the Buddha himself, believe in prophecies and gods, and tell how the gods defeated the father's precautions. One day, as Gautama was riding through the park with his charioteer, having never seen old age before, he suddenly saw an old man. In parts of the Western world, many young people are almost as well protected against such a sight as Gautama had been; such really old faces as are a common sight in India are rarely seen in the streets of most European and American countries. Gautama was startled—a psychologist might say traumatized—and asked Channa, the charioteer, about the old man. The charioteer told him that in time all of us become old. The legend claims that no old man could possibly have got into the park, and that it must have been a god—also when a few days later Gautama saw a sick man. Again, we must bring to mind a horrible image of decay. Next, Gautama beheld a dead man. Finally, he saw an ascetic, and perhaps saw in him a form of existence that was immune to old age, sickness, and death, for an ascetic has no youth and does not look healthy; he approximates death in life. Yet the ascetic looked happy. Then Gautama decided to become an ascetic.

Gautama left the palace the very night after his son, Rahula, was born. The situation brings to mind Franz Kafka's comment on the story in Genesis in which God tells Abraham to sacrifice his son, Isaac. Kierkegaard thought that most men would have refused God's commandment. Kafka said that a great many people would have said Yes willingly—but like waiters who do not say No, but: Right away, sir, only not just yet; I have something else to do first—and then something else. The Buddha, whose wife had just given birth, did not feel that he first had to attend to a few other things before departing for a life of asceticism; he went away that night. Eventually, Rahula became a member of the order founded by his father.

The legend reflects the uncompromising radicalism that, for all his mildness, is one of the most characteristic features of the Buddha. He did not compromise and was, in spite of his sublime compassion, totally free of sentimentality. Incidentally, the Buddha did not say later, as Jesus did: "Truly, I say to you, there is no man who has left house or wife or brothers or parents or children . . . who will not receive many times as much in this world, and in the world to come eternal life" (see page 113 above). Not only was the Buddha not seeking eternal life, but he knew that leaving home was but a small start and no guarantee whatever of salvation. There were many people in India in the Buddha's time who had left home to seek salvation in the woods, and he soon found that most of them were seeking in vain.

He tried asceticism as well as meditation and the lore of the Upanishads, and for six years·he surpassed the austerities of the other ascetics in the area, who admired him. He did not cease until he felt sure beyond any lingering doubt that asceticism did not lead to enlightenment. He did not opt for the opposite extreme, a life of sensuality; he chose a "middle path" and was not deterred by the gibes of the ascetics who mocked him and said that their life had evidently proved too hard for him. Like many others, he wandered about, begging for a little food, sure that his middle path was not enough. Something more was needed.

One day he sat down under a bodhi tree, now called *ficus religiosa*, and resolved not to get up again until he had found enlightenment. It was 528 B.C., about ten years after the end of the Babylonian exile, and Gautama was then thirty-five. He sat under the tree for forty-nine days before he gained enlightenment and thus became a Buddha, which means an enlightened or awakened one.

What happened during those forty-nine days? Legends say that Mara, the tempter, approached Gautama. The story of Jesus' temptation by the devil could easily have been influenced by this legend. Mara assembled a terrifying army, and when he attacked the Buddha all the gods in the ten thousand worlds who had been singing the praises of the Great Being fled, "and the Great Being was left sitting alone." Then Mara attacked him with a whirlwind, a huge rainstorm, showers of rocks, of weapons, of live coals, of hot ashes, of sand, of mud, and with a dense darkness—all to no avail. Then Mara disputed Gautama's worthiness and his right to sit there, claiming that there was none to bear witness for him. Gautama, sitting under the tree in a lotus or half lotus position, with his left hand resting on his right leg, palm up, reached down with his right hand very gently to touch the earth—a moment recaptured in many beautiful

127   Buddha images that are called either "Buddha subduing Mara" or "Buddha calling the earth to witness." The bronzes often have a simplicity that is not to be found in the texts, in which every idea is elaborated at enormous length with distracting numbers
121   and enumerations. Thus the earth is said to have "thundered, 'I bear you witness!' with a hundred, a thousand, a hundred thousand roars."

There are elements in these legends that illuminate the character of the man who inspired them; but the luxuriant belief in prodigies, the wallowing in immense numbers, the piling up of miracles, are strangely at odds with his teaching. What is doubly as-
104,123,125,   tounding is that a thousand years and more after his death, some artists caught the spirit
129,134,   of the Buddha so much better than these texts. Here indeed one image is often superior
137ff.   to a thousand words, and it makes sense to make this account of Buddhism shorter than the treatment of some of the other great religions, but to offer pictures of many Buddha images.

Mara is also said to have offered Gautama dominion "over the four great continents and their two thousand attending isles," but he replied: "I have no wish for sovereignty. I am about to make the ten thousand worlds thunder with my becoming a Buddha." He had not withdrawn from the world because it was too much for him and he could not cope with it. He had taken on its challenge, mindful of old age, sickness, and death, facing every terror instead of burying his head in distractions as most men do. Wars and famine, mutilations and diseases, floods and earthquakes, human inhumanity, ingratitude, and infidelity, brutality and callousness and drawn-out death—he faced, determined not to rise until his insight triumphed over all of it. On the forty-ninth day he found enlightenment and vanquished all the horrors of this life and of whatever other lives there might be, of this world and of any other worlds—and caused all the worlds to tremble. What was dominion over a few continents to him?

It is related further that the Buddha, having found enlightenment, remained in the same position for another forty-nine days, meditating on the truths he had discovered. What happened during those days? A legend relates that Mara approached the Buddha again and urged him to enter nirvana, but the Buddha decided to return among men and to teach them his hard-won truths. This was about one hundred fifty years before Plato argued in his *Republic* that those who have had the great vision should return to help others. Some people associate this legend about the last temptation with the Mahayana, a later form of Buddhism, and insist that early Buddhism was essentially selfish. But whether Mara tempted the Buddha or not, it is a historical fact that the Buddha did go back among men to preach indefatigably for forty-five years.

He made many converts, founded an order for monks and later also one for nuns, but admitted lay members as well. When the Buddha was young, Zarathustra was exhorting the Persians, and the Second Isaiah and Ezekiel the Jews; when he became a Buddha, Cyrus was establishing a vast empire, and Confucius was twenty-three; and when he was in his seventies, the Greeks defeated the Persians at Marathon and Greek tragedy was taking shape. Aeschylus and Sophocles were his younger contemporaries; Euripides was probably born a year before the Buddha died; Herodotus, Thucydides, and Socrates a few years later. No other age in the history of our world has seen a comparable explosion of such originality in so many widely different regions.

The forty-five years of teaching were not punctuated by dramatic events. But there is a legend that a man tried to kill the Buddha by having a mad elephant charge him. The Buddha's gentle calm soothed the elephant, who lay down at his feet. On another occasion, the tribe into which he had been born was ranged for battle against another tribe, and he walked between the armies and talked them out of fighting. The contrast with Krishna in the Gita is obvious, but it should also be noted how very different the tone of all these stories is from the atmosphere of the New Testament. It seems plain that the Buddha was worlds removed from the shrillness, the vituperation, and the hatefulness that the evangelists associated with Jesus.

A legend about the Buddha's death relates that the man to whom he came, with his disciples, on the last day of his life to beg for food, was eager to offer him something special and prepared "sweetness of pigs" (Basham, 260 n.) or "pig's soft food" (Ch'en, *sukaramaddava*, 25)—which early commentators took to mean a fine pork dish, while modern Buddhists, who assume that the Buddha must have been a vegetarian, say it was truffles. Most scholars agree that it was pork. The Buddha, realizing that the food was fatal, asked to be served all of it. Then, having eaten, he did not say "woe unto that man" or "it would be better for that man if he had never been born." He said that it was one of the two finest meals that he had ever had; the other one being his last meal before his enlightenment. Now he would enter nirvana.

It is further related that he called together his disciples, announced that he was about to enter nirvana, and urged them to ask any final questions, lest they should reproach themselves later for not having asked questions when they could. Three times he urged them, but no one asked a question. The Buddha's final words, probably not only according to legend, were: "Decay is inherent in all composite things. Work out your salvation with diligence."*

He had taught men consistently to place no faith whatever in gods, sacrifices, prayers, miracles, or idols, in sacred scriptures, or in magic. Yet as Buddhism spread, it gradually assimilated all kinds of beliefs in a vast array of gods, demons, and devils; the Buddhists came to rely not only on prayers but also on prayer wheels that one could turn to gain credit for the prayers that went round and round; relics of the Buddha were soon sought after, and stupas were built over them, although his disciples had cremated him; and in time the Buddha was worshiped, and images of him were made not only of stone but later also of gold and jade. Some Buddha images are great works of art, many are not; but even the vulgar ones are gentle.

Innumerable legends tell of the Buddha's previous incarnations. How did he behave when he was an animal, many lives back, to merit his advance to a higher level of existence? Such speculations are entirely contrary to his ethos, and yet these stories are evidence of the impression that he made on millions. As a rabbit, we are told, he once saw a hunter who was cold and hungry and had built himself a fire to warm his freezing hands. Then the Buddha-to-be jumped into the fire so that the poor man would have something to eat but took great care that his fur not be ruined by the flames, for he wished the hunter to be able to make gloves from it.

His conception of himself was simply that he was a human being who had found enlightenment and peace and could help others by communicating his truths to them. His teaching involved no appeal whatever to authority. He simply set aside the Vedas and the rich traditions that had grown up on their soil and never tried to establish any point by appealing to scripture or tradition. Nor did he polemicize against the views that others based on such authority; he did not say: You have been told, but I say to you . . . He did not appeal to any god, nor did he claim to be a god himself. In many ways, his stance resembled that of his contemporary Mahavira, the founder of Jainism, but in two important ways it seems to have been different. First, Mahavira probably claimed to be the successor of an earlier Jina, Parshva, and perhaps he himself suggested that he was the last of twenty-four tirthankaras. Although later Buddhism came to recognize previous Buddhas as well as a Buddha to come, Gautama Siddhartha seems to have taken his stand entirely upon the merits of his arguments. This brings us to the second difference. The Jina's dualistic philosophy is not ultimately based on evidence or argument. He simply offered a doctrine. The Buddha may well have been the first person in history who presented a comprehensive view of man's condition that was strikingly at variance with the religious views of his time, basing it solely on appeals to evidence and argument from that. In that sense he could be said to have been the first genuine philosopher anywhere.

82

Buddhism has assumed such diverse forms in its long history, and it has generated so many philosophies, that it would be quite impossible here to even try to cover them all. The two major divisions are the Hinayana, or small vehicle, and the Mahayana, or large vehicle. These two names are inspired by a Mahayana bias, and the adherents of

---

* Maha-Parinibbana Suttanta, 6:10; SBE, vol. 11, 114, and Warren, 109.

the Hinayana generally call it Theravada, which means the "teaching of old"—that is the old monks who were close to the Buddha. Tibetan Buddhism does not really fit into either of these two categories, nor does Zen, which needs to be understood as a reaction against the Mahayana. For all that, it seems reasonably clear what the Buddha's own teaching was. One of its most extraordinary features was its utter simplicity, which distinguishes it from all other religions. It could be stated in a very few words. But terseness was not the Indian way, and the Buddha's sermons, as recorded in the ancient Pali scriptures, are generally very long and repetitious. Nothing is said once only, briefly. In this respect one cannot fail to be reminded of the Upanishads, although the Buddha set aside their metaphysics no less than the Jina's.

It was part of his great insight under the bodhi tree that no theory about the world and the soul, about the living and the lifeless, nor any esoteric wisdom whatsoever was needed for salvation. What he had come to see was not a doctrine for initiates only, but "four noble truths" that anyone could grasp. He did not say that "whatever is more than this comes from the evil one," but he ruled out many questions that were put to him as "not tending toward edification." The bulk of his sermons is not due to any determination to cover a great deal of ground. They are meant to convey a timeless tempo, a distinctive state of mind, peace.

Here is his statement of the four noble truths in his first sermon, which he delivered in the deer park near Benares, in what now is Sarnath, where a simple stupa commemorates this sermon. Only one term he used requires explanation: "Tathagata," literally "one thus come," is a name for the Buddha.

> There are two extremes, monks, that anyone who has given up the world ought to avoid. What are these two extremes? A life given to pleasures, devoted to pleasures and lusts; this is degrading, sensual, vulgar, ignoble, and profitless. And a life given to mortifications; this is painful, ignoble, and profitless. By avoiding these two extremes, monks, the Tathagata has gained the knowledge of the middle path which leads to insight, which leads to wisdom, which conduces to calm, to knowledge, to supreme enlightenment, to nirvana.
>
> Which, monks, is this middle path the knowledge of which the Tathagata has gained, which leads to insight, which leads to wisdom, which conduces to calm, to knowledge, to supreme enlightenment, to nirvana?
>
> It is the noble eightfold path, namely: right views, right intent, right speech, right conduct, right means of livelihood, right endeavor, right mindfulness, right meditation. This, monks, is the middle path the knowledge of which the Tathagata has gained, which leads to insight, which leads to wisdom, which conduces to calm, to knowledge, to supreme enlightenment, to nirvana.
>
> This, monks, is the noble truth of suffering: birth is suffering, old age is suffering, sickness is suffering, death is suffering; sorrow, lamentation, depression, and despair are suffering; contact with things unpleasant is suffering; separation from things we love is suffering; not to get what we desire is suffering. In short, the five senses of grasping are suffering.
>
> This, monks, is the noble truth concerning the cause of suffering: that craving which leads to rebirth, combined with pleasure and lust, finding pleasure here and there; in sum, craving for pleasures, craving for existence, craving for non-existence.
>
> This, monks, is the noble truth concerning the cessation of suffering: it is passionless, cessation without remainder of this craving; the laying aside of, giving up, being free from, harboring no longer, this craving.
>
> This, monks, is the noble truth concerning the path which leads to the cessation of suffering. It is this noble eightfold path, namely, right views, right intent, right speech, right conduct, right means of livelihood, right endeavor, right mindfulness, right meditation.*

---

* Dhamma-Kakka-Ppavattana-Sutta. For another translation, see SBE, vol. 11, 146 ff.

The first noble truth calls attention to the universality of suffering. We are always apt—nowhere more so than in the modern West—to think of suffering as a mishap, an unfortunate accident that somehow was unnecessary. It is told that once a woman came to the Buddha, carrying her dead child in her arms, crazed with grief, craving his help. But he neither tried to bring the child back to life, nor did he preach to her. He asked her to go into the next village and bring back some rather ordinary spice from any family at all in which no one had ever died. This simple request provides an opportunity for tradition to elaborate the woman's visits to house after house. Whether the idea that repetition is required to make the saving truth sink in is sound, is debatable, but the first noble truth is based squarely on the evidence to which almost all of us shut our eyes. The Buddha's method in presenting it does not involve any attempt to shock, nor does he offer long descriptions of horrible suffering. There is no passion in his presentation which is heavily conceptual.

The second noble truth directs our attention to the cause of suffering, which the Buddha finds in craving or desire. This idea is developed further in many other passages. Perhaps *attachment* and *detachment* are more appropriate terms than desire and the extinction of desire, but the second truth is in any case simple enough. The death of others need not grieve us if we are not attached to them; the prospect of our own death need not cause us suffering if we are not attached to life; ingratitude need not pain us if we do not desire gratitude; loss of possessions need not sadden us if we are not attached to them; and loss of our youth, physical strength, and health will not plunge us into despair once we no longer desire these things. Often the Buddha said also that desire and attachment are rooted in ignorance. Without accepting the metaphysics of Shankara, one might also speak of illusions in a very simple and popular sense of that word. Certainly, desire often feeds on illusions, on a vast overestimation of some person or thing, on false beliefs about them, on the dream that if only we possessed someone or something we would be happy forever. Desire and attachment are rooted in ignorance of the first noble truth.

The third truth concerns the cessation of suffering. It is a very early example of scientific thinking. The removal of the cause of suffering will lead to the cessation of suffering. If we can overcome desire and attachment by rising above our illusions and our ignorance, we will cease to suffer. But this, of course, is easier said than done. What is needed is a prescription, a regimen that will lead to salvation.

The fourth truth is that the noble eightfold path will lead to the cessation of attachment and desire and hence also to redemption from suffering. The emphasis here falls on conduct, on what needs to be done, not on belief. The first of the eight elements of the path, to be sure, is right views, but what is meant is nothing like the dogmas that the Gospel according to John, the epistles of Paul, the church councils, or Martin Luther sought to define. The Buddha does not suppose that there is a god who will punish for ever and ever all those who do not believe precisely the right things about the Buddha and about his relationship to this god. The right views involve acceptance of the four noble truths, but not because it would be insubordinate or wicked to reject the Buddha's teaching. The point is rather that salvation involves no magic whatsoever, and mindless repetition of various practices will not bring about the cessation of suffering. What is indispensable is understanding. Hence there is little hope for fools. Neither is understanding enough. Right views are only the indispensable beginning.

We must fall out of love with the world. We must cease to be fooled by her charms. We must desire her no more, be attached to her no more, but not hate her either. We must grow up and feel about the world as a grown-up may feel about the toys with which he played as a child. When he was little, he may have desired some toy madly, may have been unable to sleep because he kept thinking about whether he would ever get it, and may have felt that nothing mattered more than getting this one thing; and then, having got it, he may have been attached to it passionately for a short while. Most adults still go through the same sequence of attitudes, again and again and again. What is needful is that we grow up, that we wake up, that we see what the Buddha finally saw on the forty-ninth day under the bodhi tree.

Some discipline of the intellect and indeed the whole mind is required to that end; so is some degree of asceticism, but only enough for us to gain control over the body and to cease being slaves of our desires. No advanced training in metaphysics or in yoga is needed.

The repetitious style of the Buddha's sermons may be due above all to two reasons. First, it is part of the content of his teaching that what seems enormously exciting and disturbing the first time it is experienced loses its power over us the thousandth time. The repetitions represent a deliberate attempt to make the mind dwell on the same things over and over again in order to produce detachment. It is also possible that the repetitiousness increased with repetition. The earliest Buddhist scriptures we have were put into writing centuries after the Buddha's death, and by that time the Indian love of repetition may have shaped the oral tradition. While there is no reason to doubt that the substance of the Buddha's teaching was preserved faithfully, he may well have been much briefer than the texts suggest. Still, people wanted to hear him and gathered around him to listen day after day, and he would have disappointed them if he had spoken for a mere ten or fifteen minutes. It is highly probable that he did not aim to be terse, and in the retelling everything became even much longer.

83

The oldest scriptures were written down in Pali, which is very similar to Sanskrit, and the Pali canon is common to the Theravada and the Mahayana, but the Mahayana has added many later scriptures to it, in Sanskrit. The Pali canon has three parts and is often called the *Tipitaka*, the three baskets.

The first basket, the *Vinayapitaka*, contains the rules of discipline for monks. There are over two hundred such rules, two hundred and twenty-seven in the Pali canon, two hundred and fifty in the later Chinese version, and two hundred and fifty-three in the Tibetan edition. The first of the eight sections in which these rules are presented in the Pali canon deals with the four major offenses for which one is expelled from the order: unchastity, theft, murder, and claiming miraculous powers that one does not possess. A Buddhist monk need not take any vow to remain a monk for the rest of his life; he may choose to be a monk for a time, but while he is a monk he is expected to be celibate.

Ananda, the disciple who was closest to the Buddha, is said to have asked him how a monk should behave toward women. The Buddha replied: Avoid the sight of them. Ananda persisted: But suppose we do see a woman. Replied the Buddha: Do not speak with her. Ananda: But suppose she speaks to us. Said the Buddha: Then watch out! 65,100

This obviously did not mean that the Buddha considered women evil, nor even that he considered sexual activity evil. As a youth he was married and did not leave home until he was twenty-nine. After that he was celibate, but the last food he had before attaining enlightenment was brought to him by a woman, and having become a Buddha, he willingly answered the questions of women. Eventually he also founded an order for nuns, and it is related that both his wife and his son became members of his order. Abstention from sexual relations had been a condition of ritual purity even in Vedic times, though it was required only for very short periods. In the age of the

Upanishads celibacy had become a way of life for many, but the Buddha surely did not accept this custom thoughtlessly. He evidently thought that the custom made sense for anyone who wished to fall out of love with the world and attain detachment. What had to be overcome was not sex as such but all desire, and especially the craving for pleasures.

Still, the Buddha evidently considered women inferior to men. For a long time he resisted the entreaties of Ananda and others to found an order for nuns, and when he finally did, he laid down some special rules for nuns that include at least two highly prejudicial ones: "A nun, even a hundred years old, shall arise, salute, meet humbly and behave respectfully toward a monk, even though the latter was just ordained"; and "Nuns are not allowed to reprove a nun, but a monk may reprove a nun" (Ch'en, 1968, 98).

There are very different rules in the first basket, too. One of the most memorable is this: "Brothers, you have no mother or father to care for you. If you do not care for one another, who else will? Brothers, whoever would care for me should care for the sick." Basham is surely right when he comments that "it was no doubt under the influence of such teachings" that Ashoka, the great Buddhist emperor, established free hospitals in the third century B.C., "and that Buddhist monks have at all times studied medical lore, and treated laymen as well as their own fellows" (285).

The third basket or *Abhidamma* deals with a "higher way" that need not detain us here. It is of later origin than the first two baskets and consists of seven books that deal largely with metaphysical questions. One of these books is ascribed specifically to an author who lived in the third century B.C., under the reign of Ashoka. It is the only work in the whole canon that is assigned to an individual writer.

The second basket, or *Suttapitaka*, is incomparably the most important of the three, as the Suttas are the discourses of the Buddha. They comprise five collections: the long discourses, the discourses of medium length, two collections of sayings, and the so-called minor anthologies, which include at least three that are anything but minor, namely the *Jataka*, which relates five hundred and forty-seven stories about the previous lives of the Buddha, and the *Sutta-Nipata* and *Dhammapada*, which are probably the two oldest books in the whole canon. The Dhammapada is also the most revered and most frequently quoted, and its four hundred and twenty-three stanzas "embody better than any other piece of literature the spirit of the master's teachings" (Ch'en, 1968, 216). We shall consider it at length in the next section.

As for the *Sutta-Nipata*, two suttas from the first of its five books may give at least some idea of its spirit. The third sutta is called "The Rhinoceros" and consists of forty-one four-line stanzas, the last line of every stanza being the same: "wander alone like a rhinoceros" (*eko care khaggavisanakappo*). The rhino suggests enormous strength but is not a herd animal like elephants and buffaloes.

> Have mercy on all beings,
> inflict no hurt, and seek
> no son, much less companions:
> wander alone like a rhinoceros.
>
> Togetherness breeds fondness,
> and fondness leads to pain;
> since pain issues from fondness,
> wander alone like a rhinoceros. . . .
>
> Like a huge elephant
> that quits the herd and finds
> a lotus-covered pond,
> wander alone like a rhinoceros. . . .

"Christian" rhinoceros on bronze door of Pisa cathedral, Italy, ca. 1605. / Angkor, terrace of the Leper King, ca. 1200.

> Without desire or deceit,
> attachment, jealousy, above
> illusions and fond hopes,
> wander alone like a rhinoceros.
>
> Your ties torn like a net by
> a fish, a fire that won't
> return to what it burnt,
> wander alone like a rhinoceros. . . .
>
> Not scared by sounds, a lion;
> not caught in nets, a wind;
> not stained by rain, a lotus,
> wander alone like a rhinoceros. . . .*

The eighth sutta is called "Goodwill." Here are four of its eight stanzas:

> Whatever living beings
> there are, feeble or strong,
> if great and long or medium,
> if short and small or large,
>
> if seen or never seen,
> if far away or near,
> if born or seeking birth,
> may all be blessed with peace.
>
> Let none deceive another
> or ever feel contempt,
> let none wish harm to others
> in anger or resentment.
>
> As, risking life, a mother
> cares for her only child,
> grow all-embracing thoughts
> for every living being.

Many people have found a contradiction between the supposed self-centeredness of early Buddhism and this theme of universal and boundless compassion. Some have tried to solve the problem by claiming that the selfish theme is characteristic of Theravada Buddhism, and universal love of Mahayana Buddhism. But as our two suttas show, both themes are found in the very earliest scriptures and were undoubtedly present in the Buddha's own teaching. Selfishness, however, is the wrong word. A comparison with the Gospels may prove helpful, the more so because Western critics have so often found the Buddha, or at least Theravada Buddhism, inferior in this respect to the ethic of the Gospels.

In the Gospels we found an overriding concern with one's own salvation, and the counsel to give all one has to the poor was expressly motivated by the promise of rewards in heaven. Universal love and all-embracing compassion we did not find; on the contrary, Jesus comforted his disciples by assuring them that those who would not listen to them would fare worse on the day of judgment than the worst evildoers of all time. Threats of hell and vituperation of those who did not accept his claims punctuate Jesus' teachings in the Gospels. Nowhere does he wish peace to all living beings or express regret or outrage over the eternal damnation of most human beings. Nor did

---

* Stanzas 1, 2, 19, 22, 28, 37. Different translations in *Buddha's Teachings, Being the Sutta-Nipata* . . . and in SBE, vol. 10.

Jesus show compassion for slaves or protest against the institution of slavery; Paul said expressly: "Were you a slave when called? Never mind"; and the church did not try to abolish slavery but kept slaves. The Buddha, on the other hand, set aside the caste system along with the authority of the Vedas (e.g., *Sutta-Nipata*, 141 f.).

It is possible and customary to suppose that the Buddha's teaching was predicated on the wish for release from transmigration. If we accept this view, it needs to be added that he taught that each must gain this release through his own efforts, without the help of any deity, but one could help others, as he himself tried to do, by both teaching and example. The counsel to wander alone like a rhinoceros is not an exhortation to be selfish but a way of saying that salvation is not to be found in togetherness. What is needed is the strength to go it alone, and those who wander alone like the rhino give a powerful example to their brothers and sisters. What is needed further is liberation from attachment, from desire, from selfishness. The freedom that comes of this must not be thought of in merely negative terms, as it often is; it involves universal benevolence. One can call it love if only one remembers that this kind of love does not involve any possessiveness, worry, or impatience. The state of being that the Buddha preached about and exemplified is totally free of resentment and characterized by overflowing love. The question whether the ultimate motive is not after all one's own salvation shows a lack of understanding. There is no conflict of interests; to achieve nirvana I must rise above possessiveness, selfishness, and attachment; and there is nothing better that I could do for others than to give them this example and to spread the Buddha's teachings.

Actually, the Buddha did not stress transmigration or any such metaphysical doctrines. The view just presented is not wrong, but it may lay too much stress on metaphysical assumptions that transcend experience. Nirvana, literally extinction, is not so much a metaphysical hypothesis—namely, that those who follow the noble eightfold path and attain the proper state will not be reborn—as it is that state itself. The Buddha preached for forty-five years, until he died at eighty, because he wished to help 104 as many as he could to attain nirvana. That he did not write a book instead may mean first of all that neither he nor the society in which he lived was literate. But we can hardly doubt that he also felt, rightly, that his example was quite as important as his words. In the same vein, every exposition of his teaching really needs to be supplemented with at least some pictures of a few great Buddha images that show us, face to face, the peace that passes understanding.

84

It is tempting to quote a great deal from the important "discourses of medium length" as well as some of the stories from the *Jataka*; but it must suffice here to concentrate on the *Dhammapada*. This relatively short book is regarded as highly as any Buddhist scripture throughout Theravadin southeast Asia, and "must be memorized by all novices who desire the higher ordination" (Ch'en, 216). It is also one of the two most ancient Buddhist scriptures and probably as close to the Buddha's own teaching as we can get. Finally, it is as terse as any major Indian scripture.

The book consists of four hundred and twenty-three short stanzas, divided into twenty-six chapters, and takes up a mere thirty pages in translation. Anyone interested in the Buddha cannot do better than to read the whole of it. Max Müller's nineteenth-century translation is perhaps still the best and most powerful version in English. Here is Radhakrishnan's more recent rendition of the first verse: "(The mental) natures are the result of what we have thought, are chieftained by our thoughts, are made up of our thoughts. If a man speaks or acts with an evil thought, sorrow follows him (as a consequence) even as the wheel follows the foot of the drawer (i.e., the ox which draws the cart)."

And here is Müller's version of the opening verses, which implicitly set aside all belief in supernatural powers, preclude belief in original sin, and do not permit us the excuse that we are the product of heredity and environment:

> All that we are is the result of what we have thought: it is founded on our thoughts, it is made up of our thoughts. If a man speaks or acts with an evil thought, pain follows him as the wheel follows the foot of the ox that draws a carriage.
> All that we are is the result of what we have thought: it is founded on our thoughts, it is made up of our thoughts. If a man speaks or acts with a pure thought, happiness follows him like a shadow that never leaves him.
> "He abused me, he beat me, he defeated me, he robbed me"—in those who harbor such thoughts hatred will never cease.
> "He abused me, he beat me, he defeated me, he robbed me"—in those who do not harbor such thoughts hatred will cease.
> For hatred does not ever cease by hatred: hatred ceases by love; this is an old rule.
> The world does not know that we must all come to an end here; but those who know it—their quarrels cease at once.

Millions, including even Gandhi, have associated the rule of returning love for hatred with Jesus. Actually, one of the most ancient portions of the Law of Moses commands: "If you meet your enemy's ox or his ass going astray, you shall bring it back to him. If you see the ass of one who hates you lying under its burden, you shall refrain from leaving him with it, you shall help him to lift it up" (Exodus 23:5). Yet the Jewish rule, the Christian rule, and the Buddhist rule are different.

The Jewish rule depends on God's commandment and is implicitly followed by the words: for I am the Lord your God. God has made man in his image and wants to remake man in his image by giving him laws. Man should obey to realize God's plan.

The Christian rule depends on an explicit appeal to the rewards and penalties that God will mete out after death. "For if you love those who love you, what reward have you? Do not even the tax collectors do the same?" (Matthew 5:46). In the parallel passage, Luke (6:35) reports Jesus as saying similarly: "your reward will be great." And Paul even goes a step further, by suggesting explicitly that God will not only reward those who follow this precept but also punish those whom we have refrained from punishing (Romans 12:19–20).

The "old rule" that the Buddha cites differs from both the Jewish and the Christian commandments by stating several psychological truths. (Radhakrishnan has "This is the eternal law," where Müller has "this is an old rule.") "Hatred does not ever cease by hatred: hatred ceases by love." There is a wonderful ambiguity in these words, and we need not doubt that both meanings are fully intended. First, we ourselves cannot stop hating by continuing to hate, even if we plan to hate a little less every day; what is wanted is a radical reorientation. We must adopt an altogether different attitude toward the other person and understand him instead of resenting him. We must stop dwelling on what hurt he has inflicted on us and see him as a wretch like ourselves, recalling "that we must all come to an end here." Then our hatred will cease. Moreover, our enemy's hatred will not cease as long as we return his hatred; but if he finds that we do not hate him, his hatred, too, will cease.

The Buddha's conception of love differs from most other conceptions of love, for he preaches detachment, disenchantment, a loss of interest. Those who accept the four noble truths will no longer repeat to themselves: "He abused me, he beat me, he defeated me, he robbed me." They will be free from resentment. But why should they feel love?

The serenity that the Buddha attained and wanted to help others to attain is not an inclusive resentment of this whole world, shriveled into a single point of defiant indifference. Defiance was not what the Buddha taught. He was no Stoic, and Zeno of Cyprus, who founded the Stoic school of philosophy more than two centuries later, and his Greek and Roman followers were no Buddhists.

An excellent illustration of the difference may be found by juxtaposing a Buddha image with a Roman sculpture of a man's head. Or contrast Hermann Hesse's *Siddhartha* with one of Plutarch's sketches of a Stoic. Or consider a passage from Nietzsche's discourse "On Those Who Are Sublime" in Part Two of *Thus Spoke Zarathustra*:

> One who was sublime I saw today, one who was solemn, an ascetic of the spirit . . . With a swelled chest and like one who holds in his breath, he stood there, the sublime one, silent, decked out with ugly truths, the spoil of his hunting, and rich in torn garments; many thorns, too, adorned him—yet I saw no rose.
> As yet he has not learned laughter or beauty. Gloomy this hunter returned from the woods of knowledge. He came home from a fight with savage beasts; but out of his seriousness there also peers a savage beast—one not overcome. He still stands there like a tiger who wants to leap . . .
> . . . only when he turns away from himself, will he jump over his shadow.
> . . . Contempt is still in his eyes, and nausea hides around his mouth. . . . He must still discard his heroic will; he shall be elevated, not merely sublime: the ether itself should elevate him, the will-less one. . . . As yet his knowledge has not learned to smile and to be without jealousy; as yet his torrential passion has not become still in beauty.

This passage illuminates the difference between the stern Stoic and the smiling Buddha. The Buddha's state of mind is ill characterized by such phrases as "renunciation of the world"; it is not a big No but an all-inclusive Yes.

Popular Buddhism, with its idols and prayers, ritual and relics, and its countless hells and heavens is quite remote from the spirit of the Buddha. But in many of the early scriptures—most concisely in the Dhammapada—his mind found perfect expression.

Here are a few more stanzas, in Max Müller's translation:

> 40. Knowing that this body is fragile like a jar, and making this thought firm like a fortress, one should attack Mara (the tempter) with the weapon of knowledge, one should watch him when conquered, and should never rest.
> 41. Before long, alas! this body will lie on the earth, despised, without understanding, like a useless log.
> 42. Whatever a hater may do to a hater, or an enemy to an enemy, a wrongly directed mind will do us greater mischief.
> 43. Not a mother, not a father will do so much, nor any other relative; a well-directed mind will do us greater service.
> 49. As the bee collects nectar and departs without injuring the flower, or its color or scent, so let a sage dwell in his village.
> 50. Not the perversities of others, not their sins of commission or omission, but his own misdeeds and negligences should a sage take notice of.
> 51. Like a beautiful flower, full of color, but without scent, are the fine but fruitless words of him who does not act accordingly.
> 52. But, like a beautiful flower, full of color and full of scent, are the fine and fruitful words of him who acts accordingly.
> 61. If a traveler does not meet with one who is his better, or his equal, let him firmly keep to his solitary journey; there is no companionship with a fool.

62. "These sons belong to me, and this wealth belongs to me," with such thoughts a fool is tormented. He himself does not belong to himself; how much less sons and wealth?

63. The fool who knows his foolishness, is wise at least so far. But a fool who thinks himself wise, he is called a fool indeed. [Compare Socrates.]

64. If a fool be associated with a wise man even all his life, he will perceive the truth as little as a spoon perceives the taste of soup.

65. If an intelligent man be associated for one minute only with a wise man, he will soon perceive the truth, as the tongue perceives the taste of soup.

129. All men tremble at punishment, all men fear death; remember that you are like unto them, and do not kill, nor cause slaughter.

131. He who seeking his own happiness punishes or kills beings who also long for happiness, will not find happiness after death.

141. Not nakedness, not platted hair, not dirt, not fasting, or lying on the earth, not rubbing with dust, not sitting motionless, can purify a mortal who has not overcome desires.

142. He who, though dressed in fine apparel, exercises tranquillity, is quiet, subdued, restrained, chaste, and has ceased to find fault with all other beings, he indeed is a Brahmin, an ascetic (sramana), a friar (Bhikshu).

145. Well-makers lead the water (wherever they like); fletchers bend the arrow; carpenters bend a log of wood; good people fashion themselves.

Chapter 11, on "Old Age," is short enough to be quoted entirely.

146. How is there laughter, how is there joy, as this world is always burning? Why do you not seek a light, ye who are surrounded by darkness?

147. Look at this dressed-up lump, covered with wounds, joined together, sickly, full of many thoughts, which has no strength, no hold!

148. This body is wasted, full of sickness, and frail; this heap of corruption breaks to pieces, life indeed ends in death.

149. Those white bones, like gourds thrown away in the autumn, what pleasure is there in looking at them?

150. After a stronghold has been made of the bones, it is covered with flesh and blood, and there dwell in it old age and death, pride and deceit.

151. The brilliant chariots of kings are destroyed, the body also approaches destruction, but the virtue of good people never approaches destruction—thus do the good say to the good.

152. A man who has learnt little, grows old like an ox; his flesh grows, but his knowledge does not grow.

153, 154. Looking for the maker of this tabernacle, I shall have to run through a course of many births, so long as I do not find (him); and painful is birth again and again. But now, maker of the tabernacle, thou hast been seen; thou shalt not make up this tabernacle again. All thy rafters are broken, thy ridge-pole is sundered; the mind, approaching the Eternal (visankhara, nirvana) has attained to the extinction of all desires.

155. Men who have not observed proper discipline, and have not gained treasure in their youth, perish like old herons in a lake without fish.

156. Men who have not observed proper discipline, and have not gained treasure in their youth, lie, like broken bows, sighing after the past.

Here are a few more stanzas:

266. A man is not a mendicant (Bhikshu) simply because he asks others for alms; he who adopts the whole law is a Bhikshu, not he who only begs.

267. He who is above good and evil, who is chaste, who with knowledge passes through the world, he indeed is called a Bhikshu.

320. Silently shall I endure abuse as the elephant in battle endures the arrow sent from the bow; for the world is ill-natured.

321. They lead a tamed elephant to battle, the king mounts a tamed elephant; the tamed is the best among men, he who silently endures abuse.

322. Mules are good, if tamed, and noble Sindhu horses, and elephants with large tusks; but he who tames himself is better still.

328. If a man find a prudent companion who walks with him, is wise, and lives soberly, he may walk with him, overcoming all dangers, happy, but considerate.

329. If a man find no prudent companion who walks with him, is wise, and lives soberly, let him walk alone, like a king who has left his conquered country behind—like an elephant in the forest.

330. It is better to live alone, there is no companionship with a fool; let a man walk alone, let him commit no sin, with few wishes, like an elephant in the forest.

The last chapter deals with the Arhat, the saint of Theravada Buddhism, but is called "The Brahmin." It is polemical, the point being that only an Arhat deserves the reverence that the Brahmins claimed to be their due.

389. No one should attack a Brahmin, but no Brahmin (if attacked) should let himself fly at his aggressor! Woe to him who strikes a Brahmin, more woe to him who flies at his aggressor!

390. It advantages a Brahmin not a little if he holds his mind back from the pleasures of life; when all wish to injure has vanished, pain will cease.

391. Him I call indeed a Brahmin who does not offend by body, word, or thought, and is controlled on these three points.

392. After a man has once understood the law as taught by the Well-awakened (Buddha), let him worship it carefully, as the Brahmin worships the sacrificial fire.

393. A man does not become a Brahmin by his platted hair, by his family, or by birth; in whom there is truth and righteousness, he is blessed, he is a Brahmin.

394. What is the use of platted hair, O fool! what of the raiment of goat-skins? Within you there is ravening, but the outside you make clean.

395. The man who wears dirty raiments, who is emaciated and covered with veins, who lives alone in the forest, and meditates, him I call indeed a Brahmin.

396. I do not call a man a Brahmin because of his origin or of his mother. He is indeed arrogant, and he is wealthy: but the poor, who is free from all attachments, him I call indeed a Brahmin.

397. Him I call indeed a Brahmin who has cut all fetters, who never trembles, is independent and unshackled.

405. Him I call indeed a Brahmin who finds no fault with other beings, whether feeble or strong, and does not kill nor cause slaughter.

406. Him I call indeed a Brahmin who is tolerant with the intolerant, mild with fault-finders, and free from passion among the passionate.

407. Him I call indeed a Brahmin from whom anger and hatred, pride and envy have dropped like a mustard seed from the point of a needle.

417. Him I call indeed a Brahmin who, after leaving all bondage to men, has risen above all bondage to the gods, and is free from all and every bondage.

420. Him I call indeed a Brahmin whose path the gods do not know, nor spirits (Gandharvas), nor men, whose passions are extinct, and who is an Arhat (venerable).

An earlier stanza (94) says that "even the gods envy him."

85

Although the Pali scriptures were not written down until the first century B.C. and unknown in Europe before the midnineteenth century, almost all Western scholars agree with the Theravadins that some of these books, notably the Dhammapada, bring us as close to the Buddha's teaching as we can get, while the Sanskrit scriptures of the Mahayana represent a later development. Nor do the Mahayana Buddhists question the authenticity of the Pali canon. They merely claim that what we find in these scriptures was the Buddha's exoteric teaching, while his esoteric doctrine for the more advanced disciples was transmitted orally for a much longer time before it was finally written down. Few but Mahayana Buddhists believe this. The distinctive ideas of Mahayana Buddhism are the product of a later syncretistic age. Even as the Gita represented a response to early Buddhism, the Mahayana represents a reaction to the stress on *bhakti* (fervent devotion) that found its greatest literary expression in the Gita. The Mahayana "belief in a western paradise presided over by a Buddha of boundless light and life" seems to have been "borrowed from Zoroastrianism,"* and there probably are many other borrowings as well, although in India they are difficult to prove because dates are almost impossible to come by. In China we have dates, and Chinese borrowings will be considered in the next chapter.

Kenneth Ch'en's account of *the four major differences between the Mahayana and the Theravada* is superb, and we shall follow it in the main.

First, while the Buddha of the Pali canon was a human being who had found enlightenment, the Mahayana Buddha was an eternal being who was embodied in the historical Buddha, but by no means only in him. This idea led some monks to secede at a great council in 383 B.C., a mere hundred years after the Buddha's death. They were called the Great Assembly (*Mahasanghikas*). The Mahayana, however, did not gain its separate identity before, at the earliest, the first century B.C., and "The bulk of the Mahayana Sutras appears to have been composed during the first three centuries of the Christian era." Only about "5 percent of the Mahayana Sutras have so far been reliably edited, and perhaps 2 percent intelligibly translated." Among the texts that are available, the Saddharma Pundarika Sutra ("Lotus of the True Law") is, again in the words of Conze, "a religious classic of breath-taking grandeur" (200). In the opening pages of this Sutra we see the Buddha sitting on a hilltop, surrounded by his disciples, and a ray issues from between the Buddha's eyes. Then those gathered around him recall similar occurrences in previous ages when earlier Buddhas appeared on earth. After billions of bodhisattvas have become visible in the miraculous ray, the Buddha announces that he has taught and converted all of them, and that he was from the beginning and will be forever, and since there really is neither beginning nor end, he is eternal. (The notion of bodhisattvas will be considered shortly.) To distinguish the Buddha of our age from the countless other Buddhas, he is often called Sakyamuni; and he is "just an appearance, created by the eternal Buddha who is neither born nor dies" (Ch'en, 65).

Western metaphysics at its most baroque is almost classically simple compared to the dazzling visions of many worlds in Mahayana Buddhism. Yet in some ways the Mahayana is closer to modern science than the traditional Western image of the world that is derived from the Hebrews and the Greeks. Darwin's insistence on the essential continuity of man and animal, which upset many Christians in the later nineteenth century, need not disturb either Buddhists or Hindus who, in their doctrines of transmigration, had long postulated some such continuity, and Copernicus' denial of the Western idea that the earth is the center of the universe and the one and only stage for the drama of life might strike a Mahayana Buddhist as a truism. Even the fantastic distances and time spans of modern astronomy bring to mind Mahayana Buddhism rather than the Bible. It does not follow that the mentality of the Mahayana scriptures is scientific, which it certainly is not, but their profound sense of the insignificance of what one might call "our little world" invites comparison with the ideas of twentieth-century science—ideas we know about but still have not absorbed emotionally. Of course, all these Mahayana visions of worlds upon worlds involved a depreciation of the historical Buddha.

"The facts of the master's life are no longer of great importance; what matters are

---

* Ch'en, 1968 (henceforth cited as "Ch'en"), 62. Cf. Ch'en, 1964, 15 f.

the metaphysical speculations about the eternal Buddha." And these issued in "the doctrine of the three bodies of the Buddha, the Body of Essence, the Body of Communal Enjoyment, and the Body of Transformation." Although this idea did not attain its full articulation until the fourth century A.D., at the same time that the relation of the historical Jesus to the eternal Father was defined at the Council of Nicaea, the conception of the Body of Essence, which is one and transcendent, clearly goes back to the Great Assembly of the fourth century B.C. The Body of Communal Enjoyment is perceived by the bodhisattvas as a "symphony of light and sound"; it "sits on Vulture Peak preaching the Mahayana scriptures to huge concourses of Buddhas and bodhisattvas." The third body, finally, is the fictitious phantoms that the eternal Buddha causes "to appear among ignorant and wicked mankind in order to convert it. Sakyamuni was such a phantom." The first body "is the only real body of the Buddha" (Ch'en, 65 f.).

Second, the Mahayana opposes its conception of the bodhisattva to the earlier ideal of the Arhat. When he is ready to enter nirvana, he postpones his own salvation, vowing to lead all beings to liberation first. "I will stay here to the end, even for the sake of one living soul." This compassion is associated with one bodhisattva in particular, the *Avalokiteshvara.* Because he helps so many, he is often credited with a thousand eyes and arms. In bronze and stone images he is usually identified by the presence of a small Buddha, in the lotus position, on his headdress; and he generally has only 139,140 one head with two eyes, but four arms. It is this conception that has led many people to consider the Mahayana far superior to Theravada Buddhism, and it has certainly helped to make the Mahayana so appealing to the Chinese and Japanese, who transformed the male Avalokiteshvara into *Kuanyin* (China) and *Kannon* (Japan), initially sexless and eventually feminine. It was also this ideal that led Daisetz Suzuki, the great Japanese exponent of Zen, to say (to my students in "Philosophy of Religion" at Princeton) that he could not understand how any Christian who believed in heaven and hell could possibly wish to go to heaven instead of trying to comfort the damned.

Third, the Mahayana has taken issue with Theravada Buddhism by insisting that "the path to salvation lies not in the performance of good works but in a life of faith and devotion to the Buddha Amitabha. Amitabha, or Infinite Light, is the name of the presiding Buddha of the Western Paradise, which . . . is adorned with fragrant trees and flowers, and decorated with the most beautiful jewels and gems." There is music, too, and this paradise is also often called the Pure Land. Amitabha has vowed "that anyone who has faith in him as the savior will be reborn in that Pure Land." Avalokiteshvara will escort them there. "All that the individual has to do indicate his faith is to repeat the name of Amitabha, the formula being, namo Amitabha, or homage to Amitabha. This is indeed an easy and short-cut path to salvation, and explains why the cult became so popular . . ." (Ch'en, 70). The parallel to Christianity is obvious. One could feel morally superior to the Theravada by pointing to the exalted conception of the Avalokiteshvara without having to earn one's moral superiority by one's conduct. Not all Mahayana Buddhists, any more than all Christians, took the easiest possible way out. Still, this version of the Mahayana became the most popular type of Buddhism in the Far East.

Fourth, "The Mahayana conception of nirvana is somewhat different" from the Theravada's. Existence is empty and unreal, and so is nirvana; indeed, "the phenomenal world is nirvana." One does not really leave the world of phenomena behind to enter nirvana; nirvana is "the cessation of all discriminations and dualisms and the realization that undifferentiated emptiness is the sole absolute truth. . . . The moment an individual realizes this state of mind, he is enlightened and realizes the buddhanature within himself" (Ch'en, 72 f.).

In the wake of this extraordinary doctrine, a number of subtle philosophies developed, perhaps none of them subtler than that of the *Madhyamika* school, founded by *Nagarjuna* in the second century A.D. Born a Brahmin, Nagarjuna converted to Buddhism and became a member of the *Sautrantika* school, which conceived of reality as a succession of dharmas, each of which lasts but a moment and then hands on its karma to the next *dharma*. As in a modern motion picture, the human eye is not quick enough to distinguish the separate units and interprets them as a flux. Nagajuna eventually rejected this view, subjected it to detailed criticism, and developed in its place the doctrine that there is actually nothing but the void. His relentless demonstration of contradictions in all sorts of concepts has won the admiration of some modern philosophers in the West; but one American philosopher and student of Buddhism who traveled widely in the course of his studies, James Bisset Pratt, met a Chinese who boasted that he was the only man in China to believe this doctrine (406 f.).

Western writers have often praised the Mahayana very highly at the expense of Theravada Buddhism. Yet it deprived the teachings of the Buddha of their bite. It went far toward emptying them of their moral challenge and their radical appeal to self-reliance. What was substituted for this was not always the same. Some Indian philosophers developed marvelously subtle arguments. On a more popular level the Mahayana absorbed Hindu deities, and the Hindus came to see Buddhism as a Hindu sect and the Buddha as one of Vishnu's incarnations. Mahayana Buddhism also ab-
65 sorbed pagan deities, like Hariti, who was, according to Buddhist legend, a demoness who devoured children before the Buddha converted her. When a religion without a mother goddess spreads to people who want one, they prevail, and in the case of Buddhism they introduced other goddesses as well. The irony of all this becomes evident in Buddhist art. Meanwhile, the Mahayana scriptures luxuriated in extravagant metaphysical visions, piling up huge numbers, and making a mockery of the Buddha's dismissal of questions that do not tend toward edification. One felt edified by the conception of bodhisattvas who were incarnations of boundless compassion, while feeling at the same time that all that was required of oneself was faith in them or at most *bhakti*, but certainly not works. Once again, we are led to wonder whether in conquering a large part of the world, even if that goal is achieved peacefully, a religion does not lose its soul.

86

Tantrism, which is better considered a third way and not part of the Mahayana, points in the same direction. It has actually been called Tantrayana to distinguish it from Hinayana and Mahayana (Ch'en, 1964, 325). As Buddhism encountered "wandering nomads and hardy warriors, plainsmen and mountaineers" in the age of syncretism, it quickly became apparent that such people did not find the Buddha's teachings irresistible. "The changes which crept into the religion were in part inspired by a desire to win the support of a greater number of people." To implement their ideal of universal salvation, "the Mahayana preachers sought to reach as many people as possible," and "since the uneducated and uncultured masses outnumbered all others . . . Mahayana Buddhism accepted their religious intuitions and embraced their numerous deities and occult practices. The Mahayana teachers met the masses halfway and won them over by complying with their yearning for magic and sorcery." The result was Tantrism, which was fully systematized in northern India by the seventh century.

Tantrism involved complicated practices that were supervised by gurus who transmitted their secrets orally and never fully in writing. Among the central ideas was

Hariti, Mendut temple near Borobodur, Java, late 8th century. / "Buddhist" dance, cave 7 at Aurangabad, India, 7th century.

"the transformation of the mind by significant sounds and movements," the sounds being *mantras* or mystical syllables, and the movements *mudras*, which include gestures not only of the hands and fingers but also of the body. The correct mantra and mudra were and are supposed to confer extraordinary powers.

> The most famous *mantra* is one uttered by every Tibetan, *om mani padme hum* ("O the jewel in the lotus"), and because utterance of this *mantra* can bring about a better rebirth, the Tibetans print it on banners, streamers, cylinders, prayer wheels, or barrels turned round by water. . . . All that a traveler has to do is to turn the cylinder round in passing, and he will gain just as much merit as if he had recited the *mantra* (Ch'en, 80 ff.).

If one should wonder why Tantrism flourished in Tibet, the answer is surely that Tibetan Tantrism owes at least as much to Bon as to the Buddha. Bon was the shamanism in which the Tibetans believed before they embraced and transformed Buddhism. They believed in good and evil spirits and, according to the reports of Chinese visitors, "sacrificed sheep, dogs, monkeys, horses, oxen, asses, and even human beings. The human victims were first seized by the hands and feet, then they were cut open and their hearts torn out" (Ch'en, 189). Buddhism proved to be a civilizing influence but was changed in the process.

A much more sympathetic account of Tantrism may be found in the chapter, "The Tantra, or Magical Buddhism" in Conze's *Buddhism: Its Essence and Development*. Conze refrains from criticism, and is scornful of the detractors of Tantrism. But he does not really join the issue when he says sarcastically:

> Of course, if one makes up one's mind that "original" Buddhism was a perfectly rational religion, after the heart of the "Ethical Society," without any touch of the super-natural or mysterious, then the Tantra will become an almost incomprehensible "degeneration" . . . It seems to them that in the history of Buddhism an abstract metaphysics of great sublimity has slowly given way to a preoccupation with personal deities and with witchcraft . . .

The development of the Tantra is only too easily comprehensible. Obviously the early Buddhists, too, were far from being perfectly rational. As for the Buddha himself, we cannot be sure to what extent he believed in the supernatural, and that term is far from unambiguous; but the last thing we should credit him with is "an abstract metaphysics," and the last thing we should deny is that there was something mysterious about him. Surpassing greatness is always mysterious, and that the Buddha was an extraordinarily charismatic figure is as obvious as the fact that sculptors of later ages tried hard and often successfully to capture something of his enigma. Yet the contrast between his four noble truths and most of the Dhammapada on the one side and the sight of a woman walking around a stupa, giving one prayer wheel after another a turn remains striking. Such a scene can be beautiful, and she may well feel devout. The issue is not whether she excites our contempt, which would reflect more on us than upon her, but what the Buddha might have thought of this development. The notion that Tantrism is close to the Buddha's own teaching is as implausible as it would be to suggest that Thomism is close to Jesus' teaching. It depends on the lack of any historical sense.

Any account of Tantrism must note the difference between right-handed and left-handed Tantra. The former stresses mantras, mudras, and mandalas—the magical circles, squares, or rather symbolical maps that are used as aids in meditation. An eighth-century Chinese exposition of the right-handed Tantra, which is our main source of information about it, claims that it owes a great deal to Nagarjuna. A version of it came to Japan around 800, "and as the Shin-gon (*True Word*) school is still one of the largest Japanese sects, with 8,000,000 members and 11,000 priests in 1931." Conze goes on to note:

106,107

From the third century A.D. onward, the Buddhists made an ever-increasing use of mantras for the purpose of guarding their spiritual life from interference by malignant deities. Special chapters on spells are added to some of the best known Sutras, like the *"Lotus of the Good Law"* (Chap. 21), *"The Lankavatara Sutra"* (pp. 26–262), etc. (182).

Four hundred years later the mantras became for many Buddhists the chief vehicle of salvation. Unquestionably, Tantric Buddhism turned progressively into a system of magic. Those who believe in magic may consider this progress, but they can hardly deny that it involved a radical transformation of Buddhism.

The left-handed Tantra differs from the right-handed by its emphasis on sex. As Conze sums it up:

> The chief features of the Left-handed Tantra are: 1. The worship of *Shaktis*, of female deities, with whom the male deities are united in the embrace of loving union, and from whom they derive their energy. 2. The presence of vast numbers of demons and terrifying deities, the worship of the God Bhairava (*The Terrible*), and an elaborate ritual connected with the burial ground. 3. The inclusion of sexual intercourse, and other forms of "immoral conduct," among the practices which conduce to salvation (191 f.).

Shakti means "power," and the Hindus associated it with the female consort of a god. Since Shaktism was found mainly in Shivaism, it was Parvati-Uma, the Great Mother, who represented Shakti, especially in her terrifying form of Durga-Kali. But Bharati, in his immensely erudite book, *The Tantric Tradition*, argues that the notion of Shakti "plays no role of any sort in Buddhism," although it is "the pivot of interest in Hindu 105 tantrism" (214). Bhairava was also considered a form of Shiva.

In the second century A.D. the cult of Tara entered Buddhism, and she was thought of as a female savior but also, at least by some, as the consort of Avalokiteshvara. There are many Tibetan and Nepalese bronzes of her, seated alone; there are also a great many Tibetan bronzes showing a god and goddess in the act of *maithuna* (sexual intercourse), the god usually endowed with at least four faces, often many more. The Hindu Tara is Shiva's wife and sometimes identified with Kali or Durga, but Bharati believes that the Tara of Hinduism and the Tara of Buddhism are entirely different deities (61).

Conze's reference to "immoral conduct," which he himself places in quotes, suggests that a Western reader might think of sexual intercourse in these terms. In fact, the Tantrists did. They were antinomians who deliberately sought to break taboos. Their ritual involved a kind of black mass, five sacraments that broke traditional prohibitions for those who earnestly sought salvation: "wine (*madya*), meat (*mamsa*), fish (*matsya*), parched grain (*mudra*), and sexual intercourse (*maithuna*)." The whole idea was to do "the 'five forbidden things' ('the five M's,' as they are called)" (Zimmer, 572) by way of sealing one's superiority to all moral distinctions and all dualities.

"*Mudra* in Hindu tantra means parched grain or kidney beans—any cereal aphrodisiac—or believed aphrodisiac; in Buddhist tantra it means the female partner or adept; in Hindu and Buddhist non-tantric literature it most frequently means a ritualistic gesture" (Bharati, 242). Incidentally, Bharati devotes a whole chapter (over sixty pages) to mantras.

For all his wide knowledge of Buddhism, Conze is surely unconvincing when he begins the last section of his chapter on Tantra, saying:

> It would be misleading, however, to make too much of the disagreement which separates the doctrinal formulations of the Tantra from those of the older Buddhism. In one decisive particular, the Tantra, in all its branches, has remained faithful to the spirit of Buddhist tradition. The physical body is here, as always, regarded as the chief object of all endeavour.

He goes on to point out that "the physiology of Hathayoga was accepted as authoritative," and that "the truth is within the body, and arises out of it."

One recalls the beginning of the Dhammapada and wonders whether these generalizations could possibly apply to it. But it is obviously true that early Buddhism did
concern itself with the body, teaching the monks and nuns how to subdue it. It is even
more obvious that the whole thrust of the Tantra is quite deliberately the opposite of
that of the early Pali scriptures. It is doubly remarkable that for all its antinomianism
Tantrism maintained the ancient prohibition against killing. To make Buddhism compatible with that remained for Zen.

Tara and Vasudhara (with three faces and six arms). Nepal, 18th century. Bronze.

XII

FROM CEYLON TO JAPAN

*The Emperor Ashoka and Ceylon—Indochina and Indonesia—
China Versus India—Confucius—Mo-tze—Yang-tze, Mencius,
and Chuang-tze—Lao-tze—The* TAO TEH CHING *and Taoism—
Chinese Buddhism—Chinese Ch'an and Japanese Zen—
Shinto—Soka Gakkai*

Prajnaparamita, the Buddhist Sophia and "mother of all Buddhas," with nine faces and eighteen arms. Angkor, 11th century. Bronze.

87

Except for the Buddha himself, no man deserves more credit for the spread of Buddhism than the emperor Ashoka. He was a convert, like the emperor Constantine who made Christianity the state religion of the Roman empire, but provides a striking contrast to Constantine.

Ashoka became king around 275 B.C., and in the ninth year of his reign of approximately forty years he conquered Kalinga on the east coast of India. About 100,000 people were killed in the course of his conquest, and this led him to become a Buddhist, to forswear war, and to devote himself to the practice and propagation of the teachings of the Buddha. We need not rely on legends at this point, for he erected pillars with inscriptions and also engraved his words in rocks. Before his time we have no written records of Indian history and thought, nor any architectural remains or sculptures, excepting those of the Harappa period, which came to an end in the sixteenth century B.C. In a great many ways, Ashoka marks a new beginning, and the Buddha's influence on him tells us a good deal both about the Buddha and about him.

That Ashoka provided free hospitals has already been mentioned. He was the first Indian king to provide an extensive program of social welfare. His edicts stress compassion, generosity, honesty, purity, gentleness, and tolerance; and

> they resulted in non-killing of animals, non-injury to living things, obedience to parents and elders, reverence to teachers, liberality toward friends and acquaintances, and tolerance toward other creeds. . . . All killing of animals for the royal table was stopped. At the same time he prohibited animal sacrifice in the capital and abolished the royal hunt for pleasure. . . . Castration of bulls and rams, and the caponing of cocks became unlawful.

He encouraged "almsgiving to all creeds and faiths" and "donated huge sums of money to carve out cave dwellings for the naked ascetics or to restore temples for the brahmans." In one of his inscriptions "he exhorted his people to hearken to the teachings of other creeds" (Ch'en, 113 f.). His inscriptions make no mention of the four noble truths, of arhatship, or of nirvana, which he may have associated with the life of monks. What he stressed was works for the benefit of humanity, and he believed that anyone who devoted his life to the welfare of his fellow men might be reborn in a Buddhist heaven.

One of his inscriptions proclaims that he sent missionaries to Syria, Egypt, and North Africa, as well as Macedonia; he also did much to spread Buddhism throughout his Indian empire and as far south as Ceylon. It is said that his own son and daughter converted the people of Ceylon during his reign, and the adoption of Buddhism in Ceylon during the third century B.C. proved to be immensely important. It was from here that the religion spread to Indochina, and it was also in Ceylon that the Pali scriptures were preserved and eventually discovered by Western scholars in the nine-

teenth century. It is also in Ceylon that one can still see some of the finest examples of 100,104
early Buddhist painting and sculpture.

Beginning in the sixth century, Buddhism occasionally suffered reverses when the Tamil people of southern India invaded Ceylon. Their intolerance, however, was far exceeded by that of the Portuguese who arrived in the middle of the sixteenth century, intent upon imposing Christianity on the heathen. They destroyed Buddhist monasteries and libraries, pillaged the temples, and put to death all monks wearing the yellow robe. After the expulsion of the Portuguese in 1658, the Protestant Dutch put a halt to religious persecution and allowed the surviving Buddhists to invite Burmese monks "to restore the order and to reinstate and validate the ordination ceremonies." But like the British, who replaced them in 1795, the Dutch offered rewards for conversion to Christianity, and many people forsook their old religion to acquire status and government positions. Christian missionaries had an easy time of it until a Singhalese monk challenged them to public debates in 1866, 1871, and 1873, and having studied the Bible as well as Western writings that criticized Christianity, did very well. By the end of the century, Buddhist studies were revived and began to flourish, and in 1948 Ceylon regained its independence; it is now officially called Sri Lanka.

The population exceeds 13,000,000; most are Buddhists, but about one fifth are Hindu Tamils, and Christians and Muslims number about 1,000,000 each. One of the major problems of the country is the large Hindu minority; the Hindus are resented by many of the Buddhists, who recall the Tamil invasions of the remote past. A Buddhist prime minister, Solomon West Ridgeway Dias Bandaranaike, was actually assassinated in 1959 by a Buddhist monk who considered his policies too pro-Tamil. In 1960 his widow, Mrs. Sirimavo Ratwatte Dias Bandaranaike, became prime minister, and in time she ran for re-election on a platform that included the promise that she would deport the Tamils to India. The Tamils, of course, have lived in Ceylon for centuries, and she did not try to implement her election promise.

While Ceylon enjoys a special status among countries that have accepted Theravada Buddhism, it should not be supposed that its religion is in all respects particularly close to the Pali scriptures. It is the home not only of the great ruins of Anuradhapura, the rock carvings of Polonnaruwa, and the rock paintings of Sigirya, but also of the giant tooth of the Buddha in Kandy. Many places have claimed to have teeth of the founder, 103
and the Portuguese announced that they had utterly destroyed the Kandy tooth, but the Singhalese claim that the Catholics were taken in by a fake, and the Kandy tooth is widely accepted by Buddhists as being really a tooth of the Buddha. Helmuth von Glasenapp, one of the greatest Western scholars of Buddhism, Jainism, and Hinduism, said in a lecture at Tübingen University in the spring of 1956 that, beyond a question, the great tooth was not human but an animal tooth.

88

Burma is also said to have been converted during Ashoka's reign, but the earliest conclusive evidence we have for Buddhism in Burma only goes back as far as the fifth century A.D. According to Ch'en, "Burma is the country where Theravada Buddhism is preserved in its purest form" (127). It is also the home of literally thousands of impressive old pagodas and temples at Mandalay and above all at Pagan, which was once the capital, of the enormous Shwe Dagon pagoda in Rangoon, and of many splendid 122
Buddha images. 123

Thailand was converted to Buddhism long before the Thais conquered it in the thirteenth and fourteenth centuries. Its official religion is still Theravada Buddhism.

Thai bronzes of the Buddha are probably as well known in the West as any Buddha
images, and some people consider the walking Buddhas of the Sukhodaya period
(thirteenth to fifteenth centuries) the most beautiful of all. In chapter XIV we shall
have occasion to consider some of the other styles developed in Thailand. Some of
127,129 the finest works of art in Thailand were influenced profoundly by the Khmer art of
Cambodia, but the relations between the Thais and their neighbors have been anything but friendly. The Thais invaded both Burma and Cambodia during the thirteenth
and fourteenth centuries, and it was they who destroyed Angkor. In the late eighteenth
century, the Burmese invaded Thailand, captured Ayudhaya, destroyed the temples
and the Buddha images, and melted down the gold to carry it away. Thai art never recovered from this blow. Ayudhaya was abandoned, and the capital was moved to Bang-
131 kok, but the Bangkok style, which produced many extremely colorful temples, is
hardly comparable to the achievements of the Thai Middle Ages. While Burma, like
India and Ceylon, was part of the British empire, Thailand has been independent
since it emerged from Khmer domination.

Cambodia was part of French Indochina, but gained complete independence in
1953. At that time it claimed that 99 percent of the population was Theravada Bud-
136,137 dhist. But the Khmer who built the temples of Angkor were Hindus and Mahayana
141 Buddhists. Angkor includes many temples besides Angkor Wat, which is the most
famous. All were forgotten after the Thai destruction and soon hidden by the tropical
jungle. It was only in the nineteenth century that the French rediscovered the place
and began the work of restoration, with admirable restraint. There is no more impres-
138-140 sive artistic site in the world, and the Khmer Buddha images in the Bayon style are
among the greatest creations of the human spirit.

Vietnam is a Mahayana country. Its religious thought and art have not attracted much attention, and in our time it is bound to be associated pre-eminently with the long war that ended in 1975.

145 - 61 Indonesia is now almost entirely Muslim, except for the small island of Bali, which
is still Hindu. Of Java we have noted earlier that its Islam is very different from that of
Morocco, for example, and that it is still saturated with Indian elements. In the
middle of this large island, in the vicinity of Jogjakarta, there are still two magnificent
sites, one Hindu and one Buddhist. The Hindu ruins are spread over a large area and
143 include a great temple at Prambanan. The Buddhist temple of Borobodur is the largest
142,144 Buddhist temple to be found anywhere.

89

What distinguishes China from all these countries is that it had a fully mature and enormously rich civilization of its own before it absorbed Buddhism. China and India are often lumped together by those who would like to contrast Western and Eastern religions. Even those who consider the differences between Judaism, Christianity, and Islam of great importance often generalize about "Oriental religions" as if the ways of thinking of the Indians, the Chinese, and the Japanese were very similar. Actually, China and India represent two different worlds that, before Buddhism arrived in China, had much less in common than do the three "Western" religions.

Ancient China was in many ways the antipode of ancient India. India was as metaphysical and concerned with a vast array of gods as any land ever was, while no ancient culture was less concerned with what transcends this world than China.

India, like ancient Israel and no other country, developed two major religions: one for herself and one for export. Indeed, India developed two more for her own

Thai pagoda, Chieng Mai.

population. China could also be said to have developed two religions, Confucianism and Taoism, but one may question whether these really were religions; and then China imported a third religion, Buddhism, and blended all three. Christian missionaries have often complained that, while it was not too hard to get the Chinese to accept Christianity (which actually only a small percentage did), it was next to impossible to persuade them to give up their other religions. By Western standards, the Chinese attitude toward religion is rather irreligious. For all their disagreements with each other, the early sages of China shared a profound skepticism about religious speculations and claims.

Frederick Mote has suggested that the Chinese may be "unique in having no creation myth" (17), and in his *Intellectual Foundations of China* he also reminds us of Hu Shih's observation "that centuries of Christian missionaries had been frustrated and chagrined by the apparent inability of the Chinese to take sin seriously" (24). In their organismically conceived world

> there can be no parts wrongfully present . . . The question of [man's] immortality in a future that "really counts"—if he is lucky enough or good enough to transcend the material present reality—does not even arise. This being true in the Great Tradition, countertendencies in the popular religions in China's highly congruent culture were correspondingly weakened (24 f.).

According to Chinese tradition, history begins with five legendary, semidivine emperors, followed by "Yao, the first really human ruler (supposed to have reigned 2357–2256 B.C.)" (Fung Yu-Lan, xv). Yao was succeeded by Shun, and Shun by Yü, who is supposed to have founded the first dynasty. Most historians consider Yao and Shun legendary, too, and date the Hsia dynasty from the twenty-second century B.C. The very earliest ceramic finds go back to this period and are strikingly similar to earlier ceramic finds in the Near East. The second dynasty, Shang (eighteenth to twelfth centuries), produced bronze vessels of immense sophistication, unlike anything found elsewhere in the ancient world. Still, even legend takes us back only to an age in which the pyramids of Egypt were already five hundred years old, and the Shang bronzes are probably roughly contemporary with Moses and the earliest Vedas.

90

The next dynasty, Chou (twelfth century to 249), is far better known. The bronzes of early Chou continue the superb tradition of Shang, but it was probably also during the early Chou period that the oldest parts of the *Shih Ching*, the *Shu Ching*, and the *I Ching* were composed. (Ching is pronounced "jing.") The first firm date we have is the solar eclipse of 776 B.C. But the first individual whose personality and thought are known to us is Kung-fu-tze, known in the West as Confucius, who is usually said to have lived from 551 to 479, although Richard Wilhelm (262), whose scholarly German version of the *I Ching* is the basis for the most highly regarded English translation, dates him 522–479. According to tradition, Lao-tze was his older contemporary, but the book ascribed to Lao-tze, the *Tao Teh Ching* (pronounced "dow-de-jing"), is best understood as a reaction to Confucianism. Fung Yu-Lan, in his two-volume *History of Chinese Philosophy*, argues that it could not have been composed much before 300 B.C., if then.

One sometimes gets the feeling that the Chinese were never young or crude or primitive in any sense. Like their first bronzes, their first great thinkers are extraordinarily civilized and sophisticated. The great figures of ancient Israel, Iran, Greece, and India, with their enormous capacity for intense excitement and their often passionate radicalism seem like youths compared to the earliest Chinese thinkers. Confucius and Lao-tze, Chuang-tze and Mencius almost seem to be smiling at the follies of such extreme doctrines as those of the Hebrew prophets or the Buddha, Plato or the Upanishads. Although modern historians are skeptical about Chinese traditions concerning the period before 800 B.C. and for the most part do not accept Confucius' belief that the Duke of Chou, more than five hundred years earlier, was one of the wisest and best of men, whose work Confucius was merely restoring, it seems obvious that the great sages of China, beginning with Confucius, represent the culmination of a long development.

In any case, it is agreed that Confucius edited rather than wrote four collections that were ancient even in his time: the *Shu Ching* (the Book of History, which Fung Yu-Lan characterizes as "A collection of speeches, prayers, etc., given on various historical occasions. Many of these are later forgeries, but a few may go back to the first [sic] millenium B.C."); the *Shih Ching* (The Book of Odes, which contains three hundred and five songs, including many composed as early as 1000 B.C., and perhaps even earlier); the *I Ching* (The Book of Changes, or, rather, of Divinations, again including some as old as 1000 B.C.); and the *Li Chi* (The Book of Rites). But the last collection may have been put together after Confucius' death. These four books, together with the *Ch'ün Chiu* (Spring and Autumn Annals, a brief year-by-year chronicle of the history of the small state of Lu from 722 B.C. until 481 B.C., which is said to have been written by Confucius himself) constitute the so-called Chinese classics. Often the *Hsiao Ching* (Classic of Filial Piety, put together later) is included in this canon.

In addition to these five or six "classics" there are four other books which, as a separate group, are often named together with the "classics." These "Four Books" comprised the *Ta Hsüeh* (Great Learning, concerned with morals, which also forms chapter thirty-nine of the *Li Chi*); the *Chung Yung* (Doctrine of the Mean, also concerned with morals and now chapter twenty-eight of the *Li Chi*); the *Lun Yü* (The Analects of Confucius, which is the collection of Confucius' sayings, on which any account of his ideas must draw as the main source); and the *Meng-tze* (the works of Mencius, Confucius' great successor. "Mencius" is the Latinized Western form of his name).

What can be attempted here is no more than a quick sketch of an altogether different mentality from any considered so far. We shall concentrate on a few major figures, showing how each represents a really distinctive attitude. Having done that, we shall see what happened to Buddhism when it came to China.

Kung-fu-tze, or Confucius, was not a bold innovator and heretic like the Buddha, who set aside the traditions of centuries to proclaim his own new insights. He saw himself as "a transmitter and not a creator, a believer in and lover of antiquity" (*Analects*, VII:1); and he said: "I am not one born with knowledge, but one who, loving antiquity, is diligent in seeking it there" (VII:19). He said he was "studying tirelessly and teaching others without flagging" (VII:33).*

Confucius was profoundly concerned with *li*, imperfectly rendered as ritual. He found that the music of his time was not performed properly, and tried to have the bells and drums handled as, according to tradition, they ought to be handled; and "he would not sit on his mat unless it was straight" (X:9). His concern was with *this* world: "The Master would not discuss prodigies, prowess, lawlessness, or the supernatural" (VII:20). When someone "asked about his duty to the spirits, the Master replied: When still unable to do your duty to men, how can you do your duty to the spirits? When he ventured to ask about death, Confucius answered: Not yet understanding

---

* The translations follow Fung Yu-lan, except for a few minor stylistic changes.

life, how can you understand death?" (XI:11). He felt that one could be humane only in a civilized world.

His concern with etiquette was not prompted by an exaggerated regard for the opinions of other men. Confucius believed in the saving grace of tradition. If one seeks an expression of a similar spirit in Western history, one may find it at Versailles, where style was imposed even on the trees and flowers and where during the French Revolution aristocratic refinement enabled a generation of aristocrats to go to their deaths with exquisite manners, poise, and a proud lack of anxiety in the face of the guillotine. There was a kind of piety in Confucius' attitude—a reverence not for anything supernatural but for antiquity and tradition and a high regard for graciousness and learning. When asked, "Is there any one word which could be adopted as a lifelong rule of conduct?" He replied: "Do not do to others what you do not like yourself" (XV:23).

It is also recorded that Confucius said: "My teaching contains one all pervading principle." The report continues: "When the Master had left the room the disciples asked: What did he mean? Tseng-tze replied: Our Master's teaching is loyalty (*chung*) and altruism (*shu*), and nothing else" (IV:15). On the face of it, these would appear to be two principles, not one, especially if we translate *chung* as conscientiousness, as is sometimes done. But Fung Yu-lan (71), who writes "conscientiousness," goes on to cite other passages in the Confucian Analects where this term occurs, and in three cases finds that "loyalty" yields the better meaning, while in the other two "loyalty" would plainly be at least as good as "conscientiousness." In the passage just cited, "loyalty" and "altruism" make up a single principle, and altruism evidently refers to the rule: "Do not do to others what you do not like yourself," as this is introduced with the same word.

Confucius' teaching contains "one all pervading principle" that may be characterized as altruism tempered by loyalty to tradition and to established distinctions between rulers and people, parents and children.

One of Confucius' major doctrines is said to have been the "rectification of names" (*cheng ming*). When he was asked to take over the administration of a state, he is said to have answered the question of what he would do first of all by saying: "The one thing needed is the rectification of names" (XIII:3). Asked about the principles of government by a duke, he replied: "Let the ruler be ruler, the minister minister; let the father be father, and the son son." (XII:11).

His profound conservatism—this term seems entirely appropriate when taken literally—is illuminated by another saying of his:

> When good order prevails in the world, ceremonials, music, and punitive expeditions proceed from the emperor. When good order fails in the world, ceremonials, music, and punitive expeditions proceed from the nobles. When they proceed from a noble, it is rare if his power be not lost within ten generations. When they proceed from a noble's minister, it is rare if his power be not lost within five generations. But when a minister's minister holds command in the kingdom, it is rare if his power be not lost within three generations. When there is good order in the world, its policy is not in the hands of ministers. And when there is good order in the empire, the people do not even discuss it (XVI:2).

Confucius did not believe in improvisation, experiment, and trial and error. Whatever lasts a mere ten generations was not good enough to his mind—and the society that accepted his ideas has in fact lasted twenty-five centuries. How long did the societies of the ancient Greeks endure, who were always willing to try something different? Israel, like China, endured—also owing to its conservative regard for tradition.

Confucius was not self-seeking and had no desire to found a school or religion that might bear his name. He spent his life trying to educate men to be loyal and devoted sons and subjects, ministers and nobles. He made his living, during a large part of his life, by teaching, and said: "From him who has brought his simple present of dried meat, seeking to study with me, I have never withheld instruction" (VII:7). His willingness to educate anyone who wished to learn was a major innovation. In the Analects it is said of him: "Is he not the one who knows he cannot succeed and keeps on trying?" (XIV:41).

91

Some interpreters who consider Confucius, and even Lao-tze, basically irreligious, have called Mo-tze the only indigenous religious teacher of China. This claim is based on the fact that Mo-tze preached universal love. This is closer to Buddhism than Confucius' regard for the traditional feudalism of China. But Mo-tze was as inimitably Chinese as Confucius.

> Mo-tze asked a Confucian: What is the reason for performing music? The reply was: music is performed for music's sake. Mo-tze said: You have not yet answered me. Suppose I asked: Why build houses? And you answered: It is to keep off the cold in winter, and the heat in summer, and to separate men from women. Then you would have told me the reason for building houses. Now I am asking: Why perform music? And you answer: Music is performed for music's sake. This is like saying: Why build houses? and answering: Houses are built for houses' sake (237).

Another story illustrates the same attitude. A Confucian remarked that the reason why he mourned three years after his parents' death was "in imitation of the affection that my son shows to his parents." Mo-tze replied: "The baby knows only to love its parents. Therefore, when the parents are no longer to be had, it continues to cry without ceasing. Why is this? It is the height of foolishness. And so, then, is the intelligence of the Confucian any higher than that of the baby?" (236 f.).

A third remark expresses a similar spirit: "Kung Meng-tze said: There are no ghosts and spirits. Again he said: The Superior Man should learn sacrifice and worship. Mo-tze said: To hold that there are no spirits and hold sacrificial ceremonies, is like learning the ceremonials of hospitality when there is no guest, or making fish nets when there are no fish" (236).

Clearly, Mo-tze was no idealist in the usual sense of the word. "Mo-tze said: Doctrines that can be translated into conduct may be taught frequently. Doctrines that cannot be translated into conduct should not be taught frequently. To talk frequently about what cannot be carried out is merely to tire out one's mouth" (217).

Nevertheless, he taught universal love and strongly condemned aggressive war. He was a great expert on *defensive* warfare.

For his insistence on universal love, Mo-tze gave essentially two reasons. The first argument, which is found in the fourth chapter of his book, proceeds as follows:

> Motse said: To accomplish anything whatsoever one must have standards. . . . Thus all artisans follow the standards in their work. Now, the government of the empire and that of the large states do not observe their standards. This shows the governors are even less intelligent than the artisans.
> What, then, should be taken as the proper standard in government? How will it do for everybody to imitate his parents? There are numerous parents in the world but few are magnanimous. For everybody to imitate his parents is to imitate the unmagnanimous. Imitating the unmagnanimous cannot be said to be following the proper standard.
> How will it do for everybody to follow his teacher? There are numerous teachers. . . .
> How will it do for everybody to imitate his ruler? There are many rulers. . . .

So then neither the parents nor the teacher nor the ruler should be accepted as the standard in government.

What then should be taken as the standard in government? Nothing better than following Heaven. Heaven is all-inclusive and impartial in its activities, abundant and unceasing in its blessings, and lasting and untiring in its guidance. And so, when the sage-kings had accepted Heaven as their standard, they measured every action and enterprise by Heaven. What Heaven desired they would carry out, what Heaven abominated they refrained from.

Now what is it that Heaven desires, and what does it abominate? Certainly Heaven desires to have men benefit and love one another and abominates to have them hate and harm one another. How do we know that Heaven desires to have men love and benefit one another and abominates to have them hate and harm one another? Because it loves and benefits men universally.

This first argument for universal love is obviously unsatisfactory. It may look patient and careful, seeing that several standards of behavior are considered and ruled out before the rule that we ought to imitate Heaven is introduced, and the commandment of universal love appears to be entailed by this rule. In fact, other standards of behavior are rejected because they would not entail the desired conclusion that we should magnanimously love all men. This argument is circular: all men should imitate Heaven —rather than their parents, teachers, or rulers—because Heaven benefits all alike; and we should try to benefit all alike because Heaven does.

The argument is also implausible for another reason. Surely, Heaven is *not* "unceasing in its blessings," nor does it "benefit men universally." As a matter of fact, Heaven inflicts droughts on some regions while it turns others into veritable paradises. Lightning from heaven strikes one man's barn but not his neighbor's; floods drown thousands in one valley but not in another.

What at first looked like a careful argument is no more than a little sermon; it begs the question with a pleasant illustration that breaks down as soon as we stop to examine it. The appeal to Heaven is mere rhetoric. To find what is really Mo-tze's standard we must turn to his second argument.

The second argument for universal love is found in chapter XVI, which deals at length with universal love and lacks the more religious touch of the earlier chapter.

Among all the current calamities, which are the most important? I say that the attacks on the small states by the large ones, disturbances of the small houses by the large ones, oppression of the weak by the strong, misuse of the few by the many, deception of the simple by the cunning, disdain toward the humble by the honored: these are the misfortunes in the world. . . . Also, the mutual injury and harm which the unscrupulous do to one another with weapons, poison, water and fire are still another calamity in the world.

When we come to think about the cause of all these calamities, how have they arisen? Have they arisen out of love of others and benefiting others? We must reply that this is not so. We should say that they have arisen out of hate of others and injuring others. If we should classify one by one all those who hate others and injure others, should we find them to be universal or partial (in their love)? We should have to say that they are partial. Now, since partiality against one another is the cause of the major calamities in the world, then partiality is wrong. . . .

Mo-tze said: Partiality is to be replaced by universality. But how is partiality to be replaced by universality? I say that when everyone regards the states of others as he regards his own, who would attack the others' states? Others would be regarded like self. When everyone regards the capitals of others . . . Now since universality is really the cause of the major benefits in the world, therefore Mo-tze proclaims universality to be right.

Here, in the last sentence, Mo-tze really states his standard. It is not Heaven but the promotion of what the English, 2,000 years later, were to call "the greatest possible happiness of the greatest possible number," or what Mo-tze himself calls "procuring benefits for the world and eliminating its calamities." He concludes this argument by saying: "Now we have established that universality is the cause of the great benefits in the world, and partiality is the cause of its major calamities."

Mo-tze's central demand for universal love (*chien ai*) is thus based on its utility, and he himself is reported to have said: "If it were not useful then even I would disapprove of it" (chapter XVI).

This insistence on utility helps to explain some of Mo-tze's previously cited remarks; for example, his attitude toward music. "Mo-tze said: The levy of heavy taxes on the people to construct the big bell, the sounding drum," and various other instruments "is of no help in endeavoring to procure the benefits of the world and destroy its calamities. Therefore Mo-tze said: To have music is wrong" (176 f.).

Hsün-tze, a Confucian of the third century B.C., said, understandably: "Mo-tze was blinded by utility and did not know the value of culture" (263 f.). It is obvious that Mo-tze did not esteem culture as highly as Confucius did. Like the Buddha, Mo-tze felt that the misery and suffering of humanity must be our first concern. Nevertheless, Mo-tze seems closer to Confucius, for he, too, was concerned only with this life and its pleasures. He wanted to alleviate suffering like the Buddha, but not by renouncing his attachment to this world; nor did he counsel others to cease caring about pain and pleasure and to cultivate detachment.

In the following quotation from Mo-tze's teachings, only the first sentence is reminiscent of the Buddha; what follows illustrates their difference beautifully:

> The sage does not hasten to exalt what is without use and to delight in frivolity and license. Therefore one's food should always be sufficient before one seeks to have it fine tasting; one's clothing should always be warm before one tries to make it beautiful; and one's dwelling should always be safe before one tries to make it pleasurable. . . . To put what is fundamental first and external decoration secondary: this is what the sage concerns himself with (Fung Yu-lan, 104 f.).

Mo-tze had a keen social conscience and opposed some features of the feudalism of his time that Confucius had sanctioned.

A final anecdote illustrates Mo-tze's dedication and his sense of humor:

> Wu Ma-tze said to Mo-tze: For all the righteousness that you do, men do not help you and ghosts do not bless you; yet you keep on doing it. You must be demented. Mo-tze replied: Suppose you have two employees. One of them works when he sees you, but will not work when he does not see you. The other one works whether he sees you or not. Which of the two would you value? Wu Ma-tze said that he would value the one who worked whether he saw him or not. Then Mo-tze said: Then you value him who is demented (chapter XLVI).

92

Mo-tze's greatest rival was Chuang-tze who, in the thirty-third chapter of his book, refers to a hundred schools. It was an age in which sages and thinkers abounded, but here it will suffice to mention only two besides Chuang-tze.

One of these was Yang-tze, who, in the second century B.C., took a stand diametrically opposed to Mo-tze's. Huai-nan-tze summed up the views of Confucius, Mo-tze, and Yang-tze as follows:

> The orchestra, drum and dance for the performance of music; obeisances and bowing for the cultivation of good manners; generous expenditure in funerals and protracted mourning for the obsequies of the dead: these were what Confucius established and were condemned by Mo-tze. Universal love, exaltation of the

worthy, assistance to the spirits and anti-fatalism: these were what Mo-tze established, and were condemned by Yang-tze. Completeness of living, preservation of what is genuine, and not allowing outside things to entangle one's person: these were what Yang-tze established, and were condemned by Mencius (chapter 13).

Mencius put it this way: "The principle of Yang-tze is: Each one for himself. Though he might have benefited the whole world by plucking out a single hair, he would not have done it. Mo-tze loved all alike. If by wearing away his whole body from the crown to the heel he could have benefited the world, he would have done so." (VIIa)

Mencius did not try to form a synthesis of these two opposed doctrines. He did not think that each of them embodied an important truth. Rather he considered both emphatically wrong. And the task he set himself was this: "What I desire to do is to study to be like Confucius." (IIa: 2,22)

His profound conservatism is well illustrated by his saying: "Yang's principle is, Each one for himself, which is to be without (the allegiance due to) a sovereign. Mo's principle is universal love, which is to be without (the peculiar affection for) a father. Without sovereign and without father: this is to be the same as a beast" (IIIb:9,9).

That Yang's principle is overtly opposed to any civilization is obvious: any culture depends on some restraints, some concessions, some consideration for others. That Mo-tze's demand for universal love is opposed to civilization is less obvious, but his opposition to music suggests that he considered culture a dispensable luxury that should be postponed until all human misery has been abolished. In a world in which there is so much suffering, any concern with culture involves some callousness, some partiality.

Mencius, like Confucius, was certainly not a callous man by ordinary standards, but, judged by Mo-tze's standards, he was callous. He was not an apostle of universal love, but a sage who stressed benevolence—or, to use the word that some of his translators have employed to render the Chinese *jen:* human-heartedness.

It was Mencius above all who made Confucius the most influential man in Chinese history. During his lifetime, Confucius had not been regarded as highly as he was after Mencius.

In Chuang-tze we encounter a mentality quite different from that of all the sages we have considered so far.

The tradition that places Lao-tze in the sixth century B.C. relates Chuang-tze to him, much as it relates Mencius to Confucius. Thus we read in the *Shih Chi,* the first great history of China, completed early in the first century B.C.:

> Chuang-tze . . . held a small post . . . His erudition was most varied, but his chief doctrines were based upon the saying of Lao-tze. His writings, which run to over 100,000 words, are for the most part allegorical. His literary and dialectical skill was such that the best scholars of the age [and Mencius was among his contemporaries] were unable to refute his constructive criticism of the Confucian and Mohist schools (chapter 63).

He was a man of character who turned down the offer of high public office by telling the high officials who came to him to inform him of his appointment, while he was fishing, a story of a tortoise:

> Chuang-tze went on fishing without turning his head and said: I have heard that in Ch'u there is a sacred tortoise which died when it was 3,000 years old. The prince keeps this tortoise carefully enclosed in a chest in his ancestral temple. Now would this tortoise rather be dead and have its remains venerated, or would it rather be alive and wag its tail in the mud?
>
> It would rather be alive, replied the two officials, and wag its tail in the mud.
>
> Begone! cried Chuang-tze. I, too, will wag my tail in the mud.

This story is found in the thirty-second chapter of Chuang-tze's book. Lin Yutang calls him a "mystic and humorist" and says that, "although he was probably the greatest slanderer of Confucius," he was such a brilliant writer that "no Confucian scholar has not openly or secretly admired him. People who would not openly agree with his ideas would nevertheless read him as literature." Indeed, he adds that no Chinese could really reject Chuang-tze's ideas, because Taoism—the customary name for the teachings of Lao-tze and Chuang-tze, which eventually became a popular religion—is less a doctrine than part of the typically Chinese attitude: "when a Chinese succeeds, he is always a Confucianist, and when he fails, he is always a Taoist." And since failure is so much more frequent than success, "Taoist ideas are more often at work than Confucianism" (625 f.).

About Chuang-tze's contribution to Chinese literature there can be no doubt. But the great pre-Christian history of China, quoted above, says in effect that Chuang-tze said in more than 100,000 words what the *Tao Teh Ching* said in 5,000.

In addition to the story of the tortoise, at least two others may be cited in conclusion to illustrate his manner. The first shows how he stopped at the point where a Greek philosopher might have begun. He tells how he once dreamed he was a butterfly and adds: "Now I do not know whether I was then a man dreaming I was a butterfly, or whether I am now a butterfly dreaming I am a man. Between a man and a butterfly there is necessarily a distinction. The transition is called the transformation of material things."

The second passage approximates the grotesqueness of Zen but then draws a practical moral:

> If my left arm should be transformed into a cock, I would mark with it the time of night. If my right arm should be transformed into a crossbow, I would look for a bird to bring down and roast. If my rump-bone should be transformed into a wheel, and my spirit into a horse, I would mount it and would have no need of any other steed. When we come, it is because we have the occasion to be born. When we go, we simply follow the natural course. Those who are quiet at the proper occasion and follow the course of nature cannot be affected by sorrow or joy. These men were considered by the ancients as people who are released from bondage (chapter VI).

By Western standards, Chuang-tze was no philosopher. But if philosophy is supposed to teach men how to live without fear of death, how to achieve liberation from human bondage, and how to *nil admirari*, to wonder at nothing, then Chuang-tze was a philosopher. Indeed, one could hardly ask for a better illustration of this Latin motto.

93

None of the great sages of China is more enigmatic than Lao-tze. Tradition makes him an older contemporary of Confucius, while most modern scholars place him nearer 300 B.C. He is fascinating less for what little is told about him than for the fact that one of the most wonderful books of world literature, the *Tao Teh Ching*, is ascribed to him.

Two legends about him are memorable. The first is related in many versions that have one common theme. Once Confucius and Lao-tze met, and Lao-tze, being much the older of the two, ridiculed Confucius' thoughts, endeavors, and achievements. According to one tradition, he said: "The men about whom you talk are dead, and their bones are moldered to dust. Put away your proud airs and many desires." And Confucius is said to have remarked afterward: "I know how the birds fly, how the fishes swim, how animals run. But there is the dragon. I cannot tell how it mounts on the wind through the clouds, and flies through heaven. Today I have seen Lao-tze, and I can only compare him to the dragon."

The other story is that Lao-tze, having kept archives, left the state in which he had spent most of his life when he foresaw its decay. At the frontier, a customs officer recognized the venerable old man and asked him to write a book before retiring. "Thereupon Lao-tze wrote a book of two parts, consisting of about five thousand characters, in which he discussed *Tao* and *Teh* [virtue]. Then he departed. No one knows where he died."

Scholars have urged a number of stylistic reasons against the traditional dating of the book. The matter of style is difficult, if not impossible, to judge, if one is not an expert on ancient Chinese. Evidently, many readers who are at home in ancient Chinese literature have a strong feeling, derived from reading the original, that it is part and parcel of the fourth century and not the sixth. To one who does not read ancient Chinese, another consideration may be compelling. The book is polemical from beginning to end, and what it attacks is—though most commentators do not make a point of this—Confucianism. This makes it highly unlikely that the book was written in Confucius' lifetime, for his influence became much greater after his death. Only after Mencius had inaugurated a revival of Confucianism would the attack make a great deal of sense.

How are we to account for the two legends, if we accept the later date? Since the book was anonymous, venerable, mysterious, and oracular, it would have been natural, particularly among a people who tended to equate the old and the venerable, to suppose that the book must be old. Indeed, it is in keeping with the spirit of the book to claim that, far from representing newfangled ideas, the author was older than Confucius. Also, people always like to speculate about what might have been said if two great men had met, and once it was supposed that the book had been written in Confucius' day, it was inevitable that the question should have been asked: did they ever meet, and, if so, what did they have to say to one another? The words ascribed to Lao-tze in this connection are precisely what, having read his book, one would expect him to have said.

The story of how the book came to be written was prompted by a no less natural question. That Confucius should have written a book was not puzzling, but in Lao-tze's case, it seemed inconsistent. He ridiculed book learning and self-assertion, while favoring "letting be" (*wu-wei*) and nonresistance. Why then did he write a book? What answer could have been better than the one given by the legend? When the state decayed, he did not raise his voice in protest but withdrew, and when a humble man asked him earnestly to write a book before withdrawing forever, he did not resist him but wrote a very short book, and then he left and was never heard from again. Nothing could be more in keeping with the spirit of the book than these two stories; hence, they really do not add to our knowledge but merely spell out—beautifully—implications of the book.

94

The book traditionally ascribed to Lao-tze consists of eighty-one very short poems, averaging about half a page in length. The poems are deliberately paradoxical and mysterious, and yet there is something very plain and unpretentious about them. There are a great many translations, and the translators often differ very considerably about the meaning.

Lin Yutang's version, in *The Wisdom of China and India*, is, as one would expect of him, less mysterious and more homespun than most other translations—probably too unmysterious compared with the original—but it has the great virtue that his footnotes, on the same page as the texts to which they refer, explain many of the divergencies between different translations by informing us about different readings in manuscripts and about double meanings of phrases. Once one has become baffled by different interpretations and is wondering whether different translators simply read different ideas into the book, these notes are far more helpful than the paraphrases or interpretations that are appended to the translations in some other editions.

The opening lines have given rise to a wide variety of interpretations. Here is Lin Yutang's version:

> The Tao that can be told of
> is not the absolute Tao;
> the names that can be given
> are not absolute names.

The first line, in the original, contains the word Tao twice and says that "The Tao that can be tao-ed" is not the real thing, but in classical Chinese the verb means "to be told." Some translators speak of "The Reason that can be reasoned," others of "The Way that can be trodden." Lin Yutang's version seems superior; it has the book begin with a disparagement of what can be said.

With this in mind, it would be foolhardy to attempt a definition of the Tao. It seems right not to substitute either here or in the following poems, some such word as "reason" or "way." It is far better to leave the original word standing, and to let the reader gain some feeling for it from the many contexts in which it appears.

What is reasonable for the translator will not do for us, as we cannot quote the whole book. But we need not find a single word to explain Tao. What is meant has to be gathered from reading the book again and again, but as a starting point, it may be suggested that Tao was a common word that meant "way," and that in the *Tao Teh Ching* it means something like the "way of nature." It is associated with spontaneity as opposed to the artificialities of civilization, but not with force; on the contrary, with humility, yielding, gentleness, and emptiness.

One might object that any such conception of the way of nature is quite arbitrary; that the sage projects his own preferences into the Tao, which he then wisely refuses to define; and that, even if he were right about the Tao, it would not follow that man ought to imitate it. But Lao-tze does not pretend to base his case on logical inference. He is trying to teach wisdom and speaks to the few who are ready for it. Let those who are not ready for it laugh!

The aphorisms, epigrams, and metaphors are in the main variations on a single theme, expressed especially well in poem 78:

> There is nothing weaker than water,
> but none is superior to it in overcoming the hard,
> for which there is no substitute.
> That weakness overcomes strength
> and gentleness overcomes rigidity,
> no one does not know;
> no one can put it into practice.

> Thus the sage says:
> "Who receives unto himself the calumny of the world
> is the preserver of the state.
> Who bears himself the sins of the world
> is the king of the world."
> Straight words seem crooked.

Self-assertion is consistently derided as vanity, while self-effacement is extolled. Intricate planning, whether in the form of ritual, elaborate rules of propriety, or social
engineering, is spurned; *wu-wei* (letting be) is celebrated. A state of being is thus
praised above all activity, and the example the wise man gives simply by being himself
is considered more effective in the long run than any legislation.

> Of the best rulers
> the people barely know that they exist;
> the next best they love and praise;
> the next they fear;
> and the next they revile. . . .
> But (of the best) when their task is accomplished,
> their work done,
> the people all remark:
> We have done it ourselves. (17)

In the next poem, the pervasive anti-Confucianism of the book becomes explicit,
provided one keeps in mind that "The doctrines of 'love' and 'justice' " were, to cite Lin
Yutang's footnote, "essential Confucian doctrines, usually translated (badly) as 'benevolence' and 'righteousness.' "

> On the decline of the great Tao,
> the doctrines of "love" and "justice" arose.
> When knowledge and cleverness appeared,
> great hypocrisy followed in its wake.
>
> When the six relationships no longer lived at peace,
> there was (praise of) "kind parents" and "filial sons."
> When a country fell into chaos and misrule,
> there was (praise of) "loyal ministers." (18)

Another poem comments in a similar spirit on *li*, the "Confucian doctrine of social
order and control, characterized by rituals; also courtesy, good manners" (Lin Yutang's
footnote).

> After Tao is lost, then (arises the doctrine of) kindness;
> after kindness is lost, then (arises the doctrine of) justice;
> after justice is lost, then (arises the doctrine of) *li*.
> Now *li* is the thinning out of loyalty and honesty of heart,
> and the beginning of chaos. (38)

What Lao-tze teaches is a kind of return to nature. If one compares Confucius'
outlook to that of the rococo, finding some parallels between his tastes and those of the
French eighteenth century before the Revolution, one may wonder whether Lao-tze
may be similarly compared to Rousseau. But here the differences far outweigh the
similarities, which are confined to the demand for a return to nature. Rousseau was a
would-be social reformer whose writings breathe a spirit of urgency and passion, and he
was a tormented soul who suffered from a persecution complex and published exhibi-
tionistic *Confessions*. The author of the *Tao Teh Ching* smiles at social reformers, at
urgency and passion, and veils his own personality so successfully that we do not know
who wrote the book.

It is a serious mistake to sentimentalize the *Tao Teh Ching*. Consider the beginning
of the fifth poem:

> Nature is not kind;
> it regards all things as straw dogs.
> The sage is not kind;
> he regards every Tom, Dick, and Jane as straw dogs.

My translation calls for a few explanations. The Chinese word rendered as "kind" is *jen* (pronounced "ren"), which was a cardinal virtue for Confucius and Mencius and has often been translated as "human-hearted." The Chinese term for nature is "heaven-and-earth"; that for "all things" means literally "the ten thousand things." Where I have "every Tom, Dick, and Jane," the original has "the one hundred surnames." The word I have rendered as "regards" has often been translated as "treats," which seems seriously misleading. Straw dogs were burned at funeral rites. The book is not suggesting that sages should burn people, but it says that the sage does not suppose that nature cares for us and that we are dear to it. Like nature, he regards all of us as expendable.

One should beware of attributing to Lao-tze the social conscience of the Hebrew prophets. Albert Camus's evocation of "the benign indifference of the universe," at the end of *The Stranger*, is much closer to his spirit. It remained for Zen Samurais to *treat* people like straw dogs.

Lao-tze differed with Confucius' rule: "Recompense injury with justice, and recompense kindness with kindness." (14:36,3) Lao-tze says: "Requite hatred with Virtue" (63; some translators say "kindness"). Another poem (49) is rendered by Lin Yutang as:

> The Sage has no decided opinions and feelings,
> but regards the people's opinions and feelings as his own.
>
> The good ones I declare good;
> The bad ones I also declare good.
> That is the goodness of Virtue.
> The honest ones I believe;
> The liars I also believe;
> That is the faith of Virtue.
>
> The Sage dwells in the world peacefully, harmoniously.
> The people of the world are brought into a community of heart,
> And the Sage regards them all as his own children.

In *The Sacred Books of the East*, the middle portion of this poem is rendered somewhat differently:

> To those who are good to me, I am good;
> and to those who are not good to me, I am also good;
> and thus all get to be good.
> To those who are sincere with me, I am sincere;
> and to those who are not sincere to me, I am also sincere;
> and thus all get to be sincere.

The book contains many epigrams that closely resemble lines in the Dhammapada. In the present instance, one is reminded of a line in the first poem of the Dhammapada, which has been discussed in the previous chapter: "hatred ceases by love." Like the Buddha, Lao-tze teaches and exemplifies complete freedom from resentment. But Lao-tze is more whimsical than the Buddha. Lao-tze did not even think of sending out missionaries, and the fact that he wrote a book had to be especially explained: true to his ideal of nonresistance, he did not resist the entreaties of a man who asked him for a book—and then made it as short as kindness would permit. He had no confidence in direct communication and logical argument.

> When the man of low capacity hears Tao,
> he laughs greatly at it.
> If he did not laugh
> it would not deserve to be called Tao. (41)

Stoicism was stern and heroic. Lao-tze developed a sublimely comic stoicism that delights in whimsy.

In time, Taoism became not only a philosophy, based on the *Tao Teh Ching* and on Chuang-tze's book, but also a popular religion that was not at all close to the spirit of these books. Its devotees sought a long life and eventually also immortality, took to meditation and breath control, and ate neither meat nor cereals. But above all Taoism, having no hard core of doctrine, absorbed all kinds of popular beliefs and practices. By the first century A.D., an interest in alchemy and magic had become central in Taoism, and then Chang Tao-ling is said to have discovered a magical potion to prolong his life and eventually to have ascended to heaven from a mountain on the back of a tiger. His successors, who established themselves on this same mountain, became known as Taoist popes and were thought to be reincarnations of Chang Tao-ling. Taoist priests developed a lucrative trade in pills and potions that were powerful against spirits, or conferred long life, or made one invisible, or allowed one to walk on water.

In the second century A.D. a temple was dedicated to Lao-tze, and five hundred years later the first emperor of the Tang dynasty gave official recognition to Taoism as a religion. One of the central concepts of this religion was that of the eight immortals, which came from popular belief and not from Lao-Tze. Their bodies are old, but their minds are young forever. But Taoism also came to recognize a great many gods, borrowing some of them from popular Buddhism, and repaid Buddhism with the compliment that the Buddha was a reincarnation of Lao-tze.

95

Trade contacts between India and China go back to the pre-Christian era, and Buddhism was known widely in China by the first century A.D. It was the Mahayana that spread in China, and translations of the Indian scriptures were sometimes made by Indian monks who knew little Chinese, and more often by Indians and Chinese in collaboration. The Indians would explain the text in Chinese, and the Chinese would then put the translation into writing. "The foreign monk could not compare what the Chinese wrote against the original to check the accuracy of the translation, nor could the Chinese check his written word against the foreign language of the text" (Ch'en, 1964, 365–72). Thus began the transformation of Buddhism in China.

The Buddhist term *dharma*, which is certainly hard to translate but means something like teaching, became *tao*, but *tao* was also used for *bodhi* (enlightenment), and occasionally also for *yoga*. When Christianity came to China, *tao* was naturally used to translate *logos* in the prologue to the Gospel according to John: "In the beginning was the Tao." The Buddhist *arhats* became Taoist immortals (*chen-jen*), while *nirvana* became *wu-wei* (letting be).

> The Confucian expression *hsiao-shun*, "filial submission and obedience," was used to translate the more general and abstract Sanskrit word *sila*, "morality." . . . passages and expressions deemed offensive to Confucian morality were bowdlerized or omitted. Thus words like "kiss" and "embrace" . . . were

simply eliminated. The relatively high position which Buddhism gave to women and mothers was changed in these early translations. For example, "Husband supports wife" became "The husband controls his wife," and "The wife comforts her husband" became "The wife reveres her husband" (Wright, 36 f.).

By 220 A.D., when the Han dynasty fell, more than four hundred works had been translated; during the next forty-five years, under the Wei dynasty, another two hundred and fifty-three; and between 265 and 317 almost five hundred more. Much later, in 1697, Father Bouvet, a Jesuit, said in a letter: "I do not believe that there is anything in the world more proper to dispose the spirit and the heart of the Chinese to embrace our holy religion than to make them see how it is in comformity with their ancient and legitimate philosophy" (Wright, 40). This was the liberal attitude of Jesuit missionaries not only in China, but the Buddhists had made this discovery much earlier, and it certainly does not apply to China only. What was done here by way of a deliberate policy happened elsewhere, too, less consciously. As religions spread they assimilated countless local beliefs and practices and were transformed in the process—as was the Vedic religion in India, for example.

The process also works in reverse. Thus a Roman Catholic in Germany said in 1808, speaking of the *Tao Teh Ching*, which at that time had not yet been translated in its entirety into any European language: "Many things about a Triune God are so clearly expressed that no one who has read this book can doubt that the mystery of the Holy Trinity was revealed to the Chinese five centuries before the coming of Jesus Christ."* This is again an extreme example, but surely some such falsification takes place also when *Tao* is translated "reason," or *Atman* "self," and when Indian interpreters find F. H. Bradley's "self-realization" in the Upanishads, or when Gandhi finds his own ideas in the Gita.

By about A.D. 300 the Buddhist clergy in the north of China numbered around four thousand, and "Chinese architects had begun to translate the Indian stupa form into the pagodas that were eventually to dot the landscape of the empire" (Wright, 41). As China was split into a northern and southern realm, the rulers of northern China, who were mostly Turkic or Tibetan, felt no deep loyalty to native Chinese traditions and promoted Buddhism. In the south, during the same period, it was mainly the educated classes that took an interest in Buddhism, and it was here that Buddhism and Taoism discovered their profound affinity.

In the south, Hui-yüan did not appeal only to the gentry but also, like other Buddhists of the period, built centers of devotion and teaching in the mountains. He

> was the first to teach the attainment of salvation through faith in Amitabha and thus laid the foundations for the great Pure Land sect, which was eventually to become the most popular form of Buddhism in eastern Asia. While his own writings are full of Taoist thought and terminology, he was indefatigable in his search for a sounder and fuller understanding of Indian Buddhist ideas. To this end he sent disciples to Central Asia to bring back texts (Wright, 49 f.).

He argued that monks withdrew from the world, expected nothing from princes, and therefore also should not have to pay homage to princes, but lay Buddhists "invariably first serve their parents and respect their lords." He preached accommodation with those in authority and with existing social arrangements. Syncretism levied its usual price, and in time "Buddhist monks became the priests of the ancestor cults of their patrons" (58).

It was an emperor of the Northern Wei dynasty who started the first large-scale persecution of Buddhism in 446, ordering "that all the temples, sutras, stupas, and

---

* "Lao-tsze" in the *Encyclopaedia Britannica*, 11th ed.

paintings were to be destroyed, and all the monks to be executed" (Ch'en, 147). Twenty years later, the empire made enduring amends. To symbolize repentance and the restoration of Buddhism, huge images of Buddhas and bodhisattvas were carved out of the rock of the Yün-kang caves. (For a detailed account of these caves and those at Lung-Men, see Ch'en, 1964, 166–177.) The largest of the five huge Buddhas is about seventy feet tall, and the project was influenced by the Buddha statues carved out of a cliff at Bamyan in Afghanistan, probably in the second century A.D., the tallest rising to a height of 175 feet.

By A.D. 600, China was unified again under the Sui dynasty, which in 618 gave way to the great Tang dynasty that ruled China until 907. Some of the Tang emperors offered equal opportunity to Islam and Nestorian Christianity, Zoroastrianism and Manichaeism, as well as Buddhism, and since Buddhism had by then a large headstart it flourished, at least in some ways. Under the Tang dynasty, as under the Sui before it, "imperial amnesties and particularly the remission of death sentences were justified partly in Buddhist terms. And these dynasties, continuing the Buddhist customs of earlier regimes, forbade executions, or the killing of any living thing the first, fifth, and ninth months—periods of Buddhist abstinence" (Wright, 74). But Buddhism was also used to instill a warlike spirit in the imperial armies.

The first emperor of the Sui dynasty, for example, issued a proclamation in which he said: "With a hundred victories in a hundred battles, We promote the practice of the ten Buddhist virtues. Therefore We regard the weapons of war as having become like the offerings of incense and flowers presented to Buddha." Nor did matters end with such rhetoric.

> The Chinese cult of filial piety had had a chilling effect on martial ardor. It laid upon every man a heavy obligation to return his body intact upon his death and thus to show gratitude to his parents who had given it to him; there was the further teaching that the only immortality that a man could expect was the honor paid him by his descendants in the family graveyard and ancestral temple. Warriors had a horror of disfiguring death in battle and burial far from home (Wright, 67).

Chinese Buddhism involved a different notion of immortality, and the emperors took to "building battlefield temples at the scenes of major engagements and endowing perpetual services for the repose of the souls of the war dead and their ultimate salvation" (Wright, 74 f.).

The appeal of Buddhism to the masses was enhanced, no less ironically, by its rich mythology, its colorful and interesting deities, and its glorious ceremonies. "By the eighth century, Buddhism was fully and triumphantly established throughout China" (82). But in 845, another great persecution was ordained, and imperial edicts proclaimed that 4,600 monasteries and 40,000 temples and shrines were destroyed. This, says Ch'en (156), was the beginning of the decline of Buddhism in China.

Buddhism, however, did not disappear; it merely was amalgamated more and more with native cults. "As early as the eleventh century a Buddhist monk had combined the worship of Confucius, Buddha, and Lao-tzu in a single cult, and many temples of the Sung and later periods had special halls for this worship" (Wright, 100).

Occasionally this syncretism found rather amusing expression, as a final quotation from Wright's *Buddhism in Chinese History* shows. It is, he says,

> a typical story of a peasant woman. After her death, her family inquired through a medium (not a Buddhist monk) about her status in the nether world. She replied through the medium that she had now expiated her evil karma and had applied to the proper authorities for reincarnation in human form, that her papers were in order, and that she expected an early decision.

Wright notes how "typically Chinese" this conception of the other world is (102), and there is no denying that. But one might add that the idea that God has to be approached by way of his son, and the son by way of his mother, and the mother by way of saints, as well as the whole structure of the Roman Catholic purgatory, involves quite as great a departure from the Gospels and bears the imprint of the Roman empire.

96

Of the many different schools and types of Buddhism that developed in China we shall consider only one: *Ch'an, which later became Zen in Japan.* It was introduced into China by Bodhidharma, who probably arrived from India in 520. He is generally considered an Indian, although in Chinese paintings he has Chinese features, but a virtually contemporary book by Yang Hsüan-chih, completed in 547, calls him a Persian monk (Ch'en, 1964, 351 f.) It is said that he went to the Northern Wei kingdom and sat down in front of a wall, contemplating—or not contemplating—it for nine years. He ignored a monk who asked him for instruction, but when the monk cut off one of his own arms, Bodhidharma was sufficiently impressed to teach him Ch'an, and after the master's death this monk became the second Ch'an patriarch. Many Chinese are inveterate skeptics, and some of them claimed that the arm of the second patriarch had been cut off by robbers.

Not all of Bodhidharma's instruction was oral. He also transmitted texts to his disciple, including the *Lankavatarasutra* ("Descent to the Island of Lanka"). This sutra stresses a state of enlightenment that transcends all dualities and is attainable because we have a Buddha nature within us. It also insists on the limitations of language.

Ch'an is a transliteration of the Sanskrit *dhyana*, which is a kind of meditation that leads to tranquility. Those who have mastered this technique "can keep a serenity of mind and cheerfulness of disposition even amid the world of turbulent activity"; and this appealed to "the practical nature of the Chinese" rather more than the complicated speculations of some of the other Buddhist schools (350).

Anyone who has read the *Tao Teh Ching* and Chuang-tze as well as some of the more striking Zen sayings and stories is almost bound to note that Zen owes much more to Taoism than it does to the Buddha. It hardly needs saying that this was true already of Ch'an. Wright makes the point succinctly:

> The distrust of words, the rich store of concrete metaphor and analogy, the love of paradox, the bibliophobia, the belief in direct, person-to-person, and often wordless communication of insight, the feeling that life led in close communion with nature is conducive to enlightenment—all these are colored with Taoism. Indeed Ch'an may be regarded as the reaction of a powerful tradition of Chinese thought against the verbosity, the scholasticism, the tedious logical demonstrations, of the Indian Buddhist texts (78).

It was Lao-tze and not the Buddha who had said:

He who knows does not speak;
He who speaks does not know.

This verse from the *Tao Teh Ching* (56) sums up much of Ch'an and Zen. Lao-tze and Chuang-tze, and not the Buddha or Indian Buddhism, are also the source of the whimsical touch that makes Ch'an and Zen so appealing. It was also Lao-tze and not the Buddha who inspired the quest for spontaneity and the humorous irreverence.

Actually not all branches of the Ch'an school went as far as did the *Lin-chi* (*Rinzai* in Japan) with its celebrated shock technique. It was here that the masters went out of their way to startle their pupils and often hit them. It was here that blatantly irrelevant answers were given to pious questions and that the *kung-an* (*ko-an* in Japanese) was developed as a method. Literally, the term means case or problem, but the problems that the masters gave their students to meditate on were never meant to be solved rationally; on the contrary, they were intended to prompt the discovery of the limitations of reason and language. The student must be weaned from words and be driven back into direct experience. This was the path to enlightenment (*wu*; in Japanese, *satori*).

Of course, all this was not merely a matter of going back to two books, Lao-tze's and Chuang-tze's. There was a living tradition in China that, even before Ch'an flourished, included painters and poets, including Li Po and Tu Fu, the two giants of eighth-century poetry whose verse still has the power to move us even in translation. Nobody could claim that their celebration of drinking might have been symbolical only, as some have said of Hafiz'. Li Po, now a hermit, now a drunk, addressing the moon while drifting in a boat, an enemy of all artificiality, used words to glorify experience.

Still, Ch'an and Zen have this in common with Lao-tze, that they are essentially polemical, but they go much further than he did. Thus one Ch'an master told his disciples: ". . . kill everything that stands in your way. If you should meet the Buddha, kill the Buddha. If you should meet the Patriarchs, kill the Patriarchs. If you should meet the arhats on your way, kill them too." And in the ninth century another master exhorted his disciples that what was important was the natural functions, like drinking when one is thirsty, eating when one is hungry, urinating and defecating, and resting when tired; and he added:

> There are neither Buddhas nor Patriarchs. Bodhidarma was only an old bearded barbarian. Sakyamuni and [various other worthies] . . . are only dungheap coolies. . . . Nirvana and bodhi are dead stumps to tie your donkeys. The twelve divisions of the sacred teachings are only lists of ghosts, sheets of paper fit only for wiping the pus from your boils (Ch'en, 1964, 358).

Let no one suppose that all this is *merely* symbolical. It is also a Chinese revolt against the authority of Indian scriptures and teachers. Our own age is incredibly eclectic, and the same people who turn to Zen are more likely than not also admirers of the Indian philosopher, Sri Aurobindo. Yet they would never dream of being shocked by these sayings of Zen masters. Aurobindo, on the other hand, was outraged by a far milder criticism of the *Sacred Books of the East* by Max Müller, who as the editor of the series had done more to provide scholarly translations of Asian scriptures than anyone else. Aurobindo quotes Müller's confession: "it has been for many years a problem for me, aye, and to a great extent is so still, how the *Sacred Books of the East* should, by the side of so much that is fresh, natural, simple, beautiful and true, contain so much that is not only unmeaning, artificial and silly, but even hideous and repellent." In response, Aurobindo called himself "only a poor coarse-minded Oriental." He also explained that he himself was offering in translation only those passages of the Upanishads that Western readers could hope to understand. In the case of the Chandogya Upanishad that meant a mere twenty-four verses, for how could any Western reader hope to understand more when "even the majority of Hindus" had difficulties with it? In any case, the texts were untranslatable because "in no other human tongue than Sanskrit is such grandeur and beauty possible" (53 ff.). If anyone were to answer Aurobindo after the fashion of the old Ch'an masters, nobody would be more shocked than those who admire Zen and Oriental thought in general. But when the very same people read what the Ch'an masters said about the Buddha and the Buddhist scriptures, which really need not fear comparison with Aurobindo and his books, they are simply delighted. Yet the Ch'an masters meant to shock. They meant to denigrate respect for those who write many books. They were far from feeling that all the sacred books of India were true and beautiful and never artificial and silly. The great religious figures of mankind were profoundly polemical.

Here is the reaction to Ch'an of a major Chinese writer of the late eighth century, Liang Su:

> Those who travel the path of Ch'an go so far as to teach the people that there is neither Buddha nor law, and that neither sin nor goodness has any significance. When they preach these doctrines to the average man, or men below the average, they are believed by all those who live their lives of worldly desires. Such ideas are accepted as great truths which sound so pleasing to the ear. And the people are attracted to them just as moths in the night are drawn to their burning death by the candle light. . . . Such doctrines are as injurious and dangerous as the devil (Mara) and the ancient heretics (Ch'en, 1964, 357).

How did Ch'an survive in the face of such determined opposition, while other Buddhist schools declined in influence? One reason stressed by Ch'en (363 f.) is its rule that every monk must do some productive labor every day. "The Ch'an master responsible for this rule was Huai-hai (720–814), who even in his old age insisted on working in the fields." His disciples hid his tools; he refused to eat. The rule was: no work one day, no food one day. Thus Ch'an monks were immune to the criticism generally made of Buddhist monks, that they were parasites.

Another reason for the survival of Ch'an when other forms of Buddhism declined is surely that Ch'an ceased to be Buddhist and openly attacked the Buddha, the great teachers of Buddhism, and the Buddhist scriptures. It ceased to be a foreign, Indian doctrine and became Chinese. Of course, it claimed to offer a shortcut to the state of enlightenment that had been the goal of Buddhism; it claimed to have discovered that there was no need for any eightfold path, no need to grasp four noble truths, because enlightenment could be attained without all that. That, however, would constitute good grounds for still considering Ch'an a form of Buddhism only if the state of enlightenment of the Ch'an masters were clearly the same as the Buddha's and moreover something that had distinguished the Buddha from the Jains and Vedantists and from Lao-tze and Chuang-tze. In fact, the enlightenment of the Ch'an masters was quite obviously very different from the Buddha's.

The counsel to "kill everything that stands in your way" gives expression to an aggressive spirit that permeates Ch'an and Zen. Answering a monk who asks, "All things are reducible to the One; where is this One to be reduced?" with the deliberate irrelevancy, "When I was in Tsin district I had a monk's robe made that weighed seven *chin*"—which according to Suzuki (72) is "one of the most noted sayings ever uttered by a Zen master"—is also aggressive and evinces a different state of mind from the Buddha's disparagement of questions that "tend not toward edification." But this aggressiveness is most evident when a master twists his student's nose until it is "literally out of joint" (94), or when a master becomes "furious, and finally taking hold of Hakuin gave him several slaps and pushed him off the porch. He fell several feet to the foot of a stone wall, where he remained for a while almost senseless" (128). Another story relates how a master used to lift one of his fingers by way of answering—or not answering—questions. The little boy who was his attendant took to imitating him, and when the master discovered this he cut off the boy's finger. Now when the boy tried to imitate the master, he could not do it; and "suddenly the significance of it all dawned upon him" (72). One may recall Jesus' saying, "It is better for you to enter the kingdom of God with one eye"; and one may feel that one finger was not too heavy a price for enlightenment. It still is clear that the Buddha did not twist people's noses out of joint or slap them, push them, or cut off a little boy's finger. The point is not that he was right and this is wrong, but rather that the "enlightened" state of the Ch'an and Zen masters is a very different state from that which he attained.

This becomes even clearer when we focus our attention on Japan. Here Zen succeeded because it was appreciated by the *samurai*. They had no use for the pacifism and *ahimsa* of the Buddha, but they liked the cultivation of stern discipline and spontaneity, of perfect self-control coupled with enormous verve. Many interpreters of Zen have written as if it had brought to the arts of archery and swordsmanship some utterly unheard of and mysterious quality that cannot be dissociated from a peculiar kind of mysticism. Even if this were true, it would certainly involve a radical transformation of the whole thrust of the Buddha's teaching. But in fact the mystery is no greater—and no less great—than that involved in the bowmanship of a fine cellist or violinist. He does not look at what he is doing and yet hits the strings precisely as he wishes. This takes years of training and considerable discipline, and it may be mysterious, but it is inseparable from professionalism. Seeing how Ch'an and Zen began as protests against the verbosity of the Buddhist scriptures, there is a certain irony in the verbosity of modern authors who devote book after book to disparaging the Western addiction to words while extolling Zen. After reading one or two of Suzuki's books, one is not likely to learn as much from reading more of the literature as one can learn from watching a short film that shows Pablo Casals teaching the cello. There are some splendid short stories, mostly a page or less in length, in *Zen Flesh, Zen Bones*, but none of this literature measures up to the *Tao Teh Ching*. And the torrent of words obscures the fact that Zen made Lao-tze's heritage as well as the Buddha's compatible with a life devoted to war.

Most Western admirers of Zen have simply failed to note this aspect of it, and some have actually misrepresented it as essentially antiauthoritarian and humanistic. Anyone who has stayed in a Zen monastery or studied under a master knows how deeply authoritarian Zen is, and this error is due in part to a Manichaean conception of authoritarianism that links it with gloom and everything that is considered bad. In fact, Isaiah and Micah were authoritarian when they inveighed against war and called for swords to be beaten into plowshares and spears into pruning hooks, and the Gita was authoritarian when calling for detachment in the performance of one's caste duty and for devotion to God. There is joyousness as well as terror both in the prophets and in the Gita, but the experience of life they communicate is very different. The Zen experience is different from both. The following story from *Zen Flesh, Zen Bones* has no special standing but catches something of the spirit of Zen:

A student who had studied with a Zen master since childhood wanted to visit other masters when he was twenty, but his master, instead of granting him permission, gave him a rap on the head whenever he made his request. Then the student's elder brother spoke to the master and was told that his brother could go. But when the student went to thank his master, he got another rap on the head. His elder brother was upset that the teacher should have gone back on his promise and went to speak to the master again. Then the master explained that he had not changed his mind. "I just wanted to give him one last smack over the head, for when he returns he will be enlightened and I will not be able to reprimand him again" (74).

The authoritarian atmosphere is evident, but it is lightened by a touch of whimsy, at least for the awakened who are in authority. Above all, the detachment of the enlightened is transfigured by a genuine enjoyment of the present moment. They delight in what they are doing, including very simple things, and they usually have a keen appreciation of nature. This feeling for nature was not introduced by Zen or Ch'an. In

Zen painting, Shokokuji temple compound, Kyoto. / "Ballet" in Kyoto Museum.

China we find it much earlier in Lao-tze and Chuang-tze; in Japan, in Shinto. In neither case did it come from India. Nor is the delight in the present part of the Buddha's legacy.

Detachment is compatible with the cultivation of a warrior's virtues, and so is *bhakti*; and so is a keen aesthetic sense. This aesthetic sense is one of the most distinctive features of Ch'an and Zen and found expression in fine paintings as well as superb
164   gardens. The most famous garden in Japan, the Ryoanji in Kyoto, is a Zen rock garden, and to a Westerner its originality may be astounding. But in Japan small, stylized, and exceedingly evocative gardens that invite meditation are not a peculiarity of Zen; witness the superb gardens on Mount Koya, about fifty miles from Kyoto, where the Shingon Buddhists have their monasteries. Above all, such gardens need to be compared with similar gardens in China. What is clear is that they did not originate in
165   India. Again, they express a state of mind that is closer to Shinto and to Taoism than to Indian Buddhism.

97

To judge the extent of Japanese originality, one needs to know a good deal about China and Korea. Zen has to be compared with Ch'an; Japanese temples with Korean and Chinese temples; Japanese painting, sculpture, and gardens with their prototypes on the mainland. But what is indisputable is that the best Japanese work of the Nara
172,173   period (eighth century) does not give the appearance of being copied, second-hand, or eclectic. It has a look of authenticity and spontaneity and shows such a sure aesthetic sense and has such immense vitality and verve that it seems rather ridiculous when Germans, Englishmen, or Americans speak of the Japanese as mere imitators. Buddhism came to Japan in the middle of the sixth century A.D., and prior to that time Japanese art was "primitive," using that term in a purely descriptive and comparative sense, without any pejorative overtones. Within two hundred years after the arrival of Buddhism, Japan could point to temples and sculptures that need not fear comparison with any in the world. It took France, Germany, and Great Britain a much longer time after the arrival of Christianity to produce churches or carvings of remotely comparable quality.

As for religion, Shinto had developed in Japan long before the advent of Buddhism, and since World War II a large number of new religions have sprung up in Japan. But none of these religions, not even Shinto, provide a fair measure of Japan's originality, and it is rather odd that European and American writers have occasionally spoken about Shinto with great condescension, as if their own countries had produced "higher" or "nobler" religions. Perhaps even the Greeks, whose mythology has influenced the art and literature and thinking of the West down to our own time, did not, and it is at least worth considering whether the Japanese genius is not in some ways comparable to that of the Romans and of other, younger European nations.

Unlike the religions of the ancient Romans and the Teutons, Shinto has survived to this day and therefore requires at least some attention here, the more so because it played a part in the development of Buddhism in Japan. The name "Shinto" was coined in the sixth century to distinguish the indigenous religion from Buddhism. The name comes from the Chinese and means "way of the gods," *to* being *tao*. The Japanese word is *kami* and does not quite mean "gods." It refers to what is above and might be rendered by "superior beings." The details of Shinto mythology need not detain us· here, although a good deal is known about it from old books. A Japanese history that draws on ancient oral traditions, and a volume of Japanese annals that was written in Chinese were both compiled during the first decade of the Nara period (by 720).

The old *kami* included a sun goddess, a moon god, a goddess of crops, gods of fire and water, storm and rain, rivers and sea, mountains and trees, as well as rulers and other outstanding people. The interest in nature has remained an abiding characteristic of the Japanese people. The central concern of Shinto was with pollution and purification. Western commentators have made much of the fact that Shinto did not make any sharp distinction between moral and nonmoral kinds of pollution, between disease and crime, uncleanliness and guilt, as if this distinguished Shinto from most other religions. Actually, the ancient Greeks, Indians, and Jews operated with a similar conception of the "unclean" or "polluted," although the Hebrew prophets tried hard to impress upon their people that purifications that did not involve moral regeneration were worthless. In the Gospels we also find some words of disparagement of certain rituals, but at the same time the worst fate in the afterlife is reserved for those who do not accept the right faith and the sacraments.

Whenever an emperor died, the Japanese capital was changed, apparently also in order to avoid pollution, and this custom was changed only with the founding in 710 of Nara, which remained the capital until 793. It is still one of the most impressive sights in the whole world, because of its Buddhist temples and sculptures. But there is also a fine Shinto sanctuary in Nara, the Kasuga shrine. The path that leads up to it 165 through the woods is lined with lovely stone lanterns. The gates leading to Shinto shrines have a marvelous simplicity: two round upright beams, supporting a round crossbeam that projects on both sides, not quite straight but pointing up ever so slightly at both ends, and a shorter cross-beam beneath that. In brief, the *torii* looks rather like the Greek letter *pi*. The wood is either natural or painted red. The temple itself often houses a metallic mirror that represents the sun goddess. There is a gong at the entry, and some suppose that by striking it one insures the attention of the *kami*. The *kami* are offered food and drink in the morning and in the evening. No one knows for sure whether they take more or less interest in this show of respect than do the Trinity or the Virgin Mary in the flowers on the altars of Christian churches.

According to tradition, Japanese history began with the accession of the first emperor, Jimmu, in 660 B.C. But it was only during the first century A.D. that the Yamato people invaded western Japan from Korea, and they became "the founders of the historical Japanese state" (Reischauer, 12). According to tradition, writing was introduced from Korea in A.D. 285, but some scholars would change that date to 405. We get onto firm ground only with the advent of Buddhism, and very soon Buddhism and Shinto merged.

The Japanese had buried their dead but now learned from the Buddhists to cremate them. They changed their diet to become vegetarians. They adopted the notion of retribution after death. But what is surely most interesting is the development of "Dual Shinto" (*Ryobu Shinto*). The old *kami* became Buddhist saints, if not incarnations of the Buddha; Buddhist relics and idols appeared in Shinto temples, and few Shinto temples, notably those at Ise, managed to resist this trend. Henceforth most of the Japanese accepted both Shinto and Buddhism, or rather a syncretistic religion that drew heavily on both. Something more or less like this happened in parts of Europe, notably including southern Italy, when Christianity moved in, but not so openly.

> The Tendai sect carried syncretism to extremes; it was, indeed, so comprehensive that its temples have been styled the "religious junkshops" of Buddhism. Divine favour could be sought by the austere discipline of the scholar—the Nara

tradition—or by the simple faith later stressed in the Amidist sects, or by the meditation practised by the Zen masters. . . . The Shinto traditions and rituals were only one further way of reaching the same goal. . . . Every Buddhist sect to be founded in Japan owed its origin to the influence of the temples scattered over Tendai's mountain headquarters above Kyoto. . . . Any Shinto spirit could be incorporated as an aspect of the Buddha (Bownas, 360 f.).

Shingon Buddhism, mentioned at the end of the last section, was founded by Kobo Daishi in 806, a year after Dengyo Daishi had founded the Tendai sect. There are more than one hundred Shingon monasteries on Mount Koya, and for over a thousand years no woman was allowed on the mountain. There are about 3,800 Shingon monasteries scattered all over Japan, but Koyasan is the headquarters and also the site of a Buddhist college, a seminary, and a splendid museum. *Shingon* is a translation of *mantra*, and this sect is often called esoteric. It has also been called "the sect which affected Shinto the most" and "a late form of Indian Buddhism which incorporated Hindu, Persian, Chinese and other elements" (Bownas, 359 and 361).

It was the founder of this sect who worked out the doctrine of Dual Shinto. Nothing could be more syncretistic, and as one reads about it, the complications are awesome. But such is the Japanese genius for simplicity that it is easy to remain quite unaware of this astonishing eclecticism when one stays at a Shingon monastery on Mount Koya, attending services, contemplating gardens, and walking in the woods under huge Cryptomeria trees, among thousands of old tombstones, where Shingon Buddhists believe that Kobo Daishi is still sitting somewhere in meditation. One has a sense of being close to nature, and the monastery seems austere in a beautiful way. Nothing suggests, however remotely, the Gothic or baroque complications of this form of "Buddhist gnosticism" (Moore, 127). Some rooms in the monastery look out on a garden, not large, but with a splendid mountain providing an imposing backdrop. On the way to the bath—a short walk down one corridor and then, turning right, another—one passes two small gardens, both exquisite. No hint of the great Buddha Vairocana, the sun, or the four other Dhyani Buddhas each of whom is attended by many bodhisattvas who "in turn have their satellites, and so on *in infinitum*" (Moore, 127). The historical Buddha Sakyamuni and Amida are merely two of the four satellites of Vairocana. But why go on? Not only as one reads about it but also talking to the monks at Koyasan, one wonders why all this is necessary and whether it is really more help for them than a burden. This question is pointed not only at Shingon.

98

After World War II literally hundreds of new sects and religions sprang up in Japan. *Soka Gakkai* is probably as important as any. It has millions of adherents, is growing fast, has become a political movement that has succeeded in electing candidates to the national diet, has considerable influence on Japan's politics and social life, and owns a temple complex at the foot of Fujiyama that includes the largest temple in the world.

Soka Gakkai makes much of Nichiren, a thirteenth-century Buddhist who founded a sect that was distinguished by its religious fanaticism. He spurned the tolerance and pacifism of other Buddhist sects and was a fervent nationalist. He called Pure Land Buddhism an "everlasting hell"; the practitioners of Zen, "demons"; and claimed that Shingon was ruining the nation, while the adherents of another sect were traitors.

Nationalism became popular in Japan during the nineteenth century, as it did in Europe, and attempts were made to purify Shinto of "foreign" Buddhist elements, restoring the ancient national religion. But after the crushing defeat of Japan in 1945, one might have thought that Nichiren would not have had so much appeal. What has been striking about Japan since 1945 is surely the lack of resentment and self-pity, the pride and dignity of a people that within twenty years was once again one of the strongest in the world, without having an army. But our concern here is not with politics. It is with the experience of a Christian who engaged some Soka Gakkai believers in a conversation and discovered *shakubuku* (Offner and Van Straelen).

This term has been defined as "browbeating into submission." Josei Toda (1900–1958) wrote a book *Shakubuku Kyoten* (1958) in which he quoted a writer who had argued that when Nichiren had been sentenced to death and was about to be executed, lightning struck his executioner "and instantly killed him. Thus Nichiren was saved. Christ however was killed. Therefore Nichiren Buddhism surpasses by far Christianity." Indeed, "It has an answer to all questions and thus it is the true and philosophical religion" (105 f.). Ironically, some of the arguments used against the Christian investigator are very similar to what Christians say to unbelievers.

> "In Christianity you study forever but never reach the answer." . . . "Christianity is striving for the same goal of happiness as we are, but it ends in study . . ." . . . "We are happy; Christians are all mixed up." . . .
>
> You're thinking as a Christian. You're concerned only with ideas. You think you can build your life on ideas. But you cannot receive happiness except through the Great Holy One, Nichiren.
>
> One doesn't understand a thing and then accept it. It is just the reverse. . . . You don't study electricity before you turn on a light. You don't examine all that went into making a train before you board it. Christians never get on the train. They spend all their time studying how it is made. Hence they never reach the destination—happiness. We are *happy!* (106).

To many true believers in various religions and ideologies it has never occurred that this line of "argument," which they are fond of using, might be used against them. But what are we to make of it?

Having answers to all questions is the mark of the true believer, but no warrant whatsoever of true belief. It is a warrant of conceit and lack of humility. Confronted with so many doctrines that claim to be true, we cannot base our choice between them on the self-assurance of their representatives. But suppose that the believers in Soka Gakkai were really happy; would that settle the matter? Surely, many people have found happiness in different religions. Should we choose the one that has brought happiness to more believers than any other one, regardless of the truth and moral implications of its doctrines?

These questions are much too abstract. Christianity and Islam have brought happiness to many of their adherents; they have also brought death and oppression, slavery and persecution to vast numbers of others. Hinduism, too, has brought bliss to many, but spelled misery for millions. When Karl Marx called religion the opium of the people, he was not questioning that it had brought happiness to many. It is possible to make people happy and content with their misery by promising them rewards hereafter.

Religions can be divided into two groups in a great many ways. We have found that monotheism and polytheism are not exhaustive categories; also that the so-called Oriental religions are an extremely heterogeneous group. It is tempting to suggest that it would be more useful to distinguish between religions that are predicated on the individual's search for his own salvation and those that aim at a goal for humanity. Considering the misery of so much of humanity, the boast "we are happy" bears witness to a lack of humane feeling. The Hebrew prophets did not cry, "we are happy," and this is no objection to them.

Yet this dichotomy, too, breaks down. In each religion, including Theravada as well as Mahayana Buddhism, some are concerned mainly with their own bliss, others with humanity. Nor will it do to bifurcate religions into introverted ones and extroverted ones—those stressing meditation and those emphasizing action—because many religions have found a place for both. There is no one easy conclusion, no single scheme that allows everything to fall into a neat place. But one all-important dimension still remains to be explored: religions and the arts. Perhaps this, in conjunction with the pictures in this book, will help us to gain a better understanding of the great religions.

Making a graven image, Bali.

XIII

JUDAISM, CHRISTIANITY, ISLAM, AND THE ARTS

*Religion and Art—*JUDAISM *(The Prohibition of Images—Literature—Music—Architecture—Mosaics and Painting—Influence on Gentile Painters—Religion and Talent)—*CHRISTIANITY *(Europe Versus Asia—The church of the Holy Sepulcher—What Is Christian About Christian Art?—The Gothic—Sculpture: Madonna and Child, Suffering, and the Pietà—Fra Angelico—The Church as Patron of the Arts—Literature—Music)—*ISLAM *(The Mosque—The Dome of the Rock—The Aqsa Mosque—The Fortunes of Jerusalem—Damascus and Samarra—Isfahan—The Other Arts—Northern India)*

Mosaic floor in Tiberias synagogue, ca. 300.

99

As religions spread, they often descend lower and lower, like rivers. Born in some lonely place in an exalted state of mind, they become polluted as they enter cities where large numbers of people make use of them for their own ends.

In the nineteenth century, scholars tried to understand religion in terms of evolution and sometimes confused that with progress. It became fashionable to posit crude beginnings and to trace a slow ascent—at least until the Gospels were reached. Even then, Protestant writers pointed to a sharp decline between the Hebrew prophets and Jesus, and again between Paul and Luther.

In the twentieth century it has become more and more the vogue to glorify the "primitive," to posit a superior wisdom among those who lived in the distant past, and to despair of our own ability to fathom their profundity. The uncritical faith in progress has given way to an equally naïve belief in decadence.

Intellectual fashions do not change quite as fast as those in clothes, but they do change radically. Many people are quite unaware of this and take the tastes and habits of their own time for immutable norms of decency. In the nineteenth century one could hardly discuss the history of religion at some length without speaking of "superstition"; and "magic" was a dirty word. Scholars were censorious and freely passed out marks for morals. In the twentieth century we have moved toward an eclectic reverence for the major figures of religion, and sarcastic criticism and low marks are now reserved for those who still pass judgment on the men of former ages.

This new attitude is as dogmatic as its predecessor. Both are based on preconceptions and not on the evidence. When we consider the development of the major religions that have evolved in Asia, we find that they did not all follow the same pattern. This is small wonder, for they did not all spring up at the same stage in the life of the people among whom they originated. Judaism, Hinduism, and Shintoism, though quite different from each other, all have their roots in the period when a people was born. Jainism, Buddhism, and Christianity developed in a later age, when the Indians or the Jews could look back upon an old culture. Moreover, some religions are offshoots of older religions. Nor is there any reason to assume that all the founders of religions were basically similar or at least stood in some sense on the same plane. Mary Baker Eddy, the founder of what is usually called Christian Science, and Joseph Smith, who founded the Church of Latter Day Saints, were not very much like Moses or the Buddha, and whether Jesus was profoundly similar to the Buddha has to be determined by examining the evidence. To complicate matters, some religions, notably including Hinduism, have no founder.

Religious scriptures are a form of literature, and religion is in many ways like art. Both are quests for the eternal. Both seek a triumph over time and age. They prize what endures, what moth and rust do not corrupt. To what extent religions ever succeed in this quest, we do not know for sure. Opinions differ widely. I have argued elsewhere that "it is only in some works of art that ecstasy endures" (1960, 261).

Some believe the promise of religion. Others take it to be illusory. But to some extent art offers what religion promises. Here the eternal actually enters into time and abides with us. The word is not made flesh, but the spirit is made stone, music, and poetry.

This does not imply a rivalry between art and religion. But it does mean that some Buddha images capture the spirit of the Buddha as most of the literature on him does not. The inadequacy of the literature has been one of the central points of Ch'an and Zen, but they repudiated idols, too. Much earlier, Islam made war on idols and destroyed uncounted treasures, and yet Islamic art and architecture have at times captured the spirit of Islam at its best. The opposition to idols, which is deeply ingrained in the Protestant world, goes back to the Jews. It will be best to begin our reflections on religions and the arts with the Jews, and then to proceed once again to Christianity, Islam, Hinduism, Jainism, and Buddhism.

Judaism

100

No religion furnishes a clearer example of the influence of religion on the arts than Judaism. On the face of it, the influence in this case was wholly negative; the prohibition of idolatry in the Ten Commandments inhibited the development of sculpture and painting. "You shall not make yourself a graven image or any likeness of anything that is in heaven above, or that is on the earth below, or that is in the water beneath the earth; you shall not bow down before them or serve them" (Exodus 20:4 f. and Deuteronomy 5:8 f.). No doubt, all the commandments were transgressed sometimes, and this one was so flagrantly in conflict with the spirit of Egypt and the other major cultures of the area, including that of the indigenous population, that it took some time to become firmly established. Moses himself was said to have made a bronze serpent to which people burned incense until Hezekiah, who was king in Isaiah's time, in the late eighth century, broke it into pieces (Numbers 21:8 f. and II Kings 18:4). There is also a story in the Book of Judges (chapters 17–18) about a man who gave two hundred pieces of silver to a silversmith, who made the coins into one graven and one molten image. He placed them in a shrine and hired a Levite to be his priest, but six hundred armed men of the tribe of Dan abducted the Levite and the two images and eventually set them up in their own land in the far north of Israel, where the images remained until the northern kingdom was destroyed in 722 B.C.

Incidentally, an inscription dating back to the reign of Hezekiah has been found in Jerusalem, and he is also known from the inscriptions of the kings of Assyria. What we have in the Biblical books of Judges, Samuel, and Kings is real history, antedating by many centuries the birth of historiography in Greece, not to speak of India. No doubt, that is the result in large measure of the proximity of two very ancient civilizations in Egypt and Mesopotamia, which allow us to assign firm dates, but it remains remarkable that the kings, all the way back to Saul and David in the eleventh century B.C., and even Samuel and some of the other judges, are brought to life for us as real human beings in a historical milieu that differs strikingly from the myths of ancient Greece.

A religious prohibition inhibited the development of an indigenous tradition in sculpture and painting, and the artistic impulses of the Jewish people were channeled into literature and perhaps also music. The Jews became an extraordinarily literate and literary people, and in time their religion was based on a book.

The greatest artistic achievement of the Jews is their Bible. By the third century B.C., the Torah had been translated into Greek, and since then the whole

Hebrew Bible has been translated into all major languages. Not all these versions give the reader an adequate idea of the style of the original, which is in large parts singularly terse, compact, and economical. Some people are put off by occasional genealogical lists, and others find chapters containing detailed legislation tedious, but the stories in Genesis, the histories of Saul and David in Samuel, and the account of Elijah in Kings are as gripping as they are sublime. The Book of Judges is starker fare; the earliest parts were composed in the twelfth century; but the narrative, not only in the great saga of Samson, is as taut and tense as anything in world literature. The poetry of some of the prophets and parts of Psalms and Job is unsurpassed, and Jonah, Ecclesiastes, and the Song of Songs are gems. It is no wonder that no other book has left so strong a mark on much of the world's literature, beginning with the New Testament, which was also written for the most part by Jews.

Later Jewish literature is not so easily accessible in good translations, and the Jews themselves have never felt that any of it was comparable to their Bible. Yet the Bible became the fountainhead of a rich literature that includes many Apocrypha and other "intertestamentary" works that antedate the New Testament, and the discovery of the Dead Sea Scrolls after World War II has enlarged our knowledge of the writings of that period. In addition to the two Talmuds and various collections of Midrashim, as well as the Hebrew liturgy, we also have Philo's philosophical works and Josephus' histories—and in the Middle Ages, Yudah Halevi's poetry and Maimonides' works, all obviously nourished by the Bible. This is not the place to discuss them, or Spinoza, or the tales of the Hasidim, or Heine's prose and poetry. But two twentieth-century examples may help to show how the Jewish religion had something to do with the work of some of the best Jewish writers.

Franz Kafka's influential style was modeled on the Book of Genesis. His short, simple, and straightforward sentences seem clear at first glance but, upon reflection, pose endless problems of interpretation. His short parable "Before the Law," in his novel *The Trial*, is followed by pages of alternative interpretations and is clearly modeled on Genesis and subsequent rabbinical attempts to cope with it. In this respect, the parable is a paradigm of Kafka's work.

Freud's interpretation of dreams and his psychopathology of everyday life are also derived from the way in which the rabbis dealt with texts. Every apparently trivial detail is considered significant, and Freud himself insisted in his *Traumdeutung* (1900, 184) that every neurotic symptom, every dream, and every genuine poetical creation permit more than one interpretation and require many to be fully understood. He taught modern men to read not only texts but also dreams and human behavior as the rabbis had read the Bible.

Occidental literature is unthinkable without the Bible, which helped to shape the imagination of the West, supplied countless themes, and enriched all European languages with innumerable expressions, images, and motifs. Nor was this influence confined to the West. Islam, too, is unthinkable without it and carried Jewish ideas and images into Africa and Asia.

Thus the inhibition of the development of the visual arts was not a purely negative phenomenon. It led the Jews to concentrate on language and ideas as no other people had ever done; and when a modern philosopher said, "Language is the house of Being," he spoke out of this tradition. For the Jews, the Bible first of all, and then words and concepts generally, became a home in their dispersion. Dispensing with visual aids, they developed a rare virtuosity in abstract reasoning, sharpening their intellects in argument, and eventually, when the opportunity arose in the modern world, achieved an astonishing pre-eminence in science.

Their role in *music* has been nothing like this. They cultivated it continually since at least the time of David, around 1000 B.C., and it has always played an important part in their worship, but although they have produced a number of notable composers since their emancipation in the early nineteenth century, Mendelssohn, Mahler, and Schönberg are not of the very first rank. What we do not know is how much Western music owes to Jewish music, and to what extent the Gregorian chant was derived from Jewish worship. Some of the *words* of the mass clearly come from the Jewish liturgy and from the Hebrew Bible, and much later Handel, for example, sometimes used Jewish texts for his music. The percentage of Jews among the best conductors and instrumentalists is astounding; in the middle of the twentieth century much more than half of the most renowned violinists were Jews. But there is no clear connection with the Jewish religion.

101

In *architecture*, Solomon's temple in Jerusalem may have been one of the more impressive buildings of the ancient world, but the Babylonians razed it, and the second temple, begun in the late sixth century B.C., did not compare with it. Herod beautified the temple area and built the great platform that still distinguishes the site, but the Romans did not leave one stone of the temple itself in its place. Scholarly reconstructions of the temple in the form of sketches or models suggest that the feeling for proportion that found expression in the design of the whole area was remarkable, and the sublimity of its appearance now, with the Dome of the Rock in the place where the temple once stood, may owe a good deal to the Jews.

Even while the second temple was still standing, the Jews began to build synagogues, not only in foreign lands but even in Galilee. For the Passover and other major holidays one went to the temple if possible, as Jesus did, but on the Sabbath one went to a nearby synagogue, as Jesus also did. Some of these synagogues have been dug up, and that at Kfar Nahum (the Capernaum of the Gospels) has beautiful sculptured designs, some abstract, some of floral motifs, while the architecture is Hellenistic-Roman. Since World War I many digs have also uncovered beautiful *mosaics* on synagogue floors. Those at Tiberias, a stone's throw from the sea of Galilee (early fourth century) are illustrated here; those at Bet Alpha (sixth century) are reproduced more often. These mosaics include scenes from the Bible—for example, Abraham ready to sacrifice Isaac—as well as the signs of the Zodiac. Of course, floor mosaics could not possibly be construed as objects of worship; on the contrary, one walked over them. More astonishing was the discovery, also in the twentieth century, of the synagogue of Dura Europos on the Euphrates, in Mesopotamia. Built in the third century, the walls were decorated with wall paintings illustrating Biblical stories.

Evidently, there were times when the ancient prohibition was considered perfectly compatible with the purely decorative employment of paintings and mosaics. "A Talmudic source refers to the relaxation in third-century Palestine of the ban on wall-painting, while a fourth-century reference attests to the use of mosaics"; hence these finds have only "confirmed this literary evidence" (Roth, 193. Cf. Finegan, 1959, 305).

In sum, foreign art forms gained some rather limited entry into Jewish life, but sculpture and painting were not cultivated by the Jews until modern times. Their mosaics sometimes had great charm, and by New Testament times Jews had also developed the art of illuminating manuscripts, which flourished through the Middle Ages. In the visual arts, the Jews did not develop anything like the genius that they brought to literature, but the almost five hundred illustrations in Roth's *Jewish Art*, and especially the first half, before 1700, show a wealth of fascinating material that few people would have suspected, ranging from Palestinian works in stone and bone and clay that go back to the sixth or seventh millennium B.C. to many exquisitely illuminated manuscripts. Still, what is fascinating is that work of this kind and quality is to be found here, too.

The same consideration applies to the many Jewish *painters* since the nineteenth century: Jozef Israels, Camille Pissarro, Max Liebermann, Lesser Ury, Amadeo Modigliani, Marc Chagall, and Chaim Soutine, to name a few. Jewish sculptors include Jacob Epstein and Jacques Lipchitz, and Epstein is perhaps the greatest sculptor of the century next to Rodin. Still, it is far from clear that these men have brought anything distinctively Jewish into art. Some of their works, to be sure, have a specifically Jewish content, but so do many works by Gentile artists. If instead of asking for names and numbers we look for the influence of Judaism on the visual arts, we find that the most striking influence was exerted not by Jewish artists but by the Bible upon Gentile artists.

Michelangelo's famous statue of David illustrates a Biblical theme without breathing the spirit of the Hebrew Bible and is therefore not a case in point. He might have done a statue much like that if there had never been a Jewish religion. But his paintings on the ceiling of the Sistine Chapel—the greatest single monument of Western painting —not only have the Hebrew Bible for their content but also capture much of its mood, its ethos, its sublimity.

> Recalcitrant and yet obedient, like
> the rock beneath his chisel, he abandoned
> his sculptor's calling, forced to bear his witness,
> a painter in another Nineveh.
> He saw the artless ruins of the Forum,
> the windswept walls of palaces once lit
> by human torches, and the Colosseum's
> enormous shell, where crowds had cheered when lions
> ripped captured foes to shreds.
>   Above these remnants
> of ancient outrage and the countless churches
> where kneeling men confessed their sins to priests,
> he recreated man in his own image
> and placed above the pope's most holy altar
> Jonah defying God. And with the strokes
> of his rebellious brush the Bible conquered
> the base of slavery and inquisition.

Rome is not generally seen as the base of slavery and inquisition and as another Nineveh. But Nineveh was the capital of the Assyrians who had destroyed Samaria and the northern kingdom of Israel in 722 B.C., while Rome had destroyed Jerusalem. Jonah was made to go to Nineveh against his will. Michelangelo pleaded with the pope that he had no wish to paint the ceiling of the Sistine Chapel; he was a sculptor. It was a great oddity to place Jonah, arguing with God about Nineveh, over the altar, the more so if one recalls the ethos of the Book of Jonah (see sections 12 and 29, and the last page of section 43 above). But my poem does not imply that Michelangelo was conscious of all this.

If anyone should fail to grasp the point at issue, perhaps two of Nietzsche's characteristically sharp formulations may help to clarify it, even if it should be felt that he overstated it.

> In the Jewish "Old Testament," . . . there are human beings, things, and speeches in so grand a style that Greek and Indian literature have nothing to compare with it. With terror and reverence one stands before these tremendous rem-

nants of what man once was, and will have sad thoughts about ancient Asia and its protruding little peninsula Europe, which wants by all means to signify as against Asia the "progress of man." . . . The taste for the Old Testament is a touchstone for "great" and "small" . . .

The dignity of death and a kind of *consecration* of passion has perhaps never yet been represented more beautifully . . . than by certain Jews of the Old Testament; to these even the Greeks could have gone to school!*

No Jewish artist translated this sublimity into paint or stone as Michelangelo did.

Again, the fact that Rembrandt painted a great many Jews is a minor matter, but his attitude toward the despised and shunned, the poor and oppressed goes back to the Second Isaiah and Moses. Nor was this influence indirect; Rembrandt's paintings show how he lived in the Old Testament.

Heinrich Heine—and not only he—suggested that one could trace two basically different attitudes through history: the Greek and the Hebrew. When one considers India and China, one realizes how parochial this idea is, but in Europe this dichotomy is suggestive if one does not push it too far. Rubens was surely more of a pagan than Rembrandt, and Venetian art was less Hebrew than Michelangelo's. In the same vein, Van Gogh, Rouault, and Käthe Kollwitz, with their keen sense of suffering humanity, have deep roots in the Jewish religion, while Monet, Degas, and Matisse do not.

The Jews themselves did not develop their heritage in the visual arts as some of the finest Western painters did. Perhaps a tradition that for centuries had directed them to the written word could not be set aside even in the course of a whole century. In literature, of course, as in politics, they did repeatedly express their social conscience and their feeling for those who suffer. That so many Jews have turned to medicine points to the same explanation, which is strengthened by the fact that Buddhists, too, developed a disproportionate interest in medicine.

Finally, one may wonder whether the Jewish religion has anything to do with the immense amount of talent among modern Jews. In two ways it does. That they have prized learning so highly for so long was surely one important factor, and this was reinforced by an almost deliberate breeding of intelligence. The brightest were always encouraged and all but made to devote their lives to learning; they became rabbis, they were supposed to marry young, and it was considered a privilege to have one's daughter marry a scholar. Hence the most intelligent kept having many children, while in the Christian world those who wished to study became monks and priests who were expected to be celibate and not to reproduce. Thus medieval Christendom pursued a downright dysgenic policy that tended to eliminate intelligence wherever it appeared, and the Roman Catholic church has continued to do so to this day. Bearing out this suggestion, the number of scholars and philosophers in Protestant countries who are sons or grandsons of ministers is phenomenal.

Christianity

102

The subject of Christianity and the arts is far larger than that of Judaism and the arts, but since our focus is on Asia, on the region from Mount Sinai to Fujiyama, some rather brief reflections will have to suffice. In "A Conspectus of the Eleven Living Religions of the World" (Hinduism, Judaism, Shinto, Zoroastrianism, Taoism, Jainism,

---

* *Beyond Good and Evil*, section 52, and a posthumously published note, *Gesammelte Werke*, *Musarionausgabe*, vol. xvi, 373.

Buddhism, Confucianism, Christianity, Islam, and Sikhism), Robert Ernest Hume, whose strong Christian bias is often amusing, assigns each a "Present Location." The entry for Christianity is "World"; that for Islam, "Muslim countries" (2). But if one asks oneself where in Asia there are churches or Christian works of art as important as the finest to be found in Europe—or Christian paintings, sculptures, and buildings that one might compare with the many great examples of Muslim, Hindu, Jain, or Buddhist art in Asia—one suddenly realizes that there is hardly anything except for the church of the Holy Sepulcher in Jerusalem and the church of the Nativity in Bethlehem. In both cases their historical significance far surpasses their aesthetic merit. In other words, Christianity is really more regional than one might suppose, and the primary locus of Christian art is Europe.

We shall first consider the church of the Holy Sepulcher at some length while making brief mention of some other Christian sites in the Holy Land, and then pose a more general question that is as interesting to think about as it is difficult to answer; namely, what is Christian about Christian art?

The church of the Holy Sepulcher is the most sacred and fought-over church in all of Asia. After crushing the Jews' last major revolt under Bar Kokhba in 135, the emperor Hadrian built a basilica temple of Jupiter Capitolinus on the temple mount and placed an equestrian statue of himself in front of it. Elsewhere—according to Christian tradition, on the site of Jesus' tomb—he erected a domed temple of Venus, with a marble Venus inside (Finegan, 1959, 330 and 527 ff.). Coins of the period show the Venus temple to have been round. The first Christian emperor, Constantine, had the temple razed and the polluted soil removed, and in the course of this work a tomb was discovered that was believed to be the holy sepulcher. Constantine and his mother, Helena, then sponsored three basilica churches in the Holy Land—one here, one over the cave in Bethlehem that was said to be the place where Jesus had been born, and one on the Mount of Olives to commemorate Jesus' ascent to heaven. None of these churches have survived. In the sixth century the emperor Justinian deliberately tore down the original church of the Nativity to replace it with a more splendid basilica that still stands. He also built a church at the foot of Mount Sinai that survives to this day: St. Catherine's.

The original church of the Holy Sepulcher was destroyed by the Persians in 614, but the patriarch of Jerusalem rebuilt it more modestly, in keeping with the original design. It is said that the Persians did not destroy the church in Bethlehem because a mosaic on the outside depicted the adoration of the Magi, showing them in Persian dress. The Muslims, too, respected the church of the Nativity, and initially also the church of the Holy Sepulcher. But around the year 1000 the caliph al-Hakim abandoned the traditional policy of toleration, persecuted Jews and Christians, destroyed the church, and in 1020 proclaimed himself the incarnation of God. This act of destruction did much to precipitate the Crusades, although the Byzantine emperor Constantine IX had rebuilt the church half a century before the Crusaders took Jerusalem. Their conduct after the capture of the city has been described in the chapter on post-Biblical Christianity.

The Crusaders supplemented the timber-domed rotunda built by Constantine IX by adding a basilica. In 1808 the Byzantine dome was destroyed by a fire; some rebuilding was done in the nineteenth century, but in 1935 it was found that an iron scaffolding was needed to keep the building from collapsing. Why had it been neglected to the point of ruin after having been fought for so cruelly for almost two hundred years? Largely because the Greek, Roman, and Armenian churches hated and mistrusted each other so much. *Guide to the Holy Land* by Father Eugene

Hoade, O.F.M., published by the Franciscan Press in Jerusalem in 1946 with the *imprimatur* of the Roman Catholic church, shows this very neatly.

> The door of the Basilica, closed at night, and from 11:30 to 3:30 during the day, is guarded since 1244 by two Moslem families, one of which keeps the key, while the other has the right of opening the door. . . . Every morning one of the three interested communities (Latin, Greek, and Armenian) who live within the Basilica must pay for the opening (145).
>
> The three Communities (Greek, Roman, Armenian) take care of the decoration of the Edicule: pictures, lamps and candelabra are numerically divided . . . (149).
>
> [The work of the Greeks after the fire of 1808] was one of destruction rather than reconstruction, having followed no other design than that of erasing from the edifice of the Crusaders every vestige and record of Latin civilization and Catholicism (140 f.).
>
> On April 25, 1873, a band of Greeks, monks and seculars, armed to the teeth, broke into the Sacred Grotto (Bethlehem), maltreating and wounding eight Franciscans and pillaging the Holy Place, tearing the hangings and carrying off everything that had any intrinsic value, even to the marble slabs that covered the Holy Crib (316).

Whether the claims made in the last two quotations are entirely accurate or not, they certainly reflect the inability of the three churches to agree on anything as important as the reconstruction of the church of the Holy Sepulcher.

In his sixty-page discussion of the heated arguments about the question of whether the church is actually built over the holy tomb, which must have been outside the city walls, and where exactly the wall was in Jesus' time, Dr. J. Simons, S.J., speaks of "a psychological factor, which undoubtedly plays a big part" in the debate:

> the admittedly disgraceful and unworthy conditions, prevailing for centuries at the traditional "holy places," owing to the rivalry of the resident Christian communities, the consequent division of their sanctuary into a number of strange allotments, and, as a further consequence of this, the deplorable material neglect of the structure as a whole (285).

It was "the Mandate Power [that] was finally compelled to intervene by putting up an elaborate, unsightly system of wooden and iron scaffoldings to prevent the collapse of the *basilica.*" In the 1960s a process of radical reconstruction was begun, in an effort to recapture the past by going back at least to the Crusaders, if not to Constantine. Whether there could have been a tomb in this place around A.D. 30 remains uncertain. Many Protestants doubt it, and some of them prefer the site of the so-called Garden Tomb outside the present city walls.

Neither before World War II nor during its restoration could the church be said to be particularly beautiful or impressive. Its unique distinction depends on its religious associations. These are evoked by Father Hoade as follows:

> These short minutes leave an indelible and sweet record on the soul of him whose lot it may be to cross the threshold of that mortuary chamber which held the body of the Crucified, and to kiss that sacred stone on which the hands of Joseph of Arimathea and Nicodemus piously laid the remains of their beloved Master. If he should live a thousand years, he shall never forget—to forget would be impossible—the day, the hour, the fleeting moment in which he visited the "Glorious Sepulchre" of God made Man (149).
>
> Oh, the ineffable and unforgettable sweetness of the hours here passed, where was consummated the Divine Holocaust of love . . . (157).

Of course, students of the history of architecture have found this church fascinating because it furnishes a record of so many styles and periods. But simply as a building for worship, it does not brook comparison with the great mosques of Jerusalem or Isfahan, or with the great churches of Europe.

20 The other Christian buildings that are landmarks of Jerusalem and catch the eye much more than the church of the Holy Sepulcher, which many visitors actually have trouble finding, have little merit. The Russian church in the Garden of Gethsemane on the slopes of the Mount of Olives (1888) is relatively innocuous; the Roman Catholic Basilica of the Agony just below it (1919–1924) is rather pretentious; and the Russian steeple on the top of the mountain, visible from almost everywhere, shows no feeling whatever for the landscape. Mount Zion would look more beautiful without the imitation-Romanesque Dormition Abbey (1910) that crowns it, and it is hard to see why the tallest building in the holy city should have been a Y.M.C.A. tower (1933)—until it was eclipsed by the Jerusalem Hilton (1974).

The contrast of all these highly visible buildings not only with the two great mosques and the whole temple area but also with the splendid sixteenth-century wall and its citadel, including the Migdal David, or "tower of David," is as striking as the absence of any old, impressive synagogues. The interesting remnants of the Crusaders' church of St. Anne, virtually tucked away in a backyard, have the charm one associates with Gothic ruins in a garden. But on the whole, "Christian" architecture in Jerusalem is not impressive. Asia has no churches to compare with the great churches of Europe, which seem to owe much more to the regions where they were built than to Christianity.

103

This brings us to the question of what is Christian about Christian art. First of all, the themes of countless paintings, sculptures, and reliefs are Biblical or taken from post-Biblical tradition. Second, many churches are built in the shape of a cross, with a long nave traversed by a shorter transept. Third, many churches also employ many other symbols that evoke Christian ideas, notably including a great emphasis on the number three, in honor of the Trinity. Much of this symbolism is more esoteric and can be discovered only by prolonged research.

If we ask, however, to what extent Christianity brought a new ethos into art, the question becomes far more difficult to answer. A partial answer, to be sure, has already been given in the section on Judaism, for it was Christianity that disseminated the Hebrew Bible. And if one finds the ethos of the Old Testament in Michelangelo's great frescoes on the ceiling of the Sistine Chapel, one must at least ask whether he captured something of the spirit of the New Testament when he later covered one whole wall with an immense Last Judgment.

It may be well to consider *architecture* first, and painting and sculpture after that, concluding with a brief comment on literature and music. What is most striking about the great churches of Christendom is how greatly they differ according to the regions in which they were built. In addition, a number of very different styles have succeeded each other since the early Christians adopted, and then adapted, the Roman basilica style. In some countries this was followed by the Romanesque style which, as the name suggests, was still basically Roman. Its round arches are familiar from a multitude of Roman buildings, including, for example, the Colosseum in Rome. The Romanesque style, in turn, was followed by the Gothic, which many people consider more or less *the* Christian style in architecture. In the United States, a British version of it is still widely used for churches, although in Europe it was supplanted by various other styles, notably including the baroque, which has long had its day, too. While we cannot discuss all of these styles here, some questions about the Gothic are at least worth bringing up.

First, it is a regional style, pioneered by Abbot Suger at the Abbey Church of St.-Denis in France and quickly imitated and varied elsewhere in France, in Germany, and England (see Panofsky). The Gothic of the Duomo in Milan, in northern Italy, is not very similar at all to the French Gothic, which simply did not spread through Italy, where other styles prevailed. Nor did it spread into Eastern Europe or Asia. The great churches of Rome, Florence, Siena, Venice, and Palermo, the churches of Greece and Turkey, including the immensely influential St. Sophia in Constantinople, and the churches of Russia follow utterly different styles. Thus we must ask whether the Gothic is in any sense specifically Christian, and whether there are good reasons for believing that no Gothic sanctuaries would have been built if another religion rather than Christianity had prevailed in the Roman empire.

Abbot Suger obviously thought that his church was specifically Christian, and Otto von Simson has tried to show in *The Gothic Cathedral* what ideas the Gothic embodied. But suppose we begin by noting that in Norway we find so-called stave churches, built 116 of wood, that are much more similar to Chinese pagodas than they are to Gothic churches, and we ask whether the Norwegians might have built stave sanctuaries even if some other religion had come to Norway. Not having any preconceptions about stave churches, we would not hesitate to say that this is a regional style that owes more to the people in that part of the world than it does to Christianity. Is the matter basically different when we come to the Gothic?

Once one has this question firmly in one's mind, it is surprising how little Abbot Suger and Otto von Simson say to show that the case of the Gothic is different. The abbot wanted the best and the most beautiful; "he wished to accommodate as great a crowd as possible"; "he wished to display his relics as 'nobly' and 'conspicuously' as he could."

> Nothing, he thought, would be a graver sin of omission than to withhold from the service of God and His saints what He had empowered nature to supply and man to perfect: vessels of gold or precious stone adorned with pearls and gems, golden candelabra and altar panels, sculpture and stained glass, mosaic and enamel work, lustrous vestments and tapestries.

"Christian chalices should be more gorgeous than Jewish vials," and so forth (13, 16). One feature of the Gothic that has been much stressed is the alleged brightness of the interior, which both Panofsky and von Simson discuss at length. There was much talk of the "true light," which is Christ. But in the first place the interiors of Gothic cathedrals are not really that bright, even if they were meant to be, and are, much brighter than the Romanesque churches that preceded them; in fact, it takes a while until one's eyes get used sufficiently to the darkness inside before one can really appreciate the stained glass. Moreover, the concern with light might actually have emerged sooner if another cult had come to France, England, and Germany—say, Zoroastrianism, Manichaeism, or some form of Gnosticism. The same consideration applies to the "Neoplatonic" ideas that von Simson has traced.

"St.-Denis was to become a pilgrimage center where the idea of the Crusade intermingled with the memory of Charlemagne," says von Simson (81) by way of summing up Abbot Suger's ideas. One hardly needs to say anything more after that, except perhaps to stress how great the abbot's enthusiasm for the Crusades was. Finally, it should be noted that Suger was abbot from 1122 until his death in 1151, and the Gothic developed in the wake of the conquest of Jerusalem in 1099. The Muslims had employed 22 pointed arches long before they were used in Gothic churches, and the sudden empha-

Burmese Gothic, Dhammayangyi temple, Pagan, 1160s. (*See* 402.)

sis on light also suggests Muslim influence. If it had really come from Christianity, why should it have taken so long to emerge?

It is symptomatic of the narrowness of most studies in the history of art that even book-length discussions of the Gothic fail to comment on the eighth-century cistern at Ramleh (between Jerusalem and Tel Aviv), the Friday mosque at Isfahan, and the 35ff. strikingly "Gothic" interiors of some of the temples and pagodas at Pagan, in Burma.

Perhaps one could make out a somewhat better case for the claim that St. Sophia in Istanbul is specifically Christian. The original building put up by Constantine's son and successor was destroyed by fire in 404. It was rebuilt, burned down again in 532, and then was rebuilt by Justinian. Damaged by two earthquakes in the fifties, it was repaired by Justinian, and the immense dome was raised a little (Finegan, 1959, 550. Cf. Kähler). The building was finished shortly before Muhammad was born and has survived pretty much as it was. The forms, from the arches above arches to the dome, are basically Roman, but compared with earlier basilica churches, St. Sophia is a creation of great originality. Although it invites comparison with the Pantheon in Rome, the space inside differs markedly from all earlier buildings, owing to the immense height and size of the dome and the multitude of windows, all of them fitted into Roman arches. Long before the great church became a mosque, after the Turks conquered Constantinople in 1453, it had exerted a profound influence on countless mosques, partly by way of later Byzantine churches. Eventually, it was also copied outright not only by several other mosques in Constantinople but also in Cairo. After World War I it was made a museum.

Seeing how well the building served as a mosque, one wonders whether it bears any close relation to the ethos, mood, or spirit of the Gospels or Pauline epistles. Surely, only in two ways. Its loftiness represents a highly successful attempt to create a sense of reverence for an exalted deity, and if one looks for it, one can also find some Christian symbolism, including an emphasis on the number three. But the first point is not at all distinctively Christian, while the latter is relatively esoteric and evidently did not impinge on the consciousness of the Muslims. Again one wonders whether a building very much like this one could not have been built by Justinian if he had not been a Christian. When the church was finished, he exulted that he had surpassed Solomon and his temple (Runciman, 1956, 30), and it is easier to relate St. Sophia to Justinian's personal genius than it is to relate it to the New Testament. The emperor had defeated the Goths in Italy, reconquered parts of Spain and of North Africa, and had turned the Mediterranean once again into a Roman lake. He was also the great codifier of Roman law, with a passion to master and organize diverse materials and endless details. In St. Sophia his interest in the integration of immense complexities, his taste for the grandiose that would endure, and his insistence on lucidity became stone and glass.

104

Sculpture seems altogether different from architecture because it so often presents images of man. One might expect that the Christian images of man would be quite different from the Roman. In fact, we find a sharp decline in technical mastery, and the themes and scenes are often new, but we do not see a new humanity. Buddhist Gandhara sculpture, which will be considered later, came much sooner to express a different attitude that was not Greek or Roman but the Buddha's. The contrast is instructive and makes it obvious that the early Christians did not find in Jesus a new type of humanity, a different ethos, or anything at all resembling what so many modern men attribute to him. For them he was God.

Some themes that became extremely popular in Christian art may seem to be more than mere motifs. The frequent representation of mother and child may suggest the emergence of a different attitude toward children, and the emphasis on suffering may seem to bear witness of Christian compassion. But the representation of the Madonna with the baby became popular only after a span of more than a thousand years. Moreover, representations of Isis with the little Horus on her lap, sometimes even nursing him, had been extremely popular in Hellenistic times. If some other religion had won out rather than Christianity, we might well have had more mothers with babies sooner.

Suffering was also a central theme in Hellenistic art but was submerged for more than a thousand years after the beginning of Christian art. Some late Gothic crucifixions, with their emphasis on Jesus' human suffering, certainly suggest the emergence of a new attitude toward suffering, but at the same time the portrayals of the agonized faces of the damned seem to be intended mainly as a warning. It may be difficult for us not to project our feelings into such medieval sculptures, but we should recall that the Gothic age produced the Inquisition and its terror, and we have to ask whether these sculptures were not meant by the authorities to be part of the terror. The Church expressly condemned compassion for the damned, and those not familiar with Augustine or Aquinas may perhaps recall the sermons on hell preached by Jonathan Edwards in the eighteenth century or still more recently by Catholic priests like the one whose words James Joyce recalls in *Portrait of the Artist as a Young Man.*

No doubt, Goya and some of the Expressionists of the twentieth century were influenced by the Gothic, but widespread sympathy for suffering developed only after the Reformation, when the Old Testament was read widely along with the New, and when Rembrandt, for example, came to see Jesus as a suffering Jew. In early Christian art, Christ was not our fellow man; Christian teaching had ruled out sympathy for the victims of eternal torture; and it certainly was unsafe to show compassion for the victims of temporal torment.

The theme of the pietà represents another revealing case. In the Gospels Jesus' mother is never said to have cradled his corpse. But in pre-Christian Italian art we encounter the motif of the mother holding her slain son in her lap. Actually, this interpretation of the moving sculpture in the museum at Cagliari (reproduced in Massimo Carrà's book *Italian Sculpture from Prehistory to the Etruscans,* #14) may well have been influenced by the pietà tradition. Consider the most famous pietà of all, Michelangelo's in St. Peter's. The dead "son" looks about thirty, and the "mother" is far too young to be his mother. At most, she is his age. What we are shown is not a scene from the New Testament but Isis and Osiris! Or Ishtar and Tammuz. Or Cybele and Attis. The grief of the young goddess over the death of her young husband was, no less than his resurrection, one of the central themes of many pre-Christian Mediterranean religions. Again it needs to be said that if another religion had prevailed, it might not have taken that long for such works to be created.

Still, there may seem to have been a few artists who really were specifically Christian, perhaps none more so than Fra Angelico, who became a Dominican monk around 1425. His paintings have an almost unique loveliness, and his themes are almost always Christian. Or are they? His infinitely tender angels—some dancing, some making music, some surrounding the virgin—are no more derived from the New Testament than his favorite motif, to which he returned again and again, the Coronation of the Virgin in Heaven.

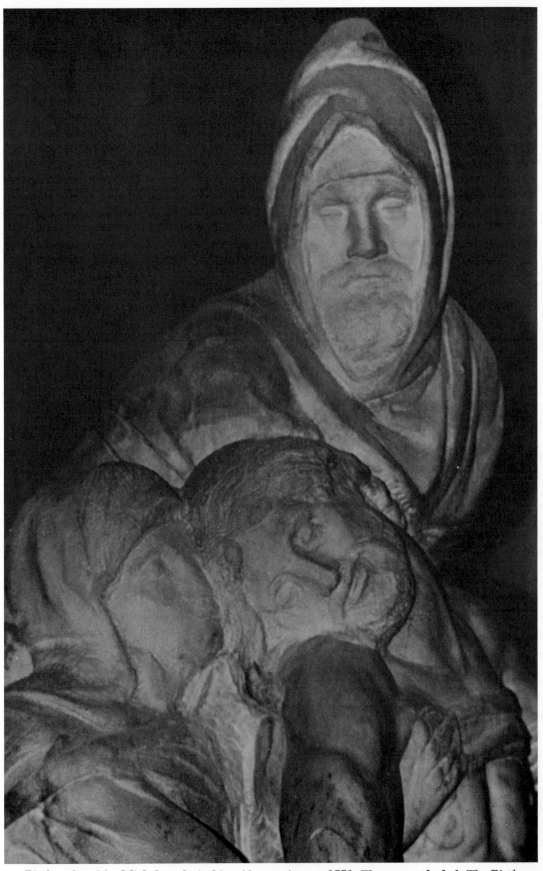

Pietà sculpted by Michelangelo in his mid-seventies, ca. 1550. Florence cathedral. The Pietà in St. Peter's was done before 1500.

Nevertheless, it is obvious that countless stories found in the Bible were portrayed by European painters, and the visual imagination of the Christian world was nourished by the Bible—the New Testament as well as the Old. But this did not happen on a large scale before the Renaissance, which involved a revival of Greek, Hellenistic, and Roman art as well as a burst of interest in the Hebrew Bible—in short, the rediscovery of the pre-Christian world.

Have we been asking too much? After all, painting, sculpture, and architecture flourished in Italy, Germany, France, and Holland, as well as some other European countries, and some of the greatest artists took their Christianity very seriously. What more could one possibly expect? We shall soon see that Islam shows how a religion can shape the architecture of its sanctuaries much more than Christianity did, and that Buddhism shows how a religion can use sculpture to convey a new human ideal. But two enormously important points can be made in favor of Christianity. First, the Church was beyond comparison the greatest patron of the arts in Europe. She lavishly supported architecture, sculpture, and painting, making medieval Europe a showcase for all three. Second, while intolerant in matters of doctrine, she gave artists considerable freedom to develop regional styles, building one type of church in one country and quite another type elsewhere. While the Jewish religion inhibited the development of the visual arts, they flourished in the Christian world.

The *literature* of the countries that became Christian is unthinkable without Christianity. That goes not only for Dante and Milton but also for Shakespeare (even if he was no Christian) and for Goethe (who called himself a pagan), for Donne and Racine, and Dostoevsky and Tolstoy. Their imagery, the range of their allusions, the world views that they held or felt it necessary to attack—all this involved Christianity and the New Testament as well as the Old. The question of whether the major works of European literature written after the advent of Christianity could also have been written if a Persian cult had dominated Europe is easy to answer. Certainly not.

Perhaps nothing produced by the Western world is more glorious than some of its *music*. From Gregorian chants to Palestrina and Monteverdi, Bach and Handel, Haydn, Mozart, and Beethoven, and many more recent masters, its ties to the liturgy are obvious, and much of the finest music is Catholic masses and Protestant passions, with the words derived from the liturgy or the Bible. Of course, one easily overestimates the significance of the words. In Mozart's *Magic Flute*, which many people consider the finest opera ever written, we encounter Sarastro, whose name is obviously derived from Zoroaster, and the opera deals with the clash between the forces of darkness and the forces of light in which "the rays of the sun" spell final victory. A prayer to "Isis and Osiris" suggests the syncretism of the Hellenistic world. Yet nobody would claim that this proves any profound Zoroastrian or Egyptian influence on Mozart, much less that his music would have been altogether different if it had not been for Zarathustra.

We cannot even say what course Western music might have taken if Haydn had died in infancy, much less what might have happened if none of the seven composers named above had ever lived, and certainly not what kind of music we might have if Christianity had died in infancy. What is clear is that Western music was not only tangentially related to the Christian liturgy but developed out of it, and the churches provided the context in which most music was composed for many centuries.

After World War II it was often said that it was simply incomprehensible how so many Germans could have done what they did and have loved German music. Thanks to Noah Greenberg we know that the music of the age of the Inquisition in Spain, for example, was exquisite.

Islam

105

Mosques do not vary as much from one region to another as do Christian churches. The great mosques of Cordoba and Isfahan, though influenced by local traditions, would never have been built in anything like their present form if it had not been for Islam. The basic architectural conception of the mosque is as distinctive and as beautiful as that of the Greek temple.

Greek temples were typically built on hills from which one could see the Mediter-   17 ranean. But even when there was no such hill, the site was chosen with some care and was usually a place where it would be beautiful to be even if there were no temple. The Greeks had a sense for nature, as the Christians for the most part did not. Early Christianity stood opposed to nature, and most great churches were built without any attempt to integrate the building with a landscape and permit the worshiper some peaceful meditation under the open sky. That was true even in Mediterranean lands, not only in the northern countries where the weather would forbid such meditation during part of the year.

The basic conception of the mosque is that of an oasis in the desert. A large court   21f.,38f. with some water and often also trees in it is part of the whole design. As soon as one enters the court, one leaves urban life behind and goes back to the desert where Islam was born. A sense of space, of spaciousness, of peace under the sun is as important as the building, and the first function of the mosque itself is that its exterior must contribute to this sense. It is meant to be seen not only from a distance as part of a skyline but also from nearby, not merely as one walks toward it to go inside but also as one sits or prays outside.

The interior provides shade and cool even on very hot days, and also a sense of space. Inside as outside there is no cluttering; the emphasis falls on emptiness. There are no idols, no sculptures, no paintings. There are old rugs on the floor, and one leaves one's shoes outside and can feel the rug's texture underfoot or sit in peace to read or think or meditate. It is a place where one can go on a brutally hot day, enjoy the cool, and study the Koran.

Mecca was and is quite different from all this. As a place of pilgrimage it attracts vast crowds. Muhammad's house in Medina, which served as a place for worship and study, is said to have influenced later mosques, but there also seem to have been two major outside influences. At least that is what the oldest extant mosque suggests.

The Dome of the Rock was completed in 691, a mere sixty years after Muhammad's   20ff. death. Its design and setting are sublime. It stands in a magnificently designed large court—the site where Solomon had built his temple in the tenth century, and where the Jews had built their second temple after the Babylonian exile. The Romans had reduced the whole area to rubble. When Jerusalem became Christian under Constantine, the temple mount was deliberately left in ruins, in keeping with the verse of Malachi that concluded the Christian Old Testament—"lest I come and smite the land with a curse"—and with some New Testament prophecies of destruction. The Christians did not even choose to live near the place; their dwellings, when the Muslims took the city, were around the church of the Holy Sepulcher and Mount Zion, though there were some monasteries and hostels south of the temple mount. The imposing site of the ancient temple was a field of stones in which pieces of masonry that had come from the temple were still recognizable. Omar, the second caliph, decided immediately to use this area for a mosque.

Before entering the city he had agreed not to destroy or take over Christian buildings, and the Christians therefore offered no resistance to him. In any case, he could scarcely have wished for a better setting; there was not even any need to quarry stones and bring them up from far away. But even as David, who had conquered the city more than sixteen centuries earlier, had to leave it to his son to build the temple, Omar did not get around to building the great mosque that many people call, erroneously, the Mosque of Omar. A pilgrim of his time reports that Omar only built a very simple mosque, and nobody knows precisely where it stood. The Dome of the Rock was built under the reign of Abd al-Malik, who appointed some Jews as guardians of the temple mount, now called Haram al-Sharif ("noble sanctuary"), and he exempted them from taxes.

One of the most striking features of the Dome of the Rock is that it makes the most of its ancient site. When the Aqsa mosque was added about twenty years after the completion of the Dome, the site was not spoiled by unseemly crowding; the second mosque was placed in the Haram but not on the platform designed for the temple; steps lead down to it. The magnificence of the Haram al-Sharif is due in large measure to the way in which the whole space has been used—or not used. Most of it has been left empty, and the Dome of the Rock looks like a perfect jewel in a simple setting. The opportunity offered by this site was unique, and the Muslims made the most of it.

The total absence of all idols and of any sculpture or painting representing any living creature—in this mosque as well as later ones—was due to Jewish influence. Whether it was Jewish influence on Muhammad, or whether the Jews who are said to have instructed Omar about the unique significance of this site also prevailed upon him to respect this ancient prohibition, is not known. Nor do we know for sure whether it was the placement of this mosque in this site that served as the great model for all later mosques. If it did, then the distinctive setting of the great mosques in a large court would have been inspired indirectly by the Jewish temple.

My speculation that the great mosques and their large courtyards are like oases may have also applied to the Jewish temple. As one entered the huge court, one returned to the desert where God had revealed himself. Four of the five books of the Torah are set in the desert of Sinai, and Jerusalem itself is perched just above the Judean desert, which can be seen from some of the hills and is but a short walk away. Occasional sandstorms all but bring the desert into the city. The theme of the desert or wilderness is one of the leitmotifs of the Hebrew Bible. The first major period of Jewish history began in the desert, at Mount Sinai, and ended in the desert, at Masada.

The desert makes for simplicity and a sense for the sublime. It is not pretty, not lovely, not charming, but vast and powerful. This does not mean that monotheism would naturally come to anyone who spent some time in the desert, but the desert provides an environment in which the austere doctrine of the One God gains some reinforcement from experience. Hence it made sense to remind those coming to the temple or the mosque of this stark simplicity and to re-create an oasis.

If the setting of the mosques and the absence of images show a strong Jewish influence, the other great outside influence was Christian. Both the octagonal shape of the Dome of the Rock and the dome surmounting it are to be found earlier in many churches. The dome was copied from that of the church of the Holy Sepulcher, down to its measurements. Both domes have been renewed a number of times since then, but that of the mosque has kept its shape, and the whole mosque has retained its basic design. The church has been destroyed again and again, and its present dome does not put one in mind of that on the mosque, nor can it be seen at all when one stands in front of the church. One cannot step back far enough, and the facade obstructs one's vision. But the dome of the church can be seen from far away and is not now particularly beautiful. The prototype for this dome, and thus indirectly also the inspiration for the Dome of the Rock, was St. Sophia. But the Muslims simplified the whole design. With their uncompromising monotheism they had no need for three domes, and again three half domes, and three tiers of this and that. The early mosques they built had *one* dome.

The octagonal shape of the Dome of the Rock did not influence later mosques and therefore strikes some viewers as unique. But this came from the Christians, too. In a book on *The Early Christian Church*, J. G. Davies includes some floor plans of octagonal structures and explains that baptistries were sometimes hexagonal because the Crucifixion had occurred on the sixth day of the week (Friday), and sometimes octagonal because Jesus had risen on the eighth day (Sunday). He also shows the floor plan of a centralized church of the sixth century at Mir'ayeh, and explains that such churches were almost invariably surmounted by a dome. This church was octagonal, with a rectangular sanctuary attached at one end. What was apparently "the central octagon of a Byzantine church of . . . the fifth century" has been excavated next to the famous ancient synagogue at Kfar Nahum (Capernaum). Finegan has published a floor plan. (1969, 56. Neither he nor Davies mentions the Dome of the Rock in this connection.) Such floor plans can be misleading. Perhaps San Vitale in Ravenna is the most famous octagonal church of the sixth century, but the outside is so cluttered and complex that one can hardly see it as an octagon.

Next to the Dome of the Rock is a very much smaller building that looks almost like a little replica, the Dome of the Chain. Actually, this dome is supported by a hexagon, while the outer structure has eleven sides and is open on ten. But while these forms —the octagon as well as the hexagon and, of course, the dome—were not original, what we see is not a complicated mixture of all kinds of disparate pieces but an overall design that is far simpler than the churches that influenced it. What is amazing about the Dome of the Rock, and also about its small dependency, is the simplicity of the design —as plain and perfect as that of a Greek temple, yet utterly different.

Even the Greek temples were adorned profusely on the outside—the Parthenon, for example, with the sculptured friezes that are now in the British Museum—and though scarcely a trace of the original paint remains, they were enormously colorful. The Dome of the Rock was covered with mosaics on the outside, but any representation was scrupulously avoided, and the ornamentation, inside as well as out, was purely decorative and abstract. In the sixteenth century, "Suleiman . . . ordered that the mosaics covering the walls of the Dome of the Rock be removed and replaced by beautiful marble tablets and facings, which adorned the building until the 1950s and were in part replaced during the repairs conducted by the Jordanian government" ("Jerusalem" in *Encyclopaedia Judaica*, 1434). The marvelous tablets and tiles of the sixteenth and seventeenth centuries were again purely decorative and non-representational. There are four doors, and while generally only one of them is used, all are decorated beautifully. There is no end of detail to delight the eye, but none of it interferes with the basic simplicity of the design.

To say that the inside of the Dome of the Rock is worthy of its outside would be true but misleading, for the problem that the builders solved was to create a structure worthy of the great rock around which the mosque was built. Roughly 51 by 58 feet, rugged and irregular in shape, and somewhat over 6 feet high, it was said to be the place where Abraham had almost sacrificed Isaac; it was the site of King David's altar in the eleventh century and had been covered by the first and second temples. Later, long after the mosque was built (Grabar, 50 ff.), it was also said that Muhammad had ascended to heaven from this rock. In time, that became the main reason why the Muslims considered Jerusalem a holy place. In the mosque, the rock is surrounded by a wooden screen that permits one to see but not to touch it. One can also go down a flight of stairs under the rock, and here some glass was placed over the rock in the late nineteen sixties to protect it from the kisses of Muslim worshipers.

As in other mosques, there are Greco-Roman columns and Oriental rugs; also marble panels and mosaics and, as on the outside, fine examples of Arabic calligraphy, mostly quotations from the Koran, that are tremendously effective as ornaments. The major inscription inside is 240 meters long and goes back to the time when the mosque was built in the seventh century. It includes many verses from the Koran deriding claims that Jesus was divine; for example: "Say: He is God, the One; God the Eternal; He has not begotten nor was He begotten; and there is none comparable to Him." And: "Praise be to God, Who has not taken unto Himself a son, and Who has no partner in Sovereignty" (Grabar, 61–64). These verses and many others like them furnish an important clue to the original purport of the mosque. The idea that it was intended as a rival to the Kaaba in Mecca and an alternative place of pilgrimage has long been refuted. And although our last quotation comes from the third verse of sura 17, the sura of the Prophet's "night journey," the inscriptions make no mention of that journey and plainly are not commemorating it. The rivalry that prompted the great building was not with Mecca; it was with the church of the Holy Sepulcher. The Muslims seized the rock and the site that the Christian builders had rejected and in effect proclaimed themselves the heirs of the promise to Abraham. They tried to build a sanctuary worthy of the temple and more splendid than the great church. They succeeded.

The building has been restored often. All the ceilings, including the inside of the dome, were redone by the Mamluks, some time after the Crusaders had converted the mosque into a church, and then again by the Ottoman Turks. In the 1950s the whole building was taken apart and rebuilt with immense care by Egyptian engineers and architects, and the Jordanian government received gifts for this work from other Muslim countries. The dome of the mosque had been black like that of the Aqsa mosque; now that of the Dome of the Rock was made golden and the far smaller one of the Aqsa-mosque silver. While there is literary evidence that the great dome over the rock was "golden" centuries ago, we do not know precisely what that means, and it is a safe assumption that it did not look as lifeless and inorganic as the new aluminum alloy. In the process of restoration, the superb old tiles were stripped away and replaced, the Crusader screen around the rock was destroyed, and the old Oriental rugs were replaced with new carpets. The unsurpassed nobility of the old design remains, and an attempt was made to re-create the old mosque as it had been long ago when everything was new. But anyone who knew the building before World War II, or who compares it with the Dome of the Chain, which in 1975 still retained its old tiles, may well feel that the mosque has been over-restored and looks gaudy now without the patina of age. Of course, the appreciation of texture and patina is not widespread, and few who see what has been done to the Dome of the Rock in the fifties and sixties, and what is being done to the Aqsa mosque in the seventies will agree with a great archaeologist who summed up his reaction in three words: "Stupid, ignorant vandals!"

23   The Aqsa mosque is essentially an old basilica. Imposing rows of polished, round marble columns used to structure the space inside, while the fine facade is divided by seven proto-Gothic arches. The variety of influences meets the eye, as it often does in mosques, but as usual the architects succeeded in giving the whole a simplicity that prevails over the multiplicity of inspirations and the interest in detail.

In August, 1969, a fire broke out in the Aqsa mosque, and charges of wanton destruction and demands for a holy war against Israel echoed through the Arab world. The culprit was caught, and the negligence of the Muslim caretakers established beyond doubt. The arsonist was a deranged Protestant fundamentalist from Australia who had thought he was obeying God's command.

The restoration of this mosque was begun before the fire and is of a kind with the restoration of the Dome of the Rock. The enterprise is under Muslim jurisdiction, and the government has kept out of it. By 1975 almost everything inside the mosque was new, and the superb old capitals, marvels of stone carving with a rich patina, were to be found outside, on the ground.

On the Haram al-Sharif there are many small structures in addition to the buildings and the arches that define the outlines of the court, but the integration of the whole large area and the lack of crowding make an overall impression that is Islamic and not Roman, Byzantine, or Christian. The way in which magnificent old trees have been used as part of the design heightens the sense of the oasis. Two towering cypresses 21 flank the fountain at the foot of the steps that lead up to the Dome of the Rock from the Aqsa mosque, and there are more great cypresses as well as a grove of olive trees.

No minaret competes with the cypresses or interferes with the solitary splendor of the Dome of the Rock. High structures are kept at a decent distance. There are four minarets, and that at the far northwest corner of the Haram, not close to the platform, 26 is especially beautiful.

We do not know at what point the Muslims began to associate the great rock on the temple mount with Muhammad's "night journey," or when they accepted from some Jews the notion that this rock marks the center of the world and that on the Day of Judgment the dead will assemble on the Mount of Olives and cross a bridge to the Haram. The ideas of the judgment and the bridge come from Zarathustra but were developed as follows: Paradise would be on one side, hell on the other, the bridge thinner than a hair and sharp as a sword, and the good would receive sweet water and shade from Pharaoh's wife and Miriam, the sister of Moses. It has been suggested that people who had such beliefs must have found some special advantage in being buried as near the place as possible, but this is not particularly plausible. It is much more likely that some Jews supposed that the eschatological bridge would span the valley in which people had been buried since time immemorial, and the Muslims accepted this notion. Eventually they considered Jerusalem the third holiest city of Islam, after Mecca and Medina. Yet the son and successor of Abd al-Malik, under whose reign the Dome of the Rock had been built, founded Ramleh and made it the capital city of the province, which it remained, while Jerusalem declined in importance. Trade routes did not reach Jerusalem, and it became a provincial town.

The Omayyads moved the capital of their empire from Mecca to Damascus, and Walid I, under whose reign the original Aqsa mosque was built, built a far larger mosque in Damascus, which he considered far more glorious than the two great mosques in Jerusalem. Before we consider that, however, let us very briefly follow the fortunes of Jerusalem.

106

When the Abbasids succeeded the Omayyad dynasty, Jerusalem decayed. Baghdad took little interest in Jerusalem, and the later Abbasids none at all. The great Harun al-Rashid, the best known of all the caliphs in Baghdad, who was a contemporary and correspondent of Charlemagne, made the pilgrimage to Mecca almost every other year and also came to nearby Syria, but never once visited Jerusalem. And Arab messengers brought Charlemagne the keys to Jerusalem.

In the ninth century Syria and Palestine had their first Turkish governor, and in the eleventh the Seljuk Turks conquered Jerusalem. A few years later the Crusaders took the city. The capture has been described in the chapter on post-Biblical Christianity. They turned the Dome of the Rock into a church, and initially their first king of Jerusalem used the Aqsa mosque as his quarters, but then the Aqsa mosque was given to the Templars, and the king moved near the citadel, at the opposite end of the town. For a while, the city was closed again to Jews and also to Muslims.

When Saladin, sultan of Egypt but a Kurd, ousted the Crusaders from Jerusalem in 1187, he turned the church of the Holy Sepulcher over to the Eastern Christians and invited Jews to settle again in Jerusalem. St. Anne's church became a *madrasa*, a Muslim seminary. But in 1229 the emperor Frederick II regained the city through negotiations, crowned himself king of Jerusalem, and turned the Haram over to the Muslims. He was an unbeliever and a consummate politician, while the motives of the earlier Crusaders were mixed. Unquestionably, religious fanaticism was part of this mixture, and that was concentrated on the church of the Holy Sepulcher. One can hardly help wondering why this site should have mattered so much to men who believed that Christ, having been buried Friday afternoon, was resurrected Sunday morning. During the reign of Frederick II, the Roman Catholic church redirected its crusading fervor against the Albigensians; later, into the Inquisition, the destruction of the "heathen" cultures of Peru and Mexico, and finally the fratricidal Thirty Years War, in which Roman Catholics and Protestants slaughtered each other. In this gruesome history, the quest for the tomb in Jerusalem was merely one gory episode.

The Crusades led the Muslims to hold Jerusalem much dearer than before, but they were slow to respond to the bloodbath of 1099, and soon after regaining the city in 1187 they turned it over to Frederick II.

In 1244 the Turks sacked Jerusalem and devastated the church of the Holy Sepulcher, but from about 1250 until 1517 the city was mostly under the rule of the Turkish Mamluks who governed Egypt. Owing to its many Muslim seminaries, the city became a minor center of Islamic studies during the later Middle Ages. It was also "the most commonly assigned place of exile" in the Mamluk empire (see Goitein's long article on Jerusalem in *Encyclopedia of Islam*, section 12).

In 1517 the Ottoman Turks conquered Jerusalem under Selim I, and it remained part of their empire for fully four hundred years. The Mamluks and Turks left their mark, although very few Turks settled in Jerusalem. Much of the present old city goes back to the Mamluk period, and Suleiman (that is, Solomon) the Magnificent followed up the conquest of 1517 by surrounding the old city with the superb wall that still stands, including the "Tower of David" (Migdal David). The wall with its many gates is not only a thing of extraordinary beauty, but also serves to separate the old city from the modern world, even as the many stepped streets and narrow lanes serve to keep out cars.

Jerusalem had been a walled city before, and Suleiman's wall and the citadel to which the Tower of David belongs embody much more ancient parts. Some of these have long been apparent, while many more have been brought to light by excavations made since 1968. In many places, notably including the citadel and the area near the
23f. Aqsa mosque and the Western Wall (once known as the Wailing Wall), archaeologists have uncovered Herodian foundations that antedate the time of Jesus, and Hasmonaean structures that are even earlier. There are many places where it is not feasible to dig, but what has been dug up is most impressive and greatly adds to the beauty of Jerusalem. So huge are the stones used by Herod that in places Suleiman's wall above them puts one in mind of filigree. Other finds include inscriptions going back to the time of King Hezekiah and the first Isaiah. Palpably and visibly, the archaeologists are recapturing the Hebrew past, but it is a past that was long known from literary evidence, and generations of Jews had lived in this past as much as in the present.

The Great Mosque of Damascus was created at the beginning of the eighth century by converting the fourth-century church of St. John the Baptist, which in turn represented a transformation of an earlier Jupiter temple. The church was said to contain the skull of St. John the Baptist. The mosque, completed in 715, dwarfed the mosques of Jerusalem. The eight sides of the Dome of the Rock measure 69 feet each; the Aqsa mosque is 262 feet long (the width has been changed since it was built by Walid I); but the mosque of Damascus is 431 feet long and was intended to be the greatest mosque in the world. Walid I is said to have told the citizens of Damascus: "You are pre-eminent over the rest of the world in four glories: light, air, gardens, and fruit. I have added the fifth: the mosque."

The mosque was ravaged by fires in 1069, 1400, 1479, and 1893, but has been rebuilt again and again. Only vestiges remain of the original building, but many decorative fragments have survived. While it would be an understatement to speak of Roman and Christian influences on this building, it was made to conform to the basic conception of the mosque described earlier.

The concept of the minaret originated at Damascus. The ancient pagan enclosure had four square watch towers at the corners, which the caliph retained and put to a new use by having the call to prayer issue from them. Only one of the four minarets of the Great Mosque remains. The call to prayer could be a very beautiful thing, but now it is usually, even in Jerusalem, an electronic blare.

The Great Mosque of Samarra in Mesopotamia, about 60 miles north of Baghdad, on the Tigris river, was built in the ninth century by the Abbasids. Its court measures about 784 feet by 512, and the outer walls, about 8 feet thick, still stand. The sanctuary, once supported by 464 columns, has not survived. But about 90 feet away stands a truly unique minaret.* The Arabs call it "the spiral," for it emulates the shape of the ancient Babylonian ziggurats that could be ascended by a spiral path along the outside. It stands on a platform in the desert, and rises to a height of 164 feet, bringing to mind the Tower of Babel. But again the enclosure and the tower and the landscape have been integrated into an organic whole. "The spiral" could obviously have been built even if there never had been any Islam, but the mosque as a whole bears the unmistakable imprint of the Muslims.

Incidentally, the great clock tower of the cathedral in Seville, in Spain, was originally a minaret, built in 1195. But the upper portion was destroyed by an earthquake in the fourteenth century and rebuilt quite differently by the Christians two hundred years later. The lower part they left substantially unchanged.

107

If one chooses a single city to conclude this discussion of mosques, none seems better for this purpose than Isfahan. It is situated a little over 200 miles due south of Teheran, almost exactly halfway to Shiraz and Persepolis. It was a provincial capital in the Parthian empire, in pre-Christian times, but did not rise to great eminence until the Seljuk Turks made it the capital of their empire in the middle of the eleventh century. They ushered in one of the great periods of art and built the Friday mosque (Masjid-i- 35f. Jami), the first and most impressive of the three superb mosques that make Isfahan one of the most beautiful cities in the world.

In *Byzantine Civilization*, Steven Runciman pictures the Muslims in general and

* Finegan (1952) has a picture (#231) of the whole complex. Du Ry offers closeups of the outer wall and the minaret (36 f.). Both also have pictures of the mosques of Mecca and Damascus.

the Turks in particular as barbarians, because they were the enemies of the Byzantine Empire. He even repeats the old legend that the Muslims consigned the great library of Alexandria to the flames (34); and when the Seljuk Turks appear on the scene, he describes them as "a primitive people" and "destructive" (43). In Arthur Upham Pope's *Persian Architecture: The Triumph of Form and Color*, on the other hand, chapter IV bears the title: "The Seljuks: Structure as Beauty." It is a large book with almost four hundred illustrations, and it certainly does not bear out Runciman's verdict. Nor do other books on Islamic art. Nor does a visit to Isfahan.

The Seljuks built the Friday mosque on the site of an earlier mosque, and construction began about twenty-five years before the Crusaders conquered Jerusalem. By no means does all of what is to be seen today go back to the end of the eleventh century. Work was continued under "a dynasty of great rulers rarely matched in history," men to whom Pope ascribed "a notable sense of ethical responsibility" (105). Pope calls the Friday mosque "one of the greatest mosques in the world," adding that it "is not purely Seljuk, but those portions which date from Seljuk times are, even today, its chief glories. More than 800 years of Persian architecture are revealed in this great mosque's twenty distinct structures, varying in date from the eleventh to eighteenth centuries" (106).

One of the major innovations of this mosque is the use of *ivans* (also known as *iwans* or *eyvans*), large vaulted niches closed on three sides but open to the central court on the fourth side. Smaller niches were also fitted into low Gothic arcs (before there was any Gothic in Europe), and fitted into upright rectangles that were later faced with colorfully decorated tiles, down to and including the arc. The four walls that bound the great court (196 by 230 feet) consist of two tiers of such *ivans*, those above being of the same width as those below but with much shorter sides, and in the middle of each wall is a large *ivan*, the great *ivan* on the south side being more than twice as high as the wall, not counting the two slender minarets that rise above it at each side. Later some of the great *ivans* were made still more splendid by the addition of stalactite vaults. All these motifs were soon used in other mosques, not only in Isfahan but also elsewhere.

The domes of the Friday mosque date from the eleventh century, and one can wander about on the roof and look at them from close up. The shapes are as superb as the construction, and there is no facing, no tile, only bare bricks. Inside, too, one sees the bricks and stones; and the spaces as well as the ways in which the light comes in and is reflected are unsurpassed.

The Mongols conquered the city in the thirteenth century but spared it. Tamerlane took it in 1388 and, after the people rebelled against him, is said to have killed 70,000 of them, building a mountain of their skulls. But the domes of the mosque survived and also weathered quakes without a crack.

The other two great mosques of Isfahan were built under the reign of Shah Abbas at the beginning of the seventeenth century, and completed while the Thirty Years War ravaged Europe. His predecessors had resided in other cities; he made Isfahan his capital and built the Shaykh Lutf Allah mosque and the huge Shah mosque. Their domes, visible from far away and also from the immense rectangular "square" on which both are situated—the Shah mosque at one end, the other to the left as one faces the Shah mosque—are very similar. Both are covered with extraordinary tile mosaics, but the Shah mosque dome is predominantly blue-green, while the other dome is more golden—subtly so, not the brand-new metallic gold of the Dome of the Rock in Jerusalem.

In 1714 what may well be the world's most beautiful *madrasa* (Muslim seminary) was completed in Isfahan, with a dome very similar to that of the Shah mosque, but here the predominant color is blue. The minarets of the madrasa and of the mosques of Isfahan are also similar—cylindrical and covered with tile.

Here were innovations, and one may wonder whether the extraordinary tiles might not have been made in Iran even if there had been no Islam. One will have to admit that the design of these mosques preserves the essential elements introduced into religious architecture by the Muslims.

The tiles, too, show the influence of Islam. What distinguishes the tile work and the other arts of Islam, including Persian rugs, from their counterparts in Europe and in India is the avoidance of representation and the virtuosity in the development of abstract decoration. The ornamental use of Arabic inscriptions is often stunning, and the tiled domes of Isfahan furnish beautiful examples.

When figures of men and animals did make their appearance in Islamic art, care was taken to dissociate them as far as possible from the slightest suggestion of idolatry. This may also help to explain the development of miniature painting. "Carpets dared to show figures because one tread upon them" (Ettinghausen, 258); but even so most carpets did not make use of images of men or beasts. And when they did, or when such figures were used elsewhere, one went out of one's way to make them look flat and to stylize them to make clear that their function was solely decorative; they were used, if at all, as elements in a design.

Muhammad's deep aversion to all luxury was another element of the desert heritage that helped to mold Islamic art. The Arab society into which he was born had borrowed Aramaic words for "potter," "carpenter," and "tailor"; the words for "window," "smith," and "bracelet" came from Ethiopic, and "silk" from Persian. To call a man a "weaver" or "son of a weaver" was an insult. An Arab was not supposed to work with his hands and be a craftsman, and when the Kaaba in Mecca, a very modest building, burned down in 605, "the Meccans called in a Greek carpenter who was then on board a ship passing through Juddah. This foreigner rebuilt the shrine with the assistance of a Coptic craftsman" (253). Thus the prophet's opposition to luxury did not go against the grain of his society, although it was also prompted by his expectation of the Day of Judgment. He succeeded in impressing on his followers that treasures on earth do not endure. According to the oral tradition (*Hadith*), he had said: "Whoever drinks from gold and silver vessels, drinks the fire of hell." Hence the Muslims did not make vessels of gold and silver, nor did they pile up treasures of precious metals and stones—not even in their mosques. Much less did they go in for such ostentatious displays of wealth as can be found in some church treasuries and in the Jain temple in Calcutta—not to speak of golden Buddha images.

What did appear in time, however, was "luxury substitutes." A film of golden luster might be applied on pottery as early as the ninth century. Later, thin pieces of gold and silver were used as inlays on bronze or brass. The same idea appears in architecture: "A thin layer of bright tilework or of faïence mosaic over a brick building" (260).

One may wonder whether at that point the whole original ethos was betrayed. Unquestionably, the splendor of the domes of Isfahan is a far cry from the rigors of the desert, and it does not bring to mind the Day of Judgment. Yet the decorations around the bases of the three great tiled domes are composed of Arabic inscriptions, and the shapes of all three are as simple as they are sublime. It is by no means far-fetched to associate a single large dome with the One God, Allah. It may be due in some measure to its current state and the merciful absence of over-restoration, but the domes of the Friday mosque are, both inside and outside, bare beauty wrought of brick and stone;

36 there is nothing precious about them, nothing opulent; they are a symphony of shape
and air and light.

<h1 style="text-align:center">108</h1>

No discussion of Islam and the arts should ignore the fact that Muslim invaders
destroyed most Indian temples and sculptures in northern India. They missed a very
few, notably including Mount Abu and Khajuraho. The major medieval monument
they built in India was the Qutb Minar outside Delhi, an enormous minaret and tower
of victory built late in the twelfth century. To the three sections built then of red
sandstone, two more were added two hundred years later. The whole Minar rises to a
height of about 240 feet, and the diameter at the bottom is over 47 feet, while that at the
top is about 9, and the slant consistent. Twenty-seven flutings, interrupted by bands
and balconies decorated with inscriptions, make the tower most impressive—much
more so than the mosque it overlooks. The Muslims used the columns of a Hindu
temple, defacing the many sculptures on them. Nearby one can also see another and
even more ambitious attempt at a similar minaret that was abandoned.

Most of the other major monuments of Muslim art in India were constructed by
the Moguls (discussed in section 65 in chapter VII). In Delhi there are Humayun's tomb
46 and the Lodi tombs, located in large parks; and the Jama Masjid, India's largest mosque,
and the Red Fort, both built by Shah Jehan in the seventeenth century. South of Delhi
there is the beautiful ghost town of Fatehpur Sikri, which Akbar built as his capital in
the sixteenth century, and a little more than 20 miles east of it, there is Agra. Both the
50 Fort, which includes the Pearl mosque, and the Taj Mahal were also built by Shah
Jehan. The Persian influence on Shah Jehan and some of the other Mogul emperors is
evident. In the mosques we still find the same basic ideas that all the great mosques
exemplify; the virtuosity in decoration is evident in many of these structures, even in
the forts—for example, in magnificently crafted screens; and the Muslim interest in
tombs reaches its apotheosis here.

These tombs could hardly be more different from the Holy Sepulcher, from
Romanesque heaviness and Gothic darkness. They are worlds removed not only from
northern Europe but also from Rome, and the church of the Holy Sepulcher surely
has absorbed nothing of the sunny clime in which it stands. The Muslim tombs of
India are wide open, airy, shady places in a spacious natural setting and do not suggest
grief. The Taj Mahal has a fairytale beauty that is just a little too sweet for some tastes,
but the design is once again strikingly simple, and this along with its brilliant ivory
color gives the building such a sense of lightness that it almost seems to float.

The dome, the *ivans*, the four minarets, and ever so much else are derived from
mosques, and the building stands squarely in the tradition of Muslim art. The Jews
could not have built it because they did not build huge monuments in honor of the
dead. The Christians could not have built it because their attitude toward death was
so different, and the whole style and feeling of the Taj Mahal are remote from theirs.
The Hindus and Jains also did not build vast structures to honor the dead, and it is
very striking that the Taj and the other Muslim buildings mentioned here owe so little,
if anything at all, to their Indian environment. The great buildings of Islam in different
countries have much more in common than do Christian churches in different countries.
Looking at Muslim art one does not get the feeling that in winning so much of the
world, Islam has lost its soul. But perhaps its architecture is the best part of Islam.

Taj Mahal.

XIV

HINDUISM, JAINISM, BUDDHISM, AND THE ARTS

HINDUISM (*Late Beginnings—Ellora—Mahabalipuram—
Khajuraho—Bhubaneshwar—Konarak—Madurai—Srirangam—
Shiva—Tanjore—Prambanan in Java—Bali—Angkor*)—
JAINISM (*Ellora—Mount Abu*)—BUDDHISM (*Early Prohibitions—
Yakshas and Yakshis—Sanchi—Gandhara—
Nagas, Naga Buddhas, and Umbrellas—Ceylon—
Borobodur in Java—Nepal and Tibet—Burma—Thailand—
Angkor—China—Korea—Japan*)

Indra Sabha Cave (#33) at Ellora, 800: Indrani, queen of the gods, on a lion, and the Jina.

If there was any Hindu art before the second century B.C., it has not survived. After the prehistoric and pre-Aryan civilization of Harappa and Mohenjo Daro had been destroyed in the sixteenth century B.C., neither the Aryan invaders nor the indigenous population of the subcontinent fashioned any works of stone, bone, clay, or metal that we know of. Before 1550 there were towns and works of art in the Indus valley, and some of the finest pieces have already been described at the beginning of chapter VIII. After that there is a gap, not even bridged by inscriptions, until we come to Ashoka, the great Buddhist emperor whom we discussed at the beginning of chapter XII. There is no Hindu or Buddhist art until well after the invasion of Alexander the Great, and then Indian art was begotten by Hellenistic art.

Thus the title of a beautiful book called *5000 Years of the Art of India* is a bit misleading, doubly so because for all we know most of the Harappan pieces that are illustrated may have been fashioned in the seventeenth century B.C. That they were found in what is now Pakistan is a relatively minor matter. In Palestine works of art have been found that go back to the sixth or seventh millennium, and the pyramids in Egypt are almost five thousand years old. It is a fact that has not been sufficiently appreciated that the people of the Vedas and Upanishads and the men and women who listened to the Buddha may not have had any temples, any sculpture, nor any idols. It is possible that they used wood; it is also possible that they were not illiterate, but if so it is remarkable that in their literature we find no mention of writing, temples, or idols, and that they should never have used durable materials when their predecessors and successors did.

Indians frequently make a point of the antiquity of their civilization, claiming that it is far older than any other. But the point here is not to score against India; it is to understand her and to realize how utterly different the Hinduism and Buddhism that we know are from pre-Hellenistic Hinduism and Buddhism. This radical transformation has gone largely unnoticed.

Obviously, there were no Buddha images in the Buddha's time, any more than there were crucifixes and madonnas in Jesus' day, and later we shall see how late the first Buddha images appeared. What is not obvious but surely worthy of note is that in the Buddha's time, and even centuries after that, both Hinduism and Buddhism seem to have dispensed with idols. With the use of that word—idols—the point may suddenly appear to be that the Indians, so far from being latecomers, declined into idolatry. In fact, no value judgment whatsoever is intended.

When one considers the head of Brahma on the cover of this book, one can scarcely help being amused at the censorious attitude of so many Christians—and even of George Bernard Shaw, who took pride in not being a Christian. In 1946, a journalist submitted to him seven written questions, one of them about "the incorporation of Hindu thought in recent English novels, like Aldous Huxley's *Time Must Have a Stop* and Somerset Maugham's *Razor's Edge.*" Shaw replied, in writing, that this was "a very good thing," and went on: "But in India the great religious sects need a Reformation. The temples are all profaned by the symbols of the crudest idolatry."* Such Protestant iconoclasm is simply blind to a whole dimension of religion—and perhaps even to more

---

* The manuscript signed and dated by Shaw, 4th June 1946, is in the author's collection.

Rameshwara cave, Ellora: Ganga, according to some the mother of Karttikeya. (*See* 229.)

than one dimension. Shaw's reference to "symbols" may voice his Puritan horror of the *lingam*, which is rarely, if ever, an expressive work of art. It is usually as simple and 77,79 stylized as the Christian cross—but sums up a diametrically opposite attitude. As a phallic symbol, it invites reverence for *this* world in general and sex in particular. This is ironical in many ways. It contrasts rather sharply with the teachings of the Upanishads and with the Gita's great commandment of detachment, and it marks the triumph of the native cults of India over the religion of the scriptures. It is doubly ironical because India has become far more puritanical than most Protestant countries, including England as well as Sweden, Denmark, and the United States.

When art in stone finally began to develop in India, beginning in the third century B.C., under the reign of Ashoka, it still took centuries before the Hindus produced major works that brook comparison with the great Buddhist sites. Applying the high standards warranted by the finest Hindu temples, one must say that there is little that one could call great before the fifth century, and little after the thirteenth. But during that period the Hindus built magnificent temples and created superb sculptures in great profusion.

It would be hopeless to try to comment on all the major sites, but it seems worthwhile to consider several briefly. First, there are the caves at *Ellora*, about 250 miles east-northeast of Bombay. (The caves at nearby Ajanta are all Buddhist.) There are more than fifty caves at Ellora, of which thirty-four are considered important, and half of these are Hindu, the others being either Buddhist or Jain. The most impressive temple at Ajanta and Ellora is number 16 at Ellora, the Kailasanatha, which is dedicated to Shiva. It is not really a cave at all, being open to the sky, and some argue that it is not a work of architecture but a sculpture, for it was hewn and carved out of the living rock, without the benefit of any scaffolding. The work was started from the top by cutting trenches into the mountainside to create a monolithic block that was more than 270 feet long, more than 150 feet wide, and 100 feet high; the temple was then fashioned out of that block. Not only can one walk around the temple at the bottom of the pit and see the sky above, one can also ascend to a higher level in the temple—and in the galleries that have been cut into the sheer rock, right and left. This temple is considerably later than most Indian Buddhist temples; work was begun late in the eighth century and finished in the ninth. It has been called one of the wonders of the world and "probably the most impressive single work of art in India" (Edwards, 75), while Zimmer has said: "This overpowering monument marks the victory of Brahmanism over Buddhism at Elura" (1960, vol. i, 291). All three judgments make good sense, even if one should find the sun temple at Konarak still more impressive, or if one should wonder why Zimmer said "at Elura" rather than "in India."

It is arguable that the finest single sculpture at Ellora is also found in a Hindu sanctuary, but there are legions of great sculptures and it would be foolish to press this point. At any rate, we show a picture of Ganga, the goddess of the Ganges river, at the Rameshwara cave (Cave XXI). It was probably carved in the seventh century.

Roughly 600 miles southeast of Ellora stands one of the oldest Hindu temples in India, built around A.D. 700. The shore temple at *Mahabalipuram*, between Madras and Pondicherry, is perhaps the loveliest temple in India, largely owing to its situation on the sea. For a famous Hindu temple it is unusually small, there is a lingam outside, 79 even closer to the water, and the spray of the waves keeps falling on it. A short walk from the temple leads to several other monuments of considerable interest, including some extraordinary reliefs depicting scenes from Hindu mythology.

The Shiva temple of Elephanta, on an island near Bombay, is a creation of the eighth century. The great stone head with three faces has already been discussed in the section on the major Hindu deities.

The greatest Hindu site in northern India is surely *Khajuraho*, roughly 200 miles

Khajuraho.

west of Benares, hidden away in the jungle, where it escaped destruction. About twenty temples survive, some of them Jain, some Hindu, most of them built in the eleventh century. The fame of these temples rests on the erotic carvings that adorn them in profusion. Actually, erotic carvings also abound in Konarak, in Bhubaneshwar, and in Nepal, showing men and women making love in various positions. At Khajuraho such carvings are especially abundant and include men standing on their heads, with the women who squat over them supported by voluptuous female attendants. How can one explain these sculptures which are so different from those adorning the outsides of Romanesque or Gothic cathedrals? The question is interesting enough to be discussed at greater length elsewhere, with many illustrations. Suffice it to note here that some interpreters claim that these sculptures merely show a more than Homeric joy in all aspects of life, which is a beautiful thought but, on reflection, scarcely plausible. Others have postulated a strange cult in which all these positions were actually adopted as a special kind of yoga. A third possibility that does not rule out either of the first two is that what we see here is a survival of very ancient native cults. To this theory we shall return when considering Buddhism and art.

Some of the salient facts about *Bhubaneshwar* have been stated in "The Third Face of India," in the poem called "Déjà Vu." Perhaps no other city in the world can boast of so many old temples. The poem expresses the occasional exasperation of a sensibility schooled on the Book of Genesis—but that mood was born of days spent wandering from temple to temple, revisiting some of them many times, always fascinated. The sense of despair comes only of imagining what endless repetition means in existential terms, translated into the lives of men, women, and children. From a purely artistic point of view, Bhubaneshwar is a kind of paradise. The Lingraja temple, built around the year 1000, is one of the few great temples to which non-Hindus still are not admitted, not even when wearing a dhoti, but there are vantage points from which one gets fine views, and there are hundreds of other temples that are smaller but for the most part endlessly interesting. The reliefs, of course, are uneven, but many of the temples are older than the Lingraja, and often the sculptures are superb. 89

Bhubaneshwar is within an easy drive from Puri, where there is another great temple that non-Hindus may not enter. It is also the gateway to the so-called Black Pagoda at *Konarak*—the remains of a thirteenth-century temple of Surya, the sun god. Some comments on it are included in "Orissa" in "The Third Face of India." But what is needed is really a whole book of pictures of Konarak and Bhubaneshwar. Here is only a single temple, or rather part of one, all that remains of it, but it is so vast, so magnificent, so beautiful that anyone who could see only one temple in India need not hesitate for a moment to choose Konarak. We show the finest of the three statues of Surya, one of 86 the wheels that suggest that the whole pagoda is his chariot, and men cleaning some of 88 the famous statues on the roof. 90

The enclosure in which the Black Pagoda stands measures 875 feet by 540. The sea is less than two miles away and rather shallow. Hence the temple used to be an important landmark for sailors, who called it the Black Pagoda, and the temple at Puri the White Pagoda. Part of the tower of the temple of Konarak was still standing in the nineteenth century and was toppled by a gale in 1848. But it has been argued that the tower had never been finished, perhaps because the technical problems proved insuperable. The long decay of the temple seems to have been precipitated by the removal of the idol in the main shrine to Puri to protect it from possible mutilation by Muslims. With the idol gone, the temple was abandoned, not only to nature but also to the greed of men who helped themselves to stones. None was more destructive than a raja who removed some of the finest sculptures early in the nineteenth century to use them for a temple of his own. A contemporary report in the *Journal of the Asiatic Society Bengal*

Some of the "thousand lingams" at Tanjore

Fragments piled up beside a temple that has lost its facing. Bhubaneshwar.

Konarak, 13th century.

(1838) describes how he "has demolished all three entrances": "the masons pick out the figures and throw them down to take their chance of being broken to pieces (which most of them are); such they leave on the spot, those that escape uninjured are taken away" (681 f.). In 1838, the government directed him to stop removing stones. Others had seriously considered using the temple stones to build a lighthouse on the shore (Mitra, 13). Conservation did not start in earnest until 1901. Almost immediately, one of the great wheels was exposed, and by 1910 much more had come to light than had been seen for centuries.

There are other interesting structures in the compound, but the center is held by what is usually called the porch of the old sun temple. Twelve pairs of wheels are carved into the sides, and in front of the porch are seven free-standing horses that pull the chariot of the sun god. Every one of the wheels is a sculptor's masterpiece; the sides of the porch are covered with carvings, and the figures on the roof are immense. The numbers are overwhelming, the attention to detail is meticulous, and the expressiveness and elegance of the carvings are superb.

110

The temples of southern India are different in style from any of those considered so far. Mahabalipuram is in the south but one of a kind. The "Indian friend" who turns up in the poem "The Cape" in "The Third Face of India" did not live very far from Konarak, which he had never seen, but said more than once: "The only temple in India that you need to see is *Madurai!*" This feeling is widely shared. The Minakshi temple in Madurai, about 150 miles north-northeast from the cape, was built in the 71f. seventeenth century and might be called an example of Indian baroque. But when India gained her independence, the temple was quite dilapidated, and the renovation generated a vast amount of public interest. Finally there was a referendum, and "it was decided to paint the gopuras (gate-towers) in the original bright colours mentioned in inscriptions" (Volwahsen, 62). To call the result gaudy would be an understatement. It is much closer to contemporary public taste in India than any other major temple. Although the Indian gurus who make their living lecturing in the West are certainly not representative of India, the popular taste is reflected quite well in the profuse and very colorful illustrations of the *Bhagavad-Gita As It Is* by "His Divine Grace A. C. Bhaktivedanta Swami Prabhupada" (quoting from the title page). Of course, Madurai is not *like that*, and while there is not much Hindu art after the thirteenth century that ranks with the best work done up to that time, the Minakshi temple is probably the most magnificent Hindu temple since 1300. Two pictures may give at least some impression of it, but they do not show the large cool spaces inside, which tend to be rather dark and not at all gaudy, and the courts where people sit and talk. Most of the temples discussed so far are old monuments or archaeological sites and not used as temples now. The Lingraja, though almost a thousand years old, is an exception. The great temple of Madurai is a center of life where people come not only to worship but also to sit in the shade.

About a hundred miles northwest of Madurai are two towns with remarkable temples: Srirangam (near Trichinopoly, alias Tiruchirapalli) and Tanjore. Trichinopoly itself is dominated by a huge rock, with a temple on top of it that affords a magnificent view of the surroundings, which include the island and town of Srirangam with its two famous temples. The huge temple of Raghunathaswami is dedicated to Vishnu and composed of seven rectangular enclosures of which the outermost measures almost 2,500 by 2,900 feet. One passes through a bazaar before coming up to the second wall, about 20 feet high. There are eight gopuras, all decorated with painted carvings, the tallest being more than 150 feet high. It has been suggested that the building was begun in the tenth century and completed by 1600. The most famous part was finished last: the so-called Hall of a Thousand Pillars. Actually, there are about 940 monoliths of granite, and the columns in the front row, which faces a large court, are carved in the shape of rearing horses, with their front hoofs high up.

Precisely because these carvings are so fine, one used to the ethos of unique events that is a legacy of the Hebrew Bible may wonder whether one such pillar might not possibly be more effective than a colonnade. Would Andrea del Verrocchio's celebrated statue of Bartolommeo Colleoni on horseback, done in bronze in the 1480s, gain anything from standing in a row of such statues?

The whole mood would be changed. Nor is the point that the Renaissance piece is a statue, while the Indian columns are part of a work of architecture. The sovereign on horseback in the cathedral of Bamberg comes closer to being an architectural ornament, and it does not tax the imagination to suppose that there were kings on dutifully tame thirteenth-century horses, similarly positioned, all over the cathedral, since after all there were legions of sovereigns, and this one is not identified. Conversely, there are cloisters in Bangkok with whole rows of Buddha statues that are more or less alike. The Colleoni is an extreme case because this statue breathes the defiant individualism of the Renaissance. The rider of Bamberg, carved during the reign of the emperor Frederick II, has the visionary quality of one ahead of his time—an individual in an age when the Gothic still forced vast numbers of people into intricate and vast designs, and it was rare for one to stand as thoroughly alone as he does. In Hindu temples such separate existence is reserved for the gods and their symbols.

In a Shiva temple there is usually a large reclining bull—just one, by himself— Nandi, Shiva's symbol, like the lingam. The gods frequently appear in larger compositions, but they also appear separately, often in bronze. The single greatest symbol of 73 Hindu art is Shiva Nataraja, Shiva as the king of the dance, celebrated in two poems in "The Third Face of India": "Shiva's Wreath" and "The Cobra."

"I would believe only in a god who could dance," said Nietzsche's Zarathustra, speaking of "Reading and Writing" and attacking "the spirit of gravity." Yet although Paul Deussen, who knew as much about Indian thought as any scholar at that time, had been Nietzsche's friend since they had studied together, Nietzsche never mentions Shiva Nataraja; only his Greek equivalent, Dionysus, whom he frequently juxtaposed with the crucified Christ. In the Christian symbol he found a curse on this life, a negation of this world; in Dionysus, an affirmation of life and a celebration of this world. It seems wholly fitting to juxtapose the dancing Shiva with the crucified Christ and to find here two almost diametrically opposite conceptions. The bull and the lingam also suggest a view of sex remarkably at odds with that of the New Testament.

In purely artistic terms, the Nataraja represents a scarcely credible achievement. He is dancing, usually in a circle of flames, his left leg raised high, one right hand raised as if to beat the rhythm, and is yet serenely unmoved. Another German philosopher, Hegel, also wrote a famous sentence that seems to have been suggested by the Nataraja, though he, too, did not know about the dancing Shiva. "The true is thus the bacchanalian whirl in which no member is not drunken; and because each, as soon as it detaches itself, dissolves immediately—the whirl is just as much transparent and simple repose." In the original German, this sentence from Hegel's preface to his first book is difficult to construe because something went wrong, and what he says is, as often, far from lucid. Yet this sentence has been quoted again and again by Hegel scholars, no doubt because the image of the Dionysian whirl that is also transparent and simple repose is so compelling. In the Shiva Nataraja it is realized in bronze.

Srirangam, Raghunathaswami temple, "Hall of 1,000 Pillars," 1600.

Verocchio's Colleoni, 1480s.

Again it is striking to see how much these idols resemble each other, and occasionally, at least in museums or in looking at pictures, one can hardly help thinking of a stencil. Truly, the similarities are far greater than those between crucifixes. At least we reserve our admiration for carvings of the Crucifixion that are different, more expressive than most, more individual in their conception. Most Natarajas are so much like each other because they follow a traditional canon that determines the proportions and details.

When he appears in a shrine, there is only one, although other bronzes may stand near him. As in Buddhist countries, it is not uncommon for the idols to be dressed, even when they are fine works of art. To a Western sensibility, the clothes may seem inappropriate. If so, Shiva's leopard skin is an exception.

The Shiva Nataraja is not the only dancing god in Indian art. Sivaramamurti's *Nataraja* is a comprehensive study of this theme with hundreds of texts and illustrations. Here it will suffice to mention that Krishna, too, is often represented in a dancing pose, supported only by his left leg, very slightly bent, the right knee raised, the right foot pointing down, the right arm bent with the hand just above the knee, and the left arm raised a little higher than horizontal. The best bronzes of this type really capture the spirit of the divine dance.

Returning once more to Srirangam, we have made mention of the great court that the colonnade of horses faces. Courts such as this one are a characteristic feature of the Hindu temples and great centers of life where they occur, which is not always. The great Vishnu temple also has a large hall supported by immense, more or less rectangular columns with carvings, where people sleep or sit, often in small groups, five women here and three men there, to chat in the relative cool on the stone floor. 74

The Jambukeshwaram temple, not far from the Vishnu temple, is dedicated to Shiva. It is smaller, but by no means small, and many writers consider it more beautiful. The poem about it, "Shiva's Wreath," makes mention of the live elephant in it. There is one in the Vishnu temple, too. Both have a chain around one leg.

The temple at *Tanjore* was built in the eleventh century and has a huge tower in the shape of a very steep pyramid that rises from a square base and is topped by a monolithic dome crowned with an ornament. The tower, which is more than 200 feet high, is not a *gopura*, a gate tower, but a *vimana* that rises over the sanctuary. There are also gopuras, but the vimana is visible from far away and totally dominates the large court that measures 415 by 800 feet. Near the entrance, inside the court, is a monolithic *nandi* of black granite, over twelve feet high and sixteen feet long. On the far right is a sanctuary, and along the right side of the court there is a long cloister with many chapels; there are additional chapels along the far side of the court. The gopuras, added in the sixteenth century when large gopuras formed part of a new style, have carvings associated with Vishnu's cult, but the shrines are Shaivite, and in the chapels there are said to be one thousand lingams. In some chapels they are arranged in four long rows, low, black cylinders with little space between them, but there are also lingams that look more like wicks rising out of ancient oil lamps, and behind these there are very interesting frescoes, covered by graffiti in all the languages of India. 77

111

Few great Hindu sites are found outside India, but there are a few that are as interesting as the major sites in India. The oldest of these three is *Prambanan* in Java, not far from Jogjakarta, in the center of the island. Here, there are many ruins of Hindu temples in a relatively small area; indeed, more than two hundred temples are said to

143   have formed part of the original design. The central group consists of a large Shiva temple, flanked by two smaller temples dedicated to Vishnu and Brahma. These temples were built in the ninth century. The exquisite friezes illustrate scenes from the *Ramayana*, the great Hindu epic, and the two great stone images of Vishnu and Brahma are among the finest anywhere. Yet Prambanan is much less famous than the vast Buddhist

139   temple at nearby Borobodur.

142   In Java, both Buddhism and Hinduism were replaced by Islam in the sixteenth century. On the smaller island of *Bali*, less than 2 miles east of Java, Hinduism has survived and is still the religion of the people. But here Hinduism has been transformed, and the religion of Bali is probably closer to the ancient indigenous religion than to Indian Hinduism. The caste system exists in Bali—but approximately nine-tenths of the Balinese are Shudras. The great Hindu "mother temple," 3,000 feet above sea level, on

148   the slopes of a volcano, Gunung Agung, which is more than 10,000 feet high, does not look like any Hindu temple in India. The pagodas seem a little closer to Buddhist

115   structures in China, Japan, and Nepal; but the "mother temple" of Besakih is *sui generis*, like Balinese Hinduism. There were temples here before Hinduism arrived in the seventh century. Bali is a tropical island, near the equator, and the Balinese love

150ff. flowers and outdoor ceremonies, grotesque masks, elaborate dances, and music. Offerings of flowers are made several times a day, and Legong dancers wear elaborate headdresses

147   made of fresh blossoms. A picture can give some idea of the beauty of such a dancer, but words are needed to add that only once during her long dance did she hold a pose for as long as one-sixtieth of a second. Her vibrancy made the music visible. Sometimes only one hand or only a thumb is in motion, but that vibration gives shape to a rhythm that pervades the whole body. It takes years of disciplined study to achieve such perfection, but during the dance nothing seems learned, nothing is mechanical, and the performance is comparable to that of a very great violinist.

        Of the many Balinese dances that involve the use of masks and resemble plays, one

161   of the most impressive is the Barong dance. The Barong is a monster, played by two men, one furnishing the front legs, the other the hind legs, which might seem clumsy though funny, but the footwork is once again of a vibrancy that makes the humor sing.

        The taste for the grotesque is evident not only in some of the dances and masks but also in many of the stone carvings, including the entrance to the Bedulu Elephant Cave. There is a light touch to it all that contrasts strongly with Indian Hinduism.

        In India misery never seems remote. Not only are old age, sickness, and death

145f. everywhere, but poverty and dirt as well. In Bali nature is beautiful both at the sea and in the mountains, and there is less dust. The humidity is so great that even newly made

149ff. graven images are covered with moss and lichen within a few months and assume the venerable beauty of old images. There is a sense of abundance that is reflected in the ubiquitous ceremonies in which beautiful women carry stunningly arranged blossoms on their heads. Here the influence of landscape on religion seems palpable. Gracious nature did its share to transform a religion.

        One feels none of the smoldering resentment that one senses so often in India and, even more so, among poor Arabs; one feels that the kindness of nature has bred a gracious freedom from resentment and brought peace to all—and then recalls how during the civil war of 1965 the Balinese ran amuck, killing members of their own families until the death toll numbered in the tens if not hundreds of thousands. A few

152   years later, the only hint of savagery was to be seen in the old frescoes of the Hall of Justice in Klungkung, which depict the punishments of the afterlife and were intended to terrify the accused—and in the favorite sport of the Balinese: cockfighting.

        The great mountains of Bali are volcanoes that look beautiful and peaceful but occasionally erupt. In 1917 Gunung Batur destroyed 65,000 homes and 2,500 temples.

In 1926 it erupted again. And in 1963 Gunung Agung erupted after having been quiet for a hundred years.

Modern Nepal is predominantly Hindu, and there are interesting Hindu temples 105–120 in Nepal, but the most celebrated buildings and bronzes of Nepal are largely Buddhist. It is arguable, however, that both Hindu and Buddhist art attained their apotheosis in Cambodia. The rediscovery of *Angkor* in the nineteenth century has already been mentioned early in chapter XII. Angkor did not become the capital of the Khmers (the Cambodians) until the tenth century, and Angkor Wat was built in the twelfth, but the artistic style that found expression at Angkor can be traced back for several centuries, and the so-called pre-Angkor period produced unquestioned masterpieces by the eighth century. Gradually, the capital was moved closer and closer to Angkor; even during the eighth century it was not very far away, and by the ninth it was in Roluos, which is part of the area called "Angkor" for short.

In this sense Angkor includes the Bakong, the earliest great temple in this area, 141 which was dedicated to Shiva and probably completed in the ninth century; Banteay Srei (tenth century), which has a distinctive style of its own; Angkor Wat (twelfth century); and the great Buddhist structures put up during the reign of Jayavarman VII (1181–1220), which will be discussed later. The Brahma on the cover of this book is a 80 superb example of the so-called Bayon style, which is named after the greatest Buddhist temple built by Jayavarman VII. It has four faces, and their expression is strikingly similar to that of the great Buddhas and bodhisattvas of that period. 138

When we ask whether Hindu art is distinctively Hindu, the answer is best given in two stages. First, confronted with a Hindu temple or statue, one is never left to wonder whether it might not be Muslim, Christian, or Jewish. Its Indian inspiration will never be in doubt. This is not merely because the stories illustrated in friezes and sculptures come from Hindu mythology; the whole "feel" of Indian art is very different from Christian, Jewish, and Islamic art—even Islamic art in India. Then, however, we must ask what, if anything, is distinctively Hindu about Hindu art when we compare it with Jain and Buddhist art, and at that point the question becomes difficult. Jainism and Buddhism borrowed a great deal from Hinduism. On the other hand, the Buddhists were the first in India to develop monumental architecture and to fashion superb sculptures, and the Jains, too, began to do great things at least as early as the Hindus. To cope with our second question, we clearly must consider Jain and Buddhist art.

Jainism

112

The major monuments of Jain art are concentrated in three places: Ellora and Khajuraho, where the Jains built their caves and temples next to the Hindus', and Mount Abu, 400 miles due north of Bombay, in Rajasthan, just across the border from the neighboring state of Gujarat. We shall concentrate on Mount Abu because it is much more distinctive than the Jain art of the other two sites. The Jain temples of Khajuraho are very similar to the nearby Hindu temples, and many of the figures are simply the same here and there.

As the very fact that the Jains and Hindus built next to one another suggests, they were more conscious at that time of what they had in common than they were obsessed with differences, at least in the visual arts. They clearly did not take offense at one another's work. The caves at Ellora—Buddhist as well as Jain and Hindu—were built beginning in the fifth century, while the Buddhists had begun to build similar caves at Ajanta several centuries earlier. Here the general mood and ethos of the Jain caves, temples, and carvings is certainly not distinctive. We show one example, Cave XXXIII, which is also called the Indra Sabha cave. Built around the year 800, it shows the Jina in meditation, and at the right of the entrance Indrani, the queen of the gods, on a lion. Indrani is a Hindu deity and seems doubly out of place next to the great ascetic, for she looks extremely sensuous. That the eroticism of her full breasts is not lost on Indians is proved by the fact that they are fondled so much that they look as if they had been oiled. This is a common sight in India and applies not only to the breasts of female nudes but also to their genitals, showing that these nudes distract attention from the meditating Buddhas and Jain Tirthankaras whom they so often flank. While India has become a much more puritan country than she once was, and bare breasts may not have attracted much attention in A.D. 800, the deliberate attempt to celebrate feminine beauty and—there is no denying it—sex appeal does furnish an odd contrast to the message of the Tirthankara, as well as that of the Buddha. Nevertheless it does not follow that this is an example of Hindu influence. When we come to Buddhist art, where this strange contrast first appears, I shall attempt a different explanation.

The meditating figure is almost sure to be mistaken by a Westerner for a Buddha. But he is nude, which is a sure indication that he is a Tirthankara. The Jain saviors are always represented in the nude, while the Buddha is never nude and usually wears a monk's robe. The presence of several large male nudes in this cave leaves no doubt about its being Jain, although the treatment of their faces as well as the protuberance on the top of the head (*ushnishi*) shows a strong Buddhist influence. In sum, the work is interesting and of high quality but not distinctively Jain.

55–63 The four Dilwara temples on Mount Abu, 4,000 feet above sea level, in a fine mountain setting, were built between the eleventh and thirteenth centuries. The two that are considered most important, the Vimala Vasihi and the Luna Vasihi, are different from any Hindu or Buddhist temples anywhere and quite astonishingly beautiful. Almost everything is white marble: the floors and the pillars, the images of the Tirthankaras, and above all the ceilings with their many small domes that are carved as delicately as if they were lace. Only a few sculptures are black, notably some elephants, and in three of the temples one Tirthankara image, the main idol, is not white either: one is black, with jeweled eyes and nipples, one brass with a brass shrine behind it, one white with jeweled eyes and nipples, and one is silver. These images are in special shrines with heavy metal doors that can be locked, while a great many white marble Tirthan-
56 karas sit in open niches and look very much alike. A guidebook, *Mount Abu: The Olympus of Rajasthan*, is properly eulogistic but admits in discussing the Vimala Vasihi that "The images in these cells are all of one pattern and stereotyped cast of features. They are . . . distinguished by their symbols placed on the pedestals." The pictures may give a better idea of the temples than a long description would. Photographs of the
60–63 four main idols have probably never been published before.

All this fairytale beauty offers a stark contrast to the austere asceticism of Mahavira. It shows more eloquently than a long essay could how the realities of the religion differ from the teachings and the ethos of the founder. We have seen in our discussion of Jainism that the strict prohibition against killing even earthworms made it impossible for the Jains to till the land and drove them into the towns where they became merchants, did well, and used some of their wealth to build resplendent temples. They have taken pride in their beautiful temples, have taken care of them, and even kept them clean. There is thus an explanation, but the irony remains. Nor is it greatly attenuated by the fact that on entering the temples on Mount Abu one must leave behind all leather, including belts and camera cases, because leather is made from animal hides.

The images of the saviors invite comparison with Buddha images. The basic posture is the same, and the seals of the Harappa culture that came to an end in 1550 B.C. suggest that it antedated the Aryan invasions. Nor is it implied by the Jain or Buddhist scriptures that the founders of these two religions discovered a new way of sitting when they meditated. On the contrary, when they went off into the forest to practice asceticism, they conformed to a traditional pattern. But the expression of the Jain idols is quite different from that of the Buddha images. The surpassing mildness and compassion that the Buddhist artists tried to capture is usually lacking. Instead the look is rather fierce, and the jeweled eyes, often quite lacking in humanity, suggest a faith in magic and the supernatural.

We shall draw our conclusions about Hindu and Jain art in the section on Buddhist art so that we can compare all three.

Buddhism

113

I use the word "idol" in a nonpejorative sense, as Indians use it. But while no Jewish or Islamic censure is intended, there is the problem that the founders of Jainism and Buddhism both suggested that man could expect no help whatsoever from the gods or from prayer and that he must rely entirely on his own efforts. Hence the worship of images poses a problem for the student of Jainism and Buddhism.

Fortunately, we know something about the development of Buddhist sculpture. Not only was there none before Alexander's invasion of India, but for several centuries after that a prohibition against all representations of the Buddha was observed. We can reconstruct what happened, stage by stage.

First, there seems to have been a prohibition against all sculpture and painting, quite as uncompromising as anything in the Bible. Then purely decorative work was allowed, but nothing having the form of any living creature. Then representations of corpses and skulls were permitted. Later also of human beings, "save for the figures of men and women coupling, all else you may paint." In a moment we shall return to this curious remark, attributed to the Buddha himself. Still later even bodhisattvas could be represented, but not the Buddha; and finally, last of all, the Buddha himself. This development took centuries and accompanied and symbolized the gradual transformation of Buddhism in India. I do not believe that it has ever before been summarized succinctly, and in the 1920s even the leading experts on the subject did not know some of this.

It is a striking fact that at the great stupa of Sanchi, roughly 400 miles south of Delhi, which was built by Ashoka in the third century B.C., enlarged to its present size in the second century, and surrounded with gates and profuse carvings through the first century A.D., representations of the historical Buddha are still scrupulously avoided. In early Buddhist art the Buddha is symbolized, for example, by a stupa or a tree with an empty place under it, and when the great departure is depicted—the Buddha leaving his palace to become an ascetic—the horse and chariot are depicted very ably, and there is an empty place in the chariot. A footprint or the wheel of the law may symbolize the 102 Buddha, but in early Buddhist art he himself does not appear.

The rationale behind all this can be reconstructed from texts quoted by Soper in an article on "Early Buddhist Attitudes Toward the Art of Painting" (1950). He found relevant passages in Chinese translations made in A.D. 404, A.D. 416, and A.D. 710 of Indian Buddhist scriptures that do not survive in the original. While the Chinese scrupulously dated their translations, there was and is no way of dating the originals.

Pagan: Gothic with later Buddha image. (*See* 368.)

The first stage is represented by the story of a nun who was scolded by the elders: "You nuns claim to have attained spiritual merit, and then you go to look at a building with paintings in it, just like a pagan woman." And then the Buddha himself said: "Henceforth I lay on you this commandment. If a nun go to look at a building with paintings in it, it is a sin that will cause her to fall into Purgatory." There is no reason to believe that the Buddha himself did say this or ever spoke of Purgatory, but the story probably goes back to a time when an influential segment of the Buddhist community still considered it sinful to as much as look at paintings, not to speak of covering their own cave temples with them as they later did at Ajanta. (All comments are mine. Soper confined his "comment on the texts to a minimum.")

The following stages are reflected in a dialogue between an elder and the Buddha. The elder pays homage to the Buddha and says: "Lord of the World, since the Lord has gone forth among men to convert them, I have ever longed to see the Buddha. I pray now that the Lord will give me some small object that I may worship." The Buddha gave him hairs and nail parings to worship, and the elder then asked for permission to raise a stupa over them. The Buddha said: "It is granted." Then the elder requested permission to paint the stupa in red, black, and white; and then to make paintings on it. At that point the Buddha says: "Save for the figures of men and women coupling, all else you may paint."

This text was translated in 404, six hundred years before such scenes were carved in Khajuraho and Bhubaneshwar, and eight hundred years before the Black Pagoda was built at Konarak. Yet modern writers have wondered what sorts of sects may have sprung up in the Middle Ages to explain these carvings. Although our story is surely apocryphal, it still makes clear that paintings of that sort were common in India at one time, and since the nun in our first story is said to have visited a "pagan" temple and was scolded for looking at its paintings, it seems safe to assume that such paintings decorated the temples of the indigenous pre-Buddhist and pre-Hindu population.

The dialogue between the elder and the Buddha continued, and the elder said: "Lord of the World, since it is not permitted to make a likeness of the Buddha's body, I pray that the Buddha will grant that I make likenesses of his attendant Bodhisattvas." And he got permission. In the 1920s, Coomaraswamy, a leading authority in the field, still denied that there had ever been such a prohibition.

In a text translated in 416, a shrine is described that was decorated with reliefs, open-work carving, and paintings, and we are told expressly: "There were no figures of coupled men and women, but instead such subjects as the figures of aged monks, grape-vines, *makara* sea-monsters, geese, corpses, and landscape scenes." There is also an interesting story, placed in the period after the Buddha's death. A councilor requests a king to protect a stupa from lawless men by covering it over with gold and silver. "Thus any who may strip away the gold and silver will leave the *stupa* itself intact." And the king followed this advice. The rationalization seems amusing, but what is fascinating is that in early times it was felt that some excuse of this sort was required for the otherwise unseemly luxury that had crept into Buddhist art.

Finally, a text translated in 710 relates that the Buddha said: "You cannot make drawings that have the form of living creatures without falling into the sin of transgression against the Law. If you draw corpses or skulls, however, there is no offense." In another story an elder is said to have been told by the Buddha to place yakshas holding maces on the two sides of a gate.

Yakshas were, in Zimmer's words, "local tutelary deities, who are the lusty guardians of the treasures of the earth" (35); and Zimmer also remarks that they, "no less than nagas, must have been very popular in the pre-Aryan tradition . . . Dwelling in the hills and mountains, they are the guardians of the precious metals, stones, and jewels in the womb of the earth, and so are bestowers of riches and prosperity. Two yakshas commonly are represented standing at either side of doors . . . " (44). Surely, the Buddha never authorized the construction of gates, flanked by deities that were bestowers of riches and prosperity. Much less did he endorse what was done at Sanchi, where Buddhist art consummated its first major triumph.

The gigantic stupa there is a simple solid hemisphere, with an ornament on top. A brick stupa was built during the reign of Ashoka but later it was made into a huge stone stupa and surrounded with a stone railing and four splendidly carved gates, adorned with elephants and with all kinds of elaborate reliefs, and flanked—not all of them but some—with luscious yakshis (female yakshas) who wear nothing but a belt. They are young and beautiful, the breasts are bulging, and the vulva is incised. One recalls the Buddha's admonition to Ananda to avoid the sight of women.

Two prohibitions are still observed at Sanchi. The Buddha himself is not represented, and—as in most Buddhist art except for that of Tantrism—there are no scenes of sexual intercourse. At Ajanta, too, the thrones are empty in the early Theravada caves, but in the later Mahayana caves we find many splendid Buddha images that for the most part succeed in conveying something of the spirit of his teaching.

The earliest Buddha images were made in Gandhara in what are now Pakistan and Afghanistan, where Alexander had been, and they are exceedingly Hellenistic in style and sometimes have a Roman look. The features usually bear the imprint of the region, and the symbolism is Buddhist—the ushnishi and the third eye between the eyes—but initially there is little promise of what was to develop later. The robe is treated with Greek finesse, the head is backed by a halo, and sometimes the Buddha has a thin moustache, but for the most part this art looks derivative and lacks any distinctive spirit. The sculptures that show the future Buddha as an utterly emaciated ascetic are the most unusual. On the whole one has the feeling that Buddhism has gone the way of "all the nations," to use a Biblical phrase.

In art we can see plainly how older cults and local traditions overwhelmed Buddhism and, we may add, Jainism and Hinduism, too. The indigenous population, conquered by the Aryans, triumphed after all. Most of the great gods of the Vedas were defeated along with the recondite mysticism of the Upanishads, as the ancient yakshis and yakshas emerged together with nagas, Nandi, and Shiva. Of course, it was not as if the Hindu and Buddhist and Jain scriptures had never been written. In Buddhist art, for example, everything was always dominated by the Buddha, whether his place was left empty, or whether he himself was represented in the center.

Before we leave India to move on to Ceylon and the East, let us consider the paradigmatic case of the nagas. They were ancient indigenous snake spirits or deities with many different associations. In one old seal of the Indus valley civilization, two serpents flank a figure seated in what may be a lotus posture. In time Hinduism, Jainism, and Buddhism absorbed the naga. There are many Hindu carvings that show a deity, often Vishnu, sitting under the multiple hood of a seven-headed cobra. This motif achieved its consummation in the Naga Buddhas, notably including splendid examples in Angkor and Thailand.

The Buddha sits on the coils of the cobra, and the cobra protects him from the weather, which he is too absorbed to notice. A myth tells the story. But here our
33 comparative perspective allows us to pick up another theme. Consider Darius the Great at Persepolis. The carving on the ancient pillar, done during the Buddha's lifetime, shows an attendant holding an umbrella over Darius. This could be rationalized as the Naga Buddha usually is by saying that the intent is to shield the king of kings from sun or rain. But consider the poem "Great God!" in "The Third Face of India" where a maharaja is followed by an umbrella—it neither rained nor was the sun particularly

Sanchi.

Sanchi.

Sanchi.

bright—and the crowd hailed him *Mahadé!* "Great god!" The umbrella is a symbol of royalty.

In this perspective, the Naga Buddha is a singularly apt symbol. The Buddha, as we saw in section 81 in chapter XI, turned down Mara's offer of sovereignty "over the four continents and their two thousand attending isles," being "about to make the ten thousand worlds thunder with my becoming a Buddha." To symbolize *his* sovereignty, an umbrella would have been peculiarly unfitting, but to have him sit, to cite the next poem, "The Cobra," "in the shadow of seven-hooded death" suggests his cosmic triumph. He is no longer daunted by the fear of old age, sickness, and death.

The umbrella, in a highly stylized form, was also used as an ornament on some stupas; for example, at Sanchi on Stupa number 3, while on the Great Stupa there is an ornament that consists of three umbrellas, the one on top being smallest, the one in the middle larger, and the disk at the bottom largest. While these early stupas have the shape of a hemisphere, and those at Sarnath and Shewaki (Afghanistan) are still extremely simple, the triple umbrella foreshadows the pagodas of the Far East, Bali, and Nepal. It does not follow that this is the origin of the pagoda. There are no ancient, pre-Buddhist buildings in China—nothing before the sixth century. But we do have pottery models of houses and watch towers that were found in tombs dating from the Han dynasty (206 B.C.–A.D. 220). Some of these are little pagodas with several stories and show that this style was used in China before the advent of Buddhism.

In Hinduism the naga turns up in many guises, none more ubiquitous than the cobra coiled around the arm of Shiva as he claps the rhythm of his cosmic dance of destruction and creation. There are also images of Vishnu under the hood of a naga, and much more rarely Ganesh and Parvati are represented that way. Parshva, the twenty-third Tirthankara of the Jains, is frequently shown under a naga hood. In sum, the art of these religions shows us vividly how older cults came back and the worship of the people did not change as much under the new religions as one might have thought. Yet at its best the art of the Hindus and the Buddhists used the ancient symbols of the native cults to express something sublime.

114

Against this background, we can be quite brief about the development of Buddhist art in other countries. Four of our pictures from *Ceylon* require a brief comment. At Sigiriya a huge monolithic rock rises out of the plain to a height of 600 feet, and part of the way up there is a gallery in the sheer face of the rock with enchanting fifth-century Buddhist paintings of twenty-one extremely attractive young women in transparent blouses. The quality of the paintings is similar to that of the Ajanta frescoes but even better, and although it has been claimed that originally there were five hundred figures, those that remain are better preserved, and one can see them in daylight. The question of whether there is anything distinctively Buddhist about these beautiful frescoes answers itself. They are more nearly anti-Buddhist—if one is thinking of the Buddha's teaching.

At Gal Vihara, near Polonnaruwa, a reclining Buddha, about 50 feet long, was carved out of the rock in the twelfth century. He has just died and entered nirvana. Near his head stands Ananda, more than 20 feet tall. There are also two great seated Buddhas nearby, both as simple and impressive as they are large. Here one does have some sense of the Buddha's teaching.

A picture of a small reclining Buddha, with a huge footprint in front of it, illustrates the popular religion of Ceylon. The footprint is an ancient symbol of the Buddha,

106

107

108

109

110

111

112

113

115

116

117

119

120

121

1

124

125

126

130

131

132

135

136

139

140

141

142

143

145

146

147

148

150

151

152

154

155

156

157

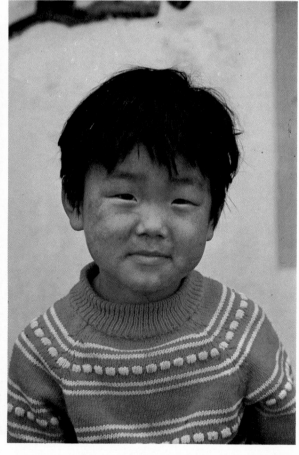

159

160

161

162

163

already in use when the prohibition against Buddha images was still observed. Here worshipers have thrown flowers and coins into the footprint. The drummer, in another 103 picture, stands in the temple in Kandy where "the Buddha's tooth" is kept.

The stupa at *Borobodur* in central Java, not far from Prambanan, is the largest Buddhist structure in the world. It was built in the eighth century, and pictures of the Mahayana reliefs that gird it, terrace after terrace, as one ascends the cosmic temple mountain that rises steeply from a square base, would fill many books. What is most imposing, however, is the sense of freedom that one gains as one reaches the last three terraces at the top, which are circular and filled with bellshaped stupas. Our two pic- 142 tures show the Buddha in the teaching pose (*dharmashakra mudra*), on the highest 144 terrace. One illustration may convey some sense of the place, with a volcano in the background; the other is a close-up of the Buddha. By the end of 1974 this lovely statue had fallen victim to the multimillion-dollar restoration of Borobodur.

The Buddhism of *Nepal* is very different and, not only geographically, much 105–120 closer to Tibet and to Tantrism. Here it is often difficult to tell what is Buddhist and what is Hindu, and the Buddha himself is rarely represented. It is interesting but hardly ever noticed—if it has been noted at all—how clearly art can show us what has happened in religion. As long as one says that the Buddhism of this part of the world seems remote from the Buddha's teaching or that the historic Buddha seems to have been all but forgotten, one expresses an opinion that may be suspect. But the art of the region shows it very plainly. The Buddha's place has been taken by all sorts of deities, many of them female with very full bare breasts, like Prajnaparamita, Vasudhara, and most often Tara; and a "Nativity of the Buddha" shows a small Buddha figure standing next to a tall woman with bare breasts, her arms raised to strike a very erotic pose (Kramrisch, plate 11, ninth century. Cf. also Waldschmidt). Even bronzes showing *mithuna* (sexual intercourse) were made in Nepal as well as Tibet. Many of these works have great beauty—and a style that clearly belongs to this region. One would rarely be in doubt as to whether a bronze is Nepalese or Indian; one may often be unsure whether it is Nepalese or Tibetan. This is also true of the mandalas that are an important part of Buddhist art in Nepal and Tibet. The pagodas point to China rather than India. Again, the visual evidence is striking. Surely, these pagodas have very little to do with the early Buddhist stupas and even less with the earlier Buddhist scriptures. Yet the Buddha was born in what is now Nepal.

Actually, the Nepalese style seems to have developed during the final flowering of Buddhist art in India, in the eighth and ninth centuries in Bengal and Bihar, near the Nepalese border. Some bronzes made in Kurkihar and a few other places in this region, and some stone images of slightly later date, evidently inspired the development of Nepalese and then also Tibetan art.

The greatest site of Burmese art is Pagan, which defies any brief discussion, in passing. In an area of approximately sixteen square miles, one can still see the remains of literally thousands of temples and pagodas built in the eleventh to thirteenth centuries—many of them magnificent.

The Shwe Dagon pagoda in Rangoon rises to a height of more than 360 feet and is shaped rather like an inverted cone, but is concave part of the way up so that it almost seems to pierce the heavens. The mood is not remotely like that of a stupa but invites comparison with the lofty single spires of some Gothic cathedrals, such as those of Freiburg and Ulm. The Shwe Dagon certainly has the heaven-storming quality that some people associate with the Gothic, but there the similarity ends. Once one sees

Sign, Sanur, Bali. / Sigirya, Ceylon.

Great stupa, Anuradhapura, Ceylon.

how this pagoda is not at all close to the spirit of early Buddhism, one may find it easier to admit that the Gothic is not close to the spirit of early Christianity.

The great sanctity of the pagoda rests on the fact that it is said to contain relics not only of the Buddha but also of the three Buddhas preceding him. It is situated on a mound that is almost 170 feet high and divided by two rectangular terraces that face east, north, west, and south, as is the rule in pagodas. The upper terrace, which is beautifully paved, measures 900 by 685 feet. Then one ascends still further, barefoot, to the platform from which the pagoda itself rises. Its circumference at the bottom is over 1,300 feet. It is solid and said to contain 25 tons of gold and 100 tons of silver—and it is completely covered with gold. Pilgrims and other worshipers, poor as well as rich, keep buying gold leaf for it.

122   The Buddha images surrounding the base defy counting. By cleaning an image one can accumulate merit, and some people keep pouring water over the same image
107 again and again, as mechanically or in some cases devoutly as pilgrims walk around stupas in Nepal, turning one prayer wheel after another.

The Burmese image of the standing Buddha shown here was carved of wood in the
123 eighteenth century. Most of the gold has worn off, though small patches remain and most of the inlaid glass is intact. The Buddha stands on a lotus, and his posture is frequently encountered in Burma. The expression, on the other hand, is most unusual and may bring to mind St. Francis of Assisi. Yet there is no ardor in this image, no ecstasy, but—as in all the finest images of the Buddha—his distinctive spirit.

The statue of the earth goddess wringing out her hair was also carved of wood in
121 the eighteenth century. This motif is rare, although bronzes of Buddha calling the earth to witness are not at all uncommon. One tradition has it that so much water came out of the hair of the goddess that the cohorts of Mara fled. What is most unusual in this sculpture is once again the sensitivity of the modeling of the face. Few Burmese sculptures have such gentle expressions.

115

Thailand has produced a rich store of images in stucco, terracotta, bronze, and stone. Many Westerners see only Bangkok and are enchanted by its beautiful temples. But these temples were built in the nineteenth century, which was not notable for its taste in architecture anywhere, and their cheerful gaudiness, which is admittedly very successful in its own way, gives one no idea of the wealth of the country's art.

The periods of art in Thailand are named after sites, but the finest sculptures are now to be found in museums and private collections. Visits to the medieval sites are worthwhile, of course, because some of the ruins are remarkable and still convey some sense of the places, but relatively little of the sculpture remains to be seen *in situ*.

The first great period was Dvaravati. Even those interested in the art of Thailand generally underestimate it. It produced faces of extraordinary expressiveness and sometimes a touch of the grotesque—mostly in stucco, sometimes in terracotta, and rarely in bronze—as early as the seventh and eighth centuries. The style continued into the eleventh century, when the Khmer conquered Dvaravati, and there are also pieces done
125 in stone and even in gold. The example shown here is a head of Buddha, with half-closed eyes, done in stucco, probably in the seventh century. The eyebrows are joined over the bridge of the nose, which is a characteristic of this style. Strictly speaking, this is not Thai art, as the Thais conquered the country later, and to give credit to the people who created this style, it is sometimes called Mon Dvaravati.

The great originality of these heads should be recognized along with their influence

Gigantic reclining Buddha, Ayudhaya, Thailand.

on Khmer art. But those who do not care for expressionism or a touch of humor in religious art can hardly be expected to admire most of the heads done in this style. All the later sculpture of Thailand bears the mark of profound influence from outside, first from Java, then, beginning in the eleventh century, of Khmer art—not to speak of India.

The ruins of Lopburi look like reduced and less vigorous versions of Angkor, and so do many Lopburi sculptures. But the best of them, though similar to Khmer work of the same period, are very fine.

During the twelfth century the so-called U Tong style developed. Again much of the work in this style immediately brings to mind Angkor and was actually made by
129 Khmer artists. The bronze head of the Buddha that we show is of this type and was made early in the twelfth century when this style first emerged. The treatment of the hair is typical of U Tong pieces, and the ushnishi is topped by a small stylized flame. In some later pieces this flame became much larger.

We also show an U Tong bronze of a seated Buddha, subduing Mara and calling
127 the earth to witness. The story has been discussed in chapter XI. The green patina is interrupted by traces of old gold. The smile somehow suffuses the whole figure. The artist has caught the gist of the ancient story, stripping it of all the repetitiousness that marks even the early Buddhist scriptures, and distilled the essential experience in a small bronze, nine inches high.

The next major style that evolved in Thailand was the Sukhodaya style. The Chiengsen style is a variant found in northern Thailand. Both were created by Thai artists, though influenced by Indian Buddha images of the Gupta period. The Buddhas of these styles, and the Ayudhaya style that succeeded them, became decidedly effeminate. Many people especially admire the type of the walking Buddha, portrayed earlier in reliefs in India and Burma and in paintings in Ceylon, but first done in the round in Thailand. The right arm hangs down in a strangely curved way, and everything is elongated, including the flame on the head and especially the fingers.
130 The solid-gold Buddha in Wat Trimitr in Bangkok belongs to the beginnings of Sukhodaya in the thirteenth century. Hundreds of years ago, it was covered with plaster to protect it against Burmese invaders, and eventually it was forgotten that it was made of solid gold. In the 1950s it was decided to move it to Bangkok to a temple that wished to install a Buddha image of that size. Since it weighed eight tons, it fell, the plaster cracked, and the gold was discovered. Despite the irony implicit in a solid-gold Buddha, the image is by no means devoid of artistic merit.

The more famous reclining Buddha in Wat Po in Bangkok, which measures about 150 feet in length, is covered with gilt lacquer over stucco and masonry, and the soles of his feet are inlaid with mother-of-pearl. It was made in the nineteenth century and
131 is an example of the Bangkok style. So is Wat Arun, the Temple of the Dawn, which stands close to the river. An illustration may give some impression of its riches. It is a great tourist attraction, as is the so-called emerald Buddha, which is actually made of a large piece of green jade, that is enshrined in another temple in Bangkok and wears various costumes, depending on the season.

Angkor has already been discussed, first near the beginning of chapter XII and then in the context of Hindu art. We can be brief about it now. The greatest single
136 monument of Buddhist art at Angkor, if not in the world, is the Bayon, an immense temple built by Jayavarman VII, who ruled from 1181 to 1220. Most of our pictures of
134 Khmer art date from his reign. The head of Buddha, with wide-open, almond-shaped eyes that do not smile, is a little older. It seems to have been a Naga Buddha, but the naga is broken off or was cut away.

Apsara, Angkor, 12th century.

Vishnu, Khmer, 12th century. Bronze.

The elongated earlobes of the Buddha are a striking feature of his images. Often, as in this case, he also wears earrings. The usual explanation is that the heavy earrings he wore as a young prince distended his earlobes. If that should seem fanciful, consider the picture of a woman in southern India, on the ferry from the temple of Vivekananda 67 back to Cape Comorin. It shows that heavy earrings can really have this effect.

We show an overall view of the Bayon as well as a partial view. All the many towers have four faces, representing the king as a bodhisattva. These faces have given the Bayon 137 style its name. The idea of the four faces at right angles to each other is surely influenced by earlier Hindu representations of Brahma. Ta Som and Prah Khan show more or less how Angkor looked when the French found it. Here they did only enough restoration to prevent collapse.

The sandstone head of Buddha that looks similar to a head of Brahma of the same 138 period has already been mentioned. Both are fine examples of the Bayon style. So is a 80 little bronze of Avalokiteshvara in a typical Khmer kilt. The ears suggest a Buddha, but 140 the Buddha himself is never represented with more than two arms, and the small seated Buddha on the headdress also serves to identify Avalokiteshvara. In his two right hands he holds a rosary and a lotus bud, in his two left hands a scroll and a flacon. It seems interesting that a slightly smaller bronze of Vishnu in the same collection, reproduced in black-and-white, holds the same symbols in his three surviving hands. Hinduism and Buddhism both flourished at Angkor as they had done earlier at Ellora.

The Bayon period represents the last great burst of creativity at Angkor. Much of the work of this period is no longer as fine and done with as much care for detail as the bronzes and carvings of the preceding period. Most of the bronzes have—by the highest standards—crude faces, and the bodies, too, are not often done with as exquisite a sense of balance as this Avalokiteshvara. The face is most unusual, and the patina with so much blue as well as green in it is also found in comparatively few pieces. In sum, the Khmer people did not produce masterpieces only, and many of their bronze and stone images have rather stiff and lifeless faces, often with small moustaches, the eyebrows firmly joined, and the expression, if any, very smug. The female bodies, usually nude above the waist, are almost always beautiful, though as a rule one is much like another, and the heads are not by any means always impressive. There are striking differences in quality. Still, the best Khmer pieces remain unsurpassed.

116

Having dealt at great length with the transformation of Buddhism in China, we shall not even try to explore Chinese Buddhist art. In line with the old adage *ex Oriente lux*, it is widely assumed that Chinese art is much older than it is in fact. Andrew Boyd set the record straight in 1962:

> When the ziggurats were being built in Mesopotamia and the drainage systems laid out at Mohenjodaro, China like Europe was deep in the stone age. Bronze, which was in use before 3000 B.C., appears in China about 1600 B.C., that is actually later than it appears in Britain. Iron, which began to be effectively used in the Mediterranean area about 1100 B.C., developed in China from the fifth to the third centuries B.C.—about the same time as in Britain.
>
> There are not even many old buildings remaining in China as in Europe . . . —no building of the age of the Parthenon or of the Pantheon, practically none of the age of San Vitale or Santa Sophia, few even of the age of Salisbury Cathedral. The Great Wall itself is lost beneath successive rebuildings.
>
> What there has been however is, straight from the brilliant flowering of the bronze age in about 1500 B.C. right up to the present, a completely continuous, individual and self-conscious civilisation of an extremely high level . . . (5).

One point about Chinese Buddhist art has already been mentioned in the account of Mahayana Buddhism in Chapter XI, when Avalokiteshvara was first introduced. In China he was transformed into Kuanyin, and then in Japan into Kannon. He first lost his definitely male character and then gradually became a goddess. When religions that have no great female deity spread into countries that would like to have one, the converts manage to have their way—as they did in Europe.

Another point can also be made very briefly and is no less paradigmatic. The Chinese created the image of the laughing pot-bellied Buddha that is found in most Chinese Buddhist temples (see Ch'en, 1964, 405–408). A greater contrast to the emaciated Gandhara ascetic is scarcely imaginable. But the difference between this image and the subtle serenity of the finest Buddhas of India and Ceylon, and then the gentle smile of the Bayon Buddhas, is also overpowering. The laughing Buddhas of China show what some of the Zen masters said in so many words: We could not care less what the Buddha himself was like or what he taught.

China's influence on the Buddhism of Korea and Japan was incalculable. While the Chinese occasionally went to India to find more scriptures and translated a vast amount of the literature of Indian Buddhism, the Japanese got their Buddhism from Korea and China.

Those intent upon disparaging the originality of the Japanese have sometimes stressed the magnitude of *Korea's influence on Japanese art*. That Buddhism came to Japan from Korea is an undisputed fact, and Japanese temples generally look very much like Korean temples. Nor is there any question of the high quality of Korean ceramics. What one sees of Korean painting in the National Museum in Seoul seems quite derivative and on the whole inferior to Chinese painting. But to come to our central concern here, "It is not easy to do justice to Korean Buddhist art, especially its sculpture, because the Chinese prototypes upon which it was directly modelled, and which served it as a guide, are all as good as lost; thus it is hard to estimate the extent to which the Korean works were imitations or original products." Dietrich Seckel (93) goes on to name and reproduce one famous Korean bodhisattva of the early seventh century which he considers specifically Korean, and this gilded bronze figure is strikingly similar to a Japanese bodhisattva of the seventh century which is made of wood and is one of the innumerable glories of Horyu-ji at Nara. (It is reproduced, for example, in Shoten, vol. 1, 34.)

There does not seem to be another case of such clear Korean influence on Japanese religious sculpture, but even this case is odd because the Nara sculpture is at least as fine and as expressive as the one in the Duksoo Palace Museum in Seoul. This is so palpable that the catalogue *Masterpieces of Korean Art: an exhibition under the auspices of the Government of the Republic of Korea*, published jointly by the National Gallery of Art in Washington and seven other American museums, said in its comments (58) on the Korean figure that the Nara statue "is so close in style and feeling as to seem a product of the same workshop in spite of the difference in medium." This would seem to be a way of saying that it is in no way inferior. The way the wood is handled to make the grain add to the effect of the figure is almost incredible. Finally, the Korean bodhisattva (the catalogue called it a Maitreya, but there is some question about that) is probably the finest example of Buddhist sculpture in Korea. The Nara bodhisattva, on the other hand, is one of a whole galaxy of great religious sculptures.

In sum, it was only in architecture that Japanese Buddhist art remained under the influence of Korea. The Japanese temples were an imitation of Korean temples, as is 162 apparent in Seoul as well as at the far older Pulkuksa temple in Kyongju, built in the 163 eighth century. But even at Kyongju the wooden structures date from the seventeenth century. Moreover, restoration is an almost continual process. But although the temples 163 we see in Korea are not nearly as old as those at Nara in Japan, it is assumed that the Koreans built in this style before the Japanese did. The question remains how much these temples were influenced by Chinese prototypes.

117

Japanese art has already been discussed briefly in chapter XII, at the beginning of section 97. Photographs of India have to be in color to give any half-way adequate idea of the country and its art and people; Japan comes across beautifully even in good photographs in black and white, and the Japanese have published many books with marvelous pictures. Hence it seemed best to concentrate on countries that have not been documented quite so well, and to discuss Japanese Buddhist art at length without pictures would not make very much sense. We shall therefore be extremely brief.

The beginning of Buddhist art in Japan is marked by a very sharp break with pre-Buddhist art. This is not the result merely of the advent of Buddhism, for Buddhism arrived together with Korean and Chinese culture. In any case, the Haniwa art of the preceding period is utterly different from the work done beginning in the seventh century and then during the Nara period (710–793). As early as the sixth century, "Japan had begun to send envoys and Buddhist monks directly to China to study Buddhist culture there," and early Buddhist art in Japan would seem to owe at least as much to direct Chinese influence as to Korean influence. (Shoten, vol. 1, 23. Vol. 1 extends through the Nara period and contains 168 superb illustrations.) The best Buddhist sculptures made in Japan during the seventh and eighth centuries are among the finest pieces of religious art anywhere, and their number is extremely large.

Europeans and Americans who would disparage this art as unoriginal or imitative ought to ask themselves whether, judged by the same standards, any medieval or Renaissance art in Europe or any American art whatever, except for pre-Columbian art, could escape the same stricture. This is not to deny Korean and Chinese influence any more than it would make sense to dispute Greek and Roman influence on medieval and Renaissance art.

The question of whether the sculptures of this period are distinctively Buddhist can readily be answered in the affirmative. Virtually all the major pieces represent the Buddha, bodhisattvas, or related subjects and succeed to an astonishing degree in conveying the states of mind—or rather the states of being—that might be held to distinguish Buddhas and bodhisattvas. It would serve little purpose to catalogue examples by referring either to the museums in Nara, Kyoto, and Tokyo or to books in which many of these pieces are illustrated, as anyone visiting these museums or looking at such books will be overwhelmed by a multitude of fine examples. But there may be some point in commenting briefly on two splendid pieces and one recurrent type that seem to furnish outstanding exceptions to the rule.

The first piece is not really an exception when one considers the whole of it. In clay, it depicts the Buddha, who has just died—the Buddha's Nirvana or Parinirvana—and he is surrounded by his disciples. The portrayal of extreme grief in some of these disciples, who evidently have not absorbed his teaching at all, is overwhelming. The work dates from 711, and there is nothing in Europe up to that time that one could compare with these figures. But one may ask whether they could not have been done even if Buddhism had not come to Japan. Perhaps they could have been, but the work as a whole depends on the contrast between these disciples and others who have achieved serenity. The triumph of the latter, expressed in some faces with extraordinary

Temple guard, Kyoto. Wood.

subtlety, is heightened by the contrast. It would be difficult to conceive of a sculpture that is more thoroughly Buddhist (Shoten, 69 f.).

A seventh-century Lady Maya (the mother of the Buddha) has a grace and verve that are almost unbelievable in a bronze but perhaps do not show any specifically Buddhist influence (Shoten, # 36 and 85). If so, it is one of the few masterpieces that do not.

That still leaves the recurrent motif of the fierce guardian. We show one of the very first examples, a clay Nio of 711, one of a pair of figures that guard the main inner gate at Horyu-ji in Nara. Not all these larger-than-life-size male figures, with expressions that are clearly meant to terrify all who look at them, are guardians, and there is even a god, Fudo, who is often represented with a frightening expression of this sort. One explanation that comes to mind is suggested by a picture of a figure of this kind in the Nara museum, with a Buddha behind it. But any attempt to deal with this type as we have dealt with the grief-stricken disciples would be strained and, on reflection, really implausible. Here are figures that the Japanese might well have fashioned even if they had not embraced Buddhism, but they found a place for them in their expanded Buddhist mythology. Their interest in such wrath and fury is familiar to people in the West from Japanese films, beginning with *Rashomon*. 172 173

What makes these magnificently angry faces so impressive is in part a profound psychological understanding that was probably nurtured by Buddhism. The fierceness was pre-Buddhist, but the keen interest in different states of mind may owe something to Buddhism. That this interest extended to a wide range of expressions is attested by an art that was developed in unique ways in Japan, the art of making masks. Balinese masks are grotesque and beautiful but altogether different. What the Japanese did with masks is distinctive. We show a Noh mask of the eighteenth century, made of wood and not lacquered as such masks usually are. It is an "Uba" mask, used by the heroine of the play *Takasago*. She is the spirit of a pine tree and symbolizes longevity and conjugal fidelity. But the surpassing interest of this mask derives from its expressiveness, and to give an adequate idea of that one has to show how the expression changes as the mask is moved. 150f.,161 168–171

Another art that was cultivated in Japan as nowhere else is that of the garden. The inspiration came from China, but the Japanese consummated this art, creating gardens unlike any seen in the rest of the world. The great gardens that are considered specifically Buddhist sanctuaries include Kinkakuji, with its Golden Pavillion Temple; Gingakuji, with the Silver Pavillion Temple; Saihoji, the great moss garden; and Ryoanji, the most celebrated rock garden—all in Kyoto. All are superb, and there are countless others as well, but the amazingly simple and small rock gardens created by Zen Buddhism are most obviously different from what are thought of as gardens elsewhere. 164,166

A picture of the path leading up to the great Shinto shrine at Nara, Kasuga, may give at least some idea of Shinto. The stone lanterns with Japanese calligraphy and two deer suggest something of the Shinto feeling for nature. 165

Daisetz Suzuki, the great apostle of Zen to the West, who was a very impressive person, would say sometimes that the Japanese, with their deep feeling for nature, quite lacked the *aggressiveness* of Europeans and Americans, who always wish to dominate, and those charmed by Zen and "the Orient" often seem to believe something like this. Intellectual fashions change fast. During World War II many Westerners thought of the Japanese as scarcely human, while the Chinese were loved dearly. After World War II, the Japanese, who had been considered aggressive brutality incarnate only a few years earlier, were suddenly thought to possess the secret of peace, while for a while the Chinese were considered devils. I have argued that precisely Zen was used centuries ago to transform Buddhism and make it compatible with a warlike ethos. But

once again art shows us vividly and clearly what scholarly prose can only try to establish
173 by slow arguments that run the risk of seeming doubtful. The photograph of the larger-
than-life-size wrathful figure with the serene Buddha behind it shows at a glance what a
more extensive study of Japanese art would bear out. There is something fiercely aggressive in the Japanese, but the sense of harmony and peace also runs deep. As long as one
sees only one or the other, one does not understand Japan.

The aggressiveness turns up in film after film and play upon play. We show a
picture of a geisha play, performed before a packed house in a huge theater. The bru-
174 tality of the man toward the woman finally drove her to hang herself. (The person in
black, with his back to the audience, is not supposed to be noticed but frequently turns
around and quickly helps the actors change their costumes.)

It also took aggressiveness for Japan to make her spectacular economic recovery
after the crushing defeat of 1945. The same determination and relentless will that, far
from living totally at peace with nature, uses strong wires to make pines grow in con-
formity with man's designs was at work in using the best Western methods to compete
successfully with Western countries in the markets of the world. In the course of this
process, Japan is changing once again as she changed after the advent of Buddhism.
Even in the short span between two visits to Japan in 1963 and 1971, the physical type
of the people changed. In 1963 most of the people were still extremely small by Western
standards, with most of the women five feet tall at most, and the men a little bigger.
With a change in their diet, that is no longer true. Kimonos have long become a rare
sight in the streets; the clothes are Western.

Tokyo, engulfed by smog and pollution, sometimes seems like a nightmarish vision
of the coming century. Not long ago, Mt. Fuji, covered with snow, but fiery inside, was
the symbol of Japan. Now one can rarely see it for the smog. Since beautiful photographs of it are so easily available, it may not be too neat a point to suggest that soon
176 we shall be able to see it only in old woodcuts, like the one by the great Hiroshige that
we show here, with a wormhole, from a book published during his lifetime, in 1848.

We began with sunrise as seen from Mt. Sinai. In some ways Israel and Japan, at
the two far ends of the great continent, are the least Asiatic countries in Asia. But our
Odyssey has not been purely geographical, from west to east. If Mt. Sinai symbolizes the
beginnings of our civilization, Japan is a harbinger of the future. And since our concern
throughout has been with human beings, it would not do to conclude with a woodcut
that shows three views of Mt. Fuji.

The final color photograph of Asia shows a Tokyo street. An older woman, dressed
178 in a kimono, passes mini-skirted mannequins with platinum-blonde hair and Western
features. That is a common sight, and we could add pictures of male mannequins with
crewcuts who wear kimonos. The advertising in the subways also suggests that the way
to look is Western, and the lesson is not lost on millions of young people who undergo
Westernizing eye operations and dye their hair. Old ways of life are vanishing, a little
faster in Japan than elsewhere, but there is a very real possibility that soon most people
everywhere will wear the same clothes and expect the same things from life. Our
pictures have for the most part shown what seems timeless—the same today as centuries ago. One may wonder whether what looks eternal will soon survive only in
pictures.

118

180   It may seem that Tokyo is unrepresentative. Then look at a picture of San Cristobal de las Casas in Chiapas in Mexico. The scene is essentially the same. The Indians
around San Cristobal de las Casas still have their own distinctive way of life, and this

little town is another world, far more different from Mexico City than Mexico City is from Madrid or any number of other large Western cities. But as one contemplates the picture of the mannequins, one wonders how much longer that can be. How long can these Indians hold out?

Having begun with sunrise on Mt. Sinai, I do not want to end with an image of mannequins. Our focus has been on humanity, especially the poor. The last color picture shows a Chamula woman at the market in San Cristobal—an Indian Hecuba. In *The Trojan Women* Euripides brings to life for us the queen who survives the destruction of her people and civilization and retains her dignity. But we also have another association with Hecuba. Shakespeare's Hamlet says: "What's Hecuba to him?" Who are the Chamulas? What is their religion?*

1–3

183

Their gods include old Indian tutelary deities that reside in the mountains, as well as Jesus Christ and various saints, the sun, the moon, the Earth Lord (a composite of a Faustian devil, a rich non-Indian, a serpent, and a thunderbolt), a variety of demons, and the cross. Christ, who died on the cross, is also the incarnate sun and the creator of the world. And the cross is not only the tree on which Christ died but also the threshold to the houses of the tutelary gods.

Chamulan folktales stress the sinfulness of Adam's and Eve's affair, while the Zinacantecs, the other major tribe that comes to market in San Cristobal de las Casas, ignore this and stress the theft of the Lord's apples. The Indians learned from Christian friars that polygamy was evil; otherwise their mores do not seem to have been influenced much by Christian teaching. They do make the sign of the cross and kiss rosaries; they also spray cane liquor at the foot of candles and sacrifice chickens.

It is easy to imagine a Christian saying that the Chamulas clearly are not Christians, the more so because the precept "Love your neighbor as yourself" is clearly not Chamulan. But then one wonders how many Christians *are* Christians, and how many Buddhists *are* Buddhists. We are not used to the Chamulan blend, and hence it seems exotic to us; but in this book we have seen that something very similar has happened as other religions spread far beyond the countries of their origin, and even to Hinduism in India.

Looking at the image of this Chamula woman, one surely does not feel like passing judgment on her for what she believes, or for her unbelief. It would make more sense to be appalled by the thought that her grandchildren may wear mini-skirts and have platinum-blonde hair. Meanwhile she sits there and has a beauty that well-groomed people almost never have. Why is it that the men and women in these pictures look incomparably more expressive than most of our fellow citizens? At first, one may think this proves that their feelings run deeper and that Western men and women have become shallow. If there is some truth in that, it is plainly not the whole story, for in an occasional unshaven drunk or beggar one can find the same sort of expressiveness, while one rarely finds it in Western poets, artists, and individuals of whom one knows that they feel deeply. We have learned to hide our feelings, to control them, and to look, as best we can, like everybody else.

There is no escaping the prospect that soon most people will look very much alike. Old age, sickness, and death will be hidden away more and more, and the humanity to which this book is an epic declaration of love will be gone.

It has often been suggested that Christianity discovered the meaningfulness of suffering. We have found reasons for doubting that Christianity had any great appreci-

---

* For what follows I am indebted to a written communication from Robert Laughlin, who knows more about the Chamulas than anyone else, and in places I quote him verbatim.

ation of that during most of its history. It has also often been suggested that the great religions that came out of India failed to appreciate the value of suffering, and it is true that Buddhism was ever so much less intent than Christianity on making people suffer. It is also true that the Indian religions concerned themselves to a considerable extent with the attainment of a state of being in which one is immune to suffering. But the ancient ascetics generated *tapas* (heat, and hence enormous power) through austerities that did involve suffering, and the bodhisattvas chose to be stretched out on the rack of life again and again to help others. In the Second Isaiah and in Judaism we find still other conceptions of meaningful suffering. But let us recall the words spoken near the end of *The Trojan Women* by Hecuba:

> Had not the gods' hand
> seized and crushed this city into the ground,
> we might have faded into darkness without giving
> a theme for music and the songs of those to come.

Now the gods, too, have died, leaving us songs and music. There are those who try officiously to keep the gods alive in a state of suspended animation; but they do neither them nor us a favor. A century ago some people thought that once the gods were dead all would be well. We know better.

CODA

So much unsaid!
I have not shown
the distant birth
of gods now dead.

Nor did I chart
the skies;
their throne
I found on earth;
their soul, in art.

From flesh and stone
they probe our worth
with human eyes.

165

166

167

168

169

170

171

172

173

174

175

176

177

178

179

180

181

182

18

EPILOGUE:
LANDSCAPE AND RELIGION

Sinai desert, near El Arish.

Of what landscape could one possibly say that it is in any way related to Hinduism? Or Buddhism? Or Confucianism? At most one might wonder whether Hinduism is the blending of a great many different cults, each of which might have owed something to a certain kind of scenery. At that point guesswork would take over. Does Buddhism owe something to the mountains of Nepal where the Buddha was born, or the plain of the Ganges where he preached, or to the totally different landscape of Ceylon where it survived after it died out in India? Does the landscape of China or Japan have anything to do with it? None of this makes sense. But there are cases in which some relation to a landscape does seem to be indicated, notably monotheism, Taoism, and Balinese Hinduism.

I have argued in this book that monotheism bears some relation to the desert, and that the mosque is a stylized oasis (at the beginning of section 105). Against this it can be argued that Islam imported monotheism before exporting it to many countries in which there are no great deserts. One might still ask why Islam imported rigorous monotheism rather than Trinitarianism or some form of polytheism, or a form of Zoroastrianism or Manichaeism involving belief in two gods. While the Bedouins did not originate monothesism, they may have felt an elective affinity for it; they may have found that it accorded well with their own experience of the austerely sublime.

An agricultural society depends on many powers and therefore often has different gods and goddesses for sun, rain, and storm, and above all fertility cults that often involve death and resurrection. A richly varied landscape may also favor nymphs and satyrs and spirits of woods and waterfalls. In the desert the one god, once proclaimed, does not meet with such distracting competition. Of course, if one remembers foreign cults that one encountered long before entering the desert, one might still be tempted to worship a golden calf, but the real competition would begin only as one entered the promised land and there found a settled agricultural society with Baalim and Ashtarot.

The doctrine of the one god that became so important for Judaism, Christianity, and Islam is associated with Moses, and we have to ask whether his association with the desert was pure coincidence, or whether there is a profound connection. It does not seem possible to resolve this question by scholarship. Hence it seems best to state the case in an admittedly impressionistic way by presenting a few poems. All of them were written before I had ever seen Mt. Sinai, though not before I had been in the desert.

Not all scholars agree about which mountain in the desert of Sinai is the historic Mt. Sinai. A few favor Mt. Serbal, which is 6,712 feet high and about 20 miles west-northwest of the peak we know today as Mt. Sinai, which is 7,363 feet in height. In one 8 of our pictures Mt. Serbal is the highest mountain in the background. Most scholars favor Mt. Sinai. It was at the foot of this mountain that the emperor Justinian built St. Catherine's monastery, at an elevation of 5,014 feet, but today the fortress walls contain an odd assortment of buildings of which by no means are all 1,400 years old. 7 Although there would be space enough for a vast cemetery, the bones of the monks buried here have been dug up and stored in the boneroom. The skulls are lined up on shelves along the wall. On the peak of Mt. Sinai there are two small chapels, one Muslim, one Christian.

Few people have ever seen a picture of Mt. Sinai, and it is quite unlikely that anyone who has never been there and never seen any pictures of it would imagine it as it is. Probably some people, on seeing a picture of the Sassolungo in the Dolomites, in the 14 Alps, would say that Mt. Sinai might well look like that. Few indeed realize that in winter Mt. Sinai is a white mountain. And who would expect such scenery as one finds near "Elijah's Well," below the summit, at a height of 6,900 feet? One cannot see the 4f. peak from St. Catherine's, but from a place close to "Elijah's Well" one can see the monastery. It could have been at such a place that Moses, seeing the people dance 6 around the golden calf, smashed the tables of the law. But the case for associating Moses with scenery of this kind does not rest upon such thoughts—and some would say, such fancies.

The poem on Moses represents an attempt to show how the desert was the fitting scenery for Moses. On climbing the mountain in the dark, approaching the summit in the dawn, and seeing the sunrise from the peak, the poem rang true to me, and it still 1–3 seems to go well with the pictures.

The First Book of Kings, Chapter 19, relates that Elijah went back to Mt. Sinai (the Bible sometimes calls it Horeb) for *his* theophany. The story could be true; it could have come down to us by way of Elijah's disciple Elisha. Again, it is wholly in character. The scenery around "Elijah's Well" goes beautifully with the portrait of the prophet in the Bible.

Nobody else in the Hebrew Bible is placed in this august company, but the Gospel according to Mark relates crisply in two sentences that after his baptism Jesus went into the desert for forty days and was tempted by Satan. The story is familiar not only from Matthew and Luke who elaborated on it (John omits it), but also from the parable of the Grand Inquisitor in Dostoevsky's *Brothers Karamazov*. The third poem here retells this story, as the second retells the story found in Kings. Both stories are usually misremembered. It is widely believed that First Kings says—as it does not—that God was in the still small voice, as if the ending were lyrical. Actually, the revelation to Elijah was quite lacking in bucolic bliss and more in keeping with the scenery of Sinai. What Elijah was told is usually repressed—as is the fact that Jesus in the Gospels did not finally refuse Satan's offers.

Elijah is a titan of one piece, and it seems wholly appropriate for him, after killing the priests of Baal, to go back to Moses' desert setting. The Jesus of the four Gospels is not of one piece but a highly ambiguous figure to whom a multitude of sayings, stories, and myths has been attributed, and the temptation story probably owes something to the legends about the Buddha's temptation by Mara. The temptation right after the calling and the refusal of the offer of empire are both found in Buddhism, and the refusal to perform miracles makes little sense when attributed to Jesus, but was an important point about the Buddha. The desert does not go particularly well with the Jesus of the Gospels, but it is not difficult to explain how it got into the story. John the Baptist was held by many, we are told, to be Elijah who had returned; he was associated with the desert and with a quotation about the desert from the Second Isaiah, and he baptized Jesus in the Jordan, at the edge of the desert. Hence, if one wanted to place Jesus in the succession of Moses and Elijah, one would have him, too, go into the desert for forty days and nights—but not the desert of Sinai. Jesus' ministry is associated with the Sea of Galilee and the surrounding towns; his passion, with Jerusalem. But 9 that is not to say that his God was all sweetness and light. The last poem pictures "God" as a "Desert-born God."*

---

* The four poems are from my *Cain and Other Poems*, 3rd enlarged edition, New York, New American Library, 1975, and reprinted here with the publisher's permission.

Moses

Not valleys, lakes, and gentle hills—
a man of mountains: when he sees
his brother scourged, he burns, and kills
the wielder of the whip, and flees

into a land of sand and rock
where courage counts, not faith or hope,
becomes a shepherd, leads his flock
up on a savage mountain slope,

and in a wilderness of stone
finds strength that feeds upon what burns,
and grows, and kindles flames. Alone,
he leaves his exile and returns

to light a fire that no scourge
consumes, a blaze whips only fan,
leads hence his people, and to purge
the dross and make the slave a man,

he drives his wretched herd into
the desert to behold what he
had seen—people who never knew
mountains, lightning, or liberty.

Days without water, hungry weeks:
what he had lit was soon consumed.
He learned the patience of the peaks,
and dying branches he relumed.

There was no trail, the climb was steep,
no man had thrilled to what he saw—
and on a flock of bleating sheep
a lonely man imposed a law,

moulding the mountain's thunderous voice
into a monumental word,
and challenged them to make a choice
that humanized a servile herd.

Where only crags stood out from sand
and life was will and not delight,
he taught them till in any land
their souls would seek the unreached height.

When only two of those he led
from slavery survived, and all
the others had been born and bred
under the challenge of his call—

triumphant past imaginings,
he blessed them, and soared out of sight,
sailing on undiminished wings,
and died, an eagle in his flight.

Elijah
I

"Years of unbroken skies and sands,
the era of the boneless crowds
that have antennae but no hands,
that live in dust and know no clouds,

were finished in one flash when I
taunted their hollow faith and feasts,
brought down white fire from the sky,
and slew four hundred fifty priests.

The land is green again, the drought
faded into a boastful tale,
no idol left, but though they shout
to God again their hearts mean Baal.

The desert I inherited:
for forty nights I walked till I
saw where a sky of burning lead
is broken by Mount Sinai;

for forty days, sand, wind, and sun,
no human voice, no human face,
and then this cleft—perhaps the one
where Moses hid from unseen grace.

But he lived in a man-sized age,
broke granite tablets, and prevailed;
mine is the day of priest and sage
and paltriness, and I have failed.

I, only I am left; and yet
I have not come here to despair:
I seek the voice of Moses; let
the jaundiced Jezebel beware!"

II

A tempest struck the crags and tore
black boulders from the rocky spires,
an earthquake split the mountain's core,
releasing serpent-bodied fires—

to man-sized men, winged seraphim
attending God's own blazing voice—
mere fire, quake, and wind to him,
nothing of God. He veiled his face

when silence fell like night, and found
his call inside his mind, at first
a whisper almost lacking sound;
but then it grew, and when it burst

like lightning from his darkness he
saw Hazael and Jehu whom
he must anoint: who bent a knee
to Baal their ruthless wars consume;

his mantle falls; Elisha slays
Baal's minions who escaped the sword;
Elijah rides—he could not raise
his people—lonely to the Lord.

Jesus' Temptation

He, too, like Moses and Elijah, dwelt
for forty days in desert solitude;
yet God did not appear to him: he felt
the presence of the devil's voice that said,

"Behold these stones: speak and they shall be bread!"
replied, "Man does not live by bread alone"—
but soon turned water into wine.

He saw himself stand on a pinnacle:
"Cast yourself down," the devil seemed to prod,
"angels will save you." To the voice from hell
Jesus replied, "You shall not tempt your God"—
but soon vied with Elisha's feats and awed
a crowd by raising Jairus' dead daughter,
withered a tree, and walked on water.

The devil promised Jesus world-wide fame
and glory that no pharaoh or king
or prophet ever equalled: yea, his name
would be like God's, and men would worship him,
if he would bow to Satan's stratagem.
He answered, "Worship none except the Lord"—
but Satan's promise was fulfilled.

Desert-Born God

Desert-born god,
sandstorm-cradled:
thine is burning,
blistering justice,
fiery darkness
that blinds and destroys.

Language, lead me not
windlike to praise him:
rhythms, swallow not
sight and memory,
lest I yield to him,
singing in darkness!

Memory, strike
through worshipful night:
rise like the sea wind,
purging the air!

Trees that are kissing
sand-whirling ground,
loving the storm that
snaps their trunks:
I shall not bow to
merciless glory.

Silvery circle,
sun rests in the storm,
the sound of the wind
is like heavy wine:
music, seduce me not
lest I forget!

Let not beauty
bury the past:
memory, marry
the flesh of god's glory!

Thine is the desert
in which you are buried,
thine is the darkness
that was your mother,
thine is the power
whose death I sing.

These poems certainly do not establish the case for a causal relationship between the desert and monotheism. What they do show is more in the nature of what is peculiarly fitting or appropriate, akin to what people sometimes call "poetic justice." This is all that can be shown, and it may be just as well to show it by using poems.

120

It would be easy to make out a similar case for the relationship of Taoism to some Chinese landscapes. One would begin with Chinese paintings, preferably of the Sung dynasty, that show strong Taoist influence—landscapes with mountains and mist and very tiny people who are easy to overlook. They are readily contrasted with Renaissance portraits by Leonardo, for example, in which the human head is large and the landscape a mere background, perhaps even with tiny mountains. Here is a wonderful juxtaposition of the spirit of the Italian Renaissance and Sung dynasty Taoism. But here the artist's world view shapes the landscape, and there is no doubt at all that this often happens. Whether the landscape shaped the world view is quite another question. Taking the affirmative, one would produce pictures of landscapes that really look like Taoist paintings, and it is one of the joys of travel in the Far East that one actually finds them. But one does not find them only in China. That one finds mountains behind mountains, behind mountains in the mist in Japan, too, is no crushing argument against the notion that Taoism owed something to the scenery of China, for Japan is nearby, Shintoism is in some ways similar to Taoism, and the Buddhism of Japan had absorbed Taoism before the Japanese embraced it as thoroughly congenial. But we find landscapes that might have produced Taoism in parts of Europe and America that never produced anything remotely like it. Instead of arguing that point, it seems better to substantiate 12–16 it with a few pictures. 117

In sum, monotheism goes well with the desert of Sinai, and Taoism goes well with certain Chinese landscapes. But somewhat similar deserts elsewhere produced no Moses, and "Chinese" landscapes in other parts of the world produced no Lao-tze. What is really hard to understand is that landscapes like those in the Dolomites and 12–14 other parts of the Alps should not have produced any great religion at all. There are times when an unbeliever, on suddenly beholding a sublime mountain landscape, feels such overpowering reverence that he thinks: Here if anywhere is the place for genuine religious awe.

The United States has produced the Church of Latter-day Saints and the Church of Christ, Scientist, which are offshoots of Christianity, and Japan is generating many new religions in our time, which are offshoots of Buddhism and Shintoism. But exceedingly few places have produced major religions that were novel and had influence beyond the place where they were born. Israel produced two, Iran one, Arabia one, northern India four, China two that were slow to become religions, and Japan one. It was surely not the landscapes of these regions that favored them above all others. But religions obviously influence our perception of nature.

This has been shown to some extent in the chapters on the arts. Judaism, with its preference for the word over the image, also extolled man over nature. Christianity tended to see nature and sex as evil, and European artists discovered nature only during and after the Renaissance. Landscape painting flourished only after the Church had lost its power, and in Islam, Hinduism, Jainism, and Buddhism it never had a place. Confucianism was too anthropocentric. Taoism is the great exception, along with Shintoism.

In the Christian West it never occurred to anybody before the Renaissance to climb a mountain for the beauty of it. But what is far stranger is that in the West no painter before Pieter Brueghel in the late sixteenth century placed human beings in nature instead of merely treating landscapes as backgrounds behind portraits, as Leonardo had still done. And it was only in Rembrandt's time that Western painters began to paint landscapes, pure and simple, without people. (Dürer had done watercolors of pure landscapes.) It took Copernicus to shatter the conceit that man was the center of the universe, and Brueghel seems to have looked askance at both Catholicism and Protestantism. It may also be relevant that by that time Dutch trade had reached the Far East. Certainly, some of Rembrandt's drawings suggest a Far Eastern influence. But for a long time after Rembrandt, Westerners still refused to see themselves as tiny specks in nature. What they saw was influenced by their beliefs.

The focus of this book is humanistic, and its pages are dominated by human beings and their sculptures and temples. One or two of the pictures of Bali are an exception, and the discussion of Bali in the context of Hindu art suggests that this beautiful island is one of the few places where a landscape has contributed very powerfully to the transformation of a religion. These concluding pages of the book and the pictures that go 1–3 with them, early in this volume, are meant to suggest a larger perspective. It was not for nothing that we began with sunrise as seen from Mount Sinai.

Olympic Peninsula, U.S.

ACKNOWLEDGMENTS

My debt to the people whose pictures appear in this book is shared by all who look at them. I hope that my feelings for these men, women, and children of the Third World will also be widely shared. None of them are white, none black, and living with their images might be some help in learning not to think in black and white, but in color.

My understanding of Judaism—and of religion—owes a great deal to Leo Baeck, Martin Buber, and Julius Seligsohn. Julius Seligsohn was a member of the small committee that represented German Jewry in its darkest hours. He returned to Germany from the United States in January 1939 as I was emigrating to the United States, and our ships passed in the night. It was not the first time he had returned from missions abroad, and he died helping others to the limits of his ability. It was in his home that I first experienced Jewish festivals. He was my mother's brother, had a delightful sense of humor, and was usually full of fun even in the grimmest of circumstances. We were very close to one another, and I have never known anyone whom I admire more.

I also feel grateful to Rabbi Rudolf Seligsohn for teaching me Hebrew, the Bible, and Jewish history, and to Ismar Elbogen whose books on Jewish history made a great impression on me. At Williams College I was exceedingly fortunate in being able to study comparative religion, as well as the psychology of religion, with James Bissett Pratt. His courses were the most valuable I ever took in college or in graduate school; he opened up for me *The Sacred Books of the East* and other texts; and he made me write thirteen long papers. Along with my teachers I should include the undergraduate and graduate students at Princeton and a few other universities who studied the philosophy of religion with me, beginning in 1948. Many have become eminent professors, but almost all of them in other fields. Religion has fallen on evil days.

Many people have given me invaluable advice and help in connection with my travels. I hope that I may be forgiven for naming only a few to whom my debt is especially great: Gillett Griffin, Marius Jansen, Jeanette Mirsky, Herbert Passin, and Khushwant Singh helped before I left home, and my wife and I also stayed with Khushwant and Kaval Singh in Delhi in 1970 and again in 1975. Of those who helped in Asia, I shall single out only Dr. Chamseddine Mofidi (Teheran), Professor Ali Shariatmadari (Isfahan), Ambassador Robert Newman (Kabul), the whole Aboody family in Bombay, Abbot and Mrs. Sohaku Ogata, with whom we stayed twice at the Shokokuji Temple (Zen) in Kyoto, in 1963 and in 1971, Professor Yoshinoro Takeuchi (Kyoto), Professor and Mrs. Hideo Mineshima (Tokyo), and Mr. Shigeharu Matsumoto and his wonderfully competent and friendly staff at the International House in Tokyo, where we also had the great pleasure of staying twice.

Seeing Pagan in 1975 with U Win Thein, who has loved and explored the stupas and temples since he was a schoolboy, was an unforgettable experience. A few months later, Pagan was devastated by an earthquake.

This book owes a great deal to some of my friends; notably Moshe Barasch, S. D. Goitein, Peter Lighte, Richard and Lanier Marius, and Ravi Ravindra. Professor Ravindra and I have been discussing Indian thought for years, and our conversations have helped me immensely. Stella Kramrisch very kindly responded to my queries about the identification of some art objects. The friendly competence of Elizabeth Boyd and Coleman Carson of the camera department at the Princeton University Store seems to know no bounds. Michael Kaufmann gave me valuable advice about photographing objects of art. And Alan Spiro assisted me daily during the crucial months of June and July, 1974, when the text was completed.

It was while I had a Fulbright research professorship at Heidelberg that I joined an academics' tour to Egypt that took us as far as Assuan, and another Fulbright professorship gave me a year of teaching at the Hebrew University in Jerusalem. A Ford

Foundation grant allowed me to return from Jerusalem by way of India, Burma, Thailand, Cambodia, Hong Kong, Taiwan, and Japan. In connection with subsequent trips to Israel I am particularly grateful to the department of philosophy at the Hebrew University and to the Jerusalem Van Leer Foundation. But the institution to which I am most beholden is Princeton University, for many reasons but above all for its generosity in granting me crucial leaves of absence. A sabbatical leave in 1974–1975 allowed me among other things to revisit Bali and Java, Thailand and Burma, India and Israel, and to check a great many things before going once more over the copy-edited manuscript.

My greatest gratitude is reserved for those to whom I have dedicated this book, and by no means confined to the reasons spelled out in the dedication.

A NOTE ON THE TRANSLATIONS

When quoting scriptures, I have generally made my own translations after comparing many scholarly versions, not only in English. Even where my versions try to capture some of the poetry of the originals, they aim to be very faithful. The "Rhinoceros Sutra" in one of the very earliest Buddhist scriptures is a case in point. Lord Chalmers published the original text of the whole *Sutta-Nipata* in scholarly transliteration, with his own translation on facing right pages, but instead of concluding each of the four-line stanzas with the refrain "Wander alone like a rhinoceros," which is the most striking feature of the original, Lord Chalmers expurgated the rhino and began most stanzas with the word "Alone!" He was a Pali scholar and I am not; yet my version is more faithful as well as, I hope, more poetic.

Most scholarly versions of the Gathas of Zarathustra are almost unreadably stiff. In a book in which part of the purpose of quoting the Gathas is to allow a comparison with the Second Isaiah, it obviously would not do to use some such version as this one:

> I who would serve you, O Mazda Ahura and Good Thought—do ye give
> through the Right the blessings of both worlds, the bodily and that of Thought,
> which set the faithful in felicity.

If it should seem presumptuous for me to offer my own versions, it should be clear why I considered it necessary.

The differences in style between different scriptures should be apparent, but nobody should think, even for a moment, that these differences include the use of "thou" and other archaisms in some but not in others. Hence it seemed essential to make some stylistic changes even when I used older translations, and it would have been pedantic and distracting to indicate such changes at every turn. It seems vastly preferable to make a plenary confession at this point.

What I aimed at was a certain uniformity of the stylistic level that would allow the genuine differences to emerge more clearly. This ruled out some very scholarly translations that are punctuated by distracting parentheses, also apologetical versions in which the translator more or less openly reads his own ideas into the texts. Although this exegetical approach may be prompted by reverence, and interpreters of this type feel that the scriptures deserve the benefit of their own most deeply cherished convictions, I find readings of this sort not reverent enough.

Unless we expose ourselves to what is really distinctive in the texts, to what we did not believe or feel before we read them, we are wasting our time. Most readers are like American travelers who stay at a Hilton Hotel wherever they go, with all the comforts of home. One wonders why they bother to go so far abroad.

The Bibliography indicates whether the translations are mine; see, for example, Buddha, *Rigveda, Upanishads,* Zarathustra.

A NOTE ON TRANSLITERATION

In the handling of names and terms from languages quite different from our own, consistency is out of the question. To write Mosheh, Yirmiyahu, and Yeshuah, instead of Moses, Jeremiah, and Jesus, would confuse most readers, but when one writes about post-Biblical figures with the very same names it is often customary to approximate the pronunciation of the Hebrew names. Another example is furnished by the name of Muhammad. Whatever transliteration you choose, you are bound to introduce different renderings of his name when you quote other authors who have written about him. Again, important terms sometimes turn up in different spellings in different quotations. There is nothing you can do about that unless you either tamper with quotations or go out of your way not to quote anyone whose spelling differs from your own, which would be silly.

I have dispensed with diacritical marks that are designed for the benefit of scholars who know Arabic or Sanskrit, for example, but often mislead other readers. Specialists will never be in doubt as to whom or what I am writing about, and nonspecialists will be helped more by my attempt to approximate the correct pronunciation. Thus I write "Shudra" and not, as is sometimes done, "Sudra." But even here consistency is not feasible. I prefer "Shiva" to "Siva," which is simply misleading, but if I went all the way and made it "Sheeva," which would be phonetically right, readers might wonder whom I meant. Again the "sh" sound in Bhubaneshwar poses no problem, but "Shrirangam" might stump those seeking further information in a reference work or gazeteer; hence I had to settle for Srirangam. Similarly, "Shri Aurobindo" would be correct phonetically, but that is not what one finds on the title pages of his books, and another compromise was called for.

Hebrew and Arabic have sounds close to the *ch* in the German word *Rauch*; English does not. Hence I have generally used an *h* to render these sounds, as is customary. "Muhammad" is a case in point. In Sanskrit, vowels are pronounced as in German or Italian but usually short, and scholars employ special marks to indicate length. The final *a* of many Sanskrit words is almost mute. As noted in the text, Brahma, the four-faced god, is one of the exceptions: the final *a* in his name is long like the vowel sound in "balm," while the first *a* is short like the vowel in "run."

In quotations from other writers I have taken the liberty of dispensing with their diacritical marks and herewith implore their forgiveness. When they quote scriptures, as when using other translations of scriptures, I have sometimes made bold to make minor stylistic changes, mostly to eliminate "thou" and archaic verb forms. The reasons for this unorthodox procedure are spelled out in the note on translation.

BIBLIOGRAPHY

Andrae, Tor. *Mohammed, The Man and His Faith*. Translated from the German by Theophil Menzel. New York, Scribner's Sons, 1936. Harper Torchbooks, 1960.

Aurobindo Ghose. *The Upanishads: Texts, Translations and Commentaries*. Pondicherry, Sri Aurobindo Ashram, 1972.

Baeck, Leo. "The Son of Man," "The Gospel as a Document of the History of the Jewish Faith," "The Faith of Paul," "Romantic Religion" in *Judaism and Christianity*, transl. with an introduction by Walter Kaufmann. Philadelphia, Jewish Publication Society of America, 1958; New York, Harper Torchbooks, 1966; New York, Atheneum Temple Books, 1970.

Barasch, Moshe. *Crusader Figural Sculpture in the Holy Land: Twelfth Century Examples from Acre, Nazareth and Belvoir Castle*. Ramat Gan, Massada Press Ltd., 1971.

Barker, Ernest. "Crusades" in *Encyclopaedia Britannica*, 11th edition.

Basham, A. L. *The Wonder That Was India: A Survey of the Culture of the Indian Subcontinent before the Coming of the Muslims*. New York, Macmillan Co., 1954; Grove Press, Evergreen edition, 1959.

Bentzen, Aage. *Introduction to the Old Testament.* 2 vols. Copenhagen, G.E.C. GAD, 1952.

Bettenson, Henry Scowcroft, ed. *Documents of the Christian Church.* London, Oxford University Press, 1943. Galaxy edition, 1947.

Bhagavad-Gītā. The translations are my own, but I have compared many versions and am indebted to the translations and commentaries listed below.

———. *The Blessed Lord's Song. Srimad-Bhagavad-Gita.* Translated by Swami Paramananda in *The Wisdom of China and India,* Lin Yutang, ed. New York, The Modern Library, 1942.

———. *Bhagavad-Gītā As It Is, Complete Edition, With Original Sanskrit Text, Roman Transliteration, English Equivalents, Translation and Elaborate Purports.* By His Divine Grace A. C. Bhaktivedanta Swami Prabhupāda, Founder—Ācārya of the International Society for Krishna Consciousness. New York, Collier Books, 1972. London, Collier-Macmillan, Ltd., 1972.

———. *A New Translation and Commentary with Sanskrit Text, Chapters 1–6,* by Maharishi Mahesh Yogi. International SRM Publications, 1967. Harmondsworth, Baltimore, Victoria, Penguin, 1971.

———. Translated by R. C. Zaehner. J. M. Dent and Sons Ltd., 1966. London, Oxford, New York, Oxford University Press, 1969. Paperback edition, 1973.

Bharati, Agehananda. *The Tantric Tradition.* Rider and Co., 1965. Garden City, New York, Anchor Books, 1970.

Bible. Translations in the text are based on the Hebrew and Greek originals; but I have consulted many versions, notably including the Revised Standard Version and N. H. Tur-Sinai's German version of the Hebrew Bible and Martin Luther's of the New Testament.

Billerbeck, Paul, and Strack, Herman L. *Kommentar zum neuen Testament aus Talmud und Midrasch.* 4 vols. München, C. H. Beck, 1922–28. 2nd ed., unchanged but with Rabbinical Index vol., 1954–56.

Bouquet, A. C. *Sacred Books of the World.* Harmondsworth, Middlesex, Pelican Books, 1954, 1955.

Bowie, Theodore, ed., Diskul, M. C. Subhadradis; Griswold, A. B. *The Sculpture of Thailand.* Catalogue of an exhibition shown in the Asia House Gallery, Fall, 1972. New York, The Asia Society, 1972. An Asia House Gallery Publication.

Bownas, G. "Shinto" in R. C. Zaehner, 1967.

Boyd, Andrew. *Chinese Architecture and Town Planning.* The University of Chicago Press, 1962.

Breasted, James Henry. *The Dawn of Conscience.* New York, London, Charles Scribner's Sons, 1933.

Brundage, James A. *The Crusades: A Documentary Survey.* Milwaukee, the Marquette University Press, 1962.

Buber, Martin. *Das Kommende, Untersuchungen zur Entstehungsgeschichte des messianischen Glaubens.* Vol. I *Königtum Gottes.* Berlin, Schocken Verlag, 1936.

———. *Die Erzählungen der Chassidim.* Zürich, Manesse Verlag, Conzett & Huber, 1949.

Buddha. The greatest collection of English translations is to be found in *The Sacred Books of the East.* The translations from the *Dhammapada* are Max Müller's from the SBE. The two long selections from the *Sutta-Nipata* are offered in my own version, made after a close comparison of the SBE version with Lord Chalmer's, listed below, and Karl Eugen Neumann's German version.

———. *Buddha's Teachings, Being the Sutta-Nipata or Discourse-Collection.* Transl. by Lord Robert Chalmers, edited in the original Pali text with an English version facing it. Volume 37 in *Harvard Oriental Series.* Ed. with the cooperation of various scholars by Charles Rockwell Lanman. Cambridge, Harvard University Press, 1932.

———. *Buddhism in Translations.* Henry Clarke Warren. Volume 3 in *Harvard Oriental Series.* Ed. with the cooperation of various scholars by Charles Rockwell Lanman. Cambridge, Harvard University Press, 1896. Eighth Issue, 1922.

Bussagli, Mario, and Sivaramamurti, Calembus. *5000 Years of the Art of India.* New York, Harry N. Abrams, Inc., n.d.

Cambridge Medieval History, The. Vol. VI. Eds. J. R. Tanner, C. W. Previté-Orton, Z. N. Brooke. New York, Macmillan Co.; Cambridge, Cambridge University Press, 1929.

Carrà, Massimo. *Italian Sculpture from Prehistory to the Etruscans.* Transl. from the Italian by Timothy Paterson. Milan, Fratelli Fabri Editori, 1966. London, New York, Sydney,

Toronto, The Hamlyn Publishing Group Ltd., 1970.

Chalmers, Lord. See Buddha.

Ch'en, Kenneth Kuan Shêng. *Buddhism in China: A Historical Survey.* Princeton, Princeton University Press, 1964.

——. *Buddhism, The Light of Asia.* Woodbury, New York, Barron's Educational Series, Inc., 1968. Usually cited simply as "Ch'en."

——. *The Chinese Transformation of Buddhism.* Princeton, Princeton University Press, 1973.

Chuang-tze. After comparing several versions, I have followed the translations in Fung Yu-lan.

Confucius. The translations are from vol. I of Fung Yu-lan. I have also consulted many other translations.

Conze, Edward. *Buddhism: Its Essence and Development.* New York, Philosophical Library, 1951. Harper Torchbooks, 1959.

Coomaraswamy, Ananda K. *History of Indian and Indonesian Art.* Karl W. Hiersemann, 1927. New York, Dover, 1965.

Coulton, G. G. *Five Centuries of Religion.* Vol. I. Cambridge, Cambridge University Press, 1923.

——. *Inquisition and Liberty.* William Heinemann Ltd., 1938. Boston, Beacon Press, 1959.

Davies, J. G. *The Early Christian Church.* New York, Chicago, San Francisco, Holt, Rinehart and Winston, 1965.

Davies, W. D. *Paul and Rabbinic Judaism: Some Rabbinic Elements in Pauline Theology.* London, S.P.C.K., 1948. 2nd ed., 1955.

——. *The Setting of the Sermon on the Mount.* Cambridge, Cambridge University Press, 1964.

Desai, Mahadev. *The Gospel of Selfless Action or the Gita According to Gandhi.* Ahmedabad, Navajivan Publishing House, 1946.

Deussen, Paul. *Das System des Vedanta nach den Brahma-Sutras des Badarayana und dem Kommentare des Cankara über dieselben als ein Kompendium der Dogmatik des Brahmanismus vom Standpunkte des Cankara aus.* 2nd ed. Leipzig, Brockhaus, 1906. *The System of the Vedanta.* Chicago, Open Court Publishing Co., 1912. New York, Dover, 1973.

Draper, Theodore. "The Road to Geneva," in *Commentary,* Vol. 57, No. 2, February 1974.

Du Ry, Carel J. *Art of Islam.* Transl. from the Dutch by Alexis Brown. New York, Harry N. Abrams, Inc., n.d.

Dutt, Nripendra Kumar. *Origin and Growth of Caste in India.* Calcutta, Firma K. L. Mukhopadhyay, 1968. 2nd edition.

Edwardes, Michael. *Great Buildings of the World: Indian Temples and Palaces.* London, New York, Sydney, Toronto, The Hamlyn Publishing Group Ltd., 1969.

Elbogen, Ismar. *Geschichte der Juden seit dem Untergang des jüdischen Staates.* Leipzig and Berlin, B. G. Teubner, 1920. Transl. by Abraham Shinedling, *History of the Jews after the Fall of the Jewish State.* Cincinnati, Union of American Hebrew Congregations, 1926.

Encyclopaedia Judaica. See "Jerusalem."

Enslin, Morton Scott. *Christian Beginnings.* New York, Harper, 1938.

Ettinghausen, Richard. "The Character of Islamic Art," in *The Arab Heritage,* Nabih Amin Faris, ed. Princeton, Princeton University Press, 1944. New York, Russell and Russell, Inc., 1963.

Farah, Caesar E. *Islam, Beliefs and Observances.* Woodbury, New York, Barron's Educational Series, Inc., 1968, 1970.

Finegan, Jack. *Archeology of World Religions. The Background of Primitivism, Zoroastrianism, Hinduism, Jainism, Buddhism, Confucianism, Taoism, Shinto, Islam, and Sikhism.* Princeton, Princeton University Press, 1952, 1966.

——. *The Archeology of the New Testament: The Life of Jesus and the Beginning of the Early Church.* Princeton, Princeton University Press, 1969.

——. *Light from the Ancient Past, the Archeological Background of Judaism and Christianity.* Princeton, Princeton University Press, 1946. 2nd edition, 1959.

Finkelstein, Louis. *Akiba: Scholar, Saint and Martyr.* New York, Covici Friede, 1936.

Fischer, Louis. *The Life of Mahatma Gandhi*. New York, Harper & Brothers, 1950. Collier Books edition, 1962.

Freud, Sigmund. *Gesammelte Werke*, 18 vols. London, Imago Publishing Co., Ltd., 1946–1968.

Frye, Richard N. *The Heritage of Persia*. Cleveland and New York, The World Publishing Company, 1963.

Fung Yu-lan. *A History of Chinese Philosophy*. Transl. by Derk Bodde. 2 vols. Peiping, H. Vetch, 1937. Princeton, Princeton University Press, 1952–1953. All references are to vol. I.

Gandhi, Mahatma. *My Non-violence*. Ahmedabad, Navajivan Publishing House, 1960.

———. *Selected Writings of Mahatma Gandhi*, ed. Ronald Duncan. London, Faber & Faber, 1951.

———. *Speeches and Writings of Mahatma Gandhi*. Madras, G. A. Natesan & Co., 4th ed., 1933.

———. Articles in *Young India*, quoted in *The Wit and Wisdom of Gandhi*, ed. Homer A. Jack. Boston, Beacon Press, 1951.

———. See also Fischer and Parulekar.

Geertz, Clifford. *Islam Observed: Religious Development in Morocco and Indonesia*. New Haven, Yale University Press, 1968. Chicago and London, University of Chicago Press, 1971.

Ghirshman, Roman. *The Arts of Ancient Iran from its Origins to the Time of Alexander the Great*. Transl. from the French by Stuart Gilbert and James Emmons. In the series *The Arts of Mankind*, edited by André Malraux and Georges Salles. Paris, Editions Gallimard, New York, Golden Press, 1964.

Gibb, H. A. R. "Islam" in R. C. Zaehner, ed., *The Concise Encyclopedia of Living Faiths*. New York, Hawthorn Books, Inc., 1959. Boston, Beacon Press, 1967, pp. 178–208.

———. *Mohammedanism: An Historical Survey*. London, Oxford University Press, 1949. New York, Mentor Books, 1955, 159 pp.

Giteau, Madeleine. *Khmer Sculpture and the Angkor Civilization*. Transl. from the French by Diana Imber. New York, Harry N. Abrams, n.d.

Glasenapp, Helmuth von. *Die Philosophie der Inder, Eine Einführung in ihre Geschichte und ihre Lehren*. Stuttgart, Ernst Klett, 1949.

Goitein, S. D. "Jerusalem" in *Encyclopedia of Islam*. 2nd ed.

———. *Jews and Arabs: Their Contacts through the Ages*. New York, Schocken Books, Inc., 1955, 1972.

Grabar, Oleg. *The Formation of Islamic Art*. New Haven and London, Yale University Press, 1973.

Griffith, Ralph T. H., transl. *Hymns of the Rigveda*. 2 vols. Varanasi, India, The Chowkhamba Sanskrit Series Office, 1963.

Hamilton, R. W. *The Structural History of the Aqsa Mosque. A Record of Archaeological Gleanings from the Repairs of 1938–1942*. London, Oxford University Press, 1949.

Harper's Bible Dictionary. See Miller.

Herford, R. Travers. *Judaism in the New Testament Period*. London, The Lindsey Press, 1928.

———. *The Pharisees*. The Macmillan Company, 1924, 1952. Boston, Beacon Press, 1962.

Hitti, Philip Khuri. *The Near East in History, A 5000 Year Story*. Princeton, Van Nostrand, 1961.

Hoade, Eugene. *Guide to the Holy Land*. Jerusalem, Franciscan Press, 1946.

Hsüntze. *The Works of Hsüntze*. Ed. and transl. from the Chinese, with notes, by Homer H. Dubs. London, A. Probsthain, 1928.

Humbach, Helmut. *Die Gathas des Zarathustra, vol. I: Einleitung, Text, Übersetzung, Paraphrase*. Heidelberg, Carl Winter, 1959.

Hume, Robert Ernest, transl. *The Thirteen Principal Upanishads*. Transl. from the Sanskrit. London, New York, Oxford University Press, 1921.

———. *The World's Living Religions: An Historical Sketch, with Special Reference to their Sacred Scriptures and in Comparison with Christianity*. New York, Charles Scribner's Sons, 1924, 1942.

James, E. O. *The Ancient Gods: The History and Diffusion of Religion in the Ancient Near East and the Eastern Mediterranean*. London, Weidenfeld and Nicolson, 1960.

"Jerusalem" in *Encyclopaedia Judaica*. Vol. 9 (1971), columns 1378–1593. 29 sections by various authors.

Jhabvala, R. Prawer. *An Experience of India.* New York, W. W. Norton & Co., Inc., 1966, 1972.

Johansson, Rune E. A. *The Psychology of Nirvana.* London, George Allen and Unwin Ltd., 1969. Garden City, New York, Anchor Books, Doubleday & Co., Inc., 1970.

Jonas, Hans. *The Gnostic Religion: The Message of the Alien God and the Beginnings of Christianity.* Boston, Beacon Press, 1958. 2nd ed., enlarged, 1963.

Jones, Henry Stuart. "Constantine I" in *Encyclopaedia Britannica,* 11th edition.

Josephus, Flavius. *The Jewish War.* The Greek original with a translation by Henry St. John Thackeray. London, W. Heinemann. New York, G. P. Putnam's Sons, 1926–1965. The translation in the text is my own; but I have compared several versions.

Jung, Carl Gustav. *Answer to Job.* Transl. R. F. C. Hull. From *The Collected Works of C. G. Jung,* vol. 11. Bollingen Series XX. New York, Bollingen Foundation, 1958. Princeton/Bollingen Paperback Edition, 1973. *Antwort auf Hiob.* Zürich, Rascher, 1952.

Kähler, Heinz. *Hagia Sophia.* Translated from the German by Ellyn Childs. New York and Washington, Praeger, 1967.

Kaufmann, Walter. *Critique of Religion and Philosophy.* Harper & Brothers, 1958; Garden City, New York, Anchor Books, 1961; Harper Torchbooks, with a new preface, 1972.

———. *The Faith of a Heretic.* Garden City, New York, Doubleday & Co., Inc., 1961; Anchor Books, 1963.

———. *From Shakespeare to Existentialism.* Boston, Beacon Press, 1959; Anchor Books, 1960.

Koran. Translations are my own, but I have always consulted *The Meaning of the Glorious Koran: An Explanatory Translation* by Mohammed Marmaduke Pickthall. New York, New American Library, Mentor Books, 1953, and *El Koran das heisst die Lesung . . . ,* transl. Lazarus Goldschmidt, Berlin, Brandussche Verlagsbuchhandlung, 1916. Rudi Paret's German version of *Der Koran,* Stuttgart, Kohlhammer, 1963–66, has valuable footnotes on every page.

Korean Art, Masterpieces of: an exhibition under the auspices of the Government of The Republic of Korea. Published by The National Gallery of Art, Washington, and seven other American museums. ". . . Harold P. Stern of The Freer Gallery of Art went to Korea to write the catalogue notes and arrange for photography of the objects . . . Robert T. Paine, Jr., of The Museum of Fine Arts, Boston, had edited and prepared the catalogue for publication . . ." (From Foreword).

Kramrisch, Stella. *The Art of India, Traditions of Indian Sculpture, Painting and Architecture.* London, Phaidon Press Ltd., 1954. Third Edition, 1965.

———. *The Art of Nepal.* New York, The Asia Society. Distributed by Harry N. Abrams, Inc. An Asia House Gallery Publication, 1964.

Krey, August C. *The First Crusade: The Accounts of Eye-Witnesses and Participants.* Princeton, Princeton University Press, 1921.

Lankāvatāra Sūtra, A Mahayana Text. Transl. from the Sanskrit by Daisetz Teitaro Suzuki. London, Routledge, 1932.

Lao-tze. *Tao Teh Ching.* See Lin Yutang. I have also consulted many other translations.

Lee, Sherman E. *A History of Far Eastern Art.* Englewood Cliffs, N.J., Prentice-Hall, Inc., and New York, Harry N. Abrams, Inc., 1964.

———. *Ancient Cambodian Sculpture.* New York, Asia Society, 1969. An Asia House Gallery Publication.

Lewis, Bernard. *The Arabs in History.* London, Hutchinson & Co., Ltd., 1950. New York, Harper Torchbooks, 1960.

———. *Race and Color in Islam.* New York, Evanston, San Francisco, London, Harper Torchbooks, 1970, 1971. Cited only in section 64.

Lin Yutang, ed. *The Wisdom of China and India.* New York, Random House, 1942. Modern Library Giant, 1955.

Lommel, Herman. *Die Religion Zarathustras.* Tübingen, Mohr, 1930. Reprographischer Nachdruck: Hildesheim and New York, 1971.

Luther, Martin. *Sämtliche Schriften,* ed. J. G. Walch, 24 vols., Halle, 1740–53. Pagination of this ed. is indicated in St. Louis reprint, 1881–1910. Only XXII, 377, and VII, 1516, refer to St. Louis ed. because this material was not included in Halle ed.

Major, H. D. A., Manson, T. W., Wright, C. J. *The Mission and Message of Jesus, An Exposition of the Gospels in the Light of Modern Research.* New York, E. P. Dutton and Co., Inc., 1938, 1947.

Majumdar, R. C., ed. *The History and Culture of the Indian People*, vol. II: *The Age of Imperial Unity*. Bombay, Bharatiya Vidya Bhavan, 1951; 2nd ed., 1953.

Manu, The Laws of. Translated with extracts from seven commentaries by G. Bühler. Oxford, Clarendon Press, 1886. (SBE, vol. XXV.) In quotations I have made many stylistic changes.

Masks: Illustrated Catalogues of Tokyo National Museum. Tokyo, 1970.

Mencius. Transl. James Legge. *The Chinese Classics*. New York, Hurd & Houghton, 1870. I have used the translations in Fung Yu-lan.

Miller, Madeleine S., and Miller, J. Lane, in consultation with eminent authorities. *Harper's Bible Dictionary*. New York, Harper & Brothers, 1952; 6th edition, 1959.

Mitra, Debala. *Konarak*. New Delhi, Director General, Archaeological Survey of India, 1968.

Montefiore, C. G., and Loewe, H., eds. *A Rabbinic Anthology*. Cleveland and New York, World Publishing Co., Greenwich Edition, 1960, Meridian, 1963.

Moore, George Foot. *History of Religions*. 2 vols. New York, Charles Scribner's Sons, 1913, 1920, 1946.

———. *Judaism in the First Centuries of the Christian Era: The Age of the Tannaim*. 3 vols. Cambridge, Harvard University Press, 1927–1930.

Mote, Frederick W. *Intellectual Foundations of China*. New York, Alfred A. Knopf, 1971.

Mo-tze. *The Ethical and Political Works of Motse*. Transl. from the Chinese by Yi-Pao Mei. London, A. Probsthain, 1929.

Munsterberg, Hugo. *Art of India and Southeast Asia*. New York, Harry N. Abrams, Inc., 1970.

Netanyahu, B., and Speiser, E. A., eds. *The World History of the Jewish People*. First Series: *Ancient Times*. Volume I: *At the Dawn of Civilization: A Background of Biblical History*. Israel, Jewish History Publications, 1961. New Brunswick, N.J., Rutgers University Press, 1964.

Nicholson, Reynold Alleyne. *The Mystics of Islam*. London, G. Bell & Sons, Ltd., 1914. Routledge & Kegan Paul, 1963.

———. "Pre-Islamic Poetry, Manners, and Religion," Chapter III of *A Literary History of the Arabs*. T. Fisher Unwin, 1907. Cambridge, Cambridge University Press, 1953.

Nietzsche, Friedrich. *Basic Writings of Nietzsche*. Transl. and ed. by Walter Kaufmann. Contains *The Birth of Tragedy, Beyond Good and Evil, On the Genealogy of Morals, The Case of Wagner*, and *Ecce Homo*. New York, Random House, Modern Library Giant, 1968.

———. *The Portable Nietzsche*. Transl. and ed. by Walter Kaufmann. Contains *Thus Spoke Zarathustra, Twilight of the Idols, The Antichrist, Nietzsche Contra Wagner*. New York, Viking, 1954; Paperback ed., 1958.

———. *The Will to Power*. Ed. Walter Kaufmann. New York, Random House, 1967; Vintage Books (Paperback), 1968.

———. *Gesammelte Werke, Musarionausgabe*, 23 vols. Munich, Musarion Verlag, 1920–29.

Noma, Seiroku. *Masks*. English adaptation from the Japanese by Meredith Weatherby. Tokyo, Kodansha. Rutland, Vermont, and Tokyo, Japan, Charles E. Tuttle Co., 1957.

Norman, James. *Terry's Guide to Mexico*. A completely revised edition of T. Philip Terry's Guidebook to Mexico. Garden City, New York, Doubleday & Co., Inc., 1909, 1972.

Offner, C. B., and Straelen, Henry Van. *Modern Japanese Religions, with Special Emphasis upon Their Doctrines of Healing*. Leiden, E. J. Brill; New York, Twayne, 1963.

Panofsky, Erwin, ed., transl. and annotated: *Abbot Suger on the Abbey Church of St.-Denis and its Art Treasures*. Princeton, Princeton University Press, 1946.

Parulekar, N. B. *The Science of the Soul Force or Mahatma Gandhi's Doctrine of Truth & Non-violence*. Bombay, Hind Kitabs Publishers, 1962.

Pirazzoli-T'Serstevens, Michèle. *Living Architecture: Chinese*. Transl. from the French by Robert Allen. New York, Grosset & Dunlap, 1971.

Pius XII, Pope, "International Penal Law: Address to the Sixth International Congress of Penal Law, October 3, 1953," in *The Catholic Mind*, Feb. 1954.

Ploetz, Karl. *Auszug aus der Geschichte*. Würzburg, A. G. Ploetz-Verlag, 26th ed., 1960.

Pope, Arthur Upham. *Persian Architecture, The Triumph of Form and Color*. New York, George Braziller, Inc., 1965.

Pratt, James Bissett. *The Pilgrimage of Buddhism and a Buddhist Pilgrimage*. New York, Macmillan, 1928.

Prawer, Joshua. *The Crusaders' Kingdom; European Colonialism in the Middle Ages*. New York, Praeger, 1972.

Pritchard, James B., ed., *Ancient Near Eastern Texts Relating to the Old Testament*. Princeton, Princeton University Press, 1950. 2nd ed., 1955.

Radhakrishnan, Sarvepalli, and Moore, Charles A., eds. *A Source Book in Indian Philosophy*. Princeton, Princeton University Press, 1957.

Rahman, Fazlur. *Islam*. New York, Holt, Rinehart, and Winston, 1966. Garden City, New York, Doubleday Anchor, 1968.

Reischauer, Edwin O. *Japan: Past and Present*. 2nd ed., rev. & enlarged, Tokyo, Tuttle, 1953.

Rigveda. I have compared many versions and usually adapted Griffith's (see above). The rhymed translation of the Creation hymn is my own.

Roth, Cecil, ed. *Jewish Art: An Illustrated History*. Tel Aviv, Massadah—P.E.C. Press Ltd., 1961.

Rowland, Jr., Benjamin. *Gandhara Sculpture from Pakistan Museums*. New York, Asia Society, Inc., 1960.

Roy Chowdhury, Subrata. *The Genesis of Bangladesh; A Study in International Legal Norms and Permissive Conscience*. Bombay, New York, Asia Publishing House, 1972.

Runciman, Steven. *Byzantine Civilization*. London, E. Arnold & Co., 1933. New York, Meridian Books, 1956.

———. *A History of the Crusades*. Vol. I: *The First Crusade*. Cambridge, Cambridge University Press, 1951.

Sacred Books of the East, The. Transl. by various Oriental scholars and ed. by F. Max Müller. 50 vols. Oxford, Clarendon Press, 1879–1910. Many impressions. Still the greatest collection of English translations.

Saunders, E. Dale. *Mudrā*. New York, Bollingen Foundation, Pantheon Books, 1960.

Schaff, Philip. *The Creeds of Christendom with a History and Critical Notes*. 3 vols., 6th rev. ed. New York, Harper & Brothers, 1877 ff., 1931.

Scholem, Gershom G. *Major Trends in Jewish Mysticism*. New York, Schocken Books, 1941. Rev. ed., 1946.

Seckel, Dietrich. *The Art of Buddhism*. Transl. from the German by Ann E. Keep. Baden-Baden, 1964. New York, Toronto, London, Greystone Press, rev. ed., 1968.

Shoten, Kadokawa, ed. *A Pictorial Encyclopedia of the Oriental Arts: Korea*, 1 vol.; *Japan*, 4 vols. New York, Crown Publishers, Inc., 1969.

Simons, J. *Jerusalem in the Old Testament, Researches and Theories*. Leiden, E. J. Brill, 1952.

Simson, Otto Georg von. *The Gothic Cathedral: Origins of Gothic Architecture and the Medieval Concept of Order*. Bollingen Series. New York, Pantheon, 1956. 2nd rev. ed., 1962.

Singh, Khushwant. *A History of the Sikhs*. 2 vols. Princeton, Princeton University Press, 1963–1966.

———. *The Sikhs Today: Their Religion, History, Culture, Customs, and Way of Life*. Bombay, Calcutta, Madras, New Delhi, Hyderabad, Dacca, Orient Lungmans Private Ltd., 1959.

Sivaramamurti, C. *Nataraja in Art, Thought and Literature*. New Delhi, National Museum, 1974.

Söderblom, Nathan. *The Living God: Basal Forms of Personal Religion*. Edinburgh, the Gifford Lectures, 1931. London, New York, Toronto, Oxford University Press, 1933, 1939.

Soper, Alexander Coburn. "Early Buddhist Attitudes Toward the Art of Painting." *The Art Bulletin* (June 1950), v. 32 no. 2.

Spear, Thomas George Percival, ed. *The Oxford History of India*. 3rd ed. by Vincent Arthur Smith. Pt. 1 revised by Mortimer Wheeler and A. L. Basham; Pt. 2 rev. by J. B. Harrison; Pt. 3 rewritten by Percival Spear. Oxford, Clarendon Press, 1958.

Staal, Frits. Review of Arthur C. Danto, *Mysticism and Morality*, in *Journal of Philosophy*, March 28, 1974.

Strayer, Joseph R. *The Albigensian Crusades*. New York, The Dial Press, 1971.

Suzuki, Daisetz Teitaro. *An Introduction to Zen Buddhism*. New York, Philosophical Library, 1949.

Tertullian. *On Spectacles* in *The Ante-Nicene Fathers down to A.D. 325.* Edited by the Reverend Alexander Roberts, and James Donaldson, in vol. 3, *Latin Christianity: Its Founder, Tertullian.* American reprint of the Edinburgh edition. Grand Rapids, Michigan, William B. Eerdmans, 1957.

Tillich, Paul. *Dynamics of Faith.* New York, Harper Torchbooks, 1958.

Troeltsch, Ernst. *Die Soziallehren der christlichen Kirchen und Gruppen.* Tübingen, J. C. B. Mohr (Paul Siebeck), 1912. *The Social Teachings of the Christian Churches,* 2 vols. Transl. Olive Wyon. New York, Harper Torchbooks, 1960.

Upanishads. I have compared many translations and am particularly indebted to those by Max Müller (see *Sacred Books*) and Robert Ernest Hume.

Volwahsen, Andreas. *Living Architecture: Indian.* New York, Grosset & Dunlap, Inc., 1969.

Waldschmidt, Ernst and Rose Lenore. *Nepal: Art Treasures from the Himalayas.* Transl. by David Wilson. New York, Universal Books, 1970.

Warren, Henry Clarke. See Buddha.

Wesendonk, O. G. von. *Das Weltbild der Iranier.* Munich, Reinhardt, 1933.

Widengren, Geo. *Mani and Manichaeism.* Transl. Charles Kessler. New York, Chicago, San Francisco, Holt, Rinehart and Winston, 1965.

Wilhelm, Richard. *A Short History of Chinese Civilization.* Transl. from the German by Joan Joshua. New York, Viking, 1929.

Williams, L. F. Rushbrook. *A Handbook for Travellers in India, Pakistan, Burma and Ceylon,* 19th ed. London, John Murray, 1962.

Wilson, R. McL. "Mani and Manichaeism" in *The Encyclopedia of Philosophy.* Vol. 5, pp. 149–150. New York, Macmillan and The Free Press, 1967. London, Collier-Macmillan Ltd., 1967.

Wright, Arthur F. *Buddhism in Chinese History.* Stanford, Stanford University Press, 1959.

Zaehner, R. C. See also *Bhagavad-Gītā.*

———. ed. *The Concise Encyclopedia of Living Faiths.* New York, Hawthorn Books, Inc., 1959. Boston, Beacon Press, 1967. The essay on Zoroastrianism was written by Zaehner.

———. *The Dawn and Twilight of Zoroastrianism.* London, Weidenfeld and Nicolson, 1961.

Zarathustra. The English versions are mine, but I am indebted to the volumes listed below, and to Humbach and Lommel.

———. *Die Gatha's des Awesta: Zarathushtra's Verspredigten. Übersetzt von Christian Bartholomae.* Strassburg, Trübner, 1905.

———. *Zarathustra, The Hymns of.* Being a translation of the Gathas together with Introduction and Commentary by Jacques Duchesne-Guillemin. Preface by Richard N. Frye. Translated from the French by Mrs. M. Henning. Boston, Beacon Press, 1963.

Zen Flesh, Zen Bones: A Collection of Zen and Pre-Zen Writings. Compiled by Paul Reps. Garden City, New York, Doubleday Anchor Books, 1961.

Zernov, Nicholas. *Eastern Christendom: A Study of the Origin and Development of the Eastern Orthodox Church.* London, Weidenfeld and Nicolson, 1961.

Zimmer, Heinrich. *The Art of Indian Asia, Its Mythology and Transformations.* 2 vols. Completed and edited by Joseph Campbell. New York, Bollingen Foundation Inc., 1955. 2nd ed., 1960.

———. *Philosophies of India.* Ed. Joseph Campbell. New York, Bollingen Foundation, Inc., 1951. Meridian, 1956.

INDEX

The index supplements the detailed table of contents. *Numbers refer to sections*, not to pages. The Prologue is included, the material after section 120 is not. Chapter X (section 78) consists of an introduction and twenty-three poems. 78.1 refers to the introduction; 78.24 to the last poem.

* Indicates that there is at least one color photograph, ** at least one black-and-white picture, and *** both. Often there are many pictures.

Most of the work on this index was done by Jill Anderson.